HARMONY &
DISSONANCE

WAYNE STATE UNIVERSITY PRESS
DETROIT

HARMONY & DISSONANCE

Voices of Jewish Identity in Detroit, 1914–1967

Sidney Bolkosky

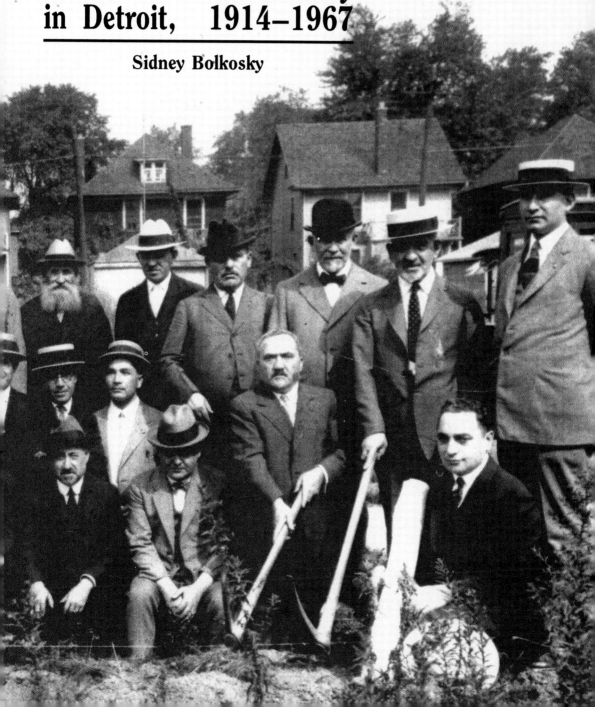

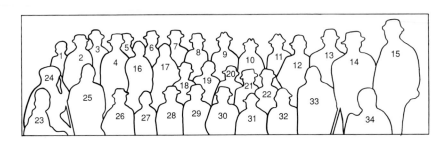

Groundbreaking for the Philadelphia-Byron branch of the United Hebrew Schools, August 31, 1923. (Courtesy of the Archives of Congregation Shaarey Zedek.)

1. Unidentified
2. Joseph Cherkose
3. Louis Medow
4. Hyman Goldberg
5. Joel Cashdan
6. Superintendent Bernard Isaacs
7. Rudolph Zuieback
8. Hyman Goldman
9. L. Granet
10. Hyman Buchhalter
11. A. Shuraytz
12. Max Rosinskey
13. I. August
14. Jacob Friedberg
15. Robert Loewenberg
16. E. Gilady
17. Leah Pike
18. S. Pollack
19. Rubin Zinder
20. J. Loewenbuck
21. Solomon Kasdan
22. J. Ariel
23. Unidentified
24. Sam Soltar
25. Louis Duscoff
26. Esser Rabinowitz
27. Shoshana Pike
28. Jacob Warren
29. M. B. Cohen
30. Morris Margolis
31. L. Dann
32. J. B. Lasky
33. David Robinson
34. I. Lewis

Library of Congress Cataloging-in-Publication Data

Bolkosky, Sidney M.
    Harmony and dissonance : voices of Jewish identity in Detroit, 1914–1967 /
Sidney Bolkosky.
        p.   cm.
    Includes bibliographical references and index.
    ISBN 0-8143-1933-5 (alk. paper)
        1. Jews—Michigan—Detroit—History.   2. Detroit (Mich.)—Ethnic relations.
I. Title.
F574.D49J52   1991
977.4'34004924—dc20   91-17287

Designer: Mary Primeau

Special acknowledgment is made to the United Jewish Charities for financial
assistance in the publication of this volume.

Contents

Preface

It has been a most exciting and rewarding task to chair the Jewish Welfare Federation History Committee, which has been responsible for the second volume of the history of the Jews in Detroit. It was not an easy task to convince the community leadership to subsidize this volume, given the many demands for the more immediate needs for the funds. However, Leonard Simons, William Avrunin, and I managed to convince our colleagues of the merits of the project.

Once we were on our way, we faced many challenges and we were not always unanimous in our decisions. But we resolved our differences, and this history represents some of those decisions. I want to thank all the members of the committee who assisted in determining some of the directions the book should follow. Besides those I have already cited, they are: Ann Chapin, Judith Cantor, Avern Cohn, Barbara Marcuse, George Stutz, and Joel Jacob. They tirelessly read a number of drafts and made valuable comments and corrections.

The committee appreciated the commitment and professionalism of our historian, Sidney Bolkosky, and the cooperation of the Wayne State University Press. We hope that the press will continue to publish books on

Judaica. Along those lines, finally, for the future: that every community write its history in order that it may keep its past and its present in perspective. Thus, future generations inherit the ability to understand their heritage. The Jewish people have always been dedicated to their history and have lived with memory. The Detroit Jewish community can do no less.

George M. Zeltzer
Chair
Jewish Welfare Federation History Committee
Detroit, Michigan

Acknowledgments

Oral histories often yield insights into a tenor of a time through personalized reactions to historical events. But, because of the fallibility of memory, or the particular perspectives of each interviewee, oral testimonies produce equivocal accuracy and, as historical resources, should be questioned—as should most resources. Taped interviews proved invaluable in this study. They offered differing accounts of events and observations from a broad variety of perspectives. I have opted to use oral testimonies for historical information when they could be confirmed by two other written or oral sources. If any doubt remained, the information was qualified or not used. A list of taped, formal interviews, appears in Appendix C.

Many Detroiters (and former Detroiters) offered advice and guidance for this book informally and not in taped interviews. Foremost among these were the members of the Jewish Welfare Federation's History Committee, chaired by George M. Zeltzer: William Avrunin, Judith Levin Cantor, Judge Avern Cohn, Joel Jacob, Barbara Marcuse, Leonard N. Simons, and George Stutz. Among the many who provided important assistance were: Joseph Faumann, Sol Drachler, Norman Drachler, Dina Greenberg, Mark Ungar, Irwin Cohen, Philip Applebaum, Morris Fine, Ronald Landau, Robert

9

Acknowledgments Rockaway, May Moskowitz, Morton Plotnik, Joan Jempel, Lee Hoffman, Miriam Shey Immerman, Evelyn Noveck, Robert Luby, Barbara Grant, Sarah and Morris Friedman, Josephine Weiner, Jewell Morris, Rosalie Kahn Butzel, Hannah Klein Wilhelm, Judy Blumenstein, Zev Davis, Regine Freund Cohane, Harold Berke, Dr. Herbert Bloom, Sarah Bell, and others too numerous to mention. Dr. Matthew Schwartz wrote sections of the first draft. To attempt to list all those who contributed to this project would be a foolish undertaking, in Thomas Mann's words, "a self-deluding quest" for thoroughness.

Stanley Moretzky, Dr. Irving Edgar, and Judy Cantor conducted some interviews. Mickey Grossman, Nina Kent, Seth Korelitz, and Jeffrey Kass provided research assistance. Alan Kandel heroically searched out hundreds of photographs from established collections, libraries, basements, and mysterious lairs. Robert Benyas' work on the photographs is also gratefully acknowledged. Colleagues who graciously read parts of the manuscript and offered suggestions included Bernard Klein, Leslie Tentler, and Bryn Roberts. Federation staff members who aided in numerous ways included Charlotte Dubin and Hazel Shackelford.

Finally, the book is dedicated to the person who gave life to it in the beginning, Anna Chapin. All of Jewish Detroit misses her.

Sidney Bolkosky

10

Introduction

Writing about Jewish history involves perils beyond the pale of other subjects. Which directions should one pursue? Should the history of Detroit consist of its Jewish success stories, its businessmen, merchants, lawyers, judges, activists, philanthropists, and rabbis? Should it consist of the sociological importance of the development of the Jewish population in a midwestern industrial city? Should it chart the progress of leading institutions? Should it address the problems that plagued Jews in other cities: difficulties of assimilation, anti-Semitism, the differences between the "little people" and the leadership? The answer to all these questions, of course, is "yes."

The Jewish population of Detroit grew more heterogeneous in the twentieth century than it had been in the previous century, and its history is thus heterogeneous. Yet patterns, trends that mirror histories of other American urban Jewish groups, may be discerned in the period from 1914 to 1967: the movement from a German to an Eastern European majority; from laborers and peddlers to merchants and businessmen; from Talmudic scholars and students to professional occupations. Dramatic social, intellectual, spiritual, and economic changes produced tensions and conflicts. 11

Like much of American Jewish history, Detroit Jewish history reflects those conflicts and the attempts to resolve them.

Abraham Cahan, in his poignantly revealing 1917 novel, *The Rise of David Levinsky,* grasped the essence of early-twentieth-century American Jewish experience in his first sentence, as Levinsky begins his narrative: "The Metamorphosis I have gone through strikes me as nothing short of a miracle." A miracle, then, characterizes Levinsky's successful American existence, a miracle and a metamorphosis that has placed him seemingly worlds away from his shtetl origins. Yet Cahan called that change "superficial" because Levinsky's "inner identity" remained frozen, somehow, although layered and masked by his American past and present: frozen, suspended in his meager, intrinsically and ineradicably Jewish identity.

In Detroit, leaders who embodied different aspects of "Jewishness" emerged from each segment of the population. Leaders or heroes to one group were ignored by another, and issues perceived by some as critical seemed unimportant to others. Within these groups, countless individuals contributed to such causes and organizations as the Allied Jewish Campaign and the Jewish Welfare Federation, the settling of Palestine and Zionism, anti-discrimination and the Jewish Community Council, education and the United Hebrew Schools, and hundreds of others. Part of the rhythm of Detroit Jewish history revolves around these different perceptions, disagreements, and divisions; and another part revolves around significant points of coalescence. In some respects, many of those leaders and heroes appear like David Levinsky: successfully American, yet haunted by ephemeral ghosts, and quintessentially Jewish.

Questions of Jewish identity loomed persistently, if often implicitly, in many of the debates and disagreements that confronted Jews in Detroit. How to define "Jewishness" occupied or preoccupied groups and individuals throughout—just as it had for centuries. Orthodox Jews, of course, brooked little discussion about what defined Jewish identity. But the others—Conservative, Reform, secular, or culturalist—seemed continually enmeshed in that tangle of issues. Detroit Jews, most frequently divided over such definitions and over more palpable issues, sought some unity of purpose in causes and in religious or secular values.

This confusion of issues presents itself to a historian who seeks some sort of order, an interpretive overview or scheme. Graham Swift opened his strange and haunting novel of history, *Waterland,* with a definition of *Historia* as a narrative inquiring into events of the past, describing what happened, when and how it happened, and, perhaps most significantly, why events "unfolded" as they did. The final definition, taken from the *Oxford English Dictionary,* is simply "a story." History then becomes an ensemble of stories and explanations, logically tracing backward, balancing variables, motives, witnesses, interpretations; weaving some tapestry of different materials, textures, and colors. No historian merely reports. A welter of events may or may not yield order or logic—no matter how hard a historian seeks them. Similarly, in *The Art of the Novel,* Milan Kundera, the brilliant Czech novelist, discussed modern literature as combining different voices or genres—fiction, essay, history, reportage, poetry—simultaneously. Drawing a musical analogy, he said literature offers us "polyphony," multiple voices that other genres fail to communicate.

In a history that has relied in part on oral testimonies, that musical analogy of simultaneous voices seems appropriate. Blending those voices and finding coherent themes in Detroit's multifarious history frequently seemed to offer a polyphonically impossible task, a task to baffle a Mozart of history. And what might appear as cacophony to those close to the fray might in retrospect sound like a modern social symphony or opera—full of voices and full of meaning.

These are heady, often bewildering, ideas that seem light years away from writing a local history of the Jews of Detroit. Yet, as this project grew, I found myself recalling just such confusing issues. At any given time the work seemed frustratingly embroiled in reportage, anecdote, historical perspective, and the sorting out of different interests. In addition, every topic of local Jewish history is overlaid with all Jewish history: the invoking of generations of religious history and tradition whenever one speaks of a particular religious observance; the calling up of multiple associations by such specific words as *Holocaust, immigration, assimilation;* and, in Detroit, the manifold associations that accompany words and names such as *Federation, Council, Labor Zionism, Coughlin,* and *Ford.*

As with Graham Swift's novel, or Kundera's analysis of literary genres, in the end are the stories, those that conflate history with History, demonstrating how individual and family lives—like small tributaries—flow into a confluence with the river of world-historical events. It will have to suffice here to recognize the polyphonic colors of Detroit's Jewish history and acknowledge that many words, names, and images evoke a myriad of others, along with different sentiments: pride, anger, hope, disappointment, joy, dignity, and self-respect. All this, composed often in dissonant and often in harmonious ways, comprises the history of the Jews of Detroit.

PART I
1914–1926

In 1914 the American Jewish Joint Distribution Committee was founded for the relief of Jews overseas. World War I began, and with it the world entered the twentieth century. The Great War transformed virtually every aspect of Detroit life and culture, and the city leaped from thirteenth in size in 1900 to become the fourth largest city in America by 1920.[1] Its physical landscape became that of a totally industrialized metropolis. Its populations were converted, almost overnight, into the epitome of the ethnic, industrial urban aggregates that would soon mark so many other American cities.

Detroit's Jewish population was in many ways—physically and socially—at the heart of these changes. Quite suddenly, for the first time in the city's history, crowded districts along the lines of New York City's enclaves appeared as huge industrial complexes grew throughout Detroit and its environs. Albert Kahn, son of a German Jewish rabbi, rebuilt the city and subtly drew attention to the German Jewish population that had established itself in Detroit from the mid-nineteenth century. In no other American city were the pressures of industrial modernization so greatly applied to Jews, and from that time Jews in Detroit would grapple with loyalties, 17 cultural trauma, religious controversies, and socioeconomic upheavals, along with the myriad problems that stimulated the formation of the Joint Distribution Committee. The American Jewish Committee and the American Jewish Congress, the rising tide of Zionism and the opposing tide of Americanization, the turbulent years of the labor movement and the Labor Zionists, the secularists, the traditionalists, and the assimilationists would all compete confusingly for the attention and loyalties of the Jews of Detroit. America's tumultuous decade of the twenties launched Jews into heightened controversies, intensified conflicts, and auspicious possibilities.

For all their differences, however, those Jews maintained a distinctive identity. Even in the Motor City, where the population had achieved a kind of homogeneity as the first to be put on wheels, members of the Jewish community, like their ancestors for millennia, sustained their separateness from non-Jews. Some Jewish Detroiters more closely resembled their non-Jewish counterparts than others, yet even these Jews acknowledged a peculiar sense of separation, or a feeling of their Jewish identity. This phenomenon, which was not unique to Detroit's Jews, manifested itself in unique ways due to the nature of Detroit's secular and non-Jewish environment. Although they were obvious sources of pride to Jews, visible leaders like Albert Kahn, who also seemed to be completely Americanized, provoked ambivalent feelings among many Jews. While Kahn and his brother Julius identified themselves as Jews—they belonged to Temple Beth El and to the Jewish elite club, the Phoenix—they were hardly Jewish leaders in the sense of leading their community.

Although they served as models of sorts, men like Kahn did not hold the community together—and neither did the anti-Semitism of the twenties and thirties. Ultimately, what Henry Feingold has called "the mystery of millenial Jewish survival" rested not upon what Jews shared with other cultures, but in what made and continues to make them different.[2]

1

A Brief Portrait:
Faces of Jewish
Identity in Detroit

It was no secret: the *Ostjuden* [East European Jews] saw the
Yahudim [German Jews] as *goyim* [non-Jews] and the *Yahudim*
saw the *Ostjuden* as ghetto Jews . . . religious zealots . . . su-
perstitious or dirty and uneducated—lower class.

Philip Slomovitz

One of the consequences of the wave of violent anti-Semitic outbursts that
swept Eastern Europe in the 1880s and after had been mass migration,
the "Great Migration" from Poland, the Ukraine, and Russia.[3] Jewish immigration to America peaked in 1910 and then slowed. In that year, the
Detroit census identified 9,986 "Yiddish-Hebrew speaking people."[4] Immigration markedly increased again because of renewed and heightened
post–World War I anti-Jewish violence and pogroms in Eastern Europe
from 1919 to 1921. In 1920, the number of Jews in Detroit had leaped to
34,727, a 247 percent increase in ten years, while the general population
of Detroit had increased by only 114 percent.[5] They composed approximately 3.7 percent of Detroit's total population. Despite continued anti-
Jewish violence in Europe, Congressional legislation curtailed and all but
halted Jewish immigration in 1924.

New restrictive immigration laws ended the waves of frightened but determined Jews seeking refuge from Russian and Polish brutality and prejudice. But if immigration to the United States diminished to a trickle,   19

immigration to Detroit continued, as Jews came from other American cities. Between 1910 and 1920, 528,000 people moved to Detroit. While the overwhelming majority of these new arrivals were foreign-born immigrants, 412,000 of them were also American migrants, that is, they had moved to Detroit from other American cities.[6] Industrial Detroit still seemed to hold out the promises that had not been fulfilled in other cities. One of the young men who made his way to Detroit from Warsaw via New York in 1914, believed that "Detroit in 1914 and 1915 had more to offer the immigrant youth than the sweatshops of the East. Industry was booming and Henry Ford's $5.00 a day in wages, regardless of skill, was also an attraction."[7]

One third of the 1920 Jewish population of Detroit was made up of proprietors of retail or manufacturing businesses; 4.4 percent were engaged in the "professions"; 29.7 percent were identified as clerical workers, salespeople, or peddlers; 29 percent were laborers. *The General Summary of the Survey of the Detroit Jewish Community* of 1923 noted that fewer than 2,000 of 5,000 workers were in labor unions. The population was overall quite prosperous, and its community fund took in some $38,000 more than it paid out.[8]

More significant, perhaps, Detroit Jewry was clearly Eastern European. By 1900, 88 percent of Detroit's Russian immigrants claimed Jewish identities; only 1.04 percent of the German immigrants could be identified as Jews. The *Survey* estimated that, after 1900, 78 percent of the Jews of Detroit hailed from Eastern Europe.[9]

By 1915, this primarily Eastern European Jewish population of Detroit had grown to some 25,000 people, with more than twenty congregations—mostly Orthodox—and a vast network of Jewish charities and organizations.[10]

In *The Jews of Detroit: From the Beginning, 1762–1914,* Robert Rockaway described Detroit's German Jews as an elite.[11] As in most American cities, the first Jews to settle in Detroit were German émigrés. Their sense of elitism, then, connects to an identity of founders; with deeper roots than latecomers, they were more thoroughly integrated into the Detroit community and were firmly established economically, socially, and educationally. The families Blitz, Butzel, Heavenrich, Heineman, Kaichen, Krolik, and others mixed socially, often married within their group, and lived in an aristocratic style unlike that of the immigrants who came in the Great Migration and settled on and around Hastings Street. Having formed Detroit's first congregation in 1850, Detroit's German Jews by 1900 claimed a sort of right of primacy.[12]

Their assimilationist views, their strong loyalty to the United States, and their sense of family and of aristocratic status derived from generations of life in the New World and indeed from German antecedents. Many German Jews succeeded quickly in businesses and in professions such as medicine and law. They built beautiful homes and sent their children to such private schools as the prestigious Liggett School and to universities in and out of Michigan, and sometimes to Europe to study or tour. Visits to Europe might also involve collecting works of art, taking the baths, or visiting relatives in Germany or Austria. Often highly cultured, they moved with ease in the worlds of art, literature, and music.

Memoirs like those of Marian Blitz Heavenrich and her sister, Helen Blitz Levy Welling, reflect this urbane and often elegant milieux:

> My own earliest recollections are from the house at 25 Bagg Street where I was born and lived until I was seven, when we moved to Woodward Terrace. . . . I remember a narrow entrance hall in which were an oak carved settee—the seat opened up for boots, etc., and an oak framed mirror above the brass hooks for cloaks, all carved by my mother, who was quite expert in this field. Her masterpiece was a cherry table with Gothic panel ends and a drawer on which were carved our father's initials . . . [and] the date. . . . Another attractive piece was a mahogany secretary . . . backed with a mirror for the display of fine pieces of Dresden . . . which stood in the parlor. . . . Another interesting piece of her artistry was a six-foot-wide and high bookcase with the motto 'Seek Knowledge and Pursue It' carved across the top.

But the elitist air Rockaway attributed to Detroit's German Jews derived from other sources as well. German Jewish attitudes in America resembled those of Europe's most proudly assimilated Jews in Germany: like them, American-German Jews became patriotic; they adopted their new country's language and culture; they were dedicated to what they perceived as American principles just as German Jews in Germany dedicated themselves to what they considered the essence of *Deutschtum,* or Germanness. To Detroit's German Jews, America mirrored the best of the German Enlightenment ideals of freedom, reason, and tolerance. America's Founding Fathers replaced such German cultural heroes as Goethe and Lessing, and assimilation appeared as a natural phenomenon.[13]

Still, following in the footsteps of German Enlightenment Jews who, like Moses Mendelssohn, were so quick to oppose prejudicial attitudes, they nevertheless looked down on the *Ostjuden,* the East European Jews. Characterizing East European Jews as coarse, crude, loud, hopelessly parochial, and dogmatically religious helped shape a markedly contrasting German-Jewish identity. Such sterotypes remained active among German-Jewish ranks in the United States.

Although they may have maintained discriminatory images of East European Jews, German Jews had not encountered them in large numbers until the Great Migration.[14]

How would the "elite," caught between *Ostjuden* and non-Jews, react to this new influx? Would a unified community emerge? Would there be an ethnically divided Jewish population? How would German Jews respond to the predictable rise of anti-Semitism? And how would the Eastern European Jews react to Detroit? Would they leap into Americanization? Would they see the alleged merits of accommodation to American religious and secular customs?

Again, like their counterparts in Germany, Detroit's German Jews sought to be an integral, indistinguishable—if distinguished—part of the greater secular society. By 1914 the process of acculturation had produced palpable results, and German Jews participated in Detroit civil society, politics, culture, and all secular aspects of the city. Even religious traditions had been bent or abandoned to accommodate Americanism. Temple Beth El, Detroit's first Jewish congregation and a national leader in the Reform movement, adopted Sunday services, abandoned Friday-night services, and became, as one Detroiter noted, like the Methodists or other Protestants. They continued a century-old German Jewish tendency that had set the majority of German Jews apart from East European Jews in Europe. It set them apart in Detroit, too.

Specific social, political, and historical conditions had produced pervasive assimilation in Germany. The ideas of equality and tolerance so tenaciously adhered to by German Jews in Germany were less controversial, more palpable, and obviously realizable in America. Because of that, the lure of Americanization, of acculturation, became as strong for many East European Jews as it had been for their predecessors from Germany. Enticed by the freedom and prospects for a good life that seemed to accompany assimilation, the children and grandchildren of those fugitive émigrés of the 1880s and 1890s began to abandon at least the social, if not the religious, trappings of their past. Thus, although many Jews maintained their old-world traditions in Detroit, by the second generation—hastened by World War I and the difficulties of maintaining traditional, cultural lifestyles—many East European Jews, like their German Jewish predecessors, had become part of the fabric of Detroit culture. Both groups, with some significant exceptions among the East European Jews, differed from the other ethnic enclaves in Detroit which clung more strongly to their traditional customs.[15] It seemed that the guidelines for Jewish-American survival in ethnic Detroit called for increased homogeneity, for indistinguishability.

Assimilation therefore inevitably entailed the gradual abandonment of certain traditional observances and practices, primarily religious but also cultural, accompanied by demonstrable increases in intermarriage and its acceptance by the younger generation. To those labeled "transformationists" by sociologist Nathan Glazer, assimilation became synonymous with changing the content of Jewishness and Judaism in America.[16] Advocates of adjustment to the gentile world were hard pressed to define the limits of this new, altered identity. Maurice Karpf, former director of the School for Jewish Social Work in New York, divided the embittered groups according to categories of "religionists," "culturists," and "assimilationists."[17] But, despite the existence of such internal dissension and disagreement on the nature of Jewish identity or definitions, Glazer has suggested that there was little threat to the "continuity of the community." In Detroit, at least, this concept was heatedly refuted. Almost all the groups carried some ambivalence regarding the future of Jewish identity in America.

Consequently, questions over Jewish identity and what would be involved in maintaining it were debated continuously and became a theme of Detroit Jewish life. The debate frequently revolved around the meaning of commitment to Jewishness and Judaism. Those labeled traditionalists and transformationists by some social historians could claim that they carried the essence of Judaism in their practices. Whatever one chose to call these antagonists, they articulated their positions through specific actions. Some continued their religious traditions without deviation from orthodoxy. Others sought to transform the Jewish mien into an American one, assimilating with a vengeance. Still others maintained a "cultural" identity through Yiddish literature, theater, and social groups. Those in the Reform movement sought to change what they considered an outdated religious system. Intent on adapting to a rapidly changing social environment, and intent on Americanizing, they were more than willing to abolish restrictive religious rules and practices: during the first quarter of the twentieth century, the *mechitzah,* the wall dividing men from women in the synagogue, was abandoned, the Sabbath was changed, bare heads were allowed and later demanded in "the temple" (as distinguished from the synagogue), and even the bar mitzvah ceremony became optional and eventually was jettisoned for a time.

As it was across the United States, Reform Judaism in Detroit was an organized attempt "to deal with the problems posed by the Americanization process."[18] Most of its adherents perceived Reformism's new rituals as saving Judaism in America. But to relinquish such ancient prescriptions and rites as the traditional Sabbath called into question the content of Jewish identity, and thus Reform Jews often sought to identify themselves as Jews through philanthropic organizations for local, national, and international problems. Through Beth El's public presence, the connection between the German Jewish tradition of patriotic assimilation and Reform Judaism's self-proclaimed mission in America became increasingly apparent.

By 1914 the sixty four-year old Temple Beth El boasted a distinguished history, a congregation that had achieved a national reputation because of its famous rabbis, and a strong local standing because of its lay leaders' prominence in the city of Detroit. Rabbi Leo M. Franklin, then forty-four years old, had arrived in Detroit in 1899. The congregation's officers included President Louis Welt, Vice-President Bernard Ginsburg, Secretary Adolph Freund, Treasurer Isaac Goldberg, and Warden Immanuel Wodec, a Civil War veteran. The religious school convened on Sunday mornings under the guidance of Rabbi Franklin and Helene Breitenbach.[19]

From 1898 to 1942 Temple Beth El, the Reform movement in Detroit, 23 and a significant part of the Jewish community was dominated by its articulate and increasingly famous rabbi, Dr. Leo M. Franklin. He passionately voiced the theme of patriotic Americanism: "Judaism is my religion; America my country. . . . As long as the Jew leads the right sort of life in the community he is as good as any man."[20] Under Franklin's guidance in 1904, Temple Beth El, for the most part willingly, replaced Friday-night services with Sunday services because the working American could rest on Saturday only with great difficulty and because Sunday, as the day of worship for their Christian neighbors, provided a general atmosphere more conducive to a feeling of spirituality and peace.[21] In his regular editorials for the *Detroit Jewish Chronicle,* Franklin continued to encourage Jews to Americanize, often explicitly apologizing for the backward life-styles displayed in the immigrant neighborhoods. He rebuked American soldiers at Fort Custer, near Battle Creek, for demanding greater privileges from the government when they had asked for religious facilities and kosher food: after all, they were in the army as Americans, not as Jews.[22] He conveyed his message of intensive Americanization not only to his own congregation and to others through his editorials in the *Chronicle,* but also reached a wider public by broadcasting his services on radio station WWJ in 1925.

Yet, just as relationships between Reform and non-Reform Jews cannot be categorized in simplistic terms as purely antagonistic, so, too, do Rabbi Franklin's relationships reflect his complex personality. He evolved into an important spokesmen for Jews in the non-Jewish world. As one of the founders of the Detroit Round Table of Catholics, Protestants and Jews, he frequently sermonized in churches ranging from imposing Catholic cathedrals to Baptist meetinghouses.[23] In 1923 Rabbi Franklin was awarded an honorary doctor of law degree from the "Catholic University of Detroit," the University of Detroit, as a show of esteem for his work in the Detroit community.[24] An editorial in the *Detroit Courier* in 1907 noted that "the Jew was to an extent ostracized in Detroit before Rabbi Franklin came. He went to Christian churches and organizations and told the story of his race."[25] The comments are curious, both for their depiction of Rabbi Franklin and for the nonchalant insensitivity of the writer, and they indicate the virtues and the dangers of Franklin's role.

As if to confound simplifiers, this paragon of Reformism established and maintained friendly relations with some of Detroit's leading Orthodox and Conservative rabbis, for example, Rabbi Judah Levin and Rabbi Abraham M. Hershman of Congregation Shaarey Zedek, newly affiliated with the national Conservative movement. In March 1918, Franklin attended the dedication of the Orthodox synagogue B'nai Moshe, and he often spoke in support of the United Hebrew Schools, although Temple Beth El's own independent school had a radically different curriculum.[26] One of his editorials in the *Chronicle* in 1921 reprimanded a writer for criticizing Orthodox Jews.[27] He was invited to officiate at weddings alongside Orthodox

colleagues, even after his retirement, as he did in 1945 when he accompanied Rabbi Joseph Ben Zion Rabinowitz and Rabbi Joshua Sperka at the
wedding of Jeffrey Strauss at B'nai David. Such interactions were typical
examples of Franklin's public liberality toward Orthodox and, later, toward
Conservative Jews. Through those social and professional relationships, he
implied certain attitudes about East European Jews, setting active examples for his congregants.[28]

Franklin, whose father was born in Prussia, was a persistent advocate of
Reform Judaism, he believed that archaic religious practices critically divided Reform and Orthodox Jews. In a burst of evangelical idealism, he
wrote that one day Reform Judaism would be the religion of the world.[29]

Franklin considered social and cultural differences among Jews reme-
diable. Under his tutelage, Temple Beth El exhibited a self-aggrandizing,
"magnanimous generosity" to East European Jewish immigrants, offering
medical services, instruction in nutrition and in English, as well as numerous social services, sports facilities, classroom space, summer camps,
and a display of charity the likes of which the city of Detroit had never
before witnessed. That long list of services, frequently initiated by such
Beth El women's groups as the Self Help Circle and the Ladies Hebrew
Sewing Circle, laid the foundation for organized Jewish charities in Detroit.[30]

With a congregation in the heart of the industrial midwest and a growing Eastern European immigrant population, Franklin sounded the first
note in response to critical questions about assimilation, Jewish identity,
and the future unity of Detroit's Jews. As usual, the leadership of Temple
Beth El took the public initiative and tried to bridge the gaps between Jews
and non-Jews and among Jews. Typically, Beth El congregants and leaders
reached "down" to new Jewish immigrants, and "up" to Detroit's gentile
leaders.

Many perceived this attitude to be the motivating force behind Rabbi
Franklin's leadership in the founding of the United Jewish Charities (UJC)
in 1899. Franklin, however, offered his rationale for the UJC in the *Free
Press* in June 1900: "The Jew is the keeper of his brother and is responsible
for him."[31] The rabbi's statement revealed the paternalistic basis for relationships between Reform and Orthodox, German and East European, or
"upper"- and "lower"-class Jews. In Detroit, the United Jewish Charities
served as the philanthropic vehicle that provided Jewish leaders with a
realistic Jewish identity. As it was founded by Dr. Franklin and staffed and
supported by members of his congregation, the UJC identified philanthropy
with Jewishness and apotheosized the philanthropic source of Jewish
identity.[32]

To many Jews in America, philanthropy consisted of charitable support
for poor Jews or perhaps assistance to Jews overseas. Charity seemed to
guarantee Jewish continuity even if all the secular and religious trappings
of Judaism were abandoned. Jewish values almost transformed themselves 25

through financial assistance. Referring to a paternal grandfather, one prominent Detroiter remembered that "it was his way to stay a Jew—he gave money to help other Jews and then went back to work. He didn't identify with religious Jews, he joined [a synagogue] but never attended. . . . But he taught [us] to give generously to other Jews—that's what being Jewish was all about." The United Jewish Charities provided a legitimized, necessary avenue to channel these impulses.

Numerous charities and philanthropic organizations already existed in Detroit in 1899. Rabbi Franklin and his cofounders of the fledgling institution aptly named it the United Jewish Charities because its pronounced purpose was to "unite various charitable groups; to widen the scope of social services; to weld Detroit Jewry into a more effective unit"; and to "form a joint association by which all charitable and educational work now being done by the various societies may be more expeditiously accomplished." Its charter noted clearly that those prominent founders entered into a voluntary association. In addition to Franklin, Martin Butzel, then-president of the Beth El Hebrew Relief Society, Sarah Berger, president of the Ladies Hebrew Sewing Circle (also of Beth El); Blanche H. Rothschild, president of the Beth El Self Help Society; and Bernard Ginsburg, president of the Jewish Relief Society, signed the charter.[33]

"From the day of its organization," wrote one Jewish Detroit chronicler, "the United Jewish Charities . . . carried on work of prevention and alleviation of poverty and disease; and of preparing young people to be good American citizens."[34] Under its rubric fell some twelve different charitable organizations, including the Fresh Air Society, which grew from the Fresh Air Camp and provided camp experiences for children; the Hebrew Free Loan Association, which granted interest-free loans to numerous Jews starting their own businesses; the Jewish House of Shelter for Jewish transients; the Jewish Home for the Aged; the Young Women's Hebrew Association; and others. Self-sufficiency for the poor—in particular the East European poor—continued to be the avowed and often-repeated aim of the UJC; a self-respect fund typified those aspirations. As a lending agency, the Self-Respect Fund offered interest-free loans to "enable people to be self-supporting and to save the self-respect of many men by preventing them from becoming recipients of charity."[35] During the depression years of 1914–15, the UJC established a plan to work out a permanent program for the unemployed. It pioneered such programs as a mothers' pension fund, tuberculosis treatments, evening English classes, and manual training classes for young Jews, all of which eventually became models for public policies of Detroit agencies.[36]

In 1899 Rabbi Franklin outlined the tasks at hand in a report to the Detroit Association of Charities: "(1) the work of direct relief, (2) the work of furnishing clothing to the poor, (3) the additional work of charity." Financial aid, as well as other types of "relief," went to the transient poor and to the resident poor "utterly unable to care for themselves."[37] There remained few doubts to whom these pronouncements referred.

American Jewish immigrants had confronted a culture more foreign to them than any they might have found in Europe. While many struggled with new institutions, established new organizations, or struck off in secular or social directions in order to fill their lives, most sought comfort in more traditional sources of Jewish life and identity. For both spiritual and social purposes, the synagogue has been a center of Jewish life through the ages. Ancient sources offer possible historical allusions to the existence of synagogues as far back as the First Commonwealth, while the prophet Ezekiel (ca. sixth century B.C.E. used the term "small sanctuary" (*mikdash me-at*) (Ezekiel 11:16). Each synagogue was an unique expression of the nature of its congregants, and synagogue officials were locally selected communal servants, not priestly intermediaries between Jews and their Creator or between Jews and the Torah. There were, in the early years of the history of the synagogue, no synagogue rabbis in the modern sense.[38]

Life without the synagogue would have been unimaginable to the Jews in ancient times. Through the ages, the synagogues served as centers for three primary activities of Jewish life: prayer, study at all levels, and meeting for social or civic purposes. Still, while Jews may have deeply respected a syngagogue and held its functions in the highest reverence, they were never so awed by its mystique or sanctity as to lose the sense of familiarity with it. Synagogues were merely physical plants, in no way similar to the mystical concept of the Roman Church. The holiness of the synagogue was in the people who used it for worship or communal functions.[39]

By 1920 there were three broad categories of Jewish places of worship in Detroit: the small Orthodox synagogues, the large, Conservative Shaarey Zedek, and the Reform Temple Beth El. A publication of the Michigan Synagogue Conference in 1940 listed fifty three synagogues founded in the Detroit area before 1928, of which about forty were then still active.[40]

Placed suddenly in the setting of an old-fashioned Orthodox synagogue, or of the Hasidic *shtibl,* a small, informal place of worship, a visitor from a church or even from Beth El might have thought he or she had entered another world. Indeed, in some ways, Orthodox synagogues had changed little from the immigrant era to the 1980s. Worshipers did not always sit quietly during services, and while the subject of a noisy discussion might well have been the scriptural reading of that day, it can also have been politics, business, or personal matters. Loud arguments about who would receive the various honors in the service were not uncommon. Synagogues tended to be small and, because of the interdiction against riding on the Sabbath, located within walking distance of their members. The mood of such synagogues was intense and individualistic. Prayers were said loudly, in Hebrew, by the entire congregation, each person at his own speed and in his own tenor of voice as most worshipers swayed back and forth (*ge-shoklt*). On Yom Kippur, congregants wept openly, and on Simchat Torah, the celebration of receiving the Torah on Mount Sinai, they danced, singing and carrying the scrolls. All men and married women covered their heads, and married men wore the *talis,* or prayer shawl. The service was not centered on a rabbi or cantor standing on a *bimah* (the front platform, which always held a snuff box). In fact, the man leading the prayers stood at a small lectern near the front of the room, usually at floor level. The Torah was read from a slightly elevated lectern near the center of the congregation.

Orthodox rabbis were traditionally scholars whose main service to their communities involved the study of Torah for its own sake. As learned men, they would be called upon to decide on questions as small as whether a blemish on a particular chicken rendered it nonkosher, or as large as those involving major political and communal issues of the day. They regularly rendered personal advice and marriage counseling. Traditional rabbis in Detroit in the 1920s continued (more or less) in that style. In particular, most remained devoted to the study of the Torah and usually wrote books of essays in the old style on the Bible, the Talmud, and Jewish Law.

A synagogue would also usually have among its members some men of learning, perhaps even ordained rabbis, alumni of European rabbinic schools who made their livings from other sorts of employment. On a Saturday or holiday such a man could present a talk, usually based on the Pentateuchal reading of the day, or teach a class. In some synagogues, there was ordinarily no sermon. Daily morning and evening services were also carried on, although they were not nearly as well attended as Sabbath or holiday services. Some of the larger and more established synagogues employed cantors, at times accompanied by choirs.

Women sat in their own section in the sanctuary and took no part in leading the services. They were separated from the men by a *mechitzah,* a partition usually about five feet high and topped by a curtain. A larger synagogue might have a balcony for the women. In many cases, especially in smaller synagogues, seats were not fixed to the floor but were provisional, possibly even bridge chairs or the like. Some synagogues used wooden benches which could become uncomfortably crowded on the High Holy Days. Since driving on the Sabbath was prohibited by traditional law, those who did ride usually parked a few blocks away.

There were no separate junior congregations or youth services in these sorts of synagogues. Children had the run of the premises until they reached the age when they could sit through services with their elders. Many Detroiters recalled fond memories of sitting, sometimes covered by a large *talis,* with grandfathers or fathers on those benches. Small children would play on the front steps, dash in to see a parent or elder sibling, and generally gallivant around the synagogue or the *succah* (booth) built for Succot (the tabernacles holiday). It was not unheard of for a child to climb onto the *succah*'s leafy roof and fall through.

Among the forty or so Orthodox synagogues was Congregation Beth David, the Russische Shul, founded in 1892 and later renamed B'nai David. In 1914, the congregation moved from a building on Adelaide Street to newly acquired premises on Winder Street which had been purchased from Shaarey Zedek. They remained on Winder only ten years. Changing neighborhoods led them to take up temporary residence at 2020–2080 Owen, and then, in 1928, the congregation relocated to a new building on Elmhurst and Fourteenth Street.[41] Ezekiel Aishishkin (1867–1935) was rabbi from 1904 until his retirement in 1933. Educated in Lithuanian *yeshivot* (rabbinical schools) in Kovno and Vilna, Rabbi Aishishkin was very much a man of the old school, pious and serious about his study of the Talmud. His published collections of rabbinic essays, *Devar Yehezkel* and *Maarei Yehezkel* were written in a *pilpul,* or debate-interpretive, style. Some of the essays had previously appeared in rabbinic journals such as *Hameasef.*[42]

In 1911 Congregation Beth Eliyahu was formed, with Aaron Holland as its first president. Services were held, in its earliest years, in rented quarters at Hastings and Winder Streets, then in the Hannah Schloss Building, and, finally, in a hall at Hastings and Brewer. In 1915, a residence on Eliot Street was purchased and used until 1919, when a permanent structure at Garfield and Beaubien was dedicated. By 1918 Beth Eliyahu, popularly known as the Hungarische Shul, was running into heavy financial problems. The four sons and three daughters of Moshe Gunsberg, who were prospering in the liquor business (still before Prohibition), pledged forty-five thousand dollars to save the synagogue and get a new building under way. Their brother, Joseph, still in Europe during World War I, had not been heard from and they feared for his safety; thus they donated the money in his honor, and renamed the synagogue B'nai Moshe after their father. In 1923 Rabbi Moses Fischer became the first permanent rabbi. Samuel Glantz was cantor from 1920 to 1922 and was succeeded by Anton Rosenfeld from 1922 to 1927.[43]

Beth Abraham, the Galicianer Shul, followed much the same pattern as the other synagogues. Founded in 1890 in a small building on Hastings, the synagogue moved several times. In 1915 Rabbi Reuben Horowitz was replaced by Rabbi Joseph Thumin, a highly accomplished Talmudist said to have been descended from forty generations of rabbis. He was active in publishing on Jewish law and in maintaining a scholarly correspondence with other rabbinic writers.[44]

B'nai Israel, founded in 1871, moved to its second permanent structure on Ferry near Hastings in 1913, when Rabbi Judah Levin became its first settled clergyman. Rabbi Levin came to Detroit in 1899, via New Haven and Rochester, from the great yeshivah of Volozhin, Lithuania. Reputedly among the most Orthodox of rabbis in America, he was at the same time quite worldly, counting many non-Orthodox Jews, including Rabbi Franklin, and non-Jews among his friends. Non-Orthodox Jews like Fred Butzel frequented his home on holidays and often sought advice from the learned scholar-rabbi. Widely respected, he often surprised people with his wide-ranging interests, on at least one occasion advising a distraught father not to interfere when his daughter became engaged to a Reform Jew.

A learned and published scholar of the Talmud, he early adopted the anti-Zionist position assumed by most Orthodox rabbis early in the twentieth century. But he soon changed his view and became one of the founders of Mizrachi, the religious Zionist movement, and included an essay praising Theodor Herzl in terms of a Talmudic parable in his two-volume collection of essays.

Rabbi Levin held several pulpits, presiding over different ones on alternate weeks, before his death in 1926. His spiritual home, however, was Beth Yehudah, although his family became influential stalwarts of Congregation Shaarey Zedek, where he had officiated from 1897 to 1904. He also became the chief rabbi of the United Hebrew Congregations of Detroit.[45]

The Mishkan Israel, founded in 1913 on Benton and St. Antoine, moved to 2625 Blaine Avenue in 1925, with Isaac Stollman as its rabbi. Beth Tefilo, served by Rabbi Joseph Eisenman, opened on 944 Napoleon in 1910 and moved to 1550 Taylor in the Twelfth Street area in 1924. Beth Yehudah, organized on Adelaide and Hastings in 1916, moved to 1600 Pingree and Twelfth Street in 1928 and was served by its rabbi, L. Landau. Shaarey Zion began in a rented store on Indiandale Avenue in 1923 and moved in 1925 to another rented store at 12407 Linwood. There was, as yet, no regular clergyman, but a Rabbi Mendel Zager came in occasionally. In 1926, Rabbi Joseph Ben-Zion Rabinowitz, scion of a noted Hasidic family, accepted a position as rabbi at the new Beth Shmuel on Twelfth Street and Blaine.[46]

By the mid-1920s, synagogues were forming in the Twelfth Street and Linwood areas as Jews moved beyond the Hastings Street neighborhood. Many synagogues faced severe financial difficulties as they were forced to relocate in order to follow their congregations. Congregations often realized the need to move after occupying new buildings in the old neighborhood for only a short time. This demographic pattern seemed to be a portent, among other fears, of a weakening of synagogue ties: the location of the institutions of prayer did not hinder moving. Other considerations besides religion, having to do with more material, social, and educational needs, seemed to take priority.[47] In the name of those needs, congregants moved; if the synagogue wanted to survive, it would have to follow them.

Small synagogues had sprouted in any area where Jews had settled in and near Detroit. The First Hebrew Congregation of Delray was organized in 1916, with Moses Fischer as rabbi. Temple Beth El of Wyandotte functioned in the early 1920s. Ahavas Achim, which served thirty-five families, was located on 9244 Delmar in the Westminster-Delmar area. Elias Horowitz and, later, Abraham Schechter were the spiritual leaders. Beth Israel, which was later called Shaar Hashomayim and widely referred to as the Muirland Shul, opened in 1925 on 15700 Muirland near Six Mile Road.[48] There was no regular rabbi, but several learned congregants helped in day-to-day matters. A typical Hasidic *shtibl* of the old style was the Stoliner Synagogue on Winder, associated with the Hasidic dynasty of the rabbis of Stolin, in White Russia. The Stoliner rabbi, Yaacov Perlow, had lived in New York by the 1920s and occasionally visited the synagogue in Detroit. When he died during one such visit years later, a controversy arose between his followers in Detroit and elsewhere about where he would be buried. When the matter finally was settled, he was buried in Detroit. His Hasidim continued to visit Detroit yearly on the anniversary of his death. The men of the Stoliner Shul were well known for the loudness of their praying and singing. Isaac Stollman was the rabbi.

Through the 1920s the Orthodox synagogues, at least within their own walls, seemed to maintain their traditional Eastern European style. Yet, as fewer young people attended services and as the Reform and Conservative movements strengthened, astute Orthodox rabbis became painfully aware of the impact of Americanization on traditional Judaism. The mean age of members of each congregation steadily, forebodingly, increased.

Through the centuries, Jews had linked the ideals of religious piety to study and education. Closely bound to religious institutions, educational institutions remained one of the primary concerns of religious and non-religious Jews. In Europe professional scholars and rabbis, as well as many laymen, devoted hours of every day to study. Jews who immigrated to Detroit, remembering old-world scholars and values, would often sit late into the night, poring over sacred books. Even those who expressed antagonism to religion or religious study clung to learning and education as ideals that seemed to be part of the air they breathed.

In Detroit, in keeping with the tradition of involving every man in study, classes were held in synagogues, often between afternoon and evening prayers. Yet Detroit began and continued as a working town, an industrial center that drew laborers from other parts of America and from Europe as well. Reinhold Niehbur, a Protestant theologian who held a pulpit in Detroit during the 1920s, wrote: "There are few cities in which wealth, suddenly acquired . . . is so little mellowed by social intelligence."[49] Niehbur observed an alarming lack of social concern among the affluent in Detroit. Concomitantly, he believed that lack accompanied a materialistic preoccupation that precluded educational pursuits. This became true, in some measure, of Detroit Jews as well. Detroit had its scholars and intellectuals, but it was no great bastion of Jewish learning. Those for whom intellectual pursuits were foremost tended to collect in cities like New York, with all   31 that that city offered to stimulate both religious and nonreligious think-ers.[50] People had come to Detroit to get jobs, not to study.

Yet Jewish education for children remained of the highest importance to most Detroit Jewish families. Several schools operated in synagogues in the afternoon or evening, after public-school classes were finished. Until 1919 the largest Jewish school was the Division Street Talmud Torah, headed by Hyman Buchhalter, a good Talmudist and respected European-born ed-ucator not unfamiliar with modern methods. Mr. Parness, a Hungarian Jew, taught at the school as well. An alumnus of Oxford and Cambridge, he loved to translate biblical texts into poetic English. Another teacher was Palestine-born Shoshana Pike. All the teachers were observant Jews.[51]

In 1919 Esser Rabinowitz and several other men joined together to im-prove and expand educational facilities for Jewish studies in Detroit. They interviewed Bernard Isaacs, then employed as a Hebrew schoolteacher in Indianapolis. Isaacs made a good impression at the interview and, after the committee checked his suitcase to see if it contained *talis* and *tefilin* (phy-lacteries), he was hired to head the new school.[52]

Born in Pilvishki, Lithuania, in 1882, Isaacs had studied in the yeshiva in Kovno. After leaving Europe, he devoted much time to the study of Hebrew literature. With the assistance of his brother and uncle, and at great risk, Isaacs had escaped serving in the Russian Army; he made his way to Germany and then to New York City, where he went on to earn a degree in engineering from Cooper Union. His first love, however, re-mained Jewish learning, and he soon began his teaching career.[53]

Isaacs organized classes in Detroit at the Wilkins Street Talmud Torah. A parade down Hastings Street with the Torah scrolls celebrated the school's opening. Soon, the Division Street school incorporated with Wilkins Street school. In 1920, the combined schools took the name United Hebrew Schools (UHS). The UHS expanded rapidly from 625 students in 1919 to 1,443 stu-dents in five buildings by 1930.[54]

A high school was soon added, and fifteen students graduated from the school's first class in 1929, after each had written a lengthy dissertation. The curriculum included courses in Bible, Hebrew literature, and Jewish history; advanced students studied Talmud. The method of "Ivrit b'Ivrit," whereby Hebrew texts were translated into spoken Hebrew, was introduced gradually over the first years. But Ivrit b'Ivrit was not a universally popular approach to teaching Hebrew; some critics thought its translation method to be tantamount to game-playing and not a solid pedagogical method. They preferred translation into Yiddish or English so that the youngsters would be sure to understand what they learned. Others felt that the method was too modern, untraditional, even antireligious.[55] Many parents thought it involved too much learning for boys who would leave Hebrew school at bar mitzvah anyway. Detroit was one of the first cities to employ the Ivrit b'Ivrit method in its Hebrew schools. Diligent UHS students could gain a

32

good knowledge of Hebrew and were able to study the great works of Hebrew literature in the original. Dr. Norval Slobin and his wife Judith, both members of the first high-school graduating class, corresponded in Hebrew during their courting days. Many students of these first classes continued to study Hebrew language and literature.

Bernard Isaacs was an accomplished writer as well as a school administrator, and he published numerous articles, mostly in Hebrew. Some of his books of short stories were translated into English from the Hebrew.[56] Isaacs wrote several plays on biblical themes that were performed entirely in Hebrew by the students. The plays demonstrated the value and success of the Ivrit b'Ivrit method of study. The first drama, the story of Esther, played to such large audiences in the school auditorium that it was decided that future plays would be presented in the twenty-five-hundred-seat Orchestra Hall, home of the Detroit Symphony Orchestra. *Saul and David,* the second play, had a musical score provided by Cantor Abraham Minkovsky, of Shaarey Zedek. Molline Weine, a twelve-year-old girl, starred in the role of David; Joe and Dora Buchhalter Ehrlich provided help with many of the practical aspects of the production. One of the singers in the production was Emma Lazaroff, later to be noted as an operatic soprano and an important supporter of Jewish causes, especially Labor Zionism. A standing-room-only crowd saw the performance and responded enthusiastically to the elaborate staging. At least one mishap occurred: a live horse, drawing a chariot, defecated on stage and, since the play could not be interrupted, Goliath (to the delight of the audience) eventually slipped into the mess. The following years saw successful productions of *Samson and Delilah* and *The Daughter of Jephthah.*

Many excellent teachers instructed students at the UHS: Aaron Markson (a devoted scholar of literature who translated *The Prince and the Pauper* into Hebrew and published several works under the pseudonym Tishbi), Joseph Chaggai, Abraham and Morris Lachover, Michael Michlin, Max Gordon, Solomon Kasdan, and Shepsel Stollman, among others. Students were expected at their UHS classes five days a week: after public shool for one and a half to two hours Monday through Thursday, and on Sunday mornings. Younger children attended the first shift of classes, older children the second. Many houses had children in both shifts and serving supper became a task of many hours for the mothers. The long hours of study provided sufficient time for serious learning, although for some children it was simply too long a day.

In many cases the support of the students' parents, for whom Jewish education was a matter of the highest priority, proved to be a great asset for the teachers. If a student came home from school complaining that a teacher had reprimanded him for misbehavior, he or she might receive twice the punishment from angered parents. Not only parents, but other adult relatives would *farherr* a child (test him on his work). The parents

33

might *shep nachas* (derive joy) from showing off a child's knowledge when friends or relatives came to visit. Such great personal interest and joy, which Jewish parents have traditionally felt toward the education of their children, was evident in the families of many UHS students.

The United Hebrew Schools provided both a social and educational milieu. Several graduates of the UHS formed the Kvutzah Ivrit (Hebrew club), which offered a chance to maintain an interest in Hebrew studies outside the school and also served as an important social facility.[57] More than one marriage came from the Kvutzah Ivrit. Among the hundreds of distinguished graduates of the UHS were Mandell (Bill) Berman, after whose mother, Esther, the main branch of the school was named; Hy Safran; Emma Lazaroff; and Max Weine, who became instrumental in forming the UHS Alumni Association.

Although some teachers at the UHS were observant, the school did not focus on religious indoctrination as a part of its curriculum. Many students came from homes where Jewish tradition was honored, and the school seemed to take for granted that most immigrant families kept kosher and respected the Sabbath—even if the father had to work on Saturday. There seemed to be no threat posed by the spread of assimilation; which increasingly was beginning to become part of the Americanization process for many Jews. Although not antireligious, the UHS in the 1920s was more "modern" than the traditional cheder school and most of its teachers were staunch Zionists. Orthodox rabbis, such as Judah Levin, Ezekiel Aishishkin, and Hyman Buchhalter, served on the UHS board alongside such community leaders as Fred Butzel. The rabbis would also visit the schools to test classes. Their support implied acceptance of the UHS, despite its modernist leanings. Rabbi Franklin also spoke in favor of the school.[58]

In 1923 new branches of the UHS began to open: first at Kirby and St. Antoine, then at Philadelphia and Byron in 1924, Parkside near Fenkell in 1926, Brush and Minnesota in the East Six Mile area in 1926, and at the D. W. Simons Branch on Holmur and Tuxedo in 1928. Several synagogue schools also cooperated with the UHS system.[59] Despite the broad community support, even new structures, like that at Philadelphia and Byron, could be overcrowded. One class had to meet in a shed where the young teacher decorated the room so the class would not seem so oppressive. Such conditions reflected the financial difficulties of the fledgling schools.

That financial outlook was much brightened in 1926, when the newly founded Jewish Welfare Federation, at the urging of lawyer Fred Butzel, undertook to help fund the UHS. Only twelve thousand dollars were available the first year, but the sum rose to seventy-five thousand dollars within a few years.[60] Still, money remained a problem. A survey conducted by Ben Rosen in 1930 stated that UHS teachers' salaries were low compared with other cities. Thirty-one teachers made only a total of $44,280; their wages ranged from $2.84 to $1.09 per hour.[61] Tuitions were not high, and poor immigrants often could not pay even the small sum. The Depression created further problems, and the Federation, with the best of intentions, could not always afford to maintain its level of support. Sometimes teachers' salaries could not be paid at all. Still, there were no strikes, classes continued on a regular schedule, and the school endured and survived the difficult years of the 1930s.

The Jewish Welfare Federation's support of this significant educational institution reflected the continued dedication of Jews to schooling for their children. With the Jewish population growing in 1919, the school had addressed the fears of parents, teachers, and community leaders that Jewish education had lapsed into chaos in Detroit. As immigration slowed and all but stopped, the schools would have to confront other problems regarding the education of Jewish children. The 1920s would offer new challenges—having to do with finances, instruction, enrollment, and attendance—and accentuate those problems associated with assimilation and the neglect of Jewish education that was increasingly evident in the more modern Jewish family. As trends in identification changed, so, too, did emphasis on learning and scholarship. Assimilation involved adapting to more secular, homogenized schooling that would jettison traditional Jewish instruction.

Like other cities, Detroit had already begun to produce identifiable Jewish lay leaders: David A. Brown, Albert and Julius Kahn, David W. Simons, Henry and Fred M. Butzel, Julian H. Krolik, Henry Wineman, James Ellman, Drs. Emil Amberg and Reuben Kahn, and Meyer Prentis were among those visibly identified as active participants in Detroit community life.[62] In 1916 D. W. Simons' son, Charles Simons, who had earlier served as a state senator, was appointed as a Republican presidential elector. And Bernard Ginsburg, former head of the Detroit Library Board, was honored by the Detroit Library Commissioners, who named a new branch library after him.[63] While Detroit Jews rarely counted them among their luminaries, scholars such as Rabbis Aishishkin and Thumin also had to be part of the list.[64] But if scholarly assiduousness and devotion had signified prominence among European Jews, new standards had already evolved for measuring accomplishment and achievement in America.

Having emigrated to New York from Lithuania in 1880, Max Jacob found the city too confining. A strapping, six-foot-two "giant," he moved to Detroit and continued the trade of his father as a bottle peddler. In 1885 Max founded his business in the midst of Detroit's German breweries (such as Stroh's), and the recycling of bottles proved lucrative. By 1900 he had begun traveling the globe, even returning to Lithuania to aid some of his family's emigration to America; and by 1910 he had entrusted the business to his sons and had begun to expand into other financial enterprises. M. Jacob and Sons, the premier bottle company among the ten in Detroit—all owned by Jews—employed Jewish émigrés from its inception. (The business grew to become the longest-lived Jewish-owned firm in Michigan in 1985).

Max Jacob, who was not a Jewish organization joiner, nevertheless began to support causes in the community and quietly developed his Zionism. A maverick in many ways, he personified those Jews of Eastern Europe who began to carve out successful business careers in Detroit while maintaining a surreptitious charitable interest in the community. His attitudes regarding public participation in Jewish causes contrasts with other Eastern European Jewish men who became visible contributors to, and actively involved in changing the nature of, the Jewish communities of Detroit.

During the first two decades of the twentieth century, the status of the Eastern European Jews in Detroit changed dramatically. The *Detroit News* on September 13, 1896, reported that were it not for the Jews from Eastern Europe "there would be hardly any need for Hebrew charitable organizations in the city . . . it is very rare that a German Israelite seeks relief from anybody."[65] Indicating a gradual transformation in American perceptions of Russian Jews, the *Detroit Free Press* in May 1903 featured an article entitled "Russian Jews in Detroit," which pointed out that while many Russian Jews "have not prospered so well in business . . . they are making their way upward." Listing specific leaders of the community, including D. W. Simons, William Saulson, Samuel Ginsburg, Dr. Noah Aronstam, and Max J. Rosenberg (the Michigan superintendent of the Industrial Removal Office), the article outlined why Russian Jews gravitated to cities, how they had flourished, what they had done to aid their "fellow countrymen" and what their "fine achievements" were. Concluding with mention of the four synagogues built by Russian Jews (among them, Shaarey Zedek), the Division Street Talmud Torah, the House of Shelter, and the Hebrew Free Loan Office, the article praised the Russian Jews of Detroit as "intelligent, sensible, hard-working people, sober and religious, of good moral character and determined to get ahead in the world. They are men with characteristics that make any nation strong."[66]

Nevertheless, in 1916 the *Jewish Chronicle* ("The Newspaper that Has Made Good") reported that "scores of Jewish children on the East side" of Detroit, with "its congestion and rush," were taken by some of the "young people of Temple Beth El" to Belle Isle. There, those unfortunate "east side kiddies got to breathe the fresh air that was in such scarce supply on Hastings Street." The *Chronicle* again praised the Beth El Fresh Air Camp, which "cannot be too highly commended for the splendid work it has done."[67] Those outings originated the Fresh Air Society, but its founding smacked of patriarchal noblesse oblige. As more *Ostjuden* became prominent in the Detroit Jewish and non-Jewish communities, the haughtiness that was identified with German Jews became more problematic. Professor Jacob

Marcus, a prominent historian of American Jewry, has suggested that German Jewish dominance in American Jewish institutions came to an end
around 1920, as Central and Eastern European Jewish cultures became
fused in Americanization. Yet organizations that had been founded by the
German Jews, the *Yahudim,* continued to exert a directive influence. That
meant that "the old differences and animosities are still in existence although they are no longer on the surface."[68]

There were, of course, continuing and deep-seated sources of unity among
the *Yahudim,* the *Ostjuden,* and the secularist factions. If philanthropy and
support for voluntary, benevolent charities was not the exclusive or primary vehicle of Jewish identity for the various factions of Jews in Detroit,
they nevertheless all shared a continuing identification as Jews that usually
focused on the concept of *tzedakah*—which they defined as "charity"—as
their major goal.[69] German Jews in Germany as well as in the United States
had expressed their commitment to Judaism through service to the Jewish
community. In the Reform tradition, the temple was often perceived as the
"house of charity." Indeed, as social worker Samuel Goldsmith maintained
in 1929, some of the concepts of Jewish social work in the United States
derived from the concept of *tzedakah* in the Bible, which Jews considered
"a human obligation." It was not only incumbent on the rich to follow the
biblical precepts of charity, but it was a fundamental issue of social justice—an issue that was, according to Goldsmith, a hallmark of Judaism.
The goal of *tzedakah* was the restoration to independence of a person in
need.[70]

As if to offer a communal example, the United Jewish Charities, with its
preponderance of founding members from Temple Beth El, selected D. W.
Simons of Congregation Shaarey Zedek as its first president in 1899. An
openly observant Jew, Simons brought with him a reputation of "understanding leadership." To him, the prime purpose of the new organization
was not charity, but "to make men and women of our dependent classes.
It is to build character." Simons's methods of character building lay in
education, and he stressed the new motto of the UJC: "Help the poor to
help themselves."[71] Regardless of the rhetoric—unquestionably sincere—
the symbolism of Simons and Franklin cooperating on behalf of the Jews
of Detroit was not lost on the communities, and the dedication to *tzedakah*
would continue as a prominent motivating factor among Jews in Detroit
that would be openly expressed and proudly heralded as part of the Detroit
Jewish heritage.

Jewish institutions, primarily devoted to charity work, continued to flourish
and came to serve as the center of Jewish communal life. For all their
idiosyncrasies and differences, Jews in Detroit cooperated in the work of
Jewish charities. Nevertheless, even as they grew less frequent and intense,
antagonisms between German Jews, the equivalent of New York's "up-
towners," and Eastern European Jews, the "downtowners," persisted.[72] One

scholar argued as late as 1938 that only the need to help suffering Jews overseas during World War I brought the two groups together.[73] Even World War I, however, would not completely unite the factions. In Detroit, the Joint Distribution Committee vied with the People's Relief in soliciting funds for the relief of suffering Jewish victims of the war. At a special meeting convened in February 1918, a reprsentative of the Hebrew Immigrant Aid Society (HIAS) asked the board of directors of the United Jewish Charities for cooperation and three thousand dollars to assist their relief efforts. The request was deferred at the regular March meeting, where the Detroit Community Union asked that all UJC contributions be funneled to the Union for a Patriotic Fund. This request, too, was deferred until another special meeting held a week later, when the Detroit Community Union's request was approved.[74]

At the same time, other Jewish societies and organizations contributed independently to the cause of refugee relief. The problem of the proliferation of organizations seemed to be endemic, and the decentralization of community efforts resulted in an inefficient duplication of efforts for helping Jews in need. These conditions had prompted the formation of the UJC, and some new action began to be discussed for the future. Those who initiated talks about "federated" charities, however, came from the leadership that this time crossed old-world national or regional boundaries and reflected a conglomerate of German and East European Jews.[75] What they shared was public prominence and economic status.

Next in importance to the UJC after philanthropic activities was the goal of Americanization. Indeed, with the United Jewish Charities' Reform Jewish leadership, the two issues of charity and Americanization were intimately linked: philanthropy was the means to achieve the goal and organized charity became the principal bridge to "make Jewish immigrants over in their [German Jewish assimilated leaders'] own image" as good Americans.[76] Making them "socially useful" citizens remained the avowed goal, so that the relative newcomers would become "better, wiser, and happier." There seemed to be an "unhappy expectation" that Yiddish-speaking Jews, the "refugees" from the uncouth regions of East Europe, would bring or come to no good "until their Orthodox notions [would] be changed." Just as it was for most Jewish organizations, from settlement houses (like the Hannah Schloss Center) to unions, the UJC's basic goal remained the modernization or transformation of the "benighted masses" into Americans, to help them prepare for participation in American and Jewish life.[77]

2

The Struggle over Americanization: Internal Conflict

As it took on the aspects of America's leading industrial urban center, with crowded residential districts, enormous factories, railroad terminals, and suburbs for a new middle class, Detroit retained its ethnic diversity and neighborhood separatism along with the old-world antagonisms these structures supported.[78] Those antagonisms and ethnicity created problems for the Jews, and they created problems for the new American leaders, such as the industrial magnate Henry Ford. His solution to the inefficiency caused by this variegated labor force was based on the concept of unification. Much of Detroit's Jewish leadership promoted an intensified pursuit of Americanization, and Detroit's non-Jewish leaders, like Henry Ford, complemented the assimilationist trend by urging ethnic Americanization programs. The Americanization Committee, formed in 1915 and dominated by Detroit industrialists, gladly accepted the models represented by Rabbi Leo Franklin and his congregants: proud in their Jewish worship, but all-American, English-speaking, educated, athletic, working paragons of American life.[79] Here there seemed to be a marriage of interests, a conjunction that produced pragmatic friendships between such apparent opposites as Rabbi Franklin and his neighbor, Henry Ford.

In 1920, under the auspices of the Americanization Committee of Detroit, mothers' classes were instituted in English and over ten thousand handbills were distributed in Italian, Polish, Hungarian, and Yiddish. That committee sought the collaboration of the UJC to encourage all Jewish immigrants to learn and to use English so that they could become naturalized. In 1920 it seemed to the business and industrial leaders of Detroit that a solid organization like the UJC might be able to weed out the Russian Jewish communists, of whose existence those leaders were certain.[80] With growing paranoia, on the brink of the Red Scare, Detroit and American leaders feared that Americanization might otherwise serve as a camouflage for insidious enemies.[81] Russian Jews, for their part, had already begun to eschew assistance which they perceived as interference from Detroit Jewish organizations. A plethora of East European immigrant organizations sprouted spontaneously, with foreign-sounding names like the Radomer Aid Society, and the various *landsmanshaftn,* associations originally founded by people (landsman) from particular cities, towns; or regions. Such groups worried and antagonized the witch-hunters, embarrassing the established Jews of Detroit—of both German and East European origin.[82]

Whether sponsored by Jewish or non-Jewish institutions, programs in linguistic and vocational education for immigrants seemed to many to have a condescending, missionizing attitude toward the Americanization of newly arrived Jews. Public relief policies, which entailed what some found to be a humiliating process of application for aid, indiciated a lack of understanding and sympathy among the leadership of the UJC, a lack the *Survey* of 1923 claimed was especially acute in regard to the "Orthodox Jewish community" and its culture.[83] In attempts to apply the latest "scientific" and American professional techniques to charitable relief, the UJC, under the direction of its superintendent, Miss Blanche Hart, adopted a series of procedures to determine how and to whom money would be dispensed.[84] To those who came from communities where such procedures were unheard or even unthought of, investigations of those applying for aid, bureaucratic account-keeping, and the processes of questioning struck many applicants as cold, unfeeling, and distinctly un-Jewish. Benevolent aid in European shtetls or larger communities had derived from primary group relationships: if support did not come from actual kin, then kinship-based structures were the rule. In such communities, where communalism permeated every aspect of life, questions about payment, need, reliability, and goodwill simply were inappropriate. Probing investigations, even those that pursued what might be deemed justifiable suspicions in cases where need was less apparent or honestly questionable, violated the accepted etiquette. So-called voluntary organizations, *chevras,* were the rule in most of the towns from which the immigrants came, and dispensing charity had rated high among their tasks in Europe.[85]

An odd mixture of what one observer called "gratitude and resentment" greeted assistance from the UJC. Insensitivity on the part of UJC staff and board was noted in the 1923 *Survey*, and many recipients of aid commented on unsympathetic treatment. The very word "charity" became an emblem for humiliation. Perhaps the root cause, if one existed, lay with the organization's failure to understand not only the financial needs of East European Jews, but their social, cultural, spiritual, and psychological needs as well. Antagonism over public relief policies, therefore, surfaced regularly and the board of directors served as a symbol of the problem: of the forty-two directors, thirty-three were from Temple Beth El, eight from Shaarey Zedek and only one from a small Orthodox congregation.[86] Twenty-two members of the board were German Jews, yet the anticipated *Yahudim-Ostjuden* antagonism receded slowly. "Uptown" Jews no longer were synonymous with German Jews as more and more East European immigrants or children of those immigrants had become successfully integrated into influential circles of Detroit Jewish life.

Although the number of applications for assistance submitted to the UJC dramatically increased from 1900 to 1923,[87] that figure reflected a correspondingly dramatic increase in population. In fact, there were proportionally far fewer applications and less than 5 percent of East European immigrants requested aid from the UJC.[88] There were other means through which impoverished or beleagured newcomers could receive help, not the least of these being the numerous small benevolent societies that attracted them. Historian Henry Feingold has even suggested that organized Jewish charities in America found themselves virtually boycotted by their potential constituents by the 1920s.[89]

In 1902, at a conference of Jewish charities that was, significantly, held in Detroit, delegates raised the subject of facilitating the relocation of immigrants who wished to leave overcrowded New York City. Thus began the Detroit Jews' involvement in the work of the Industrial Removal Office (IRO) of New York, which would prove to be of determinative importance in the nature and size of Detroit's Jewish population. In 1903 Detroit's United Jewish Charities established the Detroit office of the Industrial Removal Office, which played a critical role in redistributing and absorbing East European immigrants from New York and other cities on the eastern seaboard. With the cooperation of local factories such as Packard, Cadillac, and Chalmers and Lozier automobile plants, the IRO secured employment for thousands of applicants.[90]

The IRO procedure, however, typified "uptown" methods and attitudes in its treatment of East European Jews and echoed the UJC approach toward its applicants: ways and means were not always suitably matched, and while the records of the agencies could demonstrate success, the "successful" candidates were not always pleased.   41

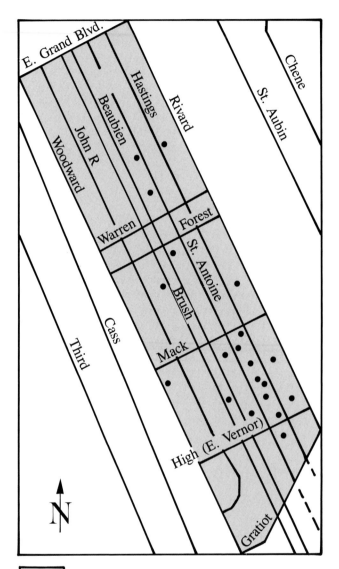

E. Grand Blvd.

Chene

St. Aubin

Hastings

Beaubien

John R

Woodward

Rivard

Warren

Forest

St. Antoine

Brush

Cass

Third

Mack

High (E. Vernor)

N

Gratiot

⬜ Highest Jewish Density

• Synagogue

The Hastings Area in 1920

Downtown Detroit, ca. 1910–1919. (From the collections of Henry Ford Museum and Greenfield Village.)

Hastings Street, between Kirby and Fredericks, Detroit, 1922. (Courtesy of the collections of Manning Brothers, Photographers.)

First Hungarian Hebrew Congregation, Garfield and Beaubien, Detroit, predecessor of Congregation B'nai Moshe, ca. 1919. (Courtesy of the collection of Manning Brothers, Photographers.)

Groundbreaking ceremony for Temple Beth El new sanctuary designed by Albert Kahn, Woodward and Gladstone, Detroit, 1921. (Courtesy of the Rabbi Leo M. Franklin Archives of Temple Beth El.)

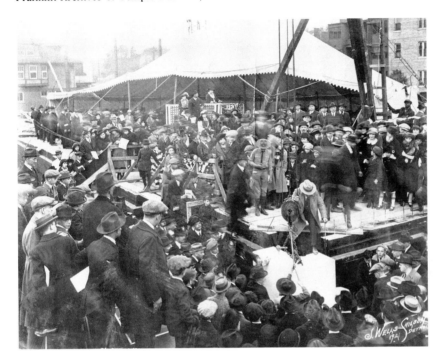

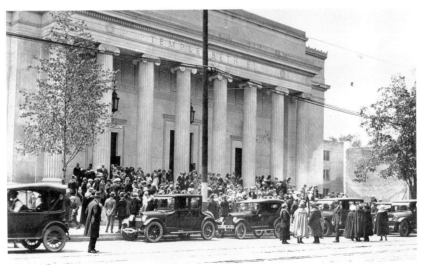

After services, in front of Temple Beth El, ca. 1922. (Courtesy of the Rabbi Leo M. Franklin Archives of Temple Beth El.)

Poster for Hastings Street, Detroit, Merchants Association War Bond Rally, ca. 1918–1920. (Courtesy of the Rabbi Leo M. Franklin Archives of Temple Beth El.)

Registering for the Jewish Legion, ca. 1917–1918: Abe Weintrobe. (Courtesy of Chana Michlin.)

First national meeting of American Orthodox Rabbis convened by Rabbi Judah Levin, assembling on steps of Congregation Shaarey Zedek, Brush and Willis, Detroit, ca. 1920. *Bottom row, eighth from left:* Rabbi Meyer Berlin, president of American Mizrachi; *tenth:* Rabbi Aaron Ashinsky; *eleventh:* Rabbi Judah Leib Levin; *twelfth:* Rabbi Abraham M. Hershman; *fourteenth:* Rabbi Ezekiel Aishiskin. *Third row, far right:* Abba Keidan. *Fourth row, third from right:* Max Jacob. (Courtesy of the Archives of Congregation Shaarey Zedek.)

Poster of the Jewish Welfare Board,
1918. (Courtesy of the collection of
the Jewish Community Center.)

Capt. Julius Berman of the Michigan National Guard with Gen. "Black Jack"
Pershing, ca. 1917. (Courtesy of the Archives of Congregation Shaarey
Zedek.)

Right: Capt. Isadore Levin with brother Samuel Levin at Fort Sheridan, ca. 1917. (Courtesy of the family of Samuel M. Levin.)

Far right: Nathan Bielfield, founder of the Jewish House of Shelter, 1905. (Courtesy of Jerry Bielfield.)

Call for lunch at the Venice Beach Camp of the Fresh Air Society, 1917. (Courtesy of the collection of the Fresh Air Society.)

Children in circle at camp of Fresh Air Society, 1919. (Courtesy of the collection of the Fresh Air Society.)

The Kinx Club of the Hannah Schloss Building, 1921. (Courtesy of the collection of the Hannah Schloss Old Timers.)

The band of the Hannah Schloss building, 1925. Professor Israel Glass, of the Grinnell Brothers Music House, conducting. (Courtesy of Rose Greenberg.)

Hannah Schloss girls basketball team, ca. 1914. (Courtesy of the Jewish Federation Apartments.)

United Hebrew Schools graduating class, 1924. (Courtesy of the Archives of Congregation Shaarey Zedek.)

Prominent Detroit Jews portrayed in the Jewish Community Blue Book, 1923. (Courtesy of the Rabbi Leo M. Franklin Archives of Temple Beth El.)

Ruda's Dry Goods store, Hastings Street, Detroit, 1914. *Behind counter:* Harry Ruda, his wife Annie, and baby Julius. Customer is Moe Raskin. (Courtesy of Jonathan D. Hyams.)

Vans of the Peoples Outfitting Co., owned by Henry Wineman. (Courtesy of the Burton Historical Collection of the Detroit Public Library.)

The Mercury Paint Co., Hastings Street, Detroit, 1922. *From left:* Max Milgrom, ———, Sam Kersh, Samuel Herman, Jack Berent. (Courtesy of the Mercury Paint Co.)

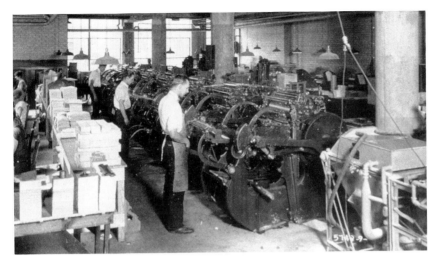

The Aronsson Printing Co., 1354 W. Lafayette, Detroit, 1927. (Courtesy of the Burton Historical Collection of the Detroit Public Library.)

The Arethusa Hotel and Bath House in Mount Clemens, ca. 1925, owned by Morris and Jacob Feldman, later by Arthur and Jerome Feldman. (Courtesy of the Local History Photo Archives of the Mount Clemens Public Library.)

Beth Tephilath Moses Synagogue, South Avenue, Mount Clemens. (Courtesy of the Local History Photo Archives of the Mount Clemens Public Library.)

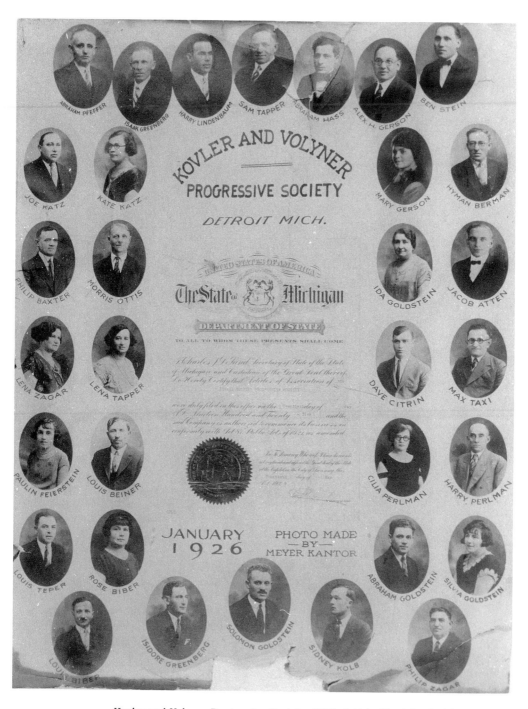

Kovler and Volyner Progressive Society, 1926. Article 11 of the Articles of Association reads: "Relief of distressed members / Visit the sick / Bury the dead / Five dollars per week sick benefit / Funeral benefit of fifty dollars." (Courtesy of Mildred Grossman.)

The Jewish Progessive Literary and Dramatic Club, 1915. *Top row, from left:*
Markov, ———, Friedland, ———, ———, Heyden, Philip Gilbert, ———,
Sam Revzin. *Second row, from left:* Ida (Jaffe) Seidler, ———, Azolin, Yehoash,
Eli Elconin, Mrs. Simon. *Third row, on floor from left:* Davis, ———, Sam
Victor, Joseph Chaggai (Hebrew teacher), ———, Wierer. (Courtesy of the
Jewish Historical Society of Michigan.)

Members of the Poale-Zion Organization
with their leader from Palestine, Jacob
Zarubevel, 1918. *Standing, from left:* M.
Ginsburg, Sadie Robinson, Dr. Raphael
Bender, Rivka Haggai, Joseph London.
Second row, from left: Dr. Meyer Glick,
Chana Weintrobe (Mrs. Michael Michlin),
Jacob Zarubavel. *First row, from left:* Joseph
Chaggai, David Zunenshine, Fannie Lifshitz
(Mrs. Theodore Levin). (Courtesy of the
Jewish Historical Society of Michigan.)

Ossip Gebrilowitsch,
second conductor of
the Detroit Symphony
Orchestra, 1918–1936.
(Courtesy of the
Archives of the Detroit
Symphony Orchestra.)

Detroiter Michael Goodman, *lower left,*
performing with the Littman's Yiddish
Theater Players, ca. 1933–1934. (Courtesy of
the collection of Michael Goodman.)

Rosters of the Jewish organizational leaders published in the Jewish Community Blue Book, 1923. (Courtesy of the Rabbi Leo M. Franklin Archives of Temple Beth El.)

David A. Brown, civic and philanthropic leader, in the 1920s. (Courtesy of Agnes Scott.)

Rosters of the leadership of the United Jewish Charities and Keren Hayesod published in the Jewish Community Blue Book, 1923. (Courtesy of the Rabbi Leo M. Franklin Archives of Temple Beth El.)

YOUNG WOMAN'S HEBREW ASSOCIATION OF THE JEWISH WOMAN'S CLUB

89 Rowena Street

MRS. SADIE C. JACOBS, Social Director
GOVERNING BOARD
MRS. OSCAR ROBINSON, Chairman

MRS. SAMUEL GLOGOWER	MRS. ISAAC GOLDBERG
MISS MILDRED SIMONS	MISS BLANCHE HART
MISS MIRIAM GOLDMAN	MRS. ADOLPH SLOMAN
MISS S. ELMINSKY	MRS. J. VICTOR ROEMER
MISS SADIE KEIDAN	MRS. HENRY WINEMAN
MRS. JOSEPH EHRLICH	MRS. JOEPH WELT
MRS. MAX MAY	MRS. MARCUS FREUD

MRS. FLORA GOODMAN

THE DETROIT ZIONIST DISTRICT

OFFICERS
JOSEPH H. EHRLICH, Chairman
A. J. KOFFMAN, Vice-Chairman
M. H. ZACKHEIM, Treasurer
WM. A. LONDON, Financial Secretary
J. MILLER, Corresponding Secretary
EXECUTIVE COMMITTEE

PHILIP SLOMOVITZ	HIMON GOLDBERG
HENRY MYERS	J. GREENBERG
DR. PHILIP BROUDO	JOS. WETSMAN
ISRAEL DAVIDSON	AARON PREGERSON
JACOB CHERKOSE	A. SRERE
ISRAEL ZILBER	LOUIS STOLL

YOUNG JUDAEA LEADERS' COUNCIL

OFFICERS
MISS ROSA COPINSKY, President
ISRAEL ZILBER, Vice-President
MARY FRIEDENBERG, Corresponding Secretary
BARNEY JAROSLOW, Recording Secretary
FAY CASHDAN, Treasurer
BOARD

MISS MARY CAPLAN	SOLOMON LEVIN
LOTTIE GANTZEVITZ	BERTHA SLOMOVITZ
SAMUEL HEYMAN	BLUMA SLOMOVITZ
DOROTHY LABRET	PHILIP SLOMOVITZ
LENA MENDELSOHN	SAMUEL ZELLMAN

AFFILIATED CLUBS
Buds of Judaea, Defenders of the White and Blue, Forget-Me-Nots of Zion, B'nos Yisroel, B'nos Rachel, Knights of Judaea, Tikvas Zion, Tiffereth Zion, Maccabees of Judaea, Sons of White and Blue, Bar Kochba Judaeans, Roses of Zion, Hadar Zion, Mogen Dovid Club, Pirchai Zion, Chaluzoth.

UNITED JEWISH CHARITIES

OFFICERS
WILLIAM FRIEDMAN, President
HENRY WINEMAN, Vice-President
WALTER M. FUCHS, Vice-President
MILTON M. ALEXANDER, Vice-President
FRED M. BUTZEL, Vice-President
DAVID W. SIMONS, Treasurer
MISS BLANCHE J. HART, Executive Secretary
DIRECTORS

JEROME ACKERMAN	ROBERT LOEWENBERG
RABBI HENRY J. BERKOWITZ	GERALD MAY
DR. PHILIP H. BROUDO	MRS. MAX MAY
HARRY Z. BROWN	JACOB NATHAN
JOSEPH S. BURAK	J. B. NIEMAN
JOSEPH H. EHRLICH	MRS. WALLACE ROSENHEIM
ADOLPH FINSTERWALD	WALLACE ROSENHEIM
RABBI LEO M. FRANKLIN	DR. HARRY SALZSTEIN
BERNARD GINSBURG	ALBERT SAMTER
MRS. SAMUEL GLOGOWER	MRS. A. SCHLESINGER
MISS EDITH HEAVENRICH	ALBERT SCHLOSS
SAMUEL HEAVENRICH	JOSEPH L. SELLING
RABBI A. M. HERSHMAN	ABE SHIFFMAN
MRS. WOLF KAPLAN	MILRED STERN
JUDGE HARRY B. KEIDAN	HARRY L. WINSTON
JULIAN H. KROLIK	DR. B. D. WELLING
J. L. LEVINE	MELVILLE S. WELT
RABBI J. L. LEVINE	MRS. HENRY WINEMAN

KEREN HAYESOD

OFFICERS
A. SRERE, Chairman
J. H. EHRLICH, First Vice-Chairman
J. LEVIN, Second Vice-Chairman
LOUIS DANN, Treasurer
J. MILLER, Secretary
EXECUTIVE BOARD

RABBI A. M. HERSHMAN	J. B. LASKY
RABBI J. L. LEVIN	E. LIGHTSTONE
RABBI E. AISHISHKIN	WM. A. LONDON
RABBI J. EISEMAN	A. J. KOFFMAN
RABBI R. HURWITZ	JUDGE H. B. KEIDAN
RABBI J. THUMIN	M. MARGOLIS
RABBI H. Z. GORDON	HENRY MEYERS
M. BLUMBERG	ROBERT MARWIL
JULIUS BRAUN	B. H. MAZURE
DR. P. M. BERNSTEIN	I. AUGUST
LOUIS BRAVER	A. PREGERSON
JOSEPH CHERKOSE	LOUIS ROBINSON
IRA COHEN	I. ROSENTHAL
ISRAEL DAVIDSON	A. SCHURAYTZ
ISRAEL ESSER	MAURICE STEINGOLD
J. FRIEDBERG	SAMUEL SCHWARTZ
H. GOLDMAN	PHILIP SLOMOVITZ
H. M. GREENBERG	M. WEISWASSER
S. GOLDSTICK	J. WARREN
M. JACOB	I. ZILBER
S. HOROWITZ	RUDOLPH ZUIEBACH
J. M. LISS	M. H. ZACKHEIM

M. KAUFMAN

Philadelphia-Byron, Detroit, branch of the United Hebrew Schools, 1925. (Courtesy of the collection of the United Hebrew Schools.)

Purim party of Mr. A. Panush's pupils at the Philadelphia-Byron branch of the United Hebrew Schools, 1933. (Courtesy of Harry Weberman.)

JULIUS DEUTELBAUM
President, 1926.

MAX EDWARDS
Vice-President, 1926.

ELIAS GOLDBERG
Secretary, 1926.

ALFRED ROSS
Past-President, 1925.

Leaders of the Pisgah Lodge, International Order of B'nai B'nith, 1925.
(Courtesy of the Midrasha—College of Jewish Studies.)

Each applicant was "examined" and "his fitness was passed upon from many angles." Only healthy men with particular skills were acceptable. If and when the individual was found to be "fit for removal," the IRO began to make arrangements to match the man with an appropriate job. Nevertheless, educated men drew manual labor positions, bank clerks became blacksmiths; these conditions prompted one deportee to write in the "Bintel Brief," the letters to the editor of the Yiddish *Daily Forward*, that "no matter how bad things were in Russia, in Detroit it is worse."[91]

As an employment bureau, the Detroit Industrial Removal Office was not an unqualified success. It managed, however, to find living quarters for its charges, and the Russian Jewish population swelled accordingly. By 1914 an estimated four thousand workers had been sent to Detroit, accounting for approximately twelve thousand Jewish newcomers. In each case, the major concerns of Detroit's Jewish leadership dealt with fears that the new immigrants would place new burdens on the Jewish (or worse, the city's) charities.[92]

Between 1914 and 1920, Detroit's East Side, with its "congestion and rush," did not resemble the "teeming tenements" of the Lower East Side of New York.[93] It was ethnically provincial enough, however, to confirm the German Jewish beliefs, and the perceptions of established East European Jews, that the shtetl, the backward rural village, had been transplanted to Detroit, and they feared that the stereotypic shtetl Jew would come with it. But because Detroit followed midwestern housing patterns, tenements were not the rule, and the congestion, real as it was, could not compare to the pushcart-laden streets of New York. While it was not the image of New York, the Hastings Street area was obviously Jewish in its sights, smells, and sounds: the small shops and bakeries, like Rosen's Bakery, where bread was "baked three times a day" and which featured "hot rolls, poppyseed horns and bagel," and the tiny delicatessens and fish stores that characterized the neighborhood.[94] Twelve synagogues were located within a half-mile radius, and the Yiddish Circle Theatre opened its doors in 1913 to visiting acting companies from New York.[95] As for the houses and apartments, they, too, were easily identifiable as Jewish-occupied. One former resident of the old neighborhood joked that "the non-Jews grew flowers, the Jews grew dirt in front of their houses." Tidy gardens with picket fences and manicured lawns seemed to be a low priority on the Jewish agenda around Hastings Street.

One- and two-family dwellings were common in Detroit. Russian Jewish émigrés, however, also lived in multiple-dwelling homes that resembled tenements. They were concentrated in the Hastings Street area, next to Stroh's on Gratiot, and bounded by St. Antoine, High, and Montcalm Streets.[96] In September 1896, the *Detroit Sunday News Tribune* had described the "Jewish Quarter . . . Detroit's ghetto" as formed by Monroe,

Watson, Brush, and Orleans Streets, which all focused on the commercial district of Hastings Street.[97] Urban neighborhood communities were cemented by the high rents that were imposed in Detroit as a result of the depressions of 1907 and 1910. Jewish institutions had already begun to establish roots in and around that neighborhood: in 1902 Henry Krolik had donated four thousand dollars toward the purchase of a site on High Street, just west of Hastings, for a building to house the United Jewish Charities. In 1903, clothing manufacturer Seligman Schloss donated $5,800 to the construction of a building in memory of his wife Hannah, who had been active in East Side Jewish charities. With the help of Bernard Ginsburg's gift of ten thousand dollars in 1910, the Hannah Schloss Building became the Jewish Institute.[98] By 1911, however, some Jews had already moved north and west of the "port of entry" of the east side around Hastings Street. Those groups and organizations with facilities for social activities recognized the demographic patterns and at least two, the Jewish Institute and the Labor Lyceum of the Workmen's Circle, opened branches in the Oakland district while maintaining their central headquarters in the Hastings Street area. Migration northward began gradually. No mass exodus swept the Jewish community from Hastings Street to the Oakland district, and the Lurie *Survey* of 1923 already noted the demographic patterns of Jewish migration to the Michigan Avenue, Twenty-ninth Street, or Twelfth Street areas.[99]

For all the external and internal pressures, not all Jewish immigrants opened their arms to Americanization. Yiddish culture continued to thrive and included such groups as the Progressive Literary Dramatic Club, which was formed by young East European immigrants who longed for more of their traditional culture. Meeting in Schreiber's Hall on Hastings Street (home of the Circle Theatre), members delivered book reviews, read short stories, or gave lectures to the general public as well as the rest of the membership. The club even arranged to bring famous Yiddish writers to Detroit, including Sholem Aleichem, who addressed a standing-room-only house at the Detroit Opera Theatre. On that May evening in 1915, the members of the Progressive Literary Dramatic Club performed Sholem Aleichem's play *The Agenten* (The Insurance Agents) and the audience, filled with representatives of all sorts of Jewish organizations, thrilled to the great humorist's reading of two of his short stories. He received five hundred dollars and was escorted back to the Elkins Hotel in Mt. Clemens.[100]

Sholem Aleichem was not the only Yiddish literary celebrity brought to Detroit by the short-lived Progressive Club: Peretz Hirshbein, Yehoash, H. Rosenblat, Abraham Reisen, and others also visited Yiddish-speaking packed houses. Indeed, on the same evening as the famous Sholem Aleichem performance, the Yiddish star Jacob Adler performed in another Detroit theater—also to a full house.[101] Yiddish theater groups, whose repertoire ranged from serious drama to burlesque, flowed into Detroit even before 1900. Performances took place at the Lyceum (which became the New Detroit Opera House), Orchestra Hall, and the Circle Theater. By 1924, the focus of Yiddish theater had become the Littman company, which was made up of local artists in residence at the Circle. What became known as Littman's People's Theatre preserved Yiddish drama and theater, and from 1924 to 1937 more than two thousand performances of over six hundred productions played to full houses. Other companies continued their tours of Detroit and the Circle Theatre even sold tickets on their behalf.[102] Yet, even Littman's became controversial, leading some to claim that it was demeaning Yiddish art by pandering to burlesque. What to some was the heart of *Yiddishkeit* in Detroit, to others was "a lot of Coca-Cola bottles on the floor, bad acting and always a happy ending." Amateur rival groups competed for the "serious" audience and Littman's stirred ambivalent reactions.

When Faygel Hoffman arrived in Detroit in 1922, she was quickly dubbed Frances Hoffman by her Uncle Joe. A wide-eyed young girl, a "greenhorn," she took English lessons in a store on Westminster and soon was invited by a young man to attend a picnic given by his "club," Dos Greene Winkel.[103] One of several Yiddish cultural groups composed of young immigrants, the club met weekly for cultural and social purposes. In each of its programs "everybody did something"—reciting, singing, reading poetry: there was a choral section, a literature and drama group, and lectures on modern Yiddish literature. Frances Hoffman was impressed by the education in letters of the members of Dos Greene Winkel and, despite the Russian and Yiddish readings she heard that day, she vowed to begin her schooling in English.

According to the 1923 Survey, Dos Greene Winkel was "almost completely 'unamericanized.' " There were no athletic activities, for example, or dancing, although the club did offer beginning English lectures.[104] Dos Greene Winkel, like numerous other cultural and social groups, recognized and feared the impending disintegration of Yiddish culture and acted to prevent it. Beyond the "culturists," many immigrants rejected or hid from any signs of integration into American culture. Indeed, many actively and consciously rejected assimilation, refusing to abandon old-world traditions, language, and values. They sought instead to recreate the ambiance of the shtetl or the village from which they had come by creating immigrant benevolent societies, the *landsmanshaftn*. Through their social and benevolent activities, these organizations "were a crucial means of supplying the basic psychic and cultural stability that was largely absent from the American experience."[105]

Unlike other voluntary organizations established by unions or the established Jewish community, membership in a *landsmanshaft* was grounded in geographical origins: all the members of the Pinsker Society theoretically were from Pinsk, all those in the Radomer Society were from Radom, and so on. (There were numerous exceptions to this geographic rule: "My parents' landlord was from Pinsk. He took them to the meetings and now they were from Pinsk, too.") At their meetings they spoke Yiddish almost exclusively as they discussed problems of life in America, reports from back home in Poland, political issues, economic worries, or the needs of the membership in terms of cemetery plots or financial support. Members of these organizations experienced virtually no dilemmas over the cultural ambiguity that plagued many American Jews. To most of them, Jewish identity had not been transformed, only their geographical locations had changed. Questions about means of survival, and the definity of their identity as Jews, infused the usually unspoken subtext of their agendas.

Frances Hoffman married Charles Driker in the Hannah Schloss Building on Hastings and High Streets. Upstairs from the wedding, the famous Yiddish poet Peretz Hirshbein struggled to be heard above the music. Members of the Odessa Progressive Society, one of the many *landsmanshaftn* in Detroit, attended the wedding. Its members called each other sisters and brothers and one of its main functions was "sociability." Like other *landsmanshaftn*, the Odessa Progressive Society had a Free Loan Association, insurance plans, medical services, and other benevolent activities to help its *landsleit*, transplanted members from the same area in Europe. An annual picnic on Belle Isle highlighted the year with much frivolity, eating and drinking. Mrs. Driker remembered the details of such events, including the unveiling held for one of the society's deceased members; the ceremony was followed by an invitation from another member for the group to join him for lunch at his home in Mt. Clemens, which in turn was followed by Frances Shayne's invitation for coffee. "They made a day out of it!"

An estimated forty *landsmanshaftn* existed in Detroit by the 1920s.[106] Some, like the United Brisker Relief Society, were branches of a network that stretched across the country. Others were tiny collections of often frightened individuals seeking to survive in close, secure, and unself-conscious relationships. In a frightening new world, "the landsmanshaftn . . . functioned as the Old World community *within* the New World."[107] One could count on "family," on *landsleit*. Emigration radically affected many Jews whose world in Europe had consisted of the conservative, traditional shtetl. *Unterstitzung*, or benevolent aid societies, allowed them to continue to speak their *mama loshen*, or mother tongue, to *talk* to others who were facing the same dilemmas and disillusionment that came with confronting the reality of American culture. Although the group might have included Orthodox Jews, their source of unity was not religion. Indeed, many of the members experienced disillusionment with their recent pasts and with the present: pogroms, suffering, loss, loneliness, and disappointment in the reality of life in the United States all tended to disabuse them of belief in God. Thus, the basis of most *landsmanshaftn* tended to be, if not antireligious, at least areligious.[108]

Landsmanshaftn meetings were conducted by means of a peculiar, club-specific interpretation of parliamentary procedures. Lively and heated debates took place; even committee reports—such as the report of the Odessa Progressive Society picnic—were controversial. Almost every meeting included reports about or from their home towns in Europe, followed by committee reports, perhaps fundraising activities for a new synagogue or school, and proposals for future activities—often the most hotly contested agenda item. Like others, the Odessa Progressive Society would engage in "surprise housewarmings," banquets, and cultural activities. At such events as the annual picnic, in order to make money for the organization, the food was donated. People like Mr. Weineman and Mr. Brusk gave food from their businesses (smoked fish, fruits, and vegetables), and the women volunteered to bake and cook.

Even within Yiddishist circles, however, there would emerge differences that resurfaced from the divisions that existed in Poland and Russia; differences derived from town versus country, secularism versus religion, socialism versus political neutrality, action versus passivity, and worker versus manager.[109] Debates might become near-violent at some *landsmanshaft* meetings, and, as one member recalled, other secular groups formed—theater or drama groups like the Dramatische Gesellschaft and the Dramstudio of the "Yikuf," as well as learning circles, or *lehnenkreise*. Foremost among secular organizations was the Workmen's Circle (*Arbeter Ring*), which grew to be the largest. While its national and local orientation stressed leftist politcs and staunch support of labor unions, many of its members joined for the same reasons they had joined the *landsmanshaftn*.[110]

Although they tended to be grouped together, an indefinite division evolved among the secular organizations that sometimes crystalized over cultural versus political issues. To some of the members of the *Dramstudio*, for example, most of the *landsmanshaftn* were *prost* or crass, engaging in petty arguments, card-playing, or noneducational pastimes. One former actress recalled that "We [in the *lehnenkreise* and the *Dramstudio*] wanted to educate ourselves—not just in English, but in the great works of Yiddish literature, old and modern." Members of the drama group, like Sarah Friedman, frequently were invited to entertain at *landsmanshaft* meetings designated for those particular nights as "cultural meetings," where they would read poetry, present dramatic excerpts, or the like. Despite the members' charitable custom of performing for free, they were nevertheless obliged to wait until the "business" of the meeting concluded only to find part of their audience less than attentive. Norman Drachler recalled that on the occasions he accompanied his father Israel, who was a teacher in the community and whom various *landsmanshaftn* had invited to speak,   63 the chairman might preface some fervent discussion by reminding the membership that "tonight is a cultural meeting and the speaker is here."

Differences in attitude and belief, goals and orientation abounded. Yet Yiddish culture in Detroit appears to have been a thickly woven quilt of activities held together by the strong ties of language and history. If life in America turned out to be less than golden, there were still places to find companionship, understanding, even old-fashioned arguments. Frequently looking back, if not with longing for Russia or Poland, then certainly with wistful yearning to bring relatives to America, the *landsmanshaftn* served as a focal point for discussions and even as a source for finances to send for *landsleit* or for family.

Culture, learning, letters, and educational advancement were not the shared goals of all elements of the Yiddishist groups, although a significant proportion of them emphasized those aspects of Jewish tradition. A sense of community was revived, and if some of its members stressed different goals, they always drew from the same cultural pool. Each of the groups fostered philanthropic and benevolent activities to aid its members; those efforts consistently permeated every one of the *landsmanshaftn*: the Bereznitzer Unterstitzung Verein, the Kiever Cooperative Association, the Kovler-Wohliner Cooperative League, the Loyaver and Chernigever, the David Horodoker Unterstitzung Verein, the Odessa Unterstitzung Verein, the Liberty Progressive Lodge, the Mezhire Unterstitzung, the Turever Verein, the Radomer (or Radimer) Verein, and numerous others.

Individually, however, each member of the *landsmanshaftn* or the clubs dreamed of educational advancement for their children. And, in the end, these laudable hopes for the next generation contributed to the undoing of the groups and, perhaps, of Yiddish culture: the *landsmanshaftn*, strong and vitally serving their members, peaked and declined—a one- or two-generation phenomenon. If Americanization loomed as a frightening or threatening prospect for Jews in Detroit, it beckoned to them for their children, who had no solid memories, no poignant or nostalgic recollections, and therefore little or no reason to want to preserve their parents' culture.

By 1923 there was an obvious decline of interest in Yiddish culture, even among the immigrant population.[111] With the gates closed to immigration, Americanization proceeded with renewed vigor and, as some observers noted, economic and material activities replaced cultural ones. Yet, the *landsmanshaftn* began and were held together by their common homes, by bonds to physical places of origin that reflected intellectual, spiritual, and psychological origins and values. The single element that explains the decline of the benevolent societies, then, is the end of European Jewish culture, the destruction of those places of origin and of the people in them. After 1945, there would be no more reports from home. The *landsmanshaftn* continued, however, some even into the 1980s.

While the *landsmanshaftn* filled certain gaps in Jewish life and allowed a clear Jewish identity to continue in the midst of the "melting pot" of industrial Detroit, numerous other organizations existed for a wide variety of purposes. They appeared to spring from nowhere, proliferating across different boundaries and eventually touching the lives of virtually every Jewish family in the city. Fraternal organizations or lodges included the Knights of Pythias Lodge No. 55, the Jericho Lodge of Oddfellows, the Perfection Lodge of the Masons, the Purity Chapter No. 359 Order of the Eastern Star, and the Detroit Lodge of Red Men. Such organizations followed a particular cycle: a non-Jewish lodge would admit Jews while others would not. This would lead the less restrictive lodges to include more Jews, until the organization became almost exclusively Jewish.[112] This phenomenon occurred among Boy Scout and Girl Scout and Camp Fire Girl troops as well as among adult lodges. Additionally, there were approximately twelve high school fraternities and sororities, some seven "more serious groups," such as debating and cultural societies, two Kadimah Clubs (both at Beth El), and several other girls' and women's groups, which included a Mother's Club. All these tended to parallel non-Jewish organizations and might be perceived as attempts "to be like everybody else, like other Americans," as one woman recalled of her childhood.

Despite these attempts, however, even the most assimilated of German Jews confronted persistent anti-Semitism in the form of exclusion. Jewish sororities, for example, while paralleling non-Jewish ones, existed so that Jewish high-school girls could emulate their peers. At the Liggett School, the prestigious educational institution in exclusive Indian Village, the young Kahn girls, daughters of the internationally known architect Albert Kahn, along with the few other primarily German Jewish girls at Liggett, remained uninvited by sororities. Even the children of that prestigious Detroit family, as fully assimilated as any Jewish family in Detroit and whose father had designed and built the new Liggett School on Burns and Charlevoix, suffered some isolation. Like their peers, the Kahn sisters boasted numerous non-Jewish friends at school.

Outstanding among the Jewish young people's groups were the Trysquare (or Tri-Square) Club and the Philomathic Debating Club. The latter, founded in 1898, declared its purpose "to train men how to think." In part because Jewish boys could not get into high school debating clubs, the club became a source of Jewish leadership into the twentieth century, producing lawyers, academicians, and community leaders who as young men met on Sunday afternoons to discuss "serious issues" in earnest. Similarly, the Trysquare Club numbered among its members its young leader, Fred Butzel, and Abe Srere, Gus D. Newman, Bernard Ginsburg, Nate Shapero, Isadore Levin, and Aaron Silberblatt. One reporter coudl write in 1940 that "every president in the Detroit Jewish community—from the Allied Jewish Campaign to the new [Jewish] Center itself—has come from that little boys' club called the Trysquare."[113] Meeting at the Jewish Institute, the Trysquares each paid their two cents a week and engaged in athletics, debates, and a wide variety of activites. (Philomathic dues were five cents.) They also became active in the Madison Athletic Club, which would serve as a center for young Jewish men. A strong committment to leadership in the Jewish community shined through in these organizations.

As these numerous organizations and institutions, social and professional, proliferated, opposing extremes, not surprisingly, emerged: on one end was the Phoenix or Phoenix Social Culb, which had been founded in 1872 and had added a golf club (the Redford Country Club) in 1914;[114] and on the other were the *landsmanshaftn* and the labor-aligned Workmen's Circle. The differences that divided those grorups were multifarious and often bitter. Yet country or golf clubs, a new phenomenon at least for East European Jews, if not for German Jews, were not necessarily composed of like-minded men and women. Nor were benevolent societies of one mind with each other or with organizations like the Workmen's Circle or the Poale Zion (Labor Zionists). What these last shared with the *landsmanshaftn* may have been economic circumstances and East European roots. Yet even those mutual concerns provided sources for disagreement.

Most of the *landsmanshaftn*, primarily areligious, were apolitical as well. Other secular Jewish groups, however, fiercely identified with the politics of the left. The Workmen's Circle, or Arbeter Ring, had its headquarters at the Labor Lyceum on Livingston near Hastings and later at the Labor Lyceum Branch on Delmar near Oakland. Many Jews and non-Jews regarded that organization as a hotbed of Jewish radicalism. Outsiders labeled all members communists, yet most of those within the organization rejected that characterization. To be an anarchist, for example, was far different from being a communist; and a Bundist might radically oppose the policies of both these groups.

All socialists were not alike and, surprisingly, over half the membership of the Workmen's Circle, which included around eight hundred dues-paying members in 1923, were not workers.[115] All members of the Workmen's Circle shared the benefits of life insurance and educational programs. Some insisted it was primarily a fraternal organization. But all had to recognize its strong political-philosophical bent, its labor orientation, and its championing of labor and socialist causes. By 1917 Detroit's Branch 156 was the largest in the United States and Canada.[116] Its school song hailed the belief that "alle Menschen seinen Brudern," all men are brothers, and its educational curriculum included the works of Marx and Engels, Ferdinand Lassalle, and Jewish radical thinkers. Among its six branches in Detroit, two were affiliates of the Communist Workers Party. Yet its membership also counted among them Orthodox Jews, Zionists, nationalists, and others. A constant source of aggravation to the Workmen's Circle leadership was noted in the 1923 *Survey*: there appeared to be "no Jewish labor class consciousness in Detroit."[117]

Most of Detroit's Jewish laborers belonged to the *landsmanshaftn*. Perhaps for this reason, those societies were lumped together with the Workmen's Circle and Poale Zion/Labor Zionists as leftist, or *linke*. Although most members of these secular organizations almost automatically belonged to *landsmanshaftn*, one former communist remembers, regarding the idea that they were leftist, that "nothing could have been further from the truth. They [the *landsmanshaftn*] were actually reactionary. They hated the unions because the members [of the societies] might be looking for cheap labor for their own businesses. So they recruited their workers from the *landsmanshaftn*. . . . We hated them." He echoed the feelings of one Bundist who wrote to the "Bintel Brief" in the *Daily Forward* of New York that none of the *linke* could trust the membership of the societies who were "just small-town Jews." In support of unions like the ILGWU (International Ladies Garment Workers Union), which encouraged workers to learn English in order to bargain with employers, the Workmen's Circle opposed the *landsmanshaftn's* adherence to Yiddish.[118] Somewhat paradoxically, then, the radical wing of Jewish organizations favored the policy of Americanization so forcefully purveyed by the "elite" in Detroit, including members of the country-club set.

3

The Emergence of Detroit Jewish Leadership

Not unlike Max Jacob, Ed Levy remained aloof from the public, institutional expressions of the Jewish community, yet contributed to what he considered to be worthy Jewish causes. Like Charles Simons, he would carefully cultivate a Republican, conservative American persona. Among the notable Jews listed in the 1914 *Book of Detroiters* were Bernard Berman, a Russian clothing manufacturer; Albert E. Bernstein, a Russian physician; David Brown, founder of the People's Ice Co. and Brown and Brown Coal Co.; Fred, Magnus, Leo, and Henry Butzel; and Henry Krolik. Each of them identified themselves in curious and revealing ways: Berman's and Bernstein's names were followed by their country of origin (Russia), either "Hebrew" or "Jewish religion," and their designation as Republicans. Both Fred and Magnus Butzel identified themselves as "Jewish religion; Republican," and David Brown listed the non-Jewish organizations with which he was connected, with no mention of religious or political affiliation.[119]

When World War I began, Detroit's 475 industries responded with a quantum leap in production.[120] The *Jewish Chronicle* seemed to be neutral, like the rest of the country, but reported intensified anti-Jewish violence on the Russian fronts. The paper also continued to run advertisements for German and Austrian firms, including Herman Eichner's Foreign Exchange and Steamship Ticket Agency, the German American Bank, and A. B. Newman Co., the "Sole Agents for the Imperial and Royal Austrian, Hungarian, Bosnia-Jerzogovinian Tobacco Monopolies." In general, the tone of the reporting and the editorials were anti-Russian and pro-German until the end of 1916.[121]

Of primary concern to American Jews was the plight of their European brethren caught between the warring countries. That the Russian and Polish authorities were harsher and more murderous in their treatment of Jews went without saying. Thus, the support for the Central Powers, Austria-Hungary and Germany, seemed more reasonable for neutrals. Word of the harassment of Jews in Russia, the increase in pogrom violence, and the murder of Jewish innocents prompted the founding of the American Jewish Joint Distribution Committee and the increase in activities of HIAS (Hebrew Immigrant Aid Society).

In November 1914, leaders of the *landsmanshaftn*, the directors of the primarily German Jewish American Jewish Committee, and representatives of the People's Relief Committee formed the Joint Distribution Committee of the American Friends of Jewish War Sufferers, soon to be renamed the American Jewish Joint Distribution Committee (JDC). Their first chairman was Felix Warburg, and their immediate task was the collection of funds to be distributed through established channels of overseas relief.[122] America's neutrality helped—so, too did the JDC's perceived neutrality among Jewish factions.

Each of the independent organizations had intitiated emergency relief programs. But each recognized the desperate plight of European Jewry and, uncharacteristically, conceded their independence. Those individual organizations, however, continued their services after the war. The Odessa Progressive Society, for example, initiated a Child Rescue Fund cochaired by two of the society's "sisters," and in 1920 the Jewish Women's European Welfare Organization was established under the leadership of Mrs. Eva Bloom. Subsequently, the Jewish Women European Welfare Organization brought over three hundred orphans to the United States and Canada, placing them in foster homes, providing clothing and care, and later reuniting them with parents and/or families.[123]

But it was the JDC that aided Jews on a grand scale, providing help to refugees on both sides of the war until April 1917, although most of their relief went to Eastern Europe. They achieved such success that Herbert Hoover described the JDC as "a major lifeline to the Jews of Poland."[124] Both HIAS and the JDC received significant support from the Jews of Detroit, who raised $100,000 in 1916 and thus began to gain their reputation as one of the most generous Jewish communities in America.[125]

When the United States entered the Great War in 1917, American Jews,   69 like their European counterparts, rushed to demonstrate their loyalty by immersing themselves in patriotic causes. At age fifteen, Harry T. Madison was among the youngest of the 250,000 Jews who served in the armed forces. He would later found the Jewish War Veterans post in Detroit and go on to become the national commander of the Jewish War Veterans. More than sixty Detroit Jews died in World War I.[126] Some of Detroit's Jewish soldiers found themselves with the Red Arrow Division in the hapless Polar Bear Expedition in 1918; the son of Rabbi Judah Levin, Lt. Isadore Levin, who was promoted in the field to the rank of captain, wrote a field artillery manual; and Nate Shapero served as a pharmaceutical mate. Detroit Jewish doctors, including Lee Cowan, fresh from UM-Medical School, Samuel Lewis, Max Ballin, David Levy, and Reuben Kahn enlisted in the Michigan medical ranks. Jewish women of the Self-Help Circle of Beth El and the women's groups from Shaarey Zedek and others formed Red Cross units to make bandages to be sent overseas.[127] Under the indefatigable command of Fred M. Butzel, who led the Detroit Patriotic Fund, the city surpassed others in Liberty Loan drive quotas and Red Cross responses. Butzel also took charge of War Camp Services, parades, and rallies.[128]

After American entry into the war, David A. Brown headed the fund-raising drive for the Joint Distribution Committee in Detroit. From a Jewish population of around 25,000 the majority of whom were immigrants with limited means, Brown set out to raise $250,000 using the slogan "Give more than your share." On May 15, 1917, at a luncheon at the Statler Hotel, Brown raised $100,000 in a half hour. Large pledges from Julius Freud and Joseph Sillman of Temple Beth El helped. When Henry Morgenthau, President Wilson's adviser, spoke at a rally in Arcadia Hall on Woodward and Stimson on June 3, $200,000 had already been collected in the Jewish War Sufferers Relief campaign. Small donors and large donors, Jews and non-Jews contributed, and when Brown convened another meeting at the Statler, the total Detroit contribution was $300,000. Only New York and Chicago collected more. Brown's remarkable capacities as a fundraiser gained him prestige in other cities and he was often called upon for advice or assistance in organizing campaigns. In 1925 he led HIAS's nationwide effort to bring relief to the Jews of the Soviet Union.[129]

If Rabbi Franklin pioneered clerical high-profile leadership in non-Jewish Detroit, David Brown became his counterpart in lay leadership. Few of the prominent Jewish Detroiters who played considerably active roles in Detroit politics, economics, and culture—distinguished leaders such as D. W. Simons, the Kahns, and the Butzels, for example—drew such national and international attention as Brown. "Pugnacious and charming," (according to his niece), he served as director general of the United War Work Campaign during World War I, became the first director of Detroit's Community Fund drive in 1918, and worked as director of the Red Cross in 1919. Members of his family remember him as a "romantic personage,"

charismatic, with white flowing hair, a gold watch, and piercing blue eyes.
In 1923, emphasizing his businessman's qualities, he ran unsuccessfully
for mayor of Detroit. Brown established standards for the Jewish leadership
even as he remained independent. In 1924 the Detroit Committee of the
Palestine Foundation Fund honored him at a dinner at the Hotel Statler.
Yet he preferred to continue identifying himself as a "non-Zionist."[130] In
1925 he toured the Soviet Union and spearheaded a campaign to resettle
Jews on land in the Crimea where a number of colonies, including the
David Brown Colony, were established.

Seemingly indefatigable, Brown worked on behalf of Irish autonomy, the
Knights of Columbus, a symphony orchestra in Detroit, Orchestra Hall,
and the Civic Music League. He assumed a high profile as a Detroit civic
leader as president of the Detroit Board of Commerce, President of the
Adcraft Club of Detroit, and as a founder of the Detroit Old Newsboys' Fund
for needly families. He climbed to national prominence and was recognized
as a brilliant financial analyst and astute observer of international affairs.
No one could surpass him in fund-raising "for the relief of suffering humanity." President Hoover, acknowledging Brown's incomparable abilities,
appointed him chairman of the China Famine Relief Fund and sent him
to that country to observe and recommend efficient means for resolving
its difficulties.[131]

David Brown's Detroit career (he moved to New York in 1929 after suffering in the stock-market crash) reflected the man's uniqueness as well
as his emblematic status: although he was clearly identified as a Jew, he
was also seen as a maverick independent "like Frank Lloyd Wright"; although he was thoroughly American in his beliefs, behavior, and initiative,
and continually involved with American causes and fund drives, he was
equally engaged in leading Jewish fund-raising—"no one did it better"—
and became known as "Do-It-Up-Brown" after the headline in a Jewish
peridical announcing his assumption of the leadership of the fourteen-million-
dollar Jewish war relief campaign of 1921.[132] According to Philip Slomovitz,
"It was the first time in history that any group, anywhere, dared to speak
in terms of so many millions as an objective in a relief campaign." Eu-
logizing Brown, Slomovitz went on to describe him as "this dedicated Jew,
patriotic American, able executive and courageous leader."[133]

Similar praise accrued to Brown's career from its explosively successful
beginnings. He seemed to attract honorary dinners, but not one of these
events could exemplify his dynamic, controversial career, nor symbolize
Detroit Jewry's relationships with the non-Jewish community, better than
the dinner that welcomed him to New York in 1929. Twenty-five hundred
men and women assembled in the Grand Ballroom of the Hotel Commo-
dore to "honor a man who, as a boy from a poverty-ridden home . . . in
the last few years has been instrumental in raising the stupendous sum of
$100,000,000 for the relief of suffering humanity." Jews and non-Jews at-

tended; messages were read from President Hoover; C. C. Wu, the Chinese Minister in Washington; and others. Henry Ford was in attendance and, indeed, seated on the dais. Ford received a standing ovation upon being introduced, but he did not speak, preferring instead to have the following encomium issued after the occasion:

> I am happy to come here tonight to pay a tribute of admiration to my good friend, David A. Brown, and through him to the great race which is proud and fortunate to count him among their own.
>
> Mr. Brown is a shining example of great benevolence of the Jewish people, their philanthropy, their eagerness to make this world better, to educate the untutored, to heal the sick, to care for the orphans; their intense and intelligent participation in all that makes for civic righteousness and social justice stamps them a great people.[134]

Like Rabbi Franklin, David Brown advocated a most strenuous involvement in American life. Both men dedicated themselves as Jews to philanthropic work, although to some, Brown's commitment to Jewish causes appeared incidental and superficial. The nature of his flamboyance sometimes seemed to foster only intermittent, if intense, involvement. Nevertheless, one Detroiter argued that, although Brown was areligious, he "built Beth El" with his fund-raising efforts. His sister, Augusta Brown, became the first president of the Fresh Air Society. "There were no shrinking violets in the family," almost all of whose members plunged into Jewish or Detroit causes like "Uncle David." Perhaps no two men did more for the philanthropic image of Detroit Jews as did Franklin and Brown.

Another prominent Detroit Jewish figure who almost literally "built Beth El," Albert Kahn, did not deny or renounce his Jewish identity, but was determined to confine it to religious matters—such as they were for a rather adamant Reform Jew whose religious practice tended to eschew traditional ritualism. Putting aside his paternal rabbinical heritage, Kahn shied away from highly visible public contributitons to or support of Jewish institutions. Kahn was perhaps the most successful architect in the United States. His credits included the Ford Highland Park Plant and Rouge Plant, the Dodge Plants, and eventually many of the exemplary structures of Detroit. He also constructed factories in the Soviet Union in collaboration with Henry Ford.[135] Both men, conservative in their economic ideologies, belived that technological efficiency would defeat communism in Russia. It was later rumored that the six-foot-thick walls of Kahn's constructions (insisted upon by Soviet authorities) partially accounted for the defeat at Stalingrad of the German armies in World War II. His buildings included Temple Beth El, constructed in 1903 on Woodward and Eliot, and the next Temple Beth El, built in 1922 on Woodward and Gladstone.[136]

This small, brilliant, and self-educated man epitomized the German Jewish mystique in Detroit. Kahn reflected Americanism. His daughter recalls that he had retained a European rigid discipline toward his children and he used that sternness to foster meticulous English: when one of his daughters used the phrase "that guy," Kahn sternly reacted with, " 'That guy?' We don't speak that way." Quiet and gentle, his goal remained integration into American society. Few achieved this goal more completely. Determined to demonstrate that Jews were the same as other Americans, Kahn joined the Bloomfield Hills Country Club, intent on impressing upon non-Jews the "honest and good qualities of Jews." He had already joined and designed the Franklin Hills Country Club and its predecessor, the Redford Country Club. Although he did not socialize with Henry Ford, he apparently remained on good terms with him throughout the period of Ford's vitriolic publications, perhaps believing that by continuing his excellent work he could "prove to Ford that [Jews] were good people." One might also surmise that Kahn protected not only himself but also the employees of his large firm by his silence on the subject of the *Independent* (see Chap. 4). There was no telling how other industrialists for whom he built would react to open opposition to Ford. Kahn did socialize with upper-crust, Grosse Pointe non-Jews, among them Edsel and Eleanor Ford, who called upon Mrs. Kahn at the death of her husband in 1943.

Typically, Kahn remained aloof from East European Jews. Indeed, he seemed distant from Jewish affairs in general. Yet his daughter averred that he "always considered himself connected to the Jewish community, giving generously to Jewish charities and the Allied Jewish Campaign." Like others among the Reform and German Jews, Kahn considered charitable contributitons necessary for *all* of Detroit—for non-Jews perhaps more than for Jews. More importantly, the Jewish community was able to point with pride to Detroit's premier architect. Like Brown and Franklin, Kahn adopted a conservative stance, equating it with Americanism and assimilation. Yet despite his obvious separation from the majority of Jews in Detroit, Kahn never renounced his identity as a Jew.

Another prominent German-Jewish family, the Butzels, adopted a similar philosophy. Kahn's daughter, Rosalie, married Martin Leo Butzel, son of Leo Martin Butzel. The two branches of the Butzel family would later boast a Michigan Supreme Court justice (Henry) and lawyers whose clients would include the most distinguished corporations and families of aristocratic Detroit: the Strohs, the Dodges, Mrs. G. Ogden Ellis, the Scripps family (owners of the *Detroit News*), and others.[137]

Like others in their community, the Butzels, in particular Leo and Martin, were always "anxious to be considered American." They seemed to hate such rituals as the bar mitzvah or even the celebration of Passover seders. And, like Albert Kahn, they continued to identify themselves as Jewish, but based their identity solely in religious (not ritualistic) terms. Their families engaged in a sort of amphibious life: moving between social worlds of Jews   73 and non-Jews. Rarely did the two mix, although Leo Butzel's daughters were given coming-out parties and announced as debutantes.

As supporters of the arts in Detroit, especially the Detroit Symphony and the Detroit Institute of Arts, the Butzels gave generously to the city— just as they gave generously to Jewish causes. Mrs. Leo Butzel sat on the boards of the Detroit Community Fund, the Franklin Street Settlement, and the Community Chest. Emma Butzel, Leo's "maiden lady" sister, took a prominent role in support of Detroit's musical society; and all the Butzel women campaigned as War Chest Women during World War I.

Many of those German Jews, who were Beth El congregants, continued to take the initiative in public leadership of Jewish affairs, Yet as they became increasingly unrepresentative of the majority of Detroit's Jews, they began to be matched in these efforts by members of Beth El's rival since 1861, Congregation Shaarey Zedek.[138] Rabbi Abraham M. Hershman, who graduated from the new Conservative rabbinical college in New York (the Jewish Theological Seminary) and was ordained by Solomon Schechter, one of Conservatism's founders, had led Shaarey Zedek's congregation since 1907. Under his guidance, the congregation had joined the United Synagogue of America almost as soon as that federation was founded in 1913. By 1914 Shaarey Zedek had become a leading force for the newly established Conservative movement.[139]

With the notable exception of Temple Beth El, Detroit synagogues still followed the Orthodox traditions even as the membership became less observant; the boundaries between Orthodox and Conservative were not then so sharp as they would later become. Prayers were identical; men and women sat separately; and few would openly drive to services on Saturday. A Shaarey Zedek constitution of 1905 declared the synagogue to be Orthodox, and to have separate seating.[140] Rabbi Hershman, however, although himself observant of religious rituals, came upon the scene with a more "modern" approach than his colleagues in Detroit. About 1920, there was a gradual beginning of mixed seating; by the time of the synagogue's move to Chicago Boulevard in 1932, a revision of the synagogue's by-laws formally allowed the change in seating. One section of the main floor remained informally set aside for men only. The Keidan family constituted the bulwark of this men-only corner as the Keidan women all sat in the balcony.[141]

Like Reform Judaism, Conservatism sought to identify itself with the life-style and language of America, to form a "new alignment with a modernist movement."[142] Conservative rabbis delivered their sermons in English; religious education adopted modern American methods. But the conservative movement attempted to preserve more of traditional faith and worship than Reformism. Under Rabbi Hershman, Shaarey Zedek tried to maintain certain traditional rituals of worship while it changed its form and function in other, more social realms. Reform and conservative differences served as subtle reminders that what impressed some American

74

Jews most was the form of worship. Shaarey Zedek's worshippers mirrored Beth El's in their attention to the proper dignity of services. Unlike the Orthodox, smaller congregations, in which prayers sometimes evoked an ecstatic cacophony of individual chants and pious independent meditation, Shaarey Zedek carved out a more uniform service that satisfied its members. Ushers, dressed in waistcoats and striped pants, maintained an unusual degree of decorum. All the men wore the same dark skullcaps. Rabbi Hershman wore black clerical robes most of the year and white on Yom Kippur—and people came to services promptly.

Almost from its beginning, Shaarey Zedek perceived itself as a self-contained society, a "way of life" that included social, athletic, and cultural events. Although that allegiance continued from generation to generation, even nostalgic recollections did not entirely cloak what Rabbi Hershman considered to be the most serious threat to the Jewish community: the lack of education and the accompanying threat of assimilation. This fear marked a pronounced difference between the vision of Hershman and that of Franklin, who advocated assimilation at almost every turn. By 1922 the *Jewish Chronicle* reported a drastic and dangerous decline and disinterest in Jewish education.[143] Afternoon schools at several synagogues, but especially at Shaarey Zedek, were rapidly losing students until the education committee of that synagogue closed the school. Hershaman warned that a synagogue without a school "is a most tragic thing," which would further aggravate the drift away from Jewish life whether families were Orthodox, Conservative, or Reform.[144] Thus Hershman identified what to him had evolved into the central issue of concern for American Jews: abandonment of Jewish learning, culture, religious training and identity.

Prominent members of each congregation cooperated in community-wide endeavors from as early as 1899, when Shaarey Zedek's D. W. Simons, president of Beth El, originated the United Jewish Charities. Along with Rabbi Franklin, Simons and others from Shaarey Zedek supported and directed the coordination of Detroit's central Jewish institution.[145] Yet it was an uneasy alliance, and perhaps spoke to the point that those two religious institutions, which were the longest-lived in Detroit, had more in common regarding social causes, despite their religious differences, than not. Simons, an Orthodox member of Shaarey Zedek, nevertheless achieved prominence in the non-Jewish world, becoming a member of Detroit's City Council. He embodied parts of the American Jewish ideal: success, integration, and recognition by the gentile world.

Following the example set by Simons was one of Detroit's most notable Jewish figures, Judge Harry B. Keidan, another member of Congregation Shaarey Zedek, who was among Detroit's most honored recorder's and later, a circuit court judge. Keidan gained a reputation as "a fair-minded, clear-thinking man" whose stiff sentences sharply contrasted with the equally famous "warmth and humanity of his heart."[146] As a crusading judge, Keidan

75

waged effective campaigns against graft and corruption. Having gained the admiration of political leaders from various camps, Keidan was offered the judgeship in the circuit court, first by Governor Alex Grossbeck in 1924 and then by Grossbeck's bitter political opponent and successor, Governor Green.[147] A successful, highly visible figure, Judge Keidan publicly identified himself as an Orthodox Jew. Among the stories about him that became popular lore were those relating his custom of walking to the courthouse on Saturday if it were necessary to release a prisoner or if there were some sort of judicial emergency. No matter what the weather, if Judge Keidan were unavoidably required downtown on the Sabbath, he would walk.[148]

The dream of such integration and acceptance by the non-Jewish world was one that members of both major congregations shared, and by 1914 their diffferences seemed to be shrinking in importance as members of the two institutions increasingly worked together on behalf of Jewish causes.

Neither group—from Beth El or from Shaarey Zedek—could speak for the great majority of Detroit Jews. Those who clung to Yiddish culture—members of the *landsmanshaftn*, or the increasingly important new secular Jewish organizations such as the Workmen's Circle, or the numerous small Orthodox synagogues—remained excluded from the levers of influence and power by the simple facts of their continued strong ethnic bent and their relative poverty. Shaarey Zedek, however, remained a prime mover of Jewish orientation and life in Detroit. In 1915 it relocated to a larger structure at Willis and Brush, a building which held a gymnasium and classrooms and would accommodate 1,432 people in its main sanctuary.[149]

Since 1910, Hastings Street, Detroit's Jewish "port of entry," had remained a Jewish enclave mainly as a center for shopping and Jewish businesses. After WWI Jews had begun to move from that center to a variety of other neighborhoods, including the East Side; areas like Delray, where Hungarian Jews established themselves; Hamtramck; and the downriver communities of River Rouge, Wyandotte, and Trenton. As the exodus slowly proceeded from Hastings Street, the most attractive areas were around Oakland Avenue, which began to develop in relation to the industris newly located there, including the Ford Motor Company Highland Park Plant and the Chrysler Corporation plant in Hamtramck. The new area attracted Jews who primarily sought new housing and business opportunities. The German Jewish population which led the way as the wealthier members of the community, as well as some non-German Jews moved to the mansions of Chicago and Boston Boulevards.[150] In 1922, a new Temple Beth El was constructed on the corner of Gladstone and Woodward. Designed by Kahn, it became a showpiece for Detroit Reform Jewry.[151]

As a result of Beth El's move, another Jewish community benefited. The old benches and accoutrements of the previous Beth El, including the holy ark, were sold to Congregation Beth Tephilath Moses, in the outlying town of Mt. Clemens, for two thousand dollars.[152] That congregation, which was founded in 1911 outside the recognized pale of Jewish communities in Detroit, for numerous, unique reasons needed expansion. Mt. Clemens's Jewish population numbered approximately one hundred families, yet in the summers, the synagogue filled to overflowing and those attending services at the Orthodox Beth Tephilath Moses had to listen from outside through the open windows.[153] Mt. Clemens had become famous for its curative mineral baths and its spas. When Morris Feldman purchased the Arethusa Hotel, he set the precedent for several other Jews who would move to Mt. Clemens as hotel-spa proprietors. Kosher kitchens, Yiddish entertainers, music, and congeniality all accompanied the fast-growing spa industry in this "boom town"—or "splash town." The "cures" lasted twenty-one days, and in its heyday (the 1920s through the 1940s), Mt. Clemens boasted thirteen baths (at least four of which were owned by Jews and which drew almost exclusively Jewish clientele from Michigan and out of state), "five blind pigs and twelve houses of ill repute." It was, wrote one late commentator, "the hottest spot on earth to relieve yourself of pain, suffering, and money."[154]

The Jews who lived in Mt. Clemens, however, were not all affiliated with the mineral baths. The town also claimed Rev. Meyer Davis as its *shochet*, or ritual slaughterer, several merchants, lawyers, junk dealers, doctors, and others who had moved to the town in pursuit of a decent life for their families.[155] Still, a summer at Mt. Clemens became a Jewish tradition that was fondly remembered by the Detroiters and other Jews (and non-Jews) who attended the baths annually. By the 1920s, celebrating Passover at one of Mt. Clemen's hotel resorts had become a sign of status.

4

Mr. Ford's Idea: The Assault

Historian Oliver Zunz has argued convincingly that in Detroit, to a much higher degree than in other industrial centers, "ethnicity [was] the major factor shaping the distribution of the population."[156] Ethnic separatism meant continued anti-Semitism. "You didn't dare walk through the next neighborhood," recalled one Jewish man of his youth, "you either took a streetcar or you walked around it or you stayed home." Russell Street marked the border between the Polish and Jewish neighborhoods. One Detroiter recalls a raging street fight between Polish and Jewish groups around 1920. Perhaps as many as one hundred young Polish men marched down Hastings to meet an equal number of Jewish men marching toward them. The two armies met between Theodore and Farnsworth Streets and battled each other to a draw with stones, sticks, and glass.

Blue-collar anti-Semitic violence was not a new phenomenon. More difficult to grasp, perhaps, was the more sophisticated variety that infected even such professions as medicine. There were, for example, rumors of quota systems at the University of Michigan Medical School, and "everyone just knew there was a 10 percent quota." That meant that only ten percent of Jewish applicants to the UM Medical School were accepted. Dr. Lee

Cowan remembered different deans and members of the faculty by their degrees of anti-Semitism. Dr. Hugh Cabot (of the distinguished Boston family), for instance, had urged a young student to "go into the business of your forefathers—selling old clothes." "My father's a doctor," replied the young man. On the other hand, Dean Walter Vaughan would lecture on Jewish medical scientists like Paul Ehrlich: "He was a Jew. Jews have produced some of the greatest scientists of the world." Vaughan seemed to be the exception, however, and his successor, when invited by Dr. Samuel Kahn on behalf of the fledgling Maimonides Medical Society to reply to questions regarding the quota system, engagingly but frankly stated that "if we would admit all qualified Jews, we would have more Jews than Christians." In 1917 no Jewish students were members of any of the honorary medical societies or fraternities.[157]

Insidious anti-Semitism stalked Detroit, from its most respected institutions to its working-class neighborhoods. On one occasion in July 1916, Rabbi Franklin and Fred Butzel refused to join President Woodrow Wilson for lunch at the Detroit Athletic Club (DAC) because it did not accept Jewish members.[158] Ironically, since he had designed it, the DAC offered Albert Kahn the rare privilege of membership which he, as had Rabbi Franklin earlier, refused because of the club's discriminatory policy toward Jews. Louis Brandeis visited Detroit two months after accepting the chairmanship of the Provisional Executive Committee for General Zionist Affairs in the United States and, based on his observation of the DAC's exclusionary policy, wrote his brother that "anti-Semitism seems to have reached its American pinnacle here."[159]

Despite the restrictive practices of the Detroit Athletic Club and the University of Michigan, a screen of polite naiveté and optimism softened the atmosphere. As if to demonstrate the age of innocence, in September 1916, four years before the *Dearborn Independent*'s anti-Semitic onslaught, Rabbi Franklin addressed a letter to Mr. E. G. Liebold, Henry Ford's personal secretary, informing him of the upcoming high holy days. The exchange of letters was described under the *Chronicle* headline "A Gracious Act on the Part of the Ford Motor Co.," as Liebold responded that permission for leave of absence had already been granted.[160] The editors of the *Chronicle* acknowledged Ford's graciousness and emphasized that his company employed several thousand Jews. Henry Ford, the editorial declared, should be an example to other Christian employers.[161]

Within two weeks yet another exchange of letters was celebrated, this time between Rabbi Franklin and Charles M. Carson, the factory manager of the Cadillac Motor Car Company. Cadillac, too, had given its Jewish employees the "opportunity to celebrate their holidays." This exchange was the subject of yet another editorial that heaped profuse praises on both motor companies.[162] The age of open anti-Semitism was about to begin, and Jewish and non-Jewish leaders in Detroit seemed locked in all-American mutual admiration and respect. Gushing letters and articles and public praise of American leaders promised the best of relations in the future. Americanism appeared to be triumphant.

In view of such apparently cordial relationships between the non-Jewish and Jewish leadership, the publication of the infamous ninety-one issues of the *Dearborn Independent* struck with particularly stunning impact. No more virulent anti-Jewish publication had appeared in the United States. In its heyday Ford's newspaper, touted as his personal expressions, sold for five cents per issue or one dollar per year and reached from 250,000 to 500,000 readers. *The International Jew,* the publication comprised of four key issues of the *Independent,* sold ten million copies; it was among the most popular books of the 1920s and was translated into sixteen languages.[163] The effects of those anti-Semitic outpourings are hard to calculate. Surprisingly, the Jews of Detroit reacted in a variety of ways: from silence to open protest. While leaders of the community vociferously expressed their outrage in public and private forums, for most Jews it meant just not buying a Ford car. But the 1923 *Survey* evaluated the publications in yet a different light: Jews in Detroit, the *Survey*'s authors contended, felt a new esprit des corps as a result of Ford's articles.[164]

The responses to Henry Ford and his publications reveal significant changes in the Jewish communities of Detroit. They reveal, too, the drastic alteration in Jewish perceptions of their position in Detroit, if not in America. That Ford was a favorite hero of Hitler's presaged even more ominous threats.[165] Groups like the Ku Klux Klan and the Black Legion became stronger in Detroit than in areas that had been traditionally racist. Dearborn became synonymous with anti-Semitism as those groups and other, less successful ones began to assert themselves in activities reminiscent of pogroms.[166] Yet the non-Jewish establishment of Detroit responded in actively supportive ways. Dr. Emil Amberg, the prominent Jewish physician, wrote to John A. Doelle, commissioner of the state fair, to protest the open sale of Ford's anti-Jewish pamphlets at the fair, asking if the sale was "in harmony with the spirit of the Constitution of the United States" and whether it was meant to "mark the progress of this state"; the commissioner moved with considerable dispatch to stop the sale of the *Dearborn Independent* article reprints.[167]

Leading the more vigorous and outspoken protests against this new tide of anti-Semitism were Jewish writers, among them Philip Slomovitz, then of the *Jewish Chronicle,* who would become editor of the *Jewish News.* Yet Slomovitz recalled that during those dark days of *the Independent,* he would receive frequent messages from Jewish employees of Ford who protested any harsh statements against the man they considered their benefactor. "They wouldn't hear of anything bad. . . . He treated them kindly, so they defended him." Ed Levy's story represents this sentiment. In 1919 Levy brashly marched into Ford's office and declared that with the opening of the Rouge Plant, Mr. Ford would need to have slag hauled from the steel manufacturing. Tall, burly, and tough, Levy already engaged in a haulage business, and he declared that his company could handle Mr. Ford's needs. Levy reported that Ford boomed to his assistant Harry Bennett that "this is just the kind of initiative we need, and just the sort of young man." It attests to the endurance of the Ford mystique in Detroit that Ed Levy and other Jews continued to defend Henry Ford against his critics—often blaming Ford's paranoia on ignorance, the media, or Jewish communists.

Indeed, Ford himself expressed chagrin and surprise when his friend Rabbi Franklin refused the new Model T offered in 1920 as an annual gift. In 1919, before the *Dearborn Independent* began its spurious series attacking Jews, Ford had been humiliated when he took the stand in a libel suit he had filed in 1916 against the *Chicago Tribune*. His statements betrayed a rural bumptiousness and publicly embarrassed the man and his company. Because of his national notoriety, over fifty newspapers covered the trial in a tiny Mt. Clemens courtroom. Somewhat stunned by Ford's ignorance, the newspapers had a proverbial field day, taking him to task on his illiteracy, his blatant unfamiliarity of even schoolboy history, and his utterly simplistic view of the American economy and world affairs.[168]

Placed in the context of both American history and Ford's personal history, this event may be perceived as shaping what followed in the next few years. American fears of communism reached new heights just after World War I, during the so-called Red Scare. Newspaper articles abounded with references to bolsheviks and Jewish revolutionaries. Theories of communist conspiracies swept irrationally across the country and found a particularly receptive audience in rural areas. Wall Street became the villain as it was seen to be, paradoxically, in the service of Jewish bolsheviks. The banks, the media—especially the newspapers, but also the budding film industry with which Ford would soon conflict—and the government were all reported to be falling prey to the insidious dealings of an international cabal.

In the midst of this intensive and widespread concern with international Jewish conspiracies, Ford became increasingly paranoid. He was convinced that banks that had refused him aid, newspapers that had attacked his intelligence and ridiculed his demeanor, and judges that had ruled against him all shared one common trait: control by Jews. It seems feasible, then, that when Ernest Liebold, Ford's anti-Semitic personal secretary, had suggested that Jewish bankers had caused him trouble, that the Jewish judge, Henry Butzel, had ruled against him in an earlier law suit filed by the Dodge Brothers, that Madame Schwimmer of the Peace Ship fiasco had caused him earlier public humiliation, or numerous other hypotheses regarding Jewish communists, union organizers, newspapers, and revolutionaries, he would have found fertile ground in Henry Ford's rather narrow mind.[169] Still, for those Jews who saw Ford as their benefactor, tolerance and the benefit of the doubt seemed most proper.

As abruptly as the articles began, they ended in January 1922. Ford's anti-Semitic campaign would resume, however, in 1927, when it would receive even more support than had this "first systematic anti-Jewish agitation in the United States." How deep the *Independent*'s editorials penetrated into Detroit remains uncertain. But the Ku Klux Klan and the Black Legion proliferated at Ford Motor Company and in the city of Dearborn. By 1921, Michigan's estimated 875,000 Klan members represented the largest group in the United States. Anti-Catholic and anti-black, organiziations such as these two hate groups fostered the views expressed on "Mr. Ford's Own Page" and villified the Jews as the international conspirators responsible for virtually everything the Klan believed evil.[170]

5

Zionism: The External Well of Jewish Identity

As the world stood on the brink of monumental events, Shaarey Zedek moved to the forefront of Jewish Detroit life regarding an external source of Jewish identity: Palestine. World War I served as the midwife of what quickly became the most hotly debated controversy in Jewish life, superseding religious, cultural, social, and economic differences.

After the United States entered World War I, Jews in Detroit, like Jews across the country, joined the armed forces. Indeed, they mirrored the patriotism of Jews in England, France, and Germany, who during and after the war would boast of Jewish losses, valor, and decorations. But the Great War, which launched the Western world into the technological atrocities of the twentieth century, also became the wellspring of twentieth-century Jewish politics. As American Jews engaged in assisting European Jewish war sufferers, some of them recognized that the European cataclysm would destroy the Turkish Ottoman Empire and open the possibilities for Jewish settlement in Palestine. Those few in Detroit who had consistently identified themselves as Zionists intensified their discussions, especially after the Balfour Declaration of November 1917 created new possibilities for Zionism. This, in turn, aggravated tensions among Zionists, non-Zionists, 83 and anti-Zionists, while it also solidified plans for action. But if no agreement seemed feasible among these warring groups, no consensus emerged from within the ranks of the Zionist groups either.

Norman Cottler and George Avrunin perhaps personified the new spirit and vigor found primarily among congregants of Shaarey Zedek when they followed the stirring, militant words of Vladimir Jabotinsky and joined the Jewish Palestine Legion.[171] Jabotinsky had recognized the prospects for Zionist advances when the Ottoman Empire allied itself with the Central Powers. With a British offensive in the Middle East imminent by the spring of 1917, Jabotinsky convinced the war office that a Jewish legion would be beneficial to Jews and British alike in order to free Palestine from Turkish rule. Thus was formed the Thirty-eighth Battalion of Royal Fusiliers, which consisted of Jewish volunteers from Europe, the Western Hemisphere, and Palestine.[172]

A recruiting office was set up on Hastings Street, featuring posters carrying such mottoes as "Enlist in the Jewish Legion Bound for Eretz Israel," and "England Offers Us Our Home—Let Us Go and Occupy It."[173] About twenty Detroiters joined the legion, and Detroit served as a collection point for many American volunteers as local Zionists helped organize them into groups and obtained transport for them to Halifax, Nova Scotia, for basic training. From there, they boarded Japanese ships for Palestine. Cottler, later owner of Dexter Davison grocery, became a sergeant and billeted in the same tent as David Ben-Gurion. Others, like Benjamin Kaplan, stayed on in Palestine. Harry Mintz, a young immigrant, went to an American army recruiting station to enlist. He dozed in the long line and dreamt that he was killed in battle in France. In his dream, soldiers were unable to identify his body and buried him in a grave topped by a cross. Mintz awoke in panic, ran out of the recruiting office and enlisted in the Jewish legion.[174]

Jewish women also volunteered for active duties. Several, including Chana Michlin, formed a Red Magen David group to support the legion and actively engage in other Zionist activities. They wore white nursing outfits with red Stars of David on their hats, aided recruits in gathering in Detroit, and prepared them to move on to Halifax.

All of these significant ventures received some notice in local Detroit newspapers. The *Detroit Jewish Chronicle,* however, gave them scant attention. This publication showed little favor toward Zionist activities in 1917. When Max Jacob had attended the Second Zionist Congress in 1898, he represented a distinct minority of Jews in Detroit and in the United States; he was almost shunned by most of American Jewry. The Reform movement took explicitly anti-Zionist stands, exemplified by Rabbi Franklin, who voiced deep antipathies toward the "nationalists," or Zionists. For Franklin "there [was] only one country, America, and but one flag, the Stars and Stripes."[175] He believed that a Jew living in the United States

should be a loyal citizen of his country and should hold no political interests anywhere else—including Zion. In his view, Judaism remained a
religion and therefore apolitical; the Balfour Declaration was not a Magna
Charta for the Yishuv, the Jewish settlement in Palestine, but simply a
political ploy by the British that might do much to disturb the peace of
Jews round the world. An openly avowed anti-Zionist (although he would
later call himself a "non-Zionist"), Franklin spoke emphatically and with
considerable authority for many Reform Jews in Detroit. He articulated the
position put forth by the Central Conference of American Reform Rabbis
in their Pittsburgh Platform.[176] Non-Zionists remained neutral on Jewish
statehood—indifferent, but not necessarily hostile. Indeed, Franklin generously supported a number of Jewish institutions in Palestine with both
his money and his work.[177]

Most Orthodox Jews opposed the Zionists as too irreligious. Some rejected the "ingathering" to Palestine before the coming of the messiah.
And factionalism was rife within the Zionist camp itself: Labor Zionists
took leftist positions, opposed by conservative convictions of religious Zionists and the extreme-rightist Revisionists led by Jabotinsky. Between the
two extremes were shades of compromise: Poale Zion, Agudat Yisrael, and
numerous others.

By the summer of 1919, American Zionists numbered about 149,000 and
were divided between two main camps: one led by Chaim Weizmann and
the other by Justice Louis Brandeis.[178] Despite the dissension, a Jewish
delegation from the Zionist Organization of America officially attended the
peace conferences convened in April 1919. Felix Frankfurter, former U.S.
labor administrator, served with the delegation and invited Capt. Isadore
Levin of Detroit to accept the office of legal adviser to the delegation during its involvement with the peace conference.[179] Young Levin, the son of
the distinguished Rabbi Judah L. Levin, had served in France since 1917
and accepted the offer. Levin was not an ardent Zionist, although he had
been president of the Intercollegiate Zionist Association of America while
he had been at Harvard. His specific assignment involved assisting in drafting the constitutional framework of a government for Palestine. On April
6, 1919, Captain Levin wrote home of two things of prime importance:
"First, the mandate, the deed of trust so to speak, from the League of
Nations and Allied and Associated powers to the particular nation that will
be the mandatory for the administration and government of Palestine. Sec-
ondly [sic], the Constitution or fundamental charter of Palestine, to be
enacted by the mandatory upon receiving Palestine." Dispatched to Jerusalem three months later, he wrote emotionally of Jewish settlements and
his assurance that the Allies would be similarly moved and convinced of
Jewish talents and goals.[180]

In part through Levin, then, Detroit became identified as a seedbed of
Zionist support. And Shaarey Zedek quickly gained a reputation as Detroit   85

Zionism's center. Rabbi Hershman, Shaarey Zedek's spiritual leader, also
acted as its Zionist leader. Hershman insisted that support of a Jewish
Palestine be one of the fundamental aspects of Jewish identity. As founder
of the Detroit chapter of the Zionist Organization of America, Hershman
saw no contradiction in his participation on the Americanization Committee. American Jews, he believed, could support Zionism while maintaining a strong American identity.[181] Just as Louis Brandeis's entrance
into the leadership of the Zionist Organization of America brought the
movement middle-class respectability that almost immediately attracted large
numbers of American Jews, Rabbi Hershman's stance, given widespread
publicity by the young Zionist journalist Philip Slomovitz, quickly attracted many Jews in Detroit.

Brandeis eloquently offered a position that Hershman echoed: "Let no
American imagine that Zionism is inconsistent with patriotism . . . multiple loyalties are objectionable only if they are inconsistent."[182] Brandeis
seemed to target the objections to American Jewish support of Zionism
raised by Reform Jewish leaders. Hershman could specifically refute the
"dual loyalty" accusations leveled by Rabbi Franklin and others in Detroit.
As if anticipating the needs of committed leaders such as Hershman, Brandeis
grew more specific: "There is no inconsistency between loyalty to America
and loyalty to Jewry. . . . The Jewish spirit, the product of our religion
. . . is essentially American . . . [and] loyalty to America demands rather
that each Jew become a Zionist."[183] In this early prouncement rings the
new definition of Jewish identity: the Jewish spirit, derived from religion,
demands support of Zionism. Brandeis had found a resolution to a Jewish-
American identity crisis in his rational yet adamant support of Palestinian
Jewry. To be a Jew meant somehow to support Zionism.

In 1916, when Hershman spoke out for Zionism in Detroit, he managed
to galvanize a small but zealous and significant portion of Detroit's Jews,
and by 1922, under the guidance of its chairman, Abraham Srere, also of
Shaarey Zedek, the Keren Hayesod (Palestine Foundation Fund), contributed sixty thousand dollars to the resettlement program.[184] Because of the
nature of those supporters, other aspects of Detroit Jewry's energies revealed themselves. Zionism metamorphosed Jewish thinking and action;
transformed traditional roles and archetypes; and revolutionized traditional
forms of Jewish thinking and comportment. Those transformations included women's roles, which altered as Jewish women entered into the
struggle for Palestine. In many respects, the shift to more open and aggressive activity merely made manifest the latent importance that Jewish
women traditionally carried.

Jewish women had long taken active roles in Jewish life, and sociological
terminology often falls short of a complete description of such traditional
terms as the *eishet chayil* (the women of valor) of every generation. Wom-
en's roles, often subtle, assumed central importance in family, community,

and culture. The transformation of Jewish life among the European immigrants threw the Jewish woman and, indeed, the entire family into a
new set of circumstances. As they had in Europe, many East European
women worked with their husbands in small stores or businesses while
they also worked in the house sewing, cooking, or taking in washing. If
the Jewish woman's place was in the home, where she was hard-working
and influential, it nevertheless appeared ignoble by modern American
standards.[185]

Young women in Detroit began to break the patterns of their ances-
tresses; they attended school and made their ways into the job market.
Teaching became the most popular profession, or the easiest avenue to
emancipation. Ida Gordon taught at Bishop School before 1920, and her
sister Rose taught first grade there after her. Other young women began
to enter clerical and social-work professions. Ida Lippman attained the rank
of sergeant in the women's division of the Detroit Police, and Dr. Rachel
Yarros presented several sex-education lectures at Temple Beth El in April
1929. Women like Rose Voss and Regine Freund Cohane began to enter
the professional world of law. These few examples all testify to the increased enrollment of Jewish women in universities. The women's suffrage
movement accompanied Americanization, attracting even Jewish women
not so young as Dr. Yarros or Rose Voss.

As early as 1917, self-proclaimed feminist Edith Greenhut, in her regular
column, "The Jewish Woman," noted a marked increase in divorce within
Jewish families. Despite her 1917-style feminism, Greenhut argued that the
fault for that increase lay with the women who no longer took care of their
children or their households but were spending too much time at luncheons and involving themselves in "women's issues."[186] Traditionalists perceived a real threat to family bonding in the emancipated environment of
the 1920s and even religious bastions were not to be exempted from what
they feared to be the feminist revolution.

One young woman attended Hebrew Union College by 1920 and a Reform rabbinical convention in New Jersey in 1922 argued in favor of ordination for women.[187] To Reform Jews in Detroit, women's active participation in public affairs had already become commonplace: the various
women's groups affiliated with Temple Beth El and Congregation Shaarey
Zedek, for example, testify to the engagement of numerous Jewish women
in Detroit in social issues. As early as 1899, Sarah Berger, president of the
Beth El Ladies Hebrew Sewing Circle; Golda Krolik; and Blanche H.
Rothschild, president of the Self Help Society, were among the founders
of the United Jewish Charities; that group would blossom into the Detroit
Chapter of the National Council of Jewish Women. With these women,
Edith Heavenrich and Lottie T. Sloman served on the original board of
directors, although no woman became president of the UJC. Those activities—the Sewing Circle, the Self Help Society, even the Yiddish *lehnen-*

87

kreise, (learning or reading groups), evinced a traditional place for women in the Jewish communities.[188] With Zionism, a different sort of activity emerged for women.

In 1916 Henrietta Szold, the founder of Hadassah (the Women's Zionist Organization), came to Detroit to start a local chapter. Her vibrancy and energy were infectious and, with the enthusiastic cooperation of Rabbi Hershman, Szold succeeded in aiding Jennie F. Gordon in founding a chapter that would prove generative for the Zionist movement.[189] Mrs. Miriam Rokeach Hershman, who had family living in Palestine, became the first president of Detroit's Hadassah, and the coterie of fervent Zionist supporters immediately began to offer support to Russian-Jewish colonizers. The Detroit chapter soon sent millions of dollars in medical supplies and clothing to women and children in Palestine, as well as a Krupp truck to serve as an ambulance. In 1918 Sarah Wetsman (Mrs. Ralph "Sally" Davidson), whose father, Joseph, had long been an active Zionist and who had hosted Henrietta Szold on her weeklong visit to Detroit, became secretary of the Zionist Organization of Detroit. Her sister, Fannie (Mrs. Morse Saulson), accompanied her to meetings at Shaarey Zedek on Willis and Brush.[190] Both women were founding members of Hadassah in Detroit, and both epitomized the egalitarianism of the movement by the nature of their work. Each would eventually become president of Hadassah—Sarah in 1933 and Fannie in 1951.

Sarah Wetsman Davidson recalled that Hadassah Hospital on Mount Scopus in Jerusalem was built on land that was purchased in 1935 by her father and D. W. Simons and which the two men later donated to Hadassah. She recalled, too, that "we [in the Detroit Hadassah] eliminated all the bake sales, rummage sales and fund raisings of that sort and went to direct pledging of funds with our honor roll system." With that, Jewish women's fund-raising joined the ranks of male-led campaigns and assumed a more direct and aggressive tone.

6

The Roaring Twenties:
On the Brink of Maturity

Post–World War I American culture seemed to explode in frantically divergent directions. Fears of Bolshevism, joy at the Armistice, desires for isolationism, puzzlement with nouveau art forms, Bohemianism, and extreme conservatism percolated uneasily together. Brimming with patriotism, many Jews assumed increasingly assimilationist attitudes. For others, Jewish identity suddenly included a Zionist dimension—a dimension that brought confusion to many and polarized Detroit's Jewish communities. Could one assimilate into American culture, assume an American identity, and simultaneously maintain a Jewish one? As Henry Ford's *Independent* began its vitriolic campaign, most Jews reacted with surprise and apprehension. Yet, for the most part, trends begun before the war continued. Some Jews stressed their Americanism, some retained their religious tradition, and others altered their position primarily with their support of a Jewish Palestine, although they rarely advocated *aliyah*, or emigration, to that country.

Among the more bizarre aspects of the 1920s in the United States was the persistence of Prohibition. Enacted in 1919 as a stark sign of the flight from modernity that had struck so painfully in 1917, it spawned bewilderment at home and abroad, while it fostered fertile soil for the wide   89 variety of crime that took on new proportions in Detroit. In 1925, for example, fifty-three bodies were fished from the Detroit River and, in all, 232 homicides were recorded.[191]

Organized gangs emerged from small, individual entrepreneurial criminal enterprises. Perhaps the best-known Jewish gang operating in Detroit was the Purple Gang. One Jewish historian suggests that Jewish involvement in organized crime during the twenties indicates the extent of Jewish assimilation. Others have argued that organized crime provided an alternative avenue to success, not unlike the entertainment business, relatively free from anti-Semitic social discrimination.[192] Detroit's Canadian border and the existence of Jewish-owned Canadian distilleries offered opportunities to Jews that rivaled organized bootlegging in cities like Chicago and New York—opportunities that eventually realized themselves in major corporate networks of vast illegal business empires.

While supplying liquor remained the principal activity of the Purple Gang, by 1927 it had infiltrated the Jewish-dominated commercial laundry and linen business. Violence in the forms of bombings and shootings became commonplace. Unlike its New York counterparts, Murder Incorporated, the Purple Gang did not involve itself in the kosher meat business and probably not in the garment industry.[193] By 1931, with the repeal of Prohibition, the Purples were declining as other, non-Jewish organized gangs forced them out. For the most part, Jewish gangsters were not heroized by Detroit's Jews. As they sat in Segal's Drug Store, where at least one gangland murder took place, or in The Cream of Michigan Restaurant, a site of other gang violence, or in the Oakland Shvitz (public baths), the meeting place for wealthy Jews in the Oakland district, or as they murdered each other and bullied their ways through Jewish merchants, they were perceived for what they were.

By the end of 1925, Jews in Detroit could be grouped into several communities. They had achieved prominence in the business world: several Jewish merchants had grown to significant positions in the dry-goods and clothing and linen businesses, including the Krolik family's Alaska Knitting Mills Co., Edwin A. Wolf's Republic Knitting Mills of Detroit, Abe Srere's Acme Mills Co. and Textile Industries, Inc., the Kuttnauer Apron Specialties Co., Louis Siegal's B. Siegal and Co., Wolf Himelhoch's clothing company, and Henry and Andrew Wineman's People's Outfitting Co. In the retail merchant field pathbreaking businesses like Sam Osnos's Sam's Cut Rate, Inc. and Nate Shapero's Economical-Cunningham Drug Stores, Inc. were among the first to pioneer chain stores.[194]

Not unlike Max Jacob, who had pursued his father's peddling profession, other Jews in Detroit evolved from related immigrant vocations into the metal industry: Max Stotter came from Cleveland in 1912 to establish the Peninsular Smelting and Refining Co., for example, and, eventually, Jews participated in the automobile industry's support services. Louis Mendelssohn

became treasurer and chairman of the board of directors of Fisher Body
Corporation, and his brother Aaron became the secretary of that company.
In 1919 Meyer Prentis became the first (and for long the only) Jew in an
executive position at the automobile companies when he was made treasurer of General Motors Corporation.[195]

The Jewish Community Blue Book of Detroit, 1923 lists numerous synagogues, including the Mogen Abraham Congregation led by Rabbi Levin,
who also guided Congregation Beth Jacob; Ahavath Achim; B'nai Moshe;
Emanuel; and B'nai Isreal; listed, too, are such famous rabbis as Rabbi
Aishiskin, Joseph Eisenman, Joseph Thumin, and Moses Fischer. In 1923,
under the leadership of Bernard Isaacs, who was recognized by the Jewish
and non-Jewish communities for his excellence as an educator, the United
Hebrew Schools merged with the Amalgamated Hebrew Schools, including
the Division Street Talmud Torah, the Wilkins Street Talmud Torah, the
Farnsworth Street Talmud Torah, and the El Moshe School to form the
United Hebrew Schools. Their faculty included Max Gordon, former principal of the Wilkins Street Talmud Torah, J. V. Ariel, S. Becker, Joel Cashdan,
Joseph Chaggai, J. Duscoff, and others of considerable educational and/or
scholarly repute.[196]

In that same year, the Fresh Air Society had established itself at a new
camp on Lake St. Clair, just four miles from Mt. Clemens, with the support
of the Friends of the Fresh Air Society, led by Seligman Schloss.[197] Under
the auspices of the United Jewish Charities, or, more specifically under the
Fresh Air Society, Dr. Harry Saltzstein opened the doors of the North End
Clinic in 1922, offering free medical and dental care to needy Jews.[198] A
Mental Hygiene Clinic followed in 1923, and it became part of the University of Michigan Hospital services the following year; the clinic was staffed,
therefore, by UM physicians but financed by the United Jewish Charities.
In a renewed effort to professionalize some of the United Jewish Charities'
work with orphans, the Jewish Social Service Bureau was organized under
the administrative guidance of Morris Waldman, whom Fred Butzel had
recruited from New York to serve as executive director of the UJC in 1923.[199]

All of these Jewish "communal philanthropic organizations" fell under
the rubric of the UJC which, since 1918, contributed its revenue to the
Detroit Community Union and submitted its budget requirements through
that organization.[200] As they seemed to proliferate "seasonally," the countless other Jewish organizations maintained a degree of independence that
continued to defeat the alleged purpose of the UJC: to centralize in order
to avoid duplication of services.

Questions about Jewish identity persisted and reverberated with new developments in Jewish life. Reacting to historical events in Europe, America,
and the Middle East, the people of Detroit, like those in other American
metropolitan areas, faced questions involving complicated and often con- 91

tradictory definitions that transcended religious considerations alone. Debates about the internal nature of Jewish identity, how Jews define themselves as Jews, ranged from religious to cultural to political topics. Divisions
within the community along the lines of German and East European, Reform, Orthodox, and Conservative; *landsmanshaftn* and United Jewish
Charities; assimilation and autonomy; "transformationist" and "assimilationist"; "integrationism" and "survivalism" derived from internal relationships: relationships visi-à-vis each other, God, non-Jews, tradition, and
American culture.

After the year 1916–17, and increasingly in the 1920s, Zionism became
an external factor in the identity debate: as the internal factors incorporated domestic relationships, this external factor was determined by
American-Jewish relationships to Palestine and to Jews overseas. Those
questions about Jewish identity revolved around how Jews related to non-
Jewish Detroit and to each other; and how they related to Palestine and
European Jewry. The two realms, internal and external, would shape Jewish identity in Detroit—as they would in the rest of America and Europe.

In 1925 the external issue of Zionism had gained nearly primary importance. More than 170,000 American Jews were affiliated in one way or
another with the Zionist cause.[201] Yet, as one prominent Detroiter remembered, "Zionism was still a dirty word among most Jews." Not a popular
cause, it nevertheless gained respectability and participants from a broad
spectrum of enthusiastic advocates. In the realm of internal affairs—that
is, in Jewish "domestic" relationships between Jews and Jews and Jews and
non-Jews—1926 marked a watershed year. In the constant striving for coordinated community efforts, for some united front, another, stronger attempt to organize the plethora of Jewish organizations gained momentum.
This effort proved to be an enormous step toward achieving some unification but, like earlier attempts, and like similar efforts in other American
cities, its unprecedented successes were matched by the creation of even
deeper divisions.

PART II
1926–1936

One Detroit observer of Jewish organizations drew the picturesque analogy of "a jigsaw puzzle whose pieces fall into place" to characterize the "different parts of the Jewish community [of Detroit]." Yet this image somehow fails to capture the nature of Detroit Jewry in the 1920s and 1930s. More appropriate, perhaps, would be another analogy: "Pieces of different puzzles with no common picture." The picture that emerges from an examination of Jewish lives in this period appears chaotic. Controversy, disagreement, and a lack of common goals all reveal a collection of Jewish "communities" rather than a single one. Some Jews coalesced around certain aspects of various organizations, but each individual had to cope with American society in relatively isolated ways. As urban American culture eroded family ties, some Jewish families clung to each other, and some organizational affiliations served to substitute for the disintegrating communal ethos of European Jewish life.[1]

Americanization meant forsaking old-world, extended family bonds. As if to compensate, then, Jews (like other ethnic groups, but seemingly more intensely) fostered a proliferation of clubs, lodges, associations, and other types of groups designed to bring Jews together as Americans. That proliferation included the Jewish Elks, the Jewish War Veterans, and fraternal lodges. Similarly, groups like the *landsmanshaftn* seemed to exist to bring Jews together as Jews.

The Jewish Welfare Federation, founded in 1926, emerges as the single organizational attempt to create order from the apparent chaos of the disorganized, contentious, and randomized community activities. Its focus was financial and social service its goal. But Federation, unlike Jewish communal organizations in Europe, remained a problematic central institution from 1926 to 1936. No united community arose under its aegis; no consensus materialized from all or even a majority of Detroit's Jews regarding Federation's leadership role; no coherent picture appeared as the pieces of the puzzle gathered around the new center. After 1936 some of Detroit's Jews still sought some sort of communal unity; others claimed it already existed with federation.

Illusory or not, Jewish unity began to grow, in part because of Federation, but more because of external pressures. The history of the decade, however, testifies to differences among Jewish groups (and within these groups) in the midst of common pressures. Secularists, religious adherents, and Federation advocates all struggled with the same socioeconomic pressures of the Depression and with anti-Semitism. A rhythm of dialogues between adversaries and a dilation of contestable issues continued and infected even those areas where there had been traditional points of agreement. Education remained a common value, but its content became a hotly debated subject. Anti-Semitic discrimination and threats escalated, but disagreements about how or even whether to react persisted. The founding of Federation in 1926, then, may have been the first attempt since 1899 at unifying the Jews of Detroit but, despite Federation's successes in particularly harsh times, it would not be the last such attempt.

7

The Neighborhoods: A Detroit Exodus

Hastings Street no longer housed the majority of Detroit Jews by the mid-twenties. Its heyday as a haven for immigrants had passed and the protracted movement of the Jewish population north and west seemed complete by 1930.[2] German Jews had led the mini-exodus as early as 1910, and others, gaining more financial stability, followed between 1915 and 1925. By 1926, a landmark year for Detroit Jewry for a number of reasons, Hastings Street still accommodated numerous Jewish stores and shops but few Jewish residences. "If you wanted authentic bagel or lox or cottage cheese," remembered one late mover from Hastings Street, "you took a streetcar back there. But almost nobody was left there by 1930." The new center of Jewish life lay in the section known as the Oakland district, with a "second front" in the area known as Twelfth Street.

Jews had left the Hastings Street area, sometimes to escape escalating neighborhood crime—which frequently served as a euphemism for their flight from the mounting black population—sometimes in pursuit of new business opportunities as they appeared. While the Oakland area quickly took on the character of the new Jewish enclave, still other Jews, persistently extending northwest, moved to the newly developed area around

Twelfth Street. Although those neighborhoods never replicated the nature of Hastings and High Streets, they evolved into distinctly Jewish domains.

Temple Beth El relocated to an Albert Kahn–built structure on Gladstone and Woodward, between the Oakland and Twelfth Street districts, in 1922. It would remain there for fifty years—the longest-lived congregational home in Detroit history. Shaarey Zedek remained at Brush and Willis from 1913 to 1926.[3] On Holbrook and Woodward, the Jewish Community Center relocated its main branch. One block north of that was Northern High School, whose student population in the 1930s was predominantly Jewish. At Holbrook and Beaubien, just west of the North End Clinic, was Congregation Ahavas Zion, which housed one of the four branches of the United Hebrew Schools. At the heart of the neighborhood, Ahavas Achim stood for years as Orthodox Jewry's best-known congregation. A short distance from Ahavas Achim was Congregation Tifereth Israel, which was constructed in 1917. Numerous other Orthodox congregations conducted services in houses reminiscent of European *shtiblach* or homemade synagogues. During the High Holidays, still other small synagogues appeared that garnered the nickname "mushroom synagogues."

Combined with the small shops that lined Westminster and Oakland Avenues, the neighborhood displayed an openly Jewish character, yet it stood in marked contrast to the Hastings Street neighborhood. Traveling down Oakland and Delmar, north and west, the two- and four-family houses seemed to transform into mansions on Chicago and Boston Boulevards and on Arden Park, where many German and other financially successful Jews had taken residence a decade before. What became an infamous institution, the Oakland Shvitz, where reputed "Purples" (members of the Purple Gang) met, served as a public meeting place on Oakland Avenue.

Further west, in the Twelfth Street area, the religious institutions also gave the neighborhood its public Jewish flavor. On Taylor and Woodrow Wilson stood Congretation Beth Tefilo Emanuel, built in 1924 and which later became the Taylor Street Shul. Congregation Beth David (later called B'nai David) was located around the corner from the Taylor Street Shul; a short distance away was Congregation Beth Abraham. As in the Oakland area, so-called mushroom synagogues abounded during the High Holidays. Along the regions known later as the Dexter-Davison area were: the first Sephardic congregation, begun sometime after 1916 by Jacob and Judith Chicorel upon their arrival from Smyrna, Turkey;[4] Young Israel; Yeshivah Beth Yehuda; Beth Jacob; the "Hungarische Shul" (Hungarian Congregation) B'nai Moshe; the Lublin Yeshiva, under the direction of Rabbi Meyer Shapero; the Stoliner Shul; and numerous others. In the midst of the neighborhood was the Chesed Shel Emes, the burial society, located on Joy Road, not far from Congregation Shaarey Zedek that was built on Chicago Boulevard in 1932.

These religious institutions burgeoned in the midst of neighborhoods that ranged from two-family houses with small front and back yards with bushes and fences around them, to larger, single-family houses located further west. In each neighborhood, a branch of the United Hebrew Schools opened, and in the Dexter-Linwood area, Central, Durfee, and Roosevelt schools rivaled Northern in their high Jewish percentages of enrollment. By 1930 Jewish neighborhoods reached beyond Broadstreet Boulevard on the west and north of Davison and even north of Six Mile Road. There was a United Hebrew School at Tuxedo and Holmur, and Congregation B'nai Moshe prepared to relocate on Dexter. The Jewish Children's Home was constructed at Petoskey and Burlingame and opened in July 1931.[5]

Here, then, were the primary locations of the Jews of Detroit in the 1920s and 1930s. There were smaller outposts in places like Trenton, Pontiac, River Rouge, Wyandotte, Michigan Avenue, and Delray (the Hungarian purlieu).[6] But these outlying regions, including the small permanent community in Mt. Clemens, remained peripheral. Indeed, during the 1930s and 1940s, many Jews from those marginal areas moved to the principal, clearly identifiable Jewish neighborhoods, often seeking community because of the rising tide of European and American anti-Semitism.

Although unique among these small, autonomous communities, Michigan Avenue also typified their qualities. According to one former resident, it consisted of over one hundred Jewish families and grew from the 1920s into one of the largest of those "outside" neighborhoods. Its heyday came in the mid-thirties. Centered around Michigan and Thirtieth, the neighborhood included a series of streets that branched off Michigan Avenue between West Grand Boulevard and Livernois. That population, comprised primarily of Jewish merchants with stores on Michigan Avenue, lived in an unusual ethnically and racially integrated environ. Because it was primarily a Polish area, those who grew up there frequently felt that they dwelled in the "real world" instead of in a sheltered Jewish world. Three of Detroit's largest theaters, the Crystal on Michigan and Thirty-first, the Kramer on Michigan and Thirty-fifth, and the largest, the Senate on Michigan just west of Livernois, were owned by a Jewish entrepreneur in the district, Sam Shevin. The neighborhood had its kosher butcher, kosher groceries, and bakeries (the Warsaw Bakery catered to Polish Jews and non-Jews). While traditional Polish myths and superstitions about Jews surfaced occasionally, Jews like Leon Cohan, who lived in the Michigan Avenue region, recalled only rare instances of anti-Semitism and few interracial or interethnic problems.

Living outside the mainstream of Jewish life also meant feeling like outsiders, and Cohan remembers taking streetcars with his mother to the Wilson Theatre to see Yiddish shows and traveling, again by streetcar, to American Zionist Association meetings to socialize with other Jewish youngsters. As Jews increasingly left the Michigan area in the late thirties and into the forties, feelings of isolation increased and Cohan's family finally moved to the Dexter Jewish area in 1948. The twin phenomenon of fear of being left behind in increasingly black neighborhoods and the desire to live among Jews penetrated the Michigan neighborhood. While not the first area to fall to these motivations, Michigan Avenue succumbed quickly, a harbinger of demographic patterns to come.

By the mid-1920s, Detroit had become America's prime industrial city. The automobile industry continued to draw workers from other parts of the country, in particular from the South. This meant a rapid influx of unemployed, usually unskilled black laborers. Attracted by such lures as the five-dollar-a-day Ford offer,[7] the increasing number of support industries attached to the car companies, and the alleged relative freedom from discrimination, black workers and their families streamed into Detroit's East Side, and Jews streamed out.[8] While many Jewish businesses, like Rosen's Bakery, the delicatessens, and the laundries, remained in the Hastings Street neighborhood, the number of Jewish residences there decreased more rapidly after 1921.

Much of Detroit's dream attractiveness seemed to evaporate for the newer immigrants from the South, just as it had for the earlier immigrants from Europe. Ford's "radical" five-dollars-a-day plan concealed horrendous labor conditions—long hours and menial jobs with little prospect of promotion. One Wayne University Jewish economist, Prof. Samuel M. Levin (another son of Rabbi Judah Levin), published his analysis of Ford's program and concluded that it rested on the bedrock of pragmatic profit-seeking rather than on humanitarian aims.[9] Black newcomers discovered the same thing.

Paradoxically, although Detroit had grown into the industrial center of the country, it nevertheless remained the least unionized city in America.[10] Unions failed to make any headway in Detroit until the dramatic encounters that took place between labor, under such union organizers as the Reuther brothers, and management in the 1930s. Union officials were dismayed over the situation that had perturbed the Workmen's Circle organizers: a near-total lack of worker consciousness and a consequent refusal, often hostile, to unionize. While this situation remained widespread among most Jews, it did not continue after the 1930s among blacks, and a number of Jews participated in the administrative organization and support of the union movement.[11] Perhaps most notable among these supporters was Maurice Sugar, the outspoken Communist lawyer whose activities in Detroit became legendary. As if to typify the relationship between Jews and the labor movement, however, Sugar—who never denied his Jewish background—hardly identified himself as a Jew, and the Jews of Detroit reciprocated. During the red-baiting years of the 1920s and thirties, even Jewish radicals generally eschewed links with the communist movement, and Sugar's apparent die-hard support of the Stalinist Soviet regime, as he lectured for the Friends of the Soviet Union, alienated them even more.[12] It would be in the 1940s that Jewish labor leaders would emerge, but, with the exceptions of people like Isador Lipsitz, who joined the Plumber's Local in 1911, Jews were rarely found among the rank and file of most of the unions. (The general exception to this phenomenon came in the Laundry and Linen Drivers Union, which became Teamsters Laundry Drivers Local 285 in 1937; see below.)

Freedom from discrimination had proved to be a myth that may have jolted newcomers, but which no longer deceived Jews, and it became an ideal of which blacks were quickly disabused. In 1926 Henry Ford's campaign against the "International Jew" in his *Dearborn Independent* seemed no more than a faded nightmare that persisted in keeping Jews from buying Ford automobiles. Most Jews accepted anti-Semitism, like racism, as a fact of American life—not as bad as in Europe, but demonstrating that the New World was no *goldene Medine* (golden country), either. Ford's renewed anti-Jewish crusade was yet to begin; yet the residual anti-Semitic effects of earlier incidents echoed still and gained impetus from groups more obviously violent. The Black Legion, for example, an organization based in Michigan and Ohio, anti-Jewish, anti-black, and anti-Catholic increased its clandestine activities with midnight raids on homes, destruction of newspaper offices, attacks on individuals, murders, and cross-burnings. The Legion even offered candidates for the Michigan legislature. They were matched by the rise in activities of the Ku Klux Klan in the 1920s.[13]

The ethnic composition of the city almost guaranteed some form of anti-Semitism and racism, and even uptown German Jews recalled housing discrimination among the upper-crust Detroit society, which continued to reflect the prejudices Brandeis had observed in the Detroit Athletic Club. Ironically, that same ethnicism promoted Protestant fundamentalist Americanism, which increasingly manifested itself through Klan and Legion rallies and augmentation. In 1924 the mayoral race threatened to produce a Klan mayor; it provided an uncommon occasion for collaborative political efforts among blacks and ethnic groups, including Jews.[14] Problems of Klan and Black Legion anti-Semitism were compounded by antagonism between Jews and other victim groups—blacks, Poles, Catholics, Irish—over economic and entrepreneurial conflicts. And if those prejudices and superstitions that fostered such conflicts were not as widespread before as they had been after 1920, the seeds nevertheless existed.

As America's fastest developing industrial center, Detroit pioneered revolutionary changes that affected virtually every aspect of life. Paved roads, middle-class suburban neighborhoods fostered by the easy access to automobiles, and closed cars all heralded faster-paced, radically different lifestyles. Such changes shook the foundations of rural America, which began to sense the death of the traditional values and conventions that had governed life for centuries. To many, the purveyors of modernity came from the city; and among those who believed that modern civilization threatened all that was good, Christian, and hallowed, "city" meant Jews.[15]

Jews in Detroit confronted these rapid changes in Detroit life with a broad variety of responses. While discrimination seemed on the rise, integration and assimilation also increased. A series of articles and letters in the *Detroit Jewish Chronicle* in 1930 found Jewish young women complaining that Jewish young men seemed to prefer dating gentile women. A number of letters seemed hostile to the idea of dating only Jews, but a significant proportion decried a lack of social groups and facilities for Jewish youth.[16] Although social assimilation usually occurred among wealthier and more educated Jews—among German Jews, in particular—the issue had broken into public discussion. Along with such troubles and fears of intermarriage, mounting assimilation meant that more and more eminent Jews became prominent Detroit citizens. As had been the case earlier, German Jews, such as the Butzels, the Kahns, the Winemans, the Kroliks, continued to gain prestige among Detroit high society, although few if any moved to Grosse Pointe, that enclave of aristocratic, gentile wealth. Jewish relief agencies, which were still run by German Jews, would join efforts with Detroit agencies, sometimes affiliating with them, as the United Jewish Charities had when they joined the Detroit Community Union. But such individual success stories as those prominent Jewish families represented heralded other successes on the communal level. If freedom had yielded success, success brought opportunities to expand community services and emulate the more effective professional agencies established by American non-Jews. Firmly convinced of their American identities, Detroit's proprietary (usually Reform) Jews, turned increasingly from religious services to community service in order to express their Jewish identity. In the eyes of some; it remained a problematic wellspring of Jewish consciousness.

8

Synagogues: Spiritual Survival under Siege

By the 1920s people drastically disagreed on the future course of Jewish religiosity. In March 1926, Rabbi Herbert Goldstein, president of the Union of Orthodox Congregations in America, predicted that the reawakening of Orthodox Judaism was not far off.[17] Yet, a *Detroit Jewish Chronicle* editorial of 1927 predicted a serious decline in Orthodoxy. As far as any serious possibility of Jews readopting traditional practices and points of view, the editorial asserted, "We may be excused for harboring a doubt as to whether it can happen again—particularly in America."[18]

In the 1927 *The Jazz Singer,* the first talking motion picture, Al Jolson, American Jewry's darling of the screen and stage, played a young man torn between his growing success as a jazz singer and a sense of obligation to his religious parents, in particular to his cantor father. The screenplay states bluntly that "Jack [the hero played by Jolson] is besieged by the old life and the new, filial duty against his life's ambition, the past against the future." Although the film offers a typical Hollywood "happy ending," with Jolson returning home to chant the Kol Nidre for his sick father, the final scene depicts him performing his famous "Mammy" before a theater audience that includes his smiling mother and, not insignificantly, his dis-   103 tinctly non-Jewish show-business fiancée, who miraculously has found acceptance by the *yiddishe mama*. Behind the joyful veneer of the film, with Jolson's exuberance and the distinction of having the first talkie include the Kol Nidre, lurked a starker authenticity.

When Jack's (Jakie's) mother comments that her son has Jewish prayers "in his head, but . . . not in his heart," she hints at those darker and deeper meanings that Jews in America could understand or at least intuit. Film historian Neal Gabler argues that the conflicted hero "can affect no resolution. His father won't let him be an American; America won't let him be a Jew."[19] Issues of religious abandonment, of the impossibility of blending Judaism with Americanism stood out in sharp relief in the film and increasingly in real life. Jews in 1927 found the young man's conflict realistic and moving.

The massive cutback in the number of Europeans immigrating to the United States in the mid-1920s emphasized American Jewry's growing physical and emotional separation from its sources. Detroit Jews began to feel more distant from a Europe that many never had seen or hardly remembered. The effect was notable in every area of religious practice. As early as 1922 Rabbi Hershman, of Congregation Shaarey Zedek, noted in an address to the Phoenix Club that most Jews were neither Orthodox nor Reform but unaffiliated.[20] Greater numbers of Jews showed increased interest in non-Jewish holidays like Halloween and Christmas. Several German Jewish families for a generation had enjoyed Christmas trees in their homes while neglecting such fundamentals of Judaism as the Passover seders. One study in the late 1920s recorded Jewish college students' lack of interest in and knowledge of their own religion.[21]

People came to synagogues less frequently, perhaps only for such special events as the High Holidays or bar-mitzvahs. Observance of the Sabbath also declined. Orthodox immigrant parents of families of eight, ten, or twelve children could rarely expect all or even any to keep the Sabbath rituals in all their details.

Yet synagogues still functioned, of course, and as the Jews migrated out of Hastings Street, the synagogues moved with them. As early as 1919 the Emanuel congregation had established temporary quarters in the northwest area, and it moved into its permanent building on Taylor, in the Twelfth Street neighborhood, in 1926. In 1931 it merged with Beth Tikvah, where Joseph Eisenman was rabbi.[22] Rabbi Rabinowitz's Beth Shmuel moved to Blaine in 1933. Congregation B'nai David (formerly Beth David) moved to Elmhurst and Fourteenth Avenue and a young American rabbi, Joshua Sperka, replaced the retiring Rabbi Aishishkin. Rabbi Sperka graduated from the Hebrew Theological College in Chicago firmly Orthodox; nevertheless he introduced some new ideas into the synagogue; including extensive youth groups, Friday-night socials, and a Sunday-morning club. He could not prevent the institution of modified mixed seating around 1934.[23] Similarly,

Max J. Wohlgelernter, an American-educated rabbi, who came to Beth Tikvah Emanuel in 1931 emphasized the role of youth and social groups in
the synagogue, as well as the prayers and the study of the Torah in the
old style. Both rabbis, Sperka and Wohlgelernter, were also active in religious Zionist affairs, as was Rabbi Isaac Stollman, who served as president
of the World Mizrachi Organization (the religious Zionists).

These men viewed their time as a time of siege and crisis; a time not
to expand and achieve gains in and for Orthodox Judaism, but to struggle
and to minimize losses. In the survey of Jewish religious life conducted by
Rabbi Sperka in 1935, he found forty-four synagogues that together had
a total of 2,497 members. They had a maximum seating capacity of about
sixteen thousand and were well attended only on the High Holidays. About
twenty-one hundred people attended Saturday-morning services. Eleven
synagogues had permanent rabbis who were generally poorly paid.[24] Older
members tended to be unaware of the problems facing American Jewry,
and younger people seemed unconcerned with retaining Jewish religious
practices and traditions. Political liberalism seemed to attract many Jews,
offering to some answers to anti-Semitism and the other problems that
faced them in America and to others, a substitute for a religious tradition
from which they believed liberal values derived.

While Jews tended to give up the strict observance of the Sabbath and
of mikvah rather quickly; many still avoided, at least to some degree, eating nonkosher food. Rabbi Aaron Ashinsky led a group that induced the
Michigan legislature to pass a law stating that food could not be sold as
kosher unless certified by the proper authorities.[25] Under the leadership of
Rabbi Ashinsky, from 1926 to 1934 recognized as Detroit's premier Orthodox sage, a Council of Orthodox Rabbis (the *Vaad* Harabonim) was organized in 1930 to supervise kashrut in Detroit. Its stated goal was to care
for Jewish matters, to help stem the decline of Judaism, especially in Detroit, and to establish a central authority for the supervision of kashrut in
the city. It would also deal with matters of marriage, divorce, conversion,
and adoption.[26] Questions of Jewish identity, then, ultimately would be
adjudicated by Orthodox sages.

Still, problems persisted: some occasionally questioned the truthfulness
of kosher butchers and of labeling of Passover foods; despite rabbinic ad-
monitions, Jewish organizations often served nonkosher meals at their public
meetings and affairs; restaurants that claimed to be kosher were usually,
in fact, "kosher style," that is, they served old Jewish favorites like chopped
liver or chicken soup with *kneidlach* but did not necessarily prepare them
according to Jewish law.[27] Efforts to organize the religious leadership met
with some success. In 1933 a *Vaad Ha-ir* that reprsented the synagogues'
leaders was formed.[28]

A group of young people who sought to maintain an Orthodox way of
life organized a Young Israel group in 1925 as part of the national Young   105

Israel movement. The first group met for Sabbath services in a room at the Jewish Center on Melbourne. Solomon Cohen, Abe Rosenshine, David Berris, and Irving Schlussel, among others, were among its early adherents.[29] A few small Young Israel groups formed, usually holding services in a side room of an established synagogue. By the early 1930s, one Young Israel group met for services on Joy Road and Linwood in a small wooden building that was hardly more than a shack. The most active group, in the Oakland neighborhood, was led by Sam Novetsky. They seemed so successful that the synagogue in which they met feared that too many adults were joining and refused them their facilities. The day was saved when the Tifereth Israel synagogue on Cameron invited the group to use their sanctuary.

Young Israel struggled through the 1920s and 1930s as most Jewish youngsters were attracted to the more liberal branches of Judaism or lost interest altogether. However, a nucleus developed and many early members remained active in Young Israel through the shifting of neighborhoods and the passing of many decades. But the majority of younger Jews, second- or third-generation Americans, seemed to view much of Jewish ritual as medieval and outmoded, although they might heartily approve of Jewish moral precepts. One often-debated proposal was whether a new Sanhedrin, a governing body, should be convened that would have the power to "modernize" Jewish law.[30]

Conservative Judaism asserted concentrated efforts to regain young people for Jewish religious practice. Thus its motives resembled those of the Reform movement and of some Orthodox groups, such as the Young Israel, yet Conservatism's rabbis refused to jettison so much Jewish tradition in favor of Americanization. Marshall Sklare has pointed out that the organizers of the Conservative movement hoped to attract young Jews but encountered the problems "of developing a service which would be traditional and at the same time modern so that the American Jew could find himself at home."[31]

In accordance with that mandate, while the Jews of Detroit moved further from their physical (European) and religious (ritual) roots, Conservative synagogues, most notably Congregation Shaarey Zedek, instituted changes in religious procedures. The first and most serious manifestation of that severance from roots had been the loss of young worshippers; and the second, an attempt to stem the tide, evolved over decades: the introduction of mixed seating (men and women together) in some of the old synagogues. This trend accompanied the building of new synagogues affiliated with the Conservative movement.

Shaarey Zedek had already begun to take the lead in attempts to entice young Jews into religious attachment. The impressive, newly constructed synagogue on Chicago stirred busily with classes, groups, and various activities. In the early 1930s, Saturday-night songfests were instituted and attracted about one hundred participants to a member's house for singing and for coffee and cake. In 1934, a consecration ceremony for girls was begun. This was a matter of some importance to Rabbi Hershman, who believed strongly in education for girls. One of the finest synagogue libraries in the city opened in 1935 under the direction of its librarian, Janet Olender.[32] Following a widespread trend in Conservative synagogues, Shaarey Zedek instituted Friday-night social programs that included singing, refreshments, and talks by Rabbi Hershman or guest speakers.[33]

Despite such changes, which struck many Orthodox members as drastic, Rabbi Hershman tried to combine the best of the old and new for his congregants. The service remained traditional. People continued to visit each other on Saturday afternoons after the Sabbath lunch, and the feeling of closeness and community that had become the hallmark of that congregation remained for those who chose to enjoy it.

As spiritual leader of Congregation Shaarey Zedek for nearly forty years (1907–1946), Rabbi A. M. Hershman was an important figure in Detroit— and not only among Jews. Born in Lithuania, he seemed to exude the scholarship of traditional rabbis. He eventually earned two doctorates from the Jewish Theological Seminary; his work toward his second degree had included a dissertation on the Jews of late-medieval Spain. From that work evolved Hershman's acclaimed biography of R. Isaac ben Sheshet Perfet, the great Sephardic rabbi of the fourteenth century. His translation of a section of Maimonides' *Mishnah Torah* for Yale University Press remains a standard work in its field. Author of several other scholarly books and articles, Hershman joined the small ranks of eminent Jewish scholars in Detroit. As a devoted supporter of Zionism who was active in the Mizrachi, the religious Zionist movement, Hershman was among Detroit's first religious supporters of a Jewish state in Palestine. The A. M. Hershman Chair at Bar Ilan University in Ramat Gan, Israel, recognizes his dedication.[34]

As time went on, a pattern emerged. As they moved from the Hastings Street neighborhood, several synagogues—particularly those whose moves coincided with the retirement of their European immigrant rabbis—gave up separate seating and joined the Conservative movement. Congregation B'nai David officially maintained its affiliation with Orthodoxy; there too, however, a modified mixed-seating plan was introduced in about 1934. (The ten front rows of the main floor were for men and the front rows of the balcony were for women. The rest was mixed.)[35]

Sociologists, historians, students of religion, and individuals who observed the immense decline of interest in Jewish religious observances and practice have offered numerous hypotheses for the phenomenon.[36] They are matched by Detroit observers who posited radically different evaluations of the virtues and vices of assimilation, American middle-class pressures, upward mobility, and other elements that contributed to changing attitudes and identities. One school of thought suggested that most learned and devout European Jews had remained in Europe, despite the pogroms and poverty, for fear that in America they and their children would become less devout. Indeed, a number of leading European rabbis openly spoke out against emigration from Europe and, in some cases, families would try to talk parents into leaving children behind so that they could continue an intense study of the Torah. Yet another suggestion claimed that public education in America offered a new, free entry into society and a freedom new to Jews. In such an environment, the traditional love of learning and emphasis on education shifted from study of Torah and Talmud to the new secular studies then available to Jewish children.[37]

Individuals repeatedly recalled, however, the difficulty of maintaining sanctity of the Sabbath in America. Jewish historians have argued that observing the Sabbath had been perceived as one of the most essential elements of Judaism, and Orthodox Jews in Detroit avowed that the diminution of that observance did irreparable damage to the practice of Orthodox Judaism in Detroit. The lure of material gain, business success as a concomitant of abandoning Sabbath observance, also attracted and sometimes overwhelmed Jewish immigrants. Frequently, old rituals seemed less attractive than business success.

In February 1922, a well-publicized incident dramatized the growing gap between the sanctification and the neglect of the Sabbath. When the girl students of a talmud torah school in Hamtramck announced plans for a Friday-night dance, an immediate controversy broke out among their parents. This dance would, of course, violate the traditional Sabbath laws. Even the New York City–based Yiddish newspaper, the *Tageblatt,* published strongly worded editorials opposing the dance. Surprised by the reaction, the girls canceled the dance.[38] The episode demonstrates the dominant trend of Detroit and American Jews away from Sabbath observance—a trend that continued and accelerated.

Other Detroit Jews have suggested that the old-style European-born rabbis could not communicate well with the American-born Jewish generation. Perhaps, like most people around them, they lacked the foresight to comprehend the hastening decline of religious Jewishness and how far it would eventually go.

Throughout this period of religious flux, Orthodox synagogues maintained their traditional Eastern European style. But the lack of young worshippers was becoming increasingly noticeable as members of the new generation joined Beth El or the burgeoning Conservative movement, or as they abandoned Jewish worship altogether. Those changes, even including that ominous abandonment, did not necessarily signify the younger Jews' abandonment of their Jewish personae; yet some of Detroit's more financially successful Jews assumed a politically conservative, Republican image with little or no visible trace of "Jewishness."[39] Others, drawn to political liberalism that sometimes seemed to lead them back to more traditional

Jewish values, assumed a more progressive, democratic, or even socialist stance, similarly deemphasizing their Jewish backgrounds.[40] For many outside the Orthodox tradition, the question remained, or resurfaced with renewed force: What did it mean to be a Jew?

9

The Jewish Welfare Federation of Detroit

Those in Detroit who had dedicated themselves to philanthropy as a vehicle to express their Jewishness also began to feel the impact of change and modernization. When Rabbi Franklin and others established the United Jewish Charities in 1899, they had hoped to reduce what they perceived as a chaotic collection of independent charities and relief societies. Each member agency had kept its identity, but the UJC seemed to have reduced the chaos by integrating those agencies and their functions into one controlling organization, with one treasury and one disbursing bureau. Directors of the individual agencies sat on the UJC board to consult on the tripartite aims of "direct relief, clothing to the poor, and charity."[41]

Yet by 1916 inefficiencies and failings were apparent. Apart from the harsh and insensitive procedures sometimes practiced by caseworkers and investigators, and even at times by members of the board of directors, the deeper structural problems of the organization were revealed by the UJC's responses to the recession of 1921, which drastically increased the number of relief requests. Miss Blanche Hart, executive director of the UJC, wrote in the 1916–1917 Yearbook that the UJC "needs to bring into its Federation all organizations whose interest is the welfare of Jews. . . . [It] must be all embracing and responsible for the support of organizations of moral, social and philanthropic endeavors. . . ." She continued her critical evaluation by pointing out deficiencies in the organization: its failure to reach all constituents not concerned with charities and its lack of coordination.[42]

A perusal of the minutes of the United Jewish Charities board of directors meetings reveals an obvious overburdening of Miss Hart. She not only took the minutes, she delivered virtually every report, presented synopses of requests for relief, and offered recommendations on those requests. Yet, despite her dedication, Hart's cynicism appeared to have mounted from 1916, as she seemed to distrust her constituents. Her criticisms of the organization should be measured in light of these factors, especially the onerous difficulties surrounding her position.

As the Jewish population grew in the 1920s, with the impact of the recession of 1921–1922, greater demands revealed that the services of the UJC were increasingly inadequate. In October 1920, Miss Mary Caplan was hired to supervise educational and recreational activities organized by the UJC.[43] In 1922 Mrs. Rose Lipson came from Boston to head the Relief Committee under the supervision of Miss Hart. That department included legal aid, medical assistance, child care, guardianship, loans, foster care for orphans, transient care, food for Passover, adoption, prison relief, and housekeeping services. It also offered relief and aid for resettling European Jewish refugees after World War I.[44] The staff's growth indicated the organization's realization of the need to expand. Unfortunately, it seemed that the UJC could not expand quickly enough; nor did it seem to expand in the appropriate directions.

With a gift from Leopold Wineman, the United Jewish Charities commissioned a panel of Jewish sociologists, social workers, and scholars to perform a self-study of the organization and of the Jews of Detroit. Directed by Harry Lurie, the *Survey* of 1923 proved disturbing in its implications; it primarily argued that the UJC, for all its accomplishments, had fallen behind the times, that it practiced outdated forms of social services and desperately needed to expand, overhaul, or somehow change its procedures and staff.[45] For Fred M. Butzel, the chairman of the board of the United Jewish Charities, the *Survey* signaled a call for significant change. If Detroit's Jews were to be a recognized power in the world of American Jewry, something would have to be altered. Butzel, who already had achieved a reputation as Detroit's premier Jewish philanthropist, received an advance copy of the *Survey* and convened executive sessions of the board of directors to discuss the implications of the report and to decide on a course of action.[46]

While the Lurie Commission acknowledged a consistent, pronounced dedication to philanthropic efforts that manifested itself through intelligent discussion, it noted, too, a rather narrow participation in those discussions. Lacking broad participation, the work and the education of directors or trustees seemed uncoordinated. Such a lack of coordination and unprofessional debate meant repeated deliberations about such topics as children's boarding, an old age home, a hospital, the Hebrew Free Loan Association facilities, and more. The *Survey* suggested, however, that discussion seemed to inhibit action. Perhaps the most significant praise offered to the UJC by the survey evaluated its integrated work with the Detroit Community Union. Successful accommodation with non-Jewish charities revealed both the strengths and the weaknesses of the UJC.[47]

The *Survey* noted several major deficiencies in the operations of the UJC, among them: an absence of cooperation among educational, relief, and medical departments; no consistent policy of case assignment and no control of caseworkers; little or no family casework except on an ad-hoc emergency basis; inadequate staffing; inadequate work for boarding homes and child care. The need to improve procedures of resettlement work, child care. The need to improve procedures of resettlement work, child care, staffing, and coordination of programs became evident throughout the document. Included, also, were blunt statements about the lack of understanding and sympathy toward the East European Jews, especially Orthodox Jews, and less blunt but clear comments about a condescending attitude that was adopted toward those segments of the Jewish population and related aspects of Jewish culture.[48]

Lurie's commission reflected contemporary trends in Jewish social work—trends that subtly altered customary approaches to philanthropic practices. Since 1920, when the Jewish Aid Society of Chicago changed its name to the Jewish Social Service Bureau of Chicago, other Jewish agencies had begun to modify their names and their styles of practice. Jewish "social service" bureaus replaced Jewish "charities" and "relief" societies. In New York, Cleveland, Baltimore, and Chicago the changes in names represented "changes in outlook and point of view, method and philosophy."[49] The word had not yet reached Detroit, where volunteer women's groups still conducted charity work among needy families, and overworked staff members divided their time between attending meetings, keeping records, minding office work, and investigating requests for assistance.

On the brink of maturity, then, the organization that had represented itself as Detroit Jewry's voice and service agency undertook a momentous transformation. Fred M. Butzel seems to have led the way in his vision and action; others, such as Henry Wineman and Julian Krolik, members of the UJC board, joined Butzel in the vanguard of the movement toward federation. Those who had served the UJC moved with this new tide, supporting the idea financially as well as intellectually: William Friedman, Judge Theodore Levin, Abraham Srere, Israel Himelhoch, Meyer Prentis, Milford Stern, Henry Meyers, Nate Shapero, Mrs. Henry Wineman, and Dora (Mrs. Joseph) Ehrlich continued their active participation in the work of Jewish social service, as did D. W. Simons, Judge Harry Keidan, and Adolph

Finsterwald. Most of them successful businessmen, they brought credibility and prestige to the new organization.[50]

In September 1923, Hart resigned her position as director of the UJC. After an extensive nationwide search, her position was filled by Morris Waldman, a professional Jewish social worker from New York who assumed his new responsibilities in Detroit in September 1924.[51] He promptly submitted a proposal for a federation of agencies, tightly organized and with specifically designated tasks, to succeed the UJC. Waldman, already experienced in Jewish social-service work in Boston, embodied new notions of professionalism and efficiency. One of his first acts in Detroit was to hire his former coworker from Boston, Esther Ruth Prussian. She would remain as a dynamic, masterful assistant director into the 1960s. In effect, she became "house executive secretary." Prussian seemed to know everyone and was repeatedly described as "efficient and hard-working." Isidore Sobeloff, who became executive director of the Jewish Welfare Federation in 1937, called Esther Prussian "the personification of . . . Federation."

At its board meeting, on May 4, 1926, the United Jewish Charities was dissolved, "and responsibility for continuing local welfare, cultural, recreational and medical services to the community" was formally turned over to a federation of Jewish agencies headed by the Jewish Welfare Federation on May 5. The UJC continued to exist as "the property-holding corporation of the Jewish Welfare Federation."[52] Waldman's plan was thus sanctioned, and invitations to join the new federation went out to the United Hebrew Schools, the Hebrew Free Loan Association, the Young Women's Hebrew Association, the Jewish Old Folks' Home, the Detroit Hebrew Orphans Home, and the Hebrew House of Shelter.[53] All of these organizations eventually affiliated with the new federation, with the Old Folks' Home coming under its aegis in 1931. The four subsidiary agencies proposed in the comprehensive Waldman Federation plan were the North End Clinic, the Fresh Air Society, the Jewish Social Service Bureau, and the Jewish Centers Association.[54] With the exception of the Fresh Air Society, these emerged as new agencies to assume efficiently organized and clearly delineated tasks.

Under the headline, "What Will Detroit Jewry Do?" the new executive director of the United Jewish Charities, Morris D. Waldman, issued a challenge to the Jews of Detroit that was published in the *Detroit Jewish Chronicle* on September 10, 1926, ten days after the articles of association were adopted:

> Within the past two years the Jewish people of this city have been awakened to the desirability of organizing their forces in such a way as to meet the larger and more complex needs of a much-increased and rapidly growing population. . . . What part shall the Jewish people take in the development of this great metropolis? Shall it be a creditable part? Shall it be an aimless drifting, a fortuitous adjustment, or shall it be a conscious organization of their capacities for their own good and the good of the city as a whole. . . .

113

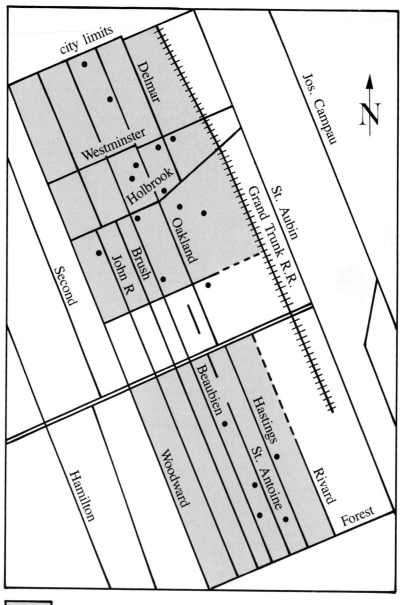

city limits

Jos. Campau

N

Delmar

Grand Trunk R.R.

St. Aubin

Westminster

Holbrook

Oakland

Second

Brush

John R

Beaubien

Woodward

Hastings

St. Antoine

Rivard

Hamilton

Forest

▧ Highest Jewish Density   ● Synagogue

Upper Hastings and Oakland in 1930

The North End Clinic, Holbrook Street, Detroit, in the 1940s. (Courtesy of the Archives of the Jewish Welfare Federation.)

Congregation B'nai Moshe, 90373 Dexter, Detroit, 1929. (Courtesy of the collection of Manning Brothers, Photographers.)

Tom's Market, forerunner of the Farmer Jack Markets, 14406 Gratiot, Detroit, in 1927. (Courtesy of the collection of Farmer Jack Markets.)

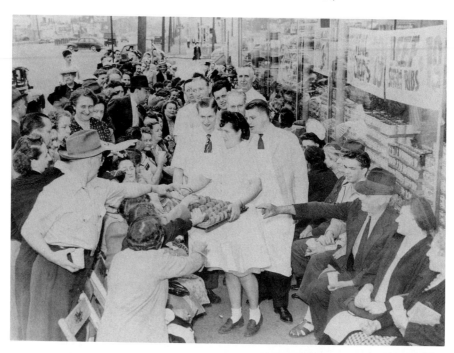

United Hebrew Schools class at the Tuxedo-Holmur branch, Detroit, led by Joseph Chaggai, 1930s. *Center:* Judith Levin. (Courtesy of the collection of the Jewish Federation Apartments.)

The Jewish Vocational Service: interviewer Anna Rose Hersh meeting with a client, 1930s. (Courtesy of the collection of the Jewish Vocational Service.)

Hebrew Free Loan president David S. Zemon interviewing client at offices at 1915 Clairmont, ca. 1930. (Courtesy of the Archives of the Jewish Welfare Federation.)

Hebrew Free Loan
Association, 9134
Linwood, Detroit, ca.
1930–1937. (Courtesy of
the Archives of the Jewish
Welfare Federation.)

Yeshiva Beth Yehuda:
opening of new building
at Sturtevant, Detroit,
1955. Susan Goldberg and
Rabbi Isaac Stollman,
dean of the Council of
Orthodox Rabbis.
(Courtesy of the collection
of Yeshiva Beth Yehuda.)

Mendelson's Atlantic Resort in South Haven, operated by Dave Mendelson, ca. 1930; later owned by Ben and Harriet Taitel. (Courtesy of the collection of Richard Appleyard and the South Haven Public Library.)

Congregation Shaarey Zedek: Celebrating the opening of the new sanctuary on Chicago Boulevard, Detroit, 1931–1932. *From right:* Rabbi A. M. Hershman of Congregation Shaarey Zedek, Rabbi Louis Finkelstein of the Jewish Theological Seminary, A. Louis Gordon, president, M. Stone, vice-president, Israel Katz, M. Bernstein. (Courtesy of the Archives of Congregation Shaarey Zedek.)

Congregation Shaarey Zedek
sunday school assembly on steps
of the synagogue, Chicago
Boulevard, Detroit, 1932.
(Courtesy of the Archives of
Congregation Shaarey Zedek.)

Morris Waldman, executive
director, Jewish Welfare
Federation, 1924–1928.
(Courtesy of the Archives of the
Jewish Welfare Federation.)

Congregation Shaarey Zedek Sisterhood on steps of Knollwood Country Club, ca.
1930. *Top row:* Bessie (Mrs. Herman) Cohen, Belle (Mrs. David) Lichtig, ———,
Rae (Mrs. A. B.) Stralser. *Second row:* Mrs. Samuel Eder, Ida (Mrs. Morris)
Blumberg, Frieda Weinstein, Rhoda (Mrs. Theodore) Levin, Miriam Hershman
(wife of Rabbi A. M. Hershman), Mary Zemon, Elizabeth (Mrs. Hyman) Kaplan,
Rose (Mrs. Abraham) Cooper, Bertha (Mrs. Saul) Saulson. *Third row:* Dora (Mrs.
Moe) Leiter, ———, Millie (Mrs. Sol) Kaufman, Rebecca "Bea" (Mrs. Maurice),
Zackheim, Hattie Gittleman, Lillian (Mrs. Charles) Smith, Jennie (Mrs. Oscar)
Blumberg. *Fourth row:* Henrietta (Mrs. A. Louis) Gordon, Lil (Mrs. David)
Diamond, Gloria (Mrs. Simon) Shetzer, Gertrude Kopel, Sadie (Mrs. Harry Z.)
Brown, Gertrude (Mrs. Herbert) Warner, Rose (Mrs. Robert) Loewenberg, Sally
(Mrs. Ralph) Davidson, Elizabeth Finley, Rose (Mrs. David) Fauman, ———.
(Courtesy of the Archives of Congregation Shaarey Zedek.)

Meyer L. Prentis with leaders of the Allied
Jewish Campaign, 1930. *Top, from left:*
Mrs. Henry Wineman, Meyer L. Prentis,
Mrs. Edwin M. Rosenthal. *Center left:*
Aaron DeRoy. *Center right:* Samuel
Summerfield. *Bottom left:* Clarence H.
Enggass. *Bottom center:* Henry Wineman.
Bottom right: Adolph Finstenwald.
(Courtesy of Jewell Morris.)

Dr. John Slawson, executive director,
Jewish Welfare Federation, 1928–1932.
(Courtesy of the Blaustein Library of the
American Jewish Committee, New York
City.)

Samuel Summerfield
1926–1931

Aaron DeRoy
1931–1934

Dora B. Ehrlich
1934–1937

Gus D. Newman
1937–1941

Irving W. Blumberg
1941–1949

Harvey H. Goldman
1949–1951

Milton K. Mahler
1951–1957

Jack O. Lefton
1957–1961

Max M. Shaye
1961–1965

George D. Keil
1965–1967

Paul Broder
1967–1971

Presidents of the Detroit Service Group of the Jewish Welfare Federation, 1926–
1971. (Courtesy of the Archives of the Jewish Welfare Federation.)

Chairman of the Allied Jewish Campaign Aaron DeRoy, *left,* congratulates
George M. Stutz, *center,* and Gus. D. Newman, 1932. (Courtesy of the Archives
of the Jewish Welfare Federation.)

Early leadership of the Jewish Welfare Federation, 1933. *Rear:* Ben B. Fenton, Harry H. Platt, Harry S. Grant, Nate S. Shapero, Irving W. Blumberg, Sidney Stone, Charles N. Agree, Alex Schreiber, Nathan Metzger, Reuben J. Rosenfeld. *Center:* Sidney L. Alexander, Harvey H. Goldman, Charles E. Feinberg, Mrs. Edwin M. Rosenthal, Barney Smith, Aaron Silberblatt. *Seated:* Meyer L. Prentis, Kurt Peiser, Aaron DeRoy, Henry Wineman, George M. Stutz, Gus D. Newman. (Courtesy of the Archives of the Jewish Welfare Federation.)

Hank Greenberg of the Detroit Tigers, ca. 1938. (Courtesy of Irwin Cohen and the Detroit Tigers.)

Joseph Zeltzer, first Jewish veterinarian in Michigan, in the 1920s. (Courtesy of George M. Zeltzer.)

Judge Harry B. Keidan, Recorders Court judge 1919–1927 and Circuit Court judge 1927–1943, in the 1920s. (Courtesy of the Archives of Congregation Shaarey Zedek.)

Halevy Musical Society, 1925. *Top row, from left:* ———, Aaron Edgar, Morris Schaver, ———, ———. *Second row:* Israel Hertz, ———, Eugene Franzlau, William Gayman, ———, ———, Max Levy. *Seated:* ———, Rose Stein, Rhoda Zahave, ———, Julius Miller, ———, ———, ———, ———. *Below:* ———, Rebecca Frohman, Emma Schaver, ———. (Courtesy of the collection of Emma Schaver.)

Ladies of the Phoenix Club, 1920s. (Courtesy of the Archives of Congregation Shaarey Zedek.)

Sholem Aleichem Institute first graduating class, 1928. *Top row, from left:* Sam Chapin, Mollie Raymon, Myra Komaroff Wolfgang, Morris Bader, Lillian F. Gold, Rose Rush, Morris Littwin. *Middle row:* ———, Shlome Bercovich, Dr. Chaim Zhitlowsky, Joseph Comay, Chaim Pomerantz. *Seated:* Joseph Cochin, Dena G. Greenberg, Amos Comay. (Courtesy of Dena Greenberg.)

The Kinder Theater, 539 Kenilworth, Detroit, under construction in 1927. *On left:* Boris Litvin. *Behind on left:* Shlome Bercovich. *Next:* Max Holtzman. (Courtesy of the Jewish Historical Society of Michigan.)

Non-Partisan Yiddish Folk School, 1930s. *Second row, from left:* Norman Drachler, Israel Drachler, Dr. Chaim Zhitlowsky, Joseph Comay, Shlome Bercovich. (Courtesy of Betty Schein.)

Albert Kahn, *left,* with Henry Ford, Glenn Martin of Martin Aviation, and Charles Sorenson of Ford Motor Co., ca. 1935–1938. (Courtesy of the collection of the Albert Kahn Associates.)

Detroit Hebrew Orphan Home, 47 Rowena, Detroit, 1937. (Courtesy of the Archives of the Jewish Welfare Federation.)

The time is past when the Jewish Community must concern itself only with its negative problems such as dependency and delinquency—charities and correction. We must deal with the positive aspects of life—with the control, so far as voluntary action can be effective, of the life of the Jewish people in all their relationships.[55]

At least in retrospect, the signing of the articles associating the Jewish Welfare Federation of Detroit must appear as a symbolic scenario. Next to such Detroit Reform leaders as Rabbi Franklin stood Esser Rabinowitz and Bernard Isaacs, the president and superintendent, respectively, of the United Hebrew Schools; alongside the Winemans and Butzels were Rabbis Ashinsky and Stollman, both leaders in the Mizrachi Orthodox Zionist movement. The concept of "one great *kehillah,*" a council responsible for the direction of the entire Jewish community, seemed within reach.[56] Despite the similarities to that old-world institution, such an idea had its detractors, and Federation leaders frequently disclaimed the *kehillah* analogy.

Assimilated and nonassimilated Jews agreed upon the signing, and the inclusion of the United Hebrew Schools (UHS) would later be viewed by Philip Slomovitz as one way that "the new Federation atoned for two sins [of the UJC]," that is, by accepting Hebrew into the educational curriculum and by including Zionists in the ranks of Detroit's Jewish leadership.[57] Pressed, apparently, by Fred Butzel, the founders of Federation funded the UHS in 1926. That allocation would increase, and then decline during the Depression. In 1939, it rose again to more than $36,000.[58] The Depression would add more arduous burdens to the continuation of Jewish education—burdens the federation obliged itself to shoulder.

As if to emphasize the distance spanned in that historic meeting, Slomovitz pointed out that some of those signers had opposed the bar mitzvah ceremony, which had been abandoned for years at Beth El (an opposition that would end in the 1950s with the presidency of Leonard N. Simons). And yet, together with Orthodox Jews, those "ultra-Reformed Jews" agreed upon the concept of the JWF.[59] Detroit entered the class of federated communities.

Although the same families moved to the forefront of Federation supervision as had governed the United Jewish Charities, leadership by 1926 became less an ethnic or national distinction and increasingly identified with economic status. Despite the diversity of the individuals who had come to its initial endorsement, Federation continued to be directed by those who were identified as "uptown" Jews, or the *Yahudim*. Perhaps unique among prominent Jews in Detroit, Fred M. Butzel and Henry Wineman consistently attempted to bridge the gaps between "uptown" and "downtown" Jews. It would be Butzel who would assume an astonishingly conciliatory position in Detroit as liaison not only between different Jewish constituencies, but between Jews and non-Jews.

131

In large part because of such efforts as Brutzel's and Wineman's, and in spite of the abiding rifts between spokesmen and the Jewish population, the Jewish Welfare Federation could soon convincingly call itself the "central community organization serving the Detroit Jewish community in three major areas: 1) central fund-raising for local, national and overseas agencies; 2) budgeting and allocation of funds raised; 3) coordinating and planning of functional programs of local social services."[60] Its goal, at least partly achieved almost immediately, reflected Waldman's professional approach to social service as he hoped to unite various agencies and their operations into "a well-ordered, cooperative system of services." While it created two new associations, the Jewish Centers Association and the Jewish Social Service Bureau (forerunner of the Jewish Family and Child Service), Federation's primary responsibilities were fund-raising, budgeting, and allocating money to member agencies and to other elements of the Jewish community of Detroit, as well as to national and overseas agencies serving Jews.[61]

Under Waldman's charge, Federation undertook its first Allied Jewish Campaign, the principal vehicle for achieving its goals. The annual campaign became the focus of Federation activities. Conducted in the fall of each year, it occupied almost all those involved with Federation throughout the entire year. The new organization from its inception offered itself, in theory at least, as a "partnership of agencies or services seeking financial support jointly through a central campaign."[62] Each agency obliged itself to give up a measure of its independence for the benefits of central planning, in particular, budgeting and allocation. Contributors to the campaign were to be included in this concept of "partnership" so that, ultimately, and again, at least in theory, Federation would be perceived as the organized Jewish community.

Each Federation agency would submit budgets to the Federation Board or to the appropriate budgetary committees, which would examine agency reports from the previous year, make projections, and then offer recommendations. As its final task, Federation would make itself responsible for coordinating and planning functional programs for local social services. The idea that, through its offices, the operations of various agencies might be united into "a well-ordered, cooperative system of services" produced a complex mixture of achievement and controversy. Yet overall, Samuel Rubiner, president of Federation in 1950, could accurately if somewhat cryptically claim at the United Jewish Charities fiftieth anniversary that in 1926, with the birth of the Jewish Welfare Federation, Jewish social services added to their central cares concerning "the needy" agencies "which were devoted to the enrichment of our lives as Jews."[63]

In the prosperous 1920s the outlook for the future of Detroit's Jewish Welfare Federation and for the Jews of Detroit seemed auspicious. The leaders of Federation apportioned the monies raised into three main categories: local, national, and international. Local needs naturally received the largest share of the revenues, with international and national shares varying as the world and national situations changed.[64] Those variations and those needs were measured differently by different people and served as still another source of internal dissension. However, the overriding purpose, aid to Jews, remained unquestioned. Federation, then, in that respect was guaranteed success.

The first campaign in 1925, overseen by Henry Wineman (chairman from 1925 to 1930), raised $150,400 from a total of 2,794 subscribers.[65] Both the campaigns and the Jews of Detroit soon would enter upon harder times that would place unexpected pressures on the services and agencies, and on every segment of the Jewish (as well as the non-Jewish) population. But in 1926, as pledges exceeded their goal by $140,000, the leaders of Federation rejoiced. (The total of $738,242 represented pledges for the years 1926–1928).[66] After a victory meeting at the prestigious Phoenix Club, David Brown proposed that the volunteer administrative group responsible for the campaign be formalized and given the name of the Detroit Service Group. Esther Prussian was appointed director of the Service Group, whose bylaws described it as "a loyal and efficient body of workers whose function is obtaining funds sufficient for the necessary general and Jewish philanthropic activities . . . in the interest of our community."[67]

After examining methods of campaign leadership in other cities, especially New York, the Detroit Service Group underwent a reorganization in 1929. Following the lead of other metropolitan areas, the Service Group transformed itself into a businessmen's council with specific divisions to lead the campaigns. Those influential volunteers each headed different trade or professional divisions and were made responsible for pledges from certain segments of the population.[68]

As they continued to set a course partially determined by the Lurie *Survey* of 1923, leaders of Federation turned to several of its other suggestions. One of the most glaring of the *Survey* criticisms had been the lack of acceptable facilities for Detroit Jewish youth—the lack, in short, of a sufficient Jewish Community Center. In 1926, responding to those criticisms, the Federation Board established the Jewish Centers Association (JCA) as part of its attempt to reorganize and dispense essential community services.[69] With considerable nostalgia, the Hannah Schloss Memorial Building was left behind, but the JCA endeavored to continue the recreational and educational activities that had brought thousands of Jewish youngsters and adults to that building ever since Seligman Schloss had donated $5,800 for the construction in 1903.[70]

Joined by the Young Women's Hebrew Association in organizing activities, the JCA administered new facilities for one year on East Philadelphia Avenue, after which it moved to the former Methodist Tabernacle on Melbourne Avenue and later opened a branch on Fenkell. With Samuel Levine as director, Milton Alexander took on the difficult assignment of President of the Jewish Center from 1926 to 1929; he was succeeded for one year by Milford Stern and then by Nate Shapero, all of whom expressed deep concern over the inadequacies of their facilities.[71] Celebrating the opening of a new center in 1933, Fred Butzel remembered the old facilities as "the frame shanties on East Philadelphia Avenue and the labyrinthine maze on Melbourne Avenue."[72] Nevertheless, in 1929 alone the center on Melbourne served over 100,000 people.[73]

Initially, the campaign allotment for a new Jewish center encountered opposition from advocates of a Jewish hospital.[74] The 1923 *Survey* called upon Detroit's Jews to give serious consideration to a hospital for Jews; and found the absence of a hospital a deficiency as serious as the lack of a center. Two camps emerged and, in effect, stalemated each other. But in 1929 Federation appointed a recreational council to seriously examine the question of new sites for a Jewish community center. A hospital fund was initiated, but no campaign allotment scheduled. A Jewish center assumed first priority, presumably for its value to young people. Judge Irving Lehman of New York City, having been consulted on the matter in Detroit, wrote to Meyer Prentis to invite him to accept the chairmanship of the Jewish Recreational Council of Detroit.[75] Prentis, treasurer of General Motors Corporation since 1919, vice-president of Federation in that year, and a highly respected member of Detroit society; accepted the invitation and brought a rigorous, if sometimes testy, businessman's enthusiasm to the commission.

At an informal dinner at David Brown's on January 30, 1930, Prentis, Wineman, and Brown engaged in frank discussions about launching the Jewish center project.[76] With firm resolve, in the teeth of the Depression, they began the project in earnest. Throughout the trying year of 1930, Prentis and his fellow committee member Henry Wineman searched for a site but, because of the Depression and the lingering debate over the equally needed hospital, they received no allocations from the Allied Jewish Campaign that year. Nevertheless, Prentis wrote to his friend Al Hecht in Hollywood in January 1931 that he was considering the northwest corner of Woodward and Taylor, which could be obtained for $100,000.[77] Painfully aware of Detroit Jewry's financial adversities, Prentis, whose thankless task as treasurer was to make decisions on collections of campaign pledges, quickly asked his friend Albert Kahn to prepare sketches for a "Y center." Within a week, Kahn completed the drawings.[78]

For all their intentions, however, the Site Committee of the Recreational Council could not proceed with plans for any new construction. As the Depression tightened its grip on the community, the campaign for 1931 fell into dire straits; it granted priority to emergency measures for relief and struggled to keep its minimal services going.[79] Having been authorized earlier by the Federation Board to place a down payment of $5,000 on the

Taylor site, the members of the Site Committee managed to withdraw the bid without losing their deposit.

Resolve remained strong, however, and when Kurt Peiser, John Slawson's successor as Executive Director of Federation, addressed the Jewish Centers Association dinner announcing the start of the Community Fund drive, he opened his remarks with a description of "conditions of want and despair."[80] But, because of such conditions, he continued, community facilities needed to be strengthened, not reduced. Detroit's Community Fund drive benefited some eighty agencies, eight of which were Jewish—the North End Clinic, the Young Women's Hebrew Association, the Jewish Centers Association, the Jewish Child Care Council, the Jewish Social Service Bureau, the Jewish Children's Home, the Fresh Air Society, and the Hebrew Free Loan Association. At the same dinner Percival Dodge, Executive Secretary of the Detroit Community Fund, complimented the Jewish community for its volunteer work and contributions. He particularly singled out the work of Julian Krolik and Fred Butzel, and promised that, while there were "no fixed goals" for 1933, the Fund would provide as much assistance as possible under those trying circumstances.[81] But in that nadir year, the Fund and most of Detroit's agencies suffered terrible losses and cutbacks. Those present at the dinner recognized that little help would come from the city.

Prentis, now paired with his friend Nate Shapero, continued his search for an appropriate and affordable location. More importantly, they needed to wait for the right moment. That moment came in January 1933, when the possibility of assuming control of a building on Holbrook and Woodward arose. For the cost of $75,000 the Federation could acquire a suitable location fit to house the Jewish Centers Association, the YWHA, and recreational and educational facilities.[82] The Site Committee received immediate approval, and plans for the remodeling of the building were implemented.[83] In May 1933, at the suggestion of Executive Director Kurt Peiser, the JCA and YWHA amalgamated to reconvene the Recreational Council, which then began planning programs for the Jewish Center. It would serve to provide a meeting place and diversified activities for Jewish youth and adults. Its central aim was "to conserve Jewish interests and ideals [in order] to gain a more meaningful Jewish community life."[84]

Fred M. Butzel, on the eve of the opening of the new Jewish Community Center, wrote a guest editorial in the *Federation News* entitled, "The New Jewish Center: Symbol of Cooperative Spirit." Butzel wryly commented that the need for a center was "about the only thing on which the Jews of Detroit have been able to agree."[85] (Although, given the debates over hospital needs, even this was tenuous agreement.) He went on to praise the new center on Holbrook for its substance. It would not appeal, he wrote, to those seeking a flashy edifice with marble fronts. But its "homey appearance" and its spaciousness offered an atmosphere "conducive to the

135

mixing of diverse groups." It would accommodate a gymnasium, club rooms, and facilities for drama, "the useful and fine arts." In short, it would provide a cultural center for Jews, a meeting place for those of all ages. With his customary insight and penchant for conciliation, Butzel concluded that "there is no one group which owns it and no one group whose interests should predominate."[86]

These remarks indicate Butzel's deep feelings for all the various components within the Jewish population. "Diverse groups" did indeed characterize the broad spectrum of Detroit Jewry; in his comment that "no one group . . . should predominate," Butzel may well have tried to allay the suspicions of the *Ostjuden* that a Federation building meant old-fashioned charity, or that it might be the exclusive domain of the wealthy. Speaking, perhaps, from fond memories of the Hannah Schloss days, he seemed to urge all sorts of cultural and practical activities and the broadest possible participation.

Nor was the Jewish Center the only challenge faced by Federation in those early years and through the Depression. In 1931, for example, Rabbi Ashinsky proposed to the Federation Board that the Mizrachi, the Orthodox Zionist organization, be included in the Allied Jewish Campaign.[87] Since many, if not most, of the board members were at best "non-Zionists," not to mention their Reform congregational affiliations, this might have proven to be a particularly sensitive or even explosive issue. Recognizing it as a potentially divisive request, Fred Butzel moved that 6 percent of the money already appropriated for the American Palestine Campaign (APC) be allotted to the local Mizrachi, pending approval of the national office of the APC. This compromise allowed Rabbi Ashinsky's request to be fulfilled without necessitating the reallotment of monies. Butzel then took it upon himself to write the national office, and he continued to do so in subsequent years.[88]

Numerous other agencies grew increasingly dependent upon Federation. The North End Clinic, housed since 1926 in the Leopold Wineman Memorial Building, was one of Detroit's finest outpatient clinics and had been a campaign budget item since 1927.[89] During the Depression, the Clinic was rescued from financial disaster by Federation loans. Similarly, agencies that fell under the rubric of the Jewish Social Service Bureau—the House of Shelter, the Jewish Home for the Aged, the Fresh Air Society and its several camps, the Jewish Children's Bureau, and the Jewish Children's Home—received both financial and moral support.[90]

Yet another institution that entered into discussions regarding affiliation with Federation from 1926 until 1935 was the Old Folks' Home (Home for the Aged), which drew more and more attention after 1930. In December 1930 Federation received a request signed by Jacob Levin, president of the Jewish Old Folks' Home. By unanimous decision, Levin wrote, the Old Folks' Home Board asked for mutual exploration of the prospects of affiliating as an agency of the Federation.[91] Spearheaded by Abraham Srere, the exploratory committee launched its investigations. In February 1931 the Home received $5,825 to settle its accrued debts, and before the year was over, the Home had become a "constituent and beneficiary" of the Jewish Welfare Federation.[92]

In the summer of 1931, a fire at the Little Sisters Home for the Poor and the Aged in Pittsburgh caused the death of forty people. That disaster drew the attention of public-safety officials in Detroit to similar institutions.[93] George Stutz, the Assistant County Prosecutor assigned to the Arson Divisions of the police and fire departments, conducted an investigation into the conditions of the Old Folks' Home, a three-story converted structure then located at John R. and Edmund Place. Because of its cramped and crowded facilities, Stutz condemned the building as a fire hazard.[94]

In the midst of the consequent heated controversy, Federation undertook a concerted effort to raise funds for new quarters. After vehement debates, which included the subject of the Jewish Children's Home, a "committee on the study of a new Jewish Old Folks Home" was formed on December 20, 1934. Chairman Abraham Srere, Federation treasurer, appointed Stutz to the committee, along with Sidney J. Allen, Maurice Aronsson, Dora (Mrs. Joseph) Ehrlich, Clarence H. Enggass, Mrs. A. M. Ferar, Marvin B. Gingold, Mrs. Fred Ginsburg, Harry S. Grant, Myron A. Keys, Henry Levitt, Herman Radner, Nate S. Shapero, Mrs. Abraham Srere, and Henry Wineman.[95]

Although the Depression had brought fund-raising to its lowest level, between 1935 and 1936 the Allied Jewish Campaign allotted $155,000 toward a new Home, which was then renamed the Jewish Home for the Aged.[96] It was located on Petoskey and Burlingame, adjacent to the Jewish Children's Home.

Of all the social services provided by various agencies in Detroit, perhaps the bitter controversy over the care of children endured the longest. A plethora of children's agencies existed before 1925, and they continued to exist until the time their control was grasped by firmer hands, like those of Harold Silver, director of the Jewish Social Service Bureau from 1933, and guided by more compassionate minds, like Fred Butzel's.[97] When, in 1928, the Federation called on Ethel D. Oberbrunner of the Jewish Child Welfare Association of Cleveland to investigate the standing of Jewish child care in Detroit, she was appalled to find a poor quality of foster homes, deplorable records, shoddy social service techniques in Detroit's two orphan institutions (the Hebrew Orphans Home and the Hebrew Infants Orphans Home), and community antagonism toward the Jewish Social Service Bureau (JSSB).[98]

As a result of her findings, the Jewish Child Care Council was established; its tasks included taking the problem of proper care in foster homes from the JSSB and acting as a clearing and coordinating center for child care in the community. It would operate as the representative group of all Jewish child care agencies.[99] Its president was Melville S. Welt and its director was Edith Bercovich, wife of the director of the Sholem Aleichem Shule.[100]

Less than two years later, Jacob Kepecs's study of the effectiveness of the Jewish Child Care Council reported that the two orphan institutions were on their way to establishing a good working rapport with the Council. But Kepecs, the director of the Jewish Home Finding Society of Chicago, found gross inadequacies in the building that housed the children. By July 1930 the Council had eighty-four children in foster home care and received some support from the Detroit Community Fund.[101] By July 1931 the two orphan institutions had merged to form the Jewish Children's Home, which assumed new lodgings in the United Jewish Charities Building on Petoskey and Burlingame in December 1932. Butzel presided at the opening ceremony, which was attended also by Mayor Frank Murphy, Dr. Robert Woodroofe, president of the Council of Social Agencies of Metropolitan Detroit, Rabbi Franklin, Rabbi Hershman, Kurt Peiser, and others. Each of them spoke hopefully about the future.[102] The new institution served children from infancy to sixteen years of age. By 1935 it housed thirty-eight children and by 1936, fifty-three. Its funding came from the Detroit Community Fund, personal donations, membership dues, and allocations from Federation.[103]

When Harold Silver arrived in Detroit in February 1933, to serve as director of the Jewish Social Service Bureau, he assumed an adversarial position toward the Jewish Child Placement Bureau. Immediately after Silver took office, Rose Lipson, one of those dedicated workers from the Blanche Hart days, resigned. Silver brought impressive professional credentials: a graduate of the University of Chicago and the Graduate School for Jewish Social Work in New York; a Phi Beta Kappa; and a member of the American Association of Social Workers and the National Conference of Jewish Social Service; he epitomized the new professionalism that began to mark the staff of the Federation agencies.[104] His presence and critical approach to the functioning of Jewish institutions in Detroit generated tension, and from this tension grew the Controversial Case Committee and, finally, the Joint Committee on Child Care, whose board included representatives of each of the four child-care agencies in Detroit.[105]

That committee was chaired by Fred Butzel from 1933 until 1944, when the JSSB subsumed child care and placement functions. Butzel's character seemed to shine most brightly when dealing with child-related issues. "We are facing a condition, not a theory," he said. Detroit's capabilities to confront the plight of Jewish orphans and impoverished children owed much to Butzel who, according to Silver, "combined the qualities of encompassing with rare understanding large communal programs while simultaneously capable of sympathetically considering the problems of a single child."[106] Detroit's foremost woman social worker, Eleonore Hutzel, commented similarly on Butzel's unique character: "Mr. Butzel has succeeded in making himself familiar with the problems of the entire field of social work. . . . He stands to other social workers in the relation of a consultant and too much cannot be said in appreciation of his, at all times, available services."[107]

By profession a lawyer, by temperament a humanitarian, and by choice a philanthropist, Butzel seemed to become everyone's ideal and clearly Detroit Jewry's premier ambassador to the non-Jewish world. He was instrumental in bringing the Boy Scouts to Detroit, aided in the establishment of the Community Chest and the Detroit Urban League, pursued a solution to the rampant truancy problem in Detroit schools in the 1920s, effected the establishment of a juvenile court in Wayne County, and joined such prominent Detroiters as J. L. Hudson and Dexter M. Ferry in founding what become one of his most cherished projects, the Detroit Boys' Home.[108] His accomplishments soared even higher regarding Jews in Detroit, and his quiet generosity toward individuals—for example, helping to send young people to college with private gifts—became legendary. Compassionate and sensitive, he opposed orphanages on principle and was instrumental in relieving the tensions surrounding the development of the Children's Department of the JSSB and the Jewish Children's Home. His constant support for the Fresh Air Society was recognized by Edith Heavenrich, President of the Society in 1927.[109]

If Butzel exhibited his finest qualities most clearly when attempting to solve the problems of child care, the Federation offered a concrete example of how it might fulfill Waldman's plan of integrating services. The Jewish Children's Home called upon a volunteer medical staff, worked with the JSSB, received medical assistance for regular health examinations from the North End Clinic (as did the Fresh Air Camp), and offered recreational programs to its children through the Jewish Community Center. Organizers within Federation successfully integrated these programs, offering a rare display of agency cooperative efforts during the Depression.

Under severely hampering financial circumstances, the Federation struggled to maintain the services under its patronage. Questions regarding emergency measures and redirection of priorities confronted board meetings throughout the period. A few prominent members of Federation disaffiliated, some after heated exchanges over contributions, some over decisions reached by the board. Loss of active and often affluent members hurt the cause of unity, especially when it meant the resignation of a committee chairman or the president of an agency. Yet no agency was discontinued, and the debates, often ardent, appeared well-intentioned and reflected the dilemmas of the times.

10

Depression:
Economic Survival

Joseph Zeltzer held the position of secretary of the Poale Zion in New York City. Aspiring to practice medicine, he learned of the educational opportunities in Michigan and moved to Detroit in 1914. Zeltzer became Michigan's first Jewish veterinarian and, because of his Yiddish background, was soon employed by the city of Detroit as an inspector of *shochtim*, kosher slaughterers and butchers.[110] The conditions under which kosher slaughtering took place (like those for slaughtering in general) were deemed appalling, and the city lacked Yiddish-speaking inspectors.[111] Zeltzer was ideally suited for the job. By 1931 the Zeltzers had lost their house and moved to smaller quarters on the West Side, but Zeltzer was still employed.

Like Zeltzer, Dr. Shmarya Kleinman had been affiliated with leftist movements in other cities before coming to Detroit in 1929. (Unlike Zeltzer, however, until 1948 Kleinman opposed Zionism from socialist-revolutionary ideological convictions.) Having arrived from Europe in New York, Dr. Kleinman, who was trained in Russian medical schools, finally settled in Detroit. With help from Fred Butzel, "Lawyer Butzel," Kleinman had been permitted to take and ultimately passed the Michigan medical exam. Although he lived in a small apartment and was poor and still struggling, he could still earn a living as a doctor. His patients paid when they could, often in kind.[112]

Both Zeltzer and Kleinman observed destitute men and women on the streets of Detroit selling apples or standing in long lines for soup. And both reflected that most Jews, poor as they might have been, escaped such a fate during the Depression. Individuals like these and organizations like the Federation strove to help Jews and keep them from selling apples on the streets or standing in soup-kitchen lines. But, as Kleinman observed, there were Jewish families that went hungry every night and Jewish men destitute on the streets of Detroit or traveling from city to city.

There are numerous speculations about why Jews in general seemed to suffer less than non-Jews during the Depression. After the American Immigration Restriction Act of 1924, the numbers of Jews entering the country fell from 120,000 in 1921 to only 10,000 in 1924.[113] Between 1925 and 1933, fewer than 100,000 Jews entered the country and from 1933 to 1945, approximately 150,000 "guaranteed risks," mostly German Jewish refugees from Nazism, found their way to America; over half of that number settled in New York City to form the intellectual ghetto often called the Fourth Reich.[114] In 1900, some 60 percent of the Jews in America earned their livings in industrial jobs. By 1930 fewer than 18 percent were engaged in industry. Correspondingly, in 1900, 25 percent of the Jews in the United States were engaged in trade, and by 1930 that number had increased to 57 percent. By the mid-thirties, approximately 35 percent were involved in manufacturing, and 34 percent might be identified as proprietors, salesmen, or providers of commercial services. White-collar workers and those in the professions (law, medicine, teaching) had increased to some 12 to 15 percent.[115]

Alongside such shifts in economic status came correlative changes in social status. Acculturation, if not assimilation, hastened and grew more intense. With the decline in their numbers, new immigrants assumed marginal roles, exerting less impact on Jewish behavior and social practices. This, in turn, produced attenuation of traditional ties. One measure of altered social mores was the pronounced decline in the birth rate among American Jews in the late 1920s and into the 1930s. The rate remained considerably lower for Jews than for other ethnic groups in the United States and provided a barometer of middle-class status.[116] The abiding Jewish social imperative of education remained, however, fueling the fires of secular assimilation and the movement toward upwardly mobile socioeconomic positions.

In the main, Jews in Detroit (as in most cities) conformed to these national patterns and had become established in the "trade" professions. Conflicting reports place the Jewish population of Detroit in 1936 between eighty-two and ninety-four thousand. They represented approximately 3.9 percent of the total population of the city and were the sixth-largest Jewish population in America.[117] When Jewish immigration to the United States had been curtailed in 1924, movement to Detroit had continued as Jews came from small towns and other cities—such as Cleveland, New York, and Pittsburgh—in search of jobs in the city that had become symbolic of the American dream.[118]

By 1935, 54.1 percent of the Jewish working population of Detroit was employed in "trade" and 49.3 percent fell under the subcategory of "wholesale and retail" workers; 26.8 percent were classified as "proprietors, managers, and officials" in such businesses as dry goods or clothing stores, food stores, junk, or rags.[119] The famous 1936 *Fortune* study, "Jews in America," estimated that 90 percent of the scrap-metal business was owned by Jews. In Detroit, they formed what became known as Detroit's "junk aristocracy." Closely connected to this vocation was the waste industry, pioneered by such men as Ed Levy.[120] Once established, those businesses tended to take in relatives and Jewish employees, insuring that the industry would remain primarily in Jewish hands. Approximately 8 percent of Detroit's Jewish population was employed in independent professions, the majority of them engaged in the law, medicine, and dentistry.[121]

Jews became proprietors of an extraordinary number of Detroit's linen and dry-goods businesses. Almost 25 percent of all the workers employed in laundries, cleaning and dyeing establishments, or clothing manufacture were Jews in 1936.[122] This Jewish labor force of linen and laundry employees owed their positions to their Jewish employers, who owned nearly 90 percent of Detroit's linen and laundry-supply industry.

As a focus of Jewish economic success, this industry became a critical vehicle for some Jews in Detroit. Divided into three categories, the linen business included damp-wash laundry, coverall manufacture, and linen supply. The first enterprise served as a domestic laundering service and involved pickups and deliveries from and to homes and small businesses. Drivers, working five-and-a-half-day weeks, would make their runs regularly, delivering the laundry to the factory, where it would be laundered in huge vats and then returned to the customers.[123] The second enterprise involved the production of industrial coveralls for local industries such as the automobile companies. Detroit's manufacturing lifeline provided such subsidiary industries with lucrative and long-lived careers. The third component in the business was linen supply: napkins, aprons, tablecloths, and whatever was needed in restaurants, hotels, or other commercial services.

The development of the cloth or clothing trades in Detroit seemed to be a logical outgrowth of the tailoring profession and the traditional European work of itinerant agents, known as *Wocher,* who collected rags and junk during the week in order to return home by Friday night for the Sabbath.[124] Among the most successful linen industry magnates, Morris Schaver began as an enterprising, determined immigrant who made laundry deliveries by carrying his bundles on streetcars. His Central Overall Supply Company would become the largest of its kind in Detroit.[125] The Lapides family owned Quality Laundry; the Milinskys owned Wayne Laundry; and Harry Schumer, owner of General Linen Supply, would become the president of the Linen Association. Dave Rosen founded Economy Linen; the Liebsons owned Domestic Linen; and others, such as Wolf Wiping Cloth Company, Kuttnauer Apron Specialties Company, Samuel Selinsky's Mohawk Overall Company, and Shlessinger's Service Garments, along with Abraham Srere's Acme Mills, Co. and the Kroliks' Alaska Knitting Mills, Co., shared origins similar to Central Overall.[126]

All of these employers—in stark contrast to Banner Linen and Marathon Coverall, which employed no Jews—hired Jewish drivers. It went without saying that this situation issued from an unwritten and unspoken policy. Proprietorship seemed to allow economic and social independence and, consequently, freedom from discrimination. Jews met non-Jews in the marketplace where goods and services were traded. Such relationships minimized noneconomic factors. Beyond that, it allowed Jews to employ Jews, thereby resulting in a kind of inbreeding in those businesses.

As if to emulate American businesses in the thirties, the Jewish laundry-linen industry became plagued by underworld figures who harassed both dry-goods store owners and laundry drivers. Members of the Purple Gang collected "dues," the traditional euphemism for protection, from their victims. Several Jews recalled the same two or three "collection agents." Most small businesses paid their monthly or weekly "dues" without protest. "It was not worth getting beaten up or losing your life or your business," recalled one woman, "so we paid [him] when he came and he left without saying anything." There was no doubt that the collectors would have resorted to violence.

Linen and laundry drivers became more deeply embroiled in Detroit-style business disputes. In 1936–1937, in the midst of what became known as the "Laundry Wars," Isaac Litwak, a feisty, intransigent union supporter who had organized the drivers into the Detroit Laundry and Linen Drivers Association in 1934, led the organization to join the Teamsters Union as Local 285. No fewer than twelve strikes ensued in 1937.[127] Picket lines were attacked and union members arrested and beaten. Litwak himself was beaten several times—once on the steps of his own home and once dragged from his car as he was en route to a picket line. He "washed the blood off and went back to the picket lines."[128] There could be no question that underworld "goons" were employed to break the union. Indeed, Litwak recalled that in the beginning a two-front battle was waged: on the one hand trying to keep the union from destruction by management; on the other hand, trying to keep out of the clutches of organized crime—both the Mafia and the Purple Gang.[129] In 1937 the union claimed victory as Litwak brought unorganized drivers earning eighteen dollars a week to contractual arrangements for ninety-five dollars a week. Arrested by the Highland Park Police for breaking a no-picketing ordinance, Litwak was accompanied to jail by Jimmy Hoffa, who was to make sure that Litwak was not beaten or killed. Teamsters Local 285 filed suit against Highland Park and won in court.[130] Litwak commanded great respect and affection from those in the union. His detractors, primarily the laundry owners and managers, accused him of arrogance and called him a "czar," an ironic epithet for one who had fled czarist persecution in Russia.[131]

For all its turmoil, the bloody street battles and corruption that riddled the linen and laundry business reflected another distressing and deep division within the Jewish population of Detroit. Here were Jews at war with Jews—Jewish management opposing Jewish labor. For all the accusations of individual culpability, the fact remained that economics had sundered Detroit's Jews, and traditional values had become clouded. In private quarters, managers were cursed in Yiddish and accused of shameful behavior; union members were similarly cursed by their antagonists, who dredged up similar shtetl designations for their adversaries. The business remained infused with internal tensions, even after the prolonged 1937 strikes were settled. Litwak retained his "prickly" attitude toward management and as late as 1971, after his retirement, he led a ten-month strike.[132]

Leaders of both sides, Teamsters and managers, would come together, uneasily but cordially, to support a cause that must have baffled non-Jews and even some Jews: Labor Zionism. This unusual show of unity was less mysterious than it may appear; its origins will be discussed further below.

Only 8.2 percent of Detroit's Jews worked in the automobile industry, comprising 1.4 percent of the auto labor force.[133] However, considerably more Jews engaged in peripheral trades, such as scrap metal, steel, or, like Ed Levy, in industrial waste (slag). Abe Srere's Acme Mills produced burlap for automobile seats and, along with Allen Industries, which was owned by Sidney Allen, manufactured materials for Ford and other auto manufacturers. One extended variation on the dry goods and laundry business pattern was the industrial cloths industry, which thrived on the auto industry and on other companies in Detroit. Benjamin Laikin, one of the more successful entrepreneurs of this industry, described the process of purchasing large amounts of rags, washing and sterilizing them, cutting them to certain specifications and selling them to companies for workers to use to clean machines or wipe their hands.[134]

Sociologist Henry J. Meyer pointed out that this employment pattern indicated a low incidence of economic insecurity and unemployment.[135] In contrast, non-Jewish Detroit suffered enormously as unemployment in the automobile industry, the bellwether for the city, rose to 35.2 percent in 1930. Mayor Frank Murphy, the liberal and popular favorite of the majority of the Jews of Detroit, struggled to alleviate the urgent conditions almost from his first day in office in September 1930. By December, the city's

144

treasury had been exhausted; the Detroit Unemployment Committee, founded in 1931, gave away baskets of apples.[136]

One historian has called this ineffectual stratagem "the last refuge of free enterprise," as the businessmen of the commission set up panhandlers on the streets of Detroit.[137] One out of seven people was on relief by the end of 1931. Children scavenged dumps and alleys. Tuberculosis reached epidemic proportions in Detroit high schools, and some four thousand children stood in bread lines daily.[138]

Samuel Baron had come to Detroit from Odessa. He gained employment at Chrysler Corporation and advanced through the ranks as an auto worker. Because of his considerable experience, in 1930 Chrysler selected Baron as one of the workers to be sent on a joint venture, with the Ford Motor Company, to help construct a plant in Nizhni Novgorod, in the Soviet Union. A confirmed supporter of the left, Baron grew disillusioned with the life he observed in Russia. Despite urgings from some members of his family in Detroit that he bring them to the Soviet Union and not return to Detroit, he was convinced that "this [Russia] is no place to raise children." Baron returned to Detroit where, a victim of the Depression, he soon lost his job with Chrysler.

Rose Baron supported the family as a seamstress. Sam remained unemployed for the remainder of his life. His daughter recalled discussions about paying the rent and hearing that "a depression is on," but there was always food on the table and a roof over her head. Her father sold apples on the streets of Detroit. At times he was reminded of the warnings he had received in Russia about not returning to Detroit. The Barons' home abounded in leaflets and talk of demonstrations to organize the workers; and Maurice Sugar, the Communist labor lawyer, was considered a Jewish hero of great dignity and intelligence. In that household, Sugar had the reputation of an idealist whose finesse, sophistication, and compassion set him apart from the ranting and raving communist street orators. Myra Kameroff Wolfgang, the colorful Jewish organizer of the waitress union, inspired equal pride. To families like the Barons, the fact that Maurice Sugar or Myra Kameroff Wolfgang, champions of the labor movement, were Jews may have been incidental; at the same time, it was not surprising.

Jews had arrived in Detroit seeking the *goldene Medine*. To many, the secret to American success lay in the land—in property. Orthodox Jews, secularists, and those seeking to integrate into American society discovered what they believed to be the economic vehicle to success in the Morris Plan. According to this scheme, an aspiring property-owner with little or no credit at a bank could receive an installment loan from the Morris Bank, a finance and loan corporation, on condition that two reliable signers vouch for him. With that, a small down payment on property could be made. This became a widespread practice, but in 1933 all those subscribers to

145

the Morris Plan lost everything—their money, property, and hopes—when the bank holiday occurred and the Morris Bank shut down.[139] The Depression struck a crushing blow to those hopes and to the illusion of the American Dream.

Recognizing the plight of poor Jews in this crisis, Mrs. Esther Gitlin, Mrs. Eva Prinzlauer, Mrs. Oscar Robinson, and others organized a group of women and men that pioneered an emergency-relief organization in 1930. They were aided by the newly appointed Assistant County Prosecutor for Wayne County, George Stutz.[140] It quickly had become apparent that the Department of Public Welfare, under the volunteer guidance of Mrs. Henry Wineman and even with its staff of professional caseworkers, could not meet the emergency-relief needs brought on by the economic catastrophe. The Federation, too, seemed ill-equipped to deal with such massive problems through its case agency, the Jewish Social Service Bureau.[141] Stutz soon became the chairman of the Detroit Jewish Emergency Relief Fund, which made direct appeals to members of the Jewish community for donations of money and goods. The generosity of the response stunned even the volunteers.

Dave Goldberg, of East Side Coal Co., president of the Retail Coal Dealers Association, prevailed on Sucher Bros. Coal Co. to join his company in providing urgently needed coal for the relief kitchens. Congregation Shaarey Zedek made its basement gymnasium available for three hundred cots to be used by Jewish indigents and the unemployed; and the House of Shelter served as one of three Jewish public kitchens. Three stores on Twelfth Street were made available as relief centers.[142] In April 1931, the Detroit Jewish Emergency Relief Fund sponsored a boxing match between Jack "Kid" Berg and Billy Wallace at Olympia Auditorium from which "proceeds [were] to go to aid the needy." Donors were offered public thanks in the *Detroit Jewish Chronicle,* which listed "Danto Fish Co. for 200 pounds of fish. Hebrew Ladies Loan Association, $11 for food. Sam Yuster . . . 50 gallons of wine for Shaarey Zedek seder. Sam Lubetsky, East Side Egg and Crate Co. . . . for baskets to pack food. Young Social Club, $20 for potatoes." Other donations ranged from one thousand dollars to fifty cents from "Anonymous" and fifty-five cents from "Unknown."[143]

After such unexpected and rapid success, Stutz began to worry about the capabilities of the volunteers to administer the program. In the spring of 1931, he met with three "giants of the Detroit Jewish Community," Fred Butzel, Abe Srere, and Julian Krolik, who discussed absorbing the Emergency Relief Fund into Federation and reorganizing it into a branch of the Jewish Social Service Bureau. Members of the Federation Board did not officially address the issue of Jewish relief until January 1931.[144] They recognized the ad hoc work of the League of Jewish Women's Organizations, which had been supplying clothes and food for the needy and, in February, appointed Milton M. Alexander as chairman of the Federation Emergency

Relief Committee to investigate how Federation might most efficiently address the crisis. At its meeting on February 10, the executive committee
voted to increase the Allied Campaign allocation for local relief from $25,000
to $35,000.[145] But it was not until June that the critical nature of the
emergency become publicly conspicuous.

At the June 30, 1931, board meeting, Aaron DeRoy proposed that at least
$53,000 of the $215,000 pledged in the campaign be allocated to local relief. He added the proviso that this sum should be appropriated regardless
of the status of the payments that might be in arrears. Of that $53,000,
he advocated that $35,000 go to Emergency Relief, $15,000 to the Old
Folks Home (only recently affiliated with Federation) and $3,000 to the
House of Shelter. DeRoy's proposal was accepted.[146] In September 1931,
Milford Stern pursued the emergency relief subject by recommending that
the Jewish Social Service Bureau of Federation form an emergency relief
department. He especially addressed the matter of "homeless men," encouraging the board to extend its support for the House of Shelter.[147] That
institution, headed by Nathan Bielfield from 1903 to 1930, had served Passover seder meals to about one hundred people in 1927. In 1932 it cared
for 665 transients and 287 local homeless unemployed men.[148] The House
of Shelter seemed to epitomize the crisis and its statistics alone could characterize the Depression.

Recognizing the urgent need for action, the board invited Harry Lurie
to act as a consultant on emergency relief in September 1931. He was to
offer some information on ways professional Jewish social service workers
in other cities, especially New York, had met the problems raised by the
Depression.[149] Later that month, it was reported that Samuel Nathanson,
president of the independent Detroit Jewish Emergency Fund represented
by George Stutz, had agreed to merge with the new projects being considered by Federation, on condition that Federation absorb the Fund's outstanding debt of $1,624. On November 12, 1931, the board voted to accept
the proposition. Thus was formed the Jewish Unemployment Relief Council.[150]

Its work, under the indefatigable direction of such people as Stutz,
Nathanson, Prinzlauer, and Gitlin, continued to keep pace with the unprecedented needs of the Jewish community. Indeed, one member averred
that the new liberal Democratic mayor, Frank Murphy, seemed to have
patterned his Mayor's Unemployment Relief Committee after the Detroit
Jewish Emergency Relief Fund model. Murphy appointed Prof. Samuel Levin,
who served as president of the JSSB, to the Unemployment Relief Committee.

Yet there still appeared shadows of differences over the nature of emergency relief. The apparent reticence on the part of Federation to subsume
much of the work of the Emergency Relief Fund; the bickering over budgetary items (the board undertook an audit of the Fund's books before
assuming the outstanding debt); and Federation's apparent unfamiliarity
with the immediacy of the emergency reflected the markedly different at-

147

titudes and values of the economic divisions of the community. By 1932, virtually every board meeting and executive committee meeting revolved around the subject of emergency relief.

Stutz became a member of the Federation Board in 1932 and in 1938 was made president of the Jewish Social Service Bureau. Shortly after the dissolution of the Fund, Stutz issued a statement to the *Chronicle* praising those men and women who had offered help to the Emergency Relief Fund and who "were unique in rendering immediate relief unhampered by organization management." Philip Slomovitz's editorial added another dimension to the effort:

> Jewish leaders in the various emergency relief movements must be careful not to confuse charity with justice. Too many make the mistake of speaking of 'charity' when they refer to relief, forgetting that the multitudes of needy in the present depression are not subjects of charity but victims of an economic calamity. . . . Relief with dignity and in justice to human beings is the important obligation of the hour.[151]

During the early years of the Depression, the organized Jewish community of Detroit, that is, the "establishment" voice of Jews in Detroit, continued to carry out what it perceived as its obligations to Jewish causes and people. Aaron DeRoy chaired the Allied Jewish Campaign in the difficult years between 1931 and 1933. Those two years signify the financial plight of Detroit Jews, as the amount collected fell from $326,017 pledged by over five thousand subscribers in 1930 to $112,913 pledged by over four thousand subscribers in 1933.[152] In March 1932 the *Federation News* noted that many of the campaign subscribers were suddenly destitute and could not deliver their pledges. Some letters of default indicated that even affluent Jews suffered multiple types of losses: "[My] husband [has] died, leaving heavy debts . . . I am working, my daughter has been stricken with heart trouble"; "I have just received a dispossess notice on my home, and I am sorry that I can't pay what I owe on the campaign"; "Have been unable to pay rent for six months and have finally received a dispossess. Having been out of a job for the same time, I must ask you to cancel what I owe"; "[dispossessed], please do not send any more bills unless you can offer me a job."[153] The difficult task of making decisions on collections in these troubled times fell to Meyer Prentis, treasurer of General Motors and treasurer of Federation, who also received a letter requesting deferment of payment from David Brown.[154]

Differences in perception of the crisis reflected differences in attitude and, finally, in pragmatic, concrete techniques for alleviating the plight of Jews in dire straits. At a decisive juncture, Kurt Peiser replaced John Slawson as executive director of Federation in 1932. He expressed his deep concern about the shift in focus brought about by the emergency. He feared, he said, that concentration on the immediate predicament would lead to the replacement of general services by a program of relief. This policy, he argued, produced deficits and placed enormously increased burdens upon Federation from the unemployed, families on relief, the ill, the aged, and other groups. Such burdens, Peiser continued, had forced Federation to accept the inadequate standards of the Department of Public Welfare on rent, food, and clothing. "There are no soup kitchens in the Jewish districts," he observed, and he pleaded for maintenance of other agencies, programs, and facilities. Peiser insisted that Federation not yield to increased relief needs at the expense of "leisure" concerns and that Federation "not be exclusively preoccupied with relief."[155]

It seemed a naive and almost insensitive reading of the situation. In the same issue of the *Federation News*, Henry Wineman, past president and past campaign chairman, emphatically asserted that "unemployment relief is the major social problem that . . . still looms before us." He insisted that Jews had always seen an obligation to care for their needy and Wineman even offered the prospect of reallocating funds from the Jewish Community Center accounts—a project central to the long-range plans of the Federation.[156] This essential debate over financial policy, of relief versus program maintenance, continued into the Depression years and would surface periodically in times of emergency.

Despite such disagreements, new agencies addressed new problems while established agencies redirected at least parts of their attention to the new situation. Along with the new Jewish Unemployment Relief Council, the long-established Hebrew Free Loan Association and the Children's Placement Bureau of the Jewish Social Service Bureau worked tirelessly to relieve a variety of crises. Between 1926 and 1939, Federation awarded special grants to the Hebrew Free Loan Association to increase its loan capital. The loan association granted almost sixteen hundred interest-free loans in 1932 in amounts that averaged eighty-three dollars. Because of the shrinking job prospects for college or high-school students, many were tuition loans.[157]

The new year of 1932 brought new hardships and challenges to all the agencies and institutions. The Children's Placement Bureau had 208 children under its supervision that year: 102 were in foster homes and 106 were in homes of relatives, with parents, or in state institutions. Forty-six children were residents at the Jewish Children's Home.[158] In January 1932 the Jewish Child Placement Bureau had 163 children under its care, ninety-eight of whom had their board paid for them. By December of that year there were 204 children, of whom eighty-seven were subsidized. Thirty percent of those children were over fifteen. Under normal circumstances they would have been discharged or "industrialized." Because of the Depression, however, the agency kept them in their care.[159] The JSSB treated an unprecedented number of emotional and mental problem cases in 1932 which the agency attributed to unemployment and business collapses. The

Family Care Department attended to 342 cases of "family disruption or delinquency" as well as to unmarried mothers. And the Unemployment Emergency Council exceeded its $35,000 allotment as it handled over 285 cases per month. In addition, Federation undertook responsibility for the Jewish Old Folks' Home, which cared for fifty-three people in that year, and for the Mother's Clinic, which had 1,159 patients.[160]

Desperate measures attended these services. The Fresh Air Society and its affiliate camps were placed on a self-support basis in 1933; the North End Clinic adopted a skeletal program of services; cutbacks from the Detroit Community Fund necessitated loans from the Reconstruction Finance Corporation; and a letter over the signatures of Kurt Peiser, Henry Wineman, and Fred Butzel went to all national agencies informing them of the Detroit Federation's financial difficulties. In that letter, the three community leaders announced that conditions compelled a moratorium on national grants for which they had budgeted funds from the previous campaign. They further informed those national agencies that the campaign that year (1933) would have "no definite goal."[161] Near the end of 1933, both the United Palestine Association (UPA) and the Joint Distribution Committee (JDC) appealed to Detroit for funds. Federation's response, with apparently little dissension among its board members, was that "the purpose of Zionism and the accomplishments of the UPA [will] be given as much publicity as any other agency participating in the [1934] Campaign." Equal participation would go to the JDC.[162] One month later, in January 1934, in recognition of the rising tide of anti-Semitism in Europe (and in America) Federation agreed to cosponsor, with the UPA, "Romance of a People," a national touring theater production whose proceeds went to relief for German Jews.[163]

With funds and students diminishing, the United Hebrew Schools continued its full curriculum of Jewish studies and Hebrew, receiving deficit support from Federation so that there were no teacher discharges and no closed schools. Adult evening classes continued and even increased in number, with subjects that included Hebrew, Yiddish, and Jewish history. Much to their annoyance, however, the three Yiddish schools, the Sholem Aleichem Institute, the Workmen's Circle Schools, and the Farband Shule, were refused assistance from Federation until 1936, when the education budget committee allotted admittedly token amounts.[164] To many Detroit Yiddishists, that allotment seemed to symbolize the breach between Federation and other elements of the Jewish population. Distrust grew, even in the face of rising anti-Semitism; indeed, that factor aggravated and highlighted the differences among the Jewish groups.

11

Secularism: The Question of Jewish Identity and Cultural Survival

For Orthodox Jews in Detroit, despite the pressure of Americanization and the metamorphosis that affected even the most pious observant Jews, questions of maintaining Jewish identity rarely, if ever, arose. "They did not trust each other," Philip Slomovitz pointed out, referring to Reform and Orthodox Jews in the 1920s and 1930s. "They were two opposite poles. The *Ostjuden* were held in contempt. To the Orthodox, the Reform Jews were *goyim* (non-Jews), *traf* (unkosher). To the Reform, *Ostjude* was the object of charity." Worries about a loss of piety and the falling away of the younger generation did not alter the way Orthodox Jews perceived themselves or Jewishness. Traditional religious practices continued in Jewish neighborhoods in Orthodox congregations and *shtiblach*. Orthodox Jews, perhaps perceiving Jewish identity to be not so much a function of integration but of survival, clung tenaciously to old-world religious practices within the constraints of American society.

Reform, Orthodox, and Conservative Jews sought and found philanthropic, social sources of identity while often maintaining connections, sometimes tenuous, to congregational membership. The leadership of Federation tended to come from Temple Beth El's ranks or from those not affiliated with any religious institution. Despite tension between Federation and congregational allegiance, constituents of these competing groups tacitly agreed that Jewish identity derived from its religious traditions. This principle enabled some Detroit Jews to continue their quest for integration into Detroit society, as they argued that Jewishness remained a personal decision of religious preference.

Yet all Jews did not concur on the role of religious Judaism in Jewish identity. Secularists argued that Jewishness lay in "value orientation" and that many essentially Jewish values readily yielded to a translation to secular realms. Detroit sociologist Joseph Faumann, for example, wrote that "the prestige of education is a function of the historical experience of Jewish life."[165] Similarly, secular groups regularly offered their principles as fundamentally Jewish or even as derived from religious origins. If religion dealt with "relationships of people: man to God; man to man; and man to self," declared a Workmen's Circle and Sholem Aleichem Institute joint statement on education, "only the first is exclusively the realm of those who believe in a supreme being . . . the other two are the concern of all thinking people."[166]

In Detroit, as in New York City and other American metropolitan areas, a singificant number of Jews, primarily of Eastern European lineage, disdained all religious ties while insisting on their abiding Jewishness. Some linked affiliations with leftist groups to Jewish values; those less palpably political embraced Diaspora traditions and clung tenaciously to Yiddish language and culture—drama, literature, lore, even "life-style"—as the wellsprings of Jewishness and Jewish identity. Yiddishists frequently joined socialist associations, like the Workmen's Circle, or else affiliated with *landsmanshaftn*. They either rebuffed or ignored the more established institutions, such as those involved with the United Jewish Charities or the newly formed Jewish Welfare Federation.

Of the vast numbers of East European Jews who, prompted by European upheavals and pogroms in the late nineteenth century, sought better lives in the United States, many had taken an active role in what became known as "socialist nationalist" movements in Eastern Europe.[167] Socialism became the vehicle for emancipation, equality, and freedom. Nationalism, arguably the dominant force of nineteenth- and twentieth-century European politics, meant the definition of the Jews of the Diaspora as a nation. Such a perception need not fix on Palestine or even be construed as Zionism, although most Jewish "nationalists" either were members of or sympathized with the Zionist movement of the early twentieth century. Those groups emphasized the vital connection between socialist ideology and ideals and Jewish national aspirations that many early Zionists had exhibited. Whether nationalist or socialist, however, their sources of Jewish identity derived from nonreligious attitudes.

152   With their secular backgrounds, those émigrés often opposed the reli-

gious hegemony over Jewish life in their native lands. Many had already broken away from the religious practices of their parents and grandparents.[168] While some welcomed the prospect of complete assimilation in American culture, with no concern for the "fate and welfare of the Jewish people," others attempted to synthesize their socialist leanings with Jewish national aspirations through the medium of what they denoted as Jewish values. Deeply attached to their "Jewishness," they abandoned religious Judaism, which they interpreted as superfluous religious doctrines and empty rites.[169]

Once again, with renewed intensity, the question of Jewish identity, commanded attention. Earlier émigrés had focused on philanthropy or the New World equivalent of *tzedakah*; by 1926, secularists centered on social and cultural values that could and frequently did include some of the same altruistic traits. Yet the secular ranks spanned a wide diversity of opinions regarding the nature of "Jewish" values and culture. Groups like the Poale Zion-Labor Zionists, the socialist-territorialists, pure Yiddishists and bilingualists (those who would accept only Yiddish and those who recognized Hebrew as an important part of the Jewish heritage, respectively), the Workmen's Circle, and a wide variety of splinter groups hotly debated not only what constituted Jewish identity, but the pragmatics of social and educational action.[170] There seemed to be no end to attempts to carve out a clear definition of the fundamental principles of Jewish secularism. Detroit's secular representatives (men and women) usually agreed upon the idea of "Jewish nationhood" based, as Irving Panush wrote, not necessarily on territory, "but on common aspirations, ethical ideals, cultural, educational and literary backgrounds and common communal institutions." He included, too, the "principle of historic Judaism," which he depicted not as a religious community but as a "people that incorporates an all-embracing world view." Finally, each secularist faction shared at least some variation on the principle of a rational approach to a secular, Jewish life.[171]

In 1925 a group of socialist-nationalist Jews in Detroit organized the Yiddishe Folkshule Farein (Jewish People's School Association). In 1929 the *farein* adopted the name of the Sholem Aleichem Folks Institute.[172] By then, the concept of secular Judaism and the formation of secular Jewish schools already possessed a checkered history. The Poale Zion had established the first Yiddish secular school in Detroit in 1915. The Workmen's Circle followed with its own school in 1919. By 1925, both these institutions had failed. But in 1925, at the request of Dr. Judah Kaufman of the Jewish Teachers Seminary of New York, members of the Poale Zion were moved to try again, this time with the expressed purpose of establishing "a Nationalist-Socialist Cultural Center" for adults, a home for the youth, and a school for children. In March 1926, they had raised enough money to purchase a two-story house on Kenilworth Street, near Oakland Avenue. In May 1926—ironically, the month of the founding of Federation—one

153

hundred children enrolled in the new school. Upon Dr. Kaufman's recommendation, Moishe Haar, of St. Louis, and Chaim Pomeranz, of New
York, were hired as teachers.[173]

Known as the Folk-shule Geselshaft (People's School Society), the organization was fueled by the enthusiasm and ambitious hopes of its leaders.
Two branches were soon opened in the Fenkell Street and Twelfth Street
neighborhoods. Chaim Bednowich, known as Bendore, joined the teaching
staff, and the first fund-raising bazaar, held in the auditorium of the United
Hebrew Schools on Kirby Street in December 1926, proved a success.[174]

With that modest triumph emerged the predictable political differences.
Some members of the Folk-shule Geselshaft were anti-Zionist or "pure"
Yiddishists. They grew increasingly disturbed by the teaching staff's obvious Zionist leanings. In the spring of 1927, Shloime Bercovich, then
affiliated with the Sholem Aleichem Institute of New York, was hired as
director and organizer of the school. At its first public gathering in April
1927, at Orchestra Hall, the children presented a performance, and Bercovich
addressed the audience with several markedly anti-Zionist remarks that
disparaged Hebrew. As a result, the Poale Zion, or Labor Zionists, seceded,
taking with them the Twelfth Street School, which then fell under the
direction of Haar and Bendore and became known as the Farband Shule.
There the orientation was Zionist, as teachers instructed students in both
Yiddish and Hebrew.[175] And on May 1, May Day, the children of the Farband
Shule sang the "Kinder Internationale," the Children's International, in
Yiddish. They openly proclaimed their socialist-nationalist or Labor Zionist
orientation.

The rump organization then took the name of the Umpartaieshe Folk-
shule Geselshaft, the Nonpartisan People's School Society, with Bercovich
as director and principal of the school on Kenilworth and the branch in
the Fenkell section. Although the name would change to the Sholem
Aleichem Institute in 1929, "umpartaiesche" remained an attribute that
the organization would cling to throughout its long life.[176] But, given its
membership, "umpartaieshe" assumed somewhat culture-specific meanings. "We were known as the Umpartaishe Shule," recalls one early student
of the Sholem Aleichem School, "but if you distinguished yourself in school,
you received a bust of Eugene V. Debs [the legendary hero of the American
labor and socialist movements]."

Frances Driker remembered that Isaac Finkelstein, the first president of
the Sholem Aleichem Institute, came to the meeting of the Odessa Progressive Society and described the new school: "They would teach the children Yiddish, literature, history *and* provide education for adults as well,
and bring to Detroit poets and writers." Convinced by his eloquence and
hopeful that Yiddish might be salvaged for their children, the Odessa Society
voted to bring fifty dollars to the bazaar. As she walked into the auditorium, Mrs. Driker heard three musicians playing on the stage.

Mr. Finkelstein and Harry Weinberg greeted everyone, and "Ida Komaroff brought out the cake." The atmosphere was electric, and members of the Odessa and other *landsmanshaftn* opted to send their children to the new Yiddish school. Yet not all of them supported its socialist orientation, and the label "umpartaieshe" seemed to make the decision easier.

Shloime Bercovich, a follower of John Dewey noted for his "progressive philosophy" of education, experimented with educational techniques. While members of the *landsmanshaftn* frequently called each other *"Bruder"* in their meetings, at the Folkshule, students called each other *"chaver"* (comrade) and even the teachers were called by that title.[177] This experimental approach to education sharply contrasted with the United Hebrew Schools' methodology, symbolized by its highly respected and erudite director, Bernard Isaacs. To many of the *Folksmenshen*, the "common people," Isaacs appeared strict and foreboding, although they generally respected him for his scholarship and learned demeanor. Isaacs, along with Bercovich and Haar, drew the esteemed appellation of "intellecutal."

Chaver Bercovich hoped to simultaneously gain the active participation of members of the *landsmanshaftn* and to raise the cultural level of the members. He brought many of them into a new-old world of learning that embodied the philosophy of the secularists.[178] Under the guidance of the "Mother of the Sholem Aleichem Institute," Ida Kamaroff, women like Frances Shayne and Frances Driker became active in fund-raising, organizing study groups, and drawing in their husbands to participate in directing the school.[179] Charles Driker and Sam Shayne became members of the board and found themselves also involved in discussion groups along with such other members of the Odessa Progressive Society as Max Holtzman.

In her description of the Sholem Aleichem Women's Division, Ida Kamarof noted that "women hand in hand with men did the most difficult tasks in raising money" and organizing the school. Not an auxiliary, but an independent part of the Sholem Aleichem Institute, the Women's Division engaged in activities to supply the school with accessories, books, a piano, or whatever was needed. They conducted a program of house calls to mothers to explain the importance of sending children to a Yiddish school. "We kept the educational institution going," recalled Mrs. Driker, "through good times and bad—door-to-door, rummage sales, study groups, educating the public, and all the time studying with teachers like Bercovich and Haar." Egalitarian precepts went beyond rhetoric among these unself-consciously feminist ranks.

Along with Moishe Haar, who was reengaged as a teacher in 1931 (and remained so until his death in 1966), Bercovich immersed thousands of Detroit's East European Jews in Yiddish culture through literature, history, and drama. Haar inaugurated the first *lehnenkreis*, reading circle, for the Women's Division of the Sholem Aleichem Institute, an institution that brought women into the world of Jewish learning and fast became a Jewish 155 tradition in Detroit. By 1939 Haar and Bercovich had founded at least twenty-six study groups.[180]

Umpartaieshe, then, might imply, in 1929, non-Zionist and noncommunist. Caught up in the swirl of political debates over communism, socialism, unionism, and Zionism, the schoolchildren of the Sholem Aleichem Institute, without discussing the issues in school, were clearly distinguished from the Labor Zionists and from the students of yet another Yiddish secularist school, the International Workers' Order (IWO) Hersh Leckert Shules—the communist schools. Like the other *Folkshules*, the Hersh Leckert Shule, named after a Jewish cobbler hero of the abortive 1905 Russian revolution, suffered continuous financial difficulties. Barely able to pay its rent, the school employed Louis Miller, a poet and teacher, and provided living quarters for him in two rooms over a nearby store. In an age when communism connoted anti-Americanism to the public at large, Jews with socialist leanings or backgrounds or vague "*linke* instincts" tried to clearly distinguish themselves from the Hersh Leckert school. It was a distinction lost on non-Jews, and on many Jews outside the secularist ranks as well.

Teachers in the five Hersh Leckert Shules taught children from ages seven to fourteen "the Yiddish language and the Yiddish revolutionary experience . . . from a cultural-political base." One alumnus of the school alleged that while their activities fell under the same genre and tone of the other secular schools, those others remained "insular," with their chief activity "being anti-Hersh Leckert." Students of this *shule*, however, learned about putting principles into action: when the Harlan County, Kentucky, miners or the Gastonia, North Carolina, textile workers struck, their children found refuge in the homes of Hersh Leckert students; those same students marched in May Day parades, in unemployment Hunger Marches, and in the 15,000-person funeral procession of the Ford Four (one of whom, Joseph Bussel, was a former Hersh Leckert student) in March 1937. They spoke on street corners, passed out leaflets, raised funds for those in need during the Depression, and worked for jailed political prisoners or causes, like the Bonus Army. Among those who gathered at the "clubrooms" were the young Borman brothers and Maurice Sugar. Coming from working-class homes, the children of the school learned to write and speak Yiddish—"no Hebrew, no bar mitzvah, no Zionist leanings and no synagogue connections."[181]

Stimulated in part by the Depression, an eclectic group of socialist-oriented Jews actively moved to "make the world a better place" in 1933. Members of the Workmen's Circle, the Poale Zion, and others of similar political and ideological persuasions, followed Joseph Cohen (a leading American anarchist thinker and former editor of *Die Freie Arbiter Stimme*, a Jewish leftist newspaper) to found the Sunrise Colony, an agricultural cooperative near Bay City, Michigan. Cohen had acquired some ten thousand acres of land from the Buhl Hardware Co. and, spurred by ideological dreams and by unemployment, he gained a following that included many Detroit Jews. The settlers tended to be antireligious; only a few observed even Yom Kippur.[182]

They raised some cattle on this experimental cooperative farm, but the main crop was peppermint, widely used by the pharmaceutical industry. Although the Sunrise Colony obtained some ten million dollars in loans from the U.S. government, pharmacy companies, fearing anarchism and communism, hesitated to deal with the farmers. One Workmen's Circle member recalled a common feeling among his comrades that anti-Semitism played no small part in those refusals to buy the Sunrise crop. But when a sympathetic University of Michigan professor persuaded Parke-Davis to buy the entire peppermint crop, success seemed imminent.[183]

This utopian dream, however, like numerous others born of the Depression, became torn by internal squabbling. A group led by Eli Greenblatt soon left the colony, and, after a few years, the Depression began to lighten, employment became more available in Detroit, and settlers left. Finally, the U.S. government bought the colony for an amount sufficient to pay off its bank loans.[184] All that remained for many were the enthusiasm, memories, and energy of that failed experiment.

In the ideologically cluttered, highly charged climate of secular Jewish Detroit, feelings ran deep and idealism permeated the various leftist movements. The Ikuf, a communist cultural organiziation, boasted between one and two hundred members and organized lectures and public discussions. The Freiheit Gesang Farein, the People's Chorus, founded in 1925, included mandolin-players and performed two concerts each year. Those concerts received audiences of between fifteen hundred and two thousand people at Orchestra Hall or at the Masonic Temple. On the program might be an oratorio, such as "Zvei Brueder," or "Judas Maccabeus," or Schubert's "Miriam's Song of Triumph." The second half of the concert typically consisted of Jewish folk songs. Rehearsals were twice a week at the Jericho Temple on Joy road, owned by the Communist organization, and faithfully attended by the entire chorus. "[We were] all *idealists*, committed and dedicated to a better world—to *Menschlichkeit* [humanness]. Monday [rehearsal night] was like a holiday for me. I was in another world—forgot about everything," recalled one member. In 1929 the name of the chorus was changed to the Jewish Folk Chorus. Another member noted that its passionate fervor continued: "It was [our] whole life; like a religion. [We] ate, slept and drank the chorus." One fervent singer in the chorus observed that, like other leftists, they had displaced religion with idealism. "[We didn't] need religion, religion is to make the world a better place. That's what [we] believed in."

As described above, ideologies had clashed in the Sunrise Colony, typifying the stormy disposition of the left in general. In Detroit, as if to dem- 157 onstrate ideological differences with the communists, the Poale Zion and the Sholem Aleichem Institute formed a competing choir, the Halevy Choir. Its founders included Morris and Emma Schaver and Rebecca and David Frohman. Both women were musicians with reputable music credentials. To many, however, despite its larger membership and the musicianship of its leaders, the Halevy remained "the *other* choir."[185]

Both singing groups considered themselves cultural organizations that promoted *Yiddishkeit*. Members of the Folk Chorus frequently attended concerts given by their counterparts in Cleveland. Established with the assistance of the Cultural Alliance in New York City—which had sent Nathan Samarov, the first of its four directors to Detroit in 1925—the Folk Chorus claimed fellow organizations in Chicago, Los Angeles, and Florida. In a world that seemed to press for the abandonment of Jewish culture, these organizations and others like them reasserted what they considered their essential Jewish identity through cultural activities.

For the *Folkshule* student, the political world seemed confusing and paradoxically simpler than for the intellectuals. One young girl who attended the *umpartaieshe shule* classified the differences through her own perceptions: "The socialists would say 'we believe that women should have equal rights,' and the communists would stand on street corners shaking their fists shouting 'we *demand* that women have equal rights.' " Yet another, a Detroiter named Emma Goldman ("but my father would never have named me after *the* Emma Goldman") recalls that "the communists stood on the street corners and yelled. As far as we [knew], all the other Jews were socialists." While this sentiment may have reflected a common feeling, it was nevertheless contradicted, even within the organizations. Membership in groups identified as *linke* might include budding or diehard "Alrightniks" or capitalists. They might include, too, members of the often conservative *landsmanshaftn*.

Most Jews, however, remained outside the flurry of ideological controversy, joining organizations for practical reasons—education for their children, companionship, family, community—and strongly identifying themselves as Jews through their cultural, ethnic background and language. By 1930 attempts to express that cultural heritage had taken to the radio. In that year, Max Blatt presented a program in Yiddish. It went off the air after about six months. He was followed by Hyman Altman, whose program on station WJLB in Detroit included news broadcasts summarizing Jewish news of the week and announcements about the activities of Jewish organizations, including the Chesed Shel Emes and the Folks Kitchen.[186]

But it was not until 1932 that the "cultural groups" of Jewish Detroit got their radio voice. In that year, at the suggestion of Shloime Bercovich, Harry Weinberg began Weinberg's Yiddish Radio Hour, which would air every Sunday from 10:30 until noon. Well-suited to cultural programming, Weinberg had long experience in the Yiddish theater and numerous connections to the New York Jewish stage. His program included music, Yiddish readings, and a situation comedy. Among the local celebrities taking part in the show were Dorothy Stollar and Cantor Jacob Sonenklar, of Congregation Shaarey Zedek. Those national and international celebrities who performed in Detroit at Littman's Yiddish Theatre on Twelfth Street frequently made appearances on Weinberg's program: Molly Picon, Jacob Kalich, Moishe Oysher, Samuel Goldenberg, and stars like Menashe Skolnik and David Romain of the national radio program "The Goldbergs" and Popele Cohen of "Abie's Irish Rose." Weinberg capitalized on those stimulating visits of scholars and poets who came to Detroit under the auspices of such groups as the Sholem Aleichem Institute and invited them to speak on his show.[187]

One of Weinberg's staunchest supporters and closest friends, Morris Schaver, had been an avid champion of Labor Zionism from the 1920s. He appealed to Weinberg early in the radio show's life to assist his performers in raising funds for the new Detroit chapter of Histadrut, the Jewish-Zionist Labor Movement. Weinberg recalled that Schaver prevailed upon him as a Warsaw landsman. Yet Weinberg, clearly steeped in Yiddish secular culture, strongly identified with Labor Zionism. He gladly offered his performers for the Histadrut cause and their help set the fledgling organization on its way.[188]

Unlike earlier attempts at Yiddish radio programming, Weinberg's show drew national and local non-Jewish, as well as Jewish, sponsors. Numbering among those were General Motors Corporation, which, combined with the continuing boycott of Ford Motor Company, virtually guaranteed that company the lion's share of Jewish automobile purchases in Detroit. Along with such non-Jewish business sponsors came others, including political announcements in election years. Many Detroiters remembered the 1940 announcement delivered by Mrs. Weinberg in English on behalf of Wendell Willkie, the Republican candiate opposing President Roosevelt's bid for an unprecedented third term. Following her announcement, Mrs. Weinberg added in Yiddish that the announcement was a paid political ad and went on to proclaim that she herself was voting for Roosevelt, as should all Jews.

The Jews of Detroit, then, debated with intensity radically different approaches to education. Virtually none, however, doubted that education remained the mainstay of Jewish life. "He who does not increase his learning decreases it," said Hillel two thousand years ago. And if the 1930s presented new problems for Jewish education and educational institutions, Hillel's injunction and the implicit warning behind it seemed to echo throughout the communities. Several of Detroit's teachers and rabbis complained that many students came to schools with less motivation and less knowledge than their predecessors. Like Esser Rabinowitz and Rabbi Hershman in the early twenties, these men seemed acutely aware that Jew- 159 ish education had grown less important in many homes. According to a 1939 study, probably fewer than 30 percent of Detroit's Jewish children received any sort of Jewish education.[189] In 1936 Bernard Isaacs criticized the increasingly common practice of hiring private tutors for children, depriving them, he said, of the benefits of a school environment.[190] Implicit in his critique was the recognition that Jewish homes and Jewish parents could no longer be counted on to convey Jewish values or learning. Even many of the major contributors to the UHS did not send their children there.

Synagogues often operated their own schools, making the creation of a unified or centralized school system difficult at best. Independent schools proliferated: the UHS grew to about eighteen hundred students in nine branches by 1939; a Kadimah school of Zionist orientation was managed by Morris Kutnick and Simon Richardson on Twelfth Street and Lawton, and there was a Carmel School as well.[191] Yeshivah Beth Yehudah offered longer class hours and a more Orthodox course of study. About twenty-five of its alumni went on to study at *yeshivot*, Jewish universities, for advanced study of Talmud in other cities.[192] The Sholem Aleichem Institute, the Workmen's Circle, the Hersh Leckert School, the Farband, and other, smaller schools rounded out a multiform collection of educational facilities. In 1927, with the combined efforts of Philip Slomovitz, Bernard Isaacs, Shlomo Bercovich, and others, Tishrei, the first month of autumn, was designated as Jewish Education Month.[193] Speeches in synagogues, newspaper articles, and even door-to-door solicitations aimed at bringing in more students and more money. In the late 1930s, the *Jewish Chronicle* devoted an entire issue each year to Jewish education.[194] These efforts were responses to the decrease in funding wrought by the Depression. Teachers in all of the schools at times went without pay. In November 1930, Federation-established relief kitchens would serve free meals to the Jewish children who went to Hebrew school after attending public school.[195] The Yeshivah Beth Yehudah chronically tottered on the brink of closing and was rescued at one point, in October 1934, by the Ladies Auxiliary dance at Congregation B'nai Moshe.[196] In 1935, 56 percent of the students attending Jewish schools paid no tuition, as fees were covered by sponsoring institutions—Federation, the Workmen's Circle, and the Sholem Aleichem Institute all subsidized those students whose parents could not afford to pay tuition.

Connections to what most secularists considered some of the most venerable traditional Jewish beliefs shined through some of the programs of Jewish secular organizations. They fostered a continued respect, bordering on worship, if not for *the* Book, then for books. Talmudic scholars and Hasidic rebbes were replaced in the eyes of the secularists by poets, novelists, and thinkers. The scholar retained a primary position of esteem. Yiddish and Hasidic melodies were retained without words. One Sholem

Aleichem writer suggested that the longing for redemption and the messiah were supplanted by the longing for egalitarianism and the fulfillment of such dreams as social revolution or the creation of a Jewish political and cultural center in Palestine.[197]

Jewish intellectuals, poets, actors, and writers were invited to Detroit by the Sholem Aleichem Institute, and one graduate of the Farband Shule remembered that during his childhood and youth "they [the nationalist poets and intellectuals] were our rabbis. We would listen to them far into the night and when they left would discuss what they said for weeks." In place of the synagogue, the centers of secular Jewish life were a few houses and the *shules* (schools).

For such a grass-roots movement, teaching Yiddish became a goal, a necessary element for the continued fostering of Yiddish culture for children and adults. Isaac Finkelstein explained that the writer Sholem Aleichem had expressed "deep love and understanding for the reality of Jewish life and for their language." Jews recognized themselves in his work, wrote Finkelstein, and could identify with his characters and ideals. Through the Sholem Aleichem Institute, secular Jewishness would be transmitted to subsequent generations, even in the midst of the melting pot.[198]

That organization, like many of the other secular groups, sought "to establish a harmonious relationship between Americanism and Jewishness" and "to maintain a specific Jewish cultural identity in America."[199] Beneath the joyful meetings, the commitment to education and learning, and the near-worship of scholars and teachers, an uneasy awareness of a threat to Jewish identity seemed to haunt Detroit's secular Jews, just as it dogged the consciousness of some religious leaders. Defining that identity became a part of secular Jewish organizations' raison d'être.

Their very existence seemed to pose again the questions of Jewish tradition and identity in America. Rejecting religion and religious ritual traditions, they nevertheless determined that Jewish culture set them apart from others. They believed that Americanism and Jewishness could strike a "harmonious balance," yet many intuited that such a balance must be threatening to their Jewish identity. All of these diverse Detroit secular Jewish groups agreed that the best medium for the transmission of Jewish culture was Yiddish. Even if, like Haar, one advocated learning Hebrew, Yiddish remained the *mama loshen*, or mother tongue, of Jews.

Not everyone agreed, of course. American-Jewish nationalism remained problematic in the 1920s and 1930s. And while the young Detroit Emma Goldman may have believed that "all other Jews were socialists," in Detroit, that was hardly the case—even among some of the socialists who were "socialists by night [at the organization meetings] and successful capitalists who fought the unions by day." Overt disagreements continued. As some active Jewish leaders seemed to sense, there lingered the fear that Detroit's Jewish organizational structure, in particular the Jewish Welfare   161

Federation, with its mystique—correctly or incorrectly perceived—of German Jewish leadership, remained insensitive to the needs of poor Jews and to the nature of *tzedakah* (philanthropy or righteousness), a term Slomovitz had used in his editorial on the Relief Council.[200]

Those referred to as *"Folksmenshen,"* the "common people," struggled through the Depression years, finding help when needed through their own organizations, which were usually outside the purview of the Jewish Welfare Federation. The talk at *landsmanshaftn*, the Workmen's Circle, the Sholem Aleichem Institute, and even the Peoples' Chorus meetings almost exclusively gravitated to economic issues—insurance, relief, loans, employment. Organizational procedures and operations—publicly, the most visible aspect of Jewish life—rarely filled the gap between constituents and leadership and remained peripheral to the mainstream of Jewish life. Particularly during the Depression, Jews toiled, like other Americans, to earn their livings, keep food on their tables, educate their children, and to be assured of proper health care, insurance, and burial. In 1935 the Jewish "working force" approximated 34,359 men and women. An estimated five thousand Jewish men and women were unemployed, some 14.7 percent of the working force. Of those unemployed, a smaller proportion of Jews, as compared to unemployed non-Jews, were to be found on the Detroit Public Welfare rolls.[201]

To many, the *landsmanshaftn* and the secular organizations like the Workmen's Circle remained, if not more trustworthy than the Detroit Public Welfare or Federation, then more understanding and therefore more approachable. Those groups, too, formed emergency-relief systems. For twenty dollars a year the Workmen's Circle offered the benefits of insurance through its membership dues; the David Horodoker Unterstitzung Verein offered similar benefits, as did the Bereznitzer Unterstitzung Verein and almost all of the nearly forty *landsmanshaftn* and/or secular groups.[202] They were not as well-endowed as Federation, but were nevertheless dedicated and determined to rescue Jews from the streets. For all their differences, as they ministered to their own brethren, this constellation of organizations, along with those of Federation that were most accessible and important to the public—the Hebrew Free Loan Association and the North End Clinic—kept the overwhelming majority of needy Jews from the municipal relief agencies.

Yet, despite the common plight of many Jews in Detroit during the Depression, ethnic divisions and the rancor that attended them continued. Not only did such divisions manifest themselves between German Jews and *Ostjuden* but between Russian Jews and Romanian Jews, Galician Jews (Galizianers) and Hungarian Jews, Lithuanian and Polish Jews. At a Federation anniversary dinner in 1986, William Avrunin, then executive vice-president emeritus of Federation, noted that sixty years earlier "the ancestors of those in attendance would have been sensitive to those who sat next to them because of their places of birth."[203] Avrunin's comment spoke volumes about the progress made in overcoming such divisions, but in 1932 or 1939, or even later, those schisms persisted.

In order to overcome such estrangements, the Jews of Detroit would need genuine rallying points, models, symbols, and positive elements of identity—recognized and recognizable leaders or heros. Such a white knight arrived in 1933 in the uniform of a Detroit Tiger baseball player. Hank Greenberg touched, sometimes personally, the lives of many of Detroit's residents, but particularly its Jews. To children and adults alike, he represented the genuine American sucess story: a big-league baseball player— and not just a pretty good one, but a great one, a star. A recognized gentleman of good character, and openly Jewish, Greenberg elicited warm smiles and pleasant memories from Jews and non-Jews alike in Detroit. People remembered seeing him in Congregation Shaarey Zedek, or walking home from services, although he was by no means a regular attender. He spoke often to Jewish youth groups.[204]

Early in its history, Detroit embodied the all-American, midwestern spirit through its sports enthusiasm. It was logical, then, for Detroit Jews who sought American identities through varying degrees of assimilation, to turn to sports figures and sports activities as acceptable vehicles. Secular, Reform, Conservative, or Orthodox Jews could all participate with little or no conflict over traditions or cultural controversies. The 1923 *Survey* recognized sports activities as a measure of Americanization, often characterizing Yiddish or Orthodox groups as "unAmericanized" if they offered no sports activities.

And many Jews excelled. Jacob Mazer, for example, a Russian Jew, organized a YMHA basketball team that won the Michigan championship in 1918. Benjamin Bagdade, a champion figure skater in 1919, went on to coach Olympic teams in 1948, 1952, and 1956. By the mid-1930s, Central High School boasted numerous athletic heroes in football, basketball, and baseball; so, too, did Northern High. In the year 1925–1926, one of the University of Michigan's leading football players was Benny Friedman. Harry Newman, another All-American Jewish quarterback, succeeded Friedman. Byron Krieger distinguished himself at Wayne University for his elegance in fencing—a skill that carried him to glory in the Pan-American Games in Argentina in 1951 and to the Olympics in 1952 and 1956.

Sports, then, often provided an arena in which conflicts among Jews and between Jews and non-Jews became quiescent. Hank Greenberg, for all the anti-Semitic taunts he endured, drew accolades from all of Detroit—and from virtually all of Detroit's Jews.

Thus, on Rosh Hashanah 1934, a doubly reverent hush fell upon the congregation attending services at Shaarey Zedek, as the giant first baseman strode quietly into the synagogue. Several people recalled that Rabbi Hershman had to call for quiet as a murmur spread throughout the sanc-   163 tuary. That day, as the Tigers were headed toward their first pennant in twenty-five years, Greenberg had to decide whether or not to play in a crucial game against the Boston Red Sox. Even most Jews who gave no attention to observing their religion during the year would go to the synagogue on Rosh Hashanah and pass the rest of the day at home enjoying the exalted mood of the holiday. What should and would Greenberg do?

By the time he ambled into Shaarey Zedek, Greenberg had already made his decision. There exist several versions of the story, with minor variations. According to *Detroit Free Press*, Hank went for advice to Jacob Thumin, the learned rabbi of the Orthodox Beth Abraham, the Galicianer shul. Rabbi Thumin pointed out a passage in the Shulchan Aruch, Orach Hayim, 518 (the Code of Jewish Law) that could be interpreted as permitting ball playing on Rosh Hashanah; he allegedly also cited a recent similar decision by a rabbi in Jerusalem.[205] Other versions of the story report Rabbi Franklin or Rabbi Hershman as the rabbinic respondent.

People gathered on the steps of Congregation Shaarey Zedek to watch Greenberg go straight from the synagogue to Navin Field. There, he hit two home runs to power the Tigers to a 2-1 victory over the Red Sox. Heading home after the game with third baseman Marv Owen, Greenberg expressed some guilt about having played. Owen replied that he himself would be glad to feel guilty anytime, if he could hit two home runs. When Greenberg decided not to play on Yom Kippur, the following week, the Tigers lost. Although they won the pennant, the Tigers did not win the World Series that year; behind the hitting of Greenberg, however, they won it the following year, as he was selected the American League's Most Valuable Player of 1935.[206]

Detroit Jews warmly and proudly accepted the New York–born-and-bred Greenberg as one of their own. Opposing ball players were not always so kind, and he would often hear a loud cry of "Jewboy" or worse coming from the opposing dugout. A mild man, Greenberg sought to answer his detractors with home runs. He remained one of the bright spots for Detroit Jews, a genuine cultural hero able to achieve what appeared nearly impossible, bringing Jews in Detroit together in agreement.

12

Palestine: Jewish Identity and the Question of National Survival

Such concordance, however, remained rare, and the more common discord assumed disturbing proportions in 1929 over what ought to have presented a clear-cut necessity for unity. In late August 1929, after a prolonged series of disputes between Arabs and Jews over religious observances at the Western Wall in Jerusalem, Arab rioters attacked Jews there, and the rioting quickly spread throughout Palestine, taking their highest toll in Hebron, where sixty Orthodox Jews were murdered and fifty more wounded. The ensuing massacres, which resulted in some 133 Jews dead and 399 wounded, stunned Jews around the world, evoking memories of such European pogroms as Kishinev and Odessa. Some referred to this most recent catastrophe as the *dritter churban,* or the third destruction of the Temple.[207] As the riots elicited statements of outrage, they also, surprisingly, roused anti-Semitism in the United States. One historian has noted that the Palestine riots of 1929 produced ominous trends of three sorts: official non-involvement, anti-Semitism and, perhaps most telling, American Jewish disunity.[208]

In Detroit anguished Detroiters, including Mrs. Isidore Cohen, whose brother and three cousins lived at the Hebron Yeshivah; Mrs. Morris Subar,   165 whose brother was in Palestine; and Mechoel Margolis, whose wife and two daughters were somewhere in Palestine; awaited some news. The *Detroit Jewish Chronicle* received phone calls inquiring about the situation for a week after the riots. At the urging of Detroit Jews, Michigan congressman Robert Clancy sent a letter to U.S. Secretary of State Henry Stimson, asking him to send American troops to restore order.[209]

Detroiter David Brown, a non-Zionist famous for fund-raising miracles, was appointed president of the Palestine Emergency Fund. Brown used his expertise and contacts to mobilize the machinery of such usually competitive organizations as the Joint Distribution Committee, the United Palestine Appeal, the Zionist Organization of America, and Hadassah; he also fully utilized his personal contacts with prominent Jews, especially in Detroit. He masterminded a campaign that netted two million dollars in six weeks. Apart from this obvious success, virtually no one argued with the choice of David Brown, despite his non-Zionist position. This indicated that "ideological differences had been set aside in favor of expertise."[210]

Yet Zionism, the question of Palestine relief, and the future and nature of the Yishuv remained explosive issues that divided Jews in the United States. Relief drives for Jews in distress abroad had succeeded before, most notably after World War I, but they had been directed by the older German Jewish establishment. Even those campaigns, as the records of the Detroit United Jewish Charities reveal, rarely proceeded without some dissent. In 1930 Louis Lipsky, then president of the Zionist Organization of America (ZOA), might have been speaking about the Detroit Jewish population when he pointed out that Jews had become more Americanized, and that they looked to refining and expanding their own lives, fixing their sights on communal centers, lodges, charitable institutions, and federations instead of on Zionist causes or relief for endangered Jews in Palestine.[211]

Indeed, although the riots in Palestine startled Jews in Detroit, prompted apprehension among those with loved ones in Palestine, and spurred relief efforts, they seem to have been ignored in the official meetings of the Federation. Continuing the pattern described in the *Survey* of 1923, Zionism attracted relatively little attention and support in Detroit. Youngsters like Danny Ginsburg, Aaron Lazaroff, Al Chafetz, Al Kramer, and George (Mike) Zeltzer, founders of Habonim, a Zionist youth group in Detroit, would participate in "tag days." On those days, they would stand on street corners trying to raise money for Histadrut, the Zionist labor organization. They received a variety of antagonistic responses. Standing in front of Littman's People's Theatre or Zeman's Bakery on Twelfth Street, various Jewish groups would compete for prime space: Habonim jostled members of Hashomer Hatzair, known as the pro-Soviet Communist youth organization. All of them confined their solicitations to Jewish neighborhoods, of course, yet drew comments like "go to Palestine where you belong" from anti-Zionist Jews. During door-to-door campaigns for

Histadrut they would experience more slammed doors than contributions.

Zionist youth groups like Habonim contributed to the sense of collective Jewish life among some young people. According to Zeltzer, one of the key creators of Habonim, the organization began as an intensely ideological one. But later, recalled another of Habonim's members, "most people didn't join out of ideology." Another affirmed that "it became a place for people who were nonreligious and wanted a Jewish organization to belong to and had good camaraderie." But if many of the members were nonideologues, they all shared a common sense of what the Zionist dream involved, and almost all of them were schooled in at least a street Marxism or socialism. Their meetings, often primarily social, nevertheless included heated and concerned discussions about the rise of Nazism, the British White Paper, new limits on immigration, and the Arab riots.

Despite the persistent antagonism toward Zionism among most Detroit Jews, many grew to support "cultural projects" in Palestine. Rabbi Franklin, for example, "never refused a donation to a cultural activity in Palestine," according to one source. The riots, however, did serve to galvanize the Zionist District of Detroit, the Poale Zion/Labor Zionists, and other pro-Zionist organizations. Reactions to the Arab violence revealed the differences in attitudes of the organized Jewish establishment and the Jewish popular mind.

Among the unanticipated supporters of Zionist activities was Detroit's premier musician, the first conductor of the Detroit Symphony Orchestra, Ossip Gabrilowitsch. Although he was not antagonistic to Judaism, this Russian-born Jewish artist seemed to hold no strong feelings about his Jewish background until 1929, when he visited Palestine before the riots. He wrote to his wife, soprano Clara Clemens (the daughter of Mark Twain), that Jewish settlers "have transformed sun-burnt sterile mountains and valleys into blooming fruit-gardens, orchards, fields of wheat and rye, also flower gardens."[212] He performed a piano concert to a packed house in Tel Aviv and donated the proceeds to the Tel Aviv School of Music. Upon his return, Gabrilowitsch and Ilya Schkolnik, his Russian-born Jewish concertmaster, became active supporters of Zionist activities, offering DSO concerts of Hebrew music even in the "non-Zionist" lair of Temple Beth El.[213]

Less surprising in her support of Zionism, Emma Lazaroff Schaver, another Detroit musician, dedicated her operatic talents to Zionist activities. She sang in Yiddish operas with such legendary stars as Tito Schipa (1933) and Jan Pierce (1939). She toured successfully in the eastern United States in 1933 and in Latin America in 1938. In 1933 Lazaroff Schaver sang the leading role in the partially Federation-supported play, "Romance of a People." With an enduring devotion to Zionism, she pursued her Jewish ideals along with her husband Morris Schaver, perhaps the most influential and tireless worker for Labor Zionism in Detroit.

In the fateful year of 1929, Morris Schaver hosted Tel Aviv mayor David Bloch at a banquet and reception fund-raiser. There, with Schaver as the Detroit Zionist District campaign leader for the Palestinian Labor Movement, seventy-five hundred dollars were raised. Fred M. Butzel, who was not famous as an apostle of Zionism, received an ovation when he rose to speak at the dinner. He expressed his concern not for "political work or agitators," but only that Jews unite in a "constructive piece of work in Palestine." Butzel later introduced Bloch to John C. Lodge, the mayor of Detroit.[214] The event, which preceded by weeks the riots in Hebron, reflected a popular—that is, East European Jewish—environment. While Butzel and Milford Stern attended as representatives of Federation, others in attendance represented the Young Poale Zion; labor-oriented organizations like the Labor-Zionist Farband (Jewish National Workers' Alliance) and the Radomer Verein. Such individuals as Rabbi Leon Fram, the young assistant to Rabbi Franklin and an openly avowed Zionist, and Irving Pokempner, an acknowledged *linke* member of the Workmen's Circle, also attended. The organizations each contributed one hundred dollars and the individuals gave twenty-five dollars.[215]

It was Schaver, however, who drove the movement. In December 1929, he was appointed chairman of the 1930 Detroit Gewerkschaften (the United Hebrew Trades movement) drive. Meeting in the social hall at Littman's Theatre, participants in the drive set their goal at ten thousand dollars, which would be used in the campaign for the purchase of land by the Jewish National Fund in order to initiate a large colonization enterprise.[216] The Gewerkschaften campaign existed to raise money for Histadrut. Founded in 1920, this Zionist labor organization had grown from a world membership of forty-four hundred members to nearly 100,000 by the mid-1930s. The organization had melded together numerous labor organizations that had been ideologically divided. "Labor" in Palestine "assumed the dignity of a religion." And it would be under the auspices of Histadrut that the various communal institutions such as the kibbutzim would take shape.[217]

There could be no question that Histadrut grew from the socialist-communist traditions and organizations of Europe. Identified with the international trade union movement, it included a Workmen's Circle Division, a Landsmanshaft Department, and a Labor Zionist section, which comprised various American branches of the Poale Zion (Workers of Zion), Habonim, and Hashomer Hatzair.[218] Its founding statutes included the following principles:

> To persist in conducting the struggle of hired workers for improved labor conditions until the complete liberation of the working class . . . to promote comradely relations with Arab workers in Palestine and foster the link between the Jewish labor movement and the International Labor movements all over the world . . . to establish and develop mutual aid institutions (Sick Fund, Life Insurance, Credit Societies, Unemployment Insurance, etc.).[219]

At the second Histadrut Convention, in 1923, David Ben-Gurion voiced his concern for the reconciliation of expanded economic activities and the preservation of "the social, proletarian and Zionist character of our economic undertakings."[220] Histadrut remained unquestionably committed to a "socialist *Yishuv*" (homeland) and included in its ranks diverse ideologies, all of which agreed on that basic commitment.

In Detroit, the majority of the support there was for Palestine went to Histadrut. Labor Zionists like Morris and Emma Schaver, the Zeltzers, Drikers, Drachlers, Harry Schumer, and Joseph Chaggai campaigned vigorously and resolutely for that cause. Yet few of them would identify themselves as members of a proletarian movement, die-hard socialists, or even trade unionists. If their sympathies were vaguely leftist, most of them remained decidedly capitalist businessmen perhaps even embarrassed by the socialist rhetoric of the Palestinian labor movement. That strange, apparent contradiction even reflected a general disparity between Detroit Jewry's multifarious organizations, their public statements, and the day-to-day life experiences of the Jews of Detroit. For all the organizational activity—Federation, *landsmanshaft*, Workmen's Circle, or the congregations—the social experiences of Jews seemed independent of each other.

Many of these businessmen began to prosper. In the late 1930s, many Jewish businesses that were primarily in the general category of "trade" (that is, retail or wholesale business) prospered in the fields of food service, scrap metal, and oil refining. Small wholesale grocery distributors and retail grocers flourished; some would emerge from their small businesses to become food magnates. Businesses like Borman Foods began with individuals peddling fruits and vegetables from carts and evolved into leading enterprises in the food trade. Abner Wolf's successful merger of his wholesale grocery supply with Grosberg's Packer's grocery chain laid the foundation for what would become another of the leading food-industry empires in the following decades.[221] Max J. Zivian's Detroit Steel, the Hamburger family's Production Steel, and Abraham Kasle's steel company in Dearborn all were developed because of the individual initiatives of Jews who grasped the opportunities provided by Detroit's unique business environment.

In the metal business, Max Stotter and Samuel J. Leve were two of the many early, successful entrepreneurs of the scrap-metal business. All of these enterprises had recast such traditional Jewish pursuits as peddling into modern, industrially productive vocations.[222]

By 1926 the Jewish population in Detroit had grown to some seventy-five thousand people. And while Federation officials looked to the thirty-two hundred people who contributed to the campaign that year, most Jews were preoccupied with the economic and social details of Detroit life. Each in their own way, too, was concerned with maintaining Jewish identity, finding ways to express it or, in some cases, to hide it. Few among those businessmen—fewer still among the owners of independent laundries and dry goods stores—thought in terms of Morris Waldman's ideological justification for the federation idea. Few concerned themselves with the ideological bases for the United Hebrew Schools or the Sholem Aleichem Institute beyond their own interests for their children. What mattered most was that a child go to school and learn what it meant to be a Jew. With significant exceptions, the philosophy behind the school mattered less.

One might view the Detroit support for Histadrut as symbolic of these disparities between organizational and individual interests. Few of Histadrut's supporters seemed ideologically committed to the socialist principles professed so unabashedly by that organization or by its affiliates, including the Poale Zion, Hashomer Hatzair, and the like. Yet they pledged their lives to that cause. Did they ignore the ideological ground? Did it matter to them? Or was their steadfast allegiance founded on some other cornerstone?

Those who recalled the invigorating yet tenuous early days of Labor Zionist campaigns in Detroit spoke of them directly and simply: support for Histadrut meant support for Palestine. And support for Palestine was good for the Jews. That organization founded *kibbutzim,* factories, and communal settlements. It established trade schools and educated children, produced Jewish laborers, and made Palestinian Jews independent and strong. Therefore, Jews in Detroit were obliged to champion, nurture, and sustain it. There were few fervent debates over communist ideals. The issue was self-evident: Jews aid Palestine.

That fact partially defined being Jewish and measured identity, exclusive of any other ideological disputations. Such patronage found its counterpart in the frequent rationale for joining youth groups for social rather than ideological motivations. As one former member of a Zionist youth organization recalled, "It was the best way to meet Jewish girls." It also served to strengthen both Jewish identification and the Zionist movement in Detroit. Jews would not accuse a man like Morris Schaver of being a Communist. However, "Mr. Histadrut," as he became known, was quintessentially Jewish.

13

Anti-Semitism: Old Stories and New Voices

Israel Drachler decided to move to Detroit and accept an administrative-teaching position at the Sholem Aleichem Schools in 1929. He believed that the Detroit community, smaller and younger than that of New York City, would offer more opportunities for creative work. Three years later he suffered a stroke, and the family opened a dry-cleaning and laundry store. The laundry and dry-goods business attracted many Jews in Detroit, in part because it seemed a logical adjunct to tailoring and in part because of the ease with which a family could maintain the business.

Charles Driker, Drachler's friend and fellow Sholem Aleichemite, also ran a dry-cleaning establishment, the Ambassador Laundry. Both were subjected to the "dues" collected by members of the Purple Gang for the so-called Laundry Association. As a common Jewish enterprise, the laundry business became a prime target for the protection business, and Driker and Drachler had the same "collection agent." Such regular costs exacerbated the already alarming economic situation, adding a new dimension of fear and anxiety. If anti-Jewish feelings had assumed an aggressive offensive in the late 1920s and early 1930s, it had also compounded rifts within the Jewish population of Detroit, which included this insidious gangsterism. 171

Estrangements between and within Jewish groups kept them fragmented and antagonistic even in exacting times. it seemed that even Eastern European Jews who had achieved financial success might continue to be looked down upon by established Jews as *arrivestes,* as "pushy" or "assertive." These time-honored attitudes lingered to create considerable difficulties for those sincerely engaged in efforts to unify the Jews of Detroit.

But economic hard times historically generated other difficulties for Jews. Anti-Semitism, sometimes subtle, sometimes dormant, but omnipresent, grew more gregarious and open as the Depression worsened. Henry Ford had ceased his anti-Jewish campaign in 1927, under some pressure from his family, financial, and legal advisers.[223] But despite his public apology, no one doubted that Ford remained if not an active enemy of the Jews, then an active supporter of their more vociferous antagonists. Still, at the New York dinner honoring David Brown, the mere mention of Ford's name and presence in 1927 drew a standing ovation from the primarily Jewish crowd.[224]

This magnanimous pardon, as ambiguous as it may have been, dissolved in the 1930s when Ford's equally ambiguous repentance became moot. *The International Jew,* Ford's infamous and frequently obscenely specious publication which he had renounced in 1927, began to appear in Europe and South America with his name on the title page and often including his photograph. In 1933, a congressional committee investigating the extent of Nazi propaganda in the United States scrutinized Ford's anti-Semitic publications and the prospect of his continued support for racist doctrines.[225] German editions appearing regularly, and a Brazilian edition based on the German translation followed. In light of these ominous developments, Rabbi Franklin called upon his erstwhile friend to ask for yet another disclaimer. Even after Ford assured Franklin that he would investigate the matter, German editions of the book continued to appear. By the end of 1933, twenty-nine German editions had been published, each bearing Ford's name and a preface praising his "great service" to America and the world by attacking the Jews. In light of the congressional committee's investigations of reports that Ford also had contributed large sums to Hitler and his party, Detroit Jews, along with Jews throughout the United States, felt that their suspicions about the industrialist's deeply rooted anti-Semitism were confirmed.[226]

The German-American Bund and other racist, anti-Semitic, and pro-Nazi groups distributed the books in the United States after 1936. Franklin had returned to Ford in August 1933, requesting that he restate unequivocally his position of 1927, repudiate once and for all *The International Jew,* and publicly sever connection with it. Ford first agreed to sign such a letter but later refused. It was not until 1937 that Ford issued a statement to the *Detroit Jewish Chronicle* "disavowing any connection whatsoever with the publication in Germany of the book known as *The International Jew.*"[227]

It was too little too late. The effect of Ford's actions undoubtedly aided Hitler and added some respectability to his campaign. As usual, rumors about Ford's anti-Semitism seemed to encourage less prominent, more populist anti-Semites in Detroit—in particular, the members of the German-American Bund from 1936 until the start of World War II.[228] Ford's involvement with Nazi anti-Semitism would deepen in 1938 before it finally ended. Its effects on the Jews of Detroit reverberated long after that; but Jewish Detroiters' immediate concerns converged more on grass-roots anti-Semitic movements.

In 1926 the *Jewish Chronicle* ran a series of articles, entitled "Easy Lessons in Anti-Semitism," which drew critical remarks from Jews and non-Jews. An ironic satire on the "new breed of scientific anti-Semitism," the series outlined what becoming anti-Semitic involved in 1926.[229] Its droll, black humor seems to have puzzled many Jews; it offended some and drew criticism from both well-meaning and anti-Semitic non-Jews. Yet Lawrence Lipton, the author of the articles, perceived, despite some heavy-handedness, the new, ominous, more subtle, pseudo-scientific strain of American anti-Semitism that had arisen in the 1920s. Myths and fantasies of Jewish world conspiracies now combined with insidious racial theories that labeled Jews as "blood pollutants." Lipton's tragic and comic series might have stood as a more serious warning had Detroit Jews in 1926 known more of European developments.

Detroit newspapers continued to publish such blatantly anti-Semitic want ads as: "Stockman—Wanted, good opportunity for advancement. Gentile. Apply F. W. Woolworth Co."; "GIRLS of good Christian character to work in a store which has a reputation for friendliness and helpfulness. . . . S.S. KRESGE COMPANY."[230] And Mr. and Mrs. H. B. Gittelman drew Philip Slomovitz's attention to stationery from the Gratiot Inn in Port Huron embossed with "The Management prefers to cater only to a Gentile clientele." Slomovitz wrote the inn and pursued the matter with legal and police authorities.[231]

Such incidents regularly occurred, often ignored or discretely passed over except by such chroniclers as Slomovitz and the Anti-Defamation League. After 1926, the task of monitoring anti-Semitism grew more dangerous as it involved overt encounters with more outspoken and violent antagonists.

The Black Legion, which numbered some 200,000 members including a minimum of 24,000 active "Night Riders" in Michigan, (it also was active in neighboring states, especially Ohio), conducted a clandestine campaign of violence and murder that continued until 1936. Its membership included the Royal Oak police chief, the mayor of Highland Park, Detroit's police commissioner, and other political figures in the Detroit metropolitan area. The Black Legion began as the elite "Black Guard" of the Ku Klux Klan (in a beginning not unlike the Nazi SS). Despite the legion's eventual antagonism toward the Ku Klux Klan, from which it split away

173

after internal dissension within the KKK, it maintained the same confused, dangerous agenda of hatred: nativism, anti-Catholicism, anticommunism, racism, and anti-Semitism.[232] In 1933 the KKK could brazenly publicize regular lectures on subjects such as "The Jews are Wrecking America." Its ads ran under the banner title of "For God and Country."[233] Fantasies of vigilantism and night-riding violence filled the arcane meetings of both groups. In 1936 Michigan's Black Legion commander devised the grandiose plot to murder one million Jews by planting bombs in every synagogue across America on Yom Kippur.[234]

Along with the activities of the KKK and numerous other newly formed groups like the Silver Shirts, echoes of European-style anti-Semitism could be heard in Detroit. Gerald L. K. Smith, the "Dean of Anti-Semites," carried on a surprising correspondence with Fred Butzel in which he urged Butzel and other Jewish leaders to "devise ways and means of disowning, criticizing, or [making] it plain" that "certain Jews" are not the "true spokesmen of American Jewry." Henry Ford instructed his secretary Ernest Liebold to allow Smith into his inner sanctum at any time. There, they presumably discussed *The International Jew* and Smith's insistence that "Christian character is the true basis of real Americanism."[235] Americanism, therefore, by definition could not apply to Jews who thus bore "the burden of proof" on their own shoulders. By 1944 Smith declared that "if someone will figure out the best way to *handle* the Jews, he will go down in history as the wisest person in all the centuries." He seemed to find no contradiction in calling the Anti-Defamation League a "Gestapo organization."[236]

Protestant rightist groups and demagogues did not reach the popularity of their Catholic counterpart. While the Silver Shirts and others clearly emulated the Nazis, the infamous Royal Oak radio priest Father Coughlin advocated a form of fascism and a corporate state; he praised Hitler and looked to a "benevolent dictator," to "save" America. As early as 1933, Detroit confronted its homegrown Nazi groups.

Slomovitz, as editor of the *Detroit Jewish Chronicle,* led the way in exposing the insidious growth of Nazi sympathies in Detroit. In August 1934, he sent an irate letter to the editor of the Detroit *Abend Post* castigating the editorial "Wer den Wind sät" as "a complete reversal of your previous policy of acting fairly with relation to the Jewish community."[237] Slomovitz had been a defender of the German newspaper as one that was "not following an anti-Semitic policy inspired by the ideas of Nazism." He had even gone so far as to recommend that Jewish merchants advertise in that paper.[238] The *Abend Post* editorial accused Jews of advocating anarchy, and, in New York, of gangsterism that was coddled by Jewish judges. In short, it mirrored Nazi accusations about Jews' infiltration of Western governments for the purpose of corrupting Western civilization.

In October 1934, Louis Zahn addressed the "Friends of New Germany" at a meeting at Carpathia Hall in Detroit. Zahn railed against "Oriental philosophy" as destroying "western civilization." In what became a flurry of rhetorical puzzles, "Oriental" was revealed as Jewish and "western" as German/Aryan. In his blatantly anti-Semitic speech, which was punctuated by cheers and applause from the audience, Zahn spoke of the connection between American Germans and the "New Germany." Referring to Hitler's support, Zahn stressed the importance of strengthening the bond between Germany and the United States. He censured the American-Jewish-led boycott of Germany—itself a reaction to the Nazi boycott of German Jewish businesses—as "taking work from the German working man" and as being communist-instigated.[239]

The publication of excerpts from that speech in the *Chronicle* augured ill tidings for Jews in Detroit: it meant, among other things, that European Jewry's plight seemed connected to American Jewry's situation. To some, it meant that the danger of more open forms of persecution than discrimination and talk might come to the streets of Detroit. Jews disagreed about how they ought to react to these new revelations. Some advocated a low profile while others, following Slomovitz's confrontational policy, demanded outspoken exposure of the rising tide of fascist anti-Jewish groups and actions. Many Detroit Jews recalled the fear inspired by Father Coughlin (whose anti-Semitic rhetoric escalated in 1937–1938) and the anger aroused by the "Gentile only" ads and "no Jews" barriers in houses and apartments. In spite of the anger and the fear, however, one Jewish lawyer noted, "We were so Jewish that we wanted to live in a Jewish neighborhood anyway."

That "luxury" of maintaining a degree of indifference and chosen separateness seemed to be dissolving in the 1930s. Most Jews may not have been aware of the significance of events like the Friends of Germany meeting or the escalating violence of anti-Semitic groups. But an increasing number expressed growing concern over local, national, and international events that seemed about to reach into Jewish lives. In 1933 Slomovitz interviewed Herr Spanknabel, who later became a leader of the German-American Bund that was founded in 1936. In his article, "Jews Beware!" Slomovitz related the stories of pogroms in Germany and of the anti-Jewish persecution about which Spanknabel had boasted. After receiving little response to the editorial, Slomovitz telephoned Secretary of State Cordell Hull, who dismissed the interview as "exaggerations of atrocity stories." Hull's response was typical of many others' refusal to believe such stories, a refusal which, coupled with the reservations of noted rabbinic leader Stephen Wise, served to quiet and mollify Jews in America.

While most Jews in America refused to accept such accounts as that of Spanknabel, news of the persecution of German Jews in the wake of Hitler's appointment as Chancellor of Germany became widely publicized common knowledge. As early as March 26, 1933, with the assistance of George Stutz

175

who managed to gain the cooperation of Police Commissioner James K. Watkins of Detroit, there were public protest meetings held at the Naval Reserve Armory.[240] A series of meetings, organized to a large extent by Slomovitz, who acted on behalf of the American Jewish Congress (which arranged such meetings across the country), continued into 1934; they included public readings of telegrams from such local and national dignitaries as Secretary of State Hull, Rep. John Dingell, and Sen. Arthur H. Vandenberg, and from organizations like the American League for Human Rights. Mayor Murphy and other prominent non-Jews participated regularly. A resolution was drafted expressing "our indignation at the atrocities perpetrated against our fellow-Jews under the Hitlerite regime"; it further stated that "likewise we protest against similar persecutions directed against all other anti-Nazi groups, regardless of race and creed"[241] Copies of the resolution went to President Roosevelt, Michigan members of Congress, and the German ambassador to the United States.

It was not until December 1933, that Federation addressed the German-Jewish crisis. At issue was the amount of money to be allocated to overseas relief in conjunction with funds for the United Palestine Association and the Joint Distribution Committee. The two rival organizations vied for funds from Federation, each demanding increased percentages for their respective causes. Taking a firm approach, the Federation Board maintained its earlier allotments, but the debate augured future entanglements of such agencies, and overseas relief became a regular item on the Federation Board meeting agenda thereafter—although not as routinely as the question of local emergency relief.[242]

By 1934 there were rumblings from non-Federation groups concerned with, ironically, the predicament of German Jews. A group of Jewish labor leaders in New York founded the Jewish Labor Committee (JLC) to act as a "labor relief agency for both Jew and non-Jew aiding the labor movement in its struggle against anti-Semitism, Nazism, and Fascism."[243] Within months, a Detroit chapter was established with the participation of such people as Shmarya Kleinman, Irving Pokempner, and Simon Shetzer. They immediately set about devising methods to enable trade unionists in Germany, especially Jews, to escape to the West. Working through underground connections with the outlawed German trade unions, they managed to help hundreds of labor leaders escape by bribery and ransom. At the same time, the JLC worked to alter restrictive immigration laws in order to allow émigrés to enter the United States. They were minimally successful in their first task, but unsuccessful in their second.

Dissatisfied with the "establishment" reticence to create any public outcry, many Jews in Detroit followed the path of others in the United States and turned to non-Jewish organizations before forming Jewish ones.[244] But in December 1935, after the passage in Germany of the infamous Nuremberg Laws of September and November, Simon Shetzer approached the Federation Board with an unprecedented request. Citing the Cleveland Federation as an example, he explained that Jews there had established the Emergency Conference of Jewish Organizations to Protest the Hitler Menace. Cleveland's Federation had funded the new organization with five thousand dollars to pay for an office and secretary. Its main function seemed to be the continuation of the boycott of German goods. The Detroit board granted money to the new organization, which was to be called the League for the Defense of Human Rights. They further commended Mr. Shetzer for his continued diligence in the local boycott effort.[245]

On the eve of European Jewry's destruction, American Jews presented a bewildered and disunited front. Detroit, like most cities, did not coalesce around the impending catastrophe; it did not consolidate its efforts or form a single-minded goal with a clear Jewish identity, as it would years later regarding the establishment of the state of Israel. Instead, many reacted with disbelief, uncertainty, or indecision. Philip Slomovitz seemed a lonely voice at times, joined only by members of the Jewish Labor Committee or the League for the Defense of Human Rights, both small and discrete organizations. When, in 1934, the Hebrew Immigrant Aid Society (HIAS) threatened to conduct their own fund-raising campaign because of the German emergency, the Federation Board told them that should such precipitous action be taken, the Federation would inform subscribers that HIAS had already been included in the 1934 Allied Jewish Campaign. The board then voted that in future, all agencies benefiting from the campaign should agree in writing not to have separate fund drives. As a result, HIAS did not conduct its own campaign but received an increased appropriation from Federation.[246]

In March 1936, Fred Butzel urged the Federation Board to add two thousand dollars for the relief of German Jews to the campaign budget, but only in 1937 would the emergency become more obvious and only then would other groups in Detroit, including the Federation, begin to respond more urgently.[247] But regardless of that urgency, few if any in the United States understood or even could imagine the scope of the danger to Jews in Europe. The general feeling regarding fascism, recalled Irwin Shaw, who became director of the Fresh Air Camp in 1936, seemed to be that "this, too, will pass. . . . [It] had to be an aberration in Germany. Germans would not tolerate Hitler for long."[248]

Such a belief in German reason seemed to deny the prospect of fascism making any headway in America. If America possessed a shorter tradition of rational thinking, it surely held a firmer, lasting tradition of tolerance and freedom. "All through Jewish history," ran the argument, "Jews had overcome anti-Semitism." Surely they would again. Shaw recalled that Dr. Franklin himself reminded Detroit Jews of Justice Felix Frankfurter's denial of widespread persecution and of the vilely false World War I propa-   177 ganda about German bayonets in French and Belgian babies.[249] Franklin spoke of his own cousin in Germany who had written that everything there in 1936 was fine. Instead of consolidating the Jews of Detroit, the impending disaster served to further divide them.

PART III
1936–1948

"We have been blessed," said one Detroit patriarch, "with the most outstanding Jewish leaders in the country." While this seems to be a rather biased evaluation, the leaders of the Detroit Jewish communities have been among the most outstanding achievers and influential spokesmen for Jews throughout the world. However one measures such an evaluation—intellectually, theologically, financially, or by other means—Detroit's Jewish leaders have excelled and stood out as significant spokesmen for American Jews. Events of the 1930s and 1940s taxed those spokespersons for Jews in Detroit and called for extraordinary actions.

Confronted by domestic and international crises of unprecedented proportions, Jewish organizations, institutions, and individuals reacted in both traditional and radical ways. With Detroit's peculiar characteristic of attracting immigrants who had already settled in other cities, the Jewish population grew more varied, accentuating centrifugal forces. Different voices seemed to cry out in disharmony for resolutions to a confusing mixture of problems and questions.

If Federation had addressed numerous crises with at least modest success, that organization seemed besieged by escalating and often contradic- 181 tory demands. As Federation leaders encountered that growing clamor and continued to enlarge their services, other groups emerged to fill what they perceived as gaps in satisfying the needs of some Jews in Detroit. Most prominent and, to Federation, most troublesome, was the Jewish Community Council with its avowed policy of "democratizing the Jewish community." Alongside Council, traditional religious organizations reached more energetically into the population, emphasizing a renewed focus on Jewish education by increasing their collaboration with Federation's United Hebrew Schools. All responded, in varying degrees, to the ominous ascendance of anti-Jewish sentiment and action in Detroit and in the world.

Few cities have matched Detroit for venomous anti-Semitism. One need only mention the infamous Father Coughlin or Henry Ford's *Dearborn Independent*. Some historians have argued that there was no significant anti-Semitic feeling in Detroit until 1920, when Henry Ford began his publication.

Yet the evidence speaks to the contrary. In a city so heavily ethnic from the nineteenth century to the present, European prejudices were bound to transfer themselves from one generation to another, and anti-Semitism permeated much of Detroit's ethnic population, making itself felt long before 1920 and before 1914 as well.

By 1936, however, anti-Semitism reached new depths as it combined with Nazi racial ideology and American nativist movements. Age-old questions of how and even whether to battle insidious and overt anti-Jewish slander and physical attacks occupied increasing space in American Jewish newspapers. By 1941, on the eve of America's entrance into World War II, Jews were divided over questions about the rescue of European refugees from Nazism and the relative allocations of funds to local and international Jewish needs. As Jewish Americans joined the war effort, bringing obvious unity among Jewish groups, divisions continued to manifest themselves along the usual lines.

Before 1936, the feelings most Detroit Jews expressed toward Zionism ranged from indifference to disquieted support to enthusiastic, devoted, and active participation for forming a Jewish state in Palestine. After 1936 Jewish opposition, neutrality, and indifference increasingly melted away. Labor Zionism in Detroit found eager patronage among labor unions—an advocacy that would flourish into the next decades. Eventually, Zionism, or the founding of the state of Israel, became the most significant issue that might unite Jews in Detroit. For some, it provided a strong focal point for Jewish identity. For others, even as they supported the state, it did not fulfil that most important function of defining Jewish consciousness. After 1945, the issue of Palestine inextricably bound itself to the aftermath of the Holocaust—an aftermath that took tangible form as some of the "saving remnant" of European Jewry, the victims of the Holocaust who sur- vived, arrived in Detroit. For a while, as they stared into the abyss, aware of the death of Jews and Jewish culture in Europe, some American Jews seemed to put aside their divisions.

14

The Neighborhoods:
The Next Exodus

By 1936, the smells of Jewish delicatessens like Sammy's (owned by Samuel Liebermann), or Liebermann's (owned by Manny Liebermann) or Boesky's and Rosen's Bakery had already extended north and west from Oakland and engulfed the Twelfth and Dexter neighborhoods bounded on the north by Davison, to the east by Twelfth and Hamilton, to the west by Livernois, and to the south by Virginia Park. According to a Federation study of 1941, approximately 80 percent of Detroit's Jewish population lived in these two (Twelfth and Dexter) districts.[1] Central High School, in the Dexter neighborhood, became known as the "Jewish school" (along with Northern High School), and in 1938 more than half its 764 graduating seniors were Jews.[2] Central offered an experimental curriculum that accounted in part for its attractiveness to upwardly aspiring Jewish parents; the rapid influx of Jewish children, however, also spurred the school on to new educational enterprises. By 1940, then, most Jews had abandoned the Oakland neighborhood to the rising black population. Thus, the pattern set earlier continued: blacks moved in, some Jewish businesses lingered in the Oakland district, but Jews moved out, in search of homes more representative of an upwardly mobile population.   185

Residents of that area recalled streets crowded with people, a high-density population, children running through alleys, and two-family houses, some with imposing second-floor porches. Along Dexter and Elmhurst one might weave or push through the crowds past Sterling Drugs, Grunt's Market, Resnick the Haberdasher, Fredson's Restaurant, the Dexter Theatre, owned first by John Brown and then by Harry Slatkin, and Dexter Chevrolet, which was owned by Slatkin's son, Joseph (one of the first Jewish car dealers in Detroit). Across the street, still enmeshed in the bustling atmosphere, were the Economical Market with its fish tank in the window, Mr. Wall's Vegetable Stand, Louis the Barber, the Esquire Deli, and the Eagle Dairy, famous for its three-scoop ice cream cones. On the corner of Joy Road and Quincy, near Dexter, Harry Dorfman and his brothers opened what would became another neighborhood institution, Dorfman Drugs, with one of the largest camera and film-processing departments in the area and a soda fountain featuring ten-cent strawberry sundaes that drew the likes of Hank Greenberg and Charlie Gehringer of the Detroit Tigers.

Unlike the inhabitants of these neighborhoods, that consisted of small residential homes or of flats, the "uptown" Jews had moved further north and west into beautifully apportioned residences on Chicago and Boston Boulevards, Russel Woods and Broadstreet Boulevard, and eventually (in the 1940s) to Six and Seven Mile Roads and Outer Drive. Often palatial, such houses displayed such novel features as large lawns, trees, clipped gardens, and garages: all of which signaled affluence. The majority of children from those homes commuted to Central High School and many went on to Wayne University or the University of Michigan.

In the 1941 survey of the Twelfth Street neighborhood, Federation officials reacted to apprehensions voiced by numerous leaders of the community that "the children of the district were exposed to a variety of unwholesome types of commercialized recreation." It further alleged that they were "enticed by means of an arts and crafts program to listen to missionary lectures sponsored by the Messianic Lecture Hall" that was situated on Twelfth Street. That study listed Buddy's Restaurant as "an all-night congregating place," and five beer gardens, two pool rooms, one dairy bar (the Eagle Dairy), Boesky's Delicatessen, the Astor Theater, Samaroff's Candy Store, the Modern Delicatessen, the Cream of Michigan Cafe (an institution in its own right that attracted suburban and downtown Jews with its barley soup and dairy dishes and which was notorious as a Jewish mobster hangout) the Bowl-O-Drome and other unsavory "congregating places." The study's conclusion regarding this list: "Wholesome recreational facilities are conspicuous by their absence."[3]

Jewish communal institutions had also begun to relocate in the Twelfth Street and Dexter areas in the 1920s. The Jewish Social Service Bureau, which existed "to preserve Jewish family life," maintained family welfare casework service. An unemployment emergency council and a child-care

investigation agency were housed in the Federation office at 51 West War-
the House of Shelter, the Sholem Aleichem Institute, the Workmen's Circle, and other organizations had relocated in the Twelfth Street neighborhood. Some fifteen Jewish schools (including the Jewish Children's School
of the Communist-aligned International Workers' Order), six Orthodox
synagogues, and five social and recreational halls for *landsmanshaftn* and
social clubs added to the compelling Jewish atmosphere of Twelfth Street.[4]

Jews in Detroit struggled with many of the same economic and social
problems as their non-Jewish neighbors during the Depression years. But
those problems seemed embedded in a web of other difficulties that historically had surrounded Jews in the Diaspora. Anti-Semitism persisted and
indeed, crept back to European modes, threatening and sometimes fulfilling violent potential. Assimilation beckoned more strongly than ever to a
generation of American Jews who knew nothing of Europe or old-world
traditions and religious observance. Dissension among Jews and Jewish
groups continued with varying levels of antagonism. An increasing number
of individuals and organizations seemed more willing to coalesce at least
once a year for Federation's Allied Jewish Campaign, but disagreements
over allotments of the revenues often aggravated groups like the secular
schools, which believed that they received only token allocations.

Beyond such community issues, however, individuals often remained ob-
livious to the organized institutions and the issues they raised and instead
concentrated on the burden of earning their livings; they watched over
their families, trying to achieve at least a comfortable life-style and perhaps
to provide a better one for their children. Some Jewish businessmen and
merchants found extraordinary opportunities in Detroit that stemmed from
the industrial complexes that grew up around the Kahn-built automobile
plants. Others, however, eked out livings in professions that were extensions of traditional occupations: the laundry and dry-goods business and
the scrap-metal industries, for example, which echoed earlier days of Jewish peddlers.

15

Varieties of Voices: The Jewish Community Council

Detroit reflected the national conditions of turmoil and uncertainty between 1926 and 1937. Within the context of those conditions, two events
dominate the institutional history of the Jews of Detroit: the founding of
the Jewish Welfare Federation in 1926 and the establishment of the Jewish
Community Council in 1937. Those two landmark events may not reflect
historic moments in the lives of the majority of Detroit's Jews. Yet, as
symbolic and institutional turning points, they still reverberate in Detroit
Jewry's past. In many respects, the multiple perspectives on the creation
of these institutions has colored subsequent attitudes toward Jewish history in Detroit.

Despite the increased participation of East European Jews in the gov-
ernance and functioning of Federation, it continued to be perceived as a
bastion of German Jewish privilege, condescension, and even, as one German Jewish participant commented, "effete snobbery." A few establishment
leaders like Fred M. Butzel and Henry Wineman had successfully reached
out to Yiddish groups, but, in the main, Federation's primary fund-raising
and allotment functions remained in the hands of those identified either
as the *Yahudim* or the *Amerikanischers*. In short, those who controlled

the levers of power in Federation fit the mold whose characteristics included Reform Judaism, assimilation into non-Jewish culture, and social
and economic distance from "the masses." As families like the Simons,
Levins, Ginsburgs, and others gained stature within the "establishment,"
it appeared that the criteria for influence was changing. Wealth, education,
and sophistication replaced, or at least augmented, the German-Jewish
standard of earlier times. Yet, to the perception of most East European
Jews—"the masses"—that establishment remained the same and was controlled by the same values if not the same people.

Other organizations, like the *landsmanshaften* or secular institutions
like the Sholem Aleichem Institute or the Workmen's Circle, served their
important functions in limited spheres, not attempting or claiming to speak
for the entire Jewish population and not engaged in the support of the
local, national, and even international enterprises that Federation could
claim. For some, these groups remained closer to real life than Federation,
addressing directly the issues of insurance, health benefits, burial, companionship, and, in some cases, politics.

Any group's claim to be the representative voice of the Jews of Detroit
seemed specious at worst, naive at best. Yet, given the political, social, and
economic climate of the 1930s, with the menacing rise of anti-Semitism
in America and the perilously worsening situation of Jewish communities
abroad, more Jews felt the need for some direct, organizational confrontation with increasingly organized forces of bigotry. "Uptown" Jews may
have ignored, or pretended to ignore, anti-Semitism, and "downtown" Jews
may have lived with and ignored it as a fact of life, but such disregard
became more problematic after 1933, and the position of benign neglect
grew increasingly tenuous. Some Jews relinquished homes in non-Jewish
neighborhoods and towns like Trenton, Dearborn, Ecorse, and Pontiac,
moving into the more conventional Jewish neighborhoods around Dexter
and Twelfth. "We felt isolated there [in Ecorse], especially after Hitler began speaking on the radio. We never felt that way before. Then there was
Coughlin and Reverend [Gerald L. K.] Smith, *verbrenter Antisemiten* [rad-
ical anti-Semites]. It felt safer being among other Jews—although my father didn't like *them* either." This recollection of the motivation to move
indicates heightened awareness of an impending threat. Anti-Semitism had
taken the offensive, and even those who had disassociated themselves from
Jewish communities in the past may have found it necessary to revert to
the safety of numbers.

Various factions of Jews in Detroit confronted the rising tide of anti-
Semitism. Communist-affiliated groups assumed what all others considered the untenable position that anti-Semitism be considered not as a Jewish
issue (or "question") but as a social issue that demonstrated the corruption
of capitalist society. In marked contrast to the communist view, the Workmen's Circle and socialist-oriented Zionist groups like Hashomer Hatzair

held public demonstrations calling for an American boycott of Germany and German goods.[5] The American Jewish Congress tried with some success to organize mass protest meetings.

Some Jews in Detroit grasped the historic nature of dangerous events after 1933. They determined to react with appropriate urgency. But two disturbing types of nonresponses alarmed them. First, the vast majority of Jews in Detroit (like those in other parts of America) appeared frightened, but unwilling to decry publicly European and American anti-Semitism. A familiar defensive pattern that may have issued from generations of impotence in the face of hostile gentile populations resurfaced. Distressed conversations commonly occurred, but within the confines of organizational or family discussions. Few would venture into the streets and gain the visibility that would come from protest marches. There still remained peaceful coexistence in the United States, but it seemed precarious. Many feared that an open demonstration against European events would draw unwanted attention to American Jews, exacerbate potential fellow-travelers of the anti-Semitic movements, and perhaps foster renewed accusations of world conspiracies—accusations that, in fact, had already begun in the preaching of Gerald L. K. Smith, Father Coughlin, and other, lesser-known demagogues.[6]

Along with this "conspiracy of silence" among the general population came what to some looked like reticence and to others deafening silence of Federation. According to a few critics, leaders of Federation conducted private meetings to limit the protests, discussing ways to defuse and reduce the pressure from such groups as the American Jewish Congress. At the very least, Federation as an institution refused to cooperate officially in any anti-anti-Semitic protests. One commentator recalled that Federation "was not geared for influencing public opinion, [it was] only there for charity."

Given these disagreements among Jews about the proper response to intensifying and unabating anti-Jewish rhetoric and behavior, it appeared to be only a question of time before some force for open reaction would emerge. Opinions differ, however, on what motivated the force that ultimately was channeled into the creation of the Jewish Community Council of Detroit. For example, Irving Pokempner, one of the staunchest supporters of the Jewish Community Council from its inception, believed that the organization was founded only in part to respond to anti-Semitism. "People who were not wealthy desired to have a say in the community. . . . *landsmanshaftn*, Labor Zionists, the Workmen's Circle, and the other left-wing organizations formed a united front." Still another die-hard champion of the council believed that it was founded "to give Jews an organized voice to speak for the Jewish community; to give Jews a voice not based on money. It was also to protect our rights and be concerned where this country was going."

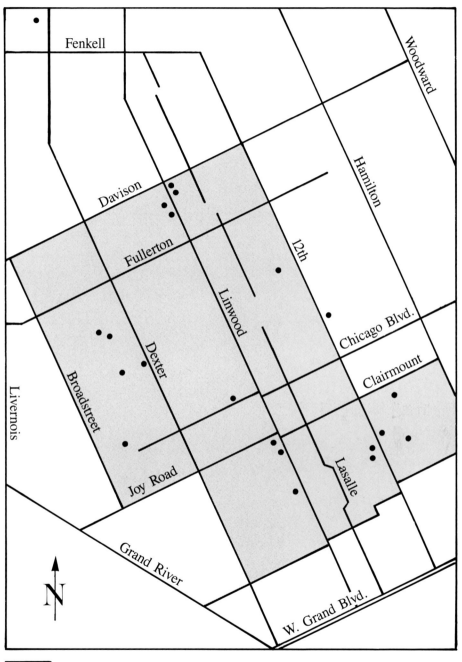

Fenkell

Woodward

Davison

Hamilton

Fullerton

12th

Linwood

Dexter

Chicago Blvd.

Broadstreet

Clairmount

Livernois

Lasalle

Joy Road

Grand River

N

W. Grand Blvd.

Highest Jewish Density   • Synagogue

12th Street–Dexter in 1940

Sam's Cut Rate, landmark store in downtown Detroit, owned by Max Osnos, 1939. (Courtesy of the Burton Historical Collection of the Detroit Public Library.)

Domestic Linen Supply and Laundry Co., 3800 18th Street, Detroit, ca. 1926. (Courtesy of the Colton family.)

Boesky's Delicatessen, 10350 Dexter, Detroit, 1939. (Courtesy of the collection of Manning Brothers, Photographers.)

Cunningham's Drugs, Sears Avenue, Highland Park, 1939. (Courtesy of the collection of Manning Brothers, Photographers.)

Winkelman's store, West Fort Street between Campbell and Cavalry, Detroit, 1930s. (Courtesy of Stanley Winkelman.)

Central Overall Co., 7043 E. Palmer, Detroit, ca. 1935–1940. (Courtesy of the collection of Emma Schaver.)

Jewish Home for Aged
11501 PETOSKEY AVENUE
DETROIT

The Jewish Home for Aged, 11501 Petoskey Avenue, Detroit, 1957. (Courtesy of the collection of the Jewish Home for Aged.)

Rabbi Leo M. Franklin of Temple Beth El, *left*, with Henry Ford, 1938. (Courtesy of the Rabbi Leo M. Franklin Archives of Temple Beth El.)

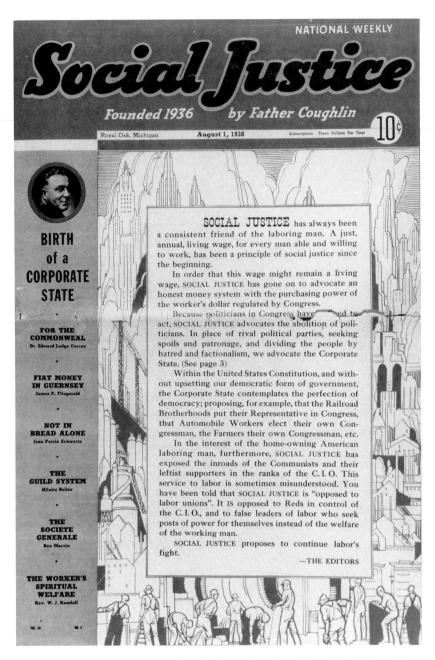

NATIONAL WEEKLY

Social Justice

Founded 1936   by Father Coughlin   10¢

Royal Oak, Michigan   August 1, 1938   Subscription: Three Dollars Per Year

BIRTH
of a
CORPORATE
STATE

FOR THE
COMMONWEAL
Dr. Edward Lodge Curran

•

FIAT MONEY
IN GUERNSEY
James P. Fitzgerald

•

NOT IN
BREAD ALONE
Jean Perrin Schwartz

•

THE
GUILD SYSTEM
Hilaire Belloc

•

THE
SOCIETE
GENERALE
Ben Marcin

•

THE WORKER'S
SPIRITUAL
WELFARE
Rev. W. J. Randall

SOCIAL JUSTICE has always been a consistent friend of the laboring man. A just, annual, living wage, for every man able and willing to work, has been a principle of social justice since the beginning.

In order that this wage might remain a living wage, SOCIAL JUSTICE has gone on to advocate an honest money system with the purchasing power of the worker's dollar regulated by Congress.

Because politicians in Congress have ___ed to act, SOCIAL JUSTICE advocates the abolition of politicians. In place of rival political parties, seeking spoils and patronage, and dividing the people by hatred and factionalism, we advocate the Corporate State. (See page 3)

Within the United States Constitution, and without upsetting our democratic form of government, the Corporate State contemplates the perfection of democracy; proposing, for example, that the Railroad Brotherhoods put their Representative in Congress, that Automobile Workers elect their own Congressman, the Farmers their own Congressman, etc.

In the interest of the home-owning American laboring man, furthermore, SOCIAL JUSTICE has exposed the inroads of the Communists and their leftist supporters in the ranks of the C.I.O. This service to labor is sometimes misunderstood. You have been told that SOCIAL JUSTICE is "opposed to labor unions". It IS opposed to Reds in control of the C.I.O., and to false leaders of labor who seek posts of power for themselves instead of the welfare of the working man.

SOCIAL JUSTICE proposes to continue labor's fight.

—THE EDITORS

Social Justice, 1938, publication founded by Father Coughlin of the Shrine of the Little Flower, Royal Oak. (Courtesy of the *Detroit Jewish News.*)

Philip Slomovitz, editor of the *Detroit Jewish News,* Zionist leader and crusader against anti-Semitism, 1940s. (Courtesy of the Archives of the Jewish Welfare Federation.)

Greetings to Dr. Chaim Weizmann, 1940. (Courtesy of Jewell Morris.)

Greetings:
Dr. Chaim Weizmann

We pay tribute to your statesmanship, to your unselfish devotion to humanitarian endeavor and to your inventive skill and genius...

The world has observed with respect and homage the contributions to scientific knowledge and progress that have come from your study and research.

Your many friends in Detroit, along with your admirers everywhere, are proud of your achievements and happy in the thought that the recognition of your position and the reflection of your glory redound to the credit of us all.

In the judgment of men, when one of us rises to heights of brilliance and of leadership, all of us rise in estimation, for your gifts to mankind may be personal in origin, but they are universal in application.

Permit us, then, within the modest limits given to us, to associate ourselves with you in your great work and particularly with the Biochemical Laboratory at Rehobot.

With this affiliation goes our warm affection and our fervent prayer that you may be granted many years of good health and continued service to mankind.

Detroit, Michigan
United States of America
The 27th Day of January, 1940

Detroit delegation to the convention of the Zionist Organization of America in Cincinnati, Ohio, in the 1940s. *Top row, from left:* Max Subar, ———, Jacob Epel, Dr. Moe Perlis, ———, ———, Judge Charles Rubiner. *Middle row:* Abe Kasle, Joseph Yolles, Philip Gilbert, Morris Jacobs, Maurice Landau, Isaac Shetzer. *Bottom row:* Walter Field, Margurite Chajes, Abraham Cooper, Anna Landau, Rabbi Morris Adler, Sadie Feldstein. (Courtesy of the Archives of Congregation Shaarey Zedek.)

Protest meeting against British injustice in Palestine, at Masonic Hall, Detroit, 1930s. (Courtesy of Evelyn Noveck.)

Federation of Polish Jews, 1930s. (Courtesy of Bessie Chase.)

The Detroit War Chest toward which Jewish organizations set records in achievements, ca. 1941. *From left:* Hale A. Clark, James I. Ellman, Fred M. Butzel, Abraham Lachover. (Courtesy of the Archives of the Jewish Welfare Federation.)

Radio station WJBK sponsors War Bond Rally in 1943, at which Jewish organizations raised $142,800. *At microphone,* Mr. and Mrs. Harry Weinberg, in charge of Jewish activities at the station. (Courtesy of Betty Schein.)

All Detroit Rabbis at historic gathering honoring Rabbi A. M. Hershman of Congregation Shaarey Zedek, 1942. *Seated, from left:* Rabbi Joseph Thumin, president of the Orthodox Rabbis Council; Rabbi Joseph Eisenman, Congregation Beth Tefile Emanuel; Rabbi Hershman; Dr. Leo M. Franklin, Rabbi Emeritus of Temple Beth El; Rabbi Moses Fischer, Congregation B'nai Moshe. *Standing, from left:* Rabbi Leizer Levin, Congregation of David W. Simons Branch of United Hebrew Schools; Rabbi B. W. Hendels, Yeshivah Chachmey Lublin; Dr. Naphtali Carlebach, Yeshivah Beth Yehudah; Rabbi Max Wohlgelernter, Congregation Beth Tefile Emanuel; Rabbi Jacob Kurland, Yeshivah Beth Yehudah; Rabbi Joshua S. Sperka, Congregation B'nai David; Dr. Samson R. Weiss, Yeshivah Beth Yehudah; Rabbi Morris Adler, Congregation Shaarey Zedek; Dr. B. Benedict Glazer, Temple Beth El; Rabbi Herschel Lymon, Temple Beth El; Rabbi Jacob Ungar, Yeshivah Beth Yehudah; Rabbi Meir Levi, director of Michigan Synagogue Conference; Rabbi Jacob Nathan, Congregation B'nai Moshe; Rabbi S. P. Wohlgelernter, Congregation Bicur Cholem, Seattle, Washington; Rabbi Jacob Hoberman, Congregation Beth Itzcheck; Rabbi Leon Fram, Temple Israel; Rabbi Joseph Rabinowitz, Congregation Beth Shmuel. (Courtesy of the Archives of Congregation Shaarey Zedek.)

Henry Meyers, president of the Jewish Community Center and chairman of the U.S.O. of Detroit during World War II, ca. 1942. *From left:* Henry Meyers, Elizabeth Meyers Klein, Hildegarde (the entertainer), Joan Meyers Jampel. (Courtesy of Joan Jampel.)

Rabbi Morris Adler saying Kiddush at a military hospital during World War II, ca. 1943. (Courtesy of the Archives of Congregation Shaarey Zedek.)

Jewish Welfare Board Annual Report cover, 1942: World War II. (Courtesy of the
Jewish Community Center.)

Last Tribute to a Hero

THE DAILY *Graphic*

SPORTS • RIPLEY
BOB TALES • CLASSIFIED DETROIT TIMES
HATLO • MARKETS , June 1948 C—13

Reburial service in 1948 for
Lt. Raymond Zussman, holder
of the Congressional Medal of
Honor for conspicuous bravery
during World War II.
(Courtesy of the Archives of
Congregation Shaarey Zedek.)

Kurt Peiser, executive director,
Jewish Welfare Federation.
(Courtesy of the Archives of
the Jewish Welfare Federation.)

David E. Heineman designed the flag of the city of Detroit, 1948. In 1984, a plaque in his memory was dedicated at the Detroit Historical Museum. *From left:* Philip Mason, director of the Walter Reuther Library, Wayne State University; Norman McCrae, member of the Detroit Historical Commission; John W. Buckbee, director of the Detroit Historical Society; Bette A. Roth, president of the Jewish Historical Society of Michigan; Solan Weeks, director of the Detroit Historical Museum; Leonard N. Simons; Philip Applebaum. (Courtesy of the Jewish Historical Society of Michigan.)

Simon Shetzer, civic leader and president of the Jewish Community Council, in the 1940s. (Courtesy of Dr. and Mrs. Harry August.)

Twelfth Street Council Center, Detroit, jointly sponsored by the Detroit Section, National Council of Jewish Women, and the Jewish Community Center, 1940s. (Courtesy of the Archives of the Jewish Welfare Federation.)

North End Clinic, Holbrook Street, Detroit, in the 1940s. (Courtesy of the Archives of the Jewish Welfare Federation.)

Fresh Air Society, "Readying the fleet," 1941. (Courtesy of Beatrice Barnett.)

Fresh Air Society, 1947: parents standing in the rain, 7:30 A.M., in front of the Aaron DeRoy Jewish Community Center, Woodward and Holbrook, Detroit, to register children for camp. (Courtesy of the collection of the Fresh Air Society.)

Edward C. Levy, civic and communal leader in the 1940s. (Courtesy of the Archives of the Jewish Welfare Federation.)

Employees of M. Jacob & Sons, 2901–13 Beaubien, Detroit, 1950, oldest continuous Jewish-owned business still operating under same family management. (Courtesy of the collection of M. Jacob & Sons.)

Himelhoch's, 1956 Woodward
Avenue, Detroit, in the 1940s.
(Courtesy of the Burton Historical
Collection of the Detroit Public
Library.)

Officers and executive members of the Ladies Auxiliary of the Korostishever Aid
Society of Detroit. *From left:* M. Fried, A. Sandler, I. Gindick, D. Harrison, G.
Burstein, B. Mellen, M. Axelrod, M. Burstein, N. Moray, S. Soppen, S. Stein, S.
Berk, B. Cutler, C. Moray, R. Friedman, president P. Chafetz. (Courtesy of the
collection of the Midrasha—College of Jewish Studies.)

Workmen's Circle Chorus directed by Dan Frohman, 1947. *Seated, from left:*
———, Sophie Shifrin, Bella Lifshitz, Lillian Newberg, Terry Schneider, Sophie
Gross, Rose Silverman, Dan Frohman, Rebecca Frohman, ———, Gussie Levitt,
Sonia Lifshitz, Mrs. Enten, ———, ———, Ruth Levitt. *Second row:* Tillie
Kaplan, Sarah Moore, Sarah Ravitz, Anne Willis, ———, Mrs. Simon, Mrs.
Smith, ———, ———, Rose Kalb, ———, ———, Alta Katz, Dora Wolfman,
Mrs. Waxman, Sam Petcherer. *Third row:* Sam Silverstein, Ben Shifrin, Mr.
Zweig, Jacob Reissman, ———, Mrs. Kalb, Frank Wolfman, Leon Cousens,
Arthur Newberg, Mr. Kaplan, Mr. Gurevitch, Morris Godhelf, Sam Singerman,
M. Schneider, Alex Levitt, ———, ———. (Courtesy of the Workmen's Circle.)

Workmen's Circle Women's Division, 1947. *Bottom row, from left:* Gisha
Reissman, Rose Segal, Anna Wolack, Anna Kass, Rose Heideman, Pauline
Luberson, Rose Lifshitz, Alta Katz, Mrs. Aronson. *Second row:* Esther Raphael,
———, Rebecca Levine, ———, ———, Dora Wolfman, Sophie Sokanoff, Sarah
Ravitz, Bessie Goodman, Sarah Moore. *Top row:* Esther Godhelf, ———, Rose
Kalb, ———, Celia Axelrod, Sonia Lifshitz, Sophie Shifrin, Mrs. Petcherer,
———, Mrs. Brownstein. (Courtesy of the Workmen's Circle.)

Jewish Labor Leaders: raising funds for Youth Center, Acre, Israel, ca. 1970. *Left:* Morris Spitzer, Amalgamated Clothing Workers of America. *Third left:* Isaac Litwak, Laundry and Linen Drivers Union. *Fifth left:* Myra Wolfgang, Hotel, Restaurant and Bartenders Union. *At center* is James P. Hoffa. (Courtesy of Arthur S. King.)

Philomathic Debating Club, 1948, photographed by Isadore Arnold Berger. *First row, from left:* Wilbur DeYoung, Louis Starfield Cohane, Dr. Irving Edgar, Albert Williams, Jack Alspector. *Second row:* Paul Goldstein, Reuben Levine, Sol J. Schwartz, Isadore Berger, Norval Slobin, Marcus Simon. *Third row:* Hyman A. Keidan, William Gordon, Jack Behrmann, Isadore G. Stone, Sol Rosenman, Harry Jacobs. *Fourth row:* Max D. Lipsitz, Howard P. Berger, Rabbi Harold Rosenthal, David Levin, Bernard Sharkey, Jack Driker, Samuel Sternberg. *Fifth row:* Morton Zieve, Norman Leemon, Philmore Leemon, Sidney DeYoung, Sam Schwartz, Albert Silber, Max Chomsky, Dr. Saul Barnet. (Courtesy of Gertrude Edgar.)

Hebrew school children arrive at Jewish Community Center, 1949. (Courtesy of the collection of the Jewish Community Center.)

Sholem Aleichem Institute, groundbreaking for new building, Seven Mile and Greenfield, Detroit, 1957. *With trowel:* Moshe Haar, director. *At right:* Dr. Lipson and Mrs. Cukerman. (Courtesy of Betty Schein.)

In his 1938 survey of Jewish community organizations, Dr. Maurice Karpf noted that the community council movement "seems to represent an interesting effort at democratizing American-Jewish community organization."[7] *Jewish Chronicle* editor Philip Slomovitz echoed part of this view by describing the Council as having been pioneered by a "group anxious to democratize the community." He and others perceived the council's creation as a vehicle that galvanized much of the anti-Federation feeling among some of the Jews of Detroit. "There was suspicion of the wealthy Jews and antagonism between the East European Jews, the *Folkstimme,* the masses, and the *Yahudim,* the German Jews." The council, then, was perceived by some as the "rebel" organization, the leftist, democratizing force exerting pressure on the establishment.

Yet there are other views regarding the inception of the council. At a fiftieth-anniversary dinner for the United Jewish Charities in 1950, Samuel Rubiner, president of Federation, related his view of the history of the UJC and Federation: "Locally," he said, "we [Federation] built the Jewish Community Council as an instrument championing equal opportunity for all." Rubiner considered the formation of the Council, a function of Federation's determination to "broaden the base of representation."[8] Curiously, Benjamin Laikin, one of the founding members of the Council, who was invited to join its planning committee as president of a branch of the Poale Zion, agreed to some extent with Rubiner's suggestion about the Federation's initiative. Recognizing that the American Jewish Congress had begun to advocate building Jewish community councils in the 1930s, Laikin noted that although the idea found sympathetic ears in Detroit (where the Congress encompassed some sixty organizations), the initiative had dissipated, as Jews in Detroit seemed to be unsure of what to do. Although he assumed a clearly defined, explicitly political and antagonistic position toward Federation, he agreed that it had taken the initiative to organize a local community council.[9]

Isidore Sobeloff, who became a dominant force in Detroit after he succeeded Kurt Peiser as executive director of Federation in 1937, believed that Federation created the Council as a community-relations agency that would deal with the non-Jewish as well as the Jewish community. He acknowledged what to him seemed to be a "hidden agenda": the creation of a "democratic forum for the masses," that is, for groups which felt unrepresented in Federation, and an avenue for expressing grievances regarding allotment of funds. For example, he said that the Council complained that Federation underfunded or refused funds for the Zionists, for a Jewish hospital, or for cultural programs. His notion of the Council was a renewed *Kehillah,* an organization that he believed "controlled" and spoke on behalf of the various groups in the community. In 1963 Sobeloff tried to indicate that the Council appeared in 1937 as all things to all men:

To some it meant the creation of a strong, unified voice in defending ourselves against our enemies. To some it meant the American equivalent of
the European Jewish Kehillah. To others it was a way to marshall larger
forces in support of the developing Palestine program and overseas relief.
And yet to others, it was to be a leavening instrument to prevent irrespon-
sible and undisciplined individuals and groups from speaking in the name
of the Jewish community. To some, it was a way of uniting the so-called
German Jews and the East European and Yiddish elements, and then there
were those who thought it would serve to break down the wall that separated
the old settlers from the "gass" mentsch, the man on the street, the Twelfth
Street Jew.[10]

In this concise summary, Soboloff substituted the euphemisms of "German
Jew" and "East European" for "Federation" and "anti-Federation." As he
addressed the Delegate Assembly of the Jewish Community Council in 1963,
however, most listeners understood the more candid implications, and most
remembered bitter exchanges between Federation and anti-Federation
adherents.

What, then, were the origins of the Jewish Community Council of Detroit? Was it formed strictly as a defense organization against anti-Semitism?
Was it to be the voice of the people, "democratizing" the community? Was
it a forum for leftist groups like the Workmen's Circle, the Labor Zionists,
and Histadrut? Or was it to embody the sentiments and ideas of Jews who
felt disenfranchised by Federation—ideas of Zionism or nationalism, and
East European Jewish culture? Or had it in fact been the brainchild of
some of the leaders of Federation?

While some aspect of each of those conflicting opinions bears truth, the
initial impetus for discussing a viable Council emerged from another quarter. It involved Federation executive director, Kurt Peiser, and several individuals who were identified with East European cultural traditions but
who drew together to discuss the serious problems of the Old Folks Home.
In his autobiography, Dr. Shmarya Kleinman claimed that even this origin
had a prehistory. As the doctor for the David Horodoker Landsmanshaft
from the 1930s on (he offered voluntary health care to most of the *landsmanshaftn*), he and several leaders of the *landsmanshaftn*, members of the
Workmen's Circle, and Joseph Bernstein, Detroit editor of the *Jewish Daily
Forward*, convened a meeting at the Jericho Temple on Joy Road to discuss
the formation of a united front, a *landsmanshaftn Kehillah*. Immediately
the discussion turned to what Kleinman called "one of the most serious
problems facing Jews in Detroit," the unsatisfactory, unsafe, and unsani-
tary conditions of the Old Folks Home. The heated deliberations of that
meeting produced a delegation charged with the task of addressing Kurt
Peiser. A separate group was authorized to carry the same message of concern to Fred Butzel.[11]

Located at Edmund Place and John R., the Old Folks Home indeed seemed
a poor excuse for a Jewish community institution. While the Home had

213

affiliated with Federation in 1931, its main financial and ideological support, as well as most of its residents, came from Orthodox and Yiddish-
speaking groups like the synagogues, *landsmanshaftn*, and secular schools.
In 1934, under Joseph Bernstein's guidance, the *Forward* had asked its
readers to offer opinions on whether a Jewish hospital or a new Old Folks
Home should take precedence on the community's agenda. A clear consensus appeared to demonstrate that the priority item for the *Forward*'s
readers was a new Home.[12] Given the readership, primarily liberal and
Yiddish-speaking, this result seemed predictable. Nevertheless, it offered a
mandate to those claiming to adhere to the demands of the Jewish population in Detroit.

Whether a delegation approached him or not, Peiser saw the significance
of the issue and convened the Conference of Jewish Organizations on January 27, 1935, at the Statler Hotel. He hoped to engender grass-roots support for a mass-based campaign as a part of the regular Allied Jewish Campaign, that is, a drive for a new Old Folks Home under Federation auspices.
Ten days before the conference, Peiser reported to the Board of Federation
that in his attempt to coordinate Jewish organizations for the Allied Jewish
Campaign he had encountered "considerable agitation" from "Yiddish-
speaking groups" regarding the Old Folks Home. He perceived this moment, the willingness to confer, as a good opportunity to bring them together to discuss the "general needs of a philanthropic program instead of
one specific piece of work." He informed the board of the impending meeting of representatives of "these Yiddish-speaking groups."[13] Thus, Peiser
seems to have viewed the Old Folks Home as a wedge for discussing more
"general needs" with the "Yiddish-speaking" groups. This particular issue,
he believed, would serve as a worthwhile vehicle to bridge the gap that
had stood between the Federation and those groups for nearly ten years.

As a result of the Conference of Jewish Organizations on January 27,
1935, funds for a new Jewish Old Folks Home were included in the Federation campaign budget. More to the point, the meeting produced the
proposal for the Committee of Twenty-One, to be composed of representatives of the organizations at the conference. This group would serve as
a liaison with Federation and would begin investigating the formation of
a Jewish community council; it would also actively monitor and discharge
the campaign's goal of funding the Home. Hyman Altman, of the Jewish
Radio Hour; Joseph Bernstein; and Jacob Levin, president of the Old Folks
Home; selected the committee.[14]

At its initial meeting on February 4, 1935, at the Old Folks Home, the
Committee of Twenty-One elected Myron A. Keys as its permanent chairman. Peiser had temporarily chaired the committee and Keys, vice-president
of the Old Folks Home and a respected lawyer in the firm of Friedman,
Meyers and Keys (William Friedman would become a judge in Detroit and
president of Federation; Henry Meyers would become the president of the

Jewish Community Center) reflected the substance of the concerns that
had led to assembling the group. Its membership and the groups represented provide some insight into the nature of the origins of the Jewish
Community Council: Henry M. Abromovitz of the Pisgah Lodge, B'nai Brith;
Irving E. Adler of the First Galician Society of Detroit; Mrs. Hyman Altman,
of the Jewish Radio Hour; Mandell Bernstein, of Congregation Beth Abraham; D. Bolotnikoff, of the Pinsker Association; David J. Cohen, of Congregation B'nai David; Mrs. George Cohen, of Eva Prenzlauer Maternity
Aid; Charles Driker, of the Odessa Progressive Aid Society; Mrs. Abraham
Ferar, of the Jewish Old Folks Home Auxiliary; Mrs. Ada Gorelick, of the
Workmen's Circle, Branch 111; Mrs. J. Harvith, of Zedakah; J. Heideman,
of the Workmen's Circle, Branch 156; Dr. A. M. Hershman, of Congre-
gation Shaarey Zedek; Myron Keys, of the Jewish Old Folks Home; Harry
Levine, of the Yiddish Folks Verein; Mrs. Max Oberfield, of the Eastern
Ladies Auxiliary; William Sandler, of Congregation Beth Tephilah Emanuel;
Mrs. A. Weisman, of the Home Relief Society; and Kurt Peiser, Hyman
Altman, Joseph Bernstein, and Jacob Levin.[15]

The task of the committee, as both Keys and Peiser had noted, was to
determine "the ways and means to conduct a campaign for funds for the
building of a new Jewish Old Folks Home."[16] Keys pointed out that one
of the suggestions for ways and means advocated conducting a drive in the
community without the assistance of Federation. The minutes, reporting
what proved to be a lengthy and volatile discussion, suggest an uneasy
truce: "It was pointed out," they begin, the speakers remaining anonymous, that the responsibility of building a Home remains a community
one." That responsibility, therefore, had been brought to the attention of
Federation by the board of the Jewish Old Folks Home. "It was further
pointed out," they continue, that the conference at the Statler Hotel "was
the first step towards bringing about a better understanding amongst the
Jews of Detroit and finally achieving a united Jewish community. It was
further hoped that proper representation in Federation activities would be
obtained by the Jewish-speaking group."[17]

These rather cryptic comments produced the unanimously passed motion that the Federation be asked to include $100,000 in its 1935 Allied
Jewish Campaign budget for a New Jewish Old Folks Home. Significantly,
however, any discussion of a community council seems attributable to Peiser.
"It was brought to the attention of the group that in the immediate future
Mr. Peiser hoped to organize a Jewish Community Council which would
have proper representation of all groups in the city and which would act
as an open forum for the discussion of all Jewish causes and the adoption
of such principles and policies as would be acceptable to the Jewish community of Detroit." Then, by unanimous approval, the group resolved that
they recommend to the February 17 meeting of organization representatives that a Jewish community council be developed. If approved by the

delegates, that resolution would be forwarded to the Jewish Welfare Federation for immediate action.[18]

Although the resolution passed, and the delegate meeting approved the suggestion, the "immediate action" of Federation would take another two years. When the Committee of Twenty-One next met, on March 25, 1935, they resolved that while they approved of the formation of a council that would represent all Jewish organizations and be "the symbol of our local, unified strength," they did not see themselves as the proper body to form such a council. That power would rest with the Conference of Jewish Organizations when it next convened.[19] The Committee of Twenty-One did not recommend that Federation initiate the council.

By April discouraging but predictable difficulties seem to have crept into the project of creating a council. At its meeting of April 21, 1935, the Committee of Twenty-One passed a motion to recommend to the conference that a mass meeting be held on April 28, at Temple Beth El, in order to create a

> spirit of loyalty and confidence between the members of the various organizations and the Federation, to acquaint groups of potential givers with the Allied Jewish Campaign and its important functions, to impress upon them the fact that a new Home for the Jewish Aged and Infirm is an urgent need, to pave the way for the solicitors who will call on the members of their organization for contributions and above all to regenerate a sense of Jewish unity and responsibility.

These last two items, unity and responsibility, seem to have flagged since February. Mandell Bernstein "decried the lack of enthusiasm" on the committee. Peiser echoed Bernstein, calling for "the feeling of enthusiasm that marked the first meeting of the Committee to be fostered and encouraged."[20]

Priorities differed. Reconstruction of the Old Folks Home remained foremost in the minds of Peiser, Federation, and some members of the Committee of Twenty-One. Peiser also argued that this project needed professional guidance, study, and careful planning. In June 1935, he raised the issue of a community council whose members would have a voice in setting policy with the Federation Board. Rabbi Leon Fram, with support from Abraham Srere, moved that a committee be set up to investigate the plan. As for the procedures on planning a new Old Folks Home, Harry Lurie, of the national Council of Jewish Federations and Welfare Funds, offered to produce a study of Jewish old folks homes and care for the chronically ill. Action on the Home would thus be deferred until the completion of the Lurie study.[21] Peiser, meanwhile, proceeded to research existing councils in Cincinnati and Cleveland, reporting back with information in late October. After completing his research, he proffered a draft of a constitution for the Jewish Community Council. The board formed a committee to study the draft.[22] In November, Peiser recommended postponement of the establishment of a community council until a professional with experience could be consulted.[23] It would be nearly a year before that occurred.

In April 1936, the board of the Jewish Old Folks Home corresponded with the Federation Board to confirm that *"Anshe Chesed Shel Emeth* (Jewish Home for the Aged) . . . relinquish[es] the undertaking of erecting a new home," for which responsibility now went to the Federation. The letters also approved the change of name to the Jewish Home for the Aged, the procedures of fund-raising, arrangements of maintenance funds, and mortgage and building costs.[24] Construction for that new facility began at Burlingame and Petoskey, next to the Children's Home. Having fulfilled a responsibility to the community in rebuilding a new home for the aged, Federation had provided a forum for the Yiddish-speaking groups to express their desires for representation in community policymaking.

In October 1936, Peiser announced to the board that William I. Boxerman had been retained as a professional consultant for the initiation of a Jewish community council.[25] At its last meeting, on January 3, 1937, Myron Keys informed the Committee of Twenty One that Federation had formed a committee of ten to organize a community council. At his insistence, the Committee of Twenty-One would provide ten others to work together with the Federation appointees. Henry Abramovitz, Charles Driker, and Nathan R. Epstein were named as a nominating committee. Those chosen to serve on the organizing committee of the Jewish Community Council were: Irving Adler, Henry Abramovitz, Maxwell Black, Charles Driker, Isaac Finkelstein, Joseph Pevin, Joseph Bernstein, Isidore Sosnick, Mrs. J. Harvith, and Samuel Lieberman. These members were matched by the ten chosen by Federation for the Committee on the Jewish Community Council which included, along with Keys, Peiser, and Boxerman: Joseph Ehrlich, Prof. Samuel M. Levin, Esther Prussian (the director of the Detroit Service Group), Simon Shetzer, and Henry Wineman.[26]

At the Committee of Twenty-One's final meeting, tensions erupted in arguments over the role of Federation. Keys assured those who were anti-Federation that no one group would dominate the new organization, which was expressly devoted to democratic representation of all Jewish groups in Detroit. It seemed logical, Keys continued, that as the most centralized institution, the Federation might inaugurate the process.[27]

Two weeks after that final meeting, on January 14, 1937, representatives of the Detroit Chapter of the American Jewish Congress (AJC) met with Federation leaders and those involved in the founding of a Jewish community council.[28] Having advocated such councils in all the larger cities in the United States, the AJC representatives seemed heartened at the prospects in Detroit, yet they expressed some chagrin over their omission from the planning to date. Some Detroit AJC members, like Benjamin Laikin, perceived Federation's assumption of a leadership role as an insidious attempt to gain control of the council at its inception. As president of the local chapter of Poale Zion, Laikin joined other representatives of AJC agencies: James Ellmann, the crusading lawyer and former president of the General Zionists in Detroit; Joseph Chaggai, a Labor Zionist; Aaron Kutnick; Anna (Mrs. Maurice) Landau; Elconin Saulson; and Sadie Feldstein. The meeting was chaired by Philip Slomovitz and attended by Boxerman, Peiser, and Simon Shetzer.[29]

Walter Klein's balanced reporting of these events intuitively discerned the importance of what the official accounts omitted as well as the tone they conveyed. As both he and Laikin pointed out in separate reminiscences that sometimes strikingly differ, the AJC faction reflected a Yiddishist, nationalistic, Zionist, and leftist slant. The group suspected Federation and the unaffiliated contingents of either disinterest or antagonism toward its perspectives on Jewish life. Incorrectly referring to Federation as "the American Jewish Committee" revealed a stereotypical identification of the American Jewish Committee as the "establishment" and therefore somehow associated with Federation. Simon Shetzer noted that although the American Jewish Congress should play a part in the formation of the Jewish Community Council because of its experience in such endeavors, its activities in other cities had proven ineffective and even disruptive. Further, he argued that in the democratic spirit of the project, the AJC ought not receive privileged or special status.[30]

Kurt Peiser broke the stalemate by offering a compromise. He suggested that the AJC receive seven seats on the organizing committee, providing these individuals represent Congress agencies, not the Congress itself. Consequently, James Ellmann, Joseph Haggai, Rabbi A. M. Hershman, Benjamin Laikin, Mrs. Anna Landau, Mrs. Sarah Levin, and Philip Slomovitz were added to the organizing committee. In stormy deliberations, however, the procedure continued. Federation asked for a council with members as individuals who would be responsible only to public opinion; the Congress faction instead sought organizational representatives, with each delegate responsible to his or her organization; a neutral faction searched for compromise.[31]

When the newly constituted group reconvened on January 17, 1937, Simon Shetzer and Myron Keys received unanimous election as chairman and cochairman, respectively. The members elected a constitution committee composed of Henry Abramovitz, Joseph Bernstein, Maxwell Black, Dora (Mrs. Joseph) Ehrlich, and Philip Slomovitz. Members of the organizing committee were canvassed to assist the constitution committee, thereby yielding unique contributions from Ellmann, the civil rights advocate who oversaw the legal aspects of the document; Haggai, the teacher and Yiddish scholar who sought to make it an "inspirational and literary" document; and Laikin, the political battler, who sought to "make sure that neither the Federation nor any other group should be able to take over control of the Council."[32] Five days earlier, Kurt Peiser had tendered his resignation to the Federation board, having accepted a position in Philadelphia.

All the additions to the Council Organizing Committee held Zionist, Workmen's Circle, or Labor Zionist views and prevented the Federation from creating a council without their vital interests and values. A widespread and trenchant suspicion of Federation motives and goals remained, along with a constant apprehension that Federation would seize control of the new institution.

In an article published in *The Reconstructionist* in November 1937, William Boxerman, the first Executive Director of the Jewish Community Council of Detroit, discussed the flowering of American Jewish community councils. He argued that their genesis signified "the need for a more inclusive organization of Jewish life." Without embroiling himself in the history of the council in Detroit, Boxerman attributed its prospects for success partly to "the vision and foresight of the Federation leadership in Detroit" and partly to "the pressure from elements who felt that the Federation itself did not embrace their major interests." The Federation, he said, proceeded cautiously and judiciously, obtaining the services of a competent professional (himself) and utilizing the media—the Anglo-Jewish and Yiddish newspapers as well as the Jewish radio programs.[33]

Boxerman alluded to Simon Shetzer's statement regarding the council, issued on the eve of the first conference of organizations. Shetzer, the chairman of the organizational committee, had spoken of a "sense of unity and a need for collective action on matters of common concern." Shetzer's inspired and inspirational declaration avowed that "the Community Council is not only a program of Jewish survival, but it is at the same time a conduit through which a positive, coordinated program of Jewish life can be carried on." He spoke, then, of the constitutional eligibility for membership in the Council, that is, to the question of which organizations might join the Council. He quoted the draft of the document, which insisted that to become a member, a group must have "a constructive interest in the preservation of some aspect of Jewish life" and must be dedicated "to maintain the dignity and integrity of the Jewish people." Shetzer proclaimed "these provisions to be the essence of the whole program—the preservation of the Jewish people *as* Jews and of Jewish values."[34]

Such language, abstract and universal, partly masked a specific, concrete concern: the admission of "political groups," or, more pointedly, communist groups. A Jewish branch of the International Workers' Order, a Communist Yiddish school, and other, smaller organizations gained prominence in the 1930s as the labor movement struggled in Detroit. Labor leaders of Jewish origin—most prominently Maurice Sugar and, more importantly, because of the predominance of Jews in the industry, Isaac Litwak, president of the Laundryman's Association—became more visible and vocal in 1937–1938.[35]

Simon Shetzer, a dedicated Labor Zionist and son of the president of 219

Shaarey Zedek, had gained a reputation as a brilliant young lawyer (graduating from Harvard Law School). His dedication to democratizing the organized Jewish community carried considerable credibility, even though he was a member of Federation's board. Shetzer, with democratic and perhaps even socialist philosophical leanings, opposed communism from the time of the split between Jewish leftist groups in the late 1920s. He firmly believed in the language he read in the draft of the Council Constitution because its specific meaning would block any communist organizations from joining.

On April 25, 1937, the first conference of organizations that would deal with the Jewish Community Council took place. According to Boxerman, three hundred people representing 180 Jewish organizations attended to discuss the proposed constitution. The meeting lasted for more than three hours and entailed fervid debates on a wide variety of subjects and language. Boxerman asserted that the delegates scrutinized every line of the document. But the most heated and caustic debate ensued over the exclusion of "organizations which are primarily political in nature" from eligibility for membership.[36] Supporters, most eloquently Simon Shetzer, argued that the primary purpose of the Council remained a "survival program." Jewish survival denoted Jewish values, goals, aspirations, and communal feeling. "Inasmuch as the chief aim of a political organization does not embrace this ideal," the argument continued, "this type of group has no place in the Council." Boxerman noted that the clause passed by a large margin of votes. Yet it troubled many of the delegates. Shmarya Kleinman, a supporter of the clause, nevertheless believed it signified a rocky start for a democratic institution. Others, also supporting the clause, seemed uneasy with such exclusionary policies.[37]

While there loomed several issues of contention, the other central stumbling block revolved around "the problem of Jewish nationalism." In 1937 Zionism could not be considered a popular philosophy among the majority of American Jews, especially among "establishment" Jews. Shetzer's preamble to the Council constitution included among the objectives of the organization the advancement and promotion of "the national and spiritual aspirations of the Jewish people."[38] The constitution committee had approved, but the organizing committee raised objections. One argument against the statement revolved around its potential offensiveness to some elements in the community. The minutes of the organizing committee record three sessions in which the issue was argued. James Ellmann had moved for acceptance of the language on the March 17, 1937, meeting of that committee. The motion passed by one vote, and the remainder of the constitution was approved for submission to the organizations that would be invited to form the Council.[39]

A second conference of organizations met to finalize the constitution on June 6, 1937, and it unanimously approved the final draft. The conference

appointed a committee to examine and evaluate organizational applications; members included Maxwell Black, Joseph Bernstein, Julian Krolik,
Samuel Lieberman, Henry Abramovitz, Simon Shetzer, and William
Boxerman. Distinctly anti-Communist yet clearly identified as Yiddish-
oriented and inclined to look favorably on Zionism, the committee reviewed each application with an eye on the political clause. The final item
on the agenda of the meeting of June 6 involved discussion of the "Polish
situation." Although the council did not yet officially exist, the delegates
designated a committee to act in conjunction with other organizations in
order to send a protest delegation to Washington.[40]

On September 29, 1937, two hundred delegates representing 155 member organizations convened at the Jewish Community Center for the first
delegate assembly of the Jewish Community Council. Simon Shetzer presided and began by classifying the meeting as a "historic event." Acknowledging that the Council would not offer the solution to all community
predicaments, Shetzer observed, however, that the Council realistically did
offer an "opportunity for a more intelligent approach" to many of the community's problems.[41]

Walter Klein recorded the categories into which each of the organizations fell: fifty philanthropic, fraternal, and benevolent organizations; thirty
synagogues and affiliates; twenty two social-service agencies; eighteen Zionist groups; twelve social groups; eleven lodges and auxiliaries; eight educational agencies; four councils of organizations. The officers, besides
President Shetzer, were Vice-Presidents Joseph Bernstein, James Ellmann,
and Julian Krolik; Secretary A. J. Lachover; and Treasurer Joseph H. Ehrlich.
The delegates elected Fred M. Butzel honorary president for life. The Executive Committee included Hyman Altman, Rabbi Franklin, Rabbi Hershman, Myron Keys, Dr. Shmarya Kleinman, Benjamin Laikin, Samuel Lieberman, Charles Rubiner, Philip Slomovitz, Isidore Sobeloff, Abe Srere,
and Henry Wineman.[42]

Sobeloff, the newly appointed successor of Kurt Peiser, addressed the
assembly and referred to the "historic event" as "a departure from the
usual Jewish practice in America . . . [which] if successful . . . will be a
model for other Jewish communities." Rabbi Fram spoke from the floor
of the delegate assembly and appealed for cooperation with the League of
Human Rights in its boycott of German goods. Thus, the public, confrontational, defense agenda of the Council emerged immediately. Yet within
moments it became clear that all the organizations, indeed, many individual delegates, had their own agendas. No certainty on the course of policy and activities could be discerned. The "suggestions" from the floor
included a plea for more recreational facilities for Jewish youth; active opposition to discrimination; a program for Jewish "self-education"
to assist Jews "to realize their own failings"; a community calendar; a
conciliation and arbitration service; and a concern from Federation dele- 221

gates that the Council might interfere with organizational fund-raising.[43]

By October 1937, 164 organizations had affiliated with the Council. William Boxerman enunciated some projected aims for the Council; borrowing from the preamble to the constitution of the Council, he listed first its primary purpose, "to maintain the dignity and integrity of Jewish life"; second, "to develop an articulate, intelligent, and effective public opinion on Jewish problems and interests." In his list of eight goals, he included the coordination of various segments of the Detroit Jewish community, the promotion of "cultural, social, economic, and philanthropic interests, and the national and spiritual aspirations of the Jewish people."[44]

Boxerman mentioned the prospect of establishing arbitration machinery to settle disputes between Jews and confirmed the commitment to the defense of civil rights. As would most adherents of the council, Boxerman stressed its democratic, functional premise—the inclusion of all elements of the Jewish population into decision-making policies and the fundamental democratic means of achieving that end. As in other democratic institutions, this goal would prove easier to theorize about than to achieve in practice.

Simon Shetzer began the preamble to the constitution by proclaiming that the Council would dedicate itself to the "coordination of the various forces of Jewish life" in Detroit. Not only would its purpose be to "preserve and maintain the dignity and integrity of the Jewish people," but also to "defend and protect its civil, political, and religious rights."

Several spokesmen touted the "survival philosophy" as they justified the clause defining membership eligibility and its requirement that the group exhibit "a constructive interest in the preservation of some aspect of Jewish life." Boxerman claimed that no other council had incorporated such a clause which, he said, recognized that "Jewish life has values common to all of its component groups . . . values worth preserving." Membership in the Council, then, was predicated upon each organization's dedication to perpetuating those values "through joint participation and group solidarity." In a clear message regarding "political," that is, communist groups, Boxerman defined what some called the "exclusion clause" as "a far cry from the assimilationist tendencies apparent among certain groups in the Jewish Community not so many years ago!"[45]

In a 1965 pamphlet outlining its history, the Council described its central purpose as establishing a cooperative process "to deal with common aims and problems . . . to enhance Jewish living and to better our relationships with each other and with the larger community." Beyond the abstract language, some of the euphemisms, and familiar maxims, lay deep concerns regarding anti-Semitism, the growing tide of assimilation, the loss of Jewish culture and tradition—religious and secular—and the fragmentation of Jews in America at a time when monumental events threatened Jewish individuals and groups. Isaac Franck, Boxerman's successor, wrote that the "Community Council Idea" arose with an awareness of "a new set of central communal problems." Franck emphatically declared that this idea symbolized the maturation of Jewish communities in America. "It [the Council idea] indicated the beginning of American Jewry's transition from inchoate agglomerations of individuals and groups whose major and often only *central* concern was philanthropy, to fully rounded communities with central community recognition of the full gamut of larger group problems which are inherent in the development of Jewish group life in America." Alongside individual and family problems, he continued, community problems had been thrust upon Jews to be confronted *"as a Jewish community, as a social organism."*[46] From philanthropy to broader matters, from individual and family to collective crises: the language thinly veiled a belief held by many that German Jews—the establishment, with its sophistication, assimilation, and wealth—would now give way to other Jewish voices that would speak to issues that included Palestine, the plight of European Jewry, and national and international defense against anti-Semitism.

Historically, federations and welfare funds met specific needs for family and individual assistance by establishing vital agencies to care for children, the old, small businesses in need of loans, and educational institutions through clinics, schools, free-loan associations, vocational services, family counseling bureaus, and community centers. Centralized fund-raising and allocation of funds logically fell into the hands of those who had organized the campaigns and seemed best qualified to determine relative needs. As the fiscal arm of the community, observed Franck, Federation in Detroit served its constituents well in its social-service planning and coordination functions.[47] And despite the much-noted lack of democratic structure, the Federation had begun to remedy that deficiency in the previous decade.

Yet the contemporary scene demanded attention to "larger group problems." In candid terms, Franck proclaimed what most knew but few admitted: that there was no unified Jewish community, but several communities "each almost hermetically sealed with very little continual interchange among them."[48] He might have added that each held considerable antagonism toward the others. Anti-Semitism forced a recognition of this state of affairs; it forced a change as well. Most Jews recognized that an attack on one Jew signified an attack on all. Some of the founders of the Council believed that this necessitated discarding the attitude that one segment of the Jewish population could serve another. Anti-Semitism compelled Jews to coalesce into one community for the sake of each member of that community.

Isaac Franck delineated several of what he considered to be critical tasks: coordination of cultural and organizational life; the expression of intelligent and articulate public opinion; the formation of a liaison with civic and governmental agencies; and the provision of a community voice and 223 structure that would guarantee the voicing of minority opinions but would maintain internal discipline as well. Franck, like some of his colleagues on the Council such as Ben Laikin, allotted fund-raising, allocations, and social-service coordination to Federation. The larger group problems demanded a representative council structure that he perceived existing in the Jewish Community Council of Detroit.

How these two organizations would collaborate remained tenuous and problematic. In 1937, however, with the creation of the Community Council, Jews of Detroit sensed that they had fashioned an institution that would respond to the unsettling spirit of the age.

Federation immediately responded favorably to the creation of a community relations committee within the Council by allocating seven thousand dollars to it. Within months the Council had appointed a public relations committee for the purpose of dealing with publicity, anti-Semitism, antidefamation, good-will work with non-Jews and "the dissemination of positive information about Jews."[49] Council immediately began actively investigating reports of discrimination. The executive committee authorized the director to begin work on a community calendar that would represent every Jewish group. Another committee began researching the prospects for a general community program. By January 1938 a committee of five had been appointed to organize Council participation in the Allied Jewish Campaign. The following month, Council formed a committee "to clarify the relationship between the Council and the Federation."[50]

To Federation, the Council's primary function was in the area of public relations and cultural programming. Thus initially there seemed little tension between the two organizations. Insofar as these activities would require significant funding, however, fiscal disagreements seemed inevitable.

224

16

The Synagogues: Varieties of Religious Experience

Detroit's largest and oldest congregations, Temple Beth El and Congregation Shaarey Zedek, withstood the Depression years fearful of losing congregants. Economic difficulties called for secular answers and increased attention to economic concerns that included education and employment. As those interests absorbed more time and energy, traditional religious concerns declined. Their religious schools lost students, yet continued under the hard times with dedicated teachers, administrators, and rabbis. Orthodox synagogues, too, suffered through the hard times but with fewer transformations, in part because of their more stable size and their intransigence regarding traditional practices and doctrine.

Reform Judaism in Detroit and other American cities went through various changes. What some deemed a "liberalizing" of religious thinking emerged in the Reform congregations. A temple in Houston, Texas, for example, made the news in 1943 by refusing to accept as members people who kept kosher or who had Zionist inclinations.[51] It was reported that a Chicago rabbi had stated that he thought of himself as a "Jewnitarian" 225 rather than simply a Jew.[52] Some Reform or unaffiliated Jews were a generation further removed and less connected to traditional practices than they had been in the 1920s.[53] At the same time, many Reform Jews were becoming deeply interested in Zionism, and the temples were filling with members of Eastern European background, some of whom had grown up in far more traditional homes where *kashrut,* Sabbath, and the like had been observed in the old manner.[54] The Columbus Platform of 1937 encouraged Reform congregations to use ritual to magnify and beautify their Judaism.[55]

In Detroit, Temple Beth El avoided such extreme actions as those of the congregations of Houston and Chicago, although it did reflect the general tide of Reform Judaism's developments. Pressure mounted to reinstitute the bar mitzvah ceremony throughout the 1940s, but only in 1953, shortly after Rabbi Hertz's arrival and at the insistence of the new president, Leonard N. Simons—who issued what was tantamount to an ultimatum—was the bar mitzvah again a part of Beth El ritual. Services continued to be conducted with organ and choir music. Organist Abraham Ray Tyler, upon reaching his twenty-fifth year with Temple Beth El, retired. He was succeeded by Jason Tickton in 1933. George Galvani directed the choir until 1942, and Julius Chajes, composer and pianist, conducted from 1942 to 1945. Friday-evening services were reintroduced in February 1936, and an earlier Friday Vespers was initiated in May 1939. Among the temple officers in the 1930s were Israel Himelhoch, Morris Garvett, Walter Heavenrich, Julius Rothschild, Harry Grossman, Herbert Kallet, and David Wilkus.[56]

Prominent figures in the worlds of politics and scholarship often came to speak at Beth El, attracting large audiences that included nonmembers. The Temple Forum series had begun in 1933 with a talk by Prof. (later Senator) Paul Douglas, of the University of Chicago. In December 1944, over eighteen hundred people came to hear newsman Drew Pearson.[57]

In 1941 the ninety-one-year-old congregation went through its second major split. In 1861, one group had left to form Shaarey Zedek. That rift derived from religious disagreements. Now, with the retirement of Rabbi Franklin, the congregation divided over the appointment of his successor. One group wanted Leon Fram, assistant rabbi and head of the Beth El educational program since 1925. But some of his opponents, who agreed on Rabbi Fram's excellent capabilities as a teacher, believed that he lacked the leadership abilities needed for so large a temple. Others saw him as too active in liberal, social, and political causes, like the former League for Human Rights, non-Jewish civic controversies having to do with labor and politics, and his continued prominence in activities of the Jewish Community Council.

Patriotic throughout his public career, Fram still sounded, to a group of Beth El members, somewhat less vigorous in his flag-waving Americanism than Rabbi Franklin. Also, Rabbi Fram's active Zionism irked some

bers, perhaps Rabbi Franklin more than most. However, this was not ultimately a decisive point, inasmuch as Franklin's eventual successor, Rabbi
B. Benedict Glazer, was also a Zionist.

On July 7, 1941, Morris Garvett, president of Beth El, presided over a meeting of about two hundred people at the Book Cadillac Hotel. After prolonged discussion, Rabbi Fram appeared and was acclaimed by those present; together they founded a new Reform congregation, Temple Israel. Apart from the personal or policy issues dividing the members of Beth El, there seemed ample room for a second Reform temple in Detroit. Garvett resigned as president of Temple Beth El and became Temple Israel's first president; Benjamin Jaffe served as its first vice-president.[58]

Rabbi Fram's new Temple Israel began holding services with fifty members in rented quarters in the Detroit Institute of Arts. Soon, there were a thousand members, most of them not drawn from existing congregations. The fledgling temple was "liberal" but more traditional than Beth El, feeling itself "friendly to the revival of beautiful traditions and symbols." It reintroduced bar mitzvah ceremonies, with Sheldon Lebret its first on May 9, 1942; it used more Hebrew in its service, and the congregation sang along with the rabbi and Cantor Robert Tulman who, along with the bar mitzvah boy, both wore prayer shawls.[59]

Fram encouraged greater attention to ritual at home, such as the lighting of candles and recital of the kiddush on Friday nights. He introduced new rituals, such as the naming of babies from the pulpit and the regular rabbinical blessings of students in the preschool. Education remained a major interest and a branch school was established in Hampton School, in the Curtis-Livernois area, in 1947, and an impressive high-school graduation ceremony was instituted. Women were becoming more active in the services. In 1943 Emma Schaver sang the Kol Nidre prayer on Yom Kippur and in February 1947, Pauline (Mrs. Harry) Jackson and a group of women led the Sabbath eve services.[60]

Temple Beth El continued to be one of America's leading Reform congregations. Its new Rabbi, B. Benedict Glazer, familiarly called "Babe," was an outspoken social activist who would openly criticize the seeming laxity of major organizations and their leaders. He was particularly active in mental-health organizations, serving as president of the Michigan Society for Mental Hygiene and of the Wayne County Chapter of the Michigan Society of Mental Health. He was also president of the Wrangler's Club, the association of Detroit clergymen.[61] For Rabbi Glazer, help for the oppressed was not merely a matter of lip service. He spoke out against antiblack discrimination as well as against anti-Semitism and brought the matter of housing discrimination before the Detroit City Council on the eve of the 1943 riots.[62]

Consistent with those stands, Glazer undertook what was nearly a one-man fight to eliminate discrimination in the tourist business. This added momentum to the passage of a Civil Liberties Law in Michigan in December 1945.[63] An active leader in the Jewish Community Council and in the Federation, Rabbi Glazer was close to Jews outside the Reform movement. Rabbi Morris Adler would say of him that he was "electric with life," and that religion to him was "a force to shake men out of the complacency and languor of the comfortable."[64]

As a scholar, Rabbi Glazer wrote an article on Rabbi Yehiel of Paris, a thirteenth-century rabbi. Much of Glazer's large library was sent to the Ponovez Yeshivah in Israel after his sudden death in 1952, affirming his commitment to Israel. That commitment, along with his dedication to social issues, placed him much closer to Rabbi Fram than Rabbi Franklin had been. Already in February 1948, the American Jewish Cavalcade was held jointly by Temple Beth El and Temple Israel, as the distinguished prewar leader of German Jewry, Rabbi Leo Baeck, spoke to a large audience composed of congregants from both temples.

Irving I. Katz joined the Beth El staff as executive secretary in 1939. Alumnus of a yeshivah in Riga, Latvia, and graduate of both Western Reserve University and Spencerian Business College, Katz was a pioneer in the field of synagogue administration, writing and lecturing prolifically on the subject and helping found the National Association of Temple Administrators in 1941.[65] For years Rabbi Franklin had been collecting materials on Michigan Jewish history; using these materials and avidly pursuing more of his own, Katz wrote hundreds of articles on the Jews of Michigan. His *History of Temple Beth El* (1954) was the first Wayne State University Press publication to win an award. He also published short histories of B'nai B'rith Pisgah Lodge, Yeshivah Beth Yehudah, several local synagogues, *Jewish Soldiers From Michigan in the Civil War* (1962), and *History of Jewish Communal Services in Detroit* (1960). Ten of his articles were contributed to the *Encyclopedia Judaica*.[66] A planned book on the history of the Jews of Detroit was left to be carried through by others. The Beth El collection was developed into a full-scale archive, masterfully organized and maintained by Mr. and Mrs. Aid and Miriam Kushner in the 1960s. Along with Allen Warsen and Irving Edgar, Katz was instrumental in founding the Jewish Historical Society of Michigan and its journal, *Michigan Jewish History,* in 1959.

Joseph Welt was president of Beth El during World War II, and about five hundred members served in the armed forces, of whom thirteen lost their lives. Sales of war bonds by the temple in 1944–1945 exceeded 10 million dollars, and war-drive leader Leonard N. Simons received a special citation from the U.S. government. The sisterhood, under the leadership of Mrs. Lawrence Freedman, Delia (Mrs. Henry) Meyers, and Bernice (Mrs. John) Hopp, collected clothing and food to send to war refugees, and in February 1945, the temple sent one of its Torah scrolls to a liberated synagogue in Europe.[67]

In 1943 Rabbi Glazer established the Annual Institute on Judaism for

Christian Clergy, a yearly symposium in which prominent Judaic scholars would come to Beth El to teach local clergymen about Judaism. In 1949 the temple's High Holiday services were televised for the first time.[68]

Having decided in 1926 to move from Willis and Brush to Chicago Boulevard and Lawton, Congregation Shaarey Zedek contracted the planning of the new building to Albert Kahn, who designed a "Moorish structure" with a dome. This elaborate experiment eventually gave way to a sloped roof, and the building became one of Detroit's Jewry's most impressive religious edifices. But complaints by local residents about the rerouting of an alley at Lawton and Wildemere led to a series of lawsuits that carried all the way to the United States Supreme Court before the synagogue, represented by attorney William Friedman, won its point.[69] The greatest damage, however, was the time involved, as the delays had pushed the completion of the new building into the Depression years and added to the serious financial threat facing Shaarey Zedek. Rabbi Hershman helped out by requesting a decrease in pay.

Throughout the 1930s, Shaarey Zedek stirred with classes, and Hershman's scholarly character asserted itself through his emphasis on Jewish education. In this respect his voice became stronger when, in 1938, Rabbi Morris Adler came from Buffalo, New York, to serve as Rabbi Hershman's assistant. Adler immediately set out to enlarge the midweek school; he added to the requirements for consecration and reorganized the Adult Institute established by Rabbi Hershman. By 1939 an adjoining building, the Kate Frank Memorial Building, was erected to house the rapidly expanding cultural and educational activities.[70]

Under the auspices of these two men, the Fortieth Annual Convention of the Rabbinical Assembly was held at Shaarey Zedek on June 25, 1940. It was the first in the midwest. Rabbis Adler and Hershman organized the Institute of Adult Jewish Studies, which affiliated with the National Academy for Adult Jewish Studies in December 1941, and offered courses on Hebrew language, literature, history, current events, and liturgy.[71] After several years overseas as an army chaplain in World War II, Rabbi Adler became full-time rabbi upon Rabbi Hershman's retirement in 1946. Much feted, Rabbi Hershman (similar, in this respect, to Rabbi Franklin) was conferred with the title of Rabbi Emeritus by a grateful congregation.

Among Shaarey Zedek's numerous active leaders in Detroit were Professor Samuel M. Levin, a longtime economist at Wayne State University; Isaac Shetzer (president from 1932 to 1936 and from 1939 to 1941), who was noted for his generosity in giving aid to immigrants; Judge Harry B. Keidan; melba and Sidney Winer, longtime supporters of Fresh Air Society; and numerous others who led Shaarey Zedek and other Jewish organizations in Detroit through difficult times during World War II. As the first congregation to officially declare itself for a Jewish state in Palestine, Shaarey

Zedek representned the gradual trend that would grow more quickly after 1944. Although it boasted several leaders of the Federation, including D. W. Simons, Abraham Srere, Joseph Wetsman, Judge Charles Rubiner, Hyman Safran, Samuel Rubiner, and others, it also claimed, through such men as Isaac Shetzer and his son and Rabbi Adler, significant leadership and participation in Council and other Jewish organizations.

17

The Rise of Anti-Semitism

"Social justice can never be achieved until the seeds of Christian charity and justice first be sowed into the hearts of men." Beneath that statement, highlighted at the base of a photograph of the statue of Christ on the cross, Father Charles Coughlin described his theologically oriented corporate state. Rooted in the "Mystical Body of Christ," the state's archenemy rested in the "mystical body of Satan," embodied in what Coughlin called Saint Paul's "synagogue of Satan." Thus his crusade for social justice fused with the Christian crusade against evil. And evil abided forever in the "combination of powers . . . which are bent not only upon deceiving the elect but upon turning this world topsy-turvy, upon destroying the plenitude and preventing the daily bread from descending into the pantries of the sons of God." Such a satanic and diabolic plan had been uncovered, insisted Coughlin, in the *Protocols of the Elders of Zion*. The plan would be perpetrated by "the" Jews.[72]

The most vocal and infamous of anti-Jewish crusaders began quietly in 1926 in a Catholic church in Royal Oak, Michigan. Ironically, before Coughlin initiated his infamous radio broadcasts and before he had come to Royal Oak, the Ku Klux Klan had burned a cross in front of the small wood-   231 frame Catholic church where Coughlin would preside. It was a quirk of history, too, that Coughlin's early assaults on the perpetrators of the Depression included a rebuke of Henry Ford for his venal capitalistic practices that Coughlin said would play into the hands of the communists. Ford, the battling adversary of "international finance," here stood publicly accused of being in cahoots with the bankers.

In 1926 Father Charles Coughlin left his parish in Flint for the small rural church in Royal Oak. As early as 1918 he had gained a reputation as an orator. One woman's organization for whom he had spoken in Detroit gushed that "a rare treat was to hear the eloquent address of Rev. Chas. Coughlin . . . beautiful thoughts, cleverly expressed, a golden tribute to Our Blessed Lady."[73] Coughlin grasped immediately the potential power inherent in mass media, particularly in radio. His Sunday-afternoon broadcasts became the center of many people's lives—Jew and non-Jew alike. Controversial almost from the start, he appealed in his early years to the working man, to the farmer, to the poor and downtrodden. His voice rang out in mellifluous tones on behalf of the masses—as if he drew together the socialist strands of his religion. So convincing and charismatic were his populist presentations, his pleas for the working man, and for the right to a decent wage, that even some Jews in Detroit sent him contributions. To them, as to tens of thousands of others, he seemed to speak for the victims of the inequities of capitalism or of an American system gone awry.[74] Their small donations added to the incredible flow of money he received from Americans across the country, especially after the Columbia Broadcasting System began carrying his programs in 1930.[75]

With the onset of the Depression, the priest's listeners multiplied and, ironically, as the poverty grew, his contributions did as well. In 1929 he undertook a massive, $500,000-campaign to build the 150-foot Charity Crucifixion Tower, which was topped with an ornately imposing statue of the crucifixion and joined by depictions of Christian saints and other holy figures. His champion, Bishop Michael Gallagher, head of the archdiocese of Detroit, appeared on the tower as the Archangel Michael. Gallagher, enthralled and even intimidated by his parish priest's powerful and hypnotic oratory, referred to him as "a national institution, invaluable to the safeguarding of genuine Americanism and true Christianity." Gallagher protected Coughlin from Catholic and non-Catholic opponents until 1937, when the bishop died.[76]

By 1931 Coughlin had become so controversial, alienating powerful individuals and groups within and without the Catholic Church, that CBS dropped his broadcasts. He promptly founded his own network and carried on, seemingly more successful than ever. An estimated forty million Americans listened to his broadcasts each week.[77]

His financial success and his apparent concern for social justice and government assistance to the unemployed drew the attention of powerful

listeners. He seemed to be speaking in sympathetic terms to some Jewish
groups concerned with the plight of the masses, and he attracted the interest of none other than Franklin Roosevelt on the eve of his 1932 campaign for the presidency. Roosevelt invited Coughlin and Detroit's liberal mayor, Frank Murphy to Hyde Park. Within weeks the radio priest identified the New Deal as "Christ's Deal," offering profuse support for Roosevelt's campaign.[78] This alliance, too, would be short-lived, as Coughlin's demagogic rhetoric seemed to know no bounds and he turned against Roosevelt by 1933.

"Christ's Deal" degenerated into the "Jew Deal" in Coughlin's extremist agenda. His sermons abandoned those fervent entreaties for social justice and turned to malevolent invectives against Roosevelt, communism, unionism, Henry Morgenthau, Jews, and money. Increasingly, he equated Jews with communism on the one hand and with parasitic Wall Street on the other. By 1934 he defied Roosevelt with his creation of the National Union for Social Justice. Beginning in 1938 his weekly journal, *Social Justice*, vilified Jews and proffered again the myths of *The Protocols of the Elders of Zion* and *The International Jew*. His broadcasts seemed to explode with increasingly frenetic references to Jewish Bolsheviks and Jewish capitalists.

In Detroit, Coughlin scurrilously attacked the Farband, the Jewish Workers' Alliance in Detroit, and the Sholem Aleichem Institute, labeling them Communist organizations.[79] (Presumably, Coughlin confused the more active political New York Sholem Aleichem Institute with the "*umparteiesche*" one in Detroit.) Every Sunday, Jews "whould gather around their radios listening for names" of organizations that Coughlin would designate as communist or evil. In 1938 he even attacked the Jewish Community council for their alleged Communist connections and their regular support of unions and Roosevelt.[80]

Alongside such inflammatory rhetoric, his speeches and *Social Justice* persisted in theorizing about relief for the common man. Thus, one issue typically began in bold print on the front page: "SOCIAL JUSTICE has always been a consistent friend of the laboring man. A just, annual, living wage, for every man able and willing to work, has been a principle of social justice since the beginning."[81] Yet, Coughlin's description of *The Protocols of the Elders of Zion*, which he admitted might be a forgery, contained the following observations: "The plotters will uproot civilization by preaching so-called liberalism. . . . Those who hold and control capital . . . which, the Protocols say, 'is entirely in our hands,' will gain control over the state." Before introducing the "First Protocol," Coughlin argued that not all Jews were necessarily involved in the nefarious conspiracy, but that "those who belong to the synagogue of Satan and who are plotting against civilization are not necessarily Jews. They are simply non-Christians in the strict sense of the word—not all non-Christians but some non-Christians   233 who despise Christianity, and are composed of both Gentile and Jew."[82]

While Coughlin expressed veiled anti-Semitism in several sermons before 1938, it was only in 1938 that *Social Justice* and his radio broadcasts took on virulent, fanatically vituperative anti-Jewish qualities. In the summer of that year, the magazine began serializing *The Protocols of the Elders of Zion* under Coughlin's by-line in his weekly column, "From the Tower."[83] His introductory interpretations of each protocol dripped with anti-Semitic rhetoric but unfailingly included some tactical disclaimer, like the one above, ultimately ignoring the historicity of the document upon which he grounded his arguments:

> Whether the *"Protocols of the Wise Men of Zion"* [sic] have any foundation in truth . . . whether these are genuine, it matters not. *It does matter that a definite plan does exist to destroy civilization and to subdue the children of men to the invisible master whose withering mind motivates the conspiracy against Christianity!*[84] (italics in original)

The first of his openly anti-Semitic broadcasts occurred on November 10, 1938. A bitter symbolism rests on the date: as Coughlin spoke about the alleged perils of religious persecution, German Jews were suffering the infamous Kristalnacht in Germany. Presumably unaware of those events, Coughlin maintained that Jews had caused the Russian Revolution and the spread of communism across the world. Avoiding open endorsement of Nazism, Coughlin told his listeners that Hitler and his colleagues had to be viewed "as a defense mechanism against the incursions of Communism."[85] With that broadcast, he launched one of the most vitriolic anti-Jewish campaigns in American history.

Detroit Jews recognized how dangerous that campaign would be, fully aware of the priest's enormous national audience, his support in such far-flung regions as Brooklyn and Boston, and the mysteriously tacit position of the Catholic Church toward his activities. Although the official Catholic publication, the *Michigan Catholic*, warned against arousing anti-Jewish feelings, suggesting that such practices defied papal directives, each of Coughlin's publications and radio broadcasts were approved by a chancery censor. Detroit's new archbishop, Edward Mooney, responded to Catholic and Jewish correspondents who objected to Coughlin's diatribes with a routine formula: " 'permission' for Father Coughlin to speak and write did not imply 'approval' of what he said." Mooney himself considered Coughlin a significant problem in the archdiocese and fundamentally disagreed with Coughlin's views, which he found "totally out of harmony with the Holy Father's leadership."[86]

The archbishop claimed that Coughlin cleverly cloaked his anti-Jewish vituperation and couched it in Christian rhetoric that included valid theological precepts. Despite these excuses, in the final analysis it seems clear that the archbishop, if not the Church, worried about offending large numbers of Coughlin's Catholic constituents. His priest thoroughly intimidated the archbishop. Worse still, mild responses to Coughlin's blatant insubordination suggest that the archbishop subscribed to much of Coughlin's propaganda that Jews were active in communist movements, or that they had been responsible for Coughlin's popularity themselves by not ignoring his attacks or by not asking for equal time to rebut his accusations.

In 1939 the archbishop, presumably bolstered by encouragement from the Vatican, confronted Coughlin on the content of *Social Justice*, formally reproving him for its "abusive language." Mooney urged Coughlin to sever his connections with the journal.[87] Finally challenged by Church authorities, Coughlin had no choice but to retreat under the apparent threat of suspension from the priesthood. In 1940 a gradual change became discernible in the policy of the Church censors. Two of them, Father John Vismara and Auxiliary Bishop Stephen Woznicki, refused to approve the text of one of Coughlin's broadcast sermons. He responded with what became known as the "silent broadcast" of February 5, 1940, in which he defiantly baffled his listeners and sponsors with a silent sermon. When the same sermon was turned down again, this time by the archbishop, Coughlin changed the sermon's topic. This event heralded the start of his decline. Most stations cancelled his 1940–1941 season, and his vocation as the "radio priest" ground to a halt.[88]

Finally, the archbishop and then the Church acted to silence Coughlin, but not until he was threatened with charges of sedition in 1942. The minimal restraints placed on him before that proved ineffectual and halfhearted at best, and even at the end Mooney believed that "some injury to the Church" could not be avoided.[89]

Stifled during the war, Father Coughlin faded into public obscurity. He retained his position as pastor of the Shrine of the Little Flower until 1966. Few figures in Detroit stimulated such adoration, devotion, and fear. His broadcasts remained vivid memories in the minds of the Jews who heard him. Those who reflected upon the meaning of his charismatic attraction feared a widespread, perfidious urge to hold Jews responsible for the socioeconomic ills of the United States. Coughlin may have been unique in his style, panache, rhetoric, and shrewdness, but others with similar urges—individuals and groups—proliferated in Detroit during the late 1930s.

From 1935 to 1942, the Black Legion, the white, Protestant, and racist organization that had separated from the Ku Klux Klan, reared its head increasingly in apparent preparation for "things to come." Exposed by a little-known newsletter published in New York and entitled "The Hour," the "terroristic band" had rallied in the late 1930s, gaining more members and becoming bolder in its Detroit activities.[90] Now connected to nativist, fascist movements, the legion began to post handbills in factories and workers' neighborhoods. In the stairwells of the Packard plant, for example, crude signs read "Jews Keep Off These Stairs." In other automobile plants stickers declared that "Jews Teach Communism, Jews Destroy Christianity, Jews Control Money." Members of the fledgling auto workers' unions received threatening notes, and one Hamtramck shopkeeper who had allowed union members to hold meetings in his store received an illiterately penciled warning that "one more meeting in this joint and out of business you go and you won't be on earth to know what business means. . . . Black Legion."[91]

Some Legion members created the Detroit National Workers League. Allegedly connected to Nazism, the League emerged in 1938 to contend with unions for worker membership. It called itself a "Nationalist political organization established on a non-partisan, non-sectarian basis." It claimed two objectives, baldly stated in its handbills: "Legal establishment of clean racial standards in the United States of America" and "legal reduction of Jewish influence in American public life to the minority position which they are entitled [sic]." Those flagrantly anti-Semitic propaganda assertions maintained that "the National Workers League is most emphatically not an anti-Semitic movement, since we neither oppose all Jews, nor most Semites."[92]

In democratically couched language, the league called for "equal rights" for non-Jews, using such terms as "common truths," which seemed to echo constitutional or patriotic rhetoric. Their vaguely stated program concluded with a call for "the first necessary democratic approach to a permanent solution of this evil in our nation"—the Depression and the control of the nation by "our Internationally controlled Jewish monetary system." That "democratic approach" meant "adopting clean racial standards which shall permanently guarantee that Americans of white European descent shall in the future direct the political and economic destiny of America." Less vocal members remained secretive about their membership, so any estimate of the strength of the organization remains speculative. Yet the organization collected dues, held meetings, openly espoused fascist doctrines, and praised Nazism. That it targeted workers proved to be its downfall. By 1940 labor-union members had infiltrated the hierarchy and crippled the organization. After America's entry into World War II, the League disbanded for fear of prosecution as a subversive group.[93] Its existence could not be ignored by Jews in Detroit, at least not by those on the Jewish Community Council or the defense agencies, including the Anti-Defamation League, the League for Human Rights, or the B'nai B'rith.

In September 1939 Philip Slomovitz wrote to former Detroit mayor Frank Murphy, then attorney general of the United States, about the League, calling his attention to one of the public meetings which, he believed, fueled "an organized movement to incite a riot against the Jewish people" of Detroit. He sent copies of the circulars to both the mayor and the FBI, requesting assistance in combatting the League. Slomovitz pointed out that besides maligning Jews, the National Workers League, at its September 3,

1939 rally, imitated the language of Fritz Kuhn of the German-American
Bund and slandered the president as well.[94]

Less vulgar but still alarming and threatening, practitioners of more
subtle forms of anti-Semitism seemed to grow more intrepid on the crest
of Father Coughlin's 1938 wave of hatred. In that year, realtors, contrac-
tors, and others in the building industry received an invitation to join a
new association, the Gentile American Realtors and Builders Association
(GARABA). Denouncing the influx of Jews and European foreigners, the
letter claimed that "the charitable indifference and overconfidence of the
unsuspecting American" allowed millions of "devious aliens" to overwhelm
the construction and real-estate industries. "Can we, the Gentile Americans, sit idly by and wait until starvation, nakedness and desperation bring
about a revolution?" The solution to this rhetorical question rests in the
hands of "those of us who profess to be red-blooded Americans."[95] Typifying the *ressentiment* of anti-Semites in Detroit, the organization seemed
to call for discrimination in hiring practices, a policy addressed almost
immediately upon its founding by the Public Relations Committee of the
Council.

In its *Bulletin* of October 1939, the Council reported on a newspaper
advertisement for clothing salesmen placed by Baumgartner Clothing
Company. The advertisement had specified that "Gentiles only" need apply.
Led by Slomovitz, the Public Relations Committee contacted Frank
Baumgartner, vice-president of the clothing company. His written response
appeared in the November *Bulletin*, in effect expressing surprise and ignorance of the advertisement. His explanation mentioned the four Jewish
salesmen employed at the company, discussion of the inadvisability of hiring more Jews, and the unfortunate initiative taken by the employee who
had written the advertisement. In an incidental defense of the employee,
Baumgartner noted that the man was Catholic and therefore "fully appre-
ciates the persecution . . . against your faith and his." In a communication to Slomovitz regarding the retraction, William Boxerman confided that
he did not believe the story and had hoped the retraction would appear in
the Anglo-Jewish press. Baumgartner had demurred, worrying that his non-
Jewish clientele would diminish. Boxerman rejected the idea of a boycott
of the store and hoped that the *Detroit News* would adhere more carefully
to its policy of refusing discriminatory ads.[96]

This single case reveals the vigilance of the Council; its methods of quiet
pursuit before public exposure (Boxerman had had several telephone conversations with Baumgartner before receiving the retraction); and the per-
nicious nature of anti-Jewish discrimination in Detroit. Even during World
War II, the Detroit Public Schools Division of Guidance and Placement
received requests for female interviewees from J.L. Hudson Company with
lists of qualifications that included: "girls of average appearance or better;
clear complexion; will consider foreign types, including Polish, Italian,

237

Hungarian, and all Nordic types (Those [sic] with a dark olive complexion, however should be eliminated, as well as those with an accent in the voice.); Gentiles."[97]

Along with the *Jewish Chronicle*, the Council's Public Relations Committee monitored discrimination against Jewish patrons of public establishments. As early as the summer of 1938, the Crystal Pool, located at Eight Mile and Greenfield Roads and one of the more notorious discriminatory establishments, drew fire from the Council. After hearing that a Jewish youth "with a slight accent" had been informed by the management of the pool that Jewish patrons were not wanted, Harold Goodman, a Jewish attorney whose family frequented that pool, wrote Philip Slomovitz. On July 14, 1938, Goodman phoned the Crystal Pool and asked if they did not desire Jewish customers. He was told that "we do not encourage it." To clarify, Goodman asked, "Then you mean that you do not want Jewish business," to which the man emphatically replied: "No."[98]

This case became a cause célèbre that was first pursued by Solomovitz, who gathered testimony from Philip Silverstein, an employee of the High Grade Laundry who had provided laundry service for the Crystal Pool in the summer of 1936. "At the beginning of the 1937 season," Silverstein's signed affidavit declared, "Mr. Rylander [the pool's owner] informed me that he did not care to do business with Jews. . . . He admitted that I gave him good service and that my laundry's price was fair and compared with anybody else's." When Silverstein bid for the contract in 1938, "Mr. Rylander was emphatic in saying that there was no use talking to him, that he would have nothing to do with Jews . . . [saying] 'there is not a decent Jew in this world.' "[99]

Slomovitz next wrote to the Crystal Swimming Pool, Inc., warning of his newspaper's intention to publish a statement advising Jews to avoid the pool. He offered his evidence, Silverstein's, other affidavits, and testimonies, and extended the opportunity to the owner to apologize and/or deny the allegations before running the article. Receiving no reply, Slomovitz published his censure of the Crystal Swimming Pool, and the Council Newsletter of August 18, 1938, reported that Mr. Rylander had refused Council's invitation to discuss the matter. A second letter sent by registered mail was returned "with the notation, 'Refused by owner.' "[100]

The Newsletter article appeared under the title "Self-Respecting Jews Will Withhold Their Patronage From the Following Two Establishments." The second establishment, the Rotunda Inn of Pine Lake, which had frequent Jewish customers, had refused to allow a Jewish woman from Detroit to enter the dining room. A guest of the hotel, the woman nevertheless was told that "they did not cater to Jews" and was requested to leave the hotel immediately. A member of the Council then wrote to inquire about accommodations and received a reply from owner George D. Brown: "Our clientele demands that we accommodate Gentiles only."[101]

Such cases did not always draw a Council-led boycott. In 1942, for example, Isaac Franck, Council executive director, pursued a complaint from
a Jewish woman regarding anti-Semitic slurs directed at her at Cliff Bell's
Restaurant on Six Mile Road. Franck wrote to Mr. Bell and received a conciliatory reply; after he visited the establishment with Rabbi Leon Fram
and they had engaged in a lengthy conversation with Mr. Bell, Franck concluded that the slurs had come from other customers and that Bell was
"a quiet, friendly gentleman . . . an honest and decent individual" who
had Jewish friends and who did business with Jewish merchants and did
not discriminate against Jewish patrons. Bell had reiterated his feelings
several times during these conversations and repeated, too, that he observed that Jews did not drink as much as non-Jews. The closest he came
to discriminatory procedures, then, was to give preferential treatment to
drinkers (Jews and non-Jews). Franck recommended no action be taken
against the restaurant and concluded "that the real moral of the story . . .
is 'If you want to be served at Cliff Bell's, go to the bar and order
drinks.' "[102]

Antidiscrimination efforts commanded Council's persistent attention.
Regardless of how one perceived the organization's origins, all agreed upon
the centrality of this issue. At its quarterly meeting on June 9, 1940, the
Council held a symposium "In Defense of Human Rights" that dealt with
anti-Jewish discrimination in Detroit. The primary purpose of the symposium, however, involved the Council's program to combat discrimination and anti-Semitism in concrete—that is, financial—terms. Simon Shetzer
presided, and the participants included Harold Silver, chairman of the subcommittee of the Committee on Economic Problems; James I. Ellmann,
chairman of the Public Relations Committee; and Louis Rosenzweig, a
member of the executive committee who also addressed the development
of a public relations program. At the conclusion of the symposium, a motion, unanimously passed, charged the executive committee with investigating "ways and means of adequately financing the public relations program." In his preface to the privately distributed pamphlet on the symposium,
Shetzer implied that Federation had not provided ample financial support.[103]

After chronicling specific examples of anti-Jewish discrimination in the
work place, the symposium discussed Council's investigation of twenty-
four employment agencies in the Detroit area. Sixteen of them recounted
that they experienced greater difficulty in placing Jewish applicants than
they did with non-Jewish applicants. Eighteen related that gentile employers indicated "distinct preferences for Gentile help. Twenty-one agencies claim that Jewish employers also practice discrimination against Jewish workers." This last, rather surprising contention, received support from
a letter to the editor of the *Jewish Chronicle* in which a prospective secretary disclosed that "Jewish businessmen themselves, when I asked them,
have admitted they do not care to hire Jewish girls." The letter continued, 239

exposing incipient resentment toward refugees as it averred "that the prominent and generous Jews, who are doing so much to help the Jewish refugees" should turn to remedy the local situation of Jewish discrimination against prospective Jewish employees.[104]

Council's study of the employment agencies sought the causes behind the discriminatory behavior. Shetzer listed some of the most common responses from employment agencies and prospective employers—including Jewish employers: "aggressiveness of Jewish employees"; "fear of competition—after a while they go out on their own after leaving your business and compete with you"; "Jews talk too much"; "they always overstep their authority"; "they are not content with their own lot"; "they don't take care of their appearance"; "they can't be trusted in their moral conduct"; "they take the Jewish holidays off"; "they are too intelligent for inferior types of manual work"; "they are labor agitators."[105]

Detroit's Council, Shetzer said, had established the Discrimination Committee in 1938. Overworked and overextended, it conducted investigations of specific cases and explored the general problem under the rubric of anti-Semitism. In some instances, he continued, after discrimination had been established based on investigations, the Council had been able to secure a change of policy by employers. In the main, however, antidiscrimination action remained too little, too random, too unprogramatic, and too disorganized.[106]

Shetzer invoked the necessity for an informational and educational program, an outreach to Jewish and non-Jewish employers, Jewish applicants, employment agencies, newspapers, colleges, and technical schools. Consistent with Council philosophy, he believed that only through such education would discrimination be curbed.

To that end, Council had requested $4,690 from the 1940 Allied Jewish Campaign. The disposition of the request still remained unknown in June 1940. In an impassioned conclusion Shetzer wrote that "the necessary funds *must* be found for an adequate discrimination program, to include the preventative, as well as the remedial measures heretofore pursued. *The work is urgently needed and must be undertaken at once—not some time in the indefinite future.*"[107] It seemed another echo of the immediacy of action that symbolized the efforts of Council constituents, versus the administrative delays, procedural debates, and budgetary encumbrances identified with Federation.

Two final, related matters emerged. Public interest had been diverted to events in Europe, Shetzer argued, and "many American Jews began to lull themselves into a false sense of security," believing that since most Americans opposed Germany, they could not " 'be anti-Hitler and anti-Semitic at the same time.' " Pointing to allegedly anti-German organizations, Shetzer reminded his readers that many of them still referred to the New Deal as the "Jew Deal," and he listed remarks from the Coughlinite organization

"America for the Americans," which insisted that "the American people [are under] the hypnotic spell of false tolerance" and must awaken to "promote the welfare of the *American-born Gentile*"[108] (italics in original).

To this realistic awareness Shetzer linked practical policy, arguing that "while it is important to send huge sums of money abroad for relief purposes, we should also recognize that we must build our fences here at home." His message to the Federation Board seemed loud and clear. Funds for the public relations, educational, and informational programs remained vital for securing Jewish life in Detroit.[109]

Concern for that security in Detroit did not preclude apprehensions about Jews in Europe. In November 1938, the Council moved to organize a committee of prominent non-Jews to "mobilize opinion" of non-Jewish groups about the plight of Jews in Germany. In January 1937, Federation president Clarence Enggass reported a meeting with Jacob Billikopf, the director of the National Coordinating Committee for Aid to Refugees, with whom he discussed what might be done "to adjust" German refugees to Detroit.[110] Almost immediately upon his arrival as new executive director of Federation, Isidore Sobeloff joined Fred Butzel in actively pursuing the resettlement of Jews from Germany.[111] Although never suspecting the true scope of the catastrophe, Detroit's Jews became increasingly aware of how grave the danger to German Jews was, and they responded with what they perceived as fitting actions.

Their alarm over the persecution of Jews in Germany heightened some Detroit Jews' awareness of the Nazi-style threats to their own well-being posed by incipient fascist groups like the Black Legion and the National Workers League, and by admittedly fascist orators like William Dudley Pelley and, worst of all, "American patriots" like Father Charles Coughlin.[112]

An explicit connection between German and American anti-Semitism surfaced in 1938, once again in Dearborn. In August 1938, on the occasion of his seventy-fifth birthday, Henry Ford accepted the Grand Cross of the Supreme Order of the German Eagle, the Third Reich's highest honor for non-Germans. Ford received the fourth such award and the first given to an American. It had been created by Hitler himself. Obviously Hitler had picked Ford, one of the rare Americans for whom he expressed admiration and the only American mentioned in *Mein Kampf*. Bestowed by German consul Karl Kapp in Ford's office, the citation accompanying the decoration read that it was given "in recognition of [Ford's] pioneering in making motor cars available for the masses." Kapp read the citation, along with Hitler's personal congratulations, at Ford's birthday dinner in front of fifteen hundred prominent Detroiters.[113]

Ford's acceptance of the medal rekindled memories of his *Dearborn Independent* escapades and touched off a national reaction. Speaking before a Hadassah meeting, entertainer Eddie Cantor declared Ford "a damn fool for permitting the world's greatest gangster to give him a citation." Cantor doubted Ford's Americanism and his Christianity.[114] The National Encampment Committee of the Jewish War Veterans of the United States, which had convened in Detroit to plan the organization's approaching Detroit convention, refused Edsel Ford's offer to supply seventy-five cars for delegates. They urged Henry Ford to return the Nazi decoration because his acceptance implied not only "endorsement of the cruel, barbarous, inhuman actions and policies of the Nazi regime," but also "endorsement of the German-American Bund and their subversive un-American activities and other anti-democratic groups subsidized here by Nazi funds."[115]

Not until December 1938, did Ford permit some tentative recantation. Rabbi Franklin paid him a visit. The two men had not spoken for years, since Ford had ignored Franklin's pleas to discontinue the publication of *The International Jew*. But Ford's aide, Harry Bennett, through Moritz Kahn (Albert's brother), arranged a meeting with Harry Newman, a Jewish car dealer and former all-American football player. Newman prevailed upon Franklin to met with Ford for the purpose of drafting a statement disavowing Nazi persecutions of Jews. Franklin agreed to write to his former neighbor requesting the meeting. They met for an hour, with Bennett and Newman present, in an atmosphere of exaggerated warmth and cordiality.[116]

Motivated, in part, by the drastic decline in sales of Lincoln and Ford automobiles, Ford offered to assist German Jewish refugees by providing employment in his factories. He suggested to Franklin that the Ford Motor Company should help the United States to "fulfill the traditional role as haven for the oppressed," adding that there were plenty of jobs available for German-Jewish refugees.[117] Seduced by this proposal, Franklin agreed to collaborate in the wording of a declaration to be issued to the newspapers. Ford then allowed the rabbi to issue an oblique statement that claimed that Ford's acceptance of the award "from the German people" did not invovle "any sympathy on my part with Nazism."[118] Ford believed, Franklin said, that "the German people were not in sympathy with their rulers in their anti-Jewish policies." He concluded the statement by reaffirming that the United States must continue to offer a haven to the oppressed, and he offered to help the victims of European oppression. Considering the past willingness of Detroit Jews to treat Ford with at least public generosity, that might have been the end of the affair.

Father Coughlin had other ideas. He attacked the statement, claiming that Franklin had authored a "totally inaccurate" communiqué in which Ford had meant to commend the German government and reject the idea of persecution in Germany.[119] The *Detroit Free Press* immediately came to Rabbi Franklin's defense, citing Ford's long-standing friendship with the rabbi and noting that "the Doctor's reputation and standing in this community is such that when he issued the statement, and said that it was authorized by Henry Ford, no newspaper in this city had any reason to question it. Nor have they now." The *Free Press* concluded its editorial by accusing Coughlin of lying ("a congenital inability to tell the truth"). Coughlin sued the newspaper, which responded with seventy pages of direct contradictory quotes from Coughlin, who then dropped the suit.[120]

To some, Ford had again duped Rabbi Franklin into affording him a credible, if clumsy, escape from a potential debacle. Committed anti-Semites who believed Ford was one of them could argue that Coughlin had been correct—after all, had Franklin not requested the meeting in writing? And Henry Ford could be perceived as a victim of Jewish conspiratorial lies. To Jews who wanted to see Ford as less malicious than innocent, drawn into anti-Semitic actions and words by his hateful lieutenants like Bennett and Ernest Liebold, the editor of the *Independent,* the statement rang true and mitigated his acceptance of the German award. Yet Ford more openly proclaimed his admiration for Hitler and the Nazis in the following three years, denouncing them only in 1942. The Ku Klux Klan continued to use his name in their anti-Semitic literature until he threatened to sue them in 1944, and *The International Jew* continued to be published with his name and sometimes his picture until 1945.[121]

These events served as a portent of things to come in Detroit and in the world. Challenges to Detroit Jews, the Jewish Community Council, and other organizations began to loom larger than ever. Henry Ford's receipt of a Nazi decoration symbolized the nascent anti-Jewish feeling in Detroit. The tone of other events and statements surfaced more menacingly, like the card received by Morton Hack, a successful Jewish businessman who frequently wrote letters to the newspapers concerning civil-rights issues:

> YOU HAVE BEEN SPOUTING OFF TOO MUCH IN THE PUBLIC LETTER BOX LATELY TO SUIT THE WHITE PEOPLE OF THIS CITY, AND NATION. IF YOU DO NOT DISCONTINUE THIS PRACTICE AT ONCE WE SHALL SEE TO IT THAT PATRONAGE IS WITHHELD FROM YOUR PLACE. SINCE THIS IS A WHITE MAN'S COUNTRY, LET THE WHITE PEOPLE DO ALL THE TALKING. WE WANT NONE OF YOU JEWS MEDDLING IN OUR AFFAIRS, NOR DO WE INTEND TO FIGHT YOUR BATTLES FOR YOU. YOU FELLOWS HAVE ASKED FOR IT, NOW TAKE IT. YOU HAVE HAD IT COMING FOR A LONG TIME. AND MORT, YOU AIN'T SEEN NOTHIN', *YET.*
>
> GOLGOTHA[122]

18

Federation: Ministering to the Communities

After only twelve years, Detroit's Federation had acquitted itself admirably in terms of its primary functions of fund-raising, planning, and budgeting. A relative late comer to the federation format, it had not achieved status as one of the five major "large federations" (New York, Cleveland, Chicago, Baltimore, and Boston), but by 1938 the Detroit organization nevertheless led all welfare funds in its population category of forty thousand or more Jews in percentage of subscribers (11 percent). Sixth in population, Detroit's raising of $445,195 made Detroit number five in campaign totals, ahead of Baltimore.[123]

Kurt Peiser left Detroit for a position in Philadelphia after five years of service. His departure from the office of Executive Director of Federation seemed to herald a new era. Harry L. Lurie, Executive Director of the Council of Jewish Federations and Welfare Funds, had had considerable involvement with Detroit since 1923. He recommended the position to a young man with experience in New Jersey, New York, and Baltimore: Isidore Sobeloff. Detroit's reputation as one of the twelve largest, rapidly growing, and most progressive federations in the United States induced Sobeloff to interview for the position of executive director. He was also familiar with the prestige of Morris Waldman, John Slawson, and Kurt Peiser. The first question put to him at his interview indicates some of the changing attitudes in Detroit: "Do you speak Yiddish, Mr. Sobeloff?"

Commended by Lurie, and based on his experience and credentials, Sobeloff got the job and launched Detroit's Federation into new challenges. With the exception of his departure during the war to work in New York, Sobeloff directed the Federation until 1967. Often gruff, Sobeloff was a brilliant administrator and organizer and gained a reputation as "this country's most outstanding [federation] fund-raiser." A man who "would not suffer fools lightly," he inspired intense loyalty and passion. In 1937 Sobeloff represented a new, more sophisticated, and mature type of leadership of the organized Jewish community.

Federation reflected its new maturity, too, in its turn from charities and relief societies to social-service bureaus and agencies. Detroit's Jewish Social Service Bureau succeeded the Family Welfare Department of the United Jewish Charities in December 1925. Since its cardinal aim remained the "preservation of Jewish family life," its work centered on combating or mitigating those social forces that disrupted Jewish families, such as domestic strife, strained relationships between family members, and behavior problems of children.

The initial plan of organization incorporated a General Family Department and a Special Investigation Department. In 1933 the bureau was reorganized and moved its headquarters to the Community Fund Building at 51 West Warren Avenue, where the central Federation offices were housed. The Bureau thus came under the same roof as the Jewish Child Placement Bureau. That same year, Harold Silver became the new executive director, and shortly thereafter, Pauline Gollub was appointed as the new agency supervisor.[124]

Friction between the Child Placement Bureau and the Social Service Bureau eventually led to the formation of the Joint Committee on Child Care, with Fred Butzel as its chairman. Between 1933 and 1944, however, under the able leadership of Butzel and Harold Silver, the Social Service Bureau subsumed more of the responsibility for child care and placement. Both men seemed to affirm the initial principle of the Child Placement Bureau, that "every child who cannot for one reason or another be cared for by its own parents, should be given a substitute home environment approximately the same as the home environment of other children in the community."[125]

In pursuit of those admirable aims, Herman Cohen, president of the Jewish Children's Home, suggested that the Joint Committee on Child Care undertake a comprehensive survey of the Jewish child-care situation in Detroit. The survey was begun in June 1940, and the resulting report, compiled by the executives of the four participating agencies, produced another significant change in Jewish children's social services, which was 245 implemented in 1941 by the amalgamation of the foster home and the institutional programs. This took the form of the Jewish Children's Bureau, with Fred M. Butzel as its president and Herman Cohen and Nathaniel Goldstick, former presidents of the Children's Home and the Child Placement Bureau, respectively, as vice-presidents. The foster-home program and the institutional elements of child care came under one executive, one staff, and one budget, with the Jewish Social Service Bureau continuing to provide the investigatory assistance. Clarice Freud became the new executive of the agency, which inherited 106 children in foster homes, twenty-eight more in the Children's Home, and nineteen refugee children.[126]

The responsibilities of the Children's Bureau expanded as it experimented with group conseling techniques. Those new methods sustained the precept of foster-home care that had informed Jewish children's social service from its inception in Detroit. Along with the traditional components of that care, the Children's Bureau added vocational counseling and guidance by cooperating with the Jewish Vocational Service, and it offered summer camp experiences at the Fresh Air Society Camp to an increased number of children. Because of the advent of "a new era in community building developments," ushered in by the unprecedented bequest of the $500,000-estate of Carrie Sittig and Joshua Cohen in 1937, the agency operated out of a building on Savery Avenue that was purchased with funds from the Carrie Sitting Cohen Fund of the United Jewish Charities. Those headquarters on Savery were later named the Solomon Cohen Memorial.[127]

As the agency constantly adjusted to the vicissitudes of social-service work and the needs of Jewish children in Detroit, yet another change seemed necessary when, in 1943, Miss Freud took a position at the University of Michigan's Institute of Social Work. She was replacd by Goldie Goldstein, a longtime member of the professional staff of the Jewish Social Service Bureau (JSSB). In 1944 the new Children's Bureau combined witht a revised Jewish Social Service Bureau to form the new Jewish Social Service Bureau, with two major departments, family welfare and child care. The tasks of resettlement of immigrants was incorporated into these two divisions as the new bureau embraced the responsibilities of the Resettlement Service. Also included in the bureau's agencies was the Mental Hygiene Clinic, which was directed by Dr. Harry August with assistance form the staff psychologist, Henry Feinberg.[128]

This newly reconstituted JSSB remained under the directorship of Harold Silver, and Goldie Goldstein became the case consultant. The purpose of the new merger seemed to be to increase efficiency in client assistance and to prevent duplication of services so that energies could be employed more judiciously.

By 1936 under the pressures of the Depression, the JSSB had incorporated the work of the Jewish Unemployment Emergency Council, the Home Service Department, and the Self-Support Program. Another of the agencies formed by the Emergency Council, the Cooperative Council of Jewish Family Welfare Organizations, continued after 1935 as the League of Jewish Women's Organizations. Under the leadership of Dora Ehrlich, the Cooperative Council served as a clearance bureau to avoid duplication of tasks, and it regularly discussed the progress of individual cases. After the Depression, all the activities of the Emergency Council passed to the Bureau which, since 1940, was fully supported on a deficit basis by the Detroit Community Fund. By 1937, the case load of the bureau was 3,697, with a budget of $49,495, and after the child-care program came under its rubric in 1944, the Community Chest campaigns included a sum of approximately $150,000 for its funding.[129]

As one of Federation's primary agencies, the JSSB served as an emblem of Jewish patterns of cooperation in Detroit. At various times it coordinated the services of the North End Clinic, the Mental Hygiene Clinic, the Jewish Children's Home, the Fresh Air society, the Jewish Center, and the House of Shelter. The JSSB undertook the responsibility of investigating applications for admission to the Jewish Home for Aged when the new home opened in 1937.[130] Among its other services, the JSSB cooperated with agencies outside Detroit, such as the National Desertion Bureau, HIAS, and the National Council of Jewish Women, to locate and/or aid relatives in Detroit. Indeed, the JSSB represented a paradigm of the Federation idea of collaborative departmental service.

In 1941 the United Jewish Charities allocated the funds for the Seymour and Albert Samter Memorial building on Second Boulevard where the JSSB and the then newly independent Jewish Vocational Service (successor to the Free Employment Bureau started in 1926) were housed. (The Vocational Service moved to other quarters in 1944, when the JSSB merged with the Jewish Children's Bureau.) Benefitting from the fortunate union of professional and lay leadership, the JSSB continued to move into new areas of social service. Among its presidents were Melville S. Welt, Abraham Srere, Judge Theodore Levin, Prof. Samuel M. Levin, George M. Stutz, Mrs. Melville Welt, Benjamin Jaffe, Mrs. Charles Lakoff, and Dr. Lawrence Seltzer. Perhaps its most active and dedicated volunteer in the 1940s was Mina (Mrs. Theodore) Bargman, whose dedicated service was acknowledged in 1949.[131]

Social services reflected the domestic crisis of the Depression. In 1937 they also began to reflect the European crisis, as German-Jewish refugees arrived in flight from Nazi persecution.[132] It fell to the Child Placement Bureau to place German Jewish children in new homes, some at regular boarding rates and others in free homes, while the agency retained supervisory responsibility and met the special needs, such as psychological counseling, of some of the children.[133] To support these children, funds were allotted from the Allied Jewish Campaign and special grants were made from the Aaron Mendelson Trust. By 1940 there were some 133 chil-   247 dren under care of the agency. They were supported by grants from the Detroit Community Fund and Wayne County.[134]

Of the approximately twenty-three thousand German-Jewish émigrés in 1937, an estimated nine thousand came to the United States.[135] Most who came to the United States under the still restrictive immigration laws needed affidavits of sponsorship from relatives or friends.[136] In Detroit, as early as January 12, 1937, Clarence Enggass, president of Federation, reported a meeting with Jacob Billikopf, the director of the National Coordinating Committee for Aid to Refugees. Billikopf had discussed procedures regarding the numbers of German-Jewish émigrés and the problems of adjusting them to life in the United States.[137] It was not until November 1937, however, that the board of Federation addressed the German-Jewish children's project. At Sobeloff's urging, only three months after his assumption of the office of executive director, the board voted six thousand dollars for the placement and care of children in Detroit. The committee to direct the project included Fred M. Butzel, Mrs. Edith Bercovich, and Nathaniel H. Goldstick (president of the Jewish Child Placement Bureau).[138]

Public discussions had begun in 1934, with the Jewish Labor Committee, and grew more insistent in 1936 after the founding of the League for Human Rights, which led the boycott of German goods in Detroit.[139] In May 1937, at the banquet to kick off the 1937 Allied Jewish Campaign, Butzel had spoken of a "double burden. . . . We must carry our share and move for American causes and for Jews abroad who are persecuted and need help in the countries which they assisted to build." At that banquet, singer and showman Eddie Cantor, a frequent visitor to Detroit, made a telephone appeal to "take care of our own."[140]

In 1938 more than 110,000 Jews fled from Germany and Austria.[141] Thousands applied for entrance into the United States. Some came under the auspices of the newly constituted National Refugee Service (NRS), which was founded in 1938 with assistance from the Joint Distribution Committee (JDC).[142] German Jewish children unaccompanied by parents found refuge with the German Jewish Children's Aid, which later became known as the European Jewish Children's Aid. All were channeled through the NRS and distributed throughout the United States on a more or less planned basis. The NRS tried to assuage those with concerns that the already large concentrations of Jews would increase in large cities like New York or Baltimore.[143]

In Detroit, sometimes with some reluctance among some segments of the Jewish (and non-Jewish) populations, Federation took an organized, active role in relocating refugees in the state of Michigan. Alongside Federation, the Jewish Community Council, the League for Human Rights, and less public organizations like the Jewish Labor Committee, devoted increasing efforts to bringing Jews out of Europe. If tensions still existed between the "uptown" and "downtown" populations, publicly the Jews of

Detroit acted as one. More than ever before, the varied voices in Detroit
Jewry grew united. The two concentric centers remained Federation
and Council, each carrying out their own programs, but cooperating to
an unprecedented extent in the brief time since the Council had been
founded.

In August 1938, under the direction of Sobeloff and Fred Butzel, Federation established the Resettlement Service.[144] Despite the service's Federation control, Sobeloff sought a broad base to represent the whole Jewish
population of Detroit and understate the Federation's principal role. Nevertheless, the Resettlement Service would undertake cooperative efforts with
such other bureaus as the JSSB, Child Placement Bureau, the National
Council of Jewish Women, the Jewish Community Center, and the Aaron
Mendelson Fund. Butzel acted as the first president, with Julian H. Krolik
as chairman of its Family Department and Mrs. Samuel R. Glowgower as
chairman of the Children's Department.[145]

Almost immediately, funding for overseas relief became a source of contention. At the November 11, 1938, board meeting, Sobeloff reported on
the work of the JDC's emergency drive for one million dollars. He recommended postponing any additional fund-raising until after the Allied
Jewish Campaign and, to hasten the process of pledge collections in this
time of emergency, Melville S. Welt was appointed chairman of an emergency collection campaign. Complementing this campaign, a women's project
was organized under the fervent guidance of Mrs. Welt, Mrs. H. J. L. Frank,
and Mrs. Fred Ginsburg.[146]

Not until November 1939 did the Federation Board take up the issue of
resettlement. Federation Executive Committee received a letter from Samuel
Schaflander, the executive secretary of the League for Human Rights, calling for cooperation from Federation and the Jewish Community Council
in their emergency rescue efforts. The Executive Committee appointed
Abraham Srere head of a committee to bring the organizations closer in
"civic-protective work." At that same meeting, the committee voted one
thousand dollars for an assistant to Anna Rose Hersh, the employment
secretary at the Jewish Community Center to do more statewide fieldwork
in placing refugees.[147]

Just as it had at the national and international levels, antagonistic competition erupted between the United Palestine Agency and the Joint Distribution Committee.[148] Each vied for money for their respective agendas:
the JDC to aid European Jews in immigrating to the United States or anywhere out of the clutches of German persecution; the UPA to aid those
same Jews in getting to Palestine. The struggle, according to one Detroit
Jewish leader, was "for leadership, money and for the hearts of the people
of each community." It grew more caustic during the war. In January 1940,
Federation agreed to give $5,250 to the Joint Distribution Committee, $2,500
to the UPA and $2,500 to the National Refugee Service.[149]

249

In the face of such antagonisms, Detroit's Resettlement Service functioned more smoothly than most others. Harold Silver directed all aspects of resettlement that fell under his bureau's aegis: family service, financial assistance where needed, employment, housing, recreation, and more. Volunteer teachers came from the National Council of Jewish Women. A committee of real-estate men helped find proper housing. The Hebrew Free Loan Association devised a loan procedure. The North End Clinic provided medical care when needed. Under the leadership of Emma Butzel; Mrs. Max Berendt, the associate chair of the Opportunity Committee; and Edith Heavenrich, vice-chair of the Family Department, some thirty women formed the Opportunity Guild in December 1939.[150] Their goals revolved around channeling the domestic talents, primarily sewing, of immigrant women in order to provide markets for their work. After supplying material, the Guild would pay for the completed work in wages and then find buyers for the products. The Jewish Community Center provided recreational and social programs and founded a social group called the German American Group, which changed its name, in 1940 to the New Americans. It numbered around 250 members.[151]

19

Organizing Jewish Education: The United Hebrew Schools

New problems confronted those concerned with Jewish education in the 1930s. As many students came to schools with less motivation and less knowledge than their predecessors, Jewish studies seemed increasingly unimportant in many homes. Ben Rosen's 1930 *Survey of the United Hebrew Schools of Detroit* praised the Detroit UHS as one of the best schools of its type and Bernard Isaacs as one of the most successful administrators. But only 20 percent of the 5,004 youngsters receiving some Jewish instruction went beyond the second grade and only 3 percent reached the high-school level, while many were not ready to respond to the heavy emphasis on Hebrew language. Students complained that they were tired after a full public school schedule and Jewish learning held no vital interest to them. Of the thirty-five UHS teachers, twenty-three were under thirty years old and salaries were low compared to other cities: the superintendent received six thousand dollars in 1930 and one of the finest teachers, three thousand dollars.[152]

Among the pioneer efforts at combined, structured schools, the UHS system included ten branches and over fifteen hundred students by the late 1930s. Its curriculum ran through kindergarten, seven years of ele-   251 mentary school, two years of junior high, and two years of high school. Students attended five days a week for one and a half hour sessions, and many came to prayer services on Saturday mornings. Its stated aims were to "prepare the child to live a Jewish life, to develop character through the profound riches of Jewish literature" and to perpetuate Jewish life "in its most meaningful sense."[153]

Three areas of emphasis composed the core of the curriculum: Hebrew language, Jewish history, and Jewish religion through study of the Bible, the prayer book, and "festivals, customs, ceremonials and institutions." These aims reflected what more traditional educators considered a "modern" approach. A more Orthodox teacher would likely have stated that a Jew must study Torah not for its social or psychological benefits, but because God commanded it. Students who could pay part or all of the tuition did so; those who could not pay were accepted without payment as Federation provided substantial subsidies that had risen to thirty six thousand dollars by 1939.[154]

Population shifts diminished the need for the UHS branches at the Delmar School in the Oakland district and the Parkside branch in the Fenkell district. In the new Dexter-Linwood area, UHS had opened in 1928 at Tuxedo and Holmur (later named after D. W. Simons), and at MacCullough public school on Buena Vista and Wildemere in 1935. UHS instilled a love of the land of Palestine from the start, and the 1931 graduation class book included a poem in honor of Lord Balfour by student Ethel Silverstein, entitled "A Friend in Need," along with several student essays in Hebrew.[155] The Kvutza Ivrit published an edition of the complete works of Aaron Markson in 1938. One of the most beloved of teachers, Markson was a man of considerable learning and wit whose lessons could mix Bible and Talmud with Shakespeare and baseball.

Although UHS tended to attract public interest for its innovations and for its Federation sponsorship, many synagogues, including Beth El and Shaarey Zedek, continued to operate their own schools. So, too, did the secular groups like the Workmen's Circle and the Sholem Aleichem Institute. For the latter group, the 1930s and 1940s proved to be their heyday, as their influence waxed along with the rise of Zionism and the adherence of the parent's generation to *Yiddishkeit*. Educators like Moishe Haar and Bercovich drew devoted audiences to lectures on Yiddish education and left lasting impressions on their students.

Morris Kutnick and Simon Richardson managed the Zionist Kadimah school on Twelfth Street and Lawton, and there was a Carmel School as well. Yeshivah Beth Yehudah, guided by Rabbi Ashinsky and later by Samuel Fine, offered longer class hours and a more Orthodox course of study than the UHS. About twenty-five of its alumni studied at yeshivahs or Talmudic schools in other cities in the late thirties.

252   All in all, few seriously considered the possibility of a unified school

system that might encompass all the varieties of Jewish education represented in Detroit. This diversity mirrored the questions about the sources and expressions of Jewish identity that may have lain beneath the surface but that consistently engaged the Jewish population of Detroit and often produced divisiveness and serious disagreement. What constituted Jewish education was a question that many Jews in Detroit recognized as part of the root of these differences. Despite these complexities, and perhaps more ominous, a 1939 survey showed that probably less than 30 percent of Detroit Jewish children were receiving any Jewish education whatsoever.[156]

Tishrei, the first autumn month, was designated by a group of concerned Jews—not all religious—as the annual Jewish Education Month. Among its strongest supporters were Judge Theodore Levin, Philip Slomovitz, Rabbis Morris Adler, and Leon Fram, who were joined by representatives from all the Jewish constituencies. Speeches in synagogues, newspaper articles, and even door-to-door solicitations aimed at bringing in more students and more money. Slomovitz's support as editor of the *Jewish Chronicle* and then of the *Jewish News* provided a critical fulcrum for the campaign to foster Jewish learning.[157]

World War II affected the UHS as it did every segment of Jewish life. Many teachers joined the armed services and some of the women teachers left Detroit to be with their husbands. Other women gave up teaching to take better-paying jobs in war industries. As changing neighborhoods slowed during the war, some of the schools stabilized. The Philadelphia-Byron school, for example, had been losing students but now seemed to stabilize. School buses still ran, but they made fewer stops. Rabbi Leizer Levin and Joseph Cashdan taught Talmud classes, and Meyer Mathis kept up publication of the Hebrew magazine *Hed Hakevutzah*. Abraham Twersky published a book of his own Yiddish poems under the title *Meschiach'n Antkegen,* which wove Hasidic traditions with hopes for tomorrow. As dedicated to Jewish study as ever, Bernard Isaacs wrote an essay in May 1943 in which he criticized schools that offered students too much song and dance and that sugarcoated the Torah without offering serious education.[158]

A 1945 Federation study by Israel B. Rappaport and Elias Picheny found that of about 25,830 Jewish children of school age in Detroit, some 5,200 were attending a Jewish school and about 62 percent of these were at a first-grade level or below.[159] Many of these children went to school only on Sundays. The dropout rate was alarmingly high; most teachers were foreign-born since young American Jews of higher ability and ambition seemed to turn to other professions. Neither the schools nor the cultural framework of Detroit had changed much in twenty years, claimed the survey. Rappaport and Picheny's recommendations included more central community encouragement for Jewish schooling and standardization of the requirements for teacher training. Adult programs were also encouraged.[160]

253

20

The Specter of Nazism

For Jews in Detroit, intimations of disaster in Europe cast their shadow in the 1930s. Ominous signs of Nazi persecution grew more insistent, demanding some sort of recognition and response. As early as July 1932, brown-shirted American supporters of Hitler marched in a parade in Washington, D.C. In January 1937, Harry H. Schaffer, commander of the Jewish War Veterans of the United States, urged a boycott of the prizefight between the American boxer, Benjamin Braddock, and the avowed Nazi, Max Schmeling.[161] In March of that same year, Fritz Kuhn, head of the German-American Bund, charged American Jews with sabotaging both the German and the American economies by boycotting German goods. He accused Jewish leaders, including Kurt Peiser, of costing the jobs of two million American workers and alleged that Jews were Soviet spies and communists.[162]

Yet no one foresaw the unprecedented implications of this newest wave of anti-Jewish activities. Rabbi Franklin, echoing sentiments of many American Jews in the 1930s, affirmed that "the Jews of Germany have suffered the tortures of hell, but it must not be forgotten that beyond counting also are the host of non-Jews who have incurred the displeasure of the despot." Still reflecting the attitudes of other Jewish leaders, Franklin, in a sermon on November 25, 1938, expressed his hope that new settlements of Jews in the United States would not be encouraged beyond the country's absorptive capacity. Such lack of foresight, he said, would lead to misunderstanding and conflict which should be avoided at all costs. This is "illustrated by what happened after the huge settlement of Eastern European Jews in this country following the Russian pogroms." New Jewish refugees must not displace native Americans. Rather, a better-organized program should be formed to find suitable places of refuge for the sufferers.[163]

In a similar vein, both national and Detroit organizations discouraged public protests against German policies. The American Jewish Committee and national leaders like Rabbi Stephen Wise opposed American Jewish Congress attempts to organize mass protest meetings, preferring, instead, to pursue a strategy of "quiet diplomacy."[164] In Detroit, even the protests organized by Rep. John Dingell against Polish anti-Semitism were not given organizational support by Federation.[165]

Leo Liffman was taken into "protective custody" and incarcerated in Buchenwald in order to protect him, the German police said, from the anger of the German people. Upon his release, he received his long-awaited American visa and came to Detroit. Yet another Detroiter, a veteran of the Austrian army, was arrested brutally that same month and imprisoned in Dachau.[166] It seemed light-years away from the announcement by Nate Shapero of new Cunningham's Drug Stores across Michigan; light-years, too, from the now familiar rhetoric of Father Coughlin, the programs at Littman's People's Theatre, or the urgent requests from Federation calling upon those who pledged to the campaign to honor their commitments so that local agencies could continue with their tasks.[167]

The Allied Jewish Campaign began its drive in April 1939, with expression of an acute awareness of the crisis in Europe and its reflections in the United States. "The *Most* We Can Give is the *Least* We Can Do!" appeared across the bottom of a solicitation letter signed by the campaign chairmen, Fred M. Butzel and Henry Wineman. The two-page folder that followed the letter bore a red background with bold black letters stating "Stand Up and FIGHT These Enemies of Democracy." It included reproductions of the front pages of such anti-Semitic newspapers as "The Free American," the official organ of the German-American Bund; Coughlin's *Social Justice,* with a photograph of Hitler at a Nazi rally with Neville Chamberlain superimposed over it; "The Canadian Nationalist," with its banner slogans "Boycott the Jews!" and "Always Buy Gentile" and swastikas prominently displayed. Superimposed on these coarse pictures were the headlines from some fifteen other anti-Semitic and/or anti-Roosevelt publications. The brochure's black-and-red back page called upon campaign contributors to "Join the Counter-Attack Against Anti-Semitism."[168]

Just as the "Stand Up and Fight" brochure chronicled domestic dangers, the May 7, 1939, "Allied Jewish Campaign News" emphasized European

255

developments. With photographs of Jews being humiliated in Memel, victims of a pogrom in Poland, and of the Hlinka Guards in Slovakia, it graphically depicted the rising threat to Jews in the world. Cochairmen Henry Wineman and Fred Butzel began their introductory statement with "six million Jews overseas face persecution, pauperization. Where, but to us, can they turn for help?" The campaign sought $790,000 to aid and support fifty two local, national and international agencies. Included in those were the UPA and the JDC. Names and photographs of the leaders of the Detroit campaign filled the remainder of the bulletin: prominently displayed was the Women's Project with its leaders Dora (Mrs. Joseph) Ehrlich, Mildred (Mrs. Joseph) Welt, and Celia (Mrs. Hyman) Broder. President of Federation, Abraham Srere, acknowledged the need to increase support overseas, but he reminded his constituents that "there still remain many essential services that we must maintain through our Jewish resources as part of the pattern of American philanthropy." Campaign heads Simon Shetzer, Gus Newman, Irv Blumberg, and Joseph Ehrlich, as well as precampaign planners like Melville Welt, Clarence Enggass, Nate Shapero, Mr. and Mrs. Harold Allen, Maurice Aronsson, Nathaniel Goldstick, Louis Blumberg, Mr. and Mrs. Leo Butzel, Mrs. Wineman, Leonard Simons, and Lawrence J. Michelson were listed with the tasks of each of their committees. Rabbi Leon Fram headed the Speakers' Bureau. Included too were separate articles about the UPA and the JDC and the National Coordinating Committee Fund, all agencies aiding the rescue of Jewish refugees from Europe.[169] It seemed that the campaign began in earnest—aware of the perils of the times—four months before the German invasion of Poland ushered in World War II.

With the advent of the war in Europe, Jews in Detroit reflected the sentiments of other American-Jewish communities: they looked to the reconstruction of Europe, "when the shattered nations begin to rebuild after the war."[170] The General Assembly of the Council of Jewish Federations held its annual meeting in Detroit in January 1940. That conference concluded with the election of Henry Wineman as vice-president and with Fred Butzel elected to the national board. Dr. Nahum Goldman's closing statement to the group urged Jewish agencies to accept the responsibility of aiding Europe's Jews *after* the war. And in Detroit, a chapter of the National Conference of Christians and Jews was initiated in April 1940 at the newly formed Detroit Council of Catholics, Jews and Protestants. Among the founding members were Leo M. Butzel, Rabbi Franklin, Charles Rubiner, and Simon Shetzer.[171]

Throughout 1940 and 1941, Sobeloff continued to report on the activities of the Joint Distribution Committee.[172] When Rabbi Abba Hillel Silver and Jonah B. Wise, national chairmen of the United Jewish Appeal, announced at the end of 1940 that the Joint Distribution Committee, United Palestine Appeal, and NRS (National Refugee Service) would conduct separate campaigns from the UJA, Sobeloff convinced the Detroit board to retain one campaign and continue to allot funds to the three agencies through the budget committee of the Federation.[173]

Local anti-Semitism, too, became an issue in 1941. Surveys conducted by the federal government between 1940 and 1941 revealed that anti-Semitism had increased sharply after the attack on Pearl Harbor. Mimeographed anti-Jewish literature, jokes, rumors, and accusations were distributed regularly in factories, war plants, and the lobbies of post offices. Jews were accused of starting labor problems, aggravating racial tensions, starting the war, and exploiting the war economy. "I think Hitler was right as far as the Jewish question," replied one respondent to a survey; "this is a Jew war," stated another; "[the Jews] are forcing Gentiles out of work," was a common refrain, along with allegations that Jews were dirty, spoke poor English, and that if Roosevelt did not send them back to Europe after the war "the Jews will be running our country."[174]

Delegates from different organizations, in particular the Jewish Community Council, insistently raised the issue of rising anti-Semitism and missionary activities in the Twelfth Street neighborhood. After considerable discussion, Mrs. Samuel Glowgower, president of the Jewish Center, was appointed chair of a committee to investigate the problems not only of anti-Semitism, but of recreational activities, juvenile delinquency, and Jewish education.[175] The B'nai B'rith sought to unify American Jewry by creating the Anti-Defamation League, which became active in Detroit also with assistance from the Council.[176]

Yet, despite general agreement among the Jewish leadership and the majority of Jews in Detroit that anti-Semitism appeared to be escalating, individual Jews tended to deny the problem and think that their particular situation remained unique. "Other" Jews may need the ADL or the defenses of the Council, but many avoided any organized group help. Some denied the existence of anti-Semitism. Some German Jews frequently identified anti-Jewish prejudice as an affliction of East European Jews. Others simply denied any effect of discrimination or prejudice on their lives. Father Coughlin and Gerald L. K. Smith preached racial anti-Semitism, factories seethed with anti-Jewish hatred, other ethnic groups ridiculed and maligned them, and many of Detroit's Jews attributed all that to scapegoating, misunderstandings, or rumors. If Coughlin frightened people, all they had to do was turn off their radios; if malicious pamphlets and leaflets offended people, they simply ignored them. More difficult, perhaps, was the plight of the Jewish factory workers who dealt with the tensions each day. In one war plant, some workers pinned a sign that said "I am a Jew" on one Jewish worker's back. No one told him about it, and he wore the sign most of the day. Descriptions of prejudicial harassment in factories were legion in the 1940s.[177]

These intermittently pressing concerns seemed to return regularly. They   257 resurfaced after some years had passed in the new neighborhoods, but were clearly aggravated by the war. They caused deep apprehensions among some Jewish leaders. Yet the realm of such educational, moral, or cultural apprehensions now belonged to the Council. Some Detroiters who had joint membership recall feelings akin to relief within the Federation agencies that this assignment of defense now rested with Council or the ADL. Jewish identity, when it went beyond combating anti-Semitism, rescuing Europe's victims, or raising money to support the philanthropic agencies, still seemed beyond the Federation pale. Offering moral support and occasional, minimal funds to organizations like the League for Human Rights (headed by Rabbi Leon Fram until its dissolution in 1940) seemed to suffice. Principal attention remained elsewhere, and the sentiment continued that these concerns with liberal or moral causes were secondary.

21

World War II

America's involvement in World War II altered the structure and purpose of the mainstream Jewish organizations in Detroit and all over the country. Words like *genocide* and *holocaust* had not yet been coined in 1941. America was attacked, and Germany and Japan had declared war, thereby resolving American dilemmas over neutrality. The Jews of Europe, despite the newspaper reports that delineated anti-Jewish actions, assumed ancillary importance to the war effort—even for most American Jews. Most Detroit Jews confronted the war as Americans first and responded patriotically. Anxieties about persecutions in Europe receded as American-Jewish young men went off to war.

As Jews in the Diaspora had for millennia, Detroiters contributed to the war effort with their work, their possessions, and their lives as they became involved in every part of the fighting and on the home front as well. Their first casualties came at Pearl Harbor, as Harold Shiffman went down with the *Arizona*. Sam Cohen got married on December 7, 1941, within hours of the attack on Pearl Harbor. Before long, he, too, was in the army and eventually fell wounded at Monte Cassino. The North End Clinic reduced its staff as dozens of Jewish doctors joined the armed forces. The Hebrew schools absorbed the shortage of trained personnel as their teachers went off to fight. The *Jewish News* weekly reported the status of Detroit Jewish servicemen, including the growing list of casualties. Included among those in active service were sixty members of Young Israel and 205 members of the Workmen's Circle by June 1944.[178]

New recruits generally were sent for basic training to military bases in the United States. Pvt. Louis Thav wrote home from Camp Forrest, Tennessee, that he woke up at five every morning to put on his phylacteries and pray. Sometimes a visiting rabbi came to conduct services on Friday night. Thav was sent on to fight in the Pacific shortly afterward. Dr. Aubrey Goldman was in England by the end of 1942. His brother, Dr. Perry Goldman, was still in California awaiting orders. Hank Greenberg's first term of service ended late in 1941, but after Pearl Harbor, the big first baseman re-enlisted. In addition to his time in battle, Greenberg also played on service baseball teams. Jeremiah Haggai, a UHS graduate and son of a UHS teacher, had settled in Palestine and enlisted with the Palestine Buffs of the British Army.

Some of the major battles of the Pacific—Midway, the Coral Sea, the Philippines—raged in 1942 as the bitter island fighting began. Sid Wolf was listed as missing in action early in that year. A year later, his family received word that he was a prisoner of the Japanese. Pvt. Sanford Blau wrote to his family from a POW camp in the Philippines. Maj. Max Weil, reported missing in action in May 1942, was also reported a Japanese prisoner a year later. He had brought down five planes with a machine gun during the fighting at Bataan. Ruben Iden was killed at Guadalcanal.

Detroit families that had men at the front awaited the arrival of the daily mail with trepidation. One black mailman would slice open important-looking envelopes on Saturdays for Orthodox Jews on his route so that they would not have to wait until nightfall to open them.

Detroit Jews participated in every theater of the war. Both Pvt. Irving Farber and Pvt. Monte Levitt saw President Roosevelt at the Casablanca Conference in 1943. Levitt was part of the president's honor guard during his stop in Casablanca in 1944. Dr. Aubrey Goldman was decorated for his work at Anzio, and his brother Perry was honored for his work fighting in the Black Sea. Jewish casualties in Europe included Herman Kasoff, who was wounded twice in Italy, and Pvt. Zalman Lopata, who had come to the United States from Poland in 1938, lost a leg at Anzio. In Northern Europe, the first casualties were Air Force men. Lt. Arthur Broat was wounded in an air battle; Lt. Marvin Schlossberg (later to become television comic weatherman Sonny Eliot) was reported missing in action over Germany after a raid on February 24, 1944. Two months later, he was reported a prisoner. Curiously, Schlossberg told his captors that he was of German background, fearing that they would single him out for harsh treatment if they knew he was Jewish. He was, in fact, treated no worse than the

others and learned after the war that on his POW papers had been written
the word *Jude*.

There were dangers other than enemy bullets and bombs. Pvt. Jay Handelsman contracted malaria; Lt. Nathan Kristall, shot down by a Japanese Zero over Truk, was endangered by sharks until rescued by a U.S. Navy flying boat. As the war intensified after D Day on June 6, 1944, the tragic list of those who lost their lives lengthened. Some of those losses were particularly poignant, like that of Flight Officer Henry Morris, who died on July 17, 1944, in France, the day after his engagement had been announced in the *Bulletin* of Temple Beth El. Ben Zion Moldawsky, "a gentle, scholarly man blessed with a melodious voice," who often led services at the Muirland Synagogue, lost one son, Chaim, in a plane crash and then a second son, Sol, was killed in action in Italy. Sigmund Moritz had escaped from Europe to America in 1940, graduated high school with honors in 1943 and returned to fight in France in 1944. He died there that same year.

As the casualty lists brought anguish to Jews in Detroit, so, too, did the articles in the *Jewish News* delineating the murder of Europe's Jews. Articles in the Anglo-American papers tended to be small and unobtrusive. Typical of this pattern, one reported the address to the Detroit Jewish Labor Committee by Magistrate Charles Solomon of the Municipal Court of New York; he declared that two million Jews had already died and five million more needed rescue. But banner headlines in the Yiddish and Anglo-Jewish papers fairly screamed the catastrophe: "Polish Jews Send Frantic Appeal to World for Food"; "Nazis Slaughter 13,000 Jews in Lwow; Report 1500 More Died in Radom of Starvation"; "7300 Greek Jews Dead of Starvation Under Nazi Rule"; "Nazis Exterminate Jews in 5 Polish Towns."[179] By April 4, 1943, Jewish Sunday schools closed so their students could attend a "Day of Sorrow" memorial ceremony at Shaarey Zedek. At that ceremony, those attending heard Rabbis Morris Adler and Leon Fram deliver moving speeches beneath the United Nations banner and the American flag.[180] The Joint Distribution Committee and the United Palestine Appeal continued their work, although thwarted by the war, and in September 1943, the Orthodox Detroit Committee for Vaad Hahatzulah appealed to the *landsmanshaftn* and fraternal organizations for money to aid five hundred Jews who had taken refuge in Shanghai and the several thousand others in Siberia and Asiatic Russia.[181]

Detroit Jews, like those all over the United States, were torn between the sorrow over the catastrophe befalling their kinsmen in Europe and the dangers to their own sons now engaged in the war. Indifference or an inability to respond to the plight of Europe's Jews may be explained, to some extent, by these dual worries. Many Detroit Jews were decorated for heroism. Sgt. Louis Miller's patrol wiped out an enemy unit of two hundred in Italy. Pvt. Benno Levi won a Silver Star at Guam. As his unit was strafed mistakenly by American planes, Levi stood up and waved the divisional flag until the planes realized their error and flew off. Among the many others was Sgt. Louis Kaminsky, who had flown seventy two missions in the South Pacific by the end of 1943 and had earned a Distinguished Flying Cross, a Purple Heart, and an Air Medal with an Oak Leaf Cluster. Capt. William J. Weinstein of the United States Marine Corps served as a company commanding officer in the Fourth Marine Division in the battles of Roi-Namur, Saipan, Tinian, and Iwo Jima. He received a Bronze Star Medal with Combat "V," the Purple Heart, and the Presidential unit citation with one bronze star. Weinstein would go on to become a major general in the Marine Corps Reserves as well as a successful attorney and director of the Detroit Bar Association.[182] Twenty-six-year-old Lt. Raymond Zussman had joined the army and was serving in France. In the Rhine Valley, in September 1944, handling a carbine and later a submachine gun, he killed eighteen German soldiers and captured another ninety two. He was awarded a Congressional Medal of Honor. The medal was awarded posthumously: Lieutenant Zussman was killed in battle only days after his extraordinary exploits.[183]

Some Jewish servicemen who were captured by the Germans were less fortunate than Lieutenant Schlossberg and reported stories of beatings and tortures. Marvin Tamaroff, for example, returned from captivity after some harrowing experiences, believing that his religious faith had been essential to his survival. Soldiers reported missing in action were sometimes found when the German POW camps were liberated by advancing Allied forces. The last Detroit Jewish casualty was Ens. Eugene Mandelberg, officially reported missing in action the day after VJ Day in a battle with Japanese planes. Reports of others finally confirmed as dead continued to come to families in Detroit for many months after the fighting had ended. More than 180 Detroit Jews lost their lives in the war. Between nine and ten thousand of Detroit's nearly ninety thousand Jews served in the armed forces.[184] Some families sent large numbers off to war, like the Nichamins of whom thirty four members were in service.

Detroit Jewish women also served in various branches of the military and more were active in the United Service Organization (USO). Caroline and Rosalie Brown, daughters of David A. Brown, served in the WAVES and in the Red Cross, respectively. About ten Detroiters served as military chaplains, including Rabbi Morris Adler, who was stationed in the Far East. Rabbi Albert Gordon conducted a Passover seder for one thousand men in New Guinea in 1944, and Chaplain Melvyn Sands presided at a seder in India. The following year, Gordon was at a seder for three thousand in Manila.

On the home front, Jews in Detroit immersed themselves in the war effort as zealously as those who fought in the field. The Jewish Community
Center, enlarged and remodeled in 1939 after Mrs. Aaron DeRoy's generous

gift of $190,000, served as the major USO lounge in Detroit. Under the guidance of Herman Jacobs after 1936, and with dedicated assistance from such volunteers as Hyman C. Broder, Morris Garvett, Mrs. Samuel Glowgower, Henry Meyers, Meyer Prentis, and Charles and Samuel Rubiner, the Center became the focus of cultural and recreational activities not only for the Jewish community, but for the general community during the war.[185]

In 1940 the Detroit Army and Navy Committee of the Jewish Welfare Board was organized, with Henry Meyers serving as first chairman. A prominent lawyer active in both the Jewish and non-Jewish realms, Meyers, president of the Jewish Community Center, was succeeded as chair of the Army and Navy Committee by Samuel Rubiner upon accepting the leadership of the entire Detroit USO program. Working closely with the State Army and Navy Committee chaired by Fred Butzel, the USO coordinated activities of all Jewish soldiers stationed in Michigan. A wide variety of recreational functions—bagel and lox brunches, dances, sports events, and regular evenings in the USO lounge on the second floor of the Center— were ceaselessly arranged by volunteer hostesses supervised by Mrs. Golda Krolik. Some five hundred young women were trained under the direction of Mrs. Samuel Glowgower and Mrs. Joseph D. Welt. Several thousand non-Jewish servicemen enjoyed their initial organized social experiences as a result of the USO and Army and Navy Committee. The joint committees also provided psychological counseling, prayer books, and occasional financial assistance.[186]

Synagogues participated in national days of prayer, like the one declared by President Roosevelt on December 31, 1943. Thousands jammed the synagogues also on D Day, and Saturday, June 10 was set aside as a day of special prayer and abstention from work.[187] Shaarey Zedek youngsters planted a victory garden on a vacant piece of land near the synagogue. Children saved scrap metals. Kosher butchers agreed to close on Fridays to help reduce meat consumption. Ben Pupko and others like him closed their businesses early Tuesday through Friday so that they could work in civil-defense units.

Jewish servicemen stationed in the Detroit area were invited to Passover seders. In 1943 Rabbi Glazer, of Temple Beth El, was able to get furloughs extended for several servicemen who were scheduled to rejoin their units right before Rosh Hashana. At the Michigan Synagogue Conference in August 1942, Rabbi Hershman, of Shaarey Zedek, outlined measures to be taken by synagogues in case of air attack during the crowded High Holiday services coming in September. The following year, the Jewish Community Center sponsored a demonstration of how to can the fruits and vegetables that people were growing in their victory gardens.[188] On September 29, 1944, the *Jewish News* reported that Chaplain Martin Perley was called to Fort Custer to minister to twenty Jews who had been taken prisoner while serving in the German army. All but one were classified by German law as *Mischlinge,* or of partial Jewish ancestry, and thus had been eligible to fight in the war.[189]

Prominent Jewish leaders ardently participated in the national War Chest campaign, raising substantial amounts of money for the war effort. Between 1942 and 1945 the War Chest supplanted the Allied Jewish Campaign, and leading fund-raisers like Isidore Sobeloff devoted themselves to the war effort.[190] (Sobeloff was assigned to the War Chest drive in New York.) As chairman of the Wayne County Retail War Savings Committee, Nate Shapero headed the war bond campaign; businesses like Boesky's Restaurant took out full-page ads for war bonds; and Jewish community leaders juggled their energies between Detroit and national campaigns and the war-related rescue of Jews in Europe.[191]

Such intense involvement in the war effort manifested a traditional public patriotism. In March 1943, the *Jewish News* began a "war records bureau" to record the "devotion of [Jewish] American soldiers, sailors and marines."[192] That sentiment echoed the Jews' dedication to defending their countries throughout the Diaspora—resonating with statements of French and German Jews after the Franco-Prussian War and World War I, and with statements by American Jews dating back to the American Revolution. No one could doubt the national identity of Jews in the United States. If World War II presented Jews with a cataclysmic destruction in Europe, it afforded American Jews another opportunity to verify their dedicated Americanism. Yet in the midst of a conflict so clearly defined in terms of freedom and good and evil, native American anti-Semites continued to flourish. American racism identified itself as patriotic and even as "Aryan," although that rhetoric faded after December 7, 1941.

22

The Detroit Riots

Government interviewers found that a significant proportion of those responding to a government survey expressed "bitter resentment toward minority groups, especially Jews." By 1943, almost one-fifth of Detroit respondents to that poll voiced anti-Semitism that revealed the persistence of anti-Jewish stereotypes. Jews, they said, were "draft dodgers" and "economic exploiters," taking advantage of the war by making excessive profits. The roots of such opinions did not lay in religious prejudice so much as in cultural, social, and economic stereotypes. A significant majority of southern whites held equal animosity for blacks and Jews and even boycotted Jewish stores. Many Jews in Detroit attributed these hostile opinions to the rise of Nazism and the attention it received in the newspapers. Nevertheless, with the escalating racism and anti-Jewish rhetoric, Jewish concerns in Detroit once again were both foreign and domestic.[193]

Ironically, Jewish respondents displayed the least prejudice of any racial or ethnic group surveyed.[194] In the increasingly tense social atmosphere of Detroit, Jewish Detroiters encountered still another crisis alongside and within the European and domestic ones. Between the attack on Pearl Harbor on December 7, 1941, and June 1943, over 350,000 people flocked to   265

Detroit seeking jobs. Ford led the way, as he had done in World War I, to show the world how American industry responded to the challenge of war.[195] Albert Kahn designed for Ford the largest of his buildings in order to mass-produce B-24 bombers. The predictable concomitant of the boom in employment and the massive immigration was an equally massive housing emergency.[196]

Once again, as in the 1920s, southern workers, black and white, poured into the south and east sides of the city, this time creating a racial powder keg. According to government surveys, southern whites in Detroit during the 1920s clung to anti-black and anti-Jewish prejudices, purveying stereotypes until they were widespread among even middle-class, northern whites in Detroit. Indeed, it appears that the only group to remain immune to anti-black sentiment was the Jews of Detroit.[197]

Although most of Detroit's eighty-five thousand Jews had moved to what some called the "Herring Belt" in the Twelfth Street and Dexter neighborhoods, many Jewish merchants maintained their businesses in the Hastings Street area, now almost exclusively black and known as "Paradise Valley." Jews, then, still owned many of the neighborhood's groceries, pawnshops, liquor stores, second-hand shops, low-cost clothing stores, and cleaners.[198]

Talk of potential black-white conflict grew between 1938 and 1941. Blacks seemed neutral toward Jews, just as Jews had exhibited the least amount of anti-black feeling. Indeed, in the areas bordering Paradise Valley, along Warren Avenue, for example, Jewish businesses were often the only ones allowing black customers.[199] (Most Jews nevertheless preferred separate residential neighborhoods; while they empathized with a persecuted minority, stereotypes still lingered.) Jewish entrepreneurs were the only white presence in the poorest black sections. This situation created ambiguous results: not only did blacks have contact with Jews, they also competed with them and, since most virulent racists like the KKK did not own businesses or would not permit blacks, an economic bitterness emerged.[200]

Detroit's city officials recognized this growing tension and took remedial steps to address a potential explosion. Jews immediately involved themselves, voluntarily and by official invitation, in some of those steps. In September 1941, the Committee on Intercultural Understanding was established "to plan and direct a state-wide program" for introducing black history and culture into school curricula. Rabbi Fram, as a principal member of that committee, urged haste in taking action rather than gradual discussions. In 1942, largely at his instigation, the committee issued a bulletin called "Toward Better Understanding and Greater Unity."[201] In May 1942, Mayor Edward Jeffries appointed a fact-finding committee to investigate discrimination in municipal services; Fred Butzel served on that committee.[202] Yet, aside from distributing the bulletin on unity, no action ensued and conditions only worsened. Some Jews, like Rabbi Fram and Rabbi Adler of Shaarey Zedek, expressed deep concerns about the blatant racist prejudices that riddled Detroit, and each of them sermonized to their congregations about it while serving on nondenominational city committees.[203]

In 1942, desperate to ease the terrible housing conditions, the city announced plans for a project for blacks. The Soujourner Truth Homes would open in Hamtramck, the Polish enclave in Detroit. Led by Rep. Rudolph G. Tenerowicz, the Poles voiced outraged opposition. The project was then declared to be white housing. On February 2, after threats of black marches on Washington, the project was reclassified as "Negro." Picketing and riots by affronted Poles followed, and a cross was burned near the project site. Father Coughlin now joined forces with the anti-Catholic KKK to oppose Sojourner Truth Homes.[204]

Racism seeped into every aspect of Detroit life. It crept into unions, factories, and businesses, and was almost tangible on the streets. Fights broke out in automobile factories when such statements as "better to let Hitler and Hirohito win than to work next to a nigger!" defied the union rules for upgrading workers on equal opportunity bases. Its problems compounded by the desperate competition for decent housing, Detroiit erupted in minor skirmishes between blacks and whites on Belle Isle. Feelings between Poles and blacks were especially volatile.[205]

Mayor Jeffries's office received regular calls blaming "the Jews" for instigating actions among the black community. Indeed, the mayor, the Wayne County prosecutor, and others attacked leaders of the NAACP as liberal instigators and continually praised the police for their conduct in handling the violent outbursts. The NAACP in Detroit, ironically, boasted one of the strongest branches in the United States because of its support by union leaders like the Reuther brothers, urban-educated blacks, and liberal Jews. It was housed in Albert Kahn's former mansion on Mack Avenue.[206]

Removed from the center of the scene in the evenings, at home in the Twelfth Street or Dexter neighborhoods, Jewish business owners seemed disconnected from the impending disasters.[207] Some Jews, however, threw themselves into the fray. Jack Raskin led the movement for a biracial Sojourner Truth Citizens' Committee. He was the lone white founding member and also served as the head of the Civil Rights Federation (accused of being a communist front). Raskin was able to get Rabbi Fram, Herman Jacobs, of the Jewish Community Center, and Fred Butzel, who already belonged to the board of the Urban League, to sign the earliest petitions in support of a black Sojourner Truth project. They did this despite their expressed fears of anti-Semitism. Raskin and Fram continued to actively speak out, maintaining the moral and often financial support of other Jews who preferred to keep a lower profile than these two.[208]

Samuel Lieberman, a merchant in Paradise Valley, gave the committee "considerable financial assistance," and in January 1941, he led the founding of the East Side Merchants Association, which initiated brotherhood dinners at the Lucy Thurman YWCA and contributed heavily to the Citizens Committee. They intended to ease tensions and to counter stereotypes by becoming involved in community development.[209] Less publicly involved in racial disputes, Rabbi Franklin nevertheless expressed his concerns over the intensification of anti-Jewish sentiment among blacks and met with five of those merchants to discuss the situation. At his suggestion, the Merchants Association sponsored scholarships for black and Jewish graduate students to study various aspects of black-Jewish relations in Detroit. This finally produced a study jointly sponsored by the Jewish Community Council and the NAACP: *Some Aspects of Negro-Jewish Relationships in Detroit, Michigan,* by Eleanor Wolf, Alvin Loving, and Donald C. Marsh. Yet the philanthropy of the association often seemed offset by black perceptions of Jewish slum landlords and economic exploitation by Jewish merchants. At the association's prodding, and as part of the effort to break such stereotypes, the organizational meeting for the Inter-Racial Council with the Detroit Roundtable of Catholics, Jews and Protestants took place at Shaarey Zedek.[210]

Despite such efforts, on Sunday, June 20, 1943, in ninety-degree heat, the bloodiest and most relentless race riots the country had seen in the twentieth century erupted in Detroit. Provoked by rumors of a "war" on Belle Isle, angry blacks burst onto Hastings Street and commenced to attack whites and to smash store windows. The rioting continued for almost three days and resulted in the deaths of nine whites and twenty-five blacks. At Governor Harry Kelly's urgent request, President Roosevelt dispatched 350 military police to the city. In the midst of the crisis, the mayor's office received numerous calls claiming that "those Jews on Joy Road are ruining the niggers and the town with them."[211]

The Detroit *Jewish News* reported numerous meetings canceled because of the state of emergency declared by the governor. "The outrageous riots," it said, had destroyed property and ruined hundreds of Jewish merchants as stores on Hastings, Oakland, and Westminster were looted and burned. A meeting of merchants was scheduled for the Beth Yehudah Synagogue on June 27, and an interracial commission had already been formed by the Detroit Council of Churches. The commission included Rabbis Adler, Franklin, and Glazer as well as Fred Butzel. Butzel was also one of twelve Detroiters appointed by the mayor to the Race Relations Committee, having been named to a similar commission in 1926.[212]

In New York City, the Central Conference of American Rabbis called for a probe of the Detroit riots. They perceived the violence as "the spirit of Hitlerism" which had "achieved a triumph on American soil." They called for "men of good will, white and Negro, to seek the roots of the evils and injustices" of these events. They declared, too, that they stood for "justice to the Negro . . . the chief victim of these un-American riots." Finally, they called upon "all Americans to eschew all racial violence and hate."

268

From their point of view, which was echoed by some voices of Jewish Detroiters, "subversive" elements had fomented the riots.[213]

The riot of 1943 stunned the city, but especially Jews—the least-prejudiced group in Detroit. As it startled unsuspecting, complacent white Detroiters, the event seemed to evoke hostility to blacks. Yet it also stimulated the increased participation of many Jewish leaders in interracial activities. Rabbis Adler, Glazer, and Fram would take the public lead in these activities, usually in conjunction with the Jewish Community Council. Several Council members traced that organization's involvement in civil rights back to the riot. Without question, it caused a business exodus to other areas— the number of Jewish merchants on Twelfth Street and Dexter increased. The riot, then, seemed to have drawn blacks and Jews together in institutional connections but had driven them apart in social and economic relations. It served as a disturbing reminder of anti-Semitism in a time of war and as a harbinger of what would come some twenty-four years later.

23

Zionism: Toward Consensus

World War II effected profound changes in attitudes regarding Palestine. The growth of Zionism had tended to further divide an already divided Jewish population in the United States. Unable to respond to crises overseas in the 1920s and throughout the 1930s, the question of one voice and joint action loomed larger than ever in the 1940s. In principle, a socialist orientation had dominated the pro-Zionist ranks in Detroit. That fact had antagonized "uptown" Jews, in particular many Reform Jews and also many Orthodox Jews. Many Jewish socialists and leftists eschewed Zionism because of their belief that the roots of anti-Semitism lay in class antagonism and not in national identity.[214] The war compounded and confused many of these already complex issues and touched off a variety of sometimes surprising responses.

Perhaps the most startling response came from the founding of the Council for American Judaism by a group of Reform rabbis in November 1942 in Philadelphia. They had originally convened in Atlantic City in June 1942 but did not announce the birth of the organization until almost six months later. Originally comprised of ninety Reform rabbis who had broken away from the Central Council of Reform Rabbis, the anti-Zionism group claimed

270

to reject Zionism because of its "secular" and "irreligious" nature. Before announcing its creation, the group had enlisted support from Orthodox rabbis and prominent Jews in New York and Philadelphia. It purportedly had close access to Secretary of State Cordell Hull's office, and its representatives had already made inroads with Secretary of the Interior Harold Ickes.[215] By January 1943, the council had drawn the condemnation of Rabbi Louis Levitsky, head of the Rabbinical Assembly of America, the Conservative rabbis organization.[216]

Rabbi Leo Franklin stood among the most renowned founders of the Council for American Judaism. His action put Detroit into an uproar. His successor, Rabbi B. Benedict Glazer (who had been hired instead of Franklin's former assistant, Rabbi Fram), openly proclaimed his pro-Zionist positions. Reform Jews in Detroit, then, were divided regarding Palestine, despite the powerful voice of one of their most venerable leaders. Franklin not only had disapproved of some of the opinions voiced by Zionist leaders like Rabbi Stephen Wise, but also complained about the infiltration of Zionist ideas into Hebrew Union College classrooms. Like his fellow Council for American Judaism members, Franklin believed that a Zionist state of Israel would be disastrous for the Jews "who have no genius for self government." Consistent with earlier statements about Judaism in America, Franklin believed that "the Jewish mission is a religious one. The American way and the ideal of religion at its best are the same." He reprised the motif of a previous confrontation with Philip Slomovitz in 1938, when the rabbi had joined with thirty-five other prominent Jewish religious leaders to reject a Jewish unity plan proposed by Rabbi Stephen Wise and the American Jewish Congress. Franklin insisted that if he had thought it fit for one organization to speak on behalf of American Jews, he "would have chosen a synagogue."[217]

Such severe opposition erupted in response to Zionism's growing support and strength in the late 1930s and 1940s. That support came from non-Jews as well as Jews in the United States. Dr. S. Ralph Harlow, chairman of the department of religion at Smith College, addressed the Flint Hadassah in January 1942. He called the colonization of Palestine by Jews a "miracle." He was baffled, he said, by any opposition to Zionism, but especially baffled by Jewish opposition: "Is there to be no place but an ocean grave or a concentration camp, no way of life but only disease and suffering and death for countless little children . . . mothers . . . fathers in this world of tomorrow?" He concluded by affirming that Arabs and Jews were friendly and would work out a satisfactory understanding "if permitted."[218]

In the midst of mounting reports of the annihilation of European Jewry, and at the same time as the Council for American Judaism was being founded, the U.S. Congress reaffirmed the promise of the "restoration of the Jewish national home" as it signed a declaration on the occasion of the twenty-fifth anniversary of the Balfour Declaration. The signers included Michigan senators Prentiss M. Brown and Arthur H. Vandenberg and Representatives Bradley, Dingell, Engel, Hook, Konkman, Woodruff, and even the Hamtramck congressman who had been elected in part on anti-Semitic slogans, Rudolph G. Tenerowicz.[219] And on the eve of the Bermuda Conference that opened on April 19, 1943—the day the Warsaw Ghetto Rebellion began— ostensibly to alleviate the "refugee question," the Zionist Organization of America took out a full-page ad in the *Jewish News* reminding the Anglo-American delegates of Winston Churchill's pledge of support in 1939 and demanding that "the doors of Palestine must be opened."[220] Despite such pressures, and despite Jewish requests for a representative voice at the conference, the Bermuda Conference accomplished nothing. By April 30, the *Jewish News* reported that the Bermuda Conference had doomed large-scale rescue for Jewish refugees. It did, however, reveal the depth of support for Zionism in America.[221]

The Jewish National Fund conducted its campaigns more successfully in Detroit than in most other cities. This may be attributed to the dynamic leadership of Detroit Jews, most notably Morris Schaver, Joseph Chaggai, Rabbi Morris Adler, Joseph Ehrlich, Abraham Srere, Henry Wineman, Fred Butzel, and Rabbi Fram. Mayor Jeffries, on the occasion of the JNF Conference at the Book Cadillac in December 1942, declared a JNF Sabbath in Detroit to indicate his own support for the movement.[222]

Among Detroit's religious leaders, Rabbi Leon Fram consistently voiced his pro-Zionist opinions and became, along with Rabbi Adler, a leading Zionist spokesman on both the Jewish Community Council and Federation boards. In 1938, the Dies Committee on Subversive Activities in Detroit had accused Rabbi Fram of acting as a "red liaison" through various Jewish organizations. The rabbi, of course, denied any affiliation with communist groups and attacked the Dies Committee for equating resisting fascism with supporting communism.[223] But Fram's outspoken support of civil and human-rights causes, his ties with the Jewish Labor Committee, the Histadrut, and other liberal organizatioons, seemed to erode his chances to succeed Rabbi Franklin when, after forty-two years of service to Temple Beth El, Franklin retired. Despite the growing pro-Zionist sentiment among some members of Beth El, the majority still seemed to oppose the movement, and most were chagrined at Fram's outspoken stand on that and other issues. There seemed to be no love lost between Franklin and his assistant.

Thus in 1941, the board of Beth El chose Rabbi B. Benedict Glazer from New York. A recognized scholar and intellectual, Glazer announced at his installation that his obligations would be to "the congregation, the Jewish community as a whole, and the American community." While this seemed to echo Franklin's farewell statement, in which he reflected on the "two major goals" of his ministry: "to maintain and keep the self respect of [my] own people" and to "establish a better understanding between Jew and non-Jew," Glazer made no bones about his own pro-Zionist convictions.[224] Fram's group, which included several prominent members of the congregation, broke away from Beth El and soon formed Temple Israel, Detroit's second Reform temple. Among those who bolted was Morris Garvett, the much-admired and respected president of Beth El. He became the first president of Temple Israel.

Although some of its most prominent patrons bore religious titles, Zionism in Detroit drew its major backing from nonreligious groups like the *landsmanshaftn,* the Workmen's Circle, the Sholem Aleichem Institute, and other secular groups. Without question Zionism in the 1930s and 1940s meant Labor Zionism to most Jews. In Detroit, the term "Labor Zionism" immediately evoked the name of Morris Schaver. He had been elected by the Poale Zion as a representative to the World Zionist Congress in Zurich in 1937; since 1929 he had led the Detroit Gewerkschaften drive for Histadrut; in 1943, the drive, headed by Schaver for the thirteenth time, raised over fifty-thousand dollars for the Jewish National Labor Committee of Palestine.[225] The announcement of that success came at a concert given at the Deroit Institute of Arts, where the audience honored "the memory of the fallen martyrs in Nazi-occupied Europe by one minute of silence." Emma Schaver, accompanied by Rebecca Frohman, was "received with tremendous applause."[226]

The movement owed much of its achievement in Detroit to Schaver. His comrades in the Labor Zionist movement contributed energetically if not as zealously as he. In April 1940, seven hundred members from six branches of the Jewish National Workers' Alliance, the Farband, held a convention at the Statler Hotel. Joseph Chaggai headed the convention committee and the members received the new six-point program of the organization which explained that it would pledge itself to: a "positive approach" to Jewish life and culture; "the rehabilitation and productivization of Jewish life"; the "democratization" of Jewish communal life; the establishment of a Jewish national homeland in Palestine "on the basis of Jewish labor"; the organization of labor "for the protection of its economic interests and . . . for the ultimate reshaping of our social order"; the "linking of the struggle of Jewish emancipation with the general struggle for a more equitable and harmonious world."[227] The program reflected the constitution of Histadrut and struck familiar chords with the founding statements of the Jewish Community Council.

By 1943 Labor Zionists no longer stood alone in support of Zionism. On April 28, Congregation Shaarey Zedek passed a strongly worded resolution at its annual meeting that identified itself as a congregation in support of the Zionist movement. The resolution called upon all members to join the Zionist Organization of America (ZOA) or some other Zionist body; it passed unanimously at the urging of Lawrence Crohn, Rabbi Adler, and Abraham

273

Cooper, president of the ZOA and a member of the congregation. Six hundred of Shaarey Zedek's 812 members were already affiliated Zionists. According to the resolution, the congregation was "moved by a sense of duty and solemn responsibility in this tragic hour in the life of our people." Following the resolution, Morris H. Blumberg was reelected president; trustees including Abraham Srere, Abe Kasle, and Judge Harry B. Keidan were elected; and Jacob H. Sonenklar was reelected cantor.[228]

Zionism unquestionably attracted more support because of the war and the staggeringly insistent news from Europe. At a luncheon honoring Simon Shetzer as director of the Zionist Organization of Detroit (ZOD) in April 1942, the executive director of the Zionist Organization of America called Detroit "a model Zionist community" that gained strength each year.[229] A year later, the Jewish National Fund opened an office on the corner of Dexter and Burlingame.[230] In June 1943 a slate of delegates to the American Jewish Conference included not only Schaver and Rabbis Glazer, Adler, and Fram, but also Joseph Ehrlich, Abraham Srere, Fred Butzel, Mrs. Dora Ehrlich, Rabbi Max Wohlgelernter, and Daniel Temchin of the Mizrachi, the religious Zionist organization.[231] A week later the ZOD advertised in the *Jewish News*: "Join the Builders of Zion . . . 'To Be A Zionist Is To Be A Loyal American' " and attached membership coupons.[232]

Members of Pioneer Women and Hadassah, both active since the 1920s, accelerated and broadened their activities. Primarily supported by the non-religious Jews in Detroit, Pioneer Women's organization for aid in the rehabilitation of Jewish life in Palestine reflected the sentiments of its 1941 guest speaker, Irma Lindheim, when she called upon Jews in America "to give up their struggle for white collar jobs at the top of the corporate ladder" and concentrate on the return to build a new life.[233] One Detroit woman remembered accompanying her mother to Pioneer Women meetings, changing streetcars twice in all kinds of weather. They dedicated themselves to raising funds for relief and rescue as well as for numerous other programs for children and mothers. Hadassah included among their number women who had been inspired by the founder of Hadassah, Henrietta Szold. Unlike Hadassah, Pioneer Women, affiliated with Labor Zionism, took a more explicit political stand and many of their members perceived themselves as antagonists of Hadassah.

In 1943 Golda Meyerson, destined for the office of prime minister of Israel as Golda Meir, was a secretary of the Pioneer Women National Office, traveling to many cities, including Detroit. Unable to afford hotels, she stayed in Detroit at the homes of different *chavarot*, or friends, like one of Detroit's Pioneer Women sparkplugs, Chana Michlin, and at Dora Kumove's, where she complained about the springs on the couch. She stayed, too, with David and Sophie Sislin, occasionally leaving her children with them for a week or ten days as she toured the United States. On one occasion she appeared at the Sislins and bluntly said: "Don't tell anyone

I'm here," and proceeded to stay in the room belonging to Evelyn, the Sislin's daughter, for two days. By the 1940s and into the 1950s, Golda and other Israeli leaders were feted by the Jewish "establishment" whenever they visited Detroit and other cities in the United States. In their search for major funding, public appearances and inspirational speeches became the order of those days. Even after her rise to political power, Meir entertained the Sislins whenever they visited Israel. David Ben-Gurion, leader of the Histadrut movement in Palestine and Israel's future first prime minister, also came to Detroit to organize and to hearten the Labor Zionists. On those occasions, Mr. Michlin and Berl Kumove would accompany Ben-Gurion on long walks on Belle Isle, discussing the prospects for statehood and the dark days of the war.

By 1945 the General Zionist Council of Detroit, led by Benjamin Laikin and including such advocates as Slomovitz, Fram, Lawrence Crohn, and Rabbi Adler, began an intense campaign to gain both Jewish and non-Jewish support. According to Laikin, "each individual was a committee" as they spoke in churches, addressed union groups, and lobbied state legislators, members of the City Council of Detroit, the mayor, the governor, senators, and congressmen. Both Sen. Arthur Vandenberg and Rep. John Dingell were approached repeatedly. Vandenberg, caught up in the cold war, shifted his focus from Palestine to the Soviet Union. Yet together Rabbi Fram and Laikin convinced Sen. Homer Ferguson to write a letter to President Truman supporting the endorsement of a Jewish state.[234]

Because of the intensification of the campaign, Palestine became a publicly debated issue in newspapers and public forums. In September 1945, Fram, as president of the ZOD, initiated a series of lectures and discussions sponsored by Temple Israel and held at the Detroit Institute of Arts. The focus of the series emphasized America's interest and included such titles as, "To Whom Does Palestine Belong?" "The Arab Problem," and "What Palestine Means to America."[235] The *Detroit News'* "Public Letter Box" began to bristle with opinions on the fate of Palestine—some supportive of a Jewish commonwealth, others suggesting an "open international state," and still others with hints of anti-Semitic denial.[236] At the core of the movement was the continuing advocacy of the Labor Zionists, who purchased land in Palestine. With Detroit stalwarts like Schaver (a delegate again to the World Zionist Congress in Switzerland in 1946) proceeding with renewed fervor, and with new patronage from businessmen like Louis Berry and others, Detroit Jews seemed to prepare for the remarkable role they would play in the years to come.

24

Unity: The Quest for the Elusive Ideal

Throughout 1942 questions about funds for relief dominated discussions at organizational meetings. The National Refugee Service, the Joint Distribution Committee, and the United Palestine Appeal competed for money. Federation's position remained consistent: the answer to divided appeals was increased giving to one fund. In Isidore Sobeloff's opinion, Detroit Jews needed to center their attentions on concrete amounts, not on percentages. The more money given to the Allied Campaign, the more money would be given to each relief organization. Nevertheless, more than half the $985,000 quota for the 1942 Allied Jewish Campaign was earmarked for overseas relief.[237] Through the JDC, 600,000 Polish Jews were to be aided in the Soviet Union, 150,000 Jews in France, and still more in Switzerland, Turkey, Spain, and Portugal. Abraham Srere, president of the Federation, called the Allied Jewish Campaign "a weapon in the fight for freedom." He recalled President Roosevelt's call for continued support of campaigns for domestic and overseas relief and quoted Churchill regarding the suffering of the Jews: "On the day of victory the Jew's suffering and his part in the struggle will not be forgotten."[238] Ads for the campaign listed the "Leaders of a Great Army of Life and Hope for Millions."[239] In an open letter to the Jews of Detroit, Fred Butzel and Isidore Sobeloff outlined the campaign budget calling it "not simply a *Jewish* cause, but an *American* cause."[240] At the official launching of the campaign, Sir Norman Angell delivered a stirring message that called for unity and praised the Jews in Palestine for their "courage and hope," referring to them as a "bastion" of hope for the future. Henry Wineman, Isidore Sobeloff, and Fred Butzel spoke, and they played a recorded message by Eddie Cantor.[241]

Despite such public appeals for unity, only after the campaign affiliated with the War Chest in 1943 did such singleness of purpose emerge. In March 1943, Leon Kay, president of the American Jewish Congress in Detroit, called upon Detroit Jews to join the American Jewish Assembly for unity of purpose and harmony.[242] Two weeks later, Fred Butzel spoke at Temple Israel on the theme of "unity and harmony."[243] And after another two weeks the executive vice-president of the JDC, J. C. Hyman, spoke at the Jewish Community Center and called for united action to save European Jewry and build up Palestine as a refuge: "There is no room for debate," he said. "Across the seas millions of our people live in anguish while we indulge in oratory and public debate and private recriminations. . . . Our greatest danger lies in our own internal divisions."[244] At the end of April, as news of the failure of the Bermuda Conference became public and as the Jewish News Agency reported that "only 350,000 Jews [are] still alive in Poland," Abe Srere's guest editorial in the *Jewish News* called upon Detroit Jews to attend the National Jewish Conference at the Jewish Community Center in order to define "an approach to unity in our ranks."[245]

Disagreements seemed put aside or at least submerged. As the Jewish Community Council expanded its organizational membership, however, the drive for "unity and harmony" was given an unexpected pause. When the International Workers' Order (IWO) applied for membership to the Council, most of the members on the committee appeared unopposed. At least one, Ben Laikin, disrupted the "unity and harmony" call and argued that although the IWO engaged in Jewish cultural work—running schools, publishing Yiddish books, and sponsoring Jewish or Yiddish programs—it was primarily a political and communist organization. The IWO's defenders contended that as a fraternal organization its membership included Zionists and religious Jews.

Some Reform Jews, members of the American Jewish Committee and B'nai B'rith, urged acceptance of the IWO for the sake of unity. Laikin and others, however, pointed out that the IWO had been founded by the American Communist Party, and that it had changed its policies with the Kremlin regarding the Arab riots in Palestine and had even supported the Nazi-Soviet Nonaggression pact of August 1939. Finally, Laikin asserted that members of the Council were obliged to put Jewish interests first. The IWO lost its bid for membership in the Council, receiving, according to Laikin, no votes.[246]

Given the climate of anti-Semitism and the frequent accusations of communist-Jewish links, sensitivities toward alliances with such blatantly left-wing groups were particularly acute. Even though it included liberal groups like the Workmen's Circle and Joseph Bernstein's Jewish Labor Committee, the Council continued to identify itself as Jewish and American. During the war, Jews in Detroit, as in other cities, felt their vulnerability to long-standing accusations identifying them with communism and voted accordingly in this representative case.

On the occasion of the fifth anniversary of the Council, a series of "institutes" took place at Temple Beth El—the site seeming to symbolize the quest for unity. After President James Ellmann's introduction, Rabbi Morris Adler, increasingly identified as a leading figure of the Council, delivered the keynote address. "American Jewry is coming of age," he declared, and "[the Council] is the expression of our needs within, not the pressure without. It is the democratizing force in Jewish life, and represents the positive, the comprehensive and the democratic in the Jewish community." The institutes that followed included "Community Relations and Anti-Defamation," "Internal Jewish Community Relations," and "Coordination of Educational and Cultural Activities"; participants included Philip Slomovitz and Joseph Bernstein, both dynamic Jewish newspaper editors and both active in local and national Jewish affairs, as well as Bernard Isaacs, Shloime Bercovich, Rabbi Wohlgelernter, Dr. Shmarya Kleinman, and others. Fred Butzel presided at a dinner following the meetings and lauded Simon Shetzer and Ellmann for their leadership; Clarence Enggass extended greetings as president of Federation.[247]

The titles of those "institutes" revealed what had emerged as the nucleus of Council activities. The term *community relations* replaced *defense* in the language of Jewish organizations, and *antidefamation* implied connection with the new agency of the B'nai B'rith. Finally, "educational and cultural activities" introduced a potentially divisive subject among the Jewish agencies in Detroit, specifically between Federation and Council. That subject would be shunted aside until after the war when, in February 1947, Council formally established the Culture Commission. Its aims, as stated in its founding resolution, were fourfold: to arouse wider awareness of the need and importance of Jewish education; to stimulate greater responsiveness to Jewish cultural values and achievements; to raise the cultural level of the programs of Council's constituent organizations; to cooperate with existing agencies to plan communitywide celebrations of Jewish Book Week, Music Week, and other important cultural anniversaries and occasions.

The Culture Commission quickly moved to introduce radio programs and art exhibits of the works of such Jewish artists as Marc Chagall. It sponsored specific Jewish programs that included the annual Warsaw Ghetto Uprising Commemoration (according to one Detroiter the oldest yearly

Holocaust memorial in the United States) and lectures from distinguished Jewish and non-Jewish scholars like Salo Baron, and Yiddish poets like Itzik Manger and Jacob Glatstein. The commission sought to provide "positive Jewish programs" instead of defensive or community relations activities. It hoped to meet the concerns of people who, like Rabbi Adler, worried about the "generation gap" that threatened Jewish traditions, values, and identity.[248] Some of the advocates of the Culture Commission embraced religious views of Jewish identity, while others were distinctly secularist. Among the religious supporters were Orthodox, Conservative, and Reform Jews. The secularists included Yiddishists, Zionists, liberals, leftists, and *umparteische* members. From the secularist group emerged Boris Joffe, the volatile executive director of Council whose European-Jewish roots lay deep in the socialist-revolutionary idealist tradition. An avid civil-rights advocate, he, along with numerous other leaders of the Culture Commission, determined Council's direction into the late 1940s and 1950s.

From 1947 on, Council took a decidedly liberal course championing civil rights and free speech, opposing the cold war, and the House Un-American Activities Committee. These issues, along with the financial concerns regarding the funding of the Culture Commission and programs of the Council, would produce a stark confrontation with Federation in the 1950s. In that same year, 1947, Federation seemed ready to respond to the unity call, and it broadened its by-laws to include representatives of "organizational groupings" like the American Jewish Congress, the B'nai B'rith, the Workmen's Circle, the Landsmanshaftn Council, the Jewish War Veterans, and, later, the Synagogue Council.[249] At the same time, Federation expanded campaign group representation to include trades and professions. In practical terms, Federation hoped to gain cooperative benefits from this "democratizing" move. Both Federation and Council advocates recognized that Federation hoped to counter Council's democratizing rhetoric regarding broad representation.

25

Public Profiles: Aspects of Jewish Success

By the mid-thirties an increasing number of Jews had become successful and prominent in Detroit professional and business life. Jews in major American urban centers had established themselves as retailers, just as they had in Detroit. But only Detroit seemed to lack a major Jewish department store like Macy's, or Gimbel's, or Filene's (Boston), or the May Company (Cleveland). With rare exceptions, including the Israel Davidson family's Federal's Department Store, Henry Wineman's People's Outfitting Company, or Sam Osnos' Sam's Cut Rate, J. L. Hudson, Inc., according to one Jewish Detroiter, monopolized that business and locked out Jews in overt and covert ways. Jewish merchants rarely dealt with Hudson's, and in the 1920s and 1930s Hudson's want ads for clerks frequently made it clear that Jewish girls need not apply.

Unlike other cities, then, Detroit's largest contributing group to the Allied Jewish Campaign was not department-store magnates, but mechanical industries, like those affiliated with the automobile companies. Between 1935 and 1940 alone the percentage of Jews involved in those industries grew from 23 percent to 47 percent.[250] These included the Edward C. Levy Company, Abe Srere's Acme Mills, Allen Industries, Max J. Zivian's Detroit

Steel, Production Steel (owned by the Hamburger family), Harry Grant's and Harry Goldman's Southern Scrap Metal, and Kasle Steel. Perhaps the most successful businessman was Max Fisher, whose father, William, founded Keystone Oil Company along with Leon Kay and Nate Epstein. It was Max, however, who brought an unusual combination of business acumen, energy, initiative, and ambition into the enterprise. Max purchased Aurora Oil Company and then bought out Keystone. Aurora then absorbed Speedway Petroleum Corporation service stations, which eventually became Marathon Oil.[251]

In 1932 Max Fisher, a struggling young businessman, contributed five dollars to the Allied Jewish Campaign. Max Fisher became Detroit's most successful business entrepreneur, a nationally and then internationally known businessman. He had been raised in a small town in Ohio among non-Jews and consequently possessed a minimal Jewish education, yet he maintained a "highly developed Jewish consciousness."[252] His wealth brought him into the heart of the non-Jewish upper classes in Detroit, and he would combine his rise to success with a recognition of his East European Jewish origins when, after 1948, he became an avid supporter of the state of Israel.

Jews gravitated to other retail businesses like the food industry, eventually developing large supermarket chains. Abner A. Wolf, whose father Joseph had run the meat department in Grossberg and Reuter's wholesale groceries, founded, along with John and Nate Lurie, Wrigley Super Market in 1935. Some Detroiters remembered seeing Tom Borman selling produce in the streets of the Jewish neighborhoods. From this beginning, Tom and Al Borman began Borman's Market, which evolved into Food Fair and then Farmer Jack's Super Markets. Along with these Jewish families, the Weisbergs and the Shayes launched Chatham and Big Bear supermarket chains, and David Goose founded the Great Scott markets that were later expanded by the Fink family. Food processors like the Slotkin family's Hygrades and the Feigenson family's Faygo joined the list of extraordinarily successful Jewish family businesses.

Jews in Detroit, like Jews in other cities, established retail specialty shops— B. Siegel and Company, Himelhoch's and Winkelman's among them—and from those positions involved themselves in civic life. Sam Osnos led the way in retail business chains after he founded Sam's Cut Rate, Inc. in 1917. Nate Shapero began his business with one store, Economical Number One, and by 1931 the Economical Drug Chain bought out the famous Cunningham's Drugs. He became one of the first Detroit businessmen to make personal gifts of baskets of food to the needy on Thanksgiving Day, and by 1933 he had offered between five hundred and eight hundred such baskets annually. Such public generosity led to Shapero's appointment to the State Welfare Commission in 1933.[253]

Men like Judge Charles C. Simons, Judge Harry Keidan, Judge Henry Butzel, State Supreme Court Chief Justice James Ellmann (twice elected associate justice in Highland Park and appointed assistant attorney general of Michigan in 1933), and Judge Theodore Levin maintained visible Jewish profiles while engaging in the public realm of jurisprudence. Their reputations as rigorous, fair-minded judges grew, and their immersion in the city's non-Jewish affairs brought them positive acclaim from their peers both locally and nationally.

Judge Charles Rubiner recalled anti-Semitic activities when he ran for reelection as common pleas judge in 1933. After he had refused to promise a delegation from the KKK that he would appoint one of their number as chief clerk, small cards were distributed throughout the district that read: "Vote for Charles Isadore Rubiner, B'nai B'rith Candidate for Common Pleas Court." He recalled other hate literature passed out in church parking lots during the campaign. It was clear, then, that anti-Semitic groups monitored Jewish candidates, and if the candidates themselves did not acknowledge their Jewishness, their opponents would.

These men, along with Judge William Friedman, contributed enormous energy to Jewish causes. Friedman had been a member of the Detroit House of Corrections since 1926 and chairman of the Wayne County Draft Appeal Board during World War II; he was appointed by Mayor Jeffries to succeed Judge Keidan as recorder's court judge in 1942.[254] Judge Charles C. Simons, of the U.S. Circuit Court of Appeals, addressed the Lawyers' Division of the Allied Jewish Campaign in 1940, urging them to campaign for rescue and relief. The son of D. W. Simons, (the first president of the United Jewish Charities), he had served as the youngest senator in the Michigan legislature, and in 1923 he was appointed by President Harding to the U.S. District Court. In 1932 he was elevated to the Sixth Circuit Court of Appeals by President Hoover. The first Detroiter—and the first Jew—appointed to that court, he became chief judge of the circuit court in 1952.[255]

Judge Levin had vigorously opposed the Michigan Alien Registration and Fingerprinting Act of 1931; he, along with Fred Butzel, denounced the cruel provisions against aliens and opposed the legislation's constitutionality in federal court. The statute was found to be unconstitutional. Nominated by President Truman to the U.S. District Court in 1946, Levin already had pursued his interests in helping the poor and unfortunate victims of the war. In 1947 Fred Butzel paid him the following tribute: "Moved by the tragedy of broken families and the uncertain status of those faced with the misery of deportation, he devoted himself . . . to the study of the law and administration of immigration and naturalization. . . . He helped in numberless cases to avoid the cruelties and rigors of the administration of our regulations." Along with numerous non-Jewish organizations, Levin actively participated in the work of the United Jewish Charities; he was president of the Federation and sat on the board of the national Council of Jewish Federation and Welfare Funds.[256]

282   In the public eye, these men represented Jewish success in the legal

profession. Lawyers like Irwin Cohn, Morris Garvett, and Nathan Milstein (who worked closely with Judge Levin on immigration problems), and judges like Henry Butzel and numerous others founded major law firms in Detroit that regularly drew propitious attention to Jewish actions in the non-Jewish world. Productive citizens, they increasingly became involved in Zionist causes as well as in work with the Council and in active participation in the Allied Jewish Campaign. Henry Meyers, who became director of the Detroit Legal Aid Bureau and a member of the Board of Governors of the Detroit Bar Association; Nathaniel H. Goldstick, who was appointed assistant corporation counsel for the City of Detroit and eventually chief corporation counsel; and law firms like Honigman, Miller, Schwartz, Butzel, Levin, Winston, and Levin, Levin, Garvett and Dill maintained public connections with their Jewish identity through support of Jewish philanthropic organizations, Council activities, or religious affiliations.[257] How those connections were perceived as Jewish remained unresolved, even controversial, among Jews. Yet, to the non-Jewish world, their Jewish identity was obvious.

26

A Saved Remnant:
The New Immigrants

In 1946 the Weintraubs arrived in Detroit. There were three of them—all teenagers. They were alone. Ruth, Jack, and Larry had survived the Lodz ghetto, Auschwitz, and several slave-labor camps. Jack had been shot in the final days of the war and regained consciousness in an Allied field hospital. Ruth struggled with nightmares, haunted by memories of her mother, her cousin, songs, death, typhus, and starvation. When Ruth returned to her family home in Lodz to search for her brothers—for anyone—she was invited in by non-Jewish neighbors and served tea on her own family's china.

There could be no choice about leaving, only a choice about where to go: Palestine or America. They came to Detroit because, while working for the army in Germany, Larry had met American soldiers from Detroit who told him it was a decent place to live and find work; a city similar to Lodz, with its industry and city college; and because in Poland, from a family of some eighty relatives, they were three of nine cousins who had survived the Holocaust.

In Detroit the Resettlement Service and the Jewish Family and Children's Service grappled with questions about procedures and appropriate actions that would serve the best interest of survivors like the Weintraubs. At first, the three found themselves separated and placed in foster homes volunteered by Jewish families like the Gellers, with whom the brothers lived. Ruth lived with Goldie Goldstein. Unaware of the full nature of the Holocaust experience, social workers tended to treat such new arrivals with professional demeanors that proved insensitive in many cases. Separation may have been the worst decision for those who clung tenaciously and fearfully to the remnants of their families.

After some agitation, especially from Ruth, the agency decided to allow them to live together; it found the three Weintraubs a flat and provided them regular domestic help, allowances, and spending money. The Jewish Vocational Service, in conjunction with the Jewish Bakers' Union, found Larry a job, and he supported the family while Jack and Ruth attended Central High School. Eventually Jack and Larry attended Wayne State University. As students, their experience heightened their gratitude to their adopted city, and they changed their name from Weintraub to Wayne. All that mattered to them, however, was staying together. The Resettlement Service, after some discussion about the advisability of allowing three immigrant, traumatized youngsters their independence, saw to it that they remained united. As a teenager, Ruth kept house for her two brothers while attending Central High School.

Before victims of the Holocaust who survived could come to the United States, they faced legal complications of immense proportions. Federal regulations demanded affidavits from sponsors in America. In Detroit, small groups of lawyers and leaders of various segments of the Jewish population began to meet in order to provide sponsorship for survivors—even for those without relatives in Detroit. Led by Judge Levin, Fred Butzel, and Julian Krolik, they undertook to cajole, persuade, or bargain with Jews in Detroit to sign affidavits for distant relatives or even strangers whose names appeared on survivor lists from the Joint Distribution Committee and HIAS. According to Nathan Milstein, a lawyer actively engaged in alleviating immigration red tape, a "complicated web of activities" involving governmental, JSSB, and Federation cooperation surreptitiously emerged. Krolik, described by Sobeloff as "one of the most able presidents of Federation, an understanding man with a feeling for other elements of the community," led a network of individuals in placing "psychological and other pressure" on individuals from government officials in the state apparatus to Jewish citizens of Detroit. This assiduous volunteer enterprise, passionately undertaken by committed men and women like the Kroliks and Fred Butzel and by professionals like Milstein and Levin, proceeded as a first step alongside the more public efforts.

As a result, survivors arrived in Detroit, usually under the auspices of a family sponsor. Many of those first arrivals, like the Weintraubs, had suffered interrupted childhoods that would never be recaptured. Simultaneously old and young, they received stipends from the Jewish Social Service Bureau, assistance from the Jewish Vocational Service, guidance from social workers, friendship through the Jewish Center, and other forms of outreach from Yiddish groups like the Sholem Aleichem Institute, the *landsmanshaftn,* and the Workmen's Circle. The Children's Service placed some of the younger survivors.[258]

All this if and when they could reach out themselves, through those lost childhoods, stark memories, and parentless lives in which everything had been torn away. Troubled youngsters like Martin Adler—who arrived in Detroit as a fifteen-year-old with no family, having survived the death camp at Auschwitz-Birkenau, the slave-labor camp of Dora, and the concentration camp at Bergen-Belsen—wrestled with the task of reaching out, silently, for a new life. Placed first in the Cleveland Jewish Children's Home, Bellefaire, with which Detroit maintained a reciprocal arrangement, Adler came to Detroit with his friend Jack Weinberger. The Children's Service placed him with a family and shortly afterward relocated him to be with his friend in another Jewish household. He received a regular stipend from the JSSB, even after he obtained a job working as a stock boy for Norman Naimark. Like the Weintraubs, he began to create a new life; unlike them, he resembled the majority of survivors who had no close family left.

Newly elected as president of Congregation B'nai Moshe, Samuel Friedman left the first board meeting over which he presided to meet his twenty-three-year-old nephew Abraham Pasternak when he arrived from New York. After being torn from his home in Betlan, Transylvania, in 1944 by Hungarian fascists, Abe endured Auschwitz, the infamous death marches, and several slave-labor camps. In 1947 he came to Detroit, where he lived in a room in his uncle's home on Chicago Boulevard. Those around him reacted to him, as they reacted to most survivors, with a mixture of incomprehension, pity, condescension, fear, and even contempt. People seemed to feel it necessary to explain how to turn on lights, flush toilets, use money, even to speak.

Pasternak recalled conflicting feelings: his longing to talk about his lost family and his experiences and to have people understand his confusion and fears; his anguish over the thought of speaking and the prospect of encountering indifferent listeners; his determination to proceed independently and make a new life; and his hope for some kind hand that would reach out to facilitate a new beginning. Employed first at Grunt's Market at twenty-five dollars a week, he was able to pay back a twenty-five-dollar loan to the Hebrew Free Loan Association, and he began to pay his uncle rent when he got a job as a stock clerk in Federal Department Store for forty-five dollars a week. There, a coworker struck a patronizing pose and told him that "when you laugh the world laughs with you; cry and you cry alone"—a clear message. "If we had only been able to tell someone how we felt," Pasternak said years later, "we could have relieved some of our burden." He recalled that the Federation sponsored Saturday-night dances for the survivors at the Jewish Community Center. By 1950 he was drafted into the army as an acting chaplain.

Jewish organizations, and a few Jewish individuals who were affiliated with them, took these wary and tormented people into their homes and lives. Just as had occurred with the earlier twentieth-century Jewish im-migration, when the immigrants stopped coming to America, they contin-ued to come to Detroit, moving there from other cities where they had located first. By the mid-fifties, Detroit's survivor population numbered between thirty-five hundred and four thousand people, and others came even into the seventies in search of work or new lives. From Beregcasz or Kapusanyi, Velky Beresny, Lodz, Crakow, Betlan, and towns from Czecho-slovakia, Greece, Poland, and Hungary, they had moved to Montreal or Galveston, Toronto or Indianapolis, Topeka or Minneapolis, New York or Cleveland. Now they came to Detroit. Approximately one-third came from Hungary, Eastern Czechoslovakia, and Rumania. Many of these, like Nathan and Edith Roth, arrived in Detroit from far-flung places like Dallas, Texas, and from small cities in Ohio, because remnants of their communities had chosen Detroit for its prospective economic possibilities. They were drawn to B'nai Moshe, the Hungarian Shul, and accepted there as they reconsti-tuted shattered lives with substitute families.

First among the institutions to give aid was the Resettlement Service (founded in 1937), which continued its work to find and to resettle these new immigrants. In September 1945, the Federation Board discussed with the Resettlement Office the prospects for Detroit's accepting responsibility for a number of Jews who had been connected with the Oswego Project since 1944.[259] After two years of struggle, the National Refugee Board es-tablished a camp in Oswego, New York, for one thousand rescued Jews. In 1945 nine hundred of the "internees" faced "release" contingent on whether private Jewish agencies would assume responsibility "for support and ad-justment" of the survivors. Federation agreed to accept "not more than thirty" of these, many of whom had been chosen by American agents for their professions.[260] Joseph Langnas, a young German Jew who, along with his family, had been rescued in Italy—virtually snatched from the hands of the SS—then placed behind wires in a camp in rural New York state, found himself as a teenager in the strange city of Detroit.

In 1947 the Resettlement Service claimed responsibility for forty-two families and five children. Its budget had grown from $16,208 in 1945 to $121,865 in 1947. By 1950, approximately 10 percent of the new immi-grants were receiving help from the Resettlement Service. In 1949 Detroit had taken in two hundred families from displaced persons camps, and Harold Silver, executive director of the service, declared that "90% . . . have no problem that cannot be solved by permanent housing and a job. . . . Their

287

health, both mental and physical, is surprisingly good. . . . They only need initial community boosts to become self-supporting, constructive residents." The 1949–1950 budget for the Resettlement Service soared to $340,000, then fell to $316,429 in 1950–1951.[261]

Part of that agency soon included an Indemnification Service, through which assistance was given to Holocaust victims to process requests for restitution for damage to "health, life and liberty under the Nazi regime." A Migration Service quickly established a center to assist in finding and bringing relatives from Europe. Beginning in 1945, the service had names of Detroit Jews searching for surviving relatives published regularly in the *Jewish News*. That paper continued to have photographs of child survivors reading, playing, and laughing and of smiling reunited families in such remote places as Oklahoma, Texas, New York, or Tel Aviv sprinkled throughout its pages.

The number of families sponsored by the Resettlement Service peaked in 1949 at 198. Yet in 1953 it brought eleven more families, and in 1957 the number had risen to thirty-five. Harold Silver wrote that "we defined our responsibility to the newcomers as material assistance at minimum levels and casework help in becoming adjusted to their new life."[262] To achieve those goals, other agencies cooperated: the Jewish Vocational Service trained new Detroiters and found jobs for them; the Jewish Community Center offered recreational, social, and educational programs like the dances Abe Pasternak recalled; the North End Clinic and, later, Sinai Hospital offered health services; the Hebrew Free Loan Association provided its services; and so it went.

In the winter of 1949 the JSSB and the Jewish Vocational Service (JVS) recommended special English classes for practical goals. With the cooperation of the Twelfth Street branch of the center, the Detroit Board of Education, and volunteers from the National Council of Jewish Women (NCJW), the classes were initiated. The teacher and supervisor, Mrs. Valerie Komives, received assistance from the NCJW. The first three-week course attracted seventy-five students and specialized in industrial English for the primarily male class. Because of its success, the center and the JSSB recommended a second course, this one for ten weeks, that drew 120 students. Hal Schneiderman, of the center staff, coordinated the classes, and a consulting committee that included Mrs. William Isenberg, of the Jewish Center board; Blanche (Mrs. David) Pollack and Mrs. Maxwell Katzen, of the Council of Jewish Women; Howard Mausner, of the JVS; and Sarah Lev, of the JSSB assisted. By 1950 the classes in industrial English were supplemented by classes in English that would prove useful to women—teaching shopping phrases, household words, and the like. When students stopped attending, Schneiderman commented, the staff knew the classes were succeeding. This educational endeavor served as a model for the cooperative work of different Jewish agencies in Detroit.[263]

Victims who survived elicited good intentions, professional social work skills, funding, and sympathy. Yet so unprecedented a catastrophe could not easily be mediated by routine procedures whose standards emerged from earlier experiences with immigrants. Much later, some survivors would reveal that they felt intimidated or patronized. In some cases, agencies did not offer them work or education that matched their own competencies. One survivor recalled that the Jewish Vocational Service offered him menial jobs working for Jewish businesses at the minimum wage of seventy-five cents an hour. Still others, like Pasternak, remember being explicitly told not to speak of their experiences: "Don't tell me or your coworkers about the terrible things you saw. That was then, this is now." And another woman, when asked about life in the ghetto, described standing in long lines for hours to obtain stale bread or rotten vegetables. The response from her Jewish coworkers: "We had to wait in lines, too, for stockings and things." Although he was among the most competent directors of social services in the country, Harold Silver seemed unaware that mental and physical health had become elusive and that these Jews would be forever marked by their experiences.

As awareness of the magnitude of the European catastrophe increased, it seemed as if the diverse elements of the Jews of Detroit drew together to give aid to the new immigrants. Yet an odd amalgam of apprehension, guilt, uncertainty, and incomprehension persisted among those who became involved with the survivors. For their part, the survivors found speaking about their trials difficult, quickly realizing how impossible any real communication about the Holocaust would be. They remained separated by that abyss, a chasm filled with confused emotions for both Detroit Jews and the European Jews who soon identified themselves as Detroiters. It would take thirty-five to forty years before they would begin to bear witness to the Holocaust—and even then only fragments of their stories filtered through the difficult task of speaking out.

Their arrival provided an opportunity for rival agencies and organizations to cooperate in their attempts at resettlement. But it would take years before the deeper needs of the survivors would come to light—too late, in many cases, to make a difference. Many survivors believed that social workers rarely offered psychological counseling or lent sympathetic and understanding ears. In general, they encouraged "new beginnings," which meant forgetting the past—or trying. Few grasped the enormity of the event and fewer still the impediments to speaking about it. If fewer immigrants came than had come in the first part of the century, the accompanying problems bore immensely more complicated consequences. Where insensitivities or misconceptions on the part of social workers in the 1920s produced one sort of aftermath, lack of information or of awareness of the unprecedented nature of the new immigrants' experiences left an aftermath that was later nearly impossible to surmount. Good intentions and the

289

most professional skills and proficiency could not have adequately countered the consequences of the Holocaust. If those who worked for the Resettlement Service and other agencies did not know that, then they shared that naiveté with virtually every Jewish American. Those consequences, however, often forced the victims who survived further into themselves and into an indescribable loneliness.

Nevertheless, the survivors would become an integral, contributing portion of Detroit Jewry, gravitating to all the various Jewish communities from the religious and Orthodox to the secular organizations. By the mid-1950s, many contributed regularly to the Allied Jewish Campaign, and by the 1960s many identified with the leadership of Federation, with Zionist supporters, especially regarding Israel bond drives, and with Council and other groups. From their ranks would emerge successful businessmen, loving parents, and forceful voices in the Jewish population of Detroit. Many would overcome religious ambivalence to lead large congregations like Shaarey Zedek and B'nai Moshe and Temple Beth El; to become members of the boards of the Federation and other agencies, and even chairmen of the Allied Jewish Campaign. They would participate prominently in organizations like the Council, the Workmen's Circle, United Hebrew Schools, and every aspect of Detroit Jewish life.

PART IV
1948–1967

Two related but separate events have profoundly determined the attitudes and actions of American Jews in the twentieth century: the Shoah (the Holocaust), and the founding of the state of Israel. Nearly 100,000 Jewish survivors of the Holocaust emigrated to the United States, and most American Jews and their organizations recognized their obligations to aid in resettlement and integration programs.[1] Those who had defined their Jewishness through Jewish philanthropy, usually Reform Jews involved with Federation, as well as Orthodox Jews, secularists, those who claimed an identity as social activists derived from Jewish traditions, or those who simply carried an unspoken consciousness of their culture, past, and European Jewish heritage, all discerned their ties to the victims who had survived. Survivors, however, presented what Elie Wiesel called a memento mori, a reminder of death: reminders, too, of the dangers that persisted as concomitants of being Jewish. Once again, then, a potential unifying force, the Shoah, ironically created confused and uneasy divisiveness.

Less so the state of Israel: "The glue which held the Jewish community together," noted one Detroiter. Yet it, too, would cause controversy and disagreement. Even before the end of World War II, in March 1945, a con-   293 ference of leading national Federation executives in New York produced two proposals in an effort to stem a new tide of contention. They perceived a three-way problem in fund requests from the United Palestine Association, the Joint Distribution Committee, and the National Refugee Service (NRS). Their suggestions included assigning an overseas commission to be sent to Europe and Palestine to study the operations of organizations supported by Federation funds and to study the needs of Jews and practical measures to be taken by American Jewry in order to implement programs. Their second proposal called for the establishment of the Inter-City Allotment Committee, through which representatives of the fifteen largest welfare funds would coordinate and organize the distribution of funds, especially regarding the UPA, JDC, and NRS. In Detroit, Abe Srere served as the Federation representative to the Inter-City Allotment Committee.[2]

These meetings anticipated problems of a new magnitude as fund-raising dilemmas loomed more agonizingly than ever before. In September 1945 Federation began a special campaign for civic-protective agencies that were not covered by the War Chest requests. They raised $180,000 for the Joint Defense Appeal, the American Jewish Congress, the Jewish Labor Committee, the Anti-Defamation League, and the Jewish Community Council.[3] The need for a separate campaign, however, portended increased demands for funds, not the least of which had to do with immigrant relief and aid to Palestine. As it had in the 1930s and 1940s, the problem of independent solicitation immediately arose: Mizrachi, the Federation of Polish Jews, the Women's ORT Federation, and the Council Round Table Project all hinted at independent fund-raising.[4] Benjamin Laikin recalled that between September and December Jews in Detroit might be besieged by requests from the Labor Zionist campaign for Farband Schools, Habonim, the *Yiddish Kempfer,* (a weekly paper), the Jewish Teacher's Seminary, and others.[5] Signposts of things to come, such solicitations prompted Isidore Sobeloff to procure from the Federation Board an allocations agreement: "No agency which is a beneficiary of the Allied Jewish Campaign may campaign locally, on an independent basis, for additional funds."[6] Federation would become adamant on this stand—yet it still did not stem the sources of discontent.

After depression, war, the Holocaust, and the birth of Israel, American Jewry would, as Irwin Shaw observed, "start over in a whole new universe with new challenges." Some would react with "guilt and fear," observed one Federation official, while others would respond with enthusiasm and exhilaration. The next twenty years witnessed intensified division and intensified drives for unity; sometimes problematic and sometimes determined identification with Jewish organizations. Old differences transformed into new issues, often carrying on their deeper and original sources of discontent. Conflict over institutions like a Jewish hospital or the nature of the Jewish Community Center; debates over kosher kitchens in those

public institutions; and ritual disagreements among different denominations emerged from earlier socioeconomic antagonisms. After 1948, however, disputes over Zionism diminished as Israel emerged as the external
unifier, coalescing divergent elements of the Jewish population into a more
harmonious whole.

Once again, as Detroit grew, so did the Jewish communities that were
part of it. But it was the launching of Israel that served as the monumental
event. Nothing would be the same after it. If they would continue competing, agencies would now compete with a dream come true, and the
focus of Jewish identity in Detroit shifted radically to an external source.

27

New Neighborhoods: Another Domestic Exodus

In a paradoxical, simultaneously erudite and unwise statement, Albert Einstein said in 1936 that "the intellectual decline brought on by a shallow materialism is a far greater menace to the survival of Jewry than numerous external foes who threaten its existence with violence." Coming on the eve of the Holocaust, such an assertion appears insensitive and uninformed. Yet it found a curious echo in a Detroit Workmen's Circle member's analysis of the loss of Jewish identity: "The tennis courts—suburban tennis courts destroyed Jewish identity."

After a century of Jewish presence in Detroit, perhaps nothing characterized that people better than its movement—mytho-biblical in its quick, successive generational wanderings and in its group cohesion. Morris Waldman, observing the rapid evacuation of the Hastings neighborhood in favor of the Westminster-Oakland area in 1924, called the phenomenon a *hegira,* or mass migration. The pattern of Jewish settlement in Detroit from 1840 to 1940 has been clearly recorded. In "Tour of Jewish Detroit," Phillip Applebaum charted the northwest exodus: from Lower Hastings to Upper Hastings, to Oakland between 1910 and 1940, to the Twelfth Street and Dexter areas just west of Oakland, to Northwest Detroit, bounded by 297

Eight Mile Road on the north, McNichols (Six Mile) on the south, Livernois on the east, and Evergreen on the west from the late 1930s to the 1960s.[7]

When correlated with generational, socioeconomic upward mobility, such a prolonged exodus seems to have sprung from a desire for larger homes, more space, and the pursuit of the symbols of economic success. Federal surveys imply that for all their tolerance, many Jews retained stereotypic views of blacks and feared living in the same neighborhoods, although they often supported civil rights and defended blacks in that arena. As black workers moved into Detroit, they occupied the areas in which Jews lived, and fears or prejudices on both sides fostered the Jewish moves. Yet another factor in the migration pattern seemed to rest with the Jewish population's tendency to follow retail markets. As the city expanded and the white middle class tended to locate further from downtown, Jewish merchants and professionals relocated.

Northwest Detroit became the new center for Jewish life in Detroit. In 1949 27 percent of the Jewish population lived there. By 1958 the number had more than doubled to 62 percent, and even as late as 1965 at least 50 percent of Detroit's Jews, close to thirteen thousand families, remained in that area. Dexter still housed 49 percent of Jewish families in 1949; but by 1958 the number had drastically decreased to only 9 percent as Northwest Detroit and the northern suburbs—especially Oak Park—began to grow. The same vibrancy that had filled the Twelfth Street neighborhood in the late 1920s and the Dexter neighborhood in the 1930s now emerged in Northwest Detroit, which quickly became the hub of Jewish residence.[8]

By 1945, as young Jewish soldiers returned home, the need for relatively low-cost housing in new areas became apparent. The promised land north of the Northwest neighborhood was Oak Park. Since the Northwest area remained the center of Jewish life in 1945, Oak Park bore the double blessing of proximity to Jewish institutions—synagogues, restaurants, butcher shops, markets—and of stability, with inexpensive new homes. Formerly a "swampy, rural community," Oak Park had already attracted some industry during the war when Vickers Corporation built an arms factory on Eight Mile and Hubbell. Along what was then Wyoming (which would become Rosewood in Oak Park as it crossed Eight Mile), some light industry had begun to develop. Real-estate developers began buying farmland and peat bogs in the 1940s, and these tracts were subdivided into blocks where houses, primarily brick ranches of five or six rooms, were built.[9]

During the 1950s, Oak Park became identified as the Jewish suburb. Having begun on farmland and woods east of Scotia, Jewish settlement eventually radiated east to Ferndale and west into Southfield. Jewish children and parents became active in the Ferndale school district, which included residents of Oak Park. Pleasant Ridge, an upper-middle-class white suburb along Ridge Road, between Nine and Ten Mile Roads, lay between Ferndale and Oak Park. Known by some as "the Dearborn of the North,"

Pleasant Ridge maintained a social aloofness for many years. At the end of Oak Park Boulevard where the street entered Pleasant Ridge and changed its name to Drayton, Pleasant Ridge erected a concrete barrier, ostensibly to keep the flow of traffic down. Some Jews in Oak Park believed the barrier represented a more symbolic separation.

Firmly established non-Jewish communities like Pleasant Ridge and, to a lesser extent, Ferndale, with generations of continuity, inhibited Jewish intrusion into those areas. Jews tended to move in clusters, as they had throughout Detroit's history (like Jewish populations in virtually all American cities), and the undeveloped area of Oak Park offered a greater opportunity for homogeneous development. Finally, Ferndale schools, like those of Berkeley, just north of Oak Park, were dominated by firmly entrenched non-Jewish administrations.[10]

Although the area east of Coolidge never assumed the comprehensive and indisputable Jewish character of the environment in the Northwest or Twelfth Street neighborhoods, the largest percentage of Jews in Detroit lived there. The area around Coolidge between Nine and Ten Mile Roads became imbued with Jewish life. By 1955 Oak Park numbered twenty eight thousand residents, of whom more than nine thousand were Jews. Forty-five percent of the school-age children were Jewish (1,330 of 2,950).[11] Based on a prudent study undertaken in 1950, the Federation purchased eighteen acres in Oak Park. In 1955 the United Hebrew Schools found the superintendent of the Board of Education most cooperative in offering the facilities of Oak Park High School for after-school Hebrew classes.[12]

Following their congregants, the synagogues moved. Conservative congregations B'nai Moshe, B'nai David, and Beth Shalom; several of the Orthodox congregations, including the Oakwood Community Center Congregation; and the newly founded Reform temple, Temple Emanuel, moved to Oak Park within a space of ten years. So, too, did the Jewish Community Center's Aaron DeRoy Memorial Building, at Woodward and Holbrook, open a branch center on Ten Mile between Coolidge and Greenfield in 1956. Three years later, the main branch moved to Curtis and Meyers. By 1960 Jewish delicatessens like the Stage, Horenstein's, and the Dexter-Davison Market—located in Northwest Detroit—either had relocated in Oak Park or had begun to contemplate it. Others, like Darby's and Boesky's remained in the Northwest area on Seven Mile. (Both were later destroyed by fires.)

Oak Park beckoned and Jews responded, because the profile of the Jewish population had continued to change. Suburban life, as it swept across urban America with its new life-styles, enticingly reflected economic developments. One study of Detroit's Jewish population maintained that it had grown from approximately 75,000 people in 1940 to 93,700 by 1956. Extrapolating from that study, the population in 1950 numbered around 85,000 people. (In an addendum to the study, Albert J. Mayer noted that the 93,700 figure represented a peak, and that the Jewish population had already begun to decline, reaching 90,000 by 1958. The birth rate had begun to decline, and many young professionals began to move to other urban areas.)[13]

An occupational profile of the Jews of Detroit after World War II reveals that a large proportion of the men held professional positions; in contrast to the non-Jews of Detroit, 38 percent of the Jews might be classified as managers, proprietors, or officials. A Federation study conducted in 1956 by Albert J. Mayer concluded that several factors accounted for the occupational distribution: what Mayer called "a tradition of taking care of themselves, a skill picked up in many centuries of precarious survival in Europe," partly accounted for the large percentage of Jews who owned their own businesses. Additionally, addressing the 18 percent of the Jewish population in the professional category, Mayer theorized that the traditional emphasis on education contributed to that obvious success. Family solidarity might account for some of the continued businesses that grew over one or two generations into major corporations or industries. Placing immigration into the historical context of Detroit's own development, Mayer argued that Jews in Detroit differed from Jews of other cities, especially New York, because they served a growing non-Jewish population and easily moved into the realm of retail businesses and services.[14]

Max Jacob began his bottle business near the turn of the century. Self-educated, ambitious, and alert, he created a significant corporation in a matter of twenty years. That business continued under the guidance of his sons, then his grandsons, and his great-grandson. Each successive generation achieved higher levels of education, became more sophisticated in marketing and production, and in technological and industrial experimentation that allowed the business of bottle recycling to evolve to bottle production then to the production of a vast variety of containers. In the same vein, Ed Levy, Sr., who was self-educated and strong-willed enough to begin his own business and present himself to Henry Ford, saw his creation expand under his college-educated son, Ed Levy, Jr. Approximately 57 percent of the Jewish business managers and proprietors handed their enterprises down to their sons. In the majority of cases, the sons enjoyed a considerably higher level of formal education than the fathers.[15] From relatively small grocery markets like Borman's came super marketchains like Farmer Jack; from wholesale dealers like Joseph Wolf came large retail businesses like Abner Wolf's and John and Nate Lurie's Wrigley's.

Similarly, 35 percent of those Jews who were white-collar workers had sons who were professionals, and 55 percent who were blue-collar workers had sons who were white-collar, managerial, or professional workers. In general, then, the American tendency toward explosive growth, the penchant for bigness to supersede small ownership found expression in the Jews of Detroit. As women entered the job markets in the 1950s, they tended toward white-collar jobs (which included professional categories), and 87 percent of those employed mark the first generation of Jewish women

to receive college educations to prepare for the marketplace. Despite this
trend, most Jewish women left their careers after marriage or after having
children.[16] This, too, would change radically by the mid-1960s.

By 1950 the younger generation of the Jews of Detroit became visibly
successful, yearning for American expansion and a suburban life that would
reflect their education and careers. First Oak Park and then Southfield,
the home of the first American shopping center, Northland, served that
purpose. In 1952 only 3 percent of the Jewish population lived in Oak Park.
The overwhelming majority still remained in the Northwest and Dexter
neighborhoods. By 1959, 28 percent had come to Oak Park, only 7 percent
remained in the Dexter area; and by 1965 46 percent resided in Oak Park,
Huntington Woods (the more affluent suburb just north of Oak Park),
Southfield, and Farmington (still further north and west). Those peripheral
Jewish enclaves like Michigan Avenue or the East Side of Mack Avenue,
which housed Jewish stores and even a synagogue, had long since disappeared as Jewish presences. But by the late 1950s, regions that had become
the hub and axis of Jewish life in Detroit were shifting. In his 1966 geographic mobility and fertility study, Mayer wrote of the years from 1950
to 1965: "Twelfth Street, as a Jewish area, is gone and forgotten. The Dexter area no longer can be considered to contain more than a trace of Jewish
households. The Northwest area . . . has gone from youth to middle age
to decline. Places whose names were not even known to most Jewish persons in 1949 have become 'marked' as Jewish sub-communities."[17]

28

Like a Magnet:
The Birth of Israel

Mary Koretz celebrated her birthday on May 16, 1948, at the athletic field of Central High School. Some twenty-two thousand exuberant celebrants joined her there for an occasion none of them would forget. They convened that Sunday at 3:30 P.M., in the "largest demonstration by Jews ever in the history of Detroit," to acclaim the birth of the state of Israel.[18] Two days earlier, British rule of Palestine had ended as a result of a United Nations vote taken in November 1947. Zionist supporters in Detroit had been "glued to [their] radios" that day as the UN roll call progressed. After the Soviet Union voted approval and when the United States cast the determining vote, cheers could be heard throughout the Northwest neighborhood and along Dexter. That momentous, consequential vote produced changes in Jewish lives all over the world, not least of all among Jews in Detroit. "Israel became like a magnet," declared one old-time Labor Zionist. It would begin to attract more and more Jews to its maintenance and sustenance. Those who had yearned for the state deepened their commitment; some of those who had opposed it became neutral, and some of them turned to its support; those who had been indifferent became Israel's champions.

Nothing before had so unified the Jews of Detroit (or America) as this day.

Eight Mile Road

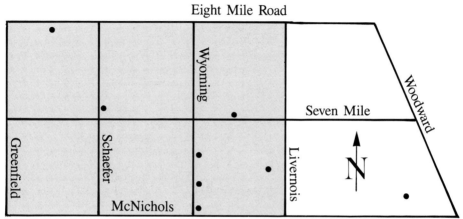

Eastern Half

Eight Mile Road

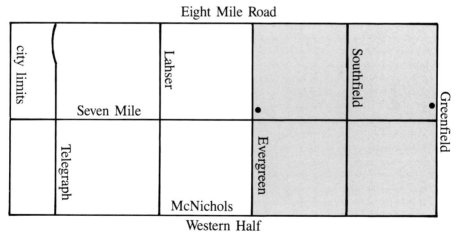

Western Half

Highest Jewish Density   • Synagogue

Northwest Detroit in 1960

Frank's Market, Joseph Campau, Detroit, predecessor of Frank's Nursery Sales, Inc., 1948. President Harry Truman's motorcade passing in front. *Extreme right:* Frank Sherr. *Center leaning forward:* I. William Sherr. *Left, with hand raised:* Max Weinberg. (Courtesy of the Sherr and Weinberg families.)

Israel Independence Day at the State Fair Grounds, 1949. (Courtesy of the collection of the Jewish Community Council.)

Governor G. Mennen Williams joins the Jewish community in celebration of Israel Independence Day at the State Fair Grounds, 1949. (Courtesy of the collection of the Jewish Community Council.)

Greeting David Ben Gurion at Detroit Airport, 1951. *From left:* Florence and Max Osnos, Paula and David Ben Gurion, Israel Davidson, Emma Schaver. (Courtesy of the collection of Emma Schaver.)

Central Overall Co., sends supplies for the Israel Defense Force, 1950s. *From left:* Morris Schaver, Ben Herold. (Courtesy of the collection of Emma Schaver.)

First National Exhibition of Jewish Ceremonial Art sponsored by the Detroit Institute of Arts, 1951. Collector Charles Feinberg showing item. (Courtesy of the collection of Congregation Shaarey Zedek.)

Detroit delegation to 13th Biennial Convention of the Pioneer Women, Washington, D.C., 1953. *Front row, from left:* Adele Mondry, Bess Berris, Chana Michlin, Helen Posner, Sophie Sislin. (Courtesy of Chana Michlin.)

Six presidents of Hadassah, 1954. *At rear, from left:* Mina Bargman, 1949–1951; Pauline Jackson, 1931–1932 and 1935–1936; Hattie Gittleman, 1923–1927; Sarah Glasier, 1940–1947. *In front:* Dora Ehrlich, 1921–1923 and 1927–1929; Sarah Davidson, 1929–1931. (Courtesy of the Jewish Historical Society of Michigan.)

"Hadassah Corners," 7 Mile and Livernois, Detroit, 1955. *From left:* Fay Moss, Bess Ravitz, Sally Jaffee, Helen Rom. (Courtesy of Hadassah.)

Adas Shalom Synagogue, Curtis Avenue at Santa Rosa, Detroit, 1945. (Courtesy of the collection of Congregation Adas Shalom.)

Congregation Ahavas Achim, 19190 Schaefer, Detroit, 1950. (Courtesy of the Burton Historical Collection of the Detroit Public Library.)

Temple Israel's Building Committee and Building Fund Committee at ceremony preparing land for new sanctuary, Manderson and Merton, Palmer Park, Detroit, 1949. *On bulldozer, from left:* Louis H. Schostak, Rabbi Leon Fram. *In front:* Sol R. Colton, Jacob I. Citrin, George M. Stutz, Edward Rose. (Courtesy of the collection of Temple Israel.)

Ira Sonnenblick, executive director of the Jewish Home for Aged, with Leonard N. Simons, in the 1960s. (Courtesy of the collection of the Jewish Home for Aged.)

Temple Israel, Manderson and Merton, Palmer Park, Detroit, 1961. (Courtesy of the collection of Temple Israel.)

Rabbi Leon Fram (*right*), founder of Temple Israel, with Rabbi M. Robert Syme of Temple Israel, ca. 1941. (Courtesy of the collection of Temple Israel.)

Rabbi Leizer Levin, leader of the Council of Orthodox Rabbis and rabbi of Congregation Beth Tefile Emanuel Tikvah, 1960s. (Courtesy of the collection of the Council of Orthodox Rabbis.)

At Temple Beth El, 1965. *From left:* Rabbi Minard Klein, Rabbi Richard C. Hertz, Philip Slomovitz, Leonard N. Simons, Irving Katz. (Courtesy of the Rabbi Leo M. Franklin Archives of Temple Beth El.)

Rabbi Jacob E. Segal of the
Northwest Hebrew
Congregation, later the Adas
Shalom Synagogue, and
founding member of the Hillel
Day School, 1960s. (Courtesy
of the Archives of the Jewish
Welfare Federation.)

Congregation Beth Abraham, 7
Mile and Greenlawn, Detroit,
1955. (Courtesy of the Burton
Historical Collection of the
Detroit Public Library.)

Program Planners Institute of the Jewish Community Council, 1949. *From left:*
Moe Kesner, Lawrence Crohn, Mrs. Max Fried, Dr. Shmarya Kleinman, Louis
Rosenzweig, James Ellman, S. Joseph Fauman, Boris M. Joffe, executive director.
(Courtesy of the collection of the Jewish Community Council.)

Proclamation on behalf of Soviet Jewry delivered by Mayor Jerome P. Cavanagh
to the Jewish Community Council, 1966. *Top row, from left:* Bernard Panush,
Rabbi Benjamin Gorelick, Rabbi Leon Fram, Edwin G. Shifrin, Benjamin Laikin.
Front row: Rabbi Chaskel Grubner, Judge Lawrence Gubow, Mayor Jerome P.
Cavanagh, Dr. Samuel Krohn, Walter E. Klein, executive director. (Courtesy of
the collection of the Jewish Community Council.)

Signing of the Absentee Voters Act, 1950. *From left:* Harry Weinberg, Rabbi Leon Fram, Rabbi Morris Adler, Larry Weinberg, State Senator Charles Blondy, Julius Goldberg. *Seated:* Governor G. Mennen Williams. (Courtesy of the Archives of the Michigan Jewish Historical Society.)

Jewish Community Council Higher Education Opportunity and Scholarship Committee, late 1960s. *From left:* Judge Theodore Levin, Judge Wade McCree, Dr. Samuel Krohn. (Courtesy of the collection of the Jewish Community Council.)

Josephine (Mrs. Leonard) Weiner, president, National Council of Jewish Women (*left*), with Nancy (Mrs. G. Mennen) Williams, 1950s. (Courtesy of the Archives of the National Council of Jewish Women, Detroit Section.)

Dora Ehrlich with Eleanor Roosevelt, 1950s. (Courtesy of Joseph B. Colten.)

Golda Krolik with Eleanor Roosevelt at Temple Beth El, ca. 1953. (Courtesy of Bess Krolik.)

Allied Jewish Campaign meeting, 1955. *From left:* Golda Meir, Julian Krolik, Gertrude Wineman, Henry Wineman. (Courtesy of Bess Krolik.)

The Jimmy Prentis Morris Branch of the Jewish Community Center, Oak Park. (Courtesy of Benyas-Kaufman Photographers.)

Groundbreaking for "New Main," the Jewish Community Center at Curtis-Meyers, Detroit, 1957. Irwin Shaw, executive vice-president, *with shovel,* and Judge Theodore Levin, *at microphone.* (Courtesy of the collection of the Jewish Community Center.)

The Jewish Community Center, Curtis-Meyers, Detroit. (Courtesy of Benyas-Kaufman Photographers.)

Survivors of the concentration camps, Larry, Ruth, and Jack Weintraub, in 1946: "Atlantic Crossing—America, My Great Country." (Courtesy of the collection of Ruth Weintraub Kent.)

Resettlement Service staff member greeting refugee family in front of the Book-Cadillac Hotel, Detroit, 1940s. (Courtesy of the Archives of the Jewish Welfare Federation.)

Survivors Israel and Paula Elpern in front of the European office of ORT (Organization for Rehabilitation through Training), 1946. (Courtesy of Joan Jampel.)

Harry T. Madison, leader of the Hannah Schloss Old Timers and national commander of the Jewish War Veterans of America, 1950s. (Courtesy of the Hannah Schloss Old Timers—Jewish Community Center.)

Fresh Air Society, dedication of Sheruth Village at Camp Tamarack, 1961. *At podium:* Anna W. Chapin, president of the Sheruth League and controller of the Jewish Welfare Federation. *At rear, from left:* Edith Heavenrich; Max M. Fisher, president of the Jewish Welfare Federation; Milton Maddin, past president of the Fresh Air Society. (Courtesy of Elyse Levinson.)

Moving out of the Chicago Boulevard sanctuary of Congregation Shaarey Zedek, 1962. *Front row, from left:* Cantor Jacob Sonenklar, Rabbi Irwin Groner, Abraham Satovsky, David Miro, Louis Berry, Rabbi Morris Adler, Abraham Salzberg, Peter Weisberg, Morris Karbal, ———, ———. *Second row:* ———, I. Murray Jacobs, Sexton Jacob Epel, ———, Reuben Himmelstein, M. Ben Lewis, Tom Borman, Hyman Keidan, Joseph Gendelman, Leonard Sidlow, Hyman Safran, Morris Fishman, Joseph Brandt, Israel Elpern. *Third row:* Abraham Srere, Charles Agree, Jack Gordon, Abraham Caplan, Harvey Weisberg, Harold Berry, Lester Satovsky, Harry Cohen, Jay Rosenthal. (Courtesy of the Archives of Congregation Shaarey Zedek).

Cornerstone-laying ceremony at new sanctuary of Congregation Shaarey Zedek, Bell Road, Southfield, 1962. *From right:* Mandell L. Berman, Dr. Samuel Krohn, Cantor Jacob Sonenklar, Max M. Fisher, Louis M. Berry, David Miro, Rabbi Morris Adler, ———, Rabbi Irwin Groner. (Courtesy of the Archives of Congregation Shaarey Zedek.)

Congregation Shaarey Zedek, Southfield, 1962. Photograph by Balthazar Koreb. (Courtesy of the Archives of Congregation Shaarey Zedek.)

Rabbi and Mrs. Morris Adler, 1950s. (Courtesy of the Archives of Congregation Shaarey Zedek.)

Viewing building plans for Sinai Hospital, 1952. *From left:* Nate Shapero, Max Osnos, Dr. Julien Priver. (Courtesy of the Archives of Sinai Hospital.)

Sinai Hospital cornerstone-laying ceremony, 1952. *From left:* Justice Henry Butzel, Nate Shapero, Rabbi B. Benedict Glazer, Samuel H. Rubiner, Max Osnos. (Courtesy of the Archives of the Jewish Welfare Federation.)

House staff of Sinai Hospital at its opening, 1953. *Seated, from left:* Drs. Edward
Salem, Howard Jacobs, Harry C. Saltzstein, George B. Easterman, Julien Priver.
Standing: Drs. Hubert Miller, Eugene Perrin, Harry Burke, Frederick Weissman,
Saul Sakwa, Gabriel Masry, Gerald Mandell, Marvin Brodie, Diab Jerius,
Raymond Zwick. (Courtesy of the Archives of the Jewish Welfare Federation.)

Three leaders of the Women's Guild of Sinai Hospital. *From left:* Mollie
Hartman, Lenore Dunsky, Tillie Martin. (Courtesy of the Women's Guild of Sinai
Hospital.)

Since the end of World War II, Jews in Detroit, as elsewhere in the United States, had increasingly advocated Jewish statehood. More people joined the intensified efforts of the Zionist Organization of Detroit behind Benjamin Laikin, Rabbi Adler, and Rabbi Fram, among others. The *Jewish News,* already a Zionist champion, more openly promoted the cause with explicitly Zionist editorials and articles that by September 1947 expressed outright hostility to Britain, demanded freedom for the displaced persons now thrown into internment camps, and focused front-page coverage on the *Exodus* in 1947, when the British seized that ship.[19] Articles about individuals who had been to Palestine and dedicated their lives to the founding of a state filled each issue.

Young Sheldon Lutz, a corporal in the Air Force, returned from Europe in August 1947 and reported about his work in the Landsberg and other DP camps where he had struggled for a year to raise funds to send Jews to Palestine. Back in Detroit, ambivalent about leaving survivors and the prospect of emigrating to Palestine, he began speaking on behalf of a Jewish state.[20] What he did not reveal in the *Jewish News* article about him was his collaboration with the Jewish underground as it strove to smuggle Jews out of Europe, past the British blockade, and into Palestine.

In Landsberg, Lutz had met another Detroiter long-pledged to Jewish statehood: Emma Lazaroff Schaver. After hearing of the dolorous condition of Jewish survivors in DP camps, she had decided to offer succor however she could. With help from the U.S. government, Mrs. Schaver toured the camps, entertaining the internees with Yiddish and Zionist songs and quietly helping whomever she could to leave for Palestine. A lifelong Labor Zionist like her husband, she represented him and Detroit's Labor Zionist commitments to the future of Israel, acting as their cultural ambassador to the remnants of European Jewry.

Yet another Detroiter who toured the DP camps and then traveled to Palestine found his commitment to Zionism forcefully strengthened. Louis Berry wrote to Rabbi Morris Adler on February 15, 1948, from Tel Aviv that "in Europe we saw darkness and shadows. Here in Israel we see light." Like Lutz, Berry was a member of Shaarey Zedek, and had formerly served as president of the congregation that had formally and publicly stated its allegiance to Zionism. He went on to describe the misery, squalor, and suffering among the "unfortunates" who had survived in Europe; he contrasted those circumstances and, tacitly, the future of Jews in Europe with the "thriving, throbbing cities. . . . Kibbutzim flourishing. . . . We see industries and factories."[21] As a result of his visit, Berry threw himself even more actively into the United Jewish Appeal, both nationally and locally, directing the 1949 campaign in Detroit with Joseph Holtzman. Together with friends and traveling companions William Avrunin and Hyman Safran, they returned to Detroit imbued with the ardor and zeal of missionaries.

Louis Berry had achieved extraordinary business success in Detroit and consequently a degree of prestige in both the Jewish and non-Jewish communities. Having begun as a salesman for Isaac Shetzer's dry-goods store (visiting other stores like that of Philip Slomovitz's father, where he would sit with his cigar and "exchange witticisms") Berry grew to become a genuine real-estate magnate, owning buildings all over the United States. By 1962 he had purchased the Fisher Building and the New Center Building from the Fisher Brothers and, with Max Fisher and others, founded the Fisher-New Center Company. Perhaps Simon Shetzer, Isaac's son, had influenced him earlier—Shetzer became national executive secretary in the Zionist Organization of America—or perhaps his involvement in the life of Shaarey Zedek had drawn him to Zionism; whatever the source, Berry brought remarkable vigor and power to fund-raising for Israel in the critical years between 1948 and 1967. His voice, along with those of his friends Joseph Holtzman, Max Fisher, and other celebrated Detroit Jewish businessmen like Paul Zuckerman, exerted strong pressures on the government and non-Jewish businessmen.

As the debate over Jewish statehood escalated, more Detroit Jews sought to pressure government representatives to vote in favor of the UN majority plan for dividing Palestine. Six weeks before the UN vote, Maurice Berdlove, commander of Michigan's department of Jewish War Veterans, wired an appeal to Secretary of State George Marshall, urging him to support the majority report. In October the American Jewish Congress organized a meeting at Central High School, where Reverend John Stanley Grauel, a non-Jewish crew member of the *Exodus,* spoke of the misery he witnessed on that ill-fated vessel. Shortly afterward, Gov. Kim Sigler and Mayor Edward Jeffries sent telegrams in support of a Jewish state to President Truman. Led by Rabbi Wohlgelernter, all of Detroit's Orthodox congregations sent similar telegrams.[22]

Impelled by newsreels and news reports from the Nuremberg trials, which revealed the extent of the catastrophe of the Holocaust, the pace quickened, support spiraled, and the ranks of those promoting Zionism began to swell with some surprising figures. The board of directors of the *Jewish News,* Maurice Aronsson, Isidore Soboloff, Fred Butzel, Judge Theodore Levin, Maurice Schwartz, Philip Slomovitz, Abe Srere, and Henry Wineman, seemed to endorse the now blatantly overt Zionist position held by the paper.[23] Most of those men (with obvious exceptions like Slomovitz, and not so obvious ones like Wineman), staunch Federation advocates, had not been known as pro-Zionist. Now, however, their association with the paper made them de facto Zionists.

Thus while more than seventy-five thousand people jammed Times Square in New York City to hear Eleanor Roosevelt and Sen. Robert Taft as they greeted the event, more than twenty-two-thousand people filled the athletic field at Central High School on May 16, 1948.[24] Along with Mary Goldman Koretz, Emma and Morris Schaver, Harry Schumer, members of

329

the Poale Zion, the Workmen's Circle, and the Sholem Aleichem Institute, all crowded onto the field to rejoice and observe the ceremonies cosponsored, significantly, by the Zionist Emergency Council of Detroit and the Jewish Community Council.

Members of Federation also joined in the extraordinary jubilation. Louis Berry, Isidore Sobeloff, Maurice Aronsson (who had presided over the 1948 campaign), past-president Abe Srere, and nearly the entire Federation board appeared. Young Cantor Hyman Adler of Congregation B'nai David blew the shofar, the ram's horn, to usher in a new era. Rabbi Isaac Stollman read from Psalms. The Detroit Police Band and the Pythias Bugle Corps provided music that included a moving memorial to Jewish martyrs.

Benjamin Laikin delivered the opening address and Rabbi Leon Fram gave the concluding, keynote speech. Between the two came statements of varying lengths from Pat McNamara of the American Federation of Labor (AFL), and from Tracy Dell and Barney Hopkins of the Congress of Industrial Organizations (CIO). Their presence signified the long-term affinity between American unions and Zionism. From 1945 on a warmly cordial relationship had existed between Zionist leaders like Golda Meir and leaders of the American labor movement like James B. Carey, secretary-treasurer of the CIO. Carey had corresponded with "Sister Myerson," reiterating his union's steadfast support of Histadrut and Zionism "from the beginning." She, in turn, had written "Brother Carey" as "Dear Comrade," and both had worked with Joseph Bernstein, Detroit's representative of the Jewish Labor Committee.[25]

Irving Bluestone arrived in Detroit in 1948 as a United Auto Workers' (UAW) organizer and assistant to Walter Reuther, president of the union. In 1945, Bluestone recalled, during the 113-day General Motors strike, the Jewish Labor Committee had become active in support of the UAW, and Bluestone already heard of one particularly daring young man, Irving Pokempner, who braved the barricades to smuggle food into the strikers. Pokempner, an avid supporter of both the Jewish Community Council and Labor Zionism, became a close friend of Bluestone's.

Such personal relationships, including the connection of Reuther's wife, Mae Wolf, whose family remained avid leftists and Workmen's Circle members, cemented the Detroit labor movement to parts of the Detroit Jewish population. Unions championed Zionism because of Histadrut, which some of its leaders and much of its rank and file saw as synonymous with socialism. They perceived the foundation of Israel as labor-oriented, liberal, and carrying a social-democratic philosophy of society. They turned out in some force on May 16, 1948, at the athletic field of Central High School.

That labor in Detroit formed close ties with Israel from its inception augured well for the state. Labor's support, which included strong patronage from the Teamsters' Union via the Laundry and Linen Drivers Union, set Detroit-Jewish philanthropic sources apart from most other American cities. Isaac Litwak, once referred to by a fellow union member as "the only real honest man in the whole Teamster Union," gathered his union together at fund-raising meetings and asked for public commitments. Friends and coworkers remembered his responses to pledges he considered too small: "I can't hear you, brother," or, "A little louder, brother, I didn't hear you." In 1950, Litwak, on behalf of the Linen and Laundry Drivers' Union, negotiated a fund-raising agreement with William Avrunin, then associate director of the Federation. Isidore Sobeloff, Harry Schumer, and Morris Schaver worked out a formula whereby 10 percent of the funds raised by the union went to the Federation for administrative costs; 60 percent of the remainder went to the Allied Jewish Campaign and 40 percent to Histadrut. By this accord, the union members were protected from a second solicitation for funds. It was, in effect, a separate Federation-Histadrut campaign that came to be feted with annual Sunday brunches steeped in at least public good-fellowship.

By the late 1950s UAW conventions regularly produced resolutions endorsing Israel. Bluestone and other labor leaders spoke to the Jewish Labor Committee in private homes and at public meetings regarding Israel; the UAW annually matched funds raised at Histadrut dinners to provide for vocational schools and other sorts of educational programs; and in the 1970s a Walter Reuther Chair was established at the Weizmann Institute. Reaffirming the ties between labor and Israel, Reuther, Bluestone, and other Detroit labor leaders became honorees at Histadrut dinners that raised funds for specific projects. Similarly, several Jews in Detroit, such as Rabbi Morris Adler, became active in the labor movement in the 1950s. Reuther had Adler appointed president of the review board of the UAW. After he was persuaded by Labor Zionist friends, Victor Reuther visited Israel with a Christian group and returned a dedicated Zionist. He would become an avid spokesman for the Jewish National Fund and a delegate to their conference in November 1950. He would speak to and on behalf of Histadrut and address Labor Zionist groups as he grew increasingly into a steadfast advocate of Israel.[26] While these relationships had already begun before 1948, May 16 marked a clear turning point in further cooperation.

Included on the lengthy list of speakers at Central High that day, Reverend Sheldon Rahn, of the Detroit Council of Churches, offered an inspiring testimonial to Israel; so, too, did George Edwards, of the Detroit City Council, Rep. Howard Coffin, long a supporter of the Zionist cause, and Rep. John Dingell who, along with Sen. Arthur J. Vandenberg, had been among the first to commend President Truman for his speedy recognition of the Jewish state. Vandenberg, who had corresponded with Philip Slomovitz affirming his endorsement of a Jewish state in Palestine since 1929, did not attend the meeting but sent the text of a speech to be read.[27] A conservative Republican, he nevertheless seemed to overlook the leftist orientation of most of the protagonists of Zionism in the 1930s and 1940s.

Predictably, the day elicited deep emotional effects: tears, laughter, and exuberant celebrations only slightly overshadowed by the fact of war that had already exploded in the Middle East. The *Jewish News* carried a two-page ad saluting Israel with photographs of an Israeli flag waving in Israel, Haganah fighters, and Dr. Chaim Weizmann (the first president of Israel) and his wife. That ad had been taken out by, among others, Claudette's Chocolates ("which now offer[ed] kosher marshmallow confection"), Central Overall Supply Co. (Morris Schaver), Kasle Steel, Schechter Furniture, Scholnick's, Harry Schumer's General Linen Supply Co., Mr. and Mrs. Philip Cutler, and the United Dairies.[28]

Another sponsor of the salute to Israel was Keystone Oil. According to some observers, the birth of Israel and the urging of his partner Leon Kay (Komisaruk) prompted Max Fisher, previously "unaffiliated and relatively uninformed," into active philanthropic participation in Jewish affairs. But Fisher recalls almost to the moment when he became dedicated to Israel and, through it, to Jewish causes in Detroit and elsewhere. In 1954 the United Jewish Appeal sent its first "mission" to the new state. Three Detroiters received invitations: William Avrunin, Max J. Zivian, and Max Fisher. An unabashed attempt to enlist the support of wealthy and influential Jews, the mission proved to be a decisive turning point in Fisher's life. He met Ben-Gurion, agriculturalist Giora Josephthal, mayor of Jerusalem Teddy Kolleck, and Golda Meir. He met, too, Jews from Iran and Iraq; he visited a Yemenite camp and heard the wailing prayer chants unlike any Jewish prayers he had encountered. It gave him, he said, a "sense of identification . . . [with] the new feeling that something [in Israel] pervaded the atmosphere." Fisher felt a sense of pride and accomplishment and an intense desire to become a part of whatever it was that "pervaded the atmosphere." Primed by earlier discussions with Leon Kay about the Holocaust and Kay's deep fidelity to Israel, Fisher now directly observed the passion of the pioneers and believed that his public Jewish identity took form in the crucible of that mission. The benefits reaped from Fisher's dynamic role in fund-raising would become incalculable.

Israeli Independence Day, *Yom Ha-Atzmaout,* seemed to galvanize Detroit's Jews and unify them solidly behind Israel. While this unity would fade, Israel would remain a mainstay, a rallying point that would attract more and more Jews—like a magnet. In the events of that day in Detroit lay the roots of the "Detroit difference" that would develop more distinctly in the next twenty years: the drawing together of groups like the Labor Zionists and the Federation; Reform, Conservative, Orthodox, and secular Jews; and individuals from diverse backgrounds, despite political, economic, or ideological differences that would otherwise appear irreconcilable. Because of such individuals and such circumstances unique to Detroit—not the least of which revolved around the automobile industry and its attendant wealth, unions, and the peripheral businesses in which Jews excelled–the Jews of Detroit would become leaders in bolstering Israel in times of need. Few cities, even those with notably larger Jewish populations, would surpass Detroit's efforts and success. It struck several of Detroit's Zionist spokespersons that this remarkable demonstration revealed that support of Israel might be the "single most important and certain source of Jewish identity." It bridged religious differences, political disagreements, and even cultural gaps. Yet the solidarity that attended May 16, 1948, began to reveal signs of erosion almost immediately.

"Internecine strife among Jews is no less a threat to the survival of our people and our faith than is the onslaught of our avowed enemies." In June 1948, Rabbi Leo Franklin concluded his letter of resignation from the anti-Zionist American Council for Judaism with those words. Referring to his previous rationale for joining the Council, and to its prospects for continuing, Franklin wrote that "for the sake of world Jewry, the American Council for Judaism, if it is to continue, must . . . shift . . . to the positive support of every legitimate effort to gain for the Jews of the world the rights of citizenship."[29] It struck some as an apology—perhaps for a career-long opposition; others viewed it as a logical transformation in light of the reality of Israel. Still others claim that Milford Stern, then president of Temple Beth El, and other leading members of the congregation convinced Rabbi Franklin of the necessity to change his stance. Whatever the reasons, this surprising move, two months before his death, echoed the sense of fellowship that had descended on American Jews because of the creation of Israel.

Yet on May 14, as the announcement of the great celebration dominated the *Jewish News,* Federation proclaimed its precampaign publicity. Ostensibly supporting the featured call to prepare for the Allied Jewish Campaign, the Zionist Council of Detroit issued a statement warning Detroit's Jews that the Allied Jewish Campaign remained the "sole agency for the collection of funds for the Jewish defense in Palestine."[30] Louis Berry declared his "wonderful feeling" about the "new look in giving," meaning that previous contributors had indicated their increased pledges. By October Associate Director William Avrunin reported that pledges had risen to nearly $5,800,000, 47 percent more than in 1947, with over thirty-thousand contributors.[31] Berry, who successfully led the United Jewish Appeal for the entire state, had proven to be a fund-raising wonder.

Avrunin wrote in the *Jewish News* that Federation sought to mainstream Jewish donations through one source rather than through individual groups. By November B'nai B'rith charged that Federation had "sabotaged" the drive for Israel. Isador Starr, president of the B'nai B'rith Council, accused Isidore Sobeloff of advising Federation officers and supporters not to contribute to the B'nai B'rith Aid to the People of Israel campaign. In an open

333

letter, Starr stated that Sobeloff had complained of B'nai B'rith extending their fund-raising to October 26, thereby violating the agreement about unilateral fund-raising during the campaign. Starr refused to acknowledge such an agreement and alleged that Federation "attempted to place strict limitations on the activities through the medium of decrees and orders."[32] The acerbic exchange foreshadowed others, equally maledictory and also over allocation of funds raised by the Allied Jewish Campaign.

One year later, on May 15, 1949, Jews in Detroit celebrated the first anniversary of the state of Israel. More than 160 congregations and community organizations joined together at the Coliseum of the State Fair on Woodward and Eight Mile Road. Principal speakers were Rabbi Morris Adler of Shaarey Zedek and Ben-Zion Ilan, former Haganah leader. The Zionist Council of Detroit, under its new president, Sidney Shevitz, cosponsored the event with the Jewish Community Council, under Aaron Droock. Twelve to fifteen thousand people attended.[33]

After the presentation of the colors—American and Israeli—by the Jewish War Veterans and by Israeli veterans together with Canadian army and navy veterans, Emma Schaver led in the singing of the national anthems, and Rabbi Leizer Levin read Hebrew prayers as spokesman for the Orthodox Vaad Harabonim. Musical selections included presentations by the Detroit Cantors' Association and some two hundred children from the United Hebrew Schools, the Farband Schools, the Sholem Aleichem Institute, the Workmen's Circle Schools, Yeshivah Beth Yehudah, Yeshivath Chachmey Lublin, Shaarey Zedek, B'nai Moshe, B'nai David, Beth El, Temple Israel, Mitttellshule, Carmel Hebrew School, Habonim, Young Judaea, Hashomer Hatzair, and Young Israel. Nominal cosponsors included the B'nai B'rith lodges, the American Jewish Congress, Jewish War Veterans, all Zionist organizations, the Workmen's Circle, the American Jewish Committee, and several of the *landsmanshaftn*.

Acting mayor George Edwards proclaimed May 15 "State of Israel Day." Sidney Shevitz, chairman of the arrangements committee, declared that "this is one occasion on which Detroit's Jews can assemble in a festive atmosphere to give thanks for the redemption that has occurred within our time."[34] Once again, long-time supporters of Zionism sponsored ads in the *Jewish News*. It seemed to be another outpouring of communal cooperation.

Nevertheless, the principal advocates were the Council and the Zionist organizations—all of which bore a distinctly Eastern European cast. There were exceptions, of course, yet the general atmosphere, the attitude, the values, and tone appeared unmistakable. Hebrew and Yiddish songs marked all the programs. Rabbi Adler and Rabbi Fram still maintained high profiles; and Sidney Shevitz and Aaron Droock, despite their involvement with the Federation, drew their main constituency from the Council.

On May 4, ten days before the official anniversary celebration, "an overflow audience of labor Zionists celebrated the first anniversary of Israel at an inspiring program." Dr. Nahum Weissman, director of the Jewish National Workers' Alliance in Detroit, presided, and Louis Levine led community singing in Yiddish and read a poem dedicated to Israel. Morris Lieberman, chairman of the Central Committee of the Detroit Labor Zionists Organization, sent a congratulatory message to Prime Minister David Ben-Gurion in Tel Aviv. Virtually everyone who attended belonged to the Farband, the Jewish National Workers Alliance.[35]

From 1949 on, a usually subtle tension existed among the major organizational factions of the Jews of Detroit. This tension assumed its most explicit expression in the endemic conflicts between Council and Federation. Smaller manifestations of such strains occasionally erupted, like the encounter between B'nai B'rith and the Federation in November 1948. But in the main, the smaller groups spoke through the Council. Ironically, both organizations shared supporters and even leaders. Sometimes that fact produced peaceful resolution to differences of opinion. Perhaps the most effective peacemaker had been Fred M. Butzel, who had supported the Council and Zionism (initially against his better judgment) and had bridged the gap between a multiplicity of groups.

When, in March 1950, Morris Lieberman told a Histadrut meeting of the successful completion of a $230,000-campaign in Detroit, Rabbi Adler spoke to the group about the continuing "Zionist ideal." After the Music Study Club Chorus entertained under the direction of Dan Frohman, Adler told those who had come to hear him at the Northwest Hebrew Congregation that "we are Jews and Americans." He averred that Israel had become the vehicle for democracy in the Middle East and that "we must continue to serve as Israel's interpreters to the outside world." His address was in Yiddish.[36]

Later that year, at the second-anniversary celebration for Israel, Mayor Cobo and Governor Williams appeared, along with twelve thousand others, at the State Fair Coliseum. There, Sidney Shevitz presided and sounded the "keynote of the meeting" when he declared that "Israel was keeping her promise of democracy in the Middle East." Shevitz echoed Rabbi Adler's comments made earlier that year, in Yiddish, at the Histadrut celebration. Israel embodied democracy, freedom, and the great American ideas. At that second-anniversary commemoration, the Central High School band, under the direction of Ben Silverstein, played both national anthems; the Jewish War Veterans presented the colors of both countries; Detroit veterans of Israel's war of independence presented the colors, too, and Leo Maizels, Peggy Leeds, Robert Leeds, Dan Bulkin, Jack Eringer, David Saferstein, Manfred Nashtalie, Herbert Hordes, David Fink, Ben Fingerroot, and Jules Doneson provided a stirring scene, with memories of glory surrounding them. Children gave greetings in Hebrew and Yiddish as each part-time and full-time Jewish school was represented. Habonim performed a dra- 335

matic sketch that concluded with the mass singing of Hatikvah and dancing of the horah.[37]

Labor Zionism, the Council, Yiddish, and an East European tone and
constituency clearly marked that occasion. Those elements of the Jewish
population of Detroit infused the speakers, the subjects, the entertainment,
and the flavor of the event. Once again, evidence of division, even over
Israel, seemed to creep into public Jewish life, even if the gap had become
considerably narrower than it had been.

One interlude of solidarity came sadly in May 1948, a week after Israel's
declaration as an independent state. Fred Butzel died, and his death oc-
casioned an outpouring of unified sorrow and loss. The full-page tribute
that appeared in the *Detroit Free Press* was cosponsored by Federation and
the United Jewish Charities, and signed by Julian H. Krolik, president of
Federation, and the Honorable Theodore Levin, president of the United
Jewish Charities. But the tribute also included endorsements from Morris
L. Schaver, president of the Farband School; Aaron Droock, president of
the Council; Abe Kasle, president of the United Hebrew Schools; Rabbi Max
J. Wohlgelernter, president of the Yeshivah Beth Yehudah; Rabbi Stephen
S. Wise, president of the American Jewish Congress; Jay Rosenshine, president of the Sholem Aleichem Institute; David Feinn, president of the
Workmen's Circle Schools; Henry Morgenthau, Jr., general chairman of
the United Jewish Appeal; and numerous other local, national, and international figures.[38] "Detroit's most valuable citizen," said the *Free Press*,
had left an unfillable gap in the community.[39] That loss brought a rare
moment of harmony to the Jews of Detroit, a moment in which they joined
many Detroit non-Jews to mourn.

Israel "had changed everything," pronounced one Council leader. And
unquestionably, the overwhelming majority of Jews in Detroit came to Israel's defense. Individuals and organizations alike, Council and Federation,
all threw their support to the new state. Yet questions remained about
what that might mean for internal or domestic policies of certain agencies.
Federation allocated large amounts from the Allied Jewish Campaign to
Israel. It still remained a source of contention, usually unexpressed but
present. At the National Planning Conference for Israel and Jewish Reconstruction held in Washington, D.C., in October 1950, more than five hundred
delegates participated in heated debates. Isidore Sobeloff, one of the more
than thirty people to attend from Detroit, raised the issue of separate campaigns during one of those debates. He challenged those delegates who
claimed that federations across the country allocated more money to local
needs than to Israel. In a particularly acrimonious exchange, some adversaries quoted figures to support their claims, to which Sobeloff argued that
they should examine concrete sums in considerable detail. Despite such
caustic arguments, the general mood of the conference seemed amicable

and became inspired when Abba Eban, Golda Meir, or Henry Montor spoke to the delegates. American Jewry, claimed Philip Slomovitz on returning from the conference, had reached a "new level of unity."[40]

To the non-Jewish world it seemed that Histadrut and Labor Zionism had become synonymous with the state of Israel. Just as he had proclaimed April 30 "Israel Day," Mayor Albert Cobo signed a proclamation on November 30, 1950, declaring that week "Histadrut Week" as Harry Schumer, Chana Michlin, Norman Cottler, Morris Lieberman, and Morris Schaver looked on.[41] U.S. Vice-president Alben W. Barkley wrote a lengthy "Tribute to Histadrut," which appeared in the Jewish News on the occasion of the labor movement's thirtieth anniversary. Franklin D. Roosevelt, Jr. wrote a similar tribute, and comparable accolades appeared from other American and European leaders. That year, Norman Cottler was declared Histadrut Man of the Year, having served as campaign treasurer in the independent Histadrut campaign. At the dedication dinner in December 1950, Histadrut delegates argued that the programs sponsored by Histadrut had never been part of the UJA because of their diverse nature.

This veiled antagonism would not begin to dissipate until the 1960s. Harold Berke, executive secretary of Histadrut, arrived in Detroit from Toronto in 1952. He found this divided situation similar to what he had left in Toronto, but worked with a board in Detroit that he found not only zealous, but extraordinary in its leadership and in its ability to inspire others to respond to the needs of Israel. He marveled at the core of volunteers, the strength of the Pioneer Women, and the commitment of virtually every member of Histadrut. Berke served a board of directors composed of "alte Kampfers," or veteran fighters: Schaver remained honorary chairman; Morris Lieberman, chairman; Harry Schumer, chairman of the executive board; Norman Cottler, treasurer; and members whose names appeared throughout the campaign; including Benjamin Laikin, Norman Naimark, Sam Rubin, Jack Malamud, and David Sislin. Chana Michlin chaired the Pioneer Women's division; Harold Silver, the communal workers' division; Irving Pokempner and Sidney Shevitz cochaired the trades and professions council; and Frank Martel and Victor Reuther cochaired the trade union council. Morris Spitzer, manager of the Detroit Joint Board of the Amalgamated Clothing Workers (of the CIO) was active in Histadrut and would represent Detroit in July 1953 as a member of the fifth Histadrut folk delegation to Israel, a fact-finding trip that involved sixty labor leaders. When he returned, Histadrut and his union organized a banquet at which he presented a Hebrew Bible to Walter Reuther from the Haifa Labor Council. Reuther spoke on behalf of Spitzer, Israel, and Histadrut that September evening, and reiterated his hopes for "a free world labor movement."[42]

Sophie Sislin boarded a bus in 1925 and set off for a Poale Zion convention in Chicago. She asked the assembled delegates there to grant De- 337 troit a charter for Pioneer Women, the women's arm of Labor Zionism. Debate followed—according to some, the men of the Labor Zionist movement feared fragmentation of efforts if women's groups proliferated; according to others, they worried that the most tireless workers, the women, would be lost to peripheral causes. Mrs. Sislin, whose husband David numbered among the most fervent of Histadrut supporters in Detroit, prevailed and brought home the first charter for a Detroit branch of Pioneer Women.

"They worked like fools," those women, running the shule (school) and the Farband Camp founded on Lake Chelsea in 1928, attending meetings, raising money, cooking for Pioneer and Histadrut or Labor Zionist gatherings. So recalled Mrs. Sislin's daughter who sometimes accompanied her mother, taking three buses and streetcars to attend the meetings. In Histadrut homes like the Sislins', workers, Zionist intellectuals, and Detroit Jewish leaders, old and young, would gather and engage in endless discussions and debates. It seemed that the consistently central activity and agenda item at meetings was arguing. What projects should they support? How? Why? Yet no question ever arose about the centrality of support for a Jewish state—not before 1948 and certainly not after.

Their politics were left-liberal and incorporated socialism in varying degrees—although they eschewed communism. They met in the Jericho Hall, the Workmen's Circle, and other *linke* groups' meeting place, on Joy and Linwood. They soon moved to Linwood, then Schaefer and Seven Mile. Detroit Histadrut and Pioneer Women, too, moved northwest—the last to go, perhaps.

In the midst of the explosion of Zionist activity in the early 1950s, Morris Schaver remained a symbol of its vitality and also of its contradictions. He had maintained warm and close friendships with all the Labor Zionists and had not severed himself from his roots, which were labor and leftist, despite his striking business accomplishments. Conflict and ill feeling lingered between Schaver, the other Labor Zionist linen owners like Schumer, and Isaac Litwak after the Local 285 struck for ten months in 1951, "almost killing some of the linen companies," according to one owner. It had proven an unfortunately bitter and even violent encounter with hired (often Jewish) hoodlums or goons engaging in bloody melees. Yet, in general, Schaver, like his fellow linen industry magnates, remained true to his principles when it came to Israel. "It was socialism for Israel and capitalism for America," said a Histadrut colleague.

On the occasion of Schaver's sixtieth birthday, his lifetime friend, Harry Schumer, sent letters to "all societies, organizations and clubs" calling for early pledges to the Histadrut campaign. Schumer hoped to present his comrade with sixty-thousand dollars at a birthday celebration dinner at the Sheraton Cadillac Hotel on December 1, 1954. He was able to do that. David Sislin, then Histadrut recording secretary, offered comments and words of praise for Schaver on behalf of the Labor Zionists in Detroit to the cheers of the six hundred who attended the dinner. The tribute was an international one: *Histadrut Foto News* recorded it and referred to Schaver's business success, which had "strengthened in Morris Schaver the faith in a better world based on cooperation and justice for the working man."[43]

There seemed no better candidate for business investment in Israel than Schaver. So, the *Histadrut Foto News* continued, he was among the first investors in the American Palestine Trading Corporation (AMPAL), the investment arm of Histadrut. Already in 1951 he had been named associate treasurer of Israel Hotels, Inc., an American corporation building a network of hotels in anticipation of American tourism. That, too, had been initiated by AMPAL. That same year he had been appointed by Abba Eban to the board of the American Financial and Development Corporation for Israel to handle its five-hundred-million-dollar bond issue.[44]

Initially controversial, the campaign for the bond issue was chaired in Detroit by Max Osnos beginning in February 1951. The planning committee included Schaver, Mrs. Ralph Davidson, Schumer, Louis Berry, Joseph Holtzman, Mrs. Theodore Bargman, Philip Slomovitz, Abe Kasle, Lawrence Crohn, Dr. Shmarya Kleinman, Judge Levin, Samuel Rubiner, and Sidney Shevitz. Eventually, with Osnos as overall chairman, Morris Jacobs became active chairman; Leon Kay served as cochair and Slomovitz, James Ellmann, and Ira Kaufman as vice-chairmen.[45]

The bond drive proclaimed that Israel could now invite investment "like any other country." Those involved, including leaders in the business community, asserted that the United Jewish Appeal contributions were inadequate for the growing economic needs of Israel; they stated clearly that they saw no conflict between the two drives since one, the campaign, involved contributions and the other, the bond drive, meant investment. Thus, according to the publicity, the two drives complemented each other.[46]

As early as the winter of 1950, Jewish business leaders in Detroit had sought to combine philanthropic support of Israel with business profit in an "effort to express ourselves" as a distinct Detroit community. Other cities had drawn upon the expertise and particular business acumen of their private entrepreneurs. In Detroit, a group of investment-minded individuals pooled their distinctive skills to invest in the new state and bring some specific benefit to it. Louis Berry, Joe Holtzman, and others conferred with Ed Levy, Sr. and Abe Kasle, and the group decided to purchase land for a rock quarry and to construct a rock-crushing plant that would aid in building new roads and highways in Israel.

Rock Products, Inc. emerged after lengthy discussions and debates. Its organizers purchased the quarry in Israel, and Avern Cohn and Richard Sloan traveled to examine the company's progress in 1951. They returned to Israel for further investigation of the rock-crushing plant in 1952. With an engineering degree from the University of Minnesota, Ben Wilk, president of the Standard Building Products Company and of Temple Beth El, and Levy also visited the site. By 1954 it had become apparent that any hope for success depended on a merger with the construction arm of Histadrut. Some of the founders refused to negotiate with Histadrut in Israel. "They saw [Histadrut] as labor and absolutely refused to deal with them," recalled one participant. After considerable discussion, the group agreed to cable Histadrut—despite the resistance of some of the leading investors.

Political and ideological disputes aside, Rock Products, Inc. represented Detroit's deep interest in the welfare of Israel. For all those involved, "Israel's security became the central issue—single-minded and all-consuming." Even before the bond issue, that security included economic stability in the eyes of many American Jews. Israel's vitality became a completely engrossing cause that crossed political boundaries, induced conservatives to consort with liberals and socialists, brought together secular Jews with religious Jews and German Jews with East European Jews, and seemed, in this one case, to force management to collaborate with labor. This episode in 1950 presaged Detroit Jewry's relationships with Israel and the changes among the Jews of Detroit that would result.

Closely related to the defense and entrepreneurial aspects of Detroit's aid to Israel came yet another source of support. In 1952 the noted soil conservationist, Walter C. Lowdermilk, addressed the annual Technion (Israel Institute of Technology) fund-raising dinner. He described in powerfully moving detail how Jews in Israel had reclaimed the land through scientific agriculture. As the appeal for funds began, Samuel Brody, a successful realtor, declared to the "thunderstruck audience" that he would match whatever was pledged that evening. Later, when his son asked him why he had made such a magnanimous gesture (which resulted in a total of over $145,000), he replied that Israel, in his view, would be dependent on the outside world for natural resources but could develop its one indigenous, major resource, "Jewish brainpower." Science-based industries would produce not only land reclamation projects, but technology of all sorts and, eventually, exports and jobs.[47]

Detroit Jews had established a unique relationship with the Technion by 1952. From the automobile industry and the Jewish engineers and scientists engaged in it, the Technion benefited from expertise as well as money. Louis Gelfand, for example, a staff engineer at General Motors, and David Segal, part of a major chemical supply firm, both directed Jewish engineers and scientists to support of the Technion and sponsored membership in the Engineering Society of Detroit, the American Chemical Society, and the Society of Automotive Engineers. Alex Taub, designer of engines for General Motors, and Louis G. Redstone, an internationally distinguished architect, both offered their energies and expertise to Detroit's chapter of the Technion Society. From its earliest years in the 1940s, the Technion

Society in Detroit drew leaders in the business and scientific community: Leon Kay, Harvey Goldman, Albert Kahn, Ben Laikin, Simon Shetzer, and Jewish leaders like Sobeloff, Saul Saulson, Bernard Cantor, Lawrence W. Crohn, and Rabbi Adler.[48]

Led by Hymie Cutler, intimate gatherings of Detroit Jews and non-Jews produced enough financial support to begin endowing programs and buildings on the Technion campus. Those gatherings provided opportunities for Jewish engineers in Detroit to socialize and to discuss professional matters. Louis Milgrom, who joined the society in the 1940s, noted that it appealed to him because of his concern for technical education, the professional camaraderie, and its apolitical position. Here, then, came a possible alternative to sponsoring Histadrut projects—although numerous members supported both organizations. Similarly, in 1956, thirty-five-year-old Dr. Joseph Epel was elected president of the chapter and recalled that the older men offered not only their friendships but became "co-workers and peers . . . [sharing] common goals, aspirations and dreams." Those aspirations and goals revolved around scientific and technical education and provided another avenue to nurture Israel's development. By the 1960s, Detroit Jews had not only offered their educational and professional cooperation, but had endowed such imposing structures and programs as the Samuel and Isabelle Friedman Auditorium, the Samuel and Isabelle Friedman Nutrition and Food Chemistry Building, the Samuel Brody Building in Agricultural Engineering, the Detroit Mechanical Engineering Complex and Equipment Fund, the Sigmund and Sophie Rohlik Energy Laboratory, the Sam Rich Processing Laboratory, the Philip Slomovitz Chair in the Hebrew Language, the Emma Schaver Research Fund, and numerous others.[49]

In 1956 border skirmishes with Arab enemies increased, and President Nasser of Egypt began to threaten Israel's existence with saber rattling and alliances with other Arab states like Saudi Arabia and Syria. On the eve of the 1956 Allied Jewish Campaign, a photograph of an Israeli watchman holding a machine gun and dramatically silhouetted against mountains appeared on the front page of the *Jewish News*. Beneath the picture, the Federation's message to the Jews of Detroit appeared in bold print:

> All Israel stands on watch today. . . . Isolated, threatened by seven saber-rattling nations, Israel looks to us for comfort and assistance. . . . Ours is the humane duty to assist in the rescue of the North African Jews who seek havens in Israel, and to encourage the young Jewish State in its economic struggle. . . . Ours also is the task of strengthening our internal structure, by continuing sound educational and health programs for Detroit Jewry. . . . This is a call to our community, through our Allied Jewish Campaign, to uphold the hands of the Israelis who are fighting for freedom and to retain the high standards of our community.

BE GENEROUS IN YOUR GIVING[50]

Detroit Jewry responded with the largest campaign since 1948, donating $5,296,804 in 1956 and transcending that the following year with $5,918,268, the largest amount ever collected in Detroit.[51] The chairman of the campaign that year, Max Fisher, had traveled a long road from his gift of five dollars in 1932. After his mission awakening in 1954, Fisher dedicated himself to preserving and strengthening "our most precious commodity," Jewish unity. Carefully avoiding ideological controversies, Fisher said he determined to draw as many contributors into the campaign as possible, stressing that "local and overseas [Israeli] needs were two sides of the same coin"—Jewish unity. Like Jews in every city in the United States, Detroit's Jews had reacted to Nasser's seizure of the Suez Canal in July 1956 and then to the demands of war when Israel undertook the Sinai Campaign in October.

29

Federation: Reorganizing to Meet New Challenges

On October 24, 1946, Julian Krolik, president of Federation, convened the first meeting of the Social Planning Committee of the Jewish Welfare Federation. He explained that the board of governors had authorized the committee "to achieve, even more effectively than in the past, communal, cross-agency thinking and planning." The Social Planning Committee consisted of subcommittees on scholarship, Yiddish schools, camping, nursery schools, resettlement, and "care of the aged and chronic sick." Its Yiddish subcommittee included Moishe Haar, Jay Rosenshine, Bendore, David Sislin, and George Stutz. The subcommittee on the aged, chaired by Stutz, also included Harold Silver, Sidney Allen, Myron Keys, Fred Butzel, Sobeloff, Abe. L. Sudran (Associate director before Avrunin took the office), Irwin Shaw, Aaron Droock, Walter Klein, and Irving Katz.[52] Both subcommittees involved a mixture of Federation and Council people.

The Social Planning Committee met annually to hear reports from its subcommittees and to establish its priorities. When it convened in December 1947, it discussed Irwin Shaw's December 1946 proposal for a subcommittee on camping. In it, Shaw described the condition of the Fresh Air Camp for 130 boys and 100 girls at Brighton and revealed that in 1946   343 the Fresh Air Society had been forced to turn away four hundred children. The two Jewish Center day camps and the mothers' and children's camp at Chelsea had, he said, "woefully inadequate facilities." Stutz's subcommittee submitted a proposal for an apartment-house project in which "those who do not need the physical or emotional protection of an institution" might live.[53]

These reports indicated a professional concern for expanding facilities and keeping pace with Jewish agencies in other parts of the country. Equally important, the Planning Committee embraced the idea of a broader representation in Federation projects. In short, the curious admixture of individuals implied an attempt to "broaden the base" of Federation involvement.

Attempts to involve groups previously unidentified with Federation in decision-making or advisory capacities took more explicit and palpable form in 1947 when Federation altered its by-laws. The new by-laws broadened the representational base of Federation as it invited representatives of "councils of organizations" to sit on its board. Delegates from the Workmen's Circle, the American Jewish Congress, Jewish War Veterans, B'nai B'rith, the Landsmanshaftn Council, the Zionist Council of Detroit and, at a later date, the Synagogue Council joined the board of Federation. In addition, representatives from the trade and professions divisions of the campaign and representatives of the Women's Division and the Junior Division of Federation were also included, along with twenty-seven "at-large" members.[54]

According to William Avrunin, who became associate director of Federation in 1948, this "broadening of its base" or "democratizing" of the campaign partially derived from the rhetoric and organizational activities of the Jewish Community Council. Striving for unity, Federation reacted to Council's claim to speak on behalf of the greater Jewish population. Abraham Sudran, Avrunin's predecessor as associate director, wrote that the by-law revision exemplified a trend toward integrating community councils and federations in American cities with more than forty-thousand Jews.[55] Apart from more pragmatic grounds for the change, this trend toward integration may have prompted Sobeloff and other leaders of Federation to attempt a similar merger. The 1950s brought this issue of amalgamation before the public. "Cooperation" or "collaboration" had been demonstrated in times of crisis—World War II, the emergency appeals from Palestine and then from Israel—but, in part because some Federation leaders continued to perceive the Council as "just another agency," merger remained politically charged. Council's most outspoken leaders argued, too, that philosophical differences about Jewish values, identity, and culture lay at the heart of their antagonism toward Federation.

Providing services for the Jewish population of Detroit continued to be

Federation's principal goal. That involvement had historically included agencies to provide family and children's services, vocational assistance, free loans, care for the aged and infirm, camps, community centers, Hebrew and Yiddish schools, and help in a wide variety of emergencies. Since 1948–1949, "the upbuilding of Israel" also increasingly occupied budgetary discussions. Planning, budgeting, and fund-raising served these preeminent purposes. To the extent that Federation's constituency benefitted from those agency services, its goals were fulfilled regularly—if necessarily incompletely—through the Allied Jewish Campaign. But as the Council spoke out more critically of what it deemed the lack of "positive Jewish content," the failure to foster Jewish identity, culture, and life beyond reacting to particular needs that bore no distinctly Jewish character, Isidore Sobeloff and Federation advocates seemed to feel the need to respond more openly, lauding the benefits of centralization and unity.

Thus in 1950, the year the new Dexter-Davison branch of the Jewish Community Center opened, Federation bought two full pages in the *Jewish News* to describe "Your Allied Jewish Campaign. What It Is and What It Does." The advertisement comprised a detailed catalogue of the procedures of the campaign and the budget allocations for 1949–1950. It listed amounts, from the total of $5,292,608, assigned to Israel and overseas ($3,639,701, of which $3,575,000 went to Israel), to the Resettlement Service ($275,527), and virtually every other agency under the Federation aegis.[56] Such a public accounting, aimed at involving all Jews in Detroit with a sense of participation and advantage, presented an impressive set of accomplishments and listed names of participants from every segment of the Jewish population, from Louis Berry and Henry Wineman (chairman and honorary chairman, respectively, of the 1949–1950 campaign), to representatives of Orthodox congregations and the *landsmanshaftn*. So many names, from so many Jewish realms in Detroit, trumpeted an inclusive participation that seemed to legitimize Federation's claim to speak for all Detroit Jewry. With explicit endorsement of Israel, Henry Ford II added his prestige to the Federation drive, intensifying a Ford policy to redress the sins of the founder, and contributed fifty-thousand dollars to the campaign in 1950.[57]

In December 1952, Detroit's Federation took a step that distinguished it in the world of American-Jewish federations by establishing the Pre-Campaign Budget Conference. This furthered its participatory tenor, as it involved from 150 to 200 people in a "community-wide conference." All members of local agency boards, donors of certain large amounts, "key community leaders," Federation board of directors and board of governors, members of the Detroit Service Group, board members of the Women's Division and the Junior Division, and all members of the budget and planning divisions convened for a full Sunday-morning session of discussions about the distribution of revenue raised in the forthcoming spring campaign.[58]

At a National Federation Agency meeting in 1957, Judge Theodore Levin 345 explained that the conference sought a "harmonious pattern" through "broad base participation" from "a cross-section of community interests, with appreciable numbers from the various religious groupings and partisans of every agency, every field of service, every geographical program, at home or abroad." Theoretically, every interest received the opportunity to influence the structuring of an allocations formula that would divide contributions into four categories: Overseas and Israel, Local Operating Funds, Local Capital Funds, and National Agencies. Each category had a budget committee that alloted money to specific agencies. Chairs of each division opened the conference with their advocacy presentations.[59] This remarkable annual gathering convened delegates from almost every conceivable corner of the Jewish population. Part of its task lay in drawing approbation from segments of the communities that did not identify with Federation; part lay in attracting those groups into the decision-making process so that they might identify their interests with those of the campaign; part lay in preventing any competitive campaigns.

Because of the innovative quality of this daring experiment, Detroit's Federation received national recognition for its efforts. Among peripheral supporters and even among opponents, the Pre-Campaign Budget Conference undoubtedly heightened awareness of the difficulties of the campaign task. It raised consciousness, too, of the claim that the campaign had become a year-round enterprise, not just a spring burst of frantic financial energies.

The conference promulgated its recommendations and passed them on to the budget and planning divisions, the executive committee, and the board of Federation. In 1956 a Survival Fund and a Rescue Fund of the United Jewish Appeal were added to the other categories, and by 1957 any amount raised beyond the regular fund was designated to the Rescue Fund. Finally, the conference allegedly provided a more flexible guide for budgeting and entailed large group involvement that indicated that the campaign would respond to broader interests of more citizens, "[making] it perfectly obvious to the people who participate that they can achieve more for the causes in which they believe only if more money is raised."[60]

Years later, Isidore Sobeloff referred to the conference as a "town meeting" and a "controlled democracy." Those who participated (and those who continue to participate) recalled heated debates, lengthy discussions, and reports—and, usually, a sense of accomplishment enhanced by the strong and encouraging conclusions of Sobeloff or Avrunin. A fundamental tenet of centrism nourished the conference: one campaign, one budget, one organization to determine which causes, agencies, and programs received what. To inquiries about Detroit's formula for distribution, especially to Israel, and about the higher percentages apportioned to Israel by other Federations, Sobeloff consistently replied: "Would you rather have a higher percentage or more money?" In short, the source of more aid to Israel or any other cause simply rested on the principle of raising more money for the central fund—not in dividing the pie differently. That insistence, in part, hindered relationships between Federation and other organizations like Council and those groups whose values and aims it claimed to embody. Yet, such determined single-mindedness created the "Detroit difference"—extraordinarily centralized, organized, and controlled success that would eventually mark Detroit as one of the outstanding contributing centers for national Jewish causes and for Israel.

Fourteen Federation agencies received the fruits of the labors of these budgetary deliberations. As one of those affiliated agencies since 1930, the Jewish Home for the Aged, for example, received regular attention. By 1949 the home boasted an impressive array of doctors who volunteered their time to serve on the Medical Committee headed by Dr. Harry Bennett. Among those assisting Bennett were Doctors Charles Lakoff, H. I. Kallett, H. S. Mellen, Morton Barnett, David Kliger, Herbert H. Cohen, Daniel E. Cohn, and E. M. Friedman. From the staff of Harper Hospital came Doctors Harry C. Saltzstein, David Sandweiss, V. Droock, J. J. Jacobs, and Edward J. Agnelly. Ira Sonnenblick served as the director of the home. By 1937, when the Old Folks' Home relocated next to the Jewish Children's Home on Petoskey Avenue, between Burlingame and Collingwood, the two Women's Auxiliaries (the northwest branch and the original one), merged, with Mrs. Rose Ferar as president, after a successful three-year membership campaign.[61]

Enticed into serving on the board of directors by his father-in-law, Max Lieberman, Leonard N. Simons became affiliated with the home in 1937, thus beginning what would become a fifty-year involvement with Federation. He recalled those dedicated people who served on the board of the home with him: Sidney Allen, Edward and Arthur Fleischman, Jack Lefton, Milton Mahler, Maurice Aronsson, Isadore Winkleman, Ben Kramer, Herman Mathias, Al Sklar, Ben Welling, Joe Kukes, Alan Schwartz, Sylvan Rapaport, Dan LeVine, Dave Miro, Dave Zack, and others. He recalled, too, the tension that existed between Federation and the Home because President Jacob Levin, one of the original incorporators of the Home in 1905, feared losing autonomy. Yet in 1937, the Home was newly incorporated by Jacob Levin, Myron Keys, Max Lieberman, Sidney J. Allen, Henry Levitt, and David Oppenheim.[62]

Gifts and memorial contributions immediately came to the Home, and the D. W. Simons Memorial Hospital Wing and the Joseph W. Allen Synagogue appeared.[63] Newly appointed board members included Gus D. Newman, Max J. Kogan, Louis Robinson, and Myron Keys, who would succeed Levin as president. Dr. Otto Hirsch, the superintendent, oversaw the 125 residents as the new home quickly filled. Because of the unexpectedly high percentage of chronically ill residents, Federation asked Dr. Frederic D. Zeman, director of the New York Home for the Aged and Infirm, to follow up the study undertaken by Harry L. Lurie of the Council of Jewish Federations which had acted as a guide for Detroit's plans after 1936.[64] Zeman's report, issued in September 1940, outlined a blueprint for "medical modernization of the Home for Aged to take better care of chronically sick aged." The report also recommended a Central Bureau for the Jewish Aged, which led to the founding of the Old Age Bureau with Federation, JSSB, Home, and North End Clinic representation. Its goal would be to coordinate the activities that would affect Jewish aged—not only those in the Home.[65] It was disbanded after three years and replaced by a Federation subcommittee that would in turn serve as a model for the committee Simons would chair to investigate housing for the aged.[66]

Just as considerations about the aged had touched off heated discussions in 1936 that culminated in the formation of the Council, so, too, did discussions of housing for the aged stimulate debate. Already in 1946, George Stutz's subcommittee on the aged had described a proposal for an "apartment house project" for "those who do not need the physical or emotional protection of an institution."[67] Leonard Simons recalled that in 1956 after returning from Denmark and Sweden where he had observed community-constructed apartment buildings for the elderly, he had broached the subject to Isidore Sobeloff, but Sobeloff had maintained that "this problem [partially subsidized housing for needy aged] didn't exist in Detroit." By 1965, however, as other cities had successfully undertaken such projects, the time seemed ripe and Simons was asked to chair a committee on housing for the elderly in 1966.

As chairman of the executive committee of the Home, Simons had distinguished himself when that committee approved his appeal to Tom and Al Borman for assistance in constructing a much-needed second building to supplement the Home for the Aged. With the understanding that the new facility would bear their family name, the Bormans gave the several-month-old fund-raising drive a considerable boost with their gift of $250,000, which Simons reported to the Committee on July 8, 1962.[68] Borman Hall opened its doors to fifty residents from the Petoskey Home in January 1966.

The Simons Committee, comprised almost exclusively of Federation people, produced an investigative report (the Simons-Cohen report) that suggested there was an "increasing population of older people in relatively good health, living alone on a modest budget." Aided by the experiences of other cities, the committee concluded, too, that many of these people lived in low-rent, often unsafe neighborhoods with inadequate transportation to services offered by Federation and other organizations.[69] Simons' committee members, along with Federation assistant director Samuel Cohen, visited other cities like Cleveland, New York, Baltimore, Philadelphia, and Pittsburgh to examine their projects. Based on their investigations, they recommended that Federation sponsor a residence project for elderly citizens; that the project should initially serve about two hundred persons who would receive "minimal assistance" in order to "maintain their dignity as accepted members of the community. The apartment house would form part of our total network of supportive social services." Both middle- and lower-income residents were to be allowed, and the facility was to offer "a semi-protective environment, but should be non-institutional in appearance and purpose."[70]

Questions of finance were to be resolved with long-term government construction loans through the federal agency for Housing and Urban Development (HUD). Federation would offer its assistance through networking, as the project would become "part of the Federation family of interrelated services."[71] Discussion of the report at the full committee meeting occurred on June 28, 1966. There, Jacob Keidan and Dr. Hyman S. Mellen argued that Federation ought not provide housing without offering necessary social services. William Avrunin responded with a definition of social services as "forms of communal assistance which . . . can be effective in retarding the institutionalization of these aged persons." After considerable discussion, the committee agreed to support the report, which Simons then presented to the executive committee in September.[72]

Opposition to the project arose from unexpected quarters. Some Federation leaders, notably Max Fisher, worried that a federally subsidized project would hinder private enterprise in Detroit. But Fisher soon joined Avrunin and others who advocated the enterprise, convinced that various cities had begun to exceed Detroit in their efforts to care for the elderly. In its final draft, the Implementation Committee, chaired by attorney Joseph Jackier in 1967, addressed such subjects as independence of the elderly, "tenants of modest means," the nature of the apartments, a one-meal-per-day plan, the amount of health service to be provided, interagency relationships, admissions procedures, budget, financing, legal questions, and location.[73] Federation Apartments formally opened in Oak Park, next to the Ten Mile Road Branch of the Jewish Community Center, in December 1971.

Along with the addition of Borman Hall on Seven Mile and Sunderland in 1965, Federation Apartments represented an example of institutional representatives coming into direct contact with the Jews of Detroit. Federation activities—often, like the apartment project, gradually developed—took tangible form in helping individual Jews. More than most other agencies, however, the Jewish Home for the Aged and Federation Apartments palpably touched the lives of Jews from almost every sector of the population.

Perhaps the only other local Federation agency to engage large numbers of people regardless of their individual religious, ideological, economic, national, or political affinities was the Jewish Community Center. From the days of the venerable Hannah Schloss/Jewish Institute on Vernor Highway near Hastings, to the expansion of branches into Oak Park and the northwestern and Dexter areas, the Center had functioned as a meeting place for activities and programs for Jews of all ages. The 1923 *Survey* had urged Detroiters to revaluate and modernize their Jewish Center, and they had followed that advice with increasing verve. As it evolved from the Jewish Women's Club (which became the Detroit chapter of the National Council of Jewish Women) to the Jewish Centers Association and, finally, to the Jewish Community Center housed in 1933 at Woodward and Holbrook (and eventually named the Aaron DeRoy Memorial Building), that agency offered great diversity and provided a place where Jewish immigrants might encounter long-established German Jews in the 1920s and 1930s and where cultural programs, meetings, lectures, and athletic facilities attracted *landsmanshaftn* and Federation, old and young, rich and poor. As Jews migrated northward in Detroit, the center followed, with the Ten Mile Branch (1956) and the new Main Building at Curtis and Meyers (1959).[74]

At the end of the 1950s, the new Jewish Community Center on Curtis and Meyers became the focus of a whirlwind of controversy that surprised many observers because of the unusual alliances it provoked and the depth of feelings that seemed to explode from unanticipated realms.

A National Jewish Welfare Board policy statement of its Jewish Community Center Division issued in June 1957, outlined a Sabbath policy regarding programming that suggested activities to be avoided and an attitude to be adopted.[75] On August 10, 1959, the Executive Committee of the Jewish Community Center of Detroit voted seven to two in favor of opening the Center on Saturdays.[76] On September 7, a group of Orthodox and Conservative rabbis met in Rabbi Adler's study and asked the president of the board to convey their objection to opening the Center, regardless of what would be included or excluded from the program on Saturdays. Two days later, the board of directors of the JCC approved the opening by a vote of twenty-two to nine and projected October 31, 1959, as the first Saturday for the policy to go into effect. That same day Irwin Shaw, director of the JCC, wrote to a friend on the National Jewish Welfare Board in New York that Rabbi Adler had expressed adamant and determined opposition to the Saturday programming.[77]

Predictably, the Orthodox rabbis staunchly opposed the new policy. Less predictably, Conservative and Reform rabbis proved as intractably hostile to the proposal. More surprising, the lay opposition mounted and grew steadily more vociferous, until the Jews and non-Jews of Detroit became aware of a serious rift within Jewish ranks. Amidst a flurry of protests, a delegation of rabbis and laymen appealed to the JCC board to reserve its decision on October 7, 1959.[78]

From September on, a flood of telegrams and letters deluged the board of directors, Sam Frankel (the president of the Center), and Shaw. In a telegram, Charles P. Gellman, president of Young Israel of Detroit, asked to "meet with you to explore every means of undoing the harm," arguing that opening the Center on Saturday would do "inestimable damage to the youth of the community";[79] in the *Jewish News* on September 18, Philip

Slomovitz dramatically editorialized against the new plan;[80] Morris J. Brandwine, president of B'nai David, called the program a "public dese-cration of the Sabbath";[81] the members of the Shaarey Zedek Sisterhood quoted "Remember the Sabbath Day to keep it Holy," and continued that it was "unthinkable for a Jewish Community Institution to . . . violate this Commandment of G-D";[82] the board of trustees of Adat Shalom, Beth Abraham, the Beth Aaron Sisterhood, Ahavas Achim, and B'nai Moshe also deplored the decision. Amidst all the others came a strong statement from the Zionist Council of Detroit. They sent a copy of their protest to Abe Kasle, who also expressed his dissatisfaction.[83]

Letters of support also poured in—fewer, but some equally adamant about the decision. Yet, of considerable concern to the board of directors were the cancellations of memberships. By the end of October the Center issued its "Statement on Sabbath Programming at the Jewish Community Cen-ter": for over a decade, it began, the Center had opened on Saturdays "for activities in consonance with the spirit of the Sabbath." Oneg Shabbat pro-grams had taken place at the Twelfth Street and Dexter-Davison Branches with Orthodox rabbis participating, but they had been discontinued be-cause of a shortage of staff. Now the center would be guided by the national Jewish Welfare Board policy developed between 1948 and 1958. Twenty-seven centers across the nation, the statement noted, had Saturday programs.[84]

Nevertheless, the initial outcry had its effect: the day the Center issued its statement, the executive committee recommended the appointment of a citizens' committee "to review the subject and bring its recommenda-tions to the Board." On November 4, 1959, the board appointed the com-mittee: Dr. Harry E. August, Tillie (Mrs. Morris J.) Brandwine, Lester S. Burton, David J. Cohen, Charles Feinberg, Mrs. Arthur I. Gould, Mrs. Lewis S. Grossman, Dr. Richard C. Hertz, Esther (Mrs. Harry L.) Jackson, Abe Kasle, Jacob L. Keidan, Louis LaMed, Rabbi Leizer Levin, Irving Pokempner, Dr. Irving Posner, Jay Rosenshine, Maurice S. Schiller, Sidney M. Shevitz, Philip Slomovitz, and Morris Garvett (who served as chairman).[85] After its first meeting on January 5, 1960, the committee settled into the second and longest of its three meetings on January 21.

In its composition the Center committee embodied Detroit Jewry. It in-cluded Orthodox, Conservative, and Reform Jews, secularists, Zionists, Federation representatives, and Council people. Garvett, prominent in Temple Beth El, Temple Israel, and the Federation, held wide-ranging respect in Detroit and had a reputation for evenhandedness and rationality. Louis LaMed was an acknowledged leader in Jewish education; Pokempner, a long-standing unionist and steadfast Council protagonist, represented a "secularist-culturalist" position on the issue and on the question of what constituted Jewishness; Shevitz, among the heroes of the Council movement, also maintained a high degree of respect; Rabbi Levin, among the most out- 351 spoken and obdurate of the Orthodox rabbis in Detroit, spoke in Yiddish; and Rosenshine, a Yiddish culturalist, represented the Sholom Aleichem Institute—and so it went, each member representing a major aspect of the Jewish population.[86]

As the meeting progressed, the question of Saturday programming took various guises, evolving into a debate over the nature of Jewishness or Jewish identity. LaMed had asked that members not become "hysterical" and related that "one community leader had told me that the Center would open over [his] dead body" and that another had invoked the Ten Commandments, saying that the Center was trying to eliminate one of the commandments. In a lengthy speech that set the tone for the meeting, LaMed appealed to reason and turned to history to chart what he identified as changes in attitude toward the Sabbath and religion in general. The term characterized as "rest" was referred to as "active rest," he said, and pointed out that men and women now sat together in many synagogues and that rabbis recognized the necessity of riding to synagogue on the Sabbath.[87]

LaMed stressed that Jewish *values* ought to inform a program that would be "in consonance with the spirit of the Sabbath" (the phrase that threatened to become a cliché throughout the controversy), a program that would include noncompetitive games, storytelling, singing, and dancing, all with "special emphasis on Jewish content and consciousness . . . and revolving around the values of the Sabbath." Given such an agenda, LaMed quoted Rabbi Ira Isenstein, that "to keep the Center closed on the Sabbath is like closing the Synagogue on a Jewish holiday." Finally, regarding dealings with the gentile community, such a program obviously would reject business-as-usual and would focus only on cultural and recreational activities.[88]

Reacting to LaMed's approach, one of the representatives from the opposition insisted that a secular institution like the Center should not teach religious values. David Cohen asserted that by its very (secular) nature, the Center could not act "in consonance with the Sabbath—it's impossible in the Center." As the tension and the subject crested, Abe Kasle declared that it was not "our task to take the children off the hands of their parents." He firmly stated that under no circumstances should the Center be open on Saturday.[89]

Antagonism between Orthodox advocates and secularists grew more open. Rabbi Levin declared that "if the Center is open it will be like hanging up a Swastika" and that "every child who will come to the Center on Saturday will be hurt to see it open." Responding to the rabbi, Sidney Shevitz compared Orthodox opposition to Saturday programming to religious opposition to the state of Israel before (and after) 1948. In a lengthy peroration, Shevitz stated that Judaism seemed in the throes of a modern crisis, and it was incumbent upon the leaders of the community to "reach out to those on the borderline of estrangement from the Jewish community and people." Shevitz hastened to add that he agreed with the sanctity of the

Sabbath and worried about it. Consequently, he deemed the content of the program critical.[90]

Dr. Harry August pursued Shevitz's line of argument and addressed his remarks to Rabbi Levin. August believed that Rabbi Levin's way of life "has not served us [Jews] well and has driven a large segment away—and we are in danger of losing them." Echoing Shevitz, he continued by referring to Detroit Jews' attempts to retrieve those who seemed disillusioned with Orthodoxy—the Jewish Parents' Institute (JPI), for example. JPI members had become "estranged from anything Jewish," August said, and questions from their children had led them to the Jewish Community Center for assistance. There, with assistance from center staff (most prominently, Irwin Shaw), they had arranged their own program. As a result, many subsequently joined synagogues and turned to studies of Jewish history, Hebrew, Yiddish, Jewish values, and philosophy.[91]

As the meeting drew to a close, Jacob Keidan asserted that "We are all Jews—each in his own way." He seemed to crystalize an issue that had surfaced from the depths of the Saturday programming controversy: What is Jewish and how is it to be defined? Almost all the contours of the Jewish-identity debates that had periodically surfaced in Detroit appeared in the arguments over the center Saturday program. They had emerged from the letters and from the arguments in the center board room, and reached beyond the building to synagogues, schools, the newspapers, Federation, and Council. They had filtered into *landsmanshaftn* meetings and social gatherings with startling intensity. When nonreligious Jews began to vehemently endorse the Orthodox position it seemed to some—especially those on the citizens' committee—that more than Saturday programming was at stake.

Perhaps most surprising in October 1959, before the formation of the citizens' committee, the stand taken by the Jewish Community Council Executive Committee; although divided, favored reversal of the Center's decision to open on Saturday. When the Internal Relations Committee of Council, chaired by Dr. Samuel Krohn, reported their recommendation to the executive committee, Louis LaMed opposed their advice. Joining him in opposition to the recommendation were Dr. Richard Hertz, Irving Pokempner, Stanley J. Winkelman, Sidney Shevitz, and others. After a stormy debate, the executive committee approved the recommendation to the Center board, adding to the voices of opposition to the Saturday opening. But Council, perceived as a bastion of religious neutrality if not downright secularism, startled some of its own membership with what appeared to be support of the Orthodox religious advocates. Among those who recognized the more subtle complexities of the debate, Meyer Schneider warned against taking a position on a religious issue. So, too, did Sidney M. Shevitz—ever the voice of reason—stating that passing judgment on this question "imposes on the council the judgement as to what is a Jew."[92]

353

Garvett's committee met for the last time on April 8, 1960, and on October 19, 1960, he wrote to Samuel Frankel, president of the Center. He reviewed the history of the controversy, the public objection, the postponement of the new policy for "further study," and the charge of his committee to "clarify the issues, to review current practices and to develop recommendations for Board consideration." He reiterated the "primary objective" of the special committee, "to help reach conclusions which will benefit the total community." Probably few, if any, had recognized what an impossible task lay before them.

They had listened to the center's proposals for programs "in consonance with the spirit of the Sabbath," Garvett said, and had discussed them and a vast sea of differences that flowed from them. But the *basic* differences, Garvett determined, "were rooted in emotion, personal background . . . and conscience." Logic had not always been apparent because such differences "were not subject to objective analysis." More questions than answers emerged: Was the opening really a "desecration of the Sabbath"? Did "in consonance with the spirit of the Sabbath" mean "in consonance with Orthodox observance of the Sabbath"? Should the total community have to conform and yield to Orthodox methods of observance? "Is 'Jewishness' synonymous with 'Judaism'?" Does a communal agency, supported by funds from the community, "have the right to conduct programs on Saturday which may be abhorrent to a minority even though these programs may be desired by the majority?" These and numerous other questions had created a quagmire in which opinions became irrational, vague, incoherent, and unproductive.

Garvett listed the arguments for and against: positive values might be created for young people; cultural programs would benefit young and old; other cities had adopted such a plan; Camp Ramah allowed recreational swimming on Saturdays, and Camp Tamarack functioned on Saturday; without such programs at the Center, young Jews turned to "public amusement"; Orthodox practices themselves had changed over the years because of modern living conditions in America; and so forth. Those against had argued that the plan would create disunity; that it would have a devastating effect on the Orthodox community; that there was symbolic value in keeping the Center closed, and a "need for 'building a fence around the law' "; that disapprobation would divorce Sabbath programs from the synagogue and the home; and, finally, that a point of religious law could not be decided by a lay group. Garvett repeated the statement about "hanging up a Swastika" and reported that at the last meeting the committee had received a statement from twenty-eight rabbis opposing the Center on Saturdays. Among those signers were Rabbis Adler, Wohlgelernter, Syme, Lehrman, Prero, Sperka, Gorelick, Arm, and, somewhat surprisingly, Fram.

Sadly the chairman of the committee reported that the meetings, although conducted in remarkably "calm and dispassionate discussions" for

354

which he commended all the participants, revealed to him "an unbridgeable chasm." In an apparent attempt to find unity somewhere in all this, Garvett praised the "high-minded spirit which animated the deliberations at all times." But in the end, they had decided (at his urging) *not* to vote on the issue. Therefore, there were no recommendations. After four months of deliberations, over eight hours of heated discussion, the responsibility for the plan remained solely with the board of directors of the Jewish Community Center—where it had begun. Garvett's final words: "Unanimity of opinion is impossible of attainment"[93]: an emblem, a representation of Jewish attitudes toward "Jewishness" or what constituted Jewish identity in Detroit.

Like such unremitting deliberations of qualities that defined Jews, the center's Saturday programming controversy persisted—indeed, grew more antagonistic, more belligerent, and even malevolent. In December 1960, the board, allegedly because of budgetary constraints, voted to postpone Saturday opening until May or June of 1961. Nevertheless, the center issued its "Tentative Plan for Saturday Afternoon Programming" on December 21, 1960. The plan called for opening at 1:00 P.M., no program or activity that would require handling of money, the closing of the business office and the switchboard (except for emergency calls), avoiding activities "which are clearly not in consonance with the spirit of the Sabbath," and making "every effort . . . to transmit an appreciation of the distinctiveness of the Sabbath and an appreciation of its basic values." No heavy equipment would be allowed, no cooking or woodworking, and no "highly structured competitive games," although art, drama, or music lessons would be permitted. The plan listed many of the cities whose centers were open with similar programs on Saturdays.[94] By March 1961, Cleveland and Cincinnati had joined those ranks, with guidance from Orthodox rabbis.[95] But the outline failed to recognize that "appreciation of basic values" only begged the question; that a committee of some of the most esteemed Jewish citizens in Detroit had thrown up their hands in frustrated deadlock.

On May 31, 1961, after hearing a Conservative and an Orthodox rabbi repeat the request of the Detroit rabbinate to keep the Center closed on the Sabbath, the board voted twenty-seven to eight to open the Center on Curtis and Meyers on Saturday afternoons after 1:00 P.M.[96] With the new policy imminent, the opposition marshaled their strongest forces. Something vital, something more than a building opening on Saturday, seemed at stake. Questions that Garvett and some other members of his committee had either confronted or observed surfacing in a sort of impotent fear of community disunity had not disappeared and loomed more ominously before them.

Abe Kasle convened a meeting at his home on June 15 to organize the opposition. It took the form of the "Committee of Fifty for the Center Closing." The following week, a lengthy letter from Kasle to the president and board members of the Center appeared on the front page of the *Jewish News*, along with a full-page ad signed by rabbis and synagogue presidents opposing the opening. In his letter, Kasle alleged that at "a historic meeting . . . 31 out of 32 [rabbis] voted to keep the Center closed on Saturday." He angrily accused the board of directors of the Center of representing only "a certain small group of our community" who do not, therefore, "have the right to take it upon themselves to desecrate the day of *Sabbath*."[97] In impassioned prose, he epitomized much of the extreme opposition to the Saturday proposal: "Members of congregations and temples will lose faith in their rabbis and probably withdraw their support from congregations and temples; or, members of congregations and temples will arise in numbers and support the rabbis and possibly cool their interest in the total support of the Community Federation." In a string of associations, Kasle foresaw the erosion of Judaism, of rabbinical and even parental authority.[98] Although his letter was hyperbolic, it spoke to the fears and uncertainties that might have vexed many religious and nonreligious Jews alike. Where could certainty lie? How could Jews identify themselves once Judaism began to slip away from its traditions? From the issue of the Center opening on Saturdays arose deeply disturbing ones that demanded attention. Kasle and those for whom he spoke seemed to recognize that as readily as less Orthodox men like Morris Garvett and Louis LaMed.

On June 23, 1961, the Center was served with a circuit court order to appear on June 30 to show cause why a restraining order should not be issued at the request of the plaintiff, Mr. Ben Wrotslavsky, who filed suit against the Center. Wrotslavsky sought an injunction "permanently barring the directors and officers from opening the Center on the Sabbath."[99] His argument included the "strong opposition" registered by twenty-eight out of twenty-nine rabbis and referred to the previous year when, he alleged, similar "vehement protests by the rabbis and other important elements of the Jewish community" had stopped the opening.[100] The plaintiff's arguments also drew upon the Jewish Community Center's Articles of Incorporation of December 7, 1933, which listed the purposes for the institution: "To provide for the spiritual, physical and social welfare of its members; to help maintain in the Jewish community a spirit of harmony and union; and to foster and develop the highest ideals of American citizenship."[101] On Saturday, June 24, the Center opened at 1:00 P.M. for its limited program.

According to one lawyer who became peripherally involved in the case, no Jewish lawyer would defend the Center. At the request of members of the Center's board, James Montante took the case. Nathan E. Shur was the plaintiff's attorney. Few if any of the protagonists in this drama to that point were pleased with this development. Jewish dissension within the ranks of the Jewish population might grow bitterly and even offensively antagonistic, but almost everyone agreed that such disagreements should remain confined to Jewish audiences. Now, Saturday programming, deep divisions among Detroit Jews, sometimes intemperate arguments became public news.

A group of five Orthodox and Conservative rabbis met with Charles H. Gershenson, the president of the Center, and expressed their chagrin at the lawsuit. Despite deploring Wrotslavsky's action, the rabbis reiterated their resolute opposition to the Saturday program and refused compromise. Judge Thomas Murphy granted several postponements, urged both parties to settle the case out of court, and suggested turning to the Jewish Community Council's Arbitration and Conciliation Committee. The rabbis refused arbitration as long as the center remained open on Saturdays. By this time, James Montante had taken a government position out of the city and Milton "Jack" Miller (of the prestigious Jewish firm of Honigman, Miller, Schwartz and Cohn) appeared on behalf of the Center.

Representatives of the Committee of Fifty for the Center Closing attended an emergency meeting with a special Center committee on July 27. They convened at Gershenson's office. Miller, Jack O. Lefton, Maurice S. Schiller, and Irwin Shaw represented the Center; Max Biber, Tom Borman, David J. Cohen, David Goldberg, Max Goldsmith, Rabbi Chaskel Grubner, and Rabbi Moses Lehrman represented the Committee of Fifty. All had agreed to explore informal discussions for unity under the cloud of a pending lawsuit and the fruitless attempts by the Council Arbitration Committee.

To open the meeting, the rabbis restated that they disapproved of the suit and had, in fact, persuaded the plaintiff to wait until August 18. Resuming the Center debate, Borman pointed out that Conservative rabbis agreed with Orthodox rabbis on this particular issue, and David Cohen added that anything Jewish had to be carried out according to Halacha, or rabbinic law. He further deemed it a remarkable concession that the rabbis were willing to arbitrate at all. Borman continued by voicing his concerns about the effect of these disputes on the campaign. David Goldberg read aloud his letter to Judge Levin, president of Federation, in which he opposed the disrespect to the rabbis and threatened to withdraw his support of the campaign. He emphasized that he himself was not an observant Jew—that he even worked on Yom Kippur. But he felt that the rabbis should be obeyed—"out of respect for his parents." Biber repeated his earlier claim that opening the Center would produce "a moral hurt to a segment of the community." Miller quipped that he preferred "to hurt Max (Biber) and benefit the children." Significantly, there appeared veiled threats to the Allied Jewish Campaign, to unity, and a persistent refusal to negotiate unless the Center remained closed. Stalemated again, but with a sense of intransigence now on both sides, Gershenson dismissed the meeting.[102]

The following day, the *Jewish News* carried a front-page article describ- 357 ing the formation of "The Detroit Committee for the Center Sabbath Closing" with Morris J. Brandwine as chairman.[103] As a public matter, unlike other internal feuds, the Center opening had evolved into quasiphilosophical, often explicit contentions about sensitive topics. Many Jews in Detroit who remained unaffiliated in similar controversies—perhaps members of small synagogues, of various *landsmanshaftn*, reading groups, lodges, or fraternal organizations—felt this dispute move closer to their lives. It touched religious Jews, it touched those who used the Center—even during the week, it touched those who read the newspapers or those who now consciously recognized that they identified their Jewishness in some way akin to the disputants. Federation leaders, campaign loyalists began to fear the effects of the battle; Orthodox Jews began to fear the effects of such rigidity. What had begun as a contentious encounter now dragged into a seemingly insoluble problem, a conundrum that threatened to abrade important sources of unity, to wind up as a debacle, suddenly and unexpectedly disastrous. Perhaps it would leave the Jews of Detroit hopelessly divided over issues of identity, religion, values, "spiritual consonance," or some amorphous principle that would expose deep-seated and irreconcilable differences.

In August, in the midst of the maelstrom, William Avrunin, Isidore Sobeloff, Rabbi Adler, and Irwin Shaw conferred with Max Fisher about the jeopardy in which the Center issue had placed Detroit Jewish unity. Fisher agreed to intercede, inviting some of the principal figures in the community to sit on a committee to be chaired by Mandell Berman.[104] The Berman Committee's charge would be to recommend to the board of the Jewish Community Center the "general nature of the Saturday afternoon program." Its members were apprised of their "solemn responsibility . . . [and] unique opportunity to render a most helpful and valuable service to our community." Advocates of each position seemed to realize the gravity of the situation and assumed the charge to "work out a pattern which makes the resources of our Jewish Community Center available to our people on the Sabbath within the framework of proper regard and reverence. . . . Such a program would evidence a community's respect for the Sabbath and would seek to communicate . . . an awareness of the role it has played in Jewish life." It would be the committee's responsibility to "counsel and help guide us" toward those objectives.[105]

Chosen for this important blue-ribbon group were Max Biber, Max M. Fisher, Rabbi Leon Fram, Samuel Frankel, Morris Garvett, Samuel Gershenson, Sidney J. Karbel, Louis LaMed, Rabbi Leizer Levin, Milton J. Miller, Rabbi Jacob E. Segal, Irwin Shaw, Abe Srere, Philip Stollman, and cochairs Mandell Berman and Stanley J. Winkelman who, as Fisher left and Berman could not attend, chaired the first meeting on September 28, 1961. Winkelman repeated the charge, but despite his caveat against debating the decision of whether to keep the Center open on Saturday, the meeting offered a forum for some of the same arguments to resurface. Introduced by Gershenson, Shaw delineated the "basic principles" for all center programming and specific rules for Saturday programs: small "friendship groups" for children up to age fourteen; no heavy programs (cooking, woodworking, or use of heavy tools), smoking, competitive team games, or transportation by bus; cultural programs of singing, drama, and storytelling led by instructors with knowledge of Judaism; the pool would be open from 1:00 to 6:00 P.M. for individual swimming; the gym would be open for "low organization games." Older adults could participate or attend cultural, Yiddish, and English programs that would include an Oneg Shabbat. Money activities—the snack bar, shoe shine, and other such profit-making operations—would be prohibited.

Max Biber stated that he still felt the center should not be open, but, for the sake of the community, he was ready to compromise on his grounds— that only children under eighteen be allowed to use the Center and that they be required to attend cultural programs before using the physical facilities. LaMed, virtually ignoring the previous speaker, emphasized that the center should provide alternatives to the non-Jewish activities that increasingly attracted Jewish youngsters on Saturdays. Since the two extreme possibilities—absolutely Orthodox content or totally secular content—were unacceptable, LaMed argued for a "modified program in consonance with the spirit of the Sabbath." Rabbi Levin, speaking in Yiddish, insisted that the parking lot be closed and that only cultural-religious programs be allowed.[106]

Despite these repeated "hard-line" positions, the meeting clearly drifted toward conciliation and compromise. Indeed, it appeared a foregone conclusion. At the conclusion of the first meeting, Winkelman appointed a drafting committee to be chaired by Rabbi Segal and including LaMed, Biber, and Miller. Rabbi Levin did not return, although his name remained on the committee, and it was noted that his group did not accept the final report that Berman and Winkelman delivered to the Center board meeting on October 25, 1961. The board voted overwhelmingly to accept the recommendations of the committee that underscored the *"importance of cultural activities"* (emphasis in minutes).[107] In effect, the Center's original "Statement on Sabbath Programming" was finally adopted. But not before wrenching emotional upheavals, anger, "even hatred" and confrontations that opened wounds that would not heal for years.

Few controversies produced such lasting and resonant discord. To some of the combatants, the issue revolved around only religious piety and the potential moral corruption (one opponent of the Center opening compared Detroit to Sodom and Gomorrah); yet to others, including some of the Orthodox spokesmen, even more was at issue. Garvett, LaMed, Keidan, and others perceived more complex symbolic values in the debate. What defined Jewishness? Who could claim to be Jewish? On what basis and how   359 should one act accordingly? Many Detroit Jews and Jewish groups regularly aired these and related questions. But now they seemed in the greater Jewish and even non-Jewish public eye. If Orthodox Jews saw no need for such discussion, firm in their belief that the answers were self-evident, the Center controversy foisted those considerations on them. Conversely, more secular Jews, like some of those on the Jewish Community Council or on the Special Citizens' Committee, could no longer avoid confronting religious adherents on the nature of Jewish culture and life.

Large numbers of American Jews may have fallen away from traditional religious practices and ritual; yet many of them obstinately defended the Orthodox stand on the Jewish Community Center, as if they perceived the rabbis as "standard-bearers" of Judaism on their behalf. Like the member of the Berman Committee who admitted working on Yom Kippur, they seemed determined to uphold the traditional obedience demanded by Orthodox rabbis—at least in advocating this position. Of concomitant importance, then, seemed the respect accorded the two other authority figures who managed to gain respect and concessions as if they were new rabbinical surrogates: Mandell L. Berman and Max Fisher. Most important, too, for his carefully organized and tactful programming and presentations offered calmly and with balance was Irwin Shaw, executive director of the center. Robert Luby, who succeeded Shaw as director of the Fresh Air Camp in Brighton, Michigan, when Shaw became head of the Center, recalled that Shaw seemed to be the model social-service professional: firm, thoughtful, attentive, widely read, and thoroughly informed of appropriate data. It was Shaw who developed the programs for Saturdays and who communicated with Fisher and Berman after drawing up the charge to the Berman Committee.

Sabbath programming at the Center demonstrated the seemingly irreconcilable approaches to Jewish identity, the lack of consensus and the intractable nature of the opinions. But it also demonstrated the ability of Detroit Jewry to reach some conciliatory compromise, to save face and observe the common agreement not to air disagreements in public. Like the divisions over the Federation Apartments, this, too, found resolution through cooperative, mediative discussions. If these two crises did not reach the amplitude of Israel's emergencies, they nevertheless exhibited some of Detroit Jewry's common ground.

On June 27, 1962, Judge Thomas J. Murphy, of the Circuit Court for the County of Wayne, dismissed the case against the Jewish Community Center and ruled for the defendant: "This is not an ecclesiastical corporation," read his decision. He argued that the Orthodox do not have to use the Center and cannot impose their view of "spiritual welfare" on others. Ignoring the Reform and Conservative rabbis who had enjoined the Center to close on Saturdays, Judge Murphy concluded that the Center had not violated the purposes for which it was organized.[108] One year after the suit had been filed, the circuit court added the secular-legal postscript to the Jewish Center debate.

By 1967, Federation separated its more than five million dollars according to fields of service (each divided into local and national) that included Health and Welfare, Culture and Education, Community Relations, and Central Services. Over half the budget was allocated to the Overseas category. These "fields" covered the Fresh Air Society, with its various children's camps like Tamarack at Ortonville and Brighton and the Center day camp, the Jewish Community Council, the Jewish Family and Children's Service (formerly the Jewish Social Service Bureau), the Home for Aged (one branch at Petoskey and one at Borman Hall on Seven Mile Road), the House of Shelter, the Jewish Vocational Service-Community Workshop, the Midrasha-College of Jewish Studies (founded in 1948 after a movement spearheaded by Louis LaMed), and the Resettlement Service, which had continued to work with Holocaust survivors into the 1960s, helped Cuban refugees in 1961, and continued to work with Soviet Jews, Sinai Hospital, and the United Hebrew Schools.[109]

In its forty-year history, Federation had evolved from an almost exclusively social-service orientation to include community service and what became known as "Jewish communal enrichment." In April 1964, the United Jewish Charities established the Jewish Community Foundation to "encourage the agencies to plan creatively for the enrichment of the Jewish community program of services." After two years, the Foundation received the William J. Schroder Memorial Award of the Council of Jewish Federations for "superior initiative and achievement of social welfare."[110] With the Foundation, Federation ventured into a broader spectrum of programs: instituting in-service training programs, engaging Jewish content specialists for the Fresh Air Society, and pioneering housing relocation projects, programs for the retarded, and teacher training for the UHS. "Community enrichment" incorporated cultural and educational projects as Federation intensified what it had begun earlier with less fanfare.

Pursuing these broader perspectives, the Health and Welfare Division, under the direction of Mrs. Esther Appelman, undertook a series of studies of current programs and needs not only of agencies under that division's auspices, but also for the B'nai B'rith Hillel Foundation at the University of Michigan, Michigan State University, and Wayne State University in 1967. Based on recommendations from the university study, Federation began to direct some of its funds toward the National Hillel Foundation for improvement of programs at the three Michigan universities.[111]

Responding to the rising complexities of life in Detroit, Federation expanded its services by 1967 to cover the needs of every age group—from children's services to the care and welfare of the aged—as it increased its committments to Israel. The Jewish Welfare Federation had become a highly professional, efficient, and responsive administrative machine. Philanthropy was no longer the focus of its activities; its fund-raising, planning, and budgeting functions became more labyrinthine and sophisticated, corresponding to the degree of sophistication of the Jewish population it served. It ranked among the most highly respected and successful federations in the United States, boasting leaders of national and international fame.

Detroit's annual Allied Jewish Campaigns owed their enormous success in part to a relatively small group of affluent contributors—approximately 80 percent of the funds pledged came from 5 percent of the contributors—a group that bore uniquely Detroit characteristics. Federation had by then organized the campaign contributors into seven divisions: mercantile, services, food, industrial and automotive, arts and crafts, professional, and real-estate and building. Each division itself contained from twenty to thirty sections with individual leadership for each section. Almost from the beginning of Detroit Jewish life in the twentieth century, business prosperity linked itself to the automotive industry, Detroit's economic lifeline. Just as Detroit's leadership in America's United Way drives could be attributed to that industry (they had always been headed by an automobile magnate before the involvement of Max Fisher) so it produced similar leadership in the Allied Jewish Campaigns.

While Jews rarely participated directly in the industry, they engaged in ancillary industries, providing vital supplies to the car companies. Reflecting this auto-connected economic prominence were some of the chairmen of the campaigns: Aaron DeRoy, automobile dealer, chaired the campaign from 1931 to 1933; Abe Kasle, steel producer, led the campaign in 1951 and 1952; Irwin Green, a tool-and-die manufacturer and supplier of the auto industry, and Sol Eisenberg, steel fabricator for the auto and appliance industries, led it in 1965 and 1966 respectively. Leading figures connected with automobile supplies included Sidney Allen and Abe Srere, both producers of material for seat covers; Max Fisher and Jack Lefton in the gasoline and oil business; and Max J. Zivian and the Jospey and Hamburger families all engaged in steel production. These extended the automobile-derived prosperity observable in the linen supply business (which provided overalls and wiping cloths for automobile and other factories); and in the scrap-metal and related industries were representatives like Harry Goldman, Jack Citrin and his son Martin, who became the largest Standard Oil distributors in Michigan, and William Sucher, who hosted "Sucher meetings" to open the campaigns.

Along with car-related industries, Jews in Detroit seemed to occupy a vanguard position in such new industries as discount stores. Alan Schwartz pioneered large discount department stores along with Israel Davidson's Federal Department Stores and David Mondry's Highland Appliance. Mondry's father, indeed, his whole family, had been longtime Labor Zionists, and the Mondrys' deep-seated involvement in Federation symbolized a prevailing movement toward collaboration between traditionally Yiddish groups and the once-estranged establishment.

So, too, did Jews become primary figures in the real-estate and construction businesses, a fact reflected, again, in campaign cochairmen like Louis Berry and Joseph Holtzman (1949), Irwin I. Cohn (1959–1960, with Leonard N. Simons), Charles Gershenson and Alfred Deutsch (1963, 1964, and 1967), and division leaders like Nathan Silverman, Sam Frankel, Phil Stollman, and Al Taubman.

Other significant industries that produced massive contributions included the food industry, from which John Lurie (Wrigley's Markets) chaired the campaign in 1955, Paul Zuckerman (Velvet Peanut Butter) was chairman in 1961 and 1962, and Abraham Borman (Farmer Jack's) in 1963 & 1964 (with Gershenson). Leaders of the Mercantile Division included Stanley Winkelman and other members of his family; Max Pincus and Israel Himelhoch, from the retail clothing business; and the Handleman family, whose business had grown from a moderate wholesale drug company to the largest recording distributor in the country. Similarly, leading the Arts and Crafts Division were printers Hy Safran and Maurice Aronsson. As the largest of the Trades and Professions groups, the Professional Division developed many campaign and Federation leaders from its ranks of attorneys, physicians, accountants, and other professional groups.

From its singular economic position, Detroit fostered an annual campaign that collected extraordinary amounts of money. As feelings for Israel strengthened, the amounts rose; as Detroit went, then, so went its Jewish leadership and so went the campaigns. Beyond financial rewards, the campaign provided another pivotal asset as it trained participants in fund-raising and social responsibility. Many of Federation's volunteer campaign workers brought their new or strengthened skills to other tasks that included leadership in synagogues, promotion of institutions like Bar Ilan or Hebrew University, and advocation of causes like the Jewish National Fund and a myriad of others.

Along those lines, Federation also developed one of the nation's most energetic and active Junior Divisions (potential leaders under age forty), as well as its preeminent Women's Division. Sol Drachler joined the Federation staff as its secretary of education in 1957; he became assistant director, overseeing the Allied Jewish Campaign's growth, and then associate director before succeeding Avrunin as executive director.

In Detroit, to many of the greater Jewish population, those Federation leaders retained an almost mythical character that enigmatically linked them to the German Jews of earlier days. Wealth still meant *Yahudim* in the eyes of some and became a euphemism for German Jews. Thus Federation leaders who were clearly not of German Jewish background, like Abe Kasle, who led the campaign in 1951 and 1952, or Max Fisher, who served as president of Federation from 1959 to 1964, nevertheless were perceived as somehow related to the founders of the United Jewish Charities and Federation. Despite its increasingly comprehensive network of service agencies, Federation came under fire during the 1950s and 1960s, from both secular and religious groups, for not addressing more positive aspects of Jewish concern and for deemphasizing or neglecting Yiddish and educational cultural programming. Aiding Jews and responding to certain needs—physical, psychological, advisory, financial, and so forth—whether for old or young, still did not present specifically Jewish content, and did not, therefore, express "Jewish consciousness or identity" in the eyes of Federation's critics.

As if acknowledging some value in such critiques, Federation began to alter its own image with subtle changes in its strategies and programs and in its rhetoric and public relations. In those respects, it reflected general trends in Jewish organizations across the country. The encounter with its critics took its most public form in heightened confrontations with the Jewish Community Council.

30

Jewish Community Council: Achievement and Conflict

In the preamble to its constitution, the founders of the Jewish Community Council included among their goals the "coordination of the various forces of Jewish life." Toward that end, Council was to "preserve and maintain the dignity and integrity of the Jewish people," "defend and protect . . . civil, political and religious rights," and "advance and promote the cultural, social, economic, and philanthropic interests and the national and spiritual aspirations of the Jewish people." With such grandiose aspirations and missions, a 1952 Council pamphlet, "Working with Our Friends," emphasized that "its [Council's] function does not reside solely in any *one* area such as community relations or internal discipline or arbitration, but is concerned with *all* facets of the life of a community."[112] In its introductory statement, as well as in its content and title, that pamphlet seemed to symbolize the ethos of the Council. Representing 303 Jewish organizations in that year, Council claimed to be the representative voice of the Jews of Detroit because of its policy of "democratic representation" through its delegate assembly. When Judge James I. Ellmann reported the results of the Council self-evaluation of 1957, he began by referring to "the basic principle of the Council idea," the maintenance of policy "through democratic representation."[113]

Although it reasonably could claim to represent virtually all the Jewish groups in Detroit through its membership, its assertion that unity had therefore been achieved was less credible. A perusal of the members of the numerous committees immediately revealed the presence of differences, some ancient and some recent. Almost every committee brought together individuals holding theoretically irreconcilable views of Jewish identity, values, religion, or politics. The Culture Commission, for example, included such secularists as Norman Drachler, Moishe Haar, and Dr. Shmarya Kleinman, together with religious spokesmen like Rabbis Max J. Kapustin, Morris Adler, Samuel Prero, Moses Lehrman, and Bernard Isaacs. Similarly, the Joint Yiddish Culture Committee, chaired by Jay Rosenshine of the Sholem Aleichem Institute, combined Shloime Bercovich, Moishe Haar, Mrs. Ida Kamaroff, and Charles Driker with generally recognized adherents of Conservative, Reform, and Orthodox Judaism.

Overtly Eastern European-Yiddishist in its cultural programming, constituency, and orientation, part of the by-laws directed that the secretary be conversant and literate in Yiddish as well as in English (this until the 1960s). Even as the diverse membership brought a multiplicity of opinions—political left and right, religious diversity—they frequently caused internal antagonisms over the function of ideology (even over whether there should be an ideological component at all), purposes, long-range goals (if any), and so forth.

"Working with Our Friends" referred to Council's cooperation with all its constituent organizations. Among its achievements within the Jewish population were numerous "arbitration and conciliation" activities by the committee of that name, assistance to the Landsmanshaftn Council in organizing some forty-one groups, and creation and maintenance of a calendar of community events that had grown from 650 listed dates in 1947 to 1,810 dates for 192 organizations in 1951–1952. It also boasted assuming the initiative in Jewish Book Month and Jewish Music Month, a Yiddish culture series at the Jewish Community Center, the Warsaw Ghetto Memorial (along with the Workmen's Circle and the Jewish Labor Committee), and attaining an extension of the absentee ballot deadline for a primary election that fell on Rosh Hashanah, producing 10,123 "religious reason" absentee ballots.[114]

Perhaps more significantly, the pamphlet described the joint efforts of Council and non-Jewish organizations and individuals. Council had actively participated in primary elections by cosponsoring, with the Catholic Archdiocese and the Detroit Council of Churches, a series of "Know Your Candidate" meetings; it had distributed fact sheets about each of the political candidates and the issues of the elections; supported the Detroit Citizens' Commission for Equal Employment Opportunities with the Michigan Council for Civil Rights; joined several groups in opposition to the racist McCarran-Walter immigration law of 1952; cosponsored, with Rabbi B. Benedict Glazer as cochairman with Bishop Richard S. Emrich, the Citizens' Committee on Group Tensions; and worked with the Midtown Neighborhood Council and the Midtown Community Council, the Mayor's Interracial Committee, and the Urban League to promote "harmonious and stabilized neighborhoods" and to combat "unscrupulous real estate dealers" who used "panic tactics" to gain cheap housing by frightening white residents.[115]

Its list continued, and the impression it produced clearly shone through to define its public persona as a civil rights–oriented, unionist, and generally liberal organization. Council leaders listed in the pamphlet added credence to that depiction: Dr. Shmarya Kleinman, long known for championing civil-rights causes and supporting the labor movement in Detroit, was outgoing president in 1952. Both Rabbi Adler and Rabbi Glazer, who had gained similar if less radical reputations, were vice-presidents (although Rabbi Glazer died just before the publication of the pamphlet and the booklet was dedicated to his memory). Defined by one of his colleagues as a member of the Socialist Revolutionary Party in Europe, Boris M. Joffe, executive director of Council since 1948, also openly supported liberal causes in Detroit and in the nation. All could boast longtime opposition to fascism and anti-Semitism during the 1930s. Many had been connected with the Jewish Labor Committee and the League for Human Rights and were early joiners of the NAACP in Detroit.

From its inception, Council displayed animated political ideology and actions. Almost every one of its committees expressed a prevalent political philosophy—although with distinct and explicit dissenting minority opinions. Its three major committees, the Community Relations Committee (CRC), the Internal Relations Committee (IRC), and the Culture Commission, regularly dealt with overlapping problems of relationships with non-Jews (primarily through the CRC) and discrimination against Jews by both non-Jews and Jews (through the IRC). By the mid-thirties, "community relations" conveyed a euphemistic code that signaled the combat of anti-Semitism. But Council's constitution defined the purpose of the IRC in Article II:

A. To help maintain the dignity and integrity of Jewish life.
B. Develop an articulate, intelligent and effective public opinion on Jewish problems and interest.
C. Coordinate . . . the activities of various segments of Detroit's Jewish community.

Toward these ends, the IRC would concern itself with community planning, the ethical conduct of Jews, the relationship between the Council and its constituent organizations, and discipline within the Jewish community.[116] Judge Ellmann's Evaluation Committee report found the IRC a critical element of the Council's activities.[117]

Yet the Evaluation Committee's conclusions represented other vital con-   367 cerns. That committee embodied a broad spectrum of opinion and included Mrs. Samuel Aaron, Rabbi Adler, William Cohen, Lawrence W. Crohn, Dr. Clarissa Fineman, Charles Goldstein, Walter E. Klein, Dr. Shmarya Kleinman, Dr. Samuel Krohn, Benjamin M. Laikin, Louis LaMed, Harry Nathan, Irving Pokempner, Samuel J. Rhodes, Louis Rosenzweig, Jacob S. Sauls, Sidney Shevitz, Harry Yudkoff, and Judge Ellmann. The report repeatedly emphasized the need for continually examining Jewish content in Council's activities in order to determine what deserved Council's attention and how it should establish priorities. Several members of the Evaluation Committee expressed their disquietude about Council's persistent forays into what they considered non-Jewish domains.[118]

In his report of the CRC to the Council Executive Committee on November 8, 1950, Sidney Shevitz listed three points from a statement drafted by Rabbi Adler, Louis Rosenzweig, and Samuel Rhodes outlining their struggle against Communist activities: (1) an educational campaign within the Jewish community to alert Jews to the dangers of Communist propaganda and to the anti-Semitic connotations of equating Jews with Communists; (2) "work with other liberal groups against Communism"; and (3) civil rights activities.[119] By 1953 the first point had become almost moot as anti-Communist paranoia subsided. The second two points, however, continued to inform Council policy and life. Meetings routinely included discussions of Fair Employment Practices legislation so that, in 1955, when Governor G. Mennen Williams attended the "housewarming" for Council's new offices, he commended the organization for its leadership toward "better communal living among religious, labor, veteran and other groups" as he praised its eleven years of support for the FEPC Bill (which became law in April 1955).[120] Regular committee reports also included activities of the National Community Relations Advisory Council (NCRAC), civil-rights activities, "Negro-Jewish relations," church-state relations, fair-housing practices, matters of tension within the Jewish population ranging from religious arguments to rent control, media coverage of Jewish activities and cultural programs, lectures, education, and cooperative ventures with secular and religious non-Jewish groups and Israel.

Those topics lay at the heart of Council's being and extended from specific, individual cases to national movements. In January 1950, for example, Harry Nathan led a subcommittee to deal with potential interracial violence in the Twelfth Street area and convened meetings with the police department, the Mayor's Interracial Committee, and the Midtown Neighborhood Council.[121] Such apprehensions were not new to the neighborhood. In 1947, for example, Council had assembled merchants and property owners to discuss problems arising "between old and new residents" and to expose "false stories about the Negro families" moving into the neighborhood. "Unscrupulous real estate dealers" proliferated such negative stereotypes in order to frighten property owners into selling, and Council hoped to defeat such malicious gossip and "bring credit to all Detroit Je-wry" in the bargain.[122]

This new action followed a violent incident in Chicago in the previous November, when several black members of the CIO met at a Jewish home. Rumors of integration flew through the neighborhood during the meeting and a crowd had gathered outside the house. Anti-Semitic and racist, the mob attacked the house and its inhabitants. Both the police and the local monsignor in the Catholic neighborhood remained uninvolved during the riot. Fearful of similar occurrences in Detroit, Council launched the discussions. Within two months, however, Boris Joffe reported on rising tensions in the neighborhood that had been stimulated by the shooting of a black passenger in a car on Hastings Street. He referred with disdain to Mayor Cobo's reactionary housing program and the ensuing crisis on the Interracial Committee on which Joffe himself sat.[123]

By April 1950, Council had joined Bishop Emrich in attempts to reform the Interracial Committee.[124] Louis Rosenzweig, chairman of the committee, outlined the details of a joint campaign to slow panicky sales of Jewish homes in the Twelfth Street–Linwood-Dexter area. Along with Bishop Emrich's church, Council had coauthored a leaflet entitled, "Neighbor Where Are You Running?" Meetings with Jewish realtors found them cooperative, and Rabbis Prero and Lehrman volunteered to begin a "pulpit campaign" to convince their congregations not to take flight from the neighborhoods; the committee recommended that block meetings be instituted.[125]

Walter Klein, then assistant director of Council, reported that the meeting of the Detroit Council for Better Housing had revealed racial tension there, too, when members of the racist Federated Property Owners of Detroit (followers of Gerald L. K. Smith), packed the meeting and jeered Roy Reuther, Judge Cody, and Tigh Woods.[126]

At that same meeting, when Joffe reported the concrete example of Harry Nathan's activities to confront "community relations" problems in a specific neighborhood, he also reported on the Civil Rights Mobilization in Washington, where four-thousand delegates had convened. Among those delegates were Meyer Silverman from the East Side Merchants Association, M. Leavitt of the Workmen's Circle, and Joffe, who sat on the Credentials Committee along with six black delegates.[127]

Members of the IRC connected their raison d'être with some of the CRC issues, such as civil rights and fair housing. A subcommittee on the East Side Merchants Association composed of Rosenzweig, Rabbi Hayim Donin, Jerome Kelman, Arthur Gould, and Joseph Edelman, recalled the 1943 riots in one of their reports. They believed that guaranteeing ethical business practices among Jews—a function of the IRC—stood as a fundamental defense against a repetition of the 1943 destruction of Jewish businesses. Beyond that, their task, according to Council's constitution, was to maintain "the dignity and integrity of Jews." Along with ethical commercial conventions, then, they perceived working for civil rights and the "mutual concern and respect of groups" as means to sustain that dignity and integrity. They concluded with another reminder that "should the economic conditions worsen, another 1943 is possible."[128]

The IRC and CRC formed a joint subcommittee on housing in 1955 which involved church, labor, civic, governmental, and racial groups interested in equal opportunity in the sale and rental of housing and in the desegregation of Detroit public housing.[129] In 1960 that subcommittee sponsored an address to the Delegate Assembly of the Jewish Community Council of Metropolitan Detroit (the name had been changed in 1955 to include "metropolitan," that is, suburban Jews) by Dr. Mel J. Ravitz, then assistant professor of sociology at Wayne State University. Already popular as a promising young liberal-Jewish political candidate (Ravitz became a member of the Detroit City Council), he spoke on the topic "Where Shall We Live?" He pointed out that since 1958 a majority of the four million people of Detroit had lived outside the city limits, the central city having lost 200,000 people in ten years. He further noted that the black population of Detroit had increased by about 300,000, so that 26 to 28 percent of the population was black. After discussing his experience with block clubs, he evaluated the neighborhoods most prone to change and outlined demographic studies and the nature of so-called protective, or "homeowner," associations; then Ravitz turned to the Jewish population.

Jews, Ravitz said, were "directly involved in this process of community change" and, in his judgment, "the Jewish Community Council has a fundamental stake in providing leadership to achieve an open housing market. The Jewish community has this responsibility for both moral and practical reasons." Listeners did not miss the irony in Ravitz, an apostate Jew at best, calling up "traditions of human dignity and social concern that are a basic element of Judaism . . . [and] a deep sensitivity to social injustice, whether it strikes them [Jews] or others." He went on to say that, in his view, "the whole ethical thrust of Judaism" had been a moral one, directed toward human decency and brotherhood "expressed . . . in tangible terms through legislation, education and community organization."

Because Ravitz recognized that moral arguments rarely moved people, he offered some practical reasons for Jewish support of open and fair housing and for stable neighborhoods. The last of his three "practical reasons" rested on the belief that any minority must protect the rights of other minorities and that the " 'liberal' or 'open' community must be the paramount goal of every minority—including and perhaps especially, the Jews." He concluded with an appeal to the Council to devote itself to "expressing the Jewish moral commitment for a just society" and to consider its work as a defense agency secondary.[130]

If Ravitz's political liberalism did not sit well with some of the delegates at the assembly, he nevertheless seemed to express the dominant philosophy of Council. Upon becoming president of Council in 1958, Lawrence W. Crohn expressed his view that the CRC and Council in general engaged in more than "putting out fires." Their original goals, he said, continued to be building better and wider understanding between the Jewish and general communities and the enhancement of Jewish living. In order to achieve those goals, Crohn declared, Council must deal with political candidates, civil rights, and education about Israel and the Middle East; it must work with the Zionist Council and promote, through its Culture Commission, the engagement of Yiddish goups through community wide celebrations, and generally look to education as a vehicle for achieving greater harmony.[131]

But this issue of changing neighborhoods persisted and would not go away. No matter how much the Council leadership entreated Detroit Jewry or expressed good faith in the powers of goodwill, negotiations, and intergroup collaboration, Jews moved, blacks moved, and sensibilities grew more aggravated each year. For whatever reasons—status, larger homes, better schools, safer neighborhoods, panic, misinformation, stereotyping—the inexorable movement northwest continued. Council fought its battles beyond 1967, but demography exposed a failure to fully represent most of Detroit's Jews. Some maintained their support for liberal causes like civil rights, equal employment, fair housing, and antidiscrimination, actively participating in such events as the marches on Washington or contributing money to the NAACP and similar organizations. Three of Council's leaders, Rabbi Adler, Dr. Kleinman, and Hoke Levin, received St. Cyprian's Protestant Episcopal Church annual award for outstanding contributions to mutual understanding in race relations during the 1950s.[132] But, as one Council administrator noted, the organizations seemed to reap more respect from non-Jews than from Jews. To many non-Jews, Council appeared to be what it claimed: the representative voice of organized Jewry.

Several of Council's founders believed that the impetus for its birth and its primary responsibility continued to be defense against anti-Semitism. Unquestionably, the leadership and a large part of its constituency believed that to be the abiding purpose of the organization; yet even that produced controversy.

Enumerating anti-Semitic incidents, threats, provocations, and any related items remained a consistent item on the Council's agenda. Thus Council regularly reported acts of vandalism, anonymous phone calls, and such items as letters from Claude Smith to Christian pastors (in which Smith equated Communism with Judaism), or the presence of the "notorious anti-Semite," Reverend William Blessing, in the area.[133] These announcements served to alert Council and the general Jewish population. Council's founders proffered cooperation with other Jewish groups to protest or combat anti-Semitic activities as one of its major functions. Yet it was not an exclusive function of the Council.

In 1955 Harry T. Madison, commander of the Jewish War Veterans in Detroit, and the Jewish Labor Committee publicly protested the planned tour of the Berlin Philharmonic Orchestra under the direction of Herbert von Karajan, known for his active participation in Nazi activities during the 1930s and 1940s. Council agreed to join the protest—but did not initiate it.[134] Similarly, when the Christian Anti-Defamation League, headed by the flagrantly anti-Semitic Lawrence Reilly, began to campaign, the CRC notified its constituents that it thought it important to watch that organization. The Anti-Defamation League of the B'nai B'rith agreed to cooperate with the CRC.[135]

Before long, however, the ADL began to resent the interference of Council in its own activities. Harry Madison continued to seek the cooperation of Council in publicizing such endeavors as monitoring VFW and American Legion meetings for anti-Semitism, and the ADL protested the duplication of projects that were their reason for being. In response, Council replied that the ADL "took its marching orders" from a national organization while the CRC directly dealt with local issues as a local organization. Nevertheless, antagonism festered over the territorial rights to lead the fight against anti-Semitism.[136]

Some of Council's most popular achievements intertwined with its stormiest controversies. At the end of 1949, Rabbi Adler, in his capacity as chairman of the Culture Commission, summarized his committee's accomplishments for the first six months of the fiscal year. Those accomplishments included a thirteen-week radio show during the previous summer on WDET, a High Holiday program that had aired on several radio stations, a Chanukah program on WWJ-TV, the publication of "Call to Jewish Parents," and a total of 249 cultural events. Adler contended that the Culture Commission's successes had been handicapped because of its problematic budget and its consequent lack of professional staff. He raised the question of Federation's persistent refusal to approve financing for cultural work[137]—the question that had become the touchstone for measuring the relationship between Council and Federation, the symbol of their disagreements and contrasting ideologies and natures.

In March of that year, as the Council Executive Committee reviewed Federation budget demands, Aaron Droock asked rhetorically if Council was an independent organization on an equal footing with Federation, at least in its own particular areas of service to the Jewish community of Detroit. Rabbi Fram answered affirmatively, and the proposition to that effect passed unanimously. Next, Droock asked if Council was master of its budget after Federation allocated its funds. Louis Rosenzweig answered affirmatively, and that proposition similarly passed. Droock opined that Council most decidedly was not "a so-called Federation agency," and moved that the two propositions be adopted as the basis for cooperative negotiations.[138]

In August Dr. Shmarya Kleinman argued again the need for funds for the Culture Commission and again Federation denied the request and a five-hundred-dollar increase for Boris Joffe that had been provided under his original contract.[139] By the time Rabbi Adler offered his synopsis in December 1949, the scene had been set for another antagonistic confrontation. Once again, all the key players appeared: Kleinman, Joffe, Rabbi Adler, Sobeloff, Julian Krolik (the president of Federation from whom the refusal letter had come), James Ellmann, and others; the issue of cultural work again assumed center stage only to evoke fundamental disparities regarding most aspects of Jewish life.

Lawrence Crohn extended the argument from the Federation's refusal of money for cultural work to the failure to agree on the scope of Council's work in general or on its "spheres of operation." He firmly believed that the Culture Commission's work "is the voice of the positive aspects of Jewish life . . . [and] an antidote to the negative defense work of the Community Relations Committee." Finally, he stated what most Council advocates believed: that Federation feared that Council would become the "overall organization" in Detroit. James Ellmann followed Crohn's statement with a description of what had occurred at a joint meeting with Federation when Joffe had been asked why cultural work was necessary and how much it was hampered by a shortage of funds. Ellmann crystallized the belief that Federation neither understood nor sympathized with the Jewish population's need for Yiddish culture.[140]

Rabbi Adler pursued this argument further. Federation allocated money to Council, he said, but that did not automatically make Council an agency of Federation, because fund-raising does not grant policymaking power. Continuing the discussion, Charles Rubiner exposed the more general, deeper realms that lay hidden beneath the surface as he declared that culture should not become the "scapegoat for the whole discussion." When Isidore Sobeloff, who attended Council Executive Committee meetings, spoke, he concurred by asserting that "sovereignty was the issue." Predictably, he argued that Detroit Jewry needed a central organization that had the power to examine all programs and their merits. He objected to the use of the term *philanthropy* (significant for the historical connotations it carried) to characterize Federation "as though Federation is the voice of philanthropy and the Council is the voice of culture and democracy." Joffe retorted that Sobeloff knew that cultural work lay at the core of Council's occupation—that it was fundamental and essential to its life. Joffe then ended the meeting, declaring (to Sobeloff) that overall organization seemed fine, but discussions about joint operations would remain fruitless until Council was able to carry on the cultural work of the Jewish community.[141]

Repressed or subterranean ideas resurfaced here: old criticisms of Federation's failure to enhance "positive aspects of Jewish life," its public persona as a philanthropic or service-oriented organization almost exclusively occupied with fund-raising, its refusal to consider the Yiddish groups, its aristocratic (that is, German Jewish) origins and continued demeanor. And, conversely, Soboloff portrayed Council as an agency whose task should remain defense; as disorganized and chaotic—tacitly conjuring up its frequently stormy, multilingual delegate assemblies and meetings—and lacking in central authority and organization for the good of the Jews of Detroit. Even the physical appearances of the protagonists seemed conflicting, according to one observer: Soboloff, tall, haughty, sophisticated, prosperous; and disciplined; Joffe and Kleinman, smaller, publicly excitable, Yiddishists, radical, somewhat disheveled, professing strong ties to grass-roots democratic movements. All struggled to speak for the Jews; each differed on who "the Jews" were or what defined them.

Regardless of their own perceptions, Soboloff had accurately captured the popular views of the two contending organizations: philanthropy versus democracy. As the decade of the fifties wore on, these basic postulates, these same fundamental issues, always kindled by discussions of cultural work coupled to budgetary debates, intensified and grew more acrimonious. In January 1950, four members of Council's Executive Committee, Adler, Ellmann, Glazer, and Shevitz, were elected to the Federation board. But the following month, Kleinman, then president of Council, revealed that the joint committee of the two groups had made no progress; that Federation representatives refused to discuss cultural work and would not allow funds for it. Council requested that the meetings resume.[142]

By September 1950, Louis Rosenzweig reported that he had met with Federation's Budget Committee under the direction of Morris Garvett, who had proceeded with a line-by-line review of their request. Everything had been approved except the issues of culture, travel, and salaries. "Line-by-line review" became the catch phrase for the confrontation. Council persisted in refusing to delineate specifics under the "culture" heading and the Federation persisted in demanding line-by-line review. To accounting heads, businessmen, and professional social-service staff, such a review seemed reasonable good sense. Some, like Morris Garvett, represented genuine desires to have Council simply follow standard procedures, and administrative rules. Others saw this procedural disagreement as masking more fundamental quarrels. Always the realist, Soboloff sent a letter stating that "no further funds [would be allocated] until we have a chance to evaluate basic relations between the Council and Federation."[143] A battle of angry correspondence ensued.[144]

Debates like this one aggravated already tense relations, and the following month, to avert what he perceived as disastrous fragmentation, Philip Slomovitz, in a *Jewish News* editorial, invited Kleinman and Samuel Rubiner, president of Federation, to discuss in writing the possibility of unifying the Jewish community under the rubric of one organization.[145] In the ensuing negotiations of the joint committee, Kleinman, Joseph Bernstein, James Ellmann, Harry Yudkoff, and Rabbis Adler and Glazer represented Council. Kleinman stated publicly that he regarded the atmosphere as inhospitable because of budget freezing. After the first meeting, Federation indicated that the differences simply revolved around money, not policy.[146] Partisans of both organizations seemed to understand, however, that money differences masked other substantive and philosophical differences.

Partly because of this, negotiations collapsed within a few months, as Federation rejected Council's plan for a unified community organization that would subscribe to the values and principles outlined in Council's constitution. As the discussions again became heated, Lawrence Crohn tried to calm the situation by observing that both groups had perhaps acted precipitously: Council plan appeared "novel" to Federation, and the Federation's plan appeared "grotesque" to Council. Rabbi Glazer, however, expressed that he "sensed a constant effort on the part of Federation's representatives to obliterate the Community Council" and felt free as a worker for both organizations to make this statement.[147]

In this prolonged debate, two attitudes toward Jewish life confronted each other. Council's characterization somehow embodied whatever distant perceptions of Federation existed among Jews who were less involved with fund-raising or agency work. Federation proponents often viewed Council as old-world, activist, liberal (or worse), the repository of East European shtetl Jewry and its *Yiddishkeit,* controlled variously by either Orthodox Jews, black-garbed and dogmatically religious, or secularist, radical antiestablishment Jews. Perhaps cultural programming offered the most blatant evidence of this view: sponsorship of Yiddish programs at the Jewish Community Center, Jewish Music Month, and Jewish Book Month, came from organizations like the Workmen's Circle or the *landsmanshaftn* and attracted almost exclusively East European Jews. Coupled with other Council actions, like the involvement of the IRC with such problems as kosher butchers, with meetings conducted in Yiddish, and the continued civil-rights pursuits (which indicated socialist and unionist leanings to politically conservative and economically successful Jews), Federation found reason to shun overtures by Council and to reject the concept that it "represented the organized Jewish community."

At the root of the melee lay serious disagreements about Jewishness, values, and identity. Rabbi Adler, a proponent of Council, believed that there was "no question . . . of the mutuality of purpose between Council and Federation, that mutuality being the best interests of the community." But the dismissal of the Council plan, he argued, "reflects a disturbing lack of earnestness on the part of Federation's representatives about developing a community and implies a lack of respect for the individuals involved and responsible for creating the plan . . . [and] injects an element of acrimony and suspicion into the negotiations."[148] Julian Krolik re-

sponded to this condemnation by denying that there had been any ultimatum or attempt to smash the Council, and he pointed out that Council's
overall budget had increased steadily.

Slomovitz's request incited a chain of reactions. Arguments against a
joint organization won the day. Joseph Bernstein referred to the confrontation as the "cold war," but most seemed to agree that the two organizations served different functions.[149]

Among the general Jewish population of Detroit, such conflict seemed
to be out of touch with their daily lives. Yet most Detroit Jews held pre-
dispositions for one side or the other. The campaign, especially with support for Israel growing, remained nearly sacrosanct. Louis LaMed, on the
heels of the cessation of negotiations, reaffirmed his belief that every effort
had to be made not to disrupt the campaign and "divide the community."
Several Council and Federation members expressed their worry that the
bitter quarrels would be aired publicly at the delegate assembly and that
the hard-liners would openly discuss their opinion that Federation insisted
on dictating Council activities. Almost humorously, in the midst of the
heated debates, Kleinman read a letter from Sobeloff (in Sobeloff's presence), inviting the Council to move to the Fred M. Butzel Memorial Building on Madison Avenue. The executive committee voted almost unanimously to postpone the decision—almost unanimously, because Sobeloff
voiced his wish to be recorded as "present."[150]

In 1950 the National Community Relations Advisory Council (NCRAC)
commissioned Dr. Robert I. MacIver, professor emeritus of sociology at
Columbia University, to direct a cooperative evaluative study of Jewish
community-relations activities. The publication of the study, which was
supported by every Jewish national agency in the country, including the
Jewish War Veterans, the Jewish Labor Committee, the Council of Jewish
Federations and Welfare Funds, and the Anti-Defamation League, struck
many as a turning point and a signal for decisive changes in the policies
of Jewish organizations.[151] The results were distributed to members of the
boards of both Federation and Council, and Sidney Shevitz reported on
possibilities for consequent action in September 1951. He quoted from
MacIver's analysis of "interagency conflict" and its detrimental affects: "Instead of getting together for the sake of their common interest, the agencies have been kept apart by mutual jealousies and suspicions, not merely
by their differences in ideology. There has been a scrambling for membership, and insistence on the merits of independence, and, on the part of
certain agencies, an exaggerated bid for exclusive credit in advancing the
course in which they are all enlisted." Shevitz noted that Rabbi Glazer, in
a local study conducted in 1947, had reached similar conclusions.[152]

MacIver's investigation of "community relations," that is, the fight against
anti-Semitism, revealed that the ADL, the American Jewish Committee,
and local groups like the community councils had overlapped and dupli-

376

cated efforts. All of them, he argued, should cooperate with non-Jewish organizations, and he urged the NCRAC to caucus on strategy. His report praised local community relations committees which, he said, needed their own autonomy. He disapproved, therefore, of funding through federations and welfare funds, suggesting that "communities should earmark funds" for a united defense appeal. Concomitantly, MacIver recommended that no ADL offices be assigned to cities where local community relations committees functioned.[153] His addition that Jews exhibited a certain "clannishness" annoyed many, but representatives of Council, like Rabbi Adler, having noted this disagreeable comment, went on to praise and endorse the MacIver Report.[154]

Those at Federation who received the evaluation reacted to it with considerably less excitement—some with indifference, some with impassive approval—although both Sobeloff and Avrunin endorsed the report enthusiastically. Given its broad scope, the report could be read by everyone as generally endorsing their own policies: Federation might point to the section on community councils that implied that they operate primarily as community relations agencies; Council, in turn, pointed to the increased role of the NCRAC in the MacIver recommendations and to the autonomy he advised for community councils. The ADL, on the other hand, issued a lengthy rejoinder to the report, refuting its proposals regarding the primacy of local community-relations work.[155] In the final Council resolution, after its special Delegate Assembly of November 18, 1951, Council applauded MacIver but added that his report had failed to address how Jewish organizations might sustain and pass on Jewish values, "positive, democratic and constructive," to a Jewish population whose "spiritual and economic growth" are impeded.[156] In short, the resolution returned to the issue of cultural programming.

According to some readers of the MacIver Report, the subject of cultural work had echoed Oscar I. Janowsky's and Salo Baron's 1948 *The Jewish Welfare Board Survey: The Report of the JWB Survey Commission,* in which the authors had concluded that cultural commissions responsible for events like Jewish book and music months should be functions of Jewish community centers. Thus, another attempt to provide organizational unity and order had encountered internal controversy and dissent.[157] Yet, partly as a result of the MacIver Report, the Council-Federation conflict peaked in a critical encounter. Remarkably, Council's leadership attempted to increase their influence and seize control of Federation's board of directors.

As the annual Federation meeting approached, several of Council's leaders, including Boris Joffe and Dr. Kleinman, decided that they had received a mandate from their constituency to gain a greater voice in determining their financial needs. On March 4, 1952, Federation elections were to take place in the Brown Chapel at Temple Beth El. Traditionally, annual meetings drew from one-hundred to two-hundred people; a slate of board members was perfunctorily elected and a synopsis of activities given by the executive director. Joffe determined to raise public consciousness to the issue of line-by-line budget review, what he considered harassment by Federation and their stifling of the Council's enacting their charge as a democratic representation of the general Jewish population. Two items were to be offered for the agenda: first, an amendment to the Federation by-laws that would recognize the status of the Jewish Community Council as a "central coordinating body in its field . . . [and] the right of the Council to decide upon its own program within its field" and would eliminate "dictation of Council activities through allocations of funds"; and, second, a separate slate of nine candidates for the Federation board, including David J. Cohen, William Cohen, Lawrence W. Crohn, Morris Lieberman, Hyman Safran, and Irving Schlussel.[158]

Fliers for the meeting bore a dual heading: "Full Support to the Allied Jewish Campaign" and "Peace in the Community." Across the "Open Letter" in large red letters was: "LET'S MEET OUR RESPONSIBILITY," followed by, "THE ISSUE IS NOT 'MORE FUNDS TO THE COUNCIL.' IT IS THIS: 'IS THE COUNCIL TO CONDUCT ITS OWN AFFAIRS WITHIN THE TOTAL AMOUNT OF FUNDS APPROPRIATED TO IT?" Sponsors of the letter were David I. Berris, Mrs. Harry Frank, Rabbi Samuel Prero, Louis Rosenzweig, and Mrs. Sophie Sislin. Those listed as "Contributors' Committee for a Democratic Jewish Community" were Dr. S. Kleinman, Dr. Lawrence Yaffa, Morris Jacobs, Phillip Stollman, I. Pokempner, William Hordes, and Mrs. Samuel A. Green. At the bottom of the ad was printed: "For a Democratic Jewish Community," and "For a Stronger and Healthier Jewish Community."[159]

Some fifteen-hundred people attended the meeting, which had to be moved to the larger sanctuary at Beth El. Sobeloff, who was adept at political maneuvers (not unlike Joffe, his Council counterpart), managed to alert Federation champions to attend the meeting. Stormy, bitter allegations flew back and forth. Sidney Shevitz delivered a speech that was "a masterful presentation of the Council's case." But the amendment and the slate suffered defeat by a 390 to 472 vote.[160] Kleinman would later call the meeting a "moral victory" because it openly presented Council's complaints and exposed, he said, Federation's obstructionist tactics.[161] Despite this claim, Federation had demonstrated strong support within the community and had shown, too, that it held the confidence of a large cross-section of Jews who concerned themselves with Jewish organizational life.

Council's agenda immediately following that decisive meeting once again contained budget questions. But the antagonism seemed to enter a new phase after 1952.[162]

In 1954 the question of Council moving its headquarters from 803 Washington Boulevard to the Butzel Memorial Building returned. A committee headed by Hy Safran recommended the move, accompanied by a set of conditions to assure the "integrity and independence of Council." Benjamin

Laikin insisted that the history of organizational conflict be made clear, but that there was no point in paying rent when a community-owned building was available. Under the watchful guidance of Stanley Winkelman, Avern Cohn, and Harold Berry, the move was effected—over the opposition of Dr. Kleinman, and with LaMed commenting that he saw it as "a step in the right direction."[163] Those opposed and those in favor of the move perceived it as symbolic, connoting a new spirit of cooperation or, conversely, of co-option.

The constituents of those two groups defined the way in which traditional discord evolved in the 1950s and 1960s. A younger generation (Berry, Winkelman, and Cohn), led by a few more conciliatory voices like Walter Klein's, Louis LaMed's, Hy Safran's, and Samuel Rhodes's, moved away from the older group (of Kleinman and Joffe) and toward more pacific relationships.

By 1955, with the Council now ensconced in the Fred M. Butzel Memorial Building, Hoke Levin reported on his first meeting as a member of the board of governors of Federation, saying that he believed that philosophical differences were of far greater importance than the small amounts of money that had become the focus of the split. Levin expressed surprise at some of the opinions he heard about Council that implied a fundamental ignorance about its workings and composition. Because of that, he proposed that three members of Federations's board sit on each of the major standing committees of Council. During the discussion of this motion, Mina (Mrs. Theodore) Bargman suggested that Council performed an intangible service to the community, one not statistically measurable. It remained difficult, she said, to present budget requests on such issues. Seemingly unremitting, the same issue of "intangible" issues returned regularly. It was unrealistic, argued Council budget-committee members, to suggest line-by-line breakdown of funds for activities that remained unreceptive to such analysis.[164] Communal, spiritual, and cultural enterprises defied quantification.

If these intangible issues—questions of values, Jewish identity, culture, and community relations—embodied the essence of Council, Federation nevertheless continued to demand more concrete budget evaluations. Still another joint committee on relations between the two organizations was initiated by Sobeloff in March 1956. When Samuel Rhodes became president of Council, he stated that his goal was to establish harmonious relations with Federation and to further Federation's understanding of Council. He followed Hoke Levin's recommendation for Federation board members to sit on standing committees.[165] Judge Theodore Levin, president of Federation, refused to submit names for the committees and instead asked for an evaluation of Council's activities. In May 1956, Rhodes read Judge Levin's letter to Council, in which Levin made what Rhodes called a "novel point . . . an attempt to equate the status of the Council with that of the service agencies of Federation . . . making the Council responsible not to the over 300 member organizations . . . but to the Federation alone." Levin had not responded to the budget evaluation questions.[166]

Sensing an escalation of hostilities again, members of both organizations, counseled by budget-committee members Berry, Safran, Winkelman, Pokempner, LaMed, Rosenzweig, Morris Lieberman, Charles Goldstein, and Shevitz, called for another joint meeting in negotiations for a merger.[167] Both organizations agreed to invite Irving Kane, a former head of the Jewish Community Council in Cleveland who had recently been appointed vice-president of the Jewish Community Federation of Cleveland—the result of the merger of a federation and council there. In the lecture hall of Sinai Hospital, the meeting was chaired by Judge Levin and Samuel Rhodes, who read the resolution of October 1950, which pledged a search for a formula to merge. Kane would address an "informational meeting" and respond to questions about the Cleveland merger. Kane began by stating that "the old Federation leadership had to open its mind to the feelings of the masses of Jews who . . . had always expressed fundamental Jewish ideals of learning, culture and social service. In turn . . . the Cleveland Council had to develop an understanding of the responsibilities of fund-raising and budgeting and an appreciation of the Federation's role in acting as provider for Jewish communal services and in having raised such tremendous amounts of money during the past years of crisis."[168]

After this tactful opening, Kane responded to questions and directed the discussion. Cultural activities, formerly the precinct of Council, he said, had been given over to the Jewish community centers. He could not, Kane said, offer any solutions or make decisions for Detroit. What he described appeared as an uneasy truce that would probably evolve into a functioning, cooperative organization. It seemed clear to everyone who listened, however, that Federation had given up none of its authority in Cleveland, but had achieved a "broader base."[169]

By the end of 1957, when the Ellmann Committee offered its evaluation of Council, some of the same concerns that had plagued the organization regarding budgeting and cultural work seemed as troublesome as they had been ten years earlier. But throughout their confrontations, Council and Federation almost imperceptibly drew closer. It became more apparent in some of the leadership's articulation of changes in focus and programs. Responding to criticisms inside and outside the Council, Walter F. Klein addressed the question, "What's Jewish about it?" As Council actively supported civil-rights causes, fair housing and employment practices, liberal speakers, and political candidates, it drew fire from Jews in Detroit as to why it took positions as a Jewish organization on non-Jewish issues, "public issues on the general American scene which seem to have no immediate or apparent connection with what we take as proper and conventional concerns as *Jews*." Klein noted that the question resembled the older one of,

"Is it good for the Jews?" He then proceeded to offer an historical rationale to provide his answer to the two related questions.

For at least a hundred years, he argued, Jews had participated in European socialist movements and had held a public affinity for liberal forces that "gave the promise of ushering in a new era" that would end oppression. In short, he connected organizational and individual Jewish support for liberal causes to the defense against anti-Semitism; in twentieth-century America, "community relations" had become the heir to that crusade. As a correlative to that legacy, Klein continued, came the conviction that if one group suffered threats of inequity, all minority groups stood susceptible to the same perils. Jewish organizational positions on American public issues, then, evolved as logical extensions of the struggle against anti-Semitism and for equality.

Klein censured those who asked the question, "What's Jewish about it?" as socially and intellectually rejecting a part of their Jewish heritage. He in effect accused those who claimed that "the job of Jewish groups is to serve the religious, cultural and welfare needs *of Jews*" of forsaking Jewish values and, therefore, Jewish identity.[170] His language—words like *welfare* and *religious*—carried a subtle rebuke of Federation-type groups that refused to adopt political stands, particularly liberal ones, and continued to narrowly identify themselves as Jews because they "served" the welfare of Jewish groups.

In a similar vein, Rabbi Adler, ever-concerned with the loss of Jewish identity, addressed the Presidents of Council Affiliated Organizations in 1959 with the announcement that there was "no greater mistake than to believe we have a community." Lacking in Detroit (and in America), he said, were those elements necessary to compose a community: common loyalties, common disciplines, common values and interests. In his view—again, in a subtle admonition to Federation—there remained too much weight on philanthropy. "Philanthropy," he said, "should be an outgrowth of common life, not a substitute for it." He discerned the beginnings of those elements in the Council of Jewish Welfare Federations newly established Foundation for Jewish Culture, thus connecting questions about the efficacy of cultural programs to the idea of Jewish community.[171]

Council activists like Klein and Adler had maintained public discussions of the nature of Jewish values and identity throughout the years, echoing secularist groups in opposition to those who advocated a less complex, philanthropic definition of Jewish identity; at the same time, Federaton began to alter its stance and address questions of "positive identity" and the nature of "Jewish content." Taking directions similar to Council's, Federation began to foster more open advocacy of strong, ethical Jewish educational content in Jewish schools and began to show more attention to the prospects of day schools and to the schools not affiliated with the UHS, like the Sholem Aleichem Institute and the Yeshivah Beth Yehudah.

Federation-sponsored Jewish Community Center cultural programs had begun under Irwin Shaw's administration and soon included conversational Hebrew classes and one of the largest and most innovative annual Jewish book fairs in America.

If, in Detroit, Federation subtly responded to prodding from Council in these educational policies, it also reflected a national trend fostered by the National Council of Jewish Federations. In urban centers across the country, organized federations took action along similar lines. Detroit, however, with its Federation development of the concept of communal schools (discussed below), became the model for American-Jewish education.

By 1962 William Avrunin, one of Federations most articulate directors, was writing about "Jewish survival," "Jewish identity," and "Jewishness." In a paper on "Jewish Communal Services and the Jewish Community," Avrunin posed the question as to whether communal services opposed or reflected Jewishness. He suggested that "the meaning of Federation and its agencies [existed] as instruments of Jewish identification." Federation manifested itself as "an acceptable instrument of Jewish identification within the American framework." While he declared that the 1960s had brought this change, his use of terms like "positive cultural programs" seemed to recognize the importance of Council's advocacy of such themes.[172] Borrowing from Arnold Gurin's "Factors that Influence Decisions in Community Planning," Avrunin discussed a "framework of values" within which functional needs could be met and decisions made.[173]

Eventually, Federation, like Council, would concentrate more of its energies on the "enrichment of Jewish life" as one of its primary objectives.[174] This attitude, stimulated partly as a response to Council's programmatic insistence on enhancing Jewish identity through education and open discussion of Jewish values and identity, represented a shift from an emphasis on individual adjustment to group identity and cohesion.[175] Council, for its part, also turned toward conciliation after the death of Joffe and the supplanting of strident voices like Kleinman's by more tempered ones like Winkelman's. This new tone seemed embodied in the close personal friendship of the two leaders of Council and Federation, Walter Klein and William Avrunin. Their mutual respect and admiration translated into a more receptive and compliant relationship between the two organizations.

At the 1971 Fortieth General Assembly of the Council of Jewish Federations and Welfare Funds in Pittsburgh, Brewster Broder, representing the Detroit Jewish Community Center, discussed planning center services. "The paramount question," he said, "is really the question of Jewish survival . . . of individuals as Jews."[176] In that question reverberated some thirty-five years of Council dialogues, institutes, and debates addressing Jewish survival, identity, culture, ethics, and similar topics that Jewish secularists had raised for a century or more. In such discussions, however, and in its written and spoken public pronouncements, Federation began to reflect a shift, or an expansion, of its considerations. In that, Detroit's organization mirrored other Jewish urban agencies, which began in the 1950s to address questions about "the effectiveness of building Jewish identity."

Council, almost from its inception, had presented a high profile in the non-Jewish world regarding social, political, and ethical controversies. Among Jews, one aspect of Council's activities assumed a more discreet and sometimes even secretive form. As a subsidiary of the Internal Relations Committee, the Arbitration and Conciliation Committee tried to police Jews for unethical practices toward non-Jews that might reflect badly on the Jewish population, and for disputes between Jews that might threaten to erupt into public scandal. As early as 1948, the IRC had appointed a subcommittee to investigate the beating of a Jewish youth and discovered that the violence had been gang-related, occuring at the infamous Bowl-O-Drome, an alleged hotbed of gambling. The committee, under the chairmanship of Gabriel Alexander, surveyed the situation and filed a discreet report that implicated the Jewish youth as more than an innocent victim. Other IRC activities involved the work of a real-estate committee, chaired by Irwin Cohn, which investigated rent gouging, discrimination, unethical actions of real-estate dealers who sought to capitalize on worries about "changing neighborhoods," and the deterioration of property that was permitted by Jewish landlords.[177]

As an often confidential committee (its minutes frequently omitted names), the Arbitration and Conciliation Committee dealt with some of the most delicate and vexatious problems within the Jewish population. By 1952, in conjunction with a Women's Consumer Action Committee and the Vaad Harabonim, it already had persuaded kosher butchers to lower their prices[178]—although kosher butchers remained a persistent problem—and had conducted hearings when one survivor of the Holocaust accused another survivor of being a *kapo* (an overseer in a concentration camp), responsible for the beatings and death of Jews. It considered, too, allegations by Jews against other Jews of usury, misappropriation of funds, and other accusations of collaboration with the Nazis brought by survivors; it effected financial reconciliations, sometimes of thousands of dollars; and persisted in its usually successful attempts to avert damaging publicity.[179]

Frequently the Arbitration Committee found itself engaged in religious controversies, such as questions of kashrut, or proper adherence to rules of kosher butchers or caterers, and in several cases responded to Orthodox charges against restaurants or meat packers of misleading or even fraudulently advertising "kosher style" when their products were not strictly kosher. The committee even became actively involved in the rabbinical accusations lodged against a *mohel,* a ritual circumciser, for unprofessional and unethical practices.[180] In 1952–1953, the Arbitration Committee arbitrated compromise arrangements among twenty-nine of the thirty Jewish furniture dealers who broke the Common Council Ordinance forbidding furniture store openings on Sundays. Assistant Corporation Counsel Nathan Goldstick acted as mediator for the Arbitration Committee and convinced the last holdout dealer to comply with the law.[181]

The services of the arbitrators, whose ranks regularly included people of a range of positions—from Orthodox rabbis to secular Jews—provided a forum for the debate between the UJA and the Israel Bond drive, which was amicably settled; and the committee offered to mediate the explosive Saturday center opening but was turned down. By 1959, when the *shochtim* (ritual slaughterers), took it upon themselves to raise their prices, Rabbi Max Kapustin, spokesman for the Arbitration Committee, called for disciplinary action on the grounds that the *shochtim* had broken an earlier agreement to consult with Council before raising prices. Now, Rabbi Kapustin said, the issue was "one of community discipline and responsibility."[182] In the stormy deliberations that followed over the course of the next six months, Max Biber chaired a subcommittee to investigate and survey prices, the Kosher Butchers' Association expressed a "hostile attitude," and the Vaad, formerly cooperative, suddenly claimed that the issue was no longer a concern of Council, but rather a rabbinical concern because of its religious connotations. Although Council aided in effecting a compromise, kosher meat and kosher butchers remained a recurrent source of controversy.[183]

With one of its primary emphases on "community relations" (the euphemism for defense against anti-Semitism), Council continued to collide with other, national organizations in Detroit. Most obvious among these rivals was the Anti-Defamation League of the B'nai B'rith, which regularly complained of Council duplication of and interference in its activities. The MacIver Report had indicated that national organizations ought not operate where local community-relations committees existed. Representatives from the CRC intermittently met with local ADL officials.[184] By 1960 a meeting with members of B'nai B'rith attempted to clarify the criteria for each organization. The B'nai B'rith representatives alleged that Council did not give them enough recognition or acknowledge their important work in combatting anti-Semitism. Discussions about the boundaries of ADL operations frequently became heated, and meetings continued into the 1960s.

As part of the new presentation of papers at executive committee meetings, Rabbi Mordecai Halpern spoke on "Who Speaks for the Jewish Community" in January 1966. That issue still seemed to hang fire in the eyes of many Council members. In June 1966, Dr. Samuel Krohn spoke on the "Meaning of the Community Council," and he outlined the basic premises of the "Council Idea" as: the "importance of the preservation of the Jewish people as a special entity," that is, the survival of Jewish cultural, religious, and group life; the "democratic approach" to community concerns; the strengthening of the "democratic way of life . . . to resist all that isolates the freedom, the equality, the justice that America holds out to all men."[185]

Krohn's speech seemed to demonstrate that in 1966 and 1967 the Council maintained the same committees, addressed the same issues, and fostered the same liberal image that it had in the 1950s. Yet by 1966 it seemed to have lost much of its popular support. Some Council diehards suggested that the rise in economic status of members of the next generation had drawn their attention to other realms, and had made them less active in civil-rights campaigns and less interested in the task of maintaining stable neighborhoods. By the mid-1960s the majority of Detroit Jews lived in Oak Park, Southfield, Huntington Woods, and Farmington. Yet Walter Klein, in April 1967, reported on the Neighborhoods Sub-Committee meeting with information of a number of Jewish merchants in the inner-city areas. The purpose of that committee now centered on determining the source and extent of tensions or problems between Jewish merchants and black clientele. Most agreed that whatever difficulties were identifiable appeared unrelated to their being Jewish, although Rabbi Syme raised the question of Jewish slum landlords, with whom Council hoped to meet.[186]

Culture Commission reports still spoke of "dramatic strides" in the quality of programs, and Krohn averred that the Culture Commission's criteria no longer revolved around the question, "Is there a Jewish stake in this issue?" but, "Can we make a significant contribution to the social environment in which we live?" As chairman of the Neighborhood Committee, Lawrence Gubow worked with other denominational and community groups—the Detroit Council of Churches, Council of Eastern Orthodox Churches, the Catholic Archdiocese—and with the NAACP in 1964–1965 to defeat the so-called Homeowner's Rights Ordinance, which was characterized as "an attempt to erect a Berlin Wall of white inclusiveness in our city."[187]

Consistent with its civil-libertarian ideals, Council added new issues to its agenda, including protests against the persecution of Soviet Jewry. A midnight vigil took place at the Jewish Community Center in April 1967, the culmination of a drive to petition Soviet authorities regarding anti-Semitism in the Soviet Union. As early as 1966, the CRC adopted a statement on the "Right of Public Protest," stimulated by overwrought reactions against anti-Vietnam War protests. In light of those reactions, a subcommittee chaired by Avern Cohn reaffirmed the original position, which decried the responses as "intemperate beyond the provocation." In their statement, the CRC affirmed "our own commitment to civil liberties."[188]

When Isidore Sobeloff addressed the Delegate Assembly of the Jewish Community Council in 1963, he dwelled at length on the social services provided by "our Jewish Welfare Federation." He concluded with a reference to the development of "a council of Jewish organizations," which he compared to the lack of any single, coordinated synagogue to speak for all Jews. Redefining the contemporary demands on community-relations organizations, Sobeloff stated that their new role involved "interpreting to the general community and . . . serving as the instrument through which the views and efforts of the Jewish community are shared with the general community on matters of common concern." References to "Jewish survival," "Jewish identity," and the American Jewish community's "finding itself" did not inspire enthusiasm in his audience members—even as he jocularly reminded them that the "Yiddish secretary of the Community Council is an office of the past" (a reference to the abandonment of the provision in Council's by-laws that the secretary be Yiddish-speaking).[189]

Despite residual estrangement, the Council and Federation drew closer in the 1960s, issuing joint statements on Israel and on some local matters. Dual allegiance became more common, as figures like Mike Zeltzer, Avern Cohn, Walter Klein, Hy Safran, Sam Rhodes, and others emerged to bridge earlier gaps. Zeltzer, the last to hold the office of Council secretary before it abandoned a Yiddish prerequisite, also became president of the UHS and of Federation; Cohn, active in Council, and once favored as Council president, became Federation president instead. That interaction affected both organizations as they increasingly shared goals, cares, rhetoric, and members. Several of those members perceived subtle and explicit changes as a function of the participation of a new generation more prosperous, educated, or sophisticated than its predecessors. If unity and single community were not achieved, at least cooperation and compromise became possible.

31

The Synagogues: Expanding Traditional Identity

As the Federation and Council sought to expand their constituent participation, they drew more Orthodox Jews into their activities. Rabbinical representatives of the Vaad Harabonim joined and sat on the board of Council and in the 1950s more Orthodox Jews participated in Federation meetings. Max Fisher, president of Federation in 1959 was unschooled in religious Judaism, yet he sought religious leaders in order to bring harmony, he said, to Federation ranks and "to the Jewish community in general." And by the 1950s, if harmony had not materialized, increased involvement had. Council's IRC, for example, included numerous Orthodox members. Federation quickly invited Orthodox rabbis like Rabbi Leizer Levin to sit on committees—even in cases when, as in the Saturday Jewish Community Center controversy, it guaranteed strife.

If the organizations pursued them, some Orthodox Jews, in turn, seemed to acknowledge the necessities of participating in the nonreligious realm. They, perhaps more than other religious denominations, feared the loss of young Jews to American culture through assimilation and intermarriage. Circumstances dictated compromise and Council, Federation, the United Hebrew Schools, the Jewish Community Center, and other organizations   387 offered more or less viable roads for excursions outside the religious, Orthodox environment. Invited to join committees, they reached out, perhaps unconcerned with questions about "survival" and "identity," but conscious of the stress of the modern world on religious commitment. Representatives of that new inclusion indicated a shift in the perspectives and strategies of all concerned, as they perhaps tacitly acknowledged mutual needs. If old differences and antagonisms were not altogether resolved, they were submerged for pragmatic as well as more abstruse reasons.

Reassessment appeared critical after the early 1940s with the annihilation of religious centers in Europe and the encroachment of the Conservative and Reform movements on the younger Orthodox population in the United States. Several new groups arriving in Detroit slowly began to strengthen and rebuild their traditional ways of life: German émigrés, well educated in both Torah and secular studies; East Europeans, still closely connected to Jewish roots (of whatever sort); and yeshivah-trained American young adults, usually from New York, Baltimore, or Cleveland, who came to teach in the day schools.

In religious terms, 1948 stood as a watershed year of sorts, marking the arrival in Detroit of effective examples of rabbis from those three types of origins. Rabbi Max Kapustin, who would become the director of the Hillel Foundation at Wayne State University, had been ordained as an Orthodox rabbi in Berlin, part of the last ordination class of Hildesheim Yeshivah in 1935. Kapustin had emigrated from Berlin and earlier taken on a rabbinic post in Virginia; he epitomized the public persona of a German Jew who maintained a "rabbinic distance," seeming rather formal and aloof. Yet his students came to know him as a warm individual in private, dedicated to propriety and scholarship in the Jewish and non-Jewish academic communities. From his position as a teacher of German literature at Wayne, he extended his instruction to Judaic studies. Uncharacteristically of German Jews, Kapustin, perhaps because of his wartime experiences, supported Zionism and became an adviser to the Israeli Students Association.

American-born Rabbi Solomon Gruskin also arrived in Detroit in 1948. Stricter than Kapustin in his Orthodoxy, he became the rabbi of B'nai Zion (the Humphrey Shul), where he attempted to bridge the gap between the generations educated in Europe and those born in America—an attempt visible in the separate Sabbath youth services conducted on the lower floor while the adults prayed upstairs. Warm and less formal than Kapustin, Gruskin was held in fond esteem by even non-Orthodox Jews. He followed Rabbi Joshua Sperka as the Jewish chaplain at Jackson State Prison and served also as rabbi to Jewish patients in mental institutions.

Ideologically between Rabbis Kapustin and Gruskin, Samuel Prero arrived in Detroit that same year as a "modern Orthodox" rabbi, destined to succeed Rabbi Leo Goldman as leader of Young Israel. He, too, taught at Wayne State University and took an active interest in the education of youngsters, determined to rescue that generation from abandonment of its Jewish identity.

According to Dr. Albert Mayer's 1956 survey of the three main branches of Judaism, Conservative Jews comprised about 46 percent of the population; Reform and Orthodox about 22 percent each. Reform Jews were almost all in professional, managerial, or white-collar jobs. Of the Orthodox, about 37 percent were in blue-collar jobs, and they were more often older and lacking in college educations. Conservatives were attracting far more of the younger generation as well as young adults. One possible conclusion, therefore, implied that children of Orthodox Jews left their parents' congregations as they attained higher socioeconomic status.[190]

Not surprisingly, regular synagogue attendance was highest among the Orthodox, with Conservative synagogues registering about 73 percent attendance on Yom Kippur and 64 percent on Passover while Reform groups noted 74 percent and 14 percent, respectively. Regular attendance for daily prayers was minimal, totaling less than 1 percent for the entire population. Place of birth also strongly affected religious affiliation. Of the Orthodox, 82 percent were foreign born, compared to 45 percent of the Conservatives and 26 percent of the Reform Jews.[191] The most notable changes in Orthodox Jewish life derived from the shifting of the neighborhoods and the founding of day schools.

The Twelfth Street and Linwood-Dexter neighborhoods supported many synagogues in the 1940s and 1950s. Congregation B'nai Israel, with Rabbi Israel Flam, opened on Linwood and Leslie in 1952. Israel Halpern came to serve as assistant to Rabbi Thumin at the still Orthodox Beth Abraham (Galicianer Shul) on Linwood and Richton in 1949. Rabbi Rabinowitz's Beth Shmuel moved onto Dexter and Fullerton in 1948. The Gemilus Chasadim Congregation was opened in 1939, largely by Orthodox refugees from Germany; Leopold Neuhaus, a survivor of the concentration camp at Theresienstadt, served as its rabbi in 1946. Like Rabbi Kapustin, Neuhaus had been ordained at the Hildesheimer rabbinic seminary and held a Ph.D. from the University of Berlin.

Rabbi Shraga Kahana was at Nusach H'ari and Rabbi Chaim Meisels presided over the Khal Charedim. M. J. Wohlgelernter served Congregation Emanuel until 1942 and later the Mogen Abraham on Dexter and Cortland. Rabbi Isaac Stollman was active both in national and local affairs, serving as head of Mizrachi in the United States and as an active leader in Young Israel, Yeshivath Beth Yehudah, the Jewish Community Council as well as on the board of Federation (at Max Fisher's suggestion). Rabbi Chaskel Grubner presided over Congregation Dovid Ben Nuchim (the Agudah) in a small room on Dexter, near Sturtevant, and later in the former quarters of the Beth Shmuel on Dexter and Fullerton. Rabbi Leizer Levin came in 1938 to the Beth Tikvah on Boston and Petoskey. Rabbi Leo Goldman came from a pulpit in Norway to serve two small congregations on Linwood.

Rabbi Phillip Rabinowitz and later Rabbi Gershon Frankel served in the Beth Moses on Linwood, near Oakman. These synagogues were far smaller than the Conservative and Reform ones, and many of their worshippers came because they were comfortable with the style, not because they were very strict in Orthodox observance.

The young Israel, led by Rabbi I. Turner, began to see some measurable success, in the later 1940s in their attempts at making traditional Judaism more palatable to modern Americans. Sermons and classes were conducted in English. In December 1944, Boy Scout group no.#210 conducted the Sabbath services. Dinners and dances provided social contact. Members began planning a new, larger building. Using a plan of architect Louis Redstone, a suitable structure was built on Dexter and Glendale. In 1959, when Samuel Prero succeeded Rabbi Leo Goldman, the Young Israel continued to expand, attracting largely a "modern Orthodox" group. A summer camp, Camp Keyuma (an Indian-sounding Hebrew word that means "establishment"), was started in 1954. The Beth Abraham building on Linwood was purchased to gain additional space when that congregation moved to the Northwest in 1955.[192]

Other Orthodox congregations began to grow in Northwest Detroit. A group holding services in a room at Bagley School affiliated formally with Young Israel in 1950.[193] In 1952 they built a permanent center on Wyoming near Santa Clara. The Beth Yehudah (Poilishe Shul), under Rabbi Joshua Spero, was one block north; Beth Joseph, associated with the Rizhiner Aid Society, was on Wyoming, near Pickford; Rabbi Leizer Levin's Beth Tefilah Emanual Tikvah opened on Margareta in 1961; Rabbi Gruskin's *shtibl* (home synagogue) was on Seven Mile and Mendota, and Rabbi Chaim Deutsch's *shtibl* moved to Seven Mile near Sorrento; Rabbi Sholom Flam's Shomrey Emunah rented a room in the Labor Zionist building on Schaefer and Seven Mile in 1956 and later moved to its own sanctuary on Schaefer and Clarita.

By the early 1950s, Orthodox Jews joined the exodus to the new suburb of Oak Park. An Orthodox *minyan,* or prayer group, began in the home of Max Nussbaum in 1953 and developed into the Young Israel of Oak Woods, with a building on Coolidge and Allen. Jacob Hominick was its first rabbi in 1955. As the Jewish settlements in the Twelfth Street and Linwood-Dexter areas were abandoned in the mid-fifties for Northwest Detroit and the suburbs, Orthodox groups began contemplating wholesale moves. Jewish life in the 1950s and 1960s centered in the Northwest suburbs and synagogues and temples continued to open: the Young Israel of Greenfield (on Ten Mile, east of Greenfield), with Joshua Sperka as rabbi; the Mogen Abraham, under the direction of Rabbi A. M. Silverstein, which shared a new building with the Yeshivah Beth Yehudah on Lincoln, west of Greenfield. Rabbi Israel Flam moved the B'nai Israel to a refurbished garage on Ten Mile, east of Greenfield, and Rabbi Leo Goldman opened the Shaarey Shomayim in 1959, housing also a catering business for weddings and bar mitzvahs.[194]

Orthodoxy flourished vigorously in Detroit. Sheer numbers indicate an exhilarating and animated religious life. One observer characterized that life as "chaotic" because of the number of organized groups; another called it a replication of shtetl (village) life in Europe; still another declared the spiritual activity in Detroit second only to Vilna (the "Jerusalem of the North" in Lithuania before its destruction by the Nazis in World War II). While these may be exaggerations, they convey a sense of vitality that may be inferred not only from numbers but also from the integrity and scholarship of some of its prominent rabbis. Although Orthodoxy suffered a crisis of membership, it would prove its endurance through the turbulent 1960s and enter a religious renaissance in the following decades.

Bright young rabbis like Morris Adler, Jacob Segal, Israel Halperin, Benjamin Gorrelik, and others who had studied both in universities and in rabbinic schools brought the Conservative movement to new heights in the 1940s and 1950s. Most new synagogues began as Conservative and some old, well-established Orthodox congregations joined the Conservative movement and adopted mixed seating, Friday-night socials, and other characteristic accoutrements of the modern synagogue.

Shaarey Zedek remained the leading Conservative synagogue, and Rabbi Morris Adler became prominent both in the synagogue and beyond it, among the Jewish and the non-Jewish communities of Detroit. For example, he worked closely with Walter Reuther and the unions, was appointed a member of the UAW Ethics Board, and served on the Michigan Fair Election Practices Commission, the Governor's Board for Higher Education, and many other community organizations.[195] He formed a warm friendship with Rabbi Glazer through their mutual involvement on the Council and, along with Rabbi Isaac Stollman, led a hard battle to install a kosher kitchen at Sinai Hospital after 1947, when the construction of the Jewish hospital became imminent. Considered a charismatic speaker, he served as professor of homiletics at the Jewish Theological Seminary during a leave of absence from Shaarey Zedek. A collection of his sermons was published posthumously under the title *The Voice Still Speaks* in 1969. Among his other writings, *The World of the Talmud* achieved widespread recognition.[196] He became known as "America's most quoted rabbi."

Succeeding Rabbi Hershman in 1946 after returning from service as a chaplain in the army, Rabbi Adler helped to add the sorts of groups and functions that typified the modern synagogue of postwar America: the Beth Hayeled nursery, a retreat called the Adult Kibbutz (1948), a Kibbutz Katon for youngsters (1954), and a summer program for children (1955), first headed by Charles Milan.[197]

Mrs. Goldie Adler represented a new sort of rabbinic wife. Blessed with a sharp mind and quick wit, she became actively involved in women's organizations and gave many public talks. On one occasion, she presented a review of a novel by Meyer Levin to a synagogue audience and, with the author sitting on the dais, she openly and cleverly castigated him for using "too much lewdness" in the novel. This new, quietly "feminist" spirit extended into active participation and leadership in Detroit's growing Jewish women's organizations, including the National Council of Jewish Women, Hadassah, and the Federation Women's Division. Mrs. Adler consistently maintained a reputation as a compassionate and forceful advocate of Jewish causes related to women.

In the 1950s Rabbi Adler began to urge the building of a new and larger synagogue in the far Northwest suburbs. Louis Berry, Mandell Berman, and Hyman Safran led the building committee, but the immensity of the project troubled some congregants. Would the community not be better off, they asked, with several smaller synagogues than one so large? Rabbi Adler persuasively argued that a synagogue like Shaarey Zedek needed a viable core of four-hundred families and would thus need facilities to accommodate a larger constituency.

Architect Percival Goodman, who had already planned forty-two synagogues, joined with Albert Kahn's office and the congregational leadership to produce one of the largest and most striking synagogue buildings in the world. After years of work, there was still some hesitation about the highly original building plan. The dean of the University of Michigan School of Architecture was consulted, and he assured the committee that the building would be years ahead of its time and "a wonderful achievement." On December 15, 1961, the congregation held its last service on Chicago Boulevard; a tearful, "simple and sentimental service," recalled Harold Berry, "a kind of reminder that the strength of our people has not been just in numbers and edifices, but in hard-core devotion and simplicity . . . the love of learning . . . devotion to our communal responsibilities." On June 17, 1962, the cornerstone was laid and the new synagogue officially dedicated in Southfield.[198]

The Northwest Hebrew Congregation and Center, soon known as Congregation Adas Shalom, incorporated in 1944. Its first services had been held on Yom Kippur of 1943 in a vacant store and had continued in private homes in the area. A larger crowd during Passover of 1944 met in a skating rink on Livernois near Six Mile, and the High Holidays found them in another rented building on Livernois near Seven Mile Road. The membership increased to four-hundred families by 1946. Services were held in the Bagley School on Curtis and Greenlawn, and ground was broken for a new building on Curtis and Santa Rosa near Livernois. In 1946 Jacob Segal became the congregation's first rabbi; Pavel Slavensky was cantor in 1947 and Nicholas Fenakel in 1949.[199]

A graduate of the Jewish Theological Seminary, Rabbi Segal came from a highly observant family, as did most Conservative rabbis of that day.

Known as an excellent preacher, Rabbi Segal's weekly sermons were laced with well-turned phrases, Hasidic stories, and a lively wit. The services were "traditional modern," as Rabbi Segal said in his speech at the dedication of the new building in 1952. Many members lived in the neighborhood in the early years and walked to synagogue on Saturday mornings. Adas Shalom's services projected a sense of warmth, community, and Sabbath serenity. There were Friday-evening programs, and on Saturday afternoons congregants took turns inviting groups to their homes for an Oneg Shabbat program.

At first, there had been some hesitancy about building the synagogue right next to the Mayflower Church on Curtis. However, the two congregations made good neighbors over the years, posting holiday greetings to each other and on occasion sharing facilities and even clergymen. In February 1950, Reverend Robert Burtt spoke at Adas Shalom's Friday-night service and Rabbi Segal spoke at the Mayflower the following Sunday.

Rabbi Segal maintained a close connection with the Jewish Theological Seminary and on several occasions brought young professors to conduct the auxiliary services on the High Holidays. One was Yohanan Muffs, who later gained note as a scholar of ancient Jewish history. Another was Fritz Rothchild, who delivered some gripping sermons woven around the life and thought of the German Jewish philosopher Franz Rosenzweig and Weimar statesman Walther Rathenau. In 1956 Adas Shalom initiated the first "Caravan," in which Rabbi Segal led a group of sixty to the Jewish Theological Seminary in New York for a weekend retreat.

Adas Shalom inaugurated dynamic and engaging youth programs. A school directed by Allen Warsen began in 1945 with seventy-five students and grew to eight-hundred by 1949, when it affiliated with the United Hebrew Schools. The school was important enough that the classroom area and social hall of the new structure on Santa Rosa were completed before the sanctuary itself.[200] Rabbi Segal viewed the synagogue generally in the traditional manner, as "a kind of People's University. . . . Indeed, learning is regarded as a basic condition of piety."[201] Under Segal's direction, Jewish religious practice reaffirmed its ancient links to Jewish learning. Building upon his Orthodox traditional background, Rabbi Segal furthered what he believed to be the active purpose of the Conservative movement: the merging of religious and cultural identities.

With one of the most successful and largest youth and education programs in Detroit—which included a junior congregation, a United Synagogue Youth chapter, a Sunday morning post–bar mitzvah club, retreats at Camp Tamarack, conventions, Chug Ivri, a youth choir, sports, and more—Adas Shalom brought in Noam Shudofsky from New York in 1958 to manage it. Great attention was focused on the summer camp, Camp Ramah, which was sponsored by the Conservative movement and offered daily classes and religious practice as well as the usual camp activities.

A good example of the numerous smaller Conservative synagogues that existed from 1940 to the mid-1960s was Beth Aaron. A few residents of the Wyoming Curtis neighborhood began to meet for prayers in private homes in 1944. They were served for short periods of time by several rabbis, including Chaim Weinstein and Pinchas Katz. In 1950 the forty members brought Benjamin Gorrelik in as rabbi, and Beth Aaron formally joined the Conservative movement. A Jewish Theological Seminary classmate of Rabbi Adler, Gorrelik had managed the Shaarey Zedek school in the previous year.

As the neighborhood filled with Jews, Beth Aaron quickly grew to about eight-hundred members and burned its mortgage seven-years later.[202] Many members were young couples who were anxious to give their children some sense of Jewish belonging and identity. The evening and Sunday schools taught over six-hundred students at their peak, and girls were confirmed after the tenth grade.[203] A Young People's League sought to attract high-school graduates through social activities aimed at transmitting some Jewish consciousness and feeling.

Several Orthodox synagogues gave up separate seating and became associated with Conservatism before they moved northwest. The change from separate to mixed seating was not always smooth—indeed, in some cases, it seemed more disruptive than the change in venue. The case of the Mt. Clemens synagogue in the mid-1950s provoked an international response and the implementation of mixed seating caused a legal battle whose litigation went all the way to the Michigan Supreme Court. In Beth Tefillah's constitution, its founders had embodied their religious principles—including the insitution of separate seating. As the older members had been replaced by the younger generation, the issue of mixed seating gained impetus. Only Baruch Litvin opposed the change. Although he had little Jewish education, in his later years he had applied himself to the study of the Torah and had embraced an Orthodox life-style.

Vigorously and alone, he carried on the opposition to the mixed seating, editing a collection of scholarly essays on the issue written by Orthodox scholars—Rabbis Aaron Kottler, Moshe Feinstein, Joseph D. Soloveichik, and others. Litvin aroused international interest in the dispute, finally filing suit to stop the change. In court, Litvin argued that the new members had no power to change the synagogue's constitution, and, after a long process of appeals, the Michigan Supreme Court decided in his favor.[204] The congregation retained its separate seating until after Litvin's death. Some have argued that the case represented a landmark in the resurgence of Orthodox Judaism.[205]

Among those Orthodox synagogues to move northwest was B'nai Moshe, which moved from Dexter and Lawrence to Ten Mile and Church in Oak Park. Replacing Rabbi Moshe Fisher in 1948, Rabbi Moses Lehrman led the exodus of the Hungarian Shul, and Shalom Ralph became sexton. David

Klein was cantor from 1937 to 1958, succeeded by Louis Klein. This new trio—Lehrman, Klein, and Ralph—became legendary for their passion, compassion, and generosity. While the congregation was in transition from Dexter to Oak Park in 1958, High Holiday services were held in the Northland Playhouse. The move was completed in time for the High Holidays of 1959.[206]

Beth Abraham, another Orthodox synagogue that shifted to mixed seating, indicating a move to Conservatism, moved to Seven Mile and Greenlawn in 1955, and Ahavas Achim (successor of the old Delmar Street Synagogue) with Rabbi Jacob Chinitz moved to Schaeffer, north of Seven Mile. Congregation B'nai David moved in 1958 to Southfield with Rabbi Jacob Donin, who had succeeded Rabbi Sperka in 1953. Rabbi Donin received considerable acclaim as two of his books became popular works among Conservative Jews: *To Be a Jew* and *To Pray as a Jew*.[207]

Conservative Judaism addressed the challenge of dwindling commitment and attendance. Marshall Sklare's study of this phenomenon reveals much about the nature of Detroit. Conservatism had originated as an attempt to hold American Jews to their religion by offering it "in what was hoped would be a palatable modernized form. By the 1960's it was clear that Conservatism had gained some success socially; i.e. some Jews were being held within the synagogue. However, it was equally clear that religious observance was declining."[208] Adherents of the Conservative movement, as they had from its inception, continued to consider it an "intermediary between the Jew and his tradition," trying to bring the two closer together or at least having them maintain contact.[209]

Like Orthodoxy, Conservativism felt the tension of fading commitment to religious Jewish life and identity. Many observers, Orthodox and Conservative alike, noted critically that materialism, typified by garishly expensive bar-mitzvah parties and gifts, had superseded traditional, religious, and family-oriented practices.

For many, the younger generation's increasingly adamant support for Israel inadequately compensated for a perceived insouciant attitude toward Judaism. Others, however, found considerable comfort in a new strong source of Jewish identity. Conservative congregations in Detroit, as in other American cities, openly identified themselves with Zionism more quickly than Orthodox or Reform groups. In the eyes of still others, any middle ground held by cultural ties or value perceptions had begun to shrink, and no amount of religious or political compromise could mitigate the loss of those sociocultural values.

Temple Beth El maintained its reputation as one of America's leading Reform congregations under the stewardship of Rabbi B. Benedict Glazer. Rabbi Glazer died suddenly in April 1952 and, in January 1953, Rabbi Richard C. Hertz left his position as associate rabbi at Sinai Temple in Chicago to head Temple Beth El.[210] Steeped in the more extreme assimilationist wing of Reformism of Rabbi Franklin and Beth El, Hertz nevertheless sensed that change was in the wind, and rabbi and congregation seemed amenable to returning to a more moderate position. At the urging of new president Leonard N. Simons, Hertz and the congregation concurred in reinstituting bar mitzvahs after a half-century hiatus, and they adopted bat mitzvahs as well. Friday-night kiddush and candle-lighting had been added to the service in 1952. What had always been called the altar or pulpit would now be referred to by its Hebrew term, *bimah,* and people were using the Hebrew *shabbat* instead of Sabbath.

Liturgical music had always been provided by an organ and a loft choir. Now, John Redfield separated from the choir and began to function on the *bimah* as a cantor. Redfield was a businessman and not a professional vocalist, but he served the temple through many years of Sabbath and holiday prayers. Music held an important place in Beth El activities under Prof. Jason Tickton's leadership. A children's choir and an adult's choir performed regularly at services. Outside choirs like Wayne State University's came in, and there were frequent cantatas and oratorios, such as Handel's *Judas Maccabeus,* at a yearly music festival. Quartets or trios from the Detroit Symphony Orchestra played on holidays.[211]

In a move designed to arouse interest in the temple, Simons in the early 1950s invited members to write essays on "what my Judaism means to me," which were published one by one in the Temple bulletins, along with congregational news. Almost always centered on philanthropy, the articles provided a picture of what Reform Jews in Detroit believed and how they conceived of themselves as Jews. Among the many writers, leaders like Nate Shapero, Max Winslow, Arthur Goulson, Benjamin Wilkus, Philip Marcuse, and Henry Wineman emphasized the importance of morality and of good character, of philanthropy and faith and strength, which they said their religion had brought them.[212]

Rituals, according to one article, are intertwined with ethics, and to separate them would destroy both.[213] However, most denied the practice of ritual as a divine mandate. Some Reform Jews did keep kosher, but for private reasons, often out of respect for the memory of parents or grandparents. An article by Rabbi Solomon Freehof, a noted scholar, claims for Reform the right to abrogate existing rituals (such as kashrut) and to introduce new ones (such as confirmation and late Friday-evening services).[214]

The May 6, 1955, issue featured an article by Nelson Glueck, president of the Hebrew Union College, in which he wrote that "Reform Judaism as taught at our own College (HUC) is based on what is known as the *Wissenschaft des Judentums,* that is, the scientific study of Judaism in all its aspects." In that term itself, Reform Judaism reaffirmed its roots in German-Jewish history, and Glueck argued that liberal Judaism was "not a corruption of traditional Judaism, but a freedom for more faith."[215]

In the 1950s and 1960s, the old guard of "aristocratic" Germans, supplemented by the "aristocracy of economic class," continued to lead Beth El. Usually members of the Franklin Hills Country Club or of the Great Lakes Club, their names are the familiar ones from earlier days: Wilkus, Butzel, Welt, Wineman, and others. Their ascendancy rested at first on cultural background, but then on style and ideology as they were joined by successful newcomers who, like Simons, were of Eastern European background. German-Jewish preeminence declined, however, in part because of intermarriage with East European Jews, the drift away from Judaism, or the traditional German Jewish antipathy toward Zionism, which persisted among some even into the 1950s. Zionist feeling strengthened throughout the Jewish population, and, fostered by Rabbi Glazer and then Rabbi Hertz, it strengthened at Beth El, too.

Like his Conservative and Reform colleagues, Rabbis Adler and Fram, Rabbi Hertz became much involved in public affairs. With them, he championed better race relations, and some have suggested that his public concern partly accounts for the temple's escape from damage during the 1967 riots. In 1959 he was sent to visit the Soviet Union by White House chief of staff Robert Merriam with the purpose of studying Jewish conditions to help President Eisenhower prepare for his meeting with Nikita Khrushchev, the premier of the USSR. This mission marked a personal turning point for Hertz, strengthening and developing his growing interest in public affairs in Detroit.[216] In 1963 he met Cardinal Augustin Bea in Rome and was the first rabbi to meet with the new Pontiff, Pope Paul VI. He maintained a close personal relationship with Archbishop John Dearden of Detroit and taught courses in Judaism at the Jesuit University of Detroit.[217] Beyond his local and congregational responsibilities, Hertz wrote prolifically.

Beth El no longer claimed to be the single seat of Reform Judaism in Detroit. After its stormy founding in 1941, Temple Israel had grown with extraordinary speed. On its twenty-fifth anniversary, Rabbi Fram wrote that "we reclaimed for the Temple and the home every Jewish symbol and ceremony still possesed of the power to inspire."[218] Thus Temple Israel represented a somewhat more traditional current in Reform Judaism in comparison to that of Temple Beth El. Its new building on Manderson Road near Palmer Park opened for Rosh Hashanah, 1950 and was formally dedicated in a two-day ceremony on April 12–13, 1951.[219] Rabbis Abba Hillel Silver and Solomon Freehof were the main speakers. In 1953 M. Robert Syme became assistant rabbi, and by then, many groups had emerged, including a youth group headed by John Shepherd and a young marrieds club first led by Ellsworth Rosten. Regular retreats to Camp Tamarack began in 1954, and a young-adult camp program was instituted in 1959.[220]

Temple Israel served a somewhat different sort of membership than did Beth El. These were not the old German families, but a group largely of Eastern European background. Some had been born in Europe (like Rabbi Fram himself) and remembered something of their cheder studies; and, for some, Yiddish was still more natural than English. Zionist feeling was strong. For these and other reasons, relations between Temples Beth El and Israel had been somewhat strained after the split in 1941. Upon moving to Detroit in 1953, Rabbi Hertz quickly visited Rabbi Fram, and the two got on well together, even occasionally substituting in each other's pulpits.[221] Both shared a commitment to the new state of Israel, and by the end of the 1950s, Zionism prompted far less controversy than it had in the 1940s.

Education was always an important concern for Rabbi Fram, and the temple school grew to almost two-thousand students by 1966. Students came on Sundays and some came also on one weekday evening. Branches opened in the Hampton and Bagley Schools in Northwest Detroit. The curriculum stressed confirmation, and students were encouraged to remain through high school. In 1966, sixty-six graduated high school at about age seventeen, and 118 were confirmed at age fourteen.[222]

As in Temple Beth El, considerable attention fell to the music of the service. Temple Israel boasted a stellar collection of experienced and talented musicians, including Julius Chajes and Dan Frohman, who conducted the Temple choir, and Karl Haas, a recent immigrant from Germany, who played the organ at services. Haas later became a popular figure around Detroit with his daily radio program of classical music. At Temple Israel's twenty-fifth anniversary celebration in 1966, an original opera by Chajes, *Out of the Desert,* premiered. Music in the service was also enhanced by Cantor Robert Tulman and then Cantor Harold Orbach, who succeeded Tulman in 1962.[223]

By the mid-1960s, Temple Israel already faced the problem of the flight to suburbia. New branches of the school opened at Clinton School in Oak Park in 1963 and at Lederle in Southfield in 1964.[224] However, Rabbi Fram still argued that there was no need to consider moving from the beautiful building on Manderson, dedicated less than fifteen years before and to which two new wings had since been added. After all, Fram contended, the Manderson location was not so far from the suburbs, and people could continue to come in for services.

By 1966 Temple Israel seemed to have proven its appeal, boasting over sixteen-hundred members.[225] Like a similar movement in Conservatism and even among some secularists, Temple Israel seemed to signify a need for fulfilling a religious and cultural gap in Jewish identity increasingly felt by some Detroiters. Despite outspoken liberal political views, the temple attracted many nonpolitical or politically conservative members who appreciated a strong identification with Israel and a ritual service more traditional than Beth El's but less Orthodox than Conservative synagogues.

As each denomination struggled with the problems of shifting demographics and the decline in Jewish identification of each successive generation, yet another group emerged to grapple with some of the same predicaments in more extreme forms. In 1963, the young former assistant rabbi at Temple Beth El who had obtained a pulpit in Windsor, Sherwin Wine, met with eight families in a home in Oak Park. They confronted some startling questions that set them apart from every other Jewish organization: Was it possible, Rabbi Wine asked, "to abolish prayer and worship and still create an institution with a clear Jewish identity?" His potential congregants perceived in him a "brilliant and charismatic leader" who might serve as a radically different Moses for Detroiters who were dissatisfied with all organized Jewish religious institutions, uneasy with even the secularist attitudes that rejected any sort of temple affiliation, and uncertain about fundamental tenets, including the existence of God.

Thirty families filled the gymnasium at Eagle Elementary School the following week and listened as Rabbi Wine read from the Reform movement's accepted text, the Union Prayer Book. Judith Goren recalled that after the newly formed ritual committee voted to eliminate the Union Prayer Book, the crown on the Torah, and even the Torah itself, they proceeded, on the advice of Wine, to eliminate, too, the use of "the three letter G-d word." The word did not appear in Wine's new meditation service. Having originally planned on locating in the Birmingham suburb of Detroit, the group took what they thought would be a temporary name, the Birmingham Temple."[226]

Rabbi Wine described the ideology the new congregation embraced. "There was no need," he wrote, "for Jews to pretend to believe what indeed they did not believe," to recite prayers that had lost meaning in the modern world, and to cling to them "simply because they [the prayers] were Jewish." Nor did Jews need to subscribe to "convictions that were incredible simply because they were traditional."[227] Plunging the group directly into the middle of the Jewish identity debates that had riddled Detroit Jewry for generations, Wine declared that "our Jewish identity was not a function of any belief system. It was independent of any creeds. It arose out of family roots and family connection." The Birmingham Temple grounded its philosophy not on antiquity, continued Wine, but on reason, morality, and human dignity; he reiterated that "the test of Jewishness was not the Bible and the Talmud; it was a sense of identification with the culture and the fate of the Jewish people."[228]

Thus emerged "that atheist temple," which would soon formulate the philosophy Rabbi Wine designated as Humanistic Judaism. As one of the temple's presidents noted, from a Sunday-night meeting came a congregation, from a congregation came a movement—an international movement. With its services filled with humanist voices from Moses to Jesus, from Heinrich Heine to Moses Mendelssohn, from Lao-tzu to feminist and avant-garde philosophers, the Birmingham Temple distinguished between "nontheistic" and "nonreligious," claiming to eschew the former but embrace the latter.

Joining the ranks of the secularists in Detroit, they often encountered skepticism and suspicion even among those kindred spirits. What, asked other secularists, made Humanistic Jews Jewish? The Birmingham Temple's sophisticated ideology appealed to upper-middle-class suburban Jews. A brief comparison of this ideology with similar attempts to define Jewish secularism by Moishe Haar in his *SA News* 1962 series "The Meaning of Secularism," or articles in that newsletter by Dr. Irving Panush and Jay Rosenshine in 1958 on "Secularism and Jewish Living," reveals both similarities and deep-seated differences. The differences emerged from a new and clearly American character that remained puzzling to old-style Yiddishists. With its emphasis on "Adam" or Man, its liberal employment of non-Jewish, often archetypally Christian sources, the Birmingham Temple battled even antireligious allies.

Yet it raised questions of critical importance to some Jews—particularly those with young children: Jews who felt alienated from all existing institutions but wanted to belong to some identifiably Jewish assemblage. Surprisingly, some of those who enlisted in its ranks came from comparatively religious—even Orthodox—backgrounds; they had attended traditional cheder, been bar mitzvahed, and raised in kosher homes. The congregation included, too, those who confessed to believing in God—who did not shrink from "the three letter G-d word"—or who called themselves agnostics or were *angst*-ridden by uncertainty. All sought to define a primarily secular Jewish identity through a rational approach to Jewish history and culture, ethical values and support of Israel. Resolutely led by Wine, the temple steered a clearly liberal political and humanistic moral course, adopting public positions on every controversial issue, from the Vietnam War to Christian (and Jewish) fundamentalism. Its members joined the ranks of Jews of all denominations who sought to combat what Rabbi Adler called "the nebulousness of our youth's idea of what 'Jewish' means . . . [and] their unsureness of their Jewish identity."[229]

32

The Schools: Education as Foundation

The day schools provided a fulcrum from which traditional Jewish practice and Talmudic learning revived in Detroit and from which the synagogues were also reinvigorated. As World War II raged in Europe, annihilating the physical and spiritual body of Jews and Judaism, a small remnant of rabbinic leaders escaped and began immediately to build yeshivahs, schools of advanced Torah study, in Israel and in the United States. Such a yeshivah was begun in 1942 in Detroit by Rabbi Moshe Rothenburg and named Chachmei Lublin after the famous school of Rabbi Meyer Shapero in Lublin, Poland. At its peak, in the early years, the school had over a hundred students, many from other cities. Rabbi Rothenburg, with the strong support of Detroiter Meilach Lifschutz, adopted the Hasidic style of study, that is, they opted for breadth of knowledge over the Lithuanian tradition of depth and careful inquiry.

In the first years after the war, the school provided a sort of gathering place for a number of yeshivah-educated men who had escaped the Holocaust and were trying to rebuild their lives in America. Most moved on after a short stay; a few settled permanently in Detroit. Internal problems undermined the school, and by the early 1950s, 401 many of its teachers had left and the student population declined.

Although only an afternoon school, the Yeshivah Beth Yehudah, founded in 1916 by Rabbi Judah Levin, had enough effect on its students so that many went on to advanced studies elsewhere. After Rabbi Levin's death in 1926, the school was led by Rabbi Aaron Ashinsky until 1932, then by Rabbi Samuel M. Fine until 1938. In 1940 Rabbi Samson R. Weiss, former director of a yeshivah in Wurzburg, Germany, came to Detroit. He remained as principal, at the urging of Henry Carlebach and David Berris, until 1944.[230]

As the Orthodox yeshivah movement gained strength on the East Coast, Rabbi Shrage Feivel Mendlowitz of New York began to send one or two of his young enthusiastic disciples to help organize and lead schools in various cities. In 1944, he sent Shubert Spero and Aibush Mendelovitz to Detroit, where they received local support from Rabbi Wohlgelernter, Wolf and Isadore Cohen, David Berris, and others. Rabbi Mendlowitz also sent two other teachers to Beth Yehudah, Rabbis A. A. Freedman (1944) and Sholom Goldstein (1946).[231] From 1944 on, the school offered a full-scale Torah-study program for half the day, under the leadership of Rabbi Simcha Wasserman (the former head of a yeshivah in Strassburg), and also a half day of secular studies for which Dr. Hugo Mendlebaum, a German émigré, was hired as principal. Classes were held in a building on Dexter and Cortland, and the school shared the facilities with Congregation Mogen Abraham, as it had in 1916.[232]

Many Detroit Jews had never seen Hasidim before. One little boy, under the influence of the television series of the 1950s, asked if the men's fur hats were Davy Crockett caps. A *Jewish News* report of 1955 noted that at a Hasidic wedding

> the dying embers of eighteenth century Hasidism were rekindled for a brief moment . . . when Rabbi Yeshiah Zev Meisels, nineteen year old son of Rabbi and Mrs. Chaim Meisels of Lawrence Avenue, took for his bride lovely eighteen year old Chaya Mindel Levin of London, England at the Beth Shmuel Synagogue on Buena Vista and Dexter.[233]

It was all quite strange for many American-born Jews in Detroit. *Jewish News* editor Philip Slomovitz criticized a local rabbi who found the whole thing degrading and embarrassing for Jews, especially for women. Educated readers, wrote Slomovitz, will not think Jewish customs abhorrent or degrading.[234] By the early 1960s such weddings were no longer unusual, as increasing numbers of Jewish day-school graduates were celebrating their nuptials in a similar manner.

Two major problems faced the school: lack of interest (and consequent difficulty in attracting students) and lack of money. Detroit Jews, even those among the Orthodox, wanted their children to become "good Americans" with some Jewish background. A heavy program of Torah study was deemed unnecessary for either aim. By 1938, Federation granted minimal support to the school with $250, which was increased in 1939 to $750.[235] By 1951 Beth Yehudah, with its two-hundred students, along with the Farband Folk Shule, the Workmen's Circle schools, and several others, received more substantial funding, but only for their afternoon schools—far from enough to keep a day school afloat.[236]

Some students were drawn in through the afternoon school; some because of the influence of observant grandparents. The summer day camp, too, was a good source of recruitment. The devotion of the Hebrew teachers extended far beyond the classroom: some would take students on outings to parks and ball games and on trips to visit out-of-town *yeshivot*. Youngsters were invited to spend Sabbath with their teachers. Still, parents frequently pulled children out, fearing that they might become "too religious."

In 1949 Rabbi Leib Bakst was brought to Beth Yehudah to head a Bais Hamedrash, a department that concentrated on teaching Talmud and rabbinic literature to high-school and college-aged young men. Rabbi Bakst was one of the students of the Mir Yeshivah of Poland who had escaped the Nazis and spent the years of World War II in Shanghai, China. Respected as one of the foremost Talmud scholars, Rabbi Bakst directed about twenty to twenty-five students in the study of Talmud from 9:00 A.M. to 1:00 P.M. six days a week.

The basic aim of Beth Yehudah was to bring students closer to the Torah, to make them all deeply knowledgeable and religiously observant Jews. Many of its students attended other yeshivahs in other cities—especially Telshe Yeshivah in Cleveland and Torah Vodaas in New York. During Thanksgiving vacation, Beth Yehudah teachers led groups of boys to Telshe Yeshivah for a weekend of sight-seeing. During their 1954 visit, Rabbis Solomon Hochler and Irving Grumer were told by Rabbi E. M. Bloch, the head of Telshe Yeshivah, that despite some of the academic insufficiencies of the Detroit students, "their spirit and intensity soon make them among our best students. I would rather have one boy from Detroit than ten from New York or New Jersey."

Beth Yehudah also trained girls, centering on preparing them for lives as observant Jewish women who would marry Torah scholars and raise observant families. By the late 1950s, a girls' school, Beth Jacob, was run separately by Rabbi Goldstein. Until the 1960s, most high-school graduates went on to university. In later years, most went on to Orthodox girls' seminaries in Israel.

By 1955 about four-hundred students attended the day school and three-hundred were registered in afternoon school. The new three-story Daniel Laven Building was opened amidst controversy. One group felt that the Dexter neighborhood was declining and that any new building should be in Northwest Detroit or in the suburbs. Others argued that the Laven building might slow up the northwest movement and keep the Dexter area Jewish. In 1964, the girls' school relocated on Seven Mile and Lesure, and in 1965 the boys' school moved into a new building on Lincoln, near Greenfield, in Southfield.[237]

A crown jewel of Conservative Judaism in Detroit was Hillel Day School. Founded in 1958, largely at the impetus of a group spearheaded by Rabbi Jacob Segal, the school offered programs of religious and secular studies in a form more palatable to some for whom Beth Yehuda seemed too old-world and the afternoon schools too weak. Students were taught the Jewish laws and prayed every day, and the boys wore *kippot* (skullcaps) and ritual fringes. But the school never tried to influence students' home lives as intrusively as did the Orthodox day schools. Love of Israel and Hebrew language and literature were emphasized.[238]

Although Hillel failed to develop a high school, the United Hebrew Schools offered a special course of study for Hillel graduates. Junior high school students studied Talmud and poets like Judah HaLevi and Chaim Bialik. The first ninth-grade graduating class in 1967 wrote impressive Hebrew essays for their class yearbook. The first principals of Hillel were Abraham Zentman and Simon Murciano. Max Goldsmith played an important role and was one of Hillel's first presidents.[239]

Significant numbers in each generation of Detroit Jews lived markedly different life-styles from those of their parents and grandparents. Each generation gained more status, more education, more economic success—and grew more affluent, more assimilated, and secularly educated. As a consequence, Jewish education and identity became more problematic: beleaguered by secular concerns perhaps best symbolized by the radically altered educational curricula and by such rituals as bar mitzvahs and the introduction of attributes that startled some Detroit Jews who adhered to more traditional ceremonies and values. Hillel School embodied—in its very name—the core of Jewish identity to its founders: the Jewish life, based on religious and ethical principles, lived in American culture.

In 1948 Albert Elazar, graduate of the David Yellin Seminary in Jerusalem and of the Sorbonne in Paris, was appointed associate superintendent of the United Hebrew Schools, assuming the head position upon Bernard Isaacs's retirement in 1956.[240] Also in 1948, a Midrasha College of Jewish Studies was added, primarily to train students as Hebrew teachers and to offer advanced studies to UHS graduates.[241] Several congregational schools, beginning with Adas Shalom in 1947, joined the UHS system. The move saved the UHS the cost of putting up new buildings in the Northwest area, and synagogues benefited from Federation's advance rent payment and the presence of a weekday school program. The UHS continued to operate separate school buildings including the Esther Berman branch on Seven Mile near Schaefer.[242]

404 One unexpected effect came out of this merger. Many synagogue mem-

bers were concerned lest their children by overly burdened with Hebrew studies and, under increasing pressure, the UHS cut the number of class hours. Students had attended Hebrew school five days a week since the 1920s. Now their schooling dropped to two weekdays plus, possibly, Sunday school. More intense instruction could be obtained for those more dedicated students. Yeshivah Beth Yehudah, the Workmen's Circle, and the Sholem Aleichem Institute operated afternoon schools as "affiliated schools" in conjunction with UHS. The fledgling Reform Temple Emanuel joined UHS, although Beth El and Israel remained independent, as did Shaarey Zedek. Several Yiddish schools intermittently attempted to merge with UHS, a collaboration that regularly brought clashes of philosophy and questions about what constituted Jewish education. Federation provided subventions to the Hayim Greenberg school.

With the new availability of day schools for Jewish youngsters who, along with their parents, seemed highly committed to Jewish studies, came a corresponding weakening of interest in the afternoon schools. The two Orthodox schools opened in the early 1940s were joined by the Conservative Hillel Day School and the Religious Zionist Yeshivat Akivah in 1958 and 1964.[243]

In the late 1940s, the feeling spread, especially among certain community leaders, that the UHS would need considerable refurbishing. Spearheaded by such strong leaders as Abe Kasle and the mitigating, even-tempered nature of Louis LaMed, Federation moved to correct what one board member called the "moribund" UHS. Recognizing that the nature of the Jewish population had altered since the 1920s wave of immigration and that students had changed visibly in numerous ways, Elazar brought his experience from Anshe Emes Synagogue in Chicago to bear on the problems of Detroit.

With Elazar's steady hand at the helm, Federation redefined its policies toward Jewish education by radically altering the structure and curriculum of the UHS. After deliberations that lasted two years, in 1952 the idea of the communal schools emerged and became a model program for American-Jewish education. Federation invited congregational schools to join the communal school education system, recommending that they adopt at least part of the UHS curriculum. A school-bus network accompanied the new scheme, and the school standardized requirements for bar-mitzvah instruction. By 1959 those who had expressed consistent chagrin over the state of Jewish education in Detroit could take heart in the success of the communal school system.[244]

Graduation ceremonies for UHS had usually been small affairs held for the students of each building in their own location. Under the new system, graduations for students of all branches now combined in Ford Auditorium, in front of several thousand guests. An impressive program involved weeks of preparation for both teachers and students. During the course of study, students visited Jewish institutions like the Jewish Family Service in order to gain interest in communal affairs, and they operated junior community organizations.

In 1951 Elazar organized a Hebrew-speaking Camp Kinneret in cooperation with the Farband Shule (United Jewish Folk Schools) and the Labor Zionist Youth Committee, and in 1963 a Hebrew-speaking unit, Kfar Ivri, began at Camp Tamarack. Continuing to expand the UHS outreach, Elazar instituted the Mina and Theodore Bargman Lecture Series, which brought outstanding scholars to offer adult classes on various Jewish topics.[245]

Elazar tried to insure the position of teachers. A salary scale had existed in earlier years, but much of the business between teachers and the administration was carried out on a more or less personal level with Bernard Isaacs. Under Elazar, teachers' salaries were raised, and teachers were given more teaching hours, again raising their salaries. They also were paid for a certain amount of self-study time.[246] Supported by such champions as Abe Kasle, who involved them in Federation's insurance plan, the teachers' situation improved through the 1950s. A teachers' union formed whose relationships with the administration became highly contentious, often entailing new UHS president Zeltzer's skills as a lawyer to break deadlocks. The union eventually quashed Elazar's request that teachers report a half hour before class in order to acclimatize themselves, and it even took one of its teachers to court for helping out with the parents' organization on a volunteer basis.

Veteran teachers gradually departed although some, like Michael Michlin, remained into the 1960s. Many Israelis, with varying degrees of Jewish knowledge and of teaching ability, served on the staff, and several well-educated German émigrés, like Alex and Iylse Roberg, Abraham Zentman, Eric Greenbaum, and Hugo Apt, began teaching in the 1940s. Among the European émigrés, Israel Elpern, a Lithuanian Holocaust survivor who had taught in the displaced persons camps after the war, became principal.

Yet another memorable teacher, Morris Noble, distinguished himself as an expert in Hebrew and Yiddish literature and in Talmud as well. Noble and Bernard Isaacs were the guiding lights of the Kvutzah Ivrit (a UHS alumni organization with a strong intellectual interest) and of a Hebrew publication, *Hed Hakvutzah.*[247]

Through the 1950s and 1960s, the UHS benefited from able administrators, both on the educational and the executive sides. Yet the UHS leadership sadly observed the decrease of commitment and Jewish knowledge among families and students, a tendency detrimental to UHS goals. The Ruffman Report of 1968 gives a positive picture of UHS, comparing it favorably to afternoon Hebrew schools in New York in terms of both administration and students. By that time, 1,767 students attended regular elementary classes with 238 in girls' or special classes—a decline from 2,402 in 1957. However, 14.5 percent went as high as fifth grade, up from 8 percent. Of those, 14 percent went on to begin high school. To the credit of the administration and the faculty, 26 percent of the teachers taught full time at perhaps the best salary scale in the country. Of those, 57 percent had over ten years of experience, 26 percent had over twenty years. On the negative side, the Midrasha had not yet attained formal national recognition as a Hebrew teachers' training college.[248]

On the whole, the Jewish afternoon schools in Detroit, as elsewhere, did not and probably could not imbue most students with a thorough knowledge and appreciation of Jewish studies. The class hours were too few, the students too often not motivated in their homes and tired after a full day in public school. Even the best of teachers and administrators faced a Herculean task. Hebrew-school education, as Jewish education had historically, became embroiled in formulating or defining Jewish survival or identity. It served as a means to mediate assimilation. Debates about education, then, focused on the nature and forms of Jewish survival and identity, not on which chapter of Mishnah or which work of poetry or philosophy the class should study next. The subtleties of properly connecting these two realms frequently eluded the educational net.

In 1954 Louis LaMed wrote about the alarmingly high dropout rate, revealing that often students remained in school no more than a year or two. The shifting of Jewish neighborhoods throughout the suburbs also contributed to the stress on the school systems.[249]

Some of those who recalled their afternoon educational experience typically remembered learning more Hebrew in one semester in college than in "all those years of Hebrew school"; quitting after a few months because "about half my friends never went"; hardly being able to read Hebrew and being unable to translate; inadequate or no answers to questions; rampant misbehavior (not uncommon even in European shtetl schools); switching from UHS to synagogue school for the more active social life; and daydreaming about baseball or other activities. Rarely did the afternoon schools include the Hebrew or Yiddish poets or mystics or the mysteries of Talmudic commentaries. Emphasis long since had shifted to trying to develop a commitment to Jewish communal life and to Israel.

Many perceived and lamented a marked and catastrophic decline in Jewish learning. According to some Jewish educators in Detroit, the highest aim was too often the bar mitzvah, the consecration, or the confirmation. Transformations in Jewish education, for millennia the heart of Jewish life and identity, reflected transformations in life-styles and accommodation to American culture. Already under way in the 1920s and 1930s, the trend away from rigorous emphasis on religious ritual and scholarly studies seemed to take a quantum leap after World War II, as socioeconomic patterns in American Jewish life propelled Jews (and non-Jews) faster and further away from tradition and the past.

The sense of the abandonment of Jewish commitment alarmed Jews in every segment of the population. Secular Jewish educators mirrored the concerns of religious schools as Jewish attachment waned among the younger generation and implied a similar abatement among their parents. Movsas Goldoftas, director and principal of the Hayim Greenberg School, which was known as the United Jewish Folk Schools (Verband Folkshule)—the Labor Zionist Organization school founded in 1915—outlined the goals of his institution annually in the school's graduation book:

> 1) the child should accept his responsibility for the welfare of the Jewish community in America and throughout the world; 2) understand his relationship to Israel, and appreciate and know the Zionist Movement; 3) Play his part in the extension of democratic rights for all people in America and throughout the world; 4) To imbue the child with an understanding of our rich Jewish culture, and an awareness of its moral and ethical values.[250]

In 1950 the school adopted Hebrew as its primary language, changing its name to the Hebrew-Yiddish Shule. Its five-year curriculum included Hebrew, Yiddish, Bible, history, music, and the "customs, rituals and traditions of our religious and national holidays," along with secular bar-mitzvah preparation. Sponsored by the LZO (Poale Zion), Pioneer Women, and the Farband (the fraternal order), the school continued to graduate about ten students each year from 1941 into the 1960s.[251]

As a continuing presence, the Hayim Greenberg Shule maintained a strong Zionist, primarily secular, program in its schools. It eschewed explicit political ideologies, unlike the Hersh Leckert Shule. While the Farband schools and the Farband Camp continued to receive minimal support from Federation and from most secularists in Detroit, other schools sought to fight the impending decline of interest in Jewish culture and history. Two such organizations began to discuss the concept of a Jewish community school as early as 1949, despite differences in their public political traditions. The Workmen's Circle and the Sholem Aleichem Institute began discussions of combined Jewish schools and produced lengthy documents propounding educational, Jewish, and ethical principles. By 1961 regular meetings took place at the Kasle High School Midrasha Lounge with representatives of the two organizations, including George Zeltzer, Albert Elazar, Moishe Haar, Harry Yudkoff, Jay Rosenshine, Lawrence Crohn, Edwin Shifrin, Morris Friedman, Phyllis Robb, and Mordechai Teiler.[252]

In their preliminary document on "Principles, Philosophy, Objectives, and Curricula," the joint committee defined Jewish secularists first as people who "approach their Jewishness as something positive which can enrich their lives." They expounded those facets of Jewishness, the boundaries that defined their identity apart from formal religious affiliation: culture, nationalism, and conscious identification of those elements that composed a community of mind and history. "Humanistic values" and a "meaningful way of life" they derived from history and cultural achievements of Jews "throughout the ages," firmly avowing that "the Jewish tradition has been a deeply ethical one, with emphasis on justice and righteousness," which secularists seek to retain.[253] Here, then, emerged another secular Jewish declaration of independence, this one with specific educational aims. As they had before, the secularists confronted the issue of the basis of Jewish identity, presenting a challenge to traditional Judaism. Within the group, debates continued on the definitions of secular Judaism, the nature of the curriculum, the roles of ritual and holidays, the questions of biblical history, and related issues. From their initial meetings in late 1961, the Inter-School Committee produced a plan for implementation by 1963 and another in 1965.[254]

These coalitions struggled to enunciate clear definitions of Jewishness couched in ethical or cultural taxonomies. Another, similar band emerged in 1947, when a handful of parents searching for "a new approach to Jewish education" turned to the advice and counsel of Harry Katz, the adult program director of the Jewish Community Center. Katz, an openly avowed *linke*, or leftist, and his wife Jeanette expressed deep commitment to Jewish secularism. They became the first supervisor and club leader of the Jewish Parent's Institute (JPI) in October 1947. Its purpose, the JPI declared, was "to develop a wholesome identification with the Jewish-American environment of today."[255] The institute's first school year lasted for thirty-five weeks and met every Sunday at the JCC. Each Sunday included two sessions: one from 9:30 to 11:00 A.M. and the second from 11:00 to 12:30 P.M.[256]

JPI's principal objectives included establishing a "strong and comfortable feeling in the children as Jews within the [American] community as well as with Jews in America and Israel." Their approach differed from the other secularists, as they saw it, because they sought to "provide a channel through which parents could learn to adjust to problems as American Jews"; in short, that meant involving parents intimately in the preparation of materials and in the teaching of their children.[257] Their concluding point in their statement of founding principles suggested this: "Because of the great diversity of religious experiences and philosophies, and because other instrumentalities and institutions can be utilized by the parents for this purpose, no religious indoctrination shall be attempted."[258]

This new coterie grew quickly and by 1951 had a waiting list of twenty-seven families. Petitioning the JCC for more assistance and space, they argued that mutual benefits would ensue from economic assistance. With the assistance of Herman Jacobs and Irwin Shaw, successive directors of the JCC, they won their point.[259] Not surprisingly, the JPI drew strong resistance from various elements of the religious communities as well as initially from the JCC board. But by 1952 it had gained concessions on space and a minimum subsidy for its supervisor. Several members of the JCC Board perceived the JPI as potentially bridging a gap between secular

Jews and the rest of the Jewish population since the JPI did include parents who belonged to synagogues and remained religiously observant Jews.

In 1951, some of the JPI's families, several of whom had left Sholem Aleichem, argued for a merger with that school. The point of contention, however, focused on what seemed to set the JPI apart: the role of parents in the education of the children. The Sholem Aleichem Institute insisted that the curricular and educational decisions reside with the principal and the professional staff. JPI, on the other hand, upheld the principle of "family learning," of participation and planning as a group. This may have guaranteed constant debate and revision of the program, yet it remained the bedrock of JPI. Some twenty-five families, however, most of whom had come from the Sholem Aleichem Institute, left JPI, dealing a crushing blow to the young organization.[260]

In 1954, a group within JPI began to press for a more formal curriculum. Cosupervisors, Sol Drachler and Dr. Sidney Radlow collaborated with parents to produce a set of units of eight clubs that included understanding Jewish holidays, Jewish and biblical history, Israel, varying patterns of Judaism, Jews in America, and secularism. That prefigured a deep source of altercation that erupted in 1961—known as "the black year" in the JPI. As one supervisor left and before another could be found to replace him, the JCC began to evaluate the viability of continuing its support for the secular organization. Eventually concluding that the JPI did indeed belong as an affiliated group, the evaluation process nevertheless created stress. In the interim, between supervisors, parents took up the slack, led by such committed educators as Robert Luby and by parents like Saul Shiefman and teachers like Mary Koretz. This time of crisis resulted in the establishment of an Institute Committee of seven people who organized a series of discussions with titles like, "What Do We Mean By Jewish Identification?," "What Do We Mean By Secularism?," and "What Are Our Jewish Values?"[261]

These discussions produced a set of written criteria for a curriculum. Among them appeared familiar secularist principles of cultural and historical identity. But the JPI also included the concept whereby Jewish children accepted their responsibilities for membership "in the total Jewish community"; providing "grounds for pride in their [children's] being secular"; recognition that religion "is a private matter to be handled by the parents at home"; and that "the sphere of competency and interest of JPI is limited to Jewishness." Saul Shiefman, one of the JPI's early presidents, voiced the group's deepest concern: "How do we handle the teaching and transmittal of ethical values to our children. . . . How do we express our Jewish identification. . . . What do we do with our Jewishness?"[262] Irving Sigel, another of JPI's early leaders, summed up the controversy by addressing the questions in a different way. In his words, the central task of

Jewish education remained promoting the Jewish experience and identity, "survival" of "ourselves and our children. Secular is merely the means we choose to do this."[263]

As it had before, debates over the content of Jewish education elicited varieties of definitions of Jewishness. Detroit's Jewish schools, from Orthodox to secularist, ran the gamut of those definitions. If members of the JPI tried to stress the similarities shared by all Jews, they and their counterparts seemed forced to dwell at length on the differences. The intensely emotional tenor of the debate indicated that questions of identity had become increasingly urgent.

33

Sinai Hospital: Conflict and Resolution

In many respects, the history of Sinai Hospital conveys significant elements of the history of Detroit Jews. In the *Survey of the Jewish Community of Detroit* undertaken by the National Bureau of Jewish Social research in 1923, Dr. Sigmund S. Goldwater, of Mt. Sinai Hospital in New York City, emphatically declared: "There is no doubt in my mind that the Jewish community of Detroit will suffer more and more . . . if Detroit does not give up the distinction of being the only first class city in the United States today without a Jewish hospital."[264] Dr. Goldwater confronted a matter that had been a factious source of debate at least since 1901. In that year Rabbi Franklin, arguably one of the most influential figures among the Jews of Detroit in 1901, declared himself "unqualifiedly averse to the encouragement of the undertaking" of a Jewish hospital, a project urged by a group of Orthodox Jews. Although a kosher kitchen appeared to be at the center of the debate,[265] the subject of a Jewish hospital would come to embody major conflicts within the Jewish population of Detroit and would not be resolved for fifty years. A hospital under Jewish auspices and all that it encompassed thus became the longest-lived, continuously palpable point of contention in Detroit Jewry's history. As such,

412

it flows throughout the years between 1914 and 1967, achieving resolution in the 1950s.

Like the history of Detroit Jewry, the hospital's began on Hastings Street. In March 1912, a group of Orthodox Jews, among them Rabbi Judah Levin, led a march down Hastings Street. They carried placards reading, "Buy a brick to save the sick." They campaigned for contributions for a Jewish hospital in the face of opposition from Rabbi Franklin and the overwhelming majority of German Jews—that is, those who might conceivably have been able to offer financial support for a hospital. The march ended with a mass rally and the formation of the Hebrew Hospital Association. A kosher kitchen remained the focus of the movement although, beyond religious considerations, that implied a particular "environment, sociability, religious atmosphere." All subsequent discussions of a hospital—conducted with the United Jewish Charities, Federation, and other groups or individuals—emphasized this apsect of the Orthodox-Jewish position. The march netted seven-thousand dollars in nickels and dimes and the association purchased a lot at St. Antoine and Hendrie Avenues, which it sold for forty-thousand dollars in 1918. Persuaded by members of the United Jewish Charities, the Hospital Association invested in government bonds—a move that rescued their money during the Depression.[266]

Here, then, came the opening salvos of what developed into a prolonged, often bitterly fought, campaign. At issue: kashrut and Jewish ambience. These would not remain the only issues around which debate would center. The 1923 *Survey* suggested that the need for a Jewish hospital not only grew from some necessity for kosher food, but, perhaps more important from the surveyors' perspective, from the need for Jewish physicians to obtain staff positions "to obviate the discriminations against Jewish physicians in non-Jewish hospitals."[267] These two considerations—the need for a kosher hospital that would provide a Jewish environment for observant and nonobservant Jews alike and the procurement of hospital staff positions for Jewish physicians—became the dual purposes advocated by pro-hospital forces. As one physician noted, a kosher kitchen may have been the "issue for Jews in the community, but now was added the issue of Jewish doctors." While each rationale carried concealed nuances, a kosher kitchen meant "poor, East European Jews" and, to non-Orthodox Jews, the mysterious minions of Orthodoxy.

Several doctors recalled the significant levels of discrimination against Jews. Quota systems existed at the University of Michigan School of Medicine in Ann Arbor in the 1920s and, more consequential still, according to Dr. Harry August, was the difficulty of obtaining internships and residencies at hospitals. At the home of Henry Wineman in 1923, August, one of the first Jewish psychiatrists in Detroit, met a doctor from Ann Arbor who invited him to work at a clinic in the Hannah Schloss Building. The clinic, he said, served "immigrants who were having trouble adjusting." 413

The Fred M. Butzel Memorial Building, 163 Madison, Detroit, headquarters of the Jewish Welfare Federation, 1952. (Courtesy of the Archives of the Jewish Welfare Federation.)

Allied Jewish Campaign meeting, ca. 1947–1948. *From left:* Abe Srere, Gertrude Wineman, Fred M. Butzel, Celia Broder, Henry Wineman, Irving Blumberg, Esther R. Prussian, Rose Cooper. (Courtesy of the Archives of the Jewish Welfare Federation.)

Allied Jewish Campaign Meeting, ca. 1948–1949. *From left:* Irving Schlussel; ———, Rabbi Isaac Halevy Herzog, chief rabbi of Israel; Rabbi Joshua Sperka; David J. Cohen. (Courtesy of the Archives of the Jewish Welfare Federation.)

Allied Jewish Campaign leaders, 1949. *From left:* Gertrude Simons, Rose Cooper, Gertrude Wineman, Henry Wineman. (Courtesy of the Archives of the Jewish Welfare Federation.)

Allied Jewish Campaign meeting, 1950. *From lower left:* Ida Cantor, Eddie Cantor, Vivian Berry, Louis Berry, Edith Sobeloff, Isidore Sobeloff, Anna Srere, Julian H. Krolik, Golda Krolik, Rabbi Leon Fram. (Courtesy of the Archives of the Jewish Welfare Federation.)

Allied Jewish Campaign meeting, 1951. *From left:* Celia Broder, Bernice Hopp, Golda Meir, Dorothy Karbel, Abe Kasle. (Courtesy of the Archives of the Jewish Welfare Federation.)

Historic mission to Israel sponsored by the United Jewish Appeal, 1954. *From left:* Max Zivian, Max M. Fisher, William Avrunin, with prime minister of Israel Moshe Sharett. (Courtesy of William Avrunin.)

Annual meeting of the Jewish Welfare Federation, 1956. *From left:* Judge Theodore Levin, Justice Henry Butzel, Max M. Fisher, Isidore Sobeloff. (Courtesy of the Archives of the Jewish Welfare Federation.)

Jewish Welfare Federation's Stag Day, 1958. *From left:* Isidore Sobeloff, Irwin I. Cohn, Judge Theodore Levin. (Courtesy of the Archives of the Jewish Welfare Federation.)

Leonard N. Simons (*far right*), on behalf of the Allied Jewish Campaign, accepts a check from Karen Ami Student Council, 1959. Albert Elazar, superintendent of the United Hebrew Schools, stands to the left of Leonard N. Simons. (Courtesy of the Archives of the Jewish Welfare Federation.)

Jewish Welfare Federation's Stag Day, 1960. *Standing, from left,* the chairmen of the Trade and Professional Division of the Allied Jewish Campaign: Alan Luckoff, David Mondry, Arthur Howard, Max Shaye, Arnold E. Frank, Arthur Schlesinger, Paul Broder, Irwin Green, George M. Zeltzer. (Courtesy of the Archives of the Jewish Welfare Federation.)

Allied Jewish Campaign Meeting, 1959. *From left:* Hyman Safran, Paul Zuckerman, Rabbi Abba Hillel Silver, Leonard N. Simons, Irwin I. Cohn. (Courtesy of the Archives of the Jewish Welfare Federation.)

Leaders of the Women's Division of the Allied Jewish Campaign, 1961. *Standing, from left:* Barbara Marcuse, Tillie Brandwine, Buena Lichter, Marion Robinson. *Seated:* Mina Bargman, Esther Jones, Helen August. (Courtesy of the Archives of the Jewish Welfare Federation.)

Officers of the Women's Division of the Allied Jewish Campaign, 1963. *Standing, from left:* Ethel Frank, Tillie Brandwine, Arlene Rhodes, Doris Priver, Sybil Jones, Ruth Broder. *Seated:* Marjorie Fisher, Marion Robinson, Shirley Harris. (Courtesy of the Archives of the Jewish Welfare Federation.)

Isidore Sobeloff (*left*), executive vice-president of the Jewish Welfare Federation, 1937–1964, with William Avrunin, executive vice-president of the Jewish Welfare Federation since 1964. (Courtesy of the Archives of the Jewish Welfare Federation.)

United Jewish Appeal National Conference, 1965. *From left:* Mr. and Mrs. Hyman Safran, Governor and Mrs. George Romney, Mr. and Mrs. Max M. Fisher, Louis Berry, Abraham Harman, Mr. and Mrs. William Avrunin. (Courtesy of the Archives of the Jewish Welfare Federation.)

Members of Detroit Israel Mission visit Detroit Friends Student Hostel, Givat Ram, Israel, 1964. *Left:* Esther Shifrin, Toby Satovsky, Esther Prussian, Esther Mellen. *Right:* Frank Bernstein, Ben Gould, Dr. Peter Shifrin, Abraham Satovsky, Dr. Hyman Mellen, Fred Ginsberg. (Courtesy of the Archives of the Jewish Welfare Federation.)

Paul Zuckerman with General Moshe Dayan, 1960s. (Courtesy of the Archives of the Jewish Welfare Federation.)

Jewish National Fund Conference to plan Michigan's Freedom Forest Campaign, 1959. *Standing:* Avern Cohn, chairman. Professor Samuel Levin is seated. (Courtesy of the University Archives, Wayne State University.)

Board of the Detroit chapter, American Society of Technion, Israel Institute of Technology, in the 1960s. *Standing, from left:* Charles Stone; D. Dan Kahn; Joseph Ami, vice-president for finance of Technion; Ben Wilk; Sam Rich, president of the Detroit chapter; Bernard J. Cantor; Charles Milan; Jerome Singer; Hymie Cutler; Jack Stone; Louis Milgrom; Louis Redstone; Albert Colman. *Seated, from left:* Peter Altman, Julius Harwood, Dr. Adrian Kantrowitz, Sam Grand, Dr. Joseph Epel, Murray Altman, Sol Lifsitz, Alex Etkin. (Courtesy of the Technion, Detroit chapter).

At the campus of the Technion, Israel Institute of Technology, Haifa, Israel, in the 1960s. *From left:* Henry Ford II, Technion president Alexander Goldberg, Max M. Fisher. (Courtesy of the Technion, Detroit chapter.)

Jewish Home for Aged, first building committee for Borman Hall, 1963. *Standing, from left:* Ira Sonnenblick, executive director; Gus D. Newman; Ben Kramer; Sylvan Rappoport; Herman Mathias; Alan E. Schwartz; Leonard N. Simons. *Bottom row, from left:* Samuel J. Greenberg; Arthur Fleischman; Jack O. Lefton; Edward Fleischman; Dr. Ben Welling. (Courtesy of the collection of the Jewish Home for Aged.)

Viewing building plans for Borman Hall of the Jewish Home for the Aged, 1962. *Left:* Tom Borman, Abraham Borman, Gus D. Newman. (Courtesy of the collection of the Jewish Home for Aged.)

Full building committee for Borman Hall of the Jewish Home for Aged, 1962.
Top row, from left: Ben Kramer, Hyman Margolis. *Second row:* Dr. David Kliger, Gus D. Newman, Harry Bielfield, David Zack. *Third row:* Saul LeVine, Herman Mathias, Jacob Schreier, Herman Cohen. *Fourth row:* Samuel J. Greenberg, Joseph Bermstein, William Avrunin, Ira Sonnenblick, ———, Jack O. Lefton, Jean Arkin, Dan LeVine. *Fifth row, bottom:* ———, ———, Tom Borman, Edward Fleischman, Abraham Borman, Arthur Fleischman, Jack Gordon. (Courtesy of the collection of the Jewish Home for Aged.)

Choral group at the Jewish Home for Aged, Petoskey Avenue, Detroit, ca. 1940s. (Courtesy of the collection of the Jewish Home for Aged.)

The Jewish community rallies at the Jewish Community Center, Curtis and Meyers, Detroit, in support of the state of Israel two days before the outbreak of the Six Day War, 1967. (Courtesy of the collection of the Jewish Community Council.)

After the riot, Twelfth Street near Clairmont, Detroit, 1967. (Courtesy of the Burton Historical Collection of the Detroit Public Library.)

Recipients (1951–1967) of the Fred M. Butzel Memorial Award, highest award annually bestowed by the Jewish Welfare Federation for distinguished communal service. (All photos courtesy of the Archives of the Jewish Welfare Federation.)

Fred M. Butzel
1877–1948

Julian H. Krolik
1951

Henry Wineman
1952

Judge William Friedmar
1953

Abraham Srere
1954

Mrs. Joseph Ehrlich
1955

Samuel H. Rubiner
1956

Hon. Henry M. Butzel
1957

Abe Kasle
1958

Sidney J. Allen
1959

Hon. Theodore Levin
1960

Irwin I. Cohn
1961

Mrs. Henry Wineman
1962

Leonard N. Simons
1963

Max M. Fisher
1964

Nate S. Shapero
1965

Morris Garvett
1966

Abraham Borman and Tom Borman
1967

Abandoned in 1924, the clinic reemerged in 1926 under the strong and forceful guidance of a young doctor, Harry C. Saltzstein, who had come from Mt. Sinai Hospital in New York; it occupied two storefronts on Westminster.[268] August became the first and only staff psychiatrist. For almost thirty years, the North End Clinic served poor Jews in Detroit, using volunteer physicians assisted by dedicated women, most of whom came from Temple Beth El.

Saltzstein had convinced Henry Wineman in 1925 to donate seventy-five-thousand dollars for an outpatient clinic in memory of Leopold Wineman. When the United Jewish Charities added thirty-thousand dollars more, a committee headed by Jesse F. Hirschman was formed, with mrs. Samuel Mendelsohn, Edith Heavenrich, Mr. and Mrs. Andrew Wineman, Jacob Neiman, and Harry Helfman as members. They hired Eleanor Ford as director of the newly opened Leopold Wineman Memorial Building at 936 Holbrook Avenue—the North End Clinic. Julian Krolik ("Mr. North End Clinic") and Edith Heavenrich headed the board. By January 1927, it boasted an outstanding professional staff that included Drs. Theodore Raphael, Harry E. August, Leon B. Cowan, Emil Amberg, Solomon G. Meyers, Louis D. Stern, and David D. Sandweiss. Immediately following that momentous opening, Saltzstein spearheaded a drive for an adjacent hospital. Federation refused to become involved.[269]

Dr. Goldwater's comments in the 1923 *Survey* included a critical evaluation of clinics similar to the North End. He believed such "isolated clinics" showed "discontinuous medical services" because they were unable to follow up treatment with hospital care and did not benefit from hospital research and teaching. Such a clinic, without a hospital affiliation, remained charity-oriented and was perceived as ministering to indigents, the poor, and to helpless immigrants. It offered no avenue of professional development for its doctors, no research capabilities, and received no serious professional consideration from other medical institutions.[270]

An energetic and dedicated staff of volunteers provided services to the clinic. Yet some significant names did not appear on the staff lists. Detroit's leading Jewish physicians, Drs. Hugo Freund, David Levy, and Norman Allen, refused to support the project of a hospital. They were joined in their reticence by Dr. Max Ballin, who worked in the clinics but opposed a hospital. From 1928 to 1945 Freund served as chief of medicine at Harper Hospital, sat on the Board of Health and on the Board of Public Welfare, and became the president of the Children's Fund of Michigan. Ballin's indefatigable service at both the Hannah Schloss and North End Clinics became legendary. As chief of surgery at Harper Hospital, he carried much prestige, and Detroit Jews turned to him (with Freund) for advice on medical matters. Like Freund and Ballin, two more of Detroit's leading Jewish doctors, Emil Amberg and David Levy opposed the idea of a Jewish hospital. Among the few Jewish physicians on hospital staffs, they argued insistently that too few Jewish doctors were qualified to staff a hospital.

Indeed, a survey commissioned by the North End medical staff in 1929 not surprisingly produced evidence that Jewish doctors seemed underrepresented on hospital staffs, especially in the private hospitals where most Jews went for treatment. That statistic might suggest that other medical personnel in Detroit agreed with the detractors. More likely, as most observers suspected, the medical profession in Detroit, as in other American urban centers, discriminated against Jewish doctors.[271]

If Jewish physicians had patients who needed hospital care, they had to refer them to a physician affiliated with one of the hospitals. Most often, then, Jewish doctors sent referrals to Freund and to the others who continued to reject the possibility of discrimination. Numerous doctors resented this opposition, believing that the leading four derived benefits from the situation and that their opposition therefore involved more than medical standards. This issue of who would allow a Jewish doctor to accompany them into an operating room or into a hospital to minister to a patient would precipitate the final drive for a hospital.

Whatever their motives, Freund, Ballin, Levy, Amberg, and a few others held more than professional sway. They held, too, the loyalty of Detroit's wealthiest Jewish families, mostly German Jews, particularly the Winemans and the Butzels.[272]

Perhaps no other issue of the twenties so clearly bears the mark of the differences between German-Jewish, or assimilationist, views and the views of those who championed some sort of separate identity. A hospital kosher kitchen symbolized how Jews were to be perceived, who they were, how they identified themselves to American society. Reform Jews, or those with assimilationist or Americanizing tendencies (German or East European) appeared to perceive religious Jews as embarrassing anachronisms in the 1920s and beyond, as this debate continued to demonstrate. They argued that "segregation" defeated the purpose of American pluralism and defeated the gains made by Jews in modern America. Orthodox Jews remained adamant about kashrut, asserting their separatism as self-evident. Ironically, some secularist Jews joined them, upholding a principle of pluralism that they believed should guarantee such separatism. Yiddishists, observant or not, tended to adhere to similar identity forms and, uncharacteristically, supported Orthodox demands.

When Dr. David Sandweiss produced his 1929 report for the North End Clinic with the intention of examining "the problem of a Jewish hospital," the "discussion was lively" and included Drs. Sandweiss, Saul Rosenzweig, Michael Davis, Freund, August, and Saltzstein. Representatives of Federation—Fred Butzel, Julian Krolik, Isadore Levin, Jacob B. Neiman, and Milford Stern—also participated.[273] Sandweiss's report concluded that "the fundamental reason for the need of a Jewish hospital is the protection of the health and welfare of the Jewish community."[274] For the first time in nearly thirty years, some agreement emerged: a fifty-bed experiment seemed feasible. But the Depression interfered, and those who might have produced results once again postponed action.

Throughout the Depression, Saltzstein and Selma Sempliner, the director of the clinic, made "continuous presentations to the Federation concerning integration with a hospital under Jewish auspices." Saltzstein referred to the "refrain about the lack of hospital facilities" that rang through the clinic.[275] But Federation leaders remained opposed. Behind the scenes as well as at public meetings, powerful voices like Judge Henry Butzel's, Fred Butzel's, and Henry Wineman's seemed adamantly opposed to a Jewish hospital. More quietly, members of other Jewish patrician families— the Welts and the Engasses, for example—apparently also resisted the idea. As successfully integrated American Jews with high public personae in greater Detroit society, they were appalled at the thought of catering to religious orthodoxy. A Jewish hospital served as a symbolic concession to what some considered empty ritual superstition. Behind their opposition, presumably, lay the advice and judgment of the aristocratic doctors (although Ballin had died in 1934).

A turning point of sorts came in 1936. On July 6, 1936, the executive committee of the clinic publicly denounced the Federation leadership for its failure to support a hospital and for its persistent refusal to allocate funds over the course of eleven years. They accused "older, established doctors" of remaining aloof. No major donors had come to their defense and the statement alleged that most Jewish doctors were resentful.[276]

That same month, the Maimonides Medical Society, founded by Jewish doctors in 1912 as a reaction to discrimination against Jews in medical societies, began to enlist support for a Jewish hospital. The president of the organization, Dr. Morris E. Bachman, appointed Dr. S. Emanuel Gould chairman of the Medical Society Hospital Committee. Gould undertook a research report, investigating the medical situations in Cleveland, Kansas City, Milwaukee, Pittsburgh, and other cities, and published his results in the *Detroit Jewish Chronicle* in January and February 1937. He concluded that every community surveyed took great pride in their hospitals and that "the needs for such a hospital must be understood by the community; other communal needs must be respected; all interested individuals and organizations should submerge their differences; and the proper auspices [meaning Federation] should initiate the movement."[277] With Gould as president, Saltzstein, Bachman, and Dr. William H. Gordon were the signatories incorporating the Detroit Jewish Hospital Association in March 1937.[278]

On May 23, 1937, a women's organization, the Mt. Sinai Hospital Association, emerged "under the indomitable force and energy of Mrs. Charles [Esther] Gitlin" (aided by Dr. Charles Gitlin) "to reawaken the enthusiasm of Jewish women." Almost immediately, Mrs. Gitlin enlisted some five-hundred members at one dollar each for dues. By November, there were one-thousand members, and by March 1938, a meeting convened at the Statler Hotel Ballroom for 2,300 members who paid three dollars each in annual dues.[279]

The Maimonides Medical Society, the Mt. Sinai Hospital Association, and the Detroit Jewish Hospital Association gained momentum. They were joined by the still-existing Hebrew Hospital Association, the North End Clinic medical staff, the two Jewish medical fraternities at the University of Michigan (Phi Delta Epsilon and Phi Lamda Chi) to form the United Jewish Hospital Committee. In spite of this rising tide, the *Chronicle* still cautioned against rash action that would ignore the enormous financial burdens that must accompany establishment of a hospital.[280]

Opposition began to dwindle, although the individuals without whose support the building of a hospital would weigh onerously remained actively or passively antagonistic. After almost unrelieved pressure from Saltzstein, the Federation Executive Committee on September 23, 1937, passed a resolution in which Federation "pledge[d] its cooperation to the end" and called for research to review the necessary financial support.[281] The result materialized in July 1938 in the form of a report supervised and written by Dr. Jacob J. Golub, director of the Hospital for Joint Diseases in New York City.[282]

The Golub report began by comparing the Jews of Detroit to Jews in other cities: Detroit Jews numbered 71,000 in 1936, sixth in Jewish population in the country. Each of the other ten largest Jewish urban centers had a Jewish hospital. Of the 344 Jewish doctors in Detroit, half had been in practice for less than ten years and desperately needed opportunities; such opportunities "are limited" outside the Jewish population.[283] Public opinion in response to the questionnaire he sent to those who might contribute modest amounts of money seemed mixed and controversial. Many respondents expressed fear over segregation and separation from the general population; others worried about costs and other needs of the community—especially the needs of the aged. Still others feared the sectarian nature of a Jewish hospital. They worried about strictly kosher food and Jewish environments; finally, many simply rejected the idea that the medical profession discriminated against Jews.[284]

In conjunction with the Golub study, Harry Lurie had conducted a feasibility investigation regarding the financial aspects of a Jewish hospital. He concluded that Detroit could and should have a Jewish hospital, but it would need the financial and moral support ofa few wealthy leaders. Lurie did not mince words: Detroit's Jewish elite—German Jews and wealthy East European Jews alike—would be needed for major contributions and for publicity.[285] By February 1939, Sobeloff reported that Federation would give strong support to advance the cause, and Abraham Srere, president of Federation, stated he was "eager to marshall our forces to see what can be done."[286] According to Sobeloff, the primary opposition of members of the Butzel family—including Fred—and of Henry Wineman had been eroded by spiraling popular enthusiasm for a hospital.

On a stormy night in February 1939, Fred Butzel, Sobeloff, Celia (Mrs. Hyman C.) Broder, Julian Krolik, Abe Srere, Dora Ehrlich, and others represented Federation at a meeting to discuss a hospital. Drs. Saltzstein, Gordon, Gould (now president of the Jewish Physicians Hospital Committee), A. Max Kohn, Rosenzweig, Sandweiss, Myers, and others attended. Over the course of three hours, the group discussed the history of the hospital movement, finances, details, and logistics. Its time had come. Srere noted the enormous and rising needs of overseas aid, and Krolik asked the doctors to concede at that time the primacy of refugee assistance; but the committee that emerged had the blessing and the financial backing of all present.[287]

The Federation joined the United Jewish Hospital Committee in inviting Dr. Morris Fishbein, editor of the *Journal of the American Medical Association,* to speak in Detroit. Addressing Detroit Jews for the third time, Fishbein argued strongly and frankly for a hospital program "which must obtain the cooperation of the wealthy element able to give in large amounts." Most of the funding, Fishbein said, would have to come from "a relatively small number of givers." His visit touched off an emotional storm once again, renewing debates over the place of Jews in America, the status of Jewish life and culture, the rejection of "clannishness and segregation," and the hopes from the other side that "Jewish institutions would distingegrate and disappear." Arguments about kashrut, Orthodox versus Reform Judaism, and the whole question of identity in America surfaced. Groups and even families divided on the issue. "The Jew must diffuse himself," argued one side; "Jews must maintain total separation of cultures and institutions," contended another.[288]

On July 30, 1941, Maurice Aronsson convened a meeting at his home on Boston Boulevard to discuss fund-raising for a hospital. Some of the twenty-five to thirty participants rehashed all the old arguments. Among those attending were Saltzstein, Leonard Simons, Max Osnos, Nathan Borin, Irving Blumberg, Harold and Sidney Allen, Charles Agree, Abraham Cooper, Irwin Cohn, Alfred Epstein, William Fisher, Nate Fishman, Harry Grant, Larry Michelson, Jacob Neiman, Leo Siegal, Barney Smith, and Abe Srere.[289] After much discussion, the group pledged to raise $125,000 by August of that year.

Those whose opposition had lingered suddenly seemed convinced that a Jewish hospital ought to receive high priority. Indeed, Fred Butzel became instrumental at the Aronsson and subsequent meetings in effecting a compromise over the kosher kitchen disagreement. Once again, fate seemed to take a hand and World War II interfered—although not before the committee had raised $125,000 by August 1941. Newly invigorated, the activities of the advocates of the hospital were forced to lay dormant during the war; not so, however, the women's organization: the Mt. Sinai Hospital Association. They went to work for the war effort, still under the spirited direction of Esther Gitlin and others like Dora Ehrlich and Mrs. Hyman Broder. They raised some $360,000 in a bond drive and purchased a B-29 named "The Spirit of Mt. Sinai, Detroit." Mrs. Gitlin pursued members to aid in the blood bank and in war hospital-supply campaigns.[290] During the war, however, because of stringent prohibitions on construction, the federal War Production Board denied the North End Clinic and Federation the priorities needed to convert the abandoned Jewish Children's Home on Petoskey and Burlingame into a hospital.[291]

It seemed only a matter of time, however, before the drive for a Jewish hospital would sweep the different elements of the Jewish population of Detroit. The final straw came on a Sunday in March 1944. Dr. Herbert Bloom received an emergency call from one of his oral surgery patients in Detroit. Dr. Bloom drove from Ann Arbor to find that he could not admit his patient to a hospital. Discrimination—in the form of barring Jewish doctors from hospital staff membership—struck home again. Enraged, Bloom went to the home of his father-in-law, Israel Davidson, where he had planned to have dinner. He complained bitterly of the situation, vowing to withdraw even from his part-time Detroit practice since he was on staff at the University of Michigan School of Medicine. Davidson took action, made several telephone calls, and arranged a luncheon for the following day.

Davidson and Bloom met with Dr. Saltzstein, Max Osnos, Nate Shapero, and Abe Srere at Sammy Sofferin's Wonder Bar on Washington Boulevard. There, Max Osnos offered $100,000 left by his father, Sam Osnos, for the purpose of a hospital, and Davidson agreed to match the sum. There were no debates. By May, the Federation had formed the Jewish Hospital Association, led by Max Osnos, to conduct another campaign. On the committee were Irving Blumberg, Abe Srere, Irwin Cohn, Maurice Aronsson, and Israel D. Davidson. They were incorporated in June 1944, with Max Osnos as president, and the hospital project seemed officially launched under Federation auspices.[292] By the end of 1945, a thirty-six acre site on West Outer Drive had been purchased. Two driving dynamos, Nate Shapero of Cunningham Drug Co. and Max Osnos of Sam's Cut Rate Stores, engaged in incessant activities, campaigning for funds, organizing, and attending meetings, as they seemed to rival each other in their zeal.

Max Osnos recalled that good hospital care at Harper Hospital had saved the lives of his brother in 1925 and his son in 1934. Dr. Willard Mayer, whom Osnos believed was the only Jewish doctor on the staff, had been their physician. His mother had been involved in the "buy a brick" campaign, and in 1937 he had convinced his father to leave a large sum for a Jewish hospital in his will. Osnos seemed to perceive the hospital as a personal crusade, and he pursued it with fervor. Shapero appeared simi- 439 larly motivated, and together they formed an irresistible team, along with men like Sidney J. Allen, Israel Davidson, and Dr. Harry Saltzstein.

Shapero became vice-president of the Greater Detroit Hospital Fund, a drive begun in 1945 to raise money for hospitals in Detroit. The project aimed at building four new hospitals, one of which would be a 222-bed Jewish hospital on the site bounded by Outer Drive, Whitcomb Avenue, McNichols Road, and Lauder Avenue. By 1945 the Jewish Hospital Association had raised over $2.5 million, but because of rising costs, its needs had doubled.[293] Federation agreed to merge their efforts with those of the city, and Shapero leaped into a leadership role. The Jews of Detroit thus agreed not to campaign separately for five years.[294] By 1950, calls for separate funding began again, and Leonard Simons assumed the associate chairmanship of the Greater Detroit Hospital Fund memorial gifts committee. Few could match Simons's and Shapero's eagerness and intensity; both seemed perfectly suited to carry out a successful campaign. As a result of this citywide drive, Sinai Hospital received $2.5 million.

None of these men advocated a kosher kitchen. Some, in fact, like Max Osnos, opposed an exclusively kosher hospital. Orthodox and Conservative rabbis like Rabbi Wohlgelenter and Rabbi Adler firmly argued for some compromise, either realizing that an exclusively kosher hospital would be impossible to achieve or opposing the idea. Yet several of the controversies that had divided Detroit Jews over the hospital lingered. In a brief history of the hospital movement, Federation took out a full page ad in the *Jewish News* headlined, "The Jewish Hospital—and You."[295] Most Jews in Detroit had remained unaware of the developments and arguments of the previous forty years.

If questions about kosher kitchens had been resolved, it seemed to some to be an uneasy resolution. To counter any reservations, then, a media campaign of sorts set out to educate the public about "its" hospital.[296] By the time of the ground-breaking ceremonies in January 1951, uncharacteristic unity had been achieved. Funds from the Hebrew Hospital Association as well as from the Mt. Sinai Hospital Association had been pooled with the understanding that there would be two kitchens and that decisions about staffing were to be determined by Harry Saltzstein and a committee of Jewish doctors. Dr. Julien Priver, the association director of Mt. Sinai Hospital in New York, was offered the position as director and arrived in Detroit in 1951. The hospital opened on January 15, 1953, as several Detroit dignitaries, including Governor G. Mennen Williams and Federation president Sam Rubiner, looked on. Present, too, was Marcus Kates, named to the board to represent the original Hebrew Hospital Association, thereby adding to the emotion-charged atmosphere.[297]

The North End Clinic moved to Sinai Hospital, where in 1959 it became the Shiffman Clinic. Under the guidance of Leonard Simons, the Designations Committee by the 1960s could boast responsibility for the Shiffman Clinic, the Fisher Wing, the Zivian Center, the Blumberg Building, the Srere Radiology Center, Slatkin Residence Hall, the Shapero School of Nursing, the Frank Family Library, and the Hamburg-Jospey Research Building. By 1960 it had grown from 238 to 351 beds and included 36 psychiatry beds under the direction of Dr. August.

As a Jewish institution, Sinai Hospital—and the hospital movement in general—illustrated patterns of conflict and resolution; debates over Jewish tradition, religion, and identity; and the differences between "uptown" (no longer only German) and "downtown" (no longer only East European) Jews. It bore within it the seeds of controversies shared by other urban Jewish communities as well as those unique to Detroit—the leadership, the staunch upper-class intransigence, and the mediation of Federation, aided by unusually powerful and influential figures. These patterns of conflict resolution involved professional experts like Golub and Fishbein, who turned to comparative attitude and demographic studies, increasing the reliance on statistical analysis and the involvement of media techniques for public education. It achieved what Jewish hospitals brought to their constituencies in other cities: a sense of pride in accomplishment.

Dr. Golub, whose report had been influential in convincing many previous opponents of the hospital, remained as a consultant. Sinai Hospital clung to those principles Golub had offered the board. He had spoken of a "three-legged stool: teaching, patient care and research." Golub insisted the hospital be "first-class" in every respect. In his view, a Jewish hospital could only justify itself if it guaranteed quality care and excellence.[298] In debates over the construction, for example, he argued strenuously over every detail—the corners on the hallways were to be round, not perpendicular, because round corners were more easily cleaned. That air of excellence, first-class quality, and research, pervaded the creation and continued practice at Sinai Hospital—the dream come true.

441

34

Detroit's Jewish Women: The Family Affair

"We were a family and our work was a family affair," declared Josephine Stern Weiner about the Detroit Section of the National Council of Jewish Women (NCJW). She had served twice as president of the section and in other offices; she had been an ambassador on the organization's behalf and a former national president, and thus spoke warmly, authoritatively, and proudly of individuals and the organization. In 1925, under the energetic leadership of Mildred (Mrs. Joseph) Welt, Temple Beth El's Jewish Women's Club became the Detroit Section of the NCJW. Referring to the divisions within the Jewish population and speaking, she said, for all Detroit Jewish women, Mrs. Welt avowed that "what unites us is much more important than what divides us."[299]

In that same year, in marked contrast, Detroit's branch of Pioneer Women, assertively Zionist, leftist, and Yiddishist, obtained its charter from the national Poale Zion in Chicago. This coincidental emergence of the two women's groups underscores again the contrasts within the Jewish population. While it aspired to unify at least Jewish women, the NCJW in Detroit emerged from philanthropic origins in Beth El when volunteers in 1891 had formed the Jewish Women's Club and reached out to East European Jewish im-

442

migrants, "elevating" them through charitable treatment and trips to the country or to Belle Isle for the children.[300] Even after 1925, its members continued to meet at Beth El, and almost all were "Beth Elniks." Pioneer Women angrily rejected such attitudes, boldly moving into the forefront of Zionist activism.

Nevertheless, Detroit's chapter of NCJW sustained a tradition of generosity and vigor even as they accepted the goals of the national organization, which also bore a distinct German-Jewish character. Insistently a volunteer organization, the NCJW acted "in the spirit of Judaism . . . dedicated to furthering human welfare in the Jewish and general communities" and aiming to advance "human welfare and the democratic way of life." Its members theoretically devoted themselves to pluralism, democracy, individual rights, political accountability, religious liberty, and public education. They focused on volunteer work for children and the aged; on the promotion of Jewish life and, by the 1950s, Israel.[301]

The NCJW bore a distinctly liberal stamp. As early as 1923 the national organization had declared itself for decent wage standards; in 1935 it had supported social security and issued a declaration on world peace in 1946. The group backed resolutions on civil rights and nondiscrimination in housing in 1943, on child care in 1941, and on school integration in 1955. It issued resolutions on the need for and nature of Jewish education in 1943, and in the 1960s, the NCJW began to discuss women's issues, introducing a 1961 resolution on women in Jewish life and law.[302] Throughout the 1930s the social welfare division, chaired by Mrs. (Joseph) Welt with the help of Mrs. Melville Welt and Mrs. Gertrude Glowgower, sponsored lectures. Their annual program at the Book Cadillac included the names of Mrs. Dora Ehrlich, who would become one of Detroit's most active women leaders, Mrs. Henry Wineman, and Regine Freund (Mrs. Louis S.) Cohane, among others.[303] Annual dues were five dollars, and with the revenue the organization funded small scholarships, fostered a committee on the blind and deaf, and, through its affiliations with the Young Women's Hebrew Association, undertook programs for education and recreation for children under sixteen, setting up clubs and classes, providing holiday programs and "mass activities"—dances, lectures, and dramatic performances. It also established a Bureau of Personal Services, "an inexhaustible source of aid for girls who come with disturbing problems," and, perhaps most important in those early years, a summer-camp program.[304]

Along with this already imposing collection of volunteer activities, the NCJW also engaged volunteer teachers for adult education, offering classes for new mothers, for example. It began a legislative committee that directed letter campaigns to congressmen and senators on such issues as the immigration bills. It sponsored six lectures on city government and formed a Peace and Arbitration Committee that addressed international subjects   443

and provided lectures, radio broadcasts, and a "Good Will Day" letter contest in schools.[305]

It stood for volunteerism and cooperation within the Jewish population
and between Jews and non-Jews. NCJW volunteers helped staff the North
End Clinic and aided in the Jewish Emergency Relief and the Federation
Unemployment Committee during the Depression. Between 1931 and 1932
the NCJW offered "mental hygiene" courses at the Jewish Community Center. In 1932 the national convention held at the Statler Hotel endorsed
birth control "in preventative and curative medicine."[306] Under the presidency of Regine Freund Cohane, the NCJW in 1933 set up a kitchen directed by Mrs. Mildred Welt, and it began the NCJW Camp at Jeddo, Michigan, to provide vacations for young women and for working women who
could not afford vacations.[307]

By 1944 the Detroit Section had aided in raising funds for "service to
[the] foreign born" during the war, had begun to work with refugee children, and had established the Twelfth Street Council Center as a joint operation with the Jewish Community Center—the first cooperative venture
of a social agency with a volunteer membership organization. Some one
thousand people a week attended the Center, a form of settlement house,
for recreational and educational programs. No fewer than 125 volunteers
served the clientele (primarily children) each week. In 1945 the Detroit
section of NCJW voluntarily increased its quota to the National Overseas
Program and Service to the Foreign Born from six-thousand dollars to ten-
thousand dollars, thereby assuming the leading role in the country.[308]

Detroit's Jewish women's groups ranged from Yiddishist *lehnenkreise,*
reading or study groups, to politically conscious Pioneer Women and Zionist charity organizations like Hadassah. From its exhilarating formative
years when the Wetsman sisters had participated in the Szold-inspired
founding of the Greater Detroit Chapter of Hadassah, that organization had
grown steadily. Uncompromising women Zionists like Jeanette Steinberg,
one of Hadassah's founders, dedicated their lives to the founding of the
state of Israel, expressing themselves through Hadassah activities and through
active support of the Zionist Organization of America. Steinberg created
the idea of organizing businesswomen into separate Hadassah units and
instituted the Business and Professional Women of Hadassah. Along with
indomitable partisans like Dora Ehrlich, Steinberg zealously pursued the
organization's goals.[309]

By 1934, Hadassah became the sole American agency for the Youth Aliyah program, which sent teenagers to Palestine. The Detroit Chapter of
Hadassah participated in publicizing and funding that program from its
inception. They also supported and publicized the parade of projects undertaken in the 1940s including the Hadassah home for disturbed, delin-
quent girls near Tel Aviv, the vocational school for girls, the Brandeis Training
444   Center for mechanical education for boys, and the first Youth Aliyah kib-

butz, Ramat Hadassah Szold, in 1949. Because of its increase in membership, in 1944, Detroit Hadassah separated into five regional groups: Central, Russell Woods, University, Huntington Woods, and B & P. In 1955,
the Detroit Chapter consisted of seventeen groups and had grown to over
six thousand members.[310]

Perhaps the two pivotal years in the chapter's history were 1948 and
1955. In the benchmark year of 1948, its membership reached five thousand, and it had begun to open its own group offices. Its activities expanded
both internationally and locally. Whatever elation Hadassah members felt
at the founding of the state of Israel became overlaid with sorrow at the
tragic murder of seventy-six Hadassah medical personnel in the Mount Scopus
Hadassah Hospital during the 1948 War of Liberation. Mount Scopus and
the hospital were lost, forcing Hadassah's energies, recruitment, and funds
into other institutions like the Hebrew University Hadassah Medical School.
Both the elation and the tragedy seemed to stimulate engagement and
membership as numbers grew in Detroit. Hadassah became one of the official representative groups for Israel, somehow gaining new legitimacy because of the new state.

In 1955, as Detroit's membership exceeded five thousand women, that
legitimacy seemed to become concrete. The group's various offices—in a
store on Linwood near Joy Road, above the Linwood post office, and above
the Avalon Theatre at Linwood and Davison—had for years been rented,
crowded, and inadequate for the growing organization's needs. Larger
quarters remained economically prohibitive. But in 1955, to a great extent
because of the urging of Dora Ehrlich, "a day dream we all indulged in"
came into reality. Theodore Bargman, Israel Davidson, Bert L. Smokler,
and Frank A. Wetsman presented the organization with Hadassah House
on Seven Mile.[311] From that "new beginning" emerged other local programs—thrift shops, fund-raising campaigns, and more sponsored activities that attracted larger numbers of people.

Alongside large national groups like Hadassah, Detroit's women's organizations included associations such as the Farband Women's Organization, which aided in sending children to the Farband Camp in summers,
and a group of Norman Thomas (the Socialist Party candidate for president) supporters, the Young Socialist League. They ran the gamut from
the popularly perceived "establishment" Women's Division of the Federation and the NCJW to smaller, less visible associations like the Sheruth
League and the Music Study Club, begun in 1924 by a group of eighteen
young women musicians, which eventually sponsored scholarships for young,
talented Jewish musicians.[312] Those groups expressed, in their very existence, dilemmas Jewish women in America faced in a rapidly changing
social and economic environment.

Incipient feminists began to question women's roles in Jewish tradition
and Judaism, although "feminism," however it might be defined after the   445

1960s, rarely grew militant among Jewish organizations. Few of Detroit's most animated women, as independent or influential as they may have been, chose to identify themselves as feminists.

Jewish women involved in communal affairs clung to the motif of family and unity. Yet some who became occupied in the NCJW in the 1960s received quizzical and critical responses from mothers and grandmothers: the NCJW was "still perceived as a German Jewish stronghold" according to one member, and not the place for daughters of Zionist-oriented, Yiddishist, East European mothers; not the place for daughters from families of modest incomes. That those daughters had not joined the more ethnically identified organizations like Farband Women or Pioneer Women indicated a shift in the economic and social status of their generation, an adjustment of attitudes and, perhaps, a loss of Yiddish roots. Apart from these residual divisions, however, loomed the more universal question of "women's place" in general.

Social historian Sydney Stahl Weinberg defined Jewish women in terms of their adherence to a "domestic religion" primarily associated with child-rearing, home, feeling, and an ensemble of qualities attached to maternal, nurturing stereotypes and practices. More or less barred from public leadership and religious scholarship in European communities, Jewish women traditionally retained authority at home. That tradition fostered feminine competence and confidence, customarily enhanced by the fulfilling of early responsibilities. Daughters learned how to "manage"—to become "mediators" and surreptitiously run the family "behind the facade of paternal authority."[313]

Family obligations, then, usually came before personal gratification, but family obligations implied a strong, dominant, directive faculty. These strong qualities, developed in earlier European generations, continued in America. They manifested themselves publicly among groups like the Pioneer Women and Hadassah. In organizations like the *landsmanshaftn,* women undertook more domestic endeavors, usually preparing refreshments for meetings and cooking for bake sales, as well as more "modern" tasks, such as organizing the Yiddish cultural circles. Among such other secular groups as the Sholem Aleichem Institute, women frequently assisted in fund-raising for the school, also cooking and baking for meetings and holidays.

German Jews frequently broke the pattern; they often perpetuated aspects of the matriarchal archetype, but with considerable differences, as their daughters received formal, secular education, sometimes traveling abroad on educational trips at young ages. Most significantly, German Jewish women dedicated themselves to communal obligations like Beth El's Jewish Women's Club and in some respects might be perceived as the origin of the organized Jewish charity agencies. From the perspective of some German Jews and some East European Jews, those volunteer projects bore the mark of noblesse oblige.

By the 1930s, Jewish women, primarily those descendants of East Eu-

ropean Jews, sought to achieve secular dreams of educational advancement in the *goldene Medine*.[314] Yet they still concentrated less on external accomplishments than on home and personal relationships. If this pattern derived from accepted internal and family traditions, it also issued from sexist attitudes among American-Jewish and non-Jewish men. Regine Freund Cohane, a young lawyer fresh from Cornell, called on a prominent Jewish attorney in the 1920s to ask for a job in his office. "I do not know of any opening in a Detroit office," he replied, "and certainly not for a woman." Although the situation changed over the course of the next three decades, and Jewish women obtained more positions as professionals, male attitudes seemed to stubbornly persist.

How Jewish women found meaning for their lives, how they expressed their talents and needs, forms a separate chapter of American-Jewish history. In the main, Detroit Jewish women followed the patterns of the urban Jews, with some significant exceptions. As the NCJW became a powerful vehicle of women's expression and activity, it evolved from a select group to a more representative one and differed from other Jewish communal agencies in its willingness to assume political positions.

In 1972 Jacqueline Levine, a vice-president of the Council of Jewish Federations and Welfare Funds (the umbrella organization for the nation's more than two-hundred local community councils and welfare federations), addressed the general assembly with a rather shocking report. Studies of women in Jewish communal life, she said, provided uncontrovertible evidence of "pervasive under-representation . . . in honorific roles and positions of influence in Jewish fund-raising organizations." She concluded with the following:

> We [women] are asking that our talents of maintaining Jewish life through the centuries—of caring for our children, of developing a volunteer cadre capable of remarkable achievement, of welding realism with compassion, of developing an understanding of the real priorities a society should have— not be set aside any longer on the grounds of a prefabricated sexual role difference. . . . so that we may be witness to and participants in the exciting challenge of creating a new and open and total Jewish community.[315]

Three years later, the Council of Jewish Federations (CJF) issued a resolution on Women in Federation Policy and Decision Making. This acknowledged that efforts had been made to incorporate women in leadership roles, but that the potential to utilize their talents as individuals had been largely untapped. A CJF study revealed that women numbered only as one of every twenty federation presidents, one of six vice-presidents, one of six members of executive committees, one of every five board members, one of four members of allocations and planning committees, and one of three chairmen of these commitees.[316] Detroit more or less reflected those statistics. 447

Golda Krolik became a directive and generative force in the activities of the NCJW. As a role model, she publicly exhibited all the qualities that she said she had learned "in [her] mother's womb" and for which the organization stood: volunteerism in the Jewish community, support of civil rights, a sense of humor, and group leadership.[317] As far as the NCJW was concerned, this last quality, leadership, meant devoting time and energy to its causes. In a domestic world of conflicting multiple demands, however, this commitment might severely limit the pool of volunteers to those who could afford to give time—they frequently, especially in the years up to the 1960s, were those whose husbands could afford to give both time and money to the male-dominated activities of Federation fund-raising.

While fund-raising preoccupied Federation officials, the NCJW declared explicitly its purposes as a volunteer community service. Those purposes included addressing social needs and ways to meet them, cooperation with unions, and public statements on women's rights and family issues. They included, too, programs to aid the elderly and infirm. By the mid-1950s, the Detroit Section had organized a placement program for older people with the Jewish Vocational Service (which won first prize in a *Detroit News* contest for "Organizational Activities in Community Service" in 1955), a procedure for high-school girls to participate in social activities and community service, a study of mental health and housing legislation, a resale shop, and a senior lounge program catering to the social and recreational needs of the aged. These activities evolved as the children's camp programs flourished, demonstrating the dual focus—on young and old—of Jewish women's volunteer activities.[318]

Before 1948 the NCJW included in its ranks pro-Zionists, non-Zionists, and anti-Zionists. As an organization, it came late to endorsing the state, perhaps betraying its lingering German-Jewish Reform leadership and character. But in 1947, Josephine (Mrs. Leonard) Weiner attended a national conference in Chicago and recalled the debate and final passing of a resolution supporting the people in Palestine. In 1959 the NCJW broke precedent and formally declared a four-year fund-raising program to build an experimental institution for teacher training: the Hebrew University High School in Israel.[319]

Detroit's NCJW excelled in support of at least two other projects, one local, the other a local expression of a national enterprise. In 1959–1960, the Greater Detroit Section of the NCJW launched Operation Friendship, a lounge program for convalescing mental patients.[320] Operation Friendship responded to national and local Jewish population surveys of needs. Cooperating with other community groups, the NCJW led the movement to help form the Receiving Hospital Service League, a women's volunteer association that undertook to furnish a lounge for the men's psychiatric ward. As it worked with the general, that is, non-Jewish community, the NCJW spearheaded the movement that culminated in 1964 when it moved to its own lounge at 17,100 Woodingham and expanded its program.[321] A Jewish women's organization had clearly and emphatically made its mark on the Detroit scene.

Demonstrating its commitment to aiding Detroit's mental health programs, the NCJW in 1962 determined that one of Detroit's greatest needs was the establishment of residential treatment centers for emotionally disturbed children—those who appeared in non-Jewish as well as Jewish agencies. The Orchards Children Service in Livonia resulted from the generosity of seventeen NCJW members and their families. It provided professional assistance for six to eight residential patients, boys with emotional problems. Aided by the chairman of Wayne State University's Social Work Program, Professor Ralph Abramowitz, Orchard House rejected treatment by drugs and practiced family therapy in conjunction with the Livonia Public Schools. Staffed by Jewish volunteers and celebrating Jewish holidays, the house maintained a distinctly "Jewish ambience." By the end of the first year, the camping program sponsored by the NCJW included a session for the Orchards children at Tamarack. During Mrs. Josephine Weiner's tenure as chair of Orchard House, the DeRoy Foundation provided an endowment for its support.[322]

Shortly after the opening of Orchard House, Mrs. Regene Freund Cohane and Mrs. Weiner, as representatives to the national board of the NCJW, attended an invitational White House Conference on Civil Rights. President John F. Kennedy had convened a meeting of the leaders of women's groups, including the entire board of the NCJW. He urged them to join the battle for civil rights to help "get [it] off the streets and into the courts."[323] Enlivened, the Detroit Section invited local affiliates of the various women's organizations in Detroit to meet at Council House to exchange ideas. As a consequence of these meetings, the Detroit section of the NCJW in 1965 allied with other women's organizations to join Women in Community Service (WICS), part of President Lyndon Johnson's "War on Poverty."[324]

Led by the NCJW, a Detroit women's coalition of the National Council of Catholic, Negro, Jewish, Church Women and the American G. I. Forum (Hispanics) emerged. Members of the NCJW in Detroit leaped into the venture, at first recruiting young women to fulfill the avowed goals of the program: to aid young people in crossing the racial, economic, and social barriers that hindered them. This took the concrete forms of serving in the Federal Job Corps, training young people in professional and skilled jobs, and providing support services for those who had completed the Job Corps courses so that they could continue their work and expand upon it in the marketplace. Volunteer social workers joined hands with other women volunteers, as "indefatigable Jewish and black women" combined in teams to interview prospective candidates in the inner city and to hold discussions on procedures.[325]

449

Unlike Federation, then, the NCJW achieved its reputation not for fund-raising and consequent aid to the Jewish population, but as a strictly volunteer service organization. Unlike Federation, it identified itself, through its national affiliation, with sociopolitical issues that were local, national, and even international. Unlike Federation (and, ironically, like Council), it expressed a liberalism that, its position papers argued, derived from Jewish values. Yet most of its leaders resolutely identified with and actively participated in Federation campaigns, usually with husbands who held committee or board positions. Those women who piloted the NCJW also assumed the initiative in the founding and development of the Federation Women's Division.

In 1946 Golda Krolik spoke at the first tea that solicited women for pledges to the Allied Jewish Campaign. One year later, the first annual meeting of the Federation Women's Division convened under the presidency of the already legendary Dora (Mrs. Joseph) Ehrlich. She addressed herself to the question, "Why a women's division?"—asserting that it offered two generations of Jewish women an opportunity to sit down "together in sincerity and integrity, just women, not representing groups or shades of opinion, but just Jewish women concerned with their responsibilities to the whole of life—not one segment—to the whole Jewish problem for survival in all its aspects—local, civic, national, and world over: just Jewish women who want to take their place as citizens, as Americans."[326]

It was a stirring speech, and it was coupled with an exhortation to avoid debates about distribution of funds and to center on the larger goal of raising more money. Mrs. Ehrlich's admonition echoed Isidore Sobeloff's philosophy of fund-raising and reflected his influence in the founding of the Women's Division. Early in 1946, he had met with Mrs. Ehrlich, Mrs. Clara Frank, Mrs. Weiner, and Mrs. Krolik to discuss what women could do. Sensing, as American Jews did, that the Holocaust and Palestine signaled new directions and greater responsibilities, their goals, with Sobeloff's guidance, included at least theoretical acknowledgement of the "problem of Jewish survival."

The "plus-gift" concept was already enunciated at that first annual meeting and, in fact, it served as the raison d'être for the Women's Division.[327] Devised by the National Council of Jewish Federations, plus-giving rested on certain assumptions about fund-raising. Federation campaigns solicited husbands as "the heads of households," presumably "with the prestige and status accompanying the contribution accorded to [them]."[328] The Women's Division provided women, primarily wives, the opportunity to make their own gifts. Yet in 1949, the organization's second president, Mrs. Frank, declared that "we want to do more than help supply funds. We want to develop responsible leadership. We want all of us to have full understanding of what we are building today."[329]

450   Serious about the formation of the division, Sobeloff employed Mrs. Pauline

Jackson as its executive director. She instilled a professionalism that brought order and discipline to the organization and set it on a course of educating young leaders, in addition to its plus-giving. A woman of "strong Jewish feelings," she assiduously trained and preened for leadership energetic and dynamic women like Mrs. Josephine Weiner, Mrs. Bernice Hopp, and Mrs. Jennie Jones.

Mrs. Jennie Jones, president from 1953 to 1955, in 1982 voiced a widely shared opinion that the Women's Division provided a vehicle for feminist expression: "We women . . . Jewish feminists before we coined such a term, expounded the position that as individuals we have rights matched with the responsibility to take our places in history and to help forge [the future] of the Jewish people."[330] Naturally enough, active and articulate leaders numbered among those who adhered to and voiced that view.

Criticisms remained, however, and they tended to come from non-Federation groups as well as from factions within. Opponents of women's volunteerism argued that such activities seemed confined to upper-middle-class women and were undertaken for organizations in which positions of influence and importance were reserved for men while women did "most of the dirty work."[331] Women seemed taken for granted and ignored or overlooked when organizations like Federation handed out recognition, prestige, and honor.

Detroit appeared less vulnerable to such criticism. By 1955, only five years after the first award, the Fred M. Butzel Memorial Award for Community Service went to Mrs. Ehrlich. Seven years later, Mrs. Henry Wineman received it. Women had served on Federation's board and principal committees since the 1920s, and few if any Federation women voiced such complaints.[332]

From its inception, the Women's Division stressed its inclusive character: Golda Krolik and Dora Ehrlich frequently declared that, at least among women, differences evaporated and a family spirit predominated. Bernice Hopp, president of the division from 1951 to 1953, declared that "when women learn, the whole family learns; when women act, the whole family is motivated."[333] Gertrude Wineman agreed that "women set the pace and establish the pattern" of Jewish behavior, and Ann Daniels noted that the membership "represents every segment of the community."[334]

Yet divisiveness persisted. The Women's Division continued to be perceived by many as the domain of the wealthy. Indeed, Jewish communal leadership, as expressed through the Federation movement, seemed to rest on substantial commitments of time and money. Many of Detroit's women leaders in the Women's Division and the NCJW attained national prominence: Mrs. Josephine Weiner, Mrs. Mildred Welt, Mrs. Ann Daniels, Mrs. B. Benedict Glazer, Mrs. Regine Freund Cohane, Mrs. Esther Jones, Mrs. Harry (Jennie) Jones, Mrs. John (Bernice) Hopp, Mrs. Celia Broder, and others.[335] As models for the community, they tended to bear the burden 451 of increasing pressure for time and money. This proved to be less the case on the local level, although even there a distinct gap continued to exist into the 1950s. As Jews climbed higher on socioeconomic scales, a broader cross-section of women participated and old rifts lessened.

By 1962, the Women's Division boasted a leadership training course, a Federation interagency conference, a cash-mobilization drive, and an informational institute. Much of this professionalized approach derived from the sharp-eyed Pauline Jackson, who inspired Detroit's Jewish women to organize in an orderly fashion and even wooed supporters of other Jewish groups into the Women's Division.[336] It offered a viable means for women to participate in and help shape the directions of Detroit's Jewish community programs and agencies. Israel's needs became more insistent and the tone of discussions about Jewish consciousness and "survival" shifted after World War II. These and other factors influenced the expansive changes in the nature of the membership. In the 1960s, it became apparent that even "the white-gloved elegance" attributed to women like Bernice Hopp had gone hand in hand with a tough-minded, serious, and effective plan to contribute to Jewish causes.

In April 1944 a small group of women not prominently affiliated with any Jewish agency in Detroit banded together to form a service organization. They met at the home of their first president, Shirley Cohen, to discuss their goals. On May 16 (four years before the great celebration of the birth of the state of Israel), as Adolf Eichmann prepared to deport the Jews of Hungary, these Detroit women sensed an emergency and adopted the name of the Sheruth "service" in Hebrew League. Their purpose would focus on such causes as "city nurseries," Russian war relief, helping Jewish asthmatic children, and sending children to camp.[337] Rabbi Hershman had suggested the name to Ruth Shapiro, and at that second meeting the members elected Cele Spector to be in charge of selling war stamps and bonds.[338] Thus began an independent grass-roots organization that would retain a relatively low profile and provide more volunteer assistance for Jewish "underprivileged children." By December, they had adopted a Yemenite child for $240 through Youth Aliyah, and by the end of the following year, members had sent five children to camp, even providing some of them with clothing for the summer.[339]

As an organization, the Sheruth League donated annually to the Allied Jewish Campaign but did not officially affiliate with Federation. Its membership remained almost exclusively descendants of East European Jews, and it was perceived as more akin to Yiddishist groups than to organizations like the Women's Division or the NCJW. Yet its quiet integrity, personified by such women as Mrs. Anna (Samuel) Chapin, comptroller of Federation, brought it the respect of virtually every element of the Jewish population. By 1954 it had built a Sheruth Lodge at Camp Tamarack; in the following year it sent fifty-seven children to that camp at a cost of five-thousand dollars and had donated a scholarship to the Michigan League for Crippled Children. In 1955 it cosponsored, with the March of Dimes and Youth Aliyah, a charity ball to benefit retarded children.[340] By 1959 the League had raised over $120,000 for charitable organizations and had dedicated a Sheruth Village at Tamarack. In 1961 it concluded an agreement with the Jewish Family and Children's Service to purchase and help staff Sheruth House. As the largest single contributor to Tamarack in 1962, Sheruth received a special tribute from the Fresh Air Society in 1963.[341]

A wide variety of supporters contributed to Sheruth's projects. Its annual yearbook, compiled for its donor luncheon, included full-page contributions from Hordes Insurance Agency, Darby's Delicatessen on Seven Mile Road, and Walter Field's Mac-O-Lac Paints, as well as from numerous non-Jewish contributors. By 1965 Sheruth had expanded its services from camp scholarships to social service, with volunteers working with over fifty families.[342] It appeared clearly differentiated from other such volunteer groups if only because its members, in the main, did not come from those other groups.

More focused than other Detroit women's organizations, the members of the Sheruth League again reflected a deep commitment to volunteerism directed toward helping Jewish children, "a women's group which accepted and fulfilled its obligations." Unlike the case among some of the men's organizations, there seemed little animosity or rivalry between the "establishment"-sponsored volunteer groups and this one. While some competitive grumbling may have occurred among some individuals, no public friction emerged. Most of Sheruth's leaders seemed satisfied with little acclaim, although their accomplishments grew each year.

35

The Year of Change, 1966–1967: Three Crises

Worries about losses of Jewish culture, education, worship, and identity persisted in Detroit from the inception of organized Jewish life. Rabbis, scholars, philanthropists, men, women, secularists, and religious Jews all addressed problems related to those losses. Among those who regularly confronted the intermittent decline of Jewish identification, Rabbi Morris Adler gained particular prominence. He discussed the subject repeatedly from the pulpit, exhorting Shaarey Zedek members, Council, Federation, and UHS to intensify Jewish learning, culture, and values as he perceived them. His powerful voice, authoritative and confident, carried conviction and influence in both the Jewish and non-Jewish worlds in and beyond Detroit.

Engaged in Detroit civic affairs ranging from union work to active participation in the Detroit Round Table of the National Conference of Christians and Jews, Adler had reached an authoritative pinnacle commensurate with his role among Detroit's Jews as leader of one of America's largest and most dynamic Conservative synagogues. The edifice seemed to symbolize this, its stained-glass peak jutting almost over the adjacent highway, with the grandeur of its foyer and sanctuary as overwhelming as a medieval cathedral. And Rabbit Adler, draped in ritual robes each Sabbath, reflected that prominence and pride, dominating the congregation and drawing attention as one of the most acclaimed spokesmen for Jews in Detroit.

On February 12, 1966, Rabbi Adler delivered an especially powerful sermon that unfolded from his theme of Abraham Lincoln's birthday. He concluded his serman deftly and dramatically, intersecting Lincoln's "hour of bitter decision" with "this hour where we too stand at a kind of crossroads." He asked for "Lincolnesque perception" to be able to "meet our problems with humility, with judgment, with faith." In a typically passionate finish, Rabbi Adler seemed to coalesce his pleas for global peace with an appeal to Detroit Jews for "healing and not suffering, understanding and not hostility, brotherhood and not conflict."[343]

As he ended the sermon, Judy Cantor and her four-year-old daughter, Ellen, entered the sanctuary. They had stood in the foyer with several other people, waiting for a proper moment to enter the service. Alongside them stood a young man who proceeded just ahead of them and then toward the left aisle as they moved to the center. The rabbi had returned to his seat on the *bimah* (altar) next to that morning's bar mitzvah boy, Steven Frank, and the president of the congregation, Louis Berry. Suddenly, the young man, whose family belonged to Shaarey Zedek and who had been counseled by Rabbi Adler on occasion, strode to the *bimah* brandishing a pistol. He ordered Berry and young Frank off the altar, fired a shot in the air, and spoke briefly, castigating the congregation for hypocrisy. He turned, fired two shots at Rabbi Adler, and then shot himself.[344] Momentary pandemonium ensued, but Mrs. Cantor remembers the horrified outcries, her fear for her daughter and for her husband and son (who sat near the front of the sanctuary), and then the quick stillness that fell over the sanctuary as Berry urged the congregation to leave quietly and go home.

The rabbi's troubled assassin died within a few days. One month later, after feverish attempts to save his life, Rabbi Adler died. On March 11, six thousand people attended the funeral service, among them Gov. George Romney, Lt. Gov. William Milliken, former governor G. Mennen Williams, Sen. Philip Hart, Mayor Jerome Cavanagh, Judges Theodore Levin, George Edwards, and Horace Gilmore, the Reuther brothers, and prominent Christian clergymen.[345] On March 13, over 15,000 attended the memorial service at Congregation Shaarey Zedek.[346] "The most quoted rabbi in the U.S." had tragically, inexplicably been struck down.

On a train to a conference in January 1966, Adler had met Elie Wiesel, the Holocaust survivor, novelist, essayist, and teacher who would become a Nobel laureate in 1986. Briefly they exchanged ideas on his foreboding ruminations about the future of American Jewry. Wiesel recalled that Adler had voiced strong disquiet about the ease of integration, the siren call "to leave the Jewish fold, to assimilate. . . . for a Jew to sit quietly, peacefully . . . rest . . . relax . . . let things happen . . . do nothing." Concurring,

455

Wiesel summarized Adler's comments: "A Jew who does not see Judaism as a constant fight is destined to assimilate."[347] In Wiesel's eyes, speaking from the depths of the Shoah, the Holocaust, indifference loomed as the sin of the twentieth century. He found Adler echoing this fear and speaking out against Jews' indifference toward their own heritage and identity.

Like his fellow Council members, from Louis LaMed to Rabbi Stollman, Adler lamented a marked decrease in attention to Jewish attitudes, practices, rituals, values, and commitment. But if he perceived indifference as a central problem, Adler also found that confusion over meaning and definitions critically beleaguered large parts of the American Jewish population. Comparing Jewish youth to the protagonists of Kenneth Kenniston's "insightful" work on America, *The Uncommitted—Alienated Youth in American Society*, he wrote that "a blurred image of Jewish selfhood is all but universal in American Jewish life, and it would be more than miraculous if our youth had a clear sense of their identity."[348] Adler discerned the harmful dilemmas at the root of this confusion over identity:

> We are in the throes of a tension between continuity and relevance; between religion and secularity; between the Jewish community and the larger society; between a yesterday that is remote and a future that is inconceivable; between reason and emotion; between the high level of our familiarity with the intellectual disciplines of our time and the low level of our knowledge of Judaism; between the ease and self-assurance which Jews have acquired in the sciences and humanities and the uneasiness and uncertainty with which they talk of Judaism because of their limited knowledge.[349]

On the day before the shooting, as he had for years, Rabbi Adler had lunched with his friend and colleague, Conservative rabbi Moses Lehrman of Congregation B'nai Moshe. As they discussed their sermon topics for the next day, Adler proferred his thoughts on Lincoln, but then he told Lehrman that "he was concerned about this age of ours; how difficult it is for everybody and particularly for youth . . . [and] that he was aware of the terrible pressures and conflicts engulfing our youth today.[350] Rabbi Lehrman implied that these apprehensions informed the topic of Rabbi Adler's sermons—perhaps they served as the wellspring for most of his addresses.

In his memorial to the rabbi, Wiesel noted that "the Jews of Detroit have been walking as if in a nightmare. They do not understand. . . . They ask: how did it happen? Why? They have no answer." He and other stunned commentators across the nation compared the rabbi's murder to John F. Kennedy's and attributed the violence to "murderous forces" loose in the twentieth century. "[Adler] lived with the Holocaust in his whole being," wrote Wiesel in a memorial article, and saw "Israel as a *reply* to slaughter, not a remedy." If the murder seemed tragic, inexplicable, to Wiesel it had far-reaching implications: "once again absurdity has been victorious."[351]

Some observers felt that Rabbi Adler's final talk resonated with his well-known worries about the quest for unity and for a meaningful content of Jewish life for Jewish youth. Among those who commented nationally, Max Lerner drew attention to Adler's abiding concern for the "uncommitted" youth and claimed that, ironically, the tormented young man "was not uncommitted but overcommitted." He had charged the congregation with abandoning its Jewish values, with hypocrisy and loss of tradition. Lerner, like Wiesel, perceived this particular tragedy as symptomatic and apocryphal: the unrest and alienation of Jewish youth, he argued, "comes not from indifference to meaning, but from a desperate search for meaning."[352] Lerner's sentiment echoed Adler's growing anxiety about the future of Jewish youth.

One chronicler of the assassination also extrapolated symbolic significance from it. T. V. LoCicero wrote that Adler had tried to address the segment of young Jews "who readily accept their Jewishness but reject the formal tenets of Judaism . . . who are alienated from middle-class Jewish life and hostile toward the religious establishment."[353] Few of those troubled searchers could be identified as fanatical or deranged or disturbed, as had been the young man who became so driven to distraction and violence. Yet the event seemed to evoke and somehow epitomize the burning questions raised by such groups as the Jewish Parents Institute or the Birmingham Temple. In a time increasingly analyzed as anxiety-ridden, where poets and other scholars discussed the insight of such ominous statements as W. B. Yeats's famous, "things fall apart: the center cannot hold," Rabbi Adler and others searched for a Jewish anchor that might rescue a potential lost generation, disenchanted with and perhaps alienated from tradition and values. How to rescue the children? Nurture them with traditions that they would question? Educate them for the success of materialism? Would they be stronger Jews? Better Americans? Wealthier citizens? Greater contributors? More fervent activists? Would they be able to identify clearly as Jews?

On the Sabbath following the shooting, Rabbi Irwin Groner, assistant rabbi at Shaarey Zedek since 1959, declared with sensitivity and strength the theme of continued life that Shaarey Zedek would explicitly set out to embody. He spoke forcefully of purpose, truth, justice, compassion, and restoration. Fearing that the congregation would bear the mark of death and tragedy, its leadership determined to publicly and intently "reaffirm the biblical challenge to choose life." After one year of mourning, during which Rabbi Adler's study remained closed and his chair on the *bimah* remained vacant, members of the congregation tried to draw closer to each other, strengthening the Shaarey Zedek image of family and community.[354]

Rabbi Adler had voiced the age-old fears of the loss of Jewish identity through assimilation, intermarriage, indifference—all internal dangers. Perhaps those inveigling attractions posed a greater threat to the contin-

457

uation of Jewish culture than the external dangers of anti-Semitism. Identification with religion, culture, values, traditions, and history seemed to be falling victim to some sort of corrosive infection as successful American life beckoned. That corruption affected youth from all elements of the Jewish population—from the Orthodox to the secular. Divisiveness over wide varieties of issues traditionally marked the Jews of Detroit (and elsewhere), but Adler, like some Orthodox, Conservative, and secular observers, sensed a graver impending crisis. To those who pondered the meaning of his death and the circumstances that surrounded it, the assassination indicated a symbolic watershed in Jewish life. In Detroit, a rallying voice—to many, an irreplaceable one—had been stilled.

A little more than a year later, a historic crisis became another rallying point, an inspiration that stunned Detroit Jewry and most of the world. Esther Jones, then president of the Women's Division, recalled that she "was awakened early that morning [June 5, 1967] by Lil Perlman, president of Hadassah, who said . . . 'It's war! All hell has broken loose!' . . . Her call was the prototype of calls coming in the rest of the day—the theme being, 'Let's work together.' "[355]

After the Sinai Campaign in 1956, Israel had incurred the approbation of even its allies for occupying Egyptian territory. President Eisenhower clung to an almost fanatical belief that the United Nations would solve the problems of the Middle East, and in private and public addresses he had insisted that Israel withdraw its forces from Sinai.[356] In Detroit, Morris Schaver led a public renunciation of the president's speech at the UN.[357] Max Fisher also privately and firmly apprised Eisenhower of his consternation at what he considered the abandonment of Israel. Yet the UN plan prevailed, as all parties agreed to grant the UNEF (United Nations Expeditionary Force) authority in the occupied areas, and Israeli forces withdrew in December 1956. This accession to diplomacy and the disregard for the requests of Israel's supporters in the West disturbed American Zionists who nevertheless had no choice but to trust to the goodwill of American diplomacy.

In Egypt, an avalanche of angry rhetoric and vituperative threats flowed from President Gamal Abdel Nasser. By 1960 his manipulation of public media and his maneuverings among Arab leaders disguised the factionalism that ran rampant throughout the Arab world. In September 1960, Nasser addressed the UN General Assembly and declared that "the only solution to Palestine is that matters should return to the condition prevailing before the error was committed—that is, the annulment of Israel's existence."[358] After the founding of the Palestine Liberation Organization in January 1964— with its explicit goal "to attain the objective of liquidating"—Nasser announced that "we swear to God that we shall not rest until we restore the Arab nation to Palestine and Palestine to the Arab nation." In March 1965 he continued his maledictions: "We shall not enter Palestine with its soil covered in sand. . . . We shall enter it with its soil saturated in blood."[359]

Between 1965 and 1967 Nasser's prestige increased in both Arab and some Western countries, and his economic, political, and social difficulties at home began to ease. His rhetoric grew still hotter, reflecting a swelling confidence. Conversely, in Syria, Col. Salah Jadid had barely withstood two armed revolts in September 1966 and February 1967. Riddled with explosive and menacing factionalism, Jadid turned to the one dependable, universally popular issue: war against Israel. Both Egypt and Syria initiated regular intermittent troop movements that edged closer to Israel's borders.[360] In April 1967 an air incident along the Israeli-Syrian border erupted into a full-scale dogfight, and Israeli jets shot down six Syrian planes and then circled freely over Damascus.[361] Nasser's forces did not move, thus implying that the highly touted Syrian-Egyptian alliance had become a dead letter. Yet troop concentrations continued following the April 7 incident.[362]

By May 15, Cairo declared a state of military emergency and sent two armored divisions over the Suez and into Sinai—it was Israeli Independence Day and Lt. Gen. Yitzchak Rabin, Commander-in-Chief of Israeli forces, received the news while reviewing his troops on the road to Jerusalem. On May 16, Nasser ordered the UNEF to leave, breaking the agreement with the UN. The next day, Cairo radio announced military preparations for "retaliatory" attacks on Israeli cities and bases. Other Arab governments made similar announcements. On May 20, the Israeli cabinet called for a general mobilization.[363]

There seemed little doubt that war would erupt. Little doubt, too, that Israel, faced with overwhelming odds, would be defeated. When Nasser sent ships to block the Strait of Tiran, in effect strangling Israeli shipping, the Israeli cabinet began round-the-clock meetings.[364] In the middle of a vacation in the Greek Islands, Max Fisher received an urgent invitation to one of those meetings. As chairman of the United Jewish Appeal, Fisher had been phoned by Prime Minister Levi Eshkol; he left his friends—Henry Ford II and Nate Cummings of Consolidated Food—aboard his boat in the Aegean and flew to Israel.

Fisher recalled sitting next to Commander Rabin, who warned of the details of the imminent war: there would be up to forty thousand casualties; they would need the financial support of the world Jewish community to the tune of one billion dollars. Then Rabin quietly whispered to Fisher, "I hope they don't rob me of the element of surprise." Fisher left and promptly convinced Henry Ford II to contribute a personal check for $100,000. His other friends—such as Cummings, who had remained reluctant to contribute to what he considered "a socialist state"—also gave. However, Rabin, who for years had maintained the necessity of preemptive strikes, for the time being lost his cabinet battle. Urged by President Lyndon Johnson and by England, as well as by Foreign Minister Abba Eban, Rabin had to restrain his insistence on a surprise attack.[365]

459

The massing of troops escalated; and the rhetoric, too, escalated. Israel found itself surrounded, impatiently awaiting an openly avowed genocidal attack on all fronts. On June 5, 1967, recognizing the inevitability of the attack, Israel struck first. Within three hours, Israeli planes had virtually demolished the entire Egyptian air force. Throughout the Jewish communities of the world the stunned response neared panic: "All hell has broken loose!" Lil Perlman voiced the universal feeling of Jews everywhere who, ignorant of events in the Middle East except for the loud, public pronouncements of the "extermination of Israel" that came from Arab governments, suddenly perceived another Holocaust looming before them.[366]

Days before the war, such slogans had begun to glean reactions from Europeans sympathetic to Israel and petitions were signed; in Sweden, members of the parliament wanted to adjourn to come to Israel's aid; in Holland, church congregations offered prayers for Israel; even in Poland, Czechoslovakia, and Rumania, before the Soviet authorities clamped down on public statements, the governments favored Israel. Volunteers all over the west lined up outside Israeli embassies to enlist in the army or to offer some bodily service.[367]

Banner headlines in the *Detroit Jewish News* proclaimed that "Israel Is Not Alone." The Zionist Council of Detroit, the Jewish Community Council, and the Allied Jewish Campaign cosponsored a rally at the Jewish Community Center on Curtis and Meyers on Sunday, June 4. There, with tension rising hourly, Philip Slomovitz spoke to an estimated six thousand people about his recent trip to Israel, and Dr. Sam Krohn, president of Council, Irwin I. Cohn, a former chairman of the Allied Jewish Campaign, and Morris Liebermann, chairman of the Zionist Council of Detroit each addressed the rally with stirring, supportive exhortations.[368] Max Fisher, the chairman of the national United Jewish Appeal, and Hyman Safran, president of Federation, sent letters to donors requesting prompt payment on pledges to the campaign. As Israel totally mobilized for war, Slomovitz announced a three-month program wherein Detroiters from age eighteen to thirty-five could serve in civilian jobs in Israel to replace the soldiers who were called up.[369] Israel mobilized—a frightening yet somehow surreal phrase that to most American Jews did not convey the reality. Exactly what "Israel is not alone" might mean remained indistinct.

As an employee of the Council, Harold Dubin helped organize the rally at the Jewish Center on June 4. One week later, on June 11, he married Charlotte Hyams, then an editor of the *Detroit Jewish News,* at Congregation Adat Shalom. Charlotte recalled that "no one cried at that wedding," which, like most weddings, bore an air of joy and hope. But that wedding might well have been celebrated by the six thousand who had attended the rally the week before and by the thousands of Jews in Detroit who had engaged in frantic activity in the week of June 5. The guests at Adat Shalom

rejoiced for the bride and groom, for their future and for Jews everywhere—most especially for those in Israel. A sense of relief permeated the
wedding, as it did the Jewish community of Detroit, fed by exhilaration,
pride, and victory. Perhaps no other week had produced such anxiety and
such consolidated action in this suddenly united Jewish community. It made
the Dubin-Hyams wedding seem like a national celebration.

Hostilities removed any doubts about what "Israel is not alone" might
mean and kindled immediate action as Detroit's premier fund-raisers began
their work. By June 9, William Avrunin, executive director of Federation,
and Hy Safran reported pledges being paid with extraordinary speed, accompanied by extra donations for the emergency fund.[370] All synagogue
services in Detroit on June 10 were devoted to fund-raising. Phillip Stollman,
in charge of the Israel Bond drive, increased the goal to two million dollars. Page after page of the *Jewish News* of June 9 demanded financial
support: "Give As You Never Gave Before"; "Help in Israel Is Needed Now!"
"You *Must* Help the People of Israel!" An Israel Emergency Dinner was
scheduled for Cobo Hall and included speeches by Slomovitz and Israeli
ambassador Arieh Eshel. Luncheons and concerts, at which such local groups
as Dan Frohman's Chorus and Mrs. Emma Schaver performed, proliferated. Headed by Mrs. Schaver, the Women's Division of Federation called
out "To All Jewish Women of Detroit! Support Israel In Her Gravest Crisis!"[371]

Under Chairman Paul Zuckerman, the Israel Emergency Fund reached
$4,700,000 within two weeks, finally totaling $5,760,000. This astonishing
sum came on the heels of Detroit's most successful campaign, headed by
Al Deutsch, which had netted $5,627,136.[372] After Fisher had returned from
the cabinet meeting prior to the war, Zuckerman had chartered an airplane
and traveled to hundreds of communities. (Zuckerman, a longtime member of the ZOA, was Detroit's "diamond in the rough" in Jewish leadership;
he was active in Federation and served as director of the Joint Distribution
Committee, as well as in numerous Michigan and Detroit institutions.) He
then mobilized ten American Jews to give one million dollars each.[373] As
he prepared to leave for Israel one week after the war, Max Fisher addressed
by telephone a meeting of volunteers convened by his friend Zuckerman.
He was joined by Esther (Mrs. Harry L.) Jones, the national UJA Women's
Division chair. Both congratulated the workers, noting the unprecedented
outpouring of time and money and energetic activities. Zuckerman emotionally declared that they had been "partners . . . in protecting our flesh
and blood."[374]

Recognizing the significance of the city, Golda Meir visited Detroit and
addressed the community on June 17. Despite her call to the Labor Zionists to lead the rebuilding efforts, Mrs. Meir joined Fisher and Zuckerman at services held at Temple Israel. With them were Rabbis Fram, Syme,
and Hertz and Cantor Harold Ohrbach.[375] Despite her deep roots in the
Histadrut-Labor Zionist movement, Mrs. Meir seemed to acknowledge that

it would be a different sort of American Jew to whom Israel would turn in times of crisis and for future support. The enormously successful collective efforts of Zuckerman and Fisher and their friends in and out of Detroit clearly demonstrated their importance and good will.

By June 10, the Six-Day War ended. Israel had performed what struck the world as a heroic miracle: recapturing the Sinai, taking the West Bank of Jerusalem and the Old City, and smashing Arab forces on all fronts. Fisher—who, along with Zuckerman and others, had virtually locked the doors on wealthy businessmen in Detroit and refused to let them out until they contributed large sums to the war effort—believed that the Six-Day War "created the idea that the Jewish state could take on the world and still win. It gave every Jew enormous pride."

Israel's Six-Day War galvanized Jews all over the world. Detroit's Jews put aside their differences and turned to aid the state with extraordinary unity. Every organization, every club, every *landsmanshaft*, agency, women's group, youth group, and congregation—Orthodox, Conservative, Reform, secular—abandoned all their disagreements and pulled together to rescue Israel. At gatherings, men and women wept openly; people donated money out of a genuine spirit of emergency that permeated every meeting. Detroit Jewry became the Detroit Jewish community.

Activities on behalf of Israel did not stop on June 10, 1967. At a near-frenetic pace, the Jews of Detroit continued to collect money, lobby, and volunteer to assist in numerous ways, including by flying to Israel to provide physical or other on-site labor. But in Detroit that summer, the city began to swelter. In sharp contrast to the animated efforts of the Jews, a lethargy settled over the metropolitan area—the "Model City" of the 1960s. With its young Kennedyesque mayor, Jerome P. Cavanagh, Detroit seemed to be in the vanguard of the Johnson administration's War on Poverty. At his second innaugural address, Cavanagh called Detroit "the City of Promise" as he hoped to bring the fruits of federal funding and thoughtful, imaginative planning to alleviate the obvious poverty and the less obvious racial tensions.[376]

Michigan led the country in civil-rights legislation. At the Michigan Constitutional Convention of 1961–1962, four Detroit Jews had been elected to represent their districts and played key roles in the drafting of the Michigan constitution of 1963. Melvin Nord, a Detroit attorney, served as vice-chair of the Committee on Legislative Organization; Jack Faxon actively participated in the Committee on Education; Samuel Ostrow, assistant attorney general of Michigan and long the mentor of Gov. G. Mennen Williams, served on the Committee on the Judicial Branch; and Harold Norris, another Detroit attorney, was vice-chair of the Committee on the Declaration of Rights, Suffrage, and Elections. Along with Richard Austin, the first black certified public accountant in Michigan who ran on an interracial ticket with Faxon, Norris, and Nord, they were intimately involved

in drafting and securing the passage of Article 5, Section 29, which created
the Michigan Civil Rights Commission—the only constitutionally established civil rights commission in the United States.[377]

According to Detroit congressman John Conyers, Jr., Norris became "a
principal architect of the bill of rights provisions" of the Michigan constitution; Governor Williams commented that Ostrow had similarly influenced Michigan legislation.[378] Norris authored the provisions that prohibited racial and religious discrimination, created rights of appeal in criminal
cases and of freedom of expression and, along with other sections, created
the "right to fair and just treatment in legislative and executive investigations and hearings" (Article I, Sec. 20). With such a document, Michigan's constitution, according to some students of constitutional law, assured the protection of civil rights and liberties better than the U.S.
Constitution.[379] Theoretically, then, Detroit's claim to the title of "model
city" rested on solid legislative ground. While other urban centers ner-
vously awaited violent outbursts, Detroit assumed a more complacent, confident air—at least as seen from outside.

Tensions within, however, grew more intense, beyond the realm of theory or of legal documents or the guarantees of civil liberties from Lansing.
On the streets of Detroit's black ghettos, face-to-face encounters between
white policemen and black young people who seemed to be more militant
each day threatened to erupt into major conflict. In the summer of 1966,
a disturbance on Kercheval, on the far East Side, had created a potentially
explosive situation as a group of black youths confronted policemen who
ordered them to disperse. Rocks and bricks were thrown, but Cavanagh
and his chief of police, Ray Girardin, called upon antipoverty and community relations groups to come to their assistance. They adopted a policy
of showing force—hundreds of policemen appeared—but avoiding mass
arrests and the use of force. This approach to the "Kercheval Incident"
proved successful and became the model for handling urban disturbances
not only in Detroit but across the country.[380]

A year later, in mid-July, a car accident on Twelfth Street revealed the
depth of tensions and anger among black Detroiters as they filled the streets
at the appearance of white policemen.[381] With antagonism between the police and the black residents of the Twelfth Street neighborhood already
heightened, militant Black Power spokesmen fueled the fires of rhetoric.
They would erupt into real fires within days.

Congregants of Shaarey Zedek had nostalgically watched as their old
synagogue on Congress and St. Antoine fell beneath a wrecker's ball on
September 20, 1930.[382] Several reflected on the double loss as they departed from Willis and Brush in May of that same year. From that time
until January 1932, when they occupied their new spiritual home on Chicago Boulevard, they conducted services in an auditorium upstairs from a
Detroit Edison substation on Twelfth Street and Clairmont. On June 27, 463

1931, Joseph Fauman's bar mitzvah was the last to be celebrated in the makeshift synagogue. By 1967, it had become a "blind pig," an illegal distillery of homemade liquor.

Blind pigs, almost exclusively black-owned and patronized, sometimes served as brothels, drug-dealing dens, or as venues for other unsavory practices. The police constantly harrassed them by trying to gain entrance as customers—a tactic not unlike the speakeasy busts of the 1920s. Around 3:00 A.M. on July 23, 1967, such a police action began in the former temporary synagogue that had been converted into a blind pig. Surprisingly, crowds gathered, a fire started, police arrived in numbers, and the orders were given to follow the procedures of the Kercheval Incident.[383]

By the following day a full-scale riot had swept over Detroit. It stunned the local and state administrations, the residents of the neighborhood, the police, the National Guard, and the white property and business owners of the neighborhood. None of those owners lived in the all-black neighborhood. But some 15 percent were Jews—a number that became inflated by popular beliefs and stereotypes. Many, but not all, of the seventy-eight Jewish-owned stores were looted. More than 27 percent of the black-owned stores suffered damage that week. More than twenty-five hundred stores were looted, burned or destroyed, including 611 supermarkets, food, and grocery stores; 537 cleaners and laundries; 326 clothing, department, and fur stores; 285 liquor stores, bars and lounges; 240 drugstores; and 198 furniture stores, along with all pawn-shops in the area (some owned by European-Jewish survivors of the Holocaust).[384] By July 25, the looting and violence had reached Seven Mile and Livernois and to the far East Side. The city mobilized sixteen hundred Detroit policemen; the governor heeded the call and sent 9,760 National Guardsmen; and the federal government sent a five-thousand-man airborne task force. Detroit looked like a war-torn city, complete with occupation troops and burning buildings that gave the appearance of having been bombed.

One historian has written that "it was Hastings Street 24 years later, Hastings Street a generation advanced in sophistication, education, and economic standing," referring to the riots of 1943 that had caused the final evacuation of Jewish businesses from that neighborhood.[385] According to an Anti-Defamation League study, there was "no real pattern of damage to Jews as Jews."[386] Yet Jewish businesses like George Victor's George V Drug Store on Dexter and Richton and Sam Lipson's Variety Store on Twelfth Street were looted and burned. Victor's black employees had hung a sign in the window saying "Soul Brother" in an attempt to divert the rioters, and pharmacist Selma Friedman insisted that hoodlums from outside the neighborhood had looted the store. Lipson—who, ironically, had long attempted to form a biracial merchants' association—lost everything and decided not to return to the neighborhood. Destroyed, too, were Robinson's Furniture on Linwood and Oakman, Gorman's Furniture at Livernois

464

and Midland, Eaton Drugs at Eaton and Livernois, and luxury stores on the Livernois–Seven Mile "Avenue of Fashion." Among those exclusive stores were Block's, Siegel's, Whalings, and Ceresnie and Offen furriers (co-owned by Sam Offen, who had come to Detroit not long after his experiences in the Holocaust). Institutions like the Jewish Home for the Aged, Congregation Beth Abraham, and the Jewish National Fund offices were untouched.[387]

Fires were frequently set to destroy credit records, especially in furniture stores and pawn shops.[388] Beyond that, the looting and destruction appeared to be random. Dr. Norman Drachler, superintendent of Detroit Public Schools, recalled the scene as he responded to Mayor Cavanagh's urgent summons to meet with him and Governor Romney on the morning of July 25: "The looting and fires were not only in areas where Jews owned property or operated businesses. I saw looting downtown . . . military men surrounded J. L. Hudson's department store to prevent looting or fires." Official reports concluded that "the looting and destruction of property was not aimed at Jewish businesses." Yet anti-Semitic epithets appeared and were heard, and some press reports argued that Jewish merchants had been singled out.[389] Deluged with telephone calls from people seeking help, Slomovitz reported that the *Jewish News* received one call which said only "Heil Hitler."

Drachler had been called in to discuss the summer schools. Cavanagh wanted reassurance that the schools would remain open for the children and that some would be available for housing incoming National Guard troops. "Summer school attendance nearly doubled," Drachler noted. "Black and white parents felt that school was the safest place for their children."

A product of Jewish secular education and politics, Drachler had inherited from his father, Israel, a commitment to education. In 1957–1958 he had been appointed director of research for the Citizen's Advisory Committee on School Needs, and from 1965 he had served as superintendent of schools. His liberal, secular Jewish background contributed to a radical revision of the Detroit school system—a revision that had reinforced the optimism for Detroit's future as he attempted to attack educational problems at their socioeconomic roots. Now, along with the rest of the administration, he watched as the dream exploded. Like Drachler, the Jewish Community Council quickly offered its services and joined with the Metropolitan Detroit Council of Churches, the Archdiocese, and the black Interdenominational Ministerial Alliance to form the Interfaith Emergency Council (IEC). The IEC established outposts in schools, churches, and neighborhood development centers to provide refuge and counseling for victims of the riot.[390] Concomitantly, the Jewish Center, the National Council of Jewish Women, the United Hebrew Schools, and Temple Beth El served as collection centers for food for victims and, along with the Jewish Family and Children's Service, offered to provide homes for those displaced by the riot.[391]

As an armed and uneasy peace came to Detroit, the mayor and the governor on July 27, convened a meeting of Detroit's leading businessmen and appointed Joseph L. Hudson, Jr., president of J. L. Hudson Company, as chairman of the newly formed New Detroit Committee, America's first urban coalition. Within weeks, its thirty-nine member board included Henry Ford II, James Roche of General Motors, Lynn Townsend of Chrysler, and virtually every powerful businessman in Detroit, along with representatives of young black organizations, welfare recipients, and other grass-roots organizations. Max Fisher and Stanley Winkelman were among the principal players—Fisher would become chairman in 1969. Included, too, were politicians like Mel Ravitz and administrators like Norman Drachler.[392] Attempting to explain what he believed to be a central position of Jews in the New Detroit effort, Fisher later argued that, because of their heritage of persecution, Jews in Detroit carried a particular sympathy for the black minority.

New Detroit struggled with defining its goals; Cavanagh had hoped to involve big business in revitalizing the city, in bringing a renaissance to Detroit, but some critics, like Rep. John Conyers, remained skeptical about a lack of adequate representation by the poor. Yet the mayor's strategy quickly began to work as the members brought substantial funds to the project and managed to raise money from the United Fund. With some guidance from Drachler, New Detroit supported summer reading programs in the inner city; they funded black arts and theater as well as businesses. "The primary focus," said Fisher, "will be to assist the community in the solution of the problems relating to the black minority." And Winkelman echoed his friend, saying, "We're here because the white community has failed . . . [to] change attitudes and institutions."[393]

Detroit's riot added the coda to the migration of Jews from Detroit to the suburbs. More than half the Jewish businesses in the Seven Mile-Livernois area and the Twelfth Street neighborhood fled the city. Jews and non-Jews who lived in Detroit, resisting the call of the suburbs, reconsidered their situations and abandoned the city for the safer pastures of the northwest. Among those who lived in Lafayette Park, high-rise apartments overlooking the Detroit River, Sidney Lutz, Allison and Abba Friedman, and Irving Tukel ventured far beyond Southfield. The Six-Day War had stirred them and touched off deep feelings that, as Max Fisher implied of others, had awakened dormant feelings of Jewish identity. In the midst of the Detroit riot, they decided to volunteer to assist Israel however they could. Perhaps there would be more fighting, and the mobilization remained active. They were willing to participate in any form of "support work"—on a kibbutz, as field hands, or perhaps Mrs. Friedman, as a nurse, could give assistance. After the travel embargo was lifted, early on the morning of July 24, the four left Lafayette Park to catch an airplane for New York. In New York, as the banks in Detroit were closed due to the riot, they completed their banking transactions, and that evening, in a stifling hot aircraft, they left for Israel.

Each came from different Jewish backgrounds and, before the war, had held divergent views about their Jewishness. Mrs. Friedman, a non-Jew, nevertheless felt the attraction of Israel's dramatic actions; Mr. Friedman had been raised in a Shaarey Zedek household that was traditional, even religious; Irving Tukel's family had been staunch Labor Zionist–Histadrut activists; and Sidney Lutz, unlike his younger brother, had drifted from his Jewish identity and, before the war, felt little allegiance to Israel. Israel's magnetic quality drew them irrepressibly, bringing them, as it did so many others, to a new type of Jewish identity: strong, proud, and national. As they drove west on I-94 to Detroit Metropolitan Airport, anxious but exhilarated and concerned about what they would find in war-torn Israel, they could see the fires of riot-torn Detroit behind them. They would find euphoria in Israel and did indeed engage in field work; Allison Friedman lent a hand as a nurse. They found, too, at dusk one evening, among crowds of visitors to the Western Wall in Jerusalem, a group of Yemenite Jews "with eyes afire," singing joyously in a "messianic" attitude.

Detroit's war, too, ended; the fires extinguished. As the events at the wall in Jerusalem determined an intensified Jewish identity for American Jews, for the Jews of Detroit—a unified Jewish community of Detroit—the "Model City" would turn to meet the challenge of deep divisions and conflict.

Appendix A

Fred M. Butzel
Memorial Award Recipients

1951	Julian H. Krolik	1967	Tom Borman
1952	Henry Wineman		Abraham Borman
1953	William Friedman	1968	Mrs. Harry L. (Jennie) Jones
1954	Abraham Srere	1969	Paul Zuckerman
1955	Mrs. Joseph H. (Dora) Ehrlich	1970	Hyman Safran
		1971	Louis Berry
1956	Samuel H. Rubiner	1972	Erwin S. Simon
1957	Henry M. Butzel	1973	Mrs. H. C. (Celia) Broder
1958	Abe Kasle	1974	Alan E. Schwartz
1959	Sidney J. Allen	1975	George M. Stutz
1960	Theodore Levin	1976	Jack O. Lefton
1961	Irwin I. Cohn	1977	Mrs. Julian H. (Golda) Krolik
1962	Mrs. Henry (Gertrude) Wineman	1978	Mandell L. Berman
		1979	Stanley J. Winkelman
1963	Leonard N. Simons	1980	Phillip Stollman
1964	Max M. Fisher		Mrs. Max (Frieda) Stollman
1965	Nate S. Shapero	1981	Irwin Green
1966	Morris Garvett	1982	Philip Slomovitz

470

Appendix B

Jewish Welfare Federation Presidents and Federation Women's Division Presidents

Jewish Welfare Federation Presidents

1926–1930	Henry Wineman	1964–1969	Hyman Safran
1931–1932	Milford Stern	1969–1972	Alan E. Schwartz
1932–1937	Clarence H. Enggass	1972–1975	Mandell L. Berman
1938–1943	Abraham Srere	1975–1978	Martin E. Citrin
1944–1945	William Friedman	1978–1981	George M. Zeltzer
1946–1949	Julian H. Krolik	1981–1983	Avern L. Cohn
1950–1954	Samuel H. Rubiner	1983–1986	Joel D. Tauber
1955–1958	Theodore Levin	1986–1989	Conrad L. Giles, M.D.
1959–1963	Max M. Fisher	1989–	Mark E. Schlussel

Women's Division Presidents

1946–1947	Dora Ehrlich	1970–1972	Frieda Stollman
1947–1949	Clara Frank	1972–1974	Tillie Brandwine
1949–1951	Josephine Weiner	1974–1976	Shirley Harris
1951–1953	Bernice Hopp	1976–1978	Carolyn Greenberg

471

Women's Division Presidents

1953–1955	Jennie Jones	1978–1980	Dulcie Rosenfeld
1955–1957	Ann Daniels	1980–1982	Shelby Tauber
1957–1959	Dorothy Karbel	1982–1983	Jane Sherman
1959–1961	Helen August	1983–1985	Ellen Labes
1961–1964	Barbara Marcuse	1985–1987	Marlene Borman
1964–1966	Esther Jones	1987–1989	Sharon Hart
1966–1968	Diane Hauser	1989–1991	Doreen Hermelin
1968–1970	Edythe Jackier	1991–	Diane Klein

Appendix C

Taped Interviews

Goldie Adler, June 11, 1987
Martin Adler, January 25, 1985
William Avrunin, June 9, 1987
Sylvia Baer, June 21, 1989
Harriet Beale, June 16, 1987
Mandell Berman, March 20, 1988
Harry Blitz, August 30, 1988
Irving Bluestone, August 16, 1988
Brewster Broder, May 12, 1988
Leon Cohan, August 17, 1988
Judge Avern Cohn, January 19, 1989
Dr. Lee Cowan, October 15, 1986
Francis Driker, May 31, 1988
Helen Dushkin, May 25, 1988
Walter Field, December 15, 1987
Margot Fleischaker, June 21 and 28, 1989
Naomi Floch, May 4, 1987
Ethel Frank, February 27, 1989
Charles Gehringer, November 8, 1987
Max and Alice Goldsmith, February 18, 1989

Appendix C   Rabbi Benjamin Gorrelik, April 12, 1989
Rabbi Chaskel Grubner, June 21, 1989
Rabbi Richard Hertz, May 18, 1989
Margaret Kaichen, October 21, 1988
Pauline Jackson, March 15, 1987
Ruth Weintraub Kent, May 2, 1982
Mary Koretz, December 25, 1986
Rabbi Leizer Levin, February 2, 1989
Ed Levy, Jr., July 10, 1987 (interview by Stanley Moretsky)
Leo Liffman, March 21, 1985
Isador Lipsitz, May 10, 1986 (interview by Dr. Saul Sugar)
Dr. Sidney Lutz, April 27, 1988
Milton Marwil, February 3, 1989
Evelyn Noveck, May 12, 1988; May 19, 1988
Samuel Novetsky, August 10, 1988
Abraham Pasternak, April 5, 1983; December 14, 1988
Irving Pokempner, March 25, 1987
Alexander Roberg, February 2, 1989
Jay Rosenthal, June 16, 1987
Nathan Roth, June 25, 1983
Edith Roth, June 28, 1983
Solomon Rothenburg, November 21, 1987
Emma and Saul Schiefman, December 25, 1986
Bernice Schiller, May 2, 1987
Zelda Selmar, June 16, 1987
Irwin Shaw, June 17, 1987
Edwin Shifrin, May 8, 1987
Leonard N. Simons, September 10, 1987, and January 21, 1988
Paul Sislin, March 24, 1988
Judith Slobin, May 4, 1987
Norval Slobin, May 4, 1987
Philip Slomovitz, December 2, 1986; December 16, 1986
Isadore Sobeloff, March 16, 1986 (interview by Sylvia Arden)
George Stutz, July 24, 1986
Jack Wayne, March 17, 1983
George M. Zeltzer, February 27, 1987; March 31, 1987
Rabbi Abraham Zentman, May 14, 1987

474

Note on Sources

Main sources for this book included materials from the Burton Collection of the Detroit Public Library, the Walter Reuther Archives of Wayne State University, the Bentley Historical Library of the University of Michigan, the library of the United Hebrew Schools and the Midrasha College of Jewish Studies, the archives of the *Detroit Jewish News,* Workmen's Circle, Jewish Community Center, Jewish Welfare Federation, Jewish Community Council, Sholem Aleichem Institute, Jewish Parents Institute, Hayim Greenberg Schools, National Council of Jewish Women, Histadrut, Temple Beth El, Congregation Shaarey Zedek, and the Michigan Jewish Historical Society as well as the archives and libraries of numerous synagogues. Also of considerable help were materials from the personal collections of Philip Slomovitz, Meyer Prentis, Dr. Jack Belen, Sylvia Baer, Chana and Michael Michlin, Abraham J. Levin, Ruth and Eiga Hershman, Jerome Silverman, Ronald Landau, Leonard Simons, George Stutz, William Avrunin, and numerous others.

Apart from standard written resources, taped oral histories were taken and used extensively. The general rule of thumb has been to use information only when confirmed by three sources (written and/or oral) and, in general, to maintain source anonymity. Interviews that were formally conducted are listed in Appendix C; those more informal conversations have not been credited except in the introductory acknowledgments.

Abbreviations:
DFP, Detroit Free Press
DJC, Detroit Jewish Chronicle
DJN   Detroit Jewish News
DN   Detroit News
MJH, Michigan Jewish History

Notes

Part I: 1914–1926

1. Eric Kocher, "Economic and Physical Growth of Detroit, 1701–1935," November 1935, Division of Economics and Statistics, Federal Housing Administration, Michigan Historical Collections, Bentley Historical Library, University of Michigan, Ann Arbor.

2. Henry L. Feingold, *A Midrash on American Jewish History* (Albany, New York: State University of New York Press, 1982), x.

3. Jacob Lestschinsky, "Jewish Migrations, 1840–1956," in L. Finkelstein, ed., *The Jews*, 3rd ed. (Philadelphia: Jewish Publication Society, 1960), 1536–96; Nathan Glazer, "New Perspectives in American Jewish Sociology," *American Jewish Year Book* 87 (1987): 3–19; Sidney Goldstein, "Jews in the U.S.: Perspectives from Deomography," *American Jewish Year Book* (1981); Sidney Goldstein and Calvin Goldscheider, *Jewish Americans* (Englewood Cliffs, N.J.: Prentice Hall, 1968).

4. Harry L. Lurie, et al., *General Summary Review of Survey of Detroit Jewish Community* (Detroit: United Jewish Charities, 1923) [page numbers obscured]; United States Department of Commerce, Bureau of Census, U.S. Census of 1910.

5. *Survey;* U.S. Department of Commerce, *Fourteenth Census of the U.S., 1920: Population* 1 (Washington, D.C.: Government Publication Office, 1921), 76–77; Kocher, "Economic and Physical Growth of Detroit, 1701–1935."

6. Detroit City Plan Commission, *Master Plan Reports: The People of Detroit* (Detroit, 1946), 5, 11–12.

7. Morton Rosenstock, "The Jews: From the Ghettos of Europe to the Suburbs of the U.S.," in Frank J. Coppa and Thomas J. Curran, eds., *The Immigrant Experience in America* (Boston: Twayne Publishers, 1976), 147–71.

8. *Survey.*

9. See also Robert Conot, *American Odyssey* (Detroit: Wayne State University Press, 1986), 177.

10. Bernard Postal and Lionel Koppman, *American Jewish Landmarks, Vol. III, The Midwest. A Travel Guide and History* (New York: Fleet Press, 1977), 120–49.

11. Robert Rockaway, *The Jews of Detroit: From the Beginning, 1762–1914* (Detroit: Wayne State University Press, 1986), 102ff.

12. Ibid.

13. Sidney M. Bolkosky, *The Distorted Image: German Jewish Perceptions of Germans and Germany, 1918–1935* (New York and Amsterdam: Elsevier, 1975).

14. Steven E. Aschheim, "The East European Jew and German Jewish Identity," *Studies in Contemporary Jewry* I (Bloomington: Indiana University Press, 1984), 3–25; Aschheim, *Brothers and Strangers: The East European Jew in German and German Jewish Consciousness, 1800–1925* (Madison: University of Wisconsin Press, 1982). See also Henry Feingold, *Zion in America* (Boston: Twayne, 1974), 142–57; Irving A. Mandel, "The Attitude of the American Jewish Community Toward East European Immigration as reflected in the Anglo-Jewish Press," *American Jewish Archives* III (June 1950), 18–20.

15. Olivier Zunz, *The Changing Face of Inequality: Urbanization, Industrial Development, and Immigrants in Detroit, 1880–1920* (Chicago: University of Chicago Press, 1982), 10, 296, passim; John Higham, *Send These to Me: Jews and Other Immigrants in Urban America* (New York: Atheneum, 1975).

16. Glazer, "New Perspectives."

17. Maurice Karpf, *Jewish Community Organization in the United States. An Outline of Types of Organizations, Activities, and Problems* (New York: Block Publishing Company, 1938), 41.

18. Henry Feingold, *A Midrash on American Jewish History* (Albany: SUNY Press, 1982), 67.

19. *Yearbook of Congregation Beth El* (1914).

20. *DFP,* January 27, 1919.

21. *DJC,* January 28, 1921.

22. Ibid., November 9, 1917.

23. Franklin letter of December 3, 1943 (Beth El Files).

24. *DFP,* June 23, 1923.

25. Beth El Files.

26. *DJC,* March 16, 1918 and February 13, 1925.

27. Ibid., April 1, 1921.

28. Some of his congregants remembered the harsher demeanor that Rabbi Franklin occasionally assumed in private. In moments of confidence, his descriptions

of East European Jews resembled those more derisive ones that he frequently condemned in public.

29. *DN,* December 25, 1910.
30. Rockaway, *The Jews of Detroit,* 102ff.
31. *DFP,* June 3, 1900.
32. Rockaway, 103; Anna W. Chapin, "Fifty Years of Organized Jewish Charity. History of the United Jewish Charities of Detroit, 1899–1949: The Story of the Jewish Welfare Federation of Detroit from 1926–1949" (Detroit, unpub. typescript, 1949), 4–9; Minutes of the United Jewish Charities, November 21, 1899.
33. Charter of the United Jewish Charities, November 21, 1899.
34. Allen A. Warsen, "The United Jewish Charities: A Pioneer in the Field of Organized Philanthropy," (Detroit, JWF File, UJC History, 1949) [no page numbers].
35. Ibid.; *DJC,* March 13, 1916.
36. Warsen, "The United Jewish Charities."
37. Charter of the UJC; Rabbi Leo M. Franklin, "Report of the United Jewish Charities," in *The 22nd Annual Report of the Board of Trustees of the Detroit Association of Charities,* (1901), 19–20.
38. Michael Avi-Youah and Zvi Baras, eds., *World History of the Jewish People* 3 (Jerusalem: Massud Publishing Co., 1977), chap. 3.
39. Ibid.
40. *Inventory of the Church and Synagogue Archives of Michigan,* Michigan Synagogue Conference, 1940.
41. *B'nai David Yearbooks.*
42. Interviews with congregants.
43. *History of Congregation B'nai Moshe,* B'nai Moshe Files.
44. Beth Abraham Synagogue Files.
45. *DN,* March 27, 1926; Eli Grad and Bette Roth, *Congregation Shaarey Zedek, 5622–5742—1861–1981* (Southfield: Congregation Shaarey Zedek, 1982), 33.
46. *Inventory of the Church and Synagogue Archives of Michigan.*
47. Ibid.
48. Ibid.
49. Reinhold Niebuhr quoted in Sidney Fine, *Frank Murphy: The Detroit Years* (Ann Arbor: University of Michigan Press, 1975), 100.
50. See, for example, the works of Irving Howe, *World of Our Fathers* (New York: Simon and Schuster, 1976) and *How We Lived: A Documentary History of Immigrant Jews in America, 1880–1930* (New York: Richard Marek Publishers, 1979).
51. *Twenty-five Years of Service: The United Hebrew Schools, 1919–1944,* pamphlet (Detroit: Jewish Welfare Federation, 1944).
52. Ibid.
53. Morris Noble, ed., *Sefer Bernard Isaacs* (New York: 1977), 82–98.
54. Ben Rosen, "Survey of the United Hebrew Schools of Detroit," (Detroit: Jewish Welfare Federation, 1930).
55. *Twenty-five Years of Service.*
56. Bernard Isaacs, *Selected Stories,* tr. by Shoshana Perla (Bat-Yam, Israel: E. Lewin-Epstein, Ltd., 1968).

57. *Twenty-five Years of Service.*

58. *DJC,* February 8, 1921.

59. *The Jewish Community Blue Book of Detroit, 1923* (Detroit: Jewish Chronicle Publishing Company, Inc., 1923), "United Hebrew Schools" and "Amalgamated Hebrew Schools."

60. *Twenty-five Years of Service.*

61. Ibid.

62. *Who's Who in Detroit, 1938* (Detroit: 1938).

63. *DJN,* April 24, 1942; *DJC,* September 15, 1916; *Detroit Jewish Society Book* (Detroit: Detroit Jewish Society Book, 1916), 285.

64. *Detroit Jewish Society Book,* 294, 297.

65. *DN,* September 13, 1896.

66. *DFP,* May 31, 1903.

67. *DJC,* September 1, 1916.

68. Karpf, 41.

69. Philip Slomovitz, "Purely Commentary," *DJN,* August 15, 1986.

70. Samuel Goldsmith, "Jewish Social Work," *Social Work Year Book, 1929* (New York: Russel Sage Foundation, 1930), 229–32.

71. Chapin, 10.

72. Henry L. Feingold, *Zion in America. The Jewish Experience from Colonial Times to the Present* (New York: Twayne Publishers, Inc., 1974), 125–6.

73. Karpf, op. cit.

74. Minutes of the UJC, February 12, 1918, March 6, 1918, March 13, 1918.

75. Chapin, 27ff.

76. Feingold, *Zion in America,* 150; Rockaway, "Ethnic Conflict in an Urban Environment: The German & Russian Jew in Detroit 1881–1914," *American Jewish Historical Quarterly* 60 (December 1970), 183–50.

77. Rockaway, "Ethnic Conflict."

78. Zunz, 10; Jonathon Schwartz, "Henry Ford's Melting Pot," in *Ethnic Groups in the City,* Otto Feinstein, ed., (New York: Heath Books, 1971), 191–98; see also Higham, *Send These to Me.*

79. Zunz, 309–17; Schwartz, "Henry Ford's Melting Pot."

80. Zunz, 317–18.

81. Conot, 204–205, 220; Zunz, 324.

82. *Detroit Jewish Society book; Survey; Directory of Jewish Clubs and Societies* (Detroit: 1934).

83. *Survey.*

84. Minutes of the UJC, 1917–1921; see, for example, minutes of June 5, 1918, where discussion occurs regarding particular cases of desertion by husbands and the directors agree that "in such cases, the wife and children are to be assisted."

85. Mark Zborowski and Elizabeth Herzog, *Life is with People: The Culture of the Shtetl* (New York: Schocken Books, 1952), 203ff; Michael R. Weisser, *A Brotherhood of Memory: Jewish Landsmanshaftn in the New World* (New York: Basic Books, Inc., 1985), 13–14. For German Jewish communal organizations, see American Joint Distribution Committee, ed., *The Structure of Jewish Emergency Relief in Germany* (Paris: 1936); *Handbuch der juedischen Gemeindverwaltung* (Berlin: Deutsche-Israelitischer Gemeindebund, 1925);

Das deutsche Juden: Seine Parteien und Organisationen (Berlin: Verlag der neuen juedischen Monatshefte, 1919).

86. Minutes, UJC, 1923; *Survey.*
87. Numbers of applicants for aid grew from under 500 in 1917 to more than 1,200 by September 1922. Minutes of the UJC, 1917–1921.
88. Mark Wischnitzer, *To Dwell in Safety: The Story of Jewish Migration Since 1900* (Philadelphia: Jewish Publication Society, 1948), 121.
89. Feingold, *Zion in America,* 127; *Survey.*
90. Robert Rockaway, "The Industrial Removal Office in Detroit," *Detroit in Perspective* 6 (Spring 1982), 40–49.
91. Ibid.; Rockaway, "Ethnic Conflict."
92. Rockaway, "Ethnic Conflict."
93. *DJC,* September 1, 1916.
94. *Detroit Sunday News Tribune,* September 13, 1896.
95. Phillip Applebaum, "A Tour of Jewish Detroit," *Tour Number 2 of Field Trip Series* (Detroit: Southeast Michigan Regional Ethnic Heritage Studies Center, 1975); see also James Albert Miller, *The Detroit Yiddish Theatre, 1920 to 1937* (Detroit: Wayne State University Press, 1967).
96. Zunz, 158.
97. *Detroit Sunday News Tribune,* September 13, 1896.
98. Chapin, 15ff.
99. *Survey;* report on the Jewish population of Detroit, Minutes of the UJC, December 12, 1923; list of "Bequests and Donations of $500 and Over Given to UJC: 1901–1946."
100. Philip J. Gilbert, "The Memorable Sholem Aleicham Reception in Detroit, Michigan, May 15, 1915," *Michigan Jewish History* (July, 1977), 11–16.
101. Ibid.
102. Miller, *The Detroit Yiddish Theatre.*
103. Frances Driker, *Live and Be Well,* unpublished ms. (Detroit, 1985).
104. *Survey.*
105. Weisser, 4; see Rosaline Schwartz and Susan Milamed, eds., *A Guide to YIVO's Landsmanshaftn Archives* (New York: YIVO, 1986).
106. *Survey; Directory of Jewish Clubs and Societies.*
107. Weisser, 27; Estelle Gilson, "The World of the Landsmanshaftn," *Congress Monthly* (May/June 1986), 13–15.
108. Weisser, 14, 148–49.
109. Feingold, *Zion in America,* 105ff.
110. Judah J. Shapiro, *The Friendly Society: A History of the Workmen's Circle* (New York: Doron Media Judaica, 1970), 11–34; Maximillian Hurwitz, *A History of the Workmen's Circle: Its History, Ideals, Organization and Institutions* (New York: The Workmen's Circle, 1936), 115–20 and "The Workmen's Circle of Detroit," (typescript).
111. *Survey.*
112. Ibid.
113. Chapin, 22; private correspondence between Jacob Berkowitz and Samuel Levin, 1918: *The Philomathian,* anniversary books of the Philomathic Debating Club, files of the Michigan Jewish Historical Society.
114. The Redford Country Club became the Franklin Hills Country Club after mov-

ing to Franklin in 1927. Leonard N. Simons, "The Sixtieth Anniversary of the Birth of Franklin Hills Country Club: 1927–1987," (Detroit: Franklin Hills Country Club, 1987).

115. *Survey.*
116. "History of the Workmen's Circle in Detroit"; *DJC,* April 11, 1947; Phyllis Lederer, "A Study of Jewish Influences in Detroit (Master's Thesis, Wayne State University, 1947).
117. *Survey.*
118. Weisser, 83, 86.
119. Albert Nelson and A. N. Marquis, eds., *Book of Detroiters: A Biographical Dictionary of Leading Living Men of the City of Detroit* (Chicago: A. N. Marquis, Inc., 1914).
120. George Fuller and George Catlin, *Historic Michigan,* 3 volumes (Chicago: Lewis Publishing Co., 1939), 732; Schwartz, "Henry Ford's Melting Pot"; Zunz, 286.
121. *DJC,* September 8, 1916, September 15, 1916, October 6, 1916.
122. Feingold, *Zion in America,* 211.
123. Program and ad book from the Forty-third Annual Banquet of the Odessa Progressive Aid Society, June 5, 1955; program of the Jewish Women European Welfare Organization Fiftieth Golden Jubilee and Annual Donor Luncheon, May 6, 1970; Harry Schneiderman, "Jewish War Relief Work," *American Jewish Year Book* (1917–1918), 194–226; Joseph Schwartz and Beatrice Vulcan, "Overseas Aid," in Oscar I. Janowsky, ed., *The American Jew: A Composite Portrait* (Philadelphia: 1964), 277–89.
124. Schwartz and Vulcan.
125. Irving I. Katz, "The Detroit Jewish Community's Generosity, 1900–1962," *Michigan Jewish History* (January 1972), 16–18.
126. "Summary of the War Record of American Jews," Department of Michigan Jewish War Veterans.
127. Lederer, 160ff.
128. *DN,* May 12, 1924; *DJN,* August 28, 1942.
129. *DN,* May 12, 1924; May 24, 1929; *DJN,* December 26, 1958.
130. *DN,* May 12, 1924.
131. *DJN,* December 26, 1958.
132. Philip Slomovitz, "Dave Brown—One of the Giants of Our Time," *DJN,* January 2, 1959.
133. Ibid.
134. *DFP,* May 24, 1929; *DN,* May 24, 1929.
135. W. Hawkins Ferry, *The Buildings of Detroit: A History* (Detroit: Wayne State University Press, 1968), 240ff; Mira Wilkins and Frank Ernest Hill, *American Business Abroad: Ford on Six Continents* (Detroit: Wayne State University Press, 1964), 208–25.
136. Malcom W. Bingay, *Detroit Is My Home Town* (New York: Bobbs Merrill, Co., 1946), 303ff; Irving I. Katz, *The Beth El Story* (Detroit: Wayne State University Press, 1955), 99, 106.
137. *Who's Who in Detroit* (1936).
138. See Rockaway, *The Jews of Detroit,* 40–42; Eli Grad and Bette Roth, *Congregation Shaarey Zedek.*

139. Grad and Roth, *Congregation Shaarey Zedek,* 40–47.

140. Shaarey Zedek Constitution (1905).

141. Shaarey Zedek By-Laws.

142. See Marshall Sklare, *Conservative Judaism: An American Religious Movement* (New York: Schocken Books, 1972); Moshe Davis, *The Emergence of Conservative Judaism* (Philadelphia: JPS, 1965); Herbert Rosenblum, *Conservative Judaism: A Contemporary History* (New York: United Synagogue of America, 1983).

143. *DJC,* September 15, 1922.

144. Shaarey Zedek Archives.

145. Minutes of the UJC, 1899–1917.

146. *DN,* August 16, 1943.

147. Ibid.; *DFP,* August 27, 1943.

148. *DJC,* August 23, 1943; *DJN,* June 25, 1943.

149. Grad and Roth, *Congregation Shaarey Zedek,* 45.

150. *Survey.*

151. Katz, *The Beth El Story.*

152. David Schwartz, "The Jewish People of Mount Clemens," undated manuscript, Midrasha Library, Southfield, Michigan; text of the address by Louis M. Davis at the dedication of Beth Tephilath Moses Synagogue, September 25, 1977.

153. Jeffrey Mandel, "Jewish Migration Patterns to Mt. Clemens—Why?" (Internal Structure of the City Urban Planning 0632, 1978).

154. Ibid.; *Detroit Free Press,* "Well, There Ain't So Many Mineral Baths in Mt. Clemens Any More, Just the One," *Detroit Magazine,* May 27, 1973.

155. Written transcript of statement by Rev. Meyer Davis, 1956.

156. Zunz, 10.

157. *Survey.*

158. *Jewish Independent,* July 28, 1916; Rockaway, "Anti-Semitism in an American City; Detroit, 1850–1914," *American Jewish Historical Quarterly,* 64 (September 1974): 42–54.

159. Rockaway, "Louis Brandeis on Detroit," *Michigan Jewish History* (July, 1977).

160. *DJC,* September 22, 1916.

161. Ibid.

162. *DJC,* September 29, 1916.

163. Albert Lee, *Henry Ford and the Jews* (New York: Stein and Day, 1980), 14.

164. *Survey.*

165. See Lee, *Henry Ford;* Conot, *American Odyssey;* and David L. Lewis, *The Public Image of Henry Ford* (Detroit: Wayne State University Press, 1976), as well as such standard biographies of Adolf Hitler as Alan Bullock, *Hitler: A Study in Tyranny* (New York: Harper and Row, 1962), for Hitler's near-adoration of Ford.

166. See below, Part II.

167. *DJC,* "Stop Sale of Ford Pamphlets at Fair," September 15, 1922.

168. Conot, 206–9; Lewis, 104–8.

169. Conot, 209ff.

170. Ibid., 228–29.

171. Franklin Lee Weinstock, "The Jewish Legion—Recollections of Harry Weinstock"; Joseph Sandweiss, "From the Diary of A Jewish Legionnaire"; Allen

A. Warsen, "Michigan Jews and the Jewish Legion," *Michigan Jewish History* (June 1968).

172. Howard M. Sachar, *A History of Israel: From the Rise of Zionism to Our Time* (New York: Alfred A. Knopf, 1979), 112–13.

173. Warsen, "Michigan Jews and the Jewish Legion."

174. "Michigan Jewish Legionnaires," *Michigan Jewish History* (January 1969).

175. Franklin File, Beth El Archives, Box 2.

176. Feingold, *A Midrash on American Jewish History*, 66–67.

177. *The Detroit Story. A History of the Detroit Chapter of the American Society for Technion Israel Institute of Technology* (Detroit Technion Society, 1989), 3.

178. Feingold, *Zion in America*, 219.

179. *DJC*, April 25, 1919.

180. *DJC*, August 1919; November 1919.

181. Ruth and Eiga Hershman, "Rabbi Abraham M. Hershman," *Michigan Jewish History* (June 1981), 16–31.

182. Louis D. Brandeis, *Brandeis on Zionism: A Collection of Addresses and Statements by Louis D. Brandeis* (Washington, D.C.: Zionist Organization of America, 1942), 28.

183. Ibid., 29.

184. *The Jewish Community Blue Book of Detroit, 1923*.

185. See Sydney Stahl Weinberg, *The World of Our Mothers* (Chapel Hill and London University of North Carolina Press, 1988), Introduction.

186. *DJC*, March 15, 1917.

187. See Nancy F. Cott, *The Grounding of Modern Feminism* (New Haven: Yale University Press, 1987); Eleanor Flexner, *Century of Struggle* (New York: Atheneum, 1968).

188. See Rockaway, *Jews of Detroit*, 100–107; Chapin, *History of UJC; The Beth El Story*.

189. *The Jewish Community Blue Book*.

190. *DFP*, 1986; *DJN*, 1976.

191. Purple Gang File, Burton Historical Collection, Detroit Public Library.

192. Albert Fried, *The Rise and Fall of the Jewish Gangster in America* (New York: Holt, 1980); see also Robert Rockaway, "Mobsters for Zion," *DJN*, June 29, 1990.

193. Purple Gang File, Burton Historical Collection.

194. *DFP*, October 8, 1939; E. G. Pipp, *Men Who Have Made Michigan* (Detroit: *Pipp's Magazine*, 1927); Clarence Burton et al., *History of Wayne County and the City of Detroit*, 5 vol. (Detroit: S. J. Clarke, 1922), 911, 993; *DN*, July 25, 1922, March 12, 1927, March 12, 1943.

195. Burton, 719, 730; *DN*, September 29, 1929; *Who's Who in American Jewry* (1938–1940); *Who's Who in Detroit* (1936).

196. *Twenty-Five Years of Service; The United Hebrew Schools, 1919–1944*, pamphlet, (Detroit: Jewish Welfare Federation, 1944).

197. Minutes of the Fresh Air Society, 1921–1923, and Venice Beach Camp-Fresh Air Society List of Contributors, files of the Jewish Welfare Federation of Detroit.

198. Harry C. Saltzstein, *Sinai Hospital and the North End Clinic* (Detroit: Wayne State University Press, 1963), 4–8, 15ff.

199. See Anna Chapin, "History of the Jewish Service Agencies," *History of the United Jewish Charities of Detroit.*

200. Ibid.

201. Louis Lipsky, *Thirty Years of American Zionism* (New York: the Nesher Publishing Co., 1927).

Part II: 1926–1936

1. Oscar I. Janowsky and Salo Baron, *The Jewish Welfare Board Survey with the Report of the JWB Survey Commission* (New York: The Dial Press, 1948).

2. Phillip Applebaum, "A Tour of Jewish Detroit," Tour Number 2 of Field Trip Series (Detroit: Southeast Michigan Regional Ethnic Heritage Studies Center, 1975).

3. See Grad and Roth, *Congregation Shaarey Zedek.*

4. *The Sephardic Community of Greater Detroit: Its Aims and Accomplishments* (Southfield: Sephardic Community, 1979).

5. Harold Silver, "Jewish Child Placement Services in Detroit, 1933–1944," *Michigan Jewish History* (November 1960), 2–14.

6. Applebaum, "A Tour of Jewish Detroit."

7. Lois Rankin, "Detroit Nationality Groups," *Michigan History Magazine* 23: 142.

8. Applebaum, "A Tour of Jewish Detroit."

9. Samuel M. Levin, *Essays on American Industrialism* (Detroit: Wayne State University Press, 1974); *DFP*, December 22, 1974.

10. Irving Howe and B. J. Widick, *The UAW and Walter Reuther* (New York: 1949), 48–50.

11. Conot, 204–5.

12. Christopher H. Johnson, *Maurice Sugar: Law, Labor and the Left in Detroit, 1912–1950* (Detroit: Wayne State University Press, 1988), 30–32, 134–35.

13. David M. Chalmers, *Hooded Americanism—The First Century of the Ku Klux Klan, 1865–1965* (Garden City, New York: Doubleday, 1965), 178ff; Peter Amann, "Vigilante Fascism: The Black Legion as an American Hybrid," *Comparative Studies in Society And History* (July 1983), 490–524.

14. Dominic J. Capeci, Jr., *Race Relations in Wartime Detroit: The Sojourner Truth Housing Controversy of 1942* (Philadelphia: Temple University Press, 1984), 5.

15. Seymour Martin Lipset and Earl Raab, *The Politics of Unreason—Right-Wing Extremism in America, 1790–1977,* 2nd ed. (Chicago and London: University of Chicago Press, 1978), 150–208. The literature on anti-Semitic movements that identified Jews as the archetypal denizens of urban and corrupt capitalist society is vast. See, for example, Norman Cohn, *Warrant for Genocide,* (New York and London: Harper and Row, 1966); George L. Mosse, *The Crisis of German Ideology* (New York: Grosset and Dunlap, 1964); Fritz Stern, *The Politics of Cultural Despair* (New York: Doubleday, 1965); George L. Mosse, *Toward the Final Solution: A History of European Racism* (Madison: University of Wisconsin Press, 1985).

16. *DJC*, January 3, 1930, and June 20, 1930.

485

17. Ibid., March 26, 1926.

18. *DJC*, December 9, 1927.

19. Neal Gabler, *An Empire of Their Own: How the Jews Invented Hollywood* (New York: Crown Publishers, Inc., 1988), 143–45.

20. Hershman, speech at Temple Beth El dedication, *DJC*, November 17, 1922.

21. See, for example, *DJC*, December 11, 1925.

22. *Inventory of Michigan Churches and Synagogues.*

23. Cantor Hyman Adler, *B'nai David Yearbook; DJC*, January 17, 1936, September 10, 1937.

24. *DJC*, July 19, 1935.

25. See, for example, *DJC*, September 10, 1930.

26. Minutes of the Council of Orthodox Rabbis.

27. *DJC*, April 5, 1935, June 17, 1938, June 5, 1939, April 19, 1940.

28. *DJC*, September 26, 1930 and March 17, 1933.

29. Records of the Young Israel.

30. *DJC*, July 19, 1935.

31. Marshall Sklare, "Aspects of Religious Worship in the Contemporary Conservative Synagogue," in Sklare, ed., *The Jews: Social Patterns of an American Group* (New York: The Free Press, 1958), 357–76.

32. Grad and Roth, *Congregation Shaarey Zedek,* 66, 77; *DJC*, June 1, 1934, September 21, 1934, and June 14, 1935.

33. *DJC*, September 19, 1934.

34. Private communication from the family of Rabbi Hershman.

35. B'nai David Archives; Sklare, "Aspects of Religious Worship in the Contemporary Conservative Synagogue."

36. Sklare, *op cit.;* see David G. Mandelbaum, *Change and Continuity in Jewish Life* (Glencoe, Ill.: Oscar Hillel Plotkin Library, 1955).

37. Nathan Glazer, "Social Characteristics of American Jews, 1654–1954," *American Jewish Year Book* (1955), 3–41; Fred L. Strodtbeck, "Family Interaction, Values and Achievement," in Sklare, ed., *The Jews,* 147–65.

38. *DJC* (each issue of February 1922).

39. See *Who's Who in Detroit* (1936–1938).

40. Lawrence H. Fuchs, "Sources of Jewish Internationalism and Liberalism," in *The Political Behavior of American Jews* (New York: The Free Press, 1956), 171–203; Werner Cohn, "The Politics of American Jews," in Sklare, ed., *The Jews,* 614–26.

41. Chapin, *History of United Jewish Charities;* Charter of the UJC.

42. UJC Yearbook, 1916–1917 (Jewish Welfare Federation File).

43. Minutes of the UJC; Chapin.

44. Chapin, op. cit.

45. *Survey.*

46. Minutes of the UJC.

47. *Survey.*

48. Ibid.

49. Karpf, 79.

50. "Federation Incorporators, Original Board and Officers," typescript (Federation files).

51. Chapin, *History of United Jewish Charities.*

52. Minutes of the UJC, May 4, 1926, and May 5, 1926.

53. Ibid.

54. Articles of Association of the Jewish Welfare Federation of Detroit, September 21, 1926.

55. Morris D. Waldman, "What Will Detroit Jewry Do?" *DJC,* September 10, 1926.

56. Philip Slomovitz, "Federation's Noteworthy Personalities Gallery," *DJN,* August 29, 1986.

57. Ibid.

58. Federation Budgetary Allotments (Federation files).

59. Slomovitz, op. cit.

60. Chapin, op. cit.

61. Articles of Association.

62. William Avrunin, "What Is Federation?—A Definition for Those Engaged in Making It Work," *Journal of Jewish Communal Service* (Spring 1981), 209–18.

63. Samuel Rubiner, address delivered at the commemoration of the 50th anniversary of the UJC (Federation files).

64. Federation Budget Allocations, 1926–1955.

65. *Fund Raising, 1925–1949* (Federation files).

66. Ibid.

67. Chapin, op. cit.; By-laws of the Detroit Service Group (Federation files).

68. Federation minutes, July 10, 1929.

69. Federation Articles of Association; Chapin, op. cit.; Fred M. Butzel, "The New Jewish Center: Symbol of Cooperative Spirit," *Federation News* (November 1933).

70. See Rockaway, *The Jews of Detroit.*

71. Chapin, op. cit.

72. Butzel, "The New Jewish Center."

73. Chapin, op. cit.

74. Butzel, "The New Jewish Center."

75. Judge Irving Lehman, letter to Meyer L. Prentis, September 27, 1929 (Papers of Meyer L. Prentis).

76. Note of January 30, 1930 (Papers of Meyer L. Prentis).

77. Prentis, letter to Al Hecht, January 24, 1931 (Papers of Meyer L. Prentis).

78. Prentis, letter to Kahn, February 27, 1931; Kahn to Prentis, March 2, 1931 (Papers of Meyer L. Prentis).

79. Federation History, 1926–1948 (typescript, author unknown, ca. 1948).

80. *Federation News,* October 1932.

81. Ibid.

82. Prentis, letter to Wineman, September 10, 1932.

83. Federation Minutes, January 5, 1933.

84. Federation Minutes, May 11, 1933; Chapin.

85. Butzel, "The New Jewish Center."

86. Ibid.

87. Federation Minutes, April 28, 1931.

88. Ibid.

89. Federation Budget Allotments, 1926–1955.

90. Federation History, 1926–1948.

487

91. Jacob Levin to Federation Executive Committee; Federation Minutes, January 7, 1931.

92. Federation Minutes, February 3, 1931.

93. *DFP,* July 28, 1931; *Detroit Evening News,* July 29, 1931.

94. *Detroit Evening News,* July 29, 1931; *DFP,* Editorial, "Pittsburgh Warns Detroit"; George Stutz, "Fifty Years of Detroit Jewish Communal Activity: A Biographical Memoir," *Michigan Jewish History* (January 1975), 5–25.

95. *DJC,* December 1, 1934; Letter from Abraham Srere to George Stutz, December 20, 1934 (Papers of George Stutz); Stutz, "Fifty Years of Detroit Communal Activity."

96. Federation Budget Allotments, 1926–1955.

97. Allen A. Warsen, "The Jewish Children's Home," *Michigan Jewish History* (January 1985), 4–5; Harold Silver, "Jewish Child Placement Services in Detroit, 1933–1944," *Michigan Jewish History* (November 1960), 2–14.

98. Ethel D. Oberbrunner, *The Jewish Child Care Situation in Detroit* (Detroit: Jewish Welfare Federation, 1928).

99. Silver, "Jewish Child Placement Services."

100. Chapin, op. cit.; see also S. D. Weinberg, *Jewish Social Services in Detroit* (in Yiddish) (Detroit: Jewish Welfare Federation, 1940).

101. Jacob Kepecs, *Report of a Study of Jewish Child Care Council of Detroit* (Detroit: Jewish Welfare Federation, 1931).

102. *Federation News* (December 1932).

103. Warsen, "The Jewish Children's Home"; *Federation News* (October 1932).

104. *Federation News* (December 1932); see also Karpf, 75–80.

105. Silver, "Jewish Child Placement."

106. Ibid.

107. *DJC,* August 24, 1927.

108. Gay Pitman Zieger, *History of the Boys Republic of Detroit* (Detroit: Boys Republic, 1988), manuscript.

109. *DJC,* August 24, 1927.

110. "Necrologies," *Michigan Jewish History* (June 1980), 29.

111. Intense arguments over and between kosher butchers regarding practices of koshering meat, pricing, and other issues persistently plagued the Jews of Detroit. Fred M. Butzel, D. W. Simons, Esser Rabinowitz, Bernard Ginsburg, and Rabbis Ashinsky and Hershman sat on a newly formed committee to adjudicate complaints and disputes about kosher butchers. See Federation Minutes, September 6, 1927; *DJC,* March 4, 11, 18, 25, 1927.

112. Dr. Shmarya Kleinman, "Autobiography" (Detroit: unpublished manuscript).

113. Stephen Thernstrom, ed., *Harvard Encyclopedia of American Ethnic Groups* (Cambridge, Mass.: Belknap Press, 1980).

114. Morton Rosenstock, "The Jews: From the Ghettos of Europe to the Suburbs of the United States," in Frank J. Coppa and Thomas J. Curran, eds., *The Immigrant Experience in America* (Boston: Twayne Publishers 1976), 147–71.

115. Thernstrom, *Harvard Encyclopedia of American Ethnic Groups.*

116. Ibid.

117. "Jewish Population in the U.S., 1986" (*American Jewish Year Book* [1987]), puts Detroit's Jewish population in 1936 at 94,000; Henry J. Meyer ("The

Economic Structure of the Jewish Community in Detroit," *Jewish Social Studies* [April 1940], 3–24), states that the Jews in Detroit in 1935 numbered 82,080.
118. *Survey.*
119. Meyer, "The Economic Structure of the Jewish Community in Detroit."
120. S. Joseph Fauman, "Occupational Selection Among Detroit Jews," *Jewish Social Studies,* vol. 14, no. 1 (1952): 17–50; "Jews in America," *Fortune Magazine,* (New York 1936); Fauman, "The Jews in the Waste Industry in Detroit," *Jewish Social Studies,* vol. 3, no. 1 (1941): 41–56; Stanley Feldstein, *The Land That I Show You* (Garden City, N.Y.: Anchor Press, 1978), 141.
121. Meyer, "The Economic Structure of the Jewish Community in Detroit."
122. Ibid.
123. For an intriguing treatment of this subject, see Leo Litwak, *Waiting for the News* (Garden City, N.Y.: Doubleday, Inc., 1969).
124. Feldstein, loc. cit.
125. *DFP,* November 28, 1954.
126. Lederer, *A Study of Jewish Influences in Detroit.*
127. *Teamster's Local 337 News* (November 1972), 1–5.
128. *DFP,* February 14, 1971.
129. Ibid; Litwak, *Waiting for the News.*
130. *Teamster's Local 337 News* (November 1972).
131. *Teamster's Local 337 News* (December 1972), 1, 4.
132. *DFP,* February 14, 1971.
133. Meyer, "The Economic Structure of the Jewish Community in Detroit."
134. Benjamin M. Laikin, *Memoirs of a Practical Dreamer: From A Russian Shtetl to an American Suburb,* trans. from the Yiddish by Murray Kass and Moshe Starkman (New York: Bloch Publishing Co., 1971), 180.
135. Meyer, op. cit.
136. Conot, *American Odyssey,* 268.
137. Ibid., 283.
138. Ibid.
139. Banking and Currency Committee, U.S. Senate, *Hearings, Practices of Stock Exchanges: Banking Operations and Practices* (Washington, D.C.: 1934), 4545–75.
140. Stutz, "Fifty Years of Detroit Jewish Communal Activity"; *DJN,* May 3, 1974.
141. Federation Minutes, January 7 and February 3, 1931.
142. Ibid.
143. *DJC,* April 3, 1931.
144. Federation Minutes, January 7 and February 3, 1931.
145. Federation Minutes (Executive Committee), February 10, 1931.
146. Federation Minutes, June 30, 1931.
147. Federation Minutes, September 4, 1931.
148. "But for the Grace of God," *Federation News* (January 1933); *Federation News* (February 1933).
149. Federation Minutes, September 4, 1931.
150. Federation Minutes, September 24 and November 12, 1931.
151. *DJC,* November 26, 1931.
152. *Allied Jewish Campaign Results, 1926–Present [1986]* (Federation files).
153. *Federation News* (March 1932).

154. Brown letter to Prentis, April 25, 1930 (Papers of Meyer Prentis).
155. *Federation News* (September 1932).
156. Ibid.
157. *Federation History, 1926–1948; Federation News* (January 1933).
158. *Federation News* (February 1933).
159. Ibid. (December 1932).
160. Ibid. (February 1933).
161. Federation Minutes, March 19 and April 4, 1933.
162. Federation Minutes, December 28, 1933.
163. Ibid., January 29, 1934.
164. *Detroit Allied Jewish Campaign Budget Allotments, 1926–1929* (Federation files).
165. Fauman, "Occupational Selection among Detroit Jews."
166. Workmen's Circle–Sholem Aleichem Institute, Joint Committee on Principles, Philosophy, Objectives and Curricula, *Preliminary Statement* (undated, Sholem Aleichem Institute files).
167. Jay Rosenshine, "History of the Sholem Aleichem Institute of Detroit, 1926–1971," *Michigan Jewish History* (June 1974), 9–20.
168. Ibid.
169. Isaac Finkelstein, "Why We Chose Sholem Aleichem for Our Name," *Emphasis* (October 1965). (Publication of the Sholem Aleichem Institute.)
170. Rosenshine, "History of the Sholem Aleichem Institute"; *Directory of Jewish Clubs and Societies* (1934).
171. Irving Panush, "Jewish Secularism," *Sholem Aleichem News* (December 1958).
172. Finkelstein, op. cit.
173. Jay Rosenshine, "Forty Years for Sholem Aleichem Institute," *Emphasis* (November 1965).
174. Rosenshine, "History of the Sholem Aleichem Institute."
175. Ibid.
176. Rosenshine, "History," *Emphasis* (October 1968), 10–12.
177. Ibid.
178. Ibid.
179. Moshe Haar, "Ida Kamaroff—The Mother-Eagle," *Emphasis* (October 1965).
180. *Yiddish Lehnenkreise in Detroit,* unpublished manuscript.
181. Irving Kroll, "The Hersh Leckert Schule," manuscript (1989).
182. Herman Levine and Benjamin Miller, *The American Jewish Farmer in Changing Times* (New York: Jewish Agricultural Society, Inc., 1966), 77–78.
183. Gabriel Davidson, *Our Jewish Farmers and the Story of the Jewish Agricultural Society* (New York: L. B. Fischer, 1943), 155–56, 161.
184. *DJC,* June 25, 1935.
185. Sarah K. Stein, "Halevy Singing Society, The Dan Frohman Chorus," *Michigan Jewish History* (November 1962).
186. Harry Weinberg, "Weinberg's Yiddish Radio Hour," *Michigan Jewish History* (November 1966), 6–9.
187. Ibid.
188. Ibid.
189. *DJC,* September 8, 1939.
190. Ibid., November 6, 1936.

191. Ibid., April 17, 1925, September 4, 1931, November 8, 1935.
192. Records of Yeshivah Beth Yehudah.
193. "Jewish Education Month," Slomonitz Files.
194. Ibid.
195. *DJC*, November 21, 1930.
196. Ibid., October 19, 1934.
197. Finkelstein, "Why We Chose Sholem Aleichem"; Moshe Haar, "The Meaning of Secularism," *Sholem Aleichem News* (April 1962), 6–7; Jay Rosenshine, "Secularism and Jewish Living," *Sholem Aleichem News* (December 1958), 2.
198. Finkelstein, op. cit.
199. Rosenshine, "Secularism and Jewish Living."
200. *DJC*, November 26, 1931.
201. Meyer, "The Economic Structure of the Jewish Community in Detroit."
202. See *Year Book, 1937* (Detroit: Jewish Welfare Federation, 1937).
203. William Avrunin, address delivered at annual dinner, 1986.
204. See Hank Greenberg, *Hank Greenberg, The Story of My Life,* Ira Berkow, ed., (New York: Times Books, 1989).
205. Ibid., 57–58, 60ff; *DFP*, September 10, 1934.
206. Greenberg, op. cit.
207. Howard M. Sachar, *A History of Israel* (New York: Alfred A. Knopf, 1978), 173–74; Naomi W. Cohen, *The Year After the Riots* (Detroit: Wayne State University Press, 1988), 11.
208. Cohen, *The Year After the Riots,* 15.
209. *DJC*, August 30, 1929.
210. Ibid.; see also Cohen, 63–65.
211. Cohen, 53.
212. Clara Clemens, *My Husband Gabrilowitsch;* see also *DJC,* September 17, 1930, October 10, 1930, April 7, 1933.
213. Beth El Archives.
214. *DJC*, July 15, 1929.
215. Ibid.
216. *DJC,*, December 13, 1929.
217. Samuel Kurland, *Cooperative Palestine: The Story of Histadrut* (New York: Sharon Books, 1947), xi–xv.
218. Ibid., xiv.
219. Ibid., 265–66.
220. Ibid., 172.
221. Merwin Grosberg, "Charles Grosberg: Super Market Pioneer," *Michigan Jewish History* (January–June 1985), 6–9.
222. Lederer, op. cit.
223. David L. Lewis, *The Public Image of Henry Ford*, 145–48.
224. *DFP*, May 24, 1929.
225. Lewis, 148.
226. Ibid., 148–49.
227. Ibid.
228. Albert Lee, *Henry Ford and the Jews*, 94–95; Sander Diamond, *The Nazi Movement in the United States, 1924–1941* (Ithaca: Cornell University Press, 1974), 155ff.

Notes to
Part III

229. *DJC,* June 18, 25, July 9, 16, 23, August 13, 1926.
230. Slomovitz Files, *Detroit Jewish News* archives.
231. Letter to Slomovitz, July 22, 1934, and correspondence following, in Slomovitz Files.
232. Amann, "Vigilante Fascism."
233. Slomovitz Files.
234. Amann, "Vigilante Fascism."
235. Leo Paul Ribufo, *Protestants on the Right: William Dudley Palley, Gerald B. Winrod, and Gerald L. K. Smith,* 2 vols. (Ph.D. dissertation, Yale University, (1976), vol. 2, 689–720.
236. Ibid.
237. *Abend Post,* August 1934.
238. Letter from Slomovitz to editor of the *Abend Post,* August 29, 1934 (Slomovitz Files).
239. Transcript of talk delivered by Louis Zahn to the Friends of New Germany meeting at Carpathia Hall, Detroit, October 18, 1934 (Slomovitz Files).
240. *DJC,* March 31, 1933.
241. Slomovitz Files.
242. Federation Minutes, December 27, 1933.
243. Herb Magidson, Jewish Labor Committee public relations release, July 1984, see also David Kranzler, "The Role in Relief and Rescue During the Holocaust by The Jewish Labor Committee," internal document of Jewish Labor Committee, undated; Statement Submitted by the Jewish Labor Committee to the President's Commission on the Holocaust, August 1979.
244. Shmarya Kleinman, "Autobiography."
245. Federation Minutes, December 4, 1935.
246. Federation Minutes, October 29, 1934.
247. Federation Minutes, March 20, 1936.
248. For comparable German Jewish reactions see Jacob Marcus, *The Rise and Destiny of the German Jew* (Cincinnati: The Union of American Hebrew Congregations, 1934), and Sidney Bolkosky, *The Distorted Image: German Jewish Perceptions of Germans and Germany, 1918–1935.*
249. For American and American Jewish denial during the Holocaust, see Deborah Lipstadt, *Beyond Belief: The American Press and the Coming of the Holocaust, 1933–1945* (New York: Free Press, 1986).

Part III: 1936–1948

1. Jewish Welfare Federation, "Services for Jewish Youth in the Twelfth Street Area," October 1941.
2. *Centralite,* Yearbook of Central High School, 1938.
3. "Services for Jewish Youth."
4. See Applebaum, "A Tour of Jewish Detroit"; and *Directory of Jewish Clubs and Societies* (1934).
5. David Kanzler, "The Role of Relief and Rescue During the Holocaust by the Jewish Labor Committee."
6. See Ribuffo, op. cit.

7. Karpf, 116.
8. Samuel Rubiner, "A Look At Tomorrow," address delivered at the fiftieth anniversary dinner of the UJC, Detroit, 1950.
9. Laikin, 220.
10. Isidore Sobeloff, Address to the Delegate Assembly, Jewish Community Council of Metropolitan Detroit, January 17, 1963.
11. Shmarya Kleinman, "Autobiography."
12. Walter Klein, "The Jewish Community Council of Metropolitan Detroit," manuscript for article published in *Michigan Jewish History* (January 1978). The manuscript was provided by Mrs. Hannah Klein Wilhelm.
13. Federation Minutes, January 17, 1935.
14. Klein, "Jewish Community Council."
15. Minutes of the Committee of Twenty-One, February 4, 1935.
16. Ibid.
17. Ibid.
18. Ibid.
19. Ibid., March 25, 1935.
20. Ibid., April 21, 1935.
21. Federation Minutes, June 11, 1935.
22. Ibid., October 31, 1935.
23. Ibid., November 27, 1935.
24. Ibid., April 25, 1936.
25. Ibid., October 13, 1936.
26. Minutes of the Committee of Twenty-One, January 3, 1937.
27. Ibid.; Klein, "Jewish Community Council."
28. Klein, "Jewish Community Council."
29. Ibid.; correspondence between Philip Slomovitz and Stephen S. Wise, president of the American Jewish Congress (Slomovitz Files).
30. Klein,; Laikin, 219 ff.
31. Klein,   .
32. Laikin, 222.
33. William I. Boxerman, "The Jewish Community Council of Detroit," *The Reconstructionist* (November 11, 1937), 11–14.
34. Ibid.
35. Johnson, *Maurice Sugar,* 153–158; Laikin, 229 ff.
36. Boxerman, op. cit.
37. Boxerman, op. cit.; Kleinman, "Autobiography."
38. Constitution of the Jewish Community Council of Detroit.
39. Klein, op. cit.
40. Boxerman, op. cit.
41. Klein, op. cit.
42. Ibid.
43. Ibid.
44. Boxerman, op. cit.
45. Ibid.
46. Isaac Franck, "The Community Council Idea," *The Jewish Social Service Quarterly* (June 1944), 191–200.
47. Ibid.

48. Ibid.
49. Minutes of the Jewish Community Council (JCC), October 12, 1937.
50. Minutes of the JCC, January 20, 1938.
51. *DJN,* December 31, 1943.
52. Ibid., June 20, 1947.
53. Jacob Rader Marcus, "Background for the History of American Jewry," in Oscar I. Janowsky, ed., *The American Jew: A Reappraisal* (Philadelphia: The Jewish Publication Society of America, 1972), 1–25.
54. Arthur Hertzberg, "The American Jew and His Religion," in Janowsky, *The American Jew,* 101–19.
55. Ibid.
56. *Yearbook of Temple Beth El,* 1931–39.
57. Ibid.
58. Files of Temple Israel.
59. Rabbi Leon Fram, "The Saga of Rabbi Leon Fram," *Michigan Jewish History* (November 1970), 23.
60. *DJN,* January 31, 1947.
61. Typed biography in Beth El Files.
62. Ibid.
63. *Beth El Bulletin,* December 23, 1945.
64. Rabbi Morris Adler's eulogy for Rabbi Glazer, Beth El Files.
65. Beth El Files, "Biography" of Rabbi Glazer.
66. Ibid.
67. *Yearbook of Congregation Beth El 1944–45*; Katz, *The Beth El Story,* 123.
68. Katz, 120, 126.
69. Grad and Roth, 51–52.
70. Ibid., 70.
71. Ibid., 72.
72. *Social Justice,* August 1, 1938, 3.
73. Leslie Tentler, *Seasons of Grace: A History of the Catholic Archdiocese of Detroit* (Detroit: Wayne State University Press, 1990), 322.
74. *Father Coughlin's Radio Sermons Complete,* October 1930–April 1931 (Baltimore: Know and Leary, 1931).
75. Leslie Tentler, *Seasons of Grace,* 323.
76. Ibid., 325–28.
77. Alan Brinkley, *Voices of Protest: Huey Long, Father Coughlin and the Great Depression* (New York: Vintage, 1982), 92–93.
78. Tentler, 324.
79. *DJC,* June 25, 1937; *DN,* June 24, 1937.
80. *DN,* November 26, 1938; *DJC,* November 25, 1938.
81. *Social Justice,* August 1, 1938, 1.
82. Ibid., 5.
83. Tentler, 335.
84. *Social Justice,* August 1, 1938.
85. Tentler, 335–36.
86. Ibid., 336.
87. Ibid., 339, 340.
88. Ibid., 338–39.

89. Ibid., 332.

90. *The Hour,* No. 36 (March 16, 1940).

91. Ibid.; Amann, op. cit.

92. Flier of the National Workers' League, undated (Slomovitz Files).

93. Dominic J. Capeci, Jr., *Race Relations in Wartime Detroit,* 118, 119–20, passim.

94. Philip Slomovitz to Frank Murphy, September 12, 1939 (Slomovitz Files).

95. Flier from the Gentile American Realtors and Builders Association, undated (Slomovitz Files).

96. *Jewish Community Council of Detroit Newsletter,* November 1939; Boxerman to Slomovitz, December 3, 1939 (Slomovitz Files).

97. Letter from Catherine E. Grindley of J. L. Hudson Company to high-school counselors of the Detroit Public Schools Division of Guidance and Placement, April 17, 1942 (Slomovitz Files).

98. Harold Goodman to Slomovitz, July 18, 1938 (Slomovitz Files).

99. Written statement from Philip Silverstein, July 18, 1938 (Slomovitz Files).

100. Slomovitz to Crystal Pool, July 12 and July 15, 1938; *Jewish Community Council Newsletter,* August 18, 1938 (Slomovitz Files).

101. Ibid.

102. Isaac Franck, "Community Relations Case—Cliff Bell," Report July 29, 1942; Cliff Bell to Isaac Franck, July 30, 1942 (Slomovitz Files).

103. Simon Shetzer and William Boxerman, eds., *In Defense of Human Rights: A Symposium* (Detroit: Jewish Community Council, 1940), 1.

104. Ibid., 3, 4–5.

105. Ibid., 6.

106. Ibid., 6–8.

107. Ibid., 9.

108. Ibid., 10, 12, 13.

109. Ibid., 24.

110. Federation Minutes, January 12, 1937.

111. Federation Minutes, November 24, 1937; Harold Silver, letter to Esther Appelman, March 13, 1963 (Federation Files).

112. Capeci, 117, 118ff, 138; see, also, Ribuffo on Pelley.

113. David Lewis, 149.

114. Ibid., 150.

115. *DN,* August 6, 1938.

116. Albert Lee, 115–18.

117. *DN* and *DFP,* December 1, 1938.

118. Lewis, 151.

119. *DN,* December 5, 1938.

120. *DFP,* December 5, 1938; Lewis, 151.

121. Lewis, 151–54.

122. Postcard postmarked May 29, 1939 (Slomovitz Files).

123. Karpf, 105.

124. Silver, "Jewish Child Placement Services."

125. Chapin, op. cit.

126. Ibid.

127. Federation History, 1926–1948.

128. Chapin, op. cit.

129. Edith B. Bercovich, "Children Under Care," report on the study made by the Federation's Joint Committee on Child Care, December 2, 1940; Chapin.

130. Federation History, op. cit.

131. Ibid.

132. See David Brody, "American Jewry, the Refugees and Immigration Restriction (1932–1942), *Publication of the American Jewish Historical Society,* 45 (June 1956), 219–47.

133. Samuel Lerner, Rose Kaplan, and Margaret Weiner, "History of Jewish Family Service," report, May 1989.

134. Chapin, op. cit.

135. Yehudah Bauer, *American Jewry and the Holocaust: The American Jewish Joint Distribution Committee, 1939–1945* (Detroit: Wayne State University Press, 1981), 26; Herbert A. Strauss, "The Immigration and Acculturation of the German Jews in the United States," *Leo Baeck Yearbook,* 16 (1971), 63–94; Maurice R. Davie, *Refugees in America: Report of the Committee for the Study of Recent Immigration from Europe* (New York: Harper Brothers Publishers, 1947); David Wyman, *Paper Walls: America and the Refugee Crisis, 1938–1941* (Amherst, Mass.: University of Massachusetts Press, 1968), 217–19.

136. Zosa Szajkowski, "The Attitude of American Jews to Refugees from Germany in the 1930's," *American Jewish Historical Quarterly,* 61 (December 1971), 101–43.

137. Federation Minutes, January 12, 1937.

138. Ibid., November 24, 1937.

139. Federation Minutes, December 4, 1935. Simon Shetzer asked for $5,000 for a secretary and an office to join the Emergency Conference on Jewish Organizations to Protest the Hitler Menace. The funds were approved and were to go to a League for the Defense of Human Rights in support of its boycott of German goods; Brody, "American Jewry."

140. *DN,* May 3, 1937.

141. Davie, *Refugees in America;* Wyman, *Paper Walls;* Strauss, "Immigration"; Bauer, 26.

142. Szajkowski, "Attitude of American Jews."

143. Ibid.; Chapin, op. cit.

144. Federation Minutes, June 21 and August 12, 1938.

145. Ibid.; June 21, 1938.

146. Ibid., November 11, 1938.

147. Ibid., November 7, 1939.

148. Bauer, 37–38.

149. Federation Minutes, January 20, 1940.

150. Chapin, op. cit.

151. Ibid.

152. Ben Rosen, *Survey of the United Hebrew Schools of Detroit,* (1930) (Federation Archives).

153. *DJC,* September 8, 1939.

154. Federation Allocations, 1937–1939 (Federation Archives).

155. UHS Yearbook, 1931.

156. *DJC,* September 8, 1939.

157. Annual articles in *DJC* and then *DJN*. "Jewish Education Month" (Slomovitz Files).
158. *DJN*, May 28, 1943.
159. Israel B. Rappoport and Elias Picheny, *The Detroit Self-Study* (Detroit: Jewish Welfare Federation, 1945).
160. Ibid.
161. *DN*, January 12, 1937.
162. *DN*, March 12, 1937.
163. Sermons of Dr. Leo Franklin, Temple Beth El Archives; see, also, Henry Feingold, "Who Shall Bear the Guilt for the Holocaust: The Human Dilemma," *American Jewish History* 68 (March 1979), 261–82; David Brody, "American Jewry, the Refugees and Immigration Restriction (1932–1942)," *Publication of the American Jewish Historical Society*, 45 (June 1956), 219–47; Herbert A. Strauss, "The Immigration and Acculturation of the German Jews in the United States," *Leo Baeck Institute Yearbook* 16 (1971), 63–94.
164. Frederick A. Lazin, "The Response of the American Jewish Committee to the Crisis of German Jewry, 1933–1939," *American Jewish History* 68 (March 1979), 284–304. See also the now standard works on the refugee rescue crisis: Henry Feingold, *The Politics of Rescue: the Roosevelt Administration and the Holocaust, 1938–1945* (New Brunswick, N.J.: Rutgers University Press, 1970); David Wyman, *Paper Walls: America and the Refugee Crisis, 1938–1941* (Amherst, Mass.: University of Massachusetts Press, 1968); Arthur D. Morse, *While Six Million Died* (New York: Random House, 1965); Wyman, *The Abandonment of the Jews: America and the Holocaust, 1941–1944* (New York: Pantheon, 1984).
165. Correspondence between Stephen W. Wise and Philip Slomovitz (Slomovitz Files).
166. *DN*, May 1, 1939.
167. *DN*, November 1, 1938.
168. Brochure of the Allied Jewish Campaign, "Stand Up And Fight," April 21, 1939.
169. "Allied Jewish Campaign News," May 7, 1939.
170. *DN*, September 24, 1939.
171. *DN*, April 17, 1940.
172. See, for example, Federation Minutes, January 20, 1940, June 24, 1940, June 10, 1941.
173. Federation Minutes, December 30, 1940.
174. Office of War Information: Bureau of Intelligence, Division of Surveys, "Anti-Semitism—A Symptom of Disaffection: Preliminary Report," October 8, 1942 (Bentley Historical Library, University of Michigan, Ann Arbor), Rensis Likert Collection, Box 9; Survey: "Ethnic Axis: The Jews," November 1942.
175. Federation Minutes, July 11, 1941.
176. Deborah Dash Moore, *B'nai B'rith and the Challenge of Ethnic Leadership* (Albany: State University of New York Press, 1981), 164–94.
177. Office of War Information, "The Ethnic Axis: The Jews," September 1942.
178. *DJN*, June 16, 1944.
179. *DJN*, April 24, 1942, May 1, 1942, May 15, 1942, March 26, 1943.
180. *DJN*, March 26 and April 9, 1943.

Notes to
Part III

181. *DJN,* September 24, 1943.
182. United States Marine Corps, Division of Information, "Major General William J. Weinstein, USMCR," November 1974; Correspondence from Ronald J. Brown, Lt. Col., USMCR, June 11, 1988.
183. Emmanuel Applebaum, "Second Lieutenant Raymond Zussman," *Michigan Jewish History,* (March 1961), 2–9.
184. Department of Michigan Jewish War Veterans, "Summary of the War Record of American Jews."
185. Federation Minutes, August 9 and November 17, 1937; Chapin, "Jewish Community Center," in *History of the UJC.*
186. Chapin, op. cit.; Federation Files on the history of the Jewish Community Center.
187. *DJN,* June 16, 1944.
188. *DJN,* September 10, 1943.
189. *DJN,* September 29, 1944.
190. "Fund-Raising, 1925–1949," report, Federation Files.
191. *DJN,* April 9, 1943, April 16, 1943.
192. *DJN,* March 26, 1943.
193. Office of War Information: Survey, "Ethnic Axis: Southerners."
194. Howard Hill, Gertrude Duncan, Herefried Dugan, A. L. Campbell, and Barbara Krenger, "Survey of Racial and Religious Conflict Forces in Detroit" (confidential, not-for-publication survey compiled by Wayne State University on "Jewish-Negro Relationships in Detroit") September 10–30, 1943.
195. Robert Shogan and Tom Craig, *The Detroit Race Riot* (Philadelphia and New York: Chilton Books, 1964), 26.
196. Conot, 376ff.
197. "Survey of Racial and Religious Forces of Conflict," *op. cit.*
198. United States Bureau of the Census, *Sixteenth Census of the U.S., 1940: Population,* vol. 2, part 3 (Washington, D.C., 1943), 889; Shogan and Craig, 35–42.
199. Donald C. Marsh, Alvin D. Loving, and Eleanor Paperno Wolf, "Some Aspects of Negro-Jewish Relationships in Detroit, Michigan: Introduction" (no date), 16–17 (Marsh Collection, Reuther Library); Capeci, 63–64.
200. Capeci, 10.
201. Ibid., 44.
202. Ibid., 40.
203. *DN,* March 21, 1942.
204. Conot, 374–75.
205. Shogan and Craig, 32; Conot, 379.
206. Conot, 378.
207. Capeci, 63.
208. Ibid., 84–85.
209. Ibid.
210. *DN,* March 21, 1942.
211. Conot, 384–85.
212. *DJN,* July 2, 1943.
213. Ibid.
214. Paul Novick, *Zionism Today: The Zionist Movement, Labor Zionism Palestine*

Realities, Questions and Answers (New York: The Jewish Buro [sic] of the Central Committee of the Communist Party of the U.S.A., 1936) a propaganda pamphlet that is an extreme example of rather malicious, leftist anti-Zionism.

215. *Independent Jewish Press Service, Inc.* (New York), December 14, 1942 (Slomovitz Files).

216. Ibid., January 25, 1943.

217. Franklin Files, Temple Beth El Archives.

218. *DJN*, January 5, 1942.

219. Ibid.

220. *DJN*, April 16, 1943.

221. Ibid., April 30, 1943.

222. *DJN*, December 10, 1943.

223. *DN*, October 15, 1938.

224. *DN*, November 8 and November 15, 1941.

225. Schaver Papers, Detroit Holocaust Memorial Center, Boxes 001/24; 001/32, 001/33; *DJC*, July 23, 1937; *DJN*, February 7, 1943.

226. *DJN*, April 16, 1943.

227. *DJC*, April 19, 1940.

228. *DJN*, May 7, 1943.

229. *DJN*, April 17, 1942.

230. Ibid., April 16, 1943.

231. Ibid., June 18, 1943.

232. Ibid., June 25, 1943.

233. *DN*, January 16, 1941.

234. Laikin, 238ff.

235. *DN*, October 6, 1945.

236. *DN*, February 23, 1946, April 1, 1946, August 26, 1946.

237. Jewish Welfare Federation Allocations, 1940–1949; *DJN*, April 17, 1942.

238. *DJN*, April 24, 1942.

239. Ibid.

240. Ibid., May 8, 1942.

241. Ibid., April 24, 1942.

242. Ibid., March 26, 1943 (report of meeting of March 17).

243. Ibid., April 2, 1943.

244. Ibid., April 16, 1943.

245. Ibid., April 30, 1943.

246. Laikin, 230–31.

247. *DJN*, April 17, 1942.

248. Irving Pokempner, "Jewish Community Council Cultural Commission" (typescript), March 18, 1963; Resolution of the Jewish Community Council Executive Committee, February, 1947.

249. Federation By-Laws.

250. Meyer, "The Economic Structure of the Jewish Community of Detroit."

251. Phillip Applebaum, *The Fishers: A Family Portrait* (Detroit: Harlo Press, 1982), 33ff. and *passim*.

252. Ibid., 81.

253. *DFP* and *DN*, October 8, 1939; *DN*, September 24, 1933.

254. *JN*, June 26, 1942.

255. *Proceedings of the Presentation of a Portrait of the Honorable Charles C. Simons*, November 29, 1965, in the United States District Court, Eastern District of Michigan.

256. *Memorial Resolution for the Honorable Theodore Levin, Judge, U. S. District Court, Eastern District of Michigan,* July 1, 1971.

257. *DFP*, July 1, 1947; *DJC*, September 8, 1939.

258. Chapin, op. cit.

259. David Wyman, *The Abandonment of the Jews* 260–76; Ruth Gruber, *Haven: The Unknown Story of One Thousand World War II Refugees* (New York: Coward, McCann and Geoghegan, 1983); Szajkowski, "Attitudes of Americans."

260. Report from Fred Butzel on the meeting of the Resettlement Service of September 6, 1945; Federation Minutes, September 11, 1945.

261. Samuel Lerner, "Historical Development and Current Program of Resettlement Service, 1937–1983," internal document; *DJN*, March 31, 1950.

262. Memorandum from Harold Silver to Esther Appelman, March 13, 1963.

263. *DJN*, April 28, 1950.

Part IV: 1948–1967

1. Raul Hilberg, *The Destruction of the European Jews* (New York: Quadrangle, 1961), 736.

2. Federation Minutes, March 14, 1945.

3. Ibid., September 11, October 17, 1945.

4. Ibid., November 9, 1945.

5. Laikin, 235ff.

6. Ibid., November 28, 1945.

7. Applebaum, *Tour.*

8. Albert J. Mayer "The Detroit Jewish Community Geographic Mobility: 1963–1965" and "Fertility—A Projection of Future Births," series 2, nos. 3 and 4, Population Report (Detroit: Jewish Welfare Federation, 1966).

9. Applebaum, op. cit.

10. Ibid.

11. Mrs. Harry L. Jones, "The Growth of Suburbs," Address at the 24th General Assemby of the Council of Jewish Federations, Chicago, November 11, 1955.

12. Ibid.

13. Albert J. Mayer, "Estimate of the Number and Age Distribution of the Jewish Population of the Detroit Metropolitan Area, 1956," report no. 5, Jewish Welfare Federation (1959).

14. Mayer, "Census Tract Study of the Jewish Population," 1956.

15. S. Joseph Fauman, "Occupational Selection Among Detroit Jews," *Jewish Social Studies* vol. 14, no. 1 (1952), 17–50.

16. Ibid.; Mayer, "Social and Economic Characteristics, 1963"; Mayer, "Place of Birth—Educational Level of the Jewish Population in the Metropolitan Detroit Area, 1956, "reports Nos. 10 and 11, Jewish Welfare Federation (1962).

17. Mayer, "Geographic Mobility: 1963–1965."

18. *DJN*, May 21, 1948.

19. Ibid., September 19, 1947.

20. Ibid.
21. Berry, letter to Adler, February 15, 1948 (Shaarey Zedek Archives); *DJN,* May 6, 1988.
22. *DJN,* October 10, 1947.
23. Ibid., September 19, 1947.
24. Ibid., May 21, 1948.
25. James B. Carey to Golda Meyerson, January 28, 1945, September 7, 1945; Meyerson to Carey, July 12, November and December 1945. Papers of the CIO Secretary Treasurer's Office, Box 22, Reuther Archives, Wayne State University.
26. *DJN,* November 10, 1950.
27. Ibid., May 21, 1948.
28. Ibid.
29. Ibid., June 11, 1948.
30. Ibid., May 14, 1948.
31. Ibid., October 1, 1948.
32. Ibid., November 5, 1948.
33. Ibid., May 13 and May 20, 1949.
34. Ibid., May 13, 1949.
35. Ibid., May 13, 1949.
36. Ibid., March 24, 1950.
37. Ibid., May 5, 1950.
38. Ibid., May 28, 1948.
39. *DFP,* May 22, 1948.
40. *DJN,* November 3, 1950.
41. Ibid., April 28, 1950, December 1, 1950.
42. Histadrut Files, Michigan Jewish Historical Society.
43. *DJN,* December 3, 1954; see also *Histadrut Foto News,* November 1954.
44. *DJN,* February 16, 1951.
45. Ibid., February 23, 1951.
46. Ibid., April 6, 1951.
47. Carl Alpert, *The Detroit Story: A History of the Detroit Chapter of the American Society for Technion Israel Institute of Technology* (Detroit: Technion Society, 1989).
48. Ibid.
49. Ibid.
50. *DJN,* March 30, 1956.
51. Allied Jewish Campaign Results, 1926–Present (1986), Federation Files.
52. Minutes of the Social Planning Committee of the Jewish Welfare Federation, October 24, 1946.
53. Ibid., December 10, 1947.
54. Federation By-Laws, 1947.
55. Abraham L. Sudran, "The Detroit Experiment," *Jewish Social Service Quarterly* (March 1947), 336–38.
56. *DJN,* April 21, 1950.
57. Ibid.
58. Theodore Levin, "Pre-Budget Campaign Conference," Address at the 26th General Assembly of the National Federation Agency, New Orleans, November 15, 1957.

501

59. Ibid.

60. Ibid.

61. Arthur Lipsitt, "Jewish Home for Aged," May 1985 (Federation Files); Chapin, op. cit.

62. Chapin, op. cit.

63. Ibid.

64. Federation Minutes, June 11, 1935, November 7, 1939.

65. Ibid., September 18, 1940; Dr. Frederic Zeman, "Study of the Jewish Aged and Chronically Ill in Detroit," Report (Detroit Jewish Welfare Federation, 1940).

66. Chapin, op. cit.

67. Minutes of the Social Planning Committee of the Jewish Welfare Federation, December 10, 1947.

68. Minutes of the Committee on Housing for the Elderly, July 8, 1962.

69. Draft of a report from Samuel Cohen to Leonard N. Simons, "Apartment House Projects for Aged in Philadelphia, Baltimore and Pittsburgh," February 16, 1966; Helen Naimark, "Jewish Federation Apartments: *Chai* Anniversary, 1967–1985," pamphlet (Detroit: Jewish Welfare Federation, 1985).

70. Report of the Committee on Housing for the Elderly, Leonard N. Simons, Chairman, Samuel Cohen, JWF Assistant Director, June 23, 1966.

71. Ibid.

72. Minutes of the Committee on Housing for the Elderly, June 28, 1966.

73. Report of the Implementation Committee on Housing for the Elderly, Joseph H. Jackier, Chairman, July 1967.

74. Irwin Shaw, "Brief History of the Jewish Community Center," Jewish Community Center Files, November 1964.

75. National Welfare Board, Jewish Community Center Division, "Digest of the Report of the Committee on the Sabbath Policy of the Jewish Community Centers Sabbath Policy on Programming," June 1957 (Jewish Community Center Files).

76. Minutes of the Board of the Jewish Community Center, August 10, 1959.

77. Ibid., September 9, 1959; Shaw, memo to Sanford Solender, September 9, 1959 (JCC Files).

78. Minutes of the Board of the JCC, October 7, 1959.

79. Telegram from Charles P. Gellman to Frankel, September 17, 1959.

80. *DJN,* September 18, 1959.

81. Morris J. Brandwine, letter to Board of JCC, October 1, 1959.

82. Mrs. Joseph H. Deutsch, president of Shaarey Zedek Sisterhood, to Board of JCC, October 26, 1959.

83. ZOD, letter to Board of JCC with copy to Abe Kasle, October 13, 1959.

84. "Statement on Sabbath Programming at the Jewish Community Center," October 28, 1959 (JCC File).

85. Minutes of the meeting of the Board of the JCC, November 4, 1959.

86. Minutes of the meeting of the Citizen's Committee, January 21, 1960.

87. Ibid.

88. Ibid.

89. Ibid.

90. Ibid.

91. Ibid.
92. Minutes of the meeting of the Jewish Community Council Executive Committee, October 22, 1959.
93. Garvett, letter to Frankel, October 19, 1960.
94. "Tentative Plan for Saturday Afternoon Programming," Jewish Community Center, December 21, 1960 (JCC Files).
95. *JWB Circle* (March 1961).
96. Minutes of the meeting of the Board of the JCC, May 31, 1961.
97. Abe Kasle, letter to the Board of Directors of the JCC, June 16, 1961 (JCC Files).
98. Ibid.
99. *DN,* June 25, 1961.
100. Letter from 28 rabbis to the Board of Directors of the JCC, April 27, 1960. Included were Rabbis Adler, Arm, Fram, Gorelick, Groner, Kapustin, Lehrman, Levin, Prero, Sperka, Stollman, Syme, and Wohlgelernter.
101. Articles of Incorporation, Jewish Community Center of Detroit, December 7, 1933.
102. Minutes of the meeting of the Special Center Committee with Representatives of the "Committee of 50 for Center Closing," July 27, 1961.
103. *DJN,* July 28, 1961.
104. Memorandum from Shaw to Max Fisher, September 28, 1961.
105. "Charge for Berman Committee," September 28, 1961.
106. Minutes of the meeting of the Berman Committee, September 28, 1961.
107. Minutes of the meeting of the Board of Directors of the JCC, October 25, 1961.
108. Honorable Thomas J. Murphy, Circuit Court for the County of Wayne, Decision in Wrotlovsky vs. Jewish Community Center of Detroit, June 27, 1962.
109. 1966–1967 Allocations to Beneficiary Agencies (Federation Files).
110. "Jewish Community Foundation. A Program of Innovation and Service," (Detroit: Jewish Welfare Federation, 1979).
111. "Current Programs and Needs—B'nai B'rith Hillel Foundation," Federation study chaired by Esther Appelman (Federation Files, 1967).
112. Jewish Community Council of Detroit, "Working with Our Friends: Biennial Report, 1950–1952," (Detroit: 1952), 6.
113. Minutes of the Jewish Community Council Executive Committee, December 4, 1957.
114. "Working With Our Friends," 8, 20, 23, *passim*; *DJN,* September 15, 1950.
115. "Working With Our Friends," 17ff.
116. Jewish Community Council Constitution and By-Laws.
117. "Summary Report of Views of Evaluation Committee of Jewish Community Council," chaired by James I. Ellmann, November 7, 1957; Minutes of the IRC, December 23, 1953.
118. Ellmann Report.
119. Minutes of Council Executive Committee, November 8, 1950.
120. Council minutes, March 30, 1955.
121. Ibid., January 18, 1950.
122. *DJN,* October 3, 1947.
123. Council minutes, March 30, 1950.

124. Ibid., April 26, 1950.
125. Ibid., June 8, 1950.
126. Ibid., April 26, 1950.
127. Ibid., January 18, 1950.
128. Minutes of the IRC, May 25, 1954.
129. Council minutes, November 30, 1955.
130. Mel J. Ravitz, "Where Shall We Live?" Address delivered to the Delegate Assembly of the Jewish Community Council of Metropolitan Detroit, October 20, 1960.
131. Council minutes, May 27, 1958.
132. *DJN*, September 29, 1950.
133. Council minutes, October 12, 1950.
134. Ibid., February 28, 1955.
135. Ibid., February 14, 1952.
136. Ibid., February 27, 1956.
137. Ibid., December 22, 1949.
138. Ibid., March 24, 1949.
139. Ibid., August 24, 1949.
140. Ibid., December 22, 1949.
141. Ibid.
142. Ibid., February 20, 1950.
143. Ibid., September 14, 1950.
144. Ibid.
145. Ibid., October 12, 1950; *DJN*, October 20, 1950.
146. Council minutes, November 8, 1950.
147. Ibid., January 18, 1951.
148. Ibid.
149. Ibid., March 23, 1954.
150. Ibid., December 19, 1951.
151. NCRAC, Confidential digest of "Report on the Jewish Community Relations Agencies, Section I," by R. M. MacIver; NCRAC Special Committee on Evaluative Studies," "Summary of Comments by Professor R. M. MacIver in reply to questions of clarification regarding "Report . . .," Jewish Community Relations Agencies Conference, June 12–13, 1951.
152. Council minutes, September 20, 1951.
153. Digest of "Report"; C. Bezahl Sherman, "The MacIver Report," *Jewish Frontier* (December 1951), 6–11.
154. Council minutes, September 20, 1951.
155. "Statement of Views of the Anti-Defamation League of the B'nai B'rith on the 'Report on the Jewish Community Relations Agencies' by Professor Robert M. MacIver," October 21, 1951.
156. Resolution on the MacIver Report unanimously Adopted by 271 Delegates at the Delegate Assembly on November 18, 1951, Council Archives.
157. Oscar I. Janowsky and Salo Baron, *The Jewish Welfare Board Survey with the Report of the JWB Survey Commission* (New York: The Dial Press, 1948).
158. "An Open Letter to the Detroit Jewish Community," flier of the Jewish Community Council, undated [1952].
159. Ibid.

160. Minutes of the Annual Meeting of the Jewish Welfare Federation, March 4, 1952.
161. Council minutes, March 27, 1952.
162. Ibid., April 22, 1952.
163. Ibid., September 20, 1954.
164. Ibid., December 29, 1955.
165. Ibid., April 26, 1956.
166. Ibid., May 21, 1956.
167. Ibid., December 26, 1956.
168. Minutes of joint meeting of the Council and the Federation, January 31, 1957.
169. Ibid., January 31, 1957.
170. Walter Klein, "What's Jewish About It?" *Jewish Digest* (April 1977), 3–7.
171. Notes of Address of Rabbi Morris Adler at the Third Annual Conference and Brunch for Presidents of Council Affiliated Organizations, December 13, 1959.
172. William Avrunin, "Jewish Communal Services and the Jewish Community," paper delivered at the Intermediate and Small City Executive Institute, Council of Jewish Federations and Welfare Funds, August 1961.
173. Arnold Gurin, "Factors that Influence Decisions in Community Planning," paper presented at the Annual Meeting of the National Conference of Jewish Communal Service, May 28, 1961.
174. Avrunin, "Jewish Communal Services."
175. Gurin, "Factors."
176. Brewster Broder, "Current Issues in Planning Center Services," paper delivered at the Fortieth General Assembly of Council of Jewish Federations and Welfare Funds, Pittsburgh, November 10–14, 1971.
177. Minutes of the IRC, October 26, 1948.
178. Ibid., 1950–1953; May 1951.
179. Ibid., December 1954, February 2, 1955.
180. Ibid., October 26, 1948, February 2, 1955, March 30, 1955, December 1954.
181. Ibid., November 26, 1952, May 13, 1953, December 23, 1957.
182. Ibid., November 16, 1959.
183. Ibid., March 16, 1960.
184. Council minutes, February 27, 1956, November 14, 1960.
185. Council minutes, January 5, 1966; June 21, 1966.
186. Ibid., April 28, 1967.
187. Jewish Community Council, "Report to the Delegates, 1964–1965."
188. Ibid., February 16, 1966.
189. Isidore Sobeloff, "History of Jewish Community Services," address to the Delegate Assembly of the Jewish Community Council, January, 1963.
190. Albert J. Mayer, "Branches of Judaism, Synagogue and Temple Membership, Attendance at Religious Services," Population Report no. 9 (Jewish Welfare Federation, 1956).
191. Ibid.
192. Beth Abraham Synagogue Files; *DJN,* May 13, 1955.
193. Files of the Young Israel.
194. Ibid.
195. See Grad and Roth, 68–122.

196. Morris J. Adler, *The Voice Still Speaks* (New York: Bloch Publishing Co., 1969); *The World of the Talmud* (New York: Schocken, 1963).

197. Grad and Roth, 78, 84; *DJN,* September 10, 1948.

198. Grad and Roth, 93–105.

199. Files of Adat Shalom; *DJN,* July 11, 1947, July 8, 1949.

200. Files of Adat Shalom.

201. *The Voice,* November 3, 1950.

202. Papers of Beth Aaron.

203. Ibid.

204. Baruch Litvin, ed., *The Sanctity of the Synagogue: The Case for the Mechitzah—Separation Between Men and Women in the Synagogue—Based on Jewish Law, History and Philosophy From Sources Old and New* (Mt. Clemens, 1959).

205. Samson Raphael Weiss, *Jewish Action* (December 1988).

206. "A Journey Through B'nai Moshe's History," *Seventy-fifth Anniversary: Congregation B'nai Moshe: The Jubilee Year* (1988), files of B'nai Moshe.

207. Jacob Donin, *To Be a Jew* (New York: Basic Books, 1972); *To Pray As a Jew* (New York: Basic Books, 1980).

208. Sklare, *Conservative Judaism* (1972).

209. Herbert Rosenblum, *Conservative Judaism. A Contemporary History* (New York: United Synagogue of America, 1983), 100.

210. Katz, *The Beth El Story,* 142–43.

211. Beth El Bulletins.

212. Beth El Bulletins (from October 1952).

213. Beth El Bulletin, May 11, 1953.

214. Temple Bulletin, 1954.

215. Beth El Bulletin, May 6, 1955.

216. Beth El Files.

217. Ibid.

218. Rabbi Leon Fram, "The Story of Temple Israel," and Reuben Levine, "A Bicentennial Glance at Temple Israel," in *Twenty-fifth Anniversary Book* (1966).

219. Ibid.

220. Ibid.; *DJN,* November 20, 1953.

221. Temple Israel Files.

222. Fram, op. cit.

223. Ibid.

224. Annual Report of Rabbi Fram, 1964–65, in Temple Israel Files.

225. Levine, op. cit.

226. *The Jewish Humanist: The Birmingham Temple 25th Anniversary* (1989), 15.

227. Ibid., 2.

228. Ibid., 2–3.

229. Morris Adler, "American Jewish Youth: A Profile," *Jewish Heritage* (Summer 1966), 14–18.

230. Turo histories in Yeshivah Beth Yehudah Files.

231. Ibid.

232. Ibid.

233. *DJN,* July 1, 1955.

234. Ibid.

235. Allocations to Federation Beneficiary Agencies, 1926–1939.

236. Ibid., 1950–1951.

237. Yeshivah Beth Yehudah Files.

238. Hillel Yearbook, 1967.

239. Ibid.

240. "The United Hebrew Schools: 65 Years of Accomplishment," pamphlet of the Jewish Welfare Federation (1985); "The History of the United Hebrew Schools," Midrasha Files.

241. Ibid.

242. Ibid.

243. Louis Ruffman, "A Qualitative Study of the United Hebrew Schools, 1967," Jewish Welfare Federation Files.

244. Lawrence Crohn, "Detroit's Communal School System," *Reconstructionist Magazine* (November 27, 1959); "Federation Policy for Financing Jewish Education" (Self Study, submitted by Mandell L. Berman/George M. Zeltzer Committee, May 1979).

245. "History of the United Hebrew Schools."

246. Ibid.

247. Morris Nobel, ed., *Sefer Bernard Isaacs* (New York: Shulsinger Bros., Inc., 1977).

248. Ruffman, op. cit.

249. Jewish Welfare Federation Files.

250. "The Labor Zionist Movement of Detroit," pamphlet, 1961 (Files of the Hayim Greenberg School).

251. Yearbooks of the Hayim Greenberg School; *School Jubilee: Hayim Greenberg Hebrew—Yiddish School, 1915–1965*, 19.

252. Minutes of the Board of the United Jewish Folk Schools, January 1956–December 1961 (Files of the Hayim Greenberg School and the Sholom Aleichem Institute).

253. Minutes of the Inter-School Committee Meeting, December 18, 1961; Moishe Haar, "Proposals for Consideration by the Executive Board of the Combined Jewish Schools of the Sholem Aleichem Institute and Arbeiter Ring in Detroit, Michigan," 1965 (Files of the Sholem Aleichem Institute).

254. Ibid.; Plan of Implementation of the Combined Schools, 1963.

255. Correspondence, Jack Stein, March 23, 1987; See also *DJN*, October 13, 1950.

256. Stein, March 23, 1987; *DJN*, October 24, 1947.

257. Stein, March 23, 1987.

258. Ibid.

259. Ibid.

260. Irving Sigel, "Jewish Parents Institute: How J.P.I. Arrived At Its Definition of Secular—History of a Controversy" (JPI Files, 1961–1962).

261. Ibid.

262. JPI Curriculum, section on "What Secular Jews Believe" (JPI Files).

263. Sigel, op. cit.

264. *Survey.*

265. Harry C. Saltzstein, *Sinai Hospital and the North End Clinic: Reminiscences of the History of the Jewish Hospital Movement in Detroit* (Detroit: Wayne State University Press, 1963), 5.

266. Ibid., 7–9.
267. *Survey.*
268. Chapin, op. cit.
269. Saltzstein, 14–20.
270. *Survey.*
271. Saltzstein, 28–30.
272. Ibid., 29f.
273. Ibid.
274. Chapin, op. cit.
275. Saltzstein, *Sinai Hospital,* 36–37.
276. Sinai Hospital Files.
277. *DJC,* February 6 and 7, 1937.
278. Saltzstein, 41.
279. Ibid.
280. Ibid., 42–53.
281. Federation Minutes, September 23, 1937.
282. Saltzstein, 43.
283. Dr. Jacob J. Golub, "The Detroit Hospital Survey," July 1938 (Federation Files).
284. Saltzstein, 44.
285. Harry Lurie and J. Golub, "The Jewish Hospital Situation in Detroit," November 1938 (Federation Files).
286. Minutes of the meeting of the Jewish Hospital Association and the Federation Hospital Survey Committee, February 9, 1939 (Federation Files).
287. Ibid.
288. Saltzstein, 45–47.
289. Saltzstein, 48–49.
290. Saltzstein, 48–49.
291. Federation Minutes, July 23, 1943.
292. Federation Minutes, May 9 and June 21, 1944.
293. *DJN,* May 19, 1950.
294. Ibid., May 26, 1950.
295. *DJN,* October 27, 1950.
296. Ibid., November 3, 1950.
297. Saltzstein, op. cit.
298. Golub, op. cit.
299. Greater Detroit Section of the National Council of Jewish Women, Historical Highlights (NCJW Files).
300. Ibid.; Rockaway, *The Jews of Detroit,* 129.
301. NCJW's Mission Statement (NCJW Files).
302. *National Council of Jewish Women: National Resolutions* (Washington, D.C., 1987).
303. *DJC,* April 25, 1930.
304. NCJW Bulletin, "What Your Local Council Is Doing with Its Modest Income," April 1931 (NCJW Files).
305. Ibid.
306. *DJC,* March 27 and April 3, 1932.
307. *Detroit Times,* August 6, 1933.
308. NCJW Historical Highlights.

309. Files of the Detroit Chapter of Hadassah.

310. Ibid.

311. "The Hadassah Story," internal document, files of Detroit Chapter of Hadassah.

312. Correspondence from the Music Study Club of Metropolitan Detroit, May 30, 1990.

313. Sydney Stahl Weinberg, *The World of Our Mothers: The Lives of Jewish Immigrant Women* (Chapel Hill and London: University of North Carolina Press, 1988), 148.

314. Ibid., 63, 151.

315. Jacqueline Levine, quoted in Elizabeth Koltun, ed., *The Jewish Woman: New Perspectives* (New York: Schocken Books, 1976), 193.

316. Stephen M. Cohen, Susan Dessel, Michael Pelavin, "The Changing (?) Role of Women in Jewish Communal Affairs: A Look into the UJA," in Koltun, ed., *The Jewish Woman* 193–201.

317. Chapin, op. cit.

318. NCJW Historical Highlights; *DN,* September 9, 1955; NCJW Bulletin, October, 1955.

319. *NCJW: National Resolutions.*

320. NCJW Historical Highlights.

321. Ibid.

322. Ibid.

323. Ibid.

324. Ibid.

325. WICS Files.

326. Dora Ehrlich, President's Report of the First Annual Meeting of Federation Women's Division, October 1947.

327. Ibid.

328. Cohen, Dessel, and Pelavin, op. cit.

329. Clara Frank, President's Report, October 1949.

330. Jenny Jones, Address at the Annual Meeting of Women's Division, May 12, 1982.

331. Cohen, Dessen, and Pelavin, *op. cit.*

332. Carolyn Greenberg and Shelby Tauber, "Our Present, Our Future," Federation Survey of Women's Division leadership (Federation Files, 1982).

333. Bernice Hopp, President's Report, 1953.

334. Ann Daniels, "Women in Communal Service," Workshop delivered at the 27th General Assembly of CJFWF, Washington, D.C., November 13, 1959; also in Daniels, Address at Annual Meeting of Women's Division, May 12, 1982.

335. Detroit Leaders in the Big Picture (NCJW Files).

336. Barbara Marcuse, Address at the Annual Meeting of Women's Division, May 12, 1982.

337. Minutes of Sheruth League, April 18, 1944 (Michigan Jewish Historical Society Files).

338. Ibid., May 16, 1944.

339. Ibid., December 26, 1944; "Reflections from our minutes as we approach the end of our twentieth year, on the story of a women's group which accepted and fulfilled its obligations, built on a broad base of community activity," *Annual Yearbook,* December 4, 1963.

340. Summary of Minutes of Sheruth League, 1954–1955; 1955–1956.
341. "Reflections from our minutes," op. cit.
342. Sheruth League, *Nineteenth Annual Year Book,* December 8, 1965.
343. Morris Adler, "The Last Sermon," in *The Voice Still Speaks: Message of the Torah for Contemporary Man* (New York: Bloch Publishing Co., 1969), 431–36.
344. Ibid., 349–56.
345. *Congregation Shaarey Zedek Recorder,* March 24, 1966.
346. Ibid.
347. Elie Wiesel, "Brief Encounter," in *In Memoriam Rabbi Morris Adler, Jewish Heritage* (Spring 1966), 4–6.
348. Adler, "American Jewish Youth."
349. Ibid.
350. T. V. LoCicero, *Murder in the Synagogue* (Engelwood Cliffs, N.J.: Prentice Hall, Inc., 1970), 348–49.
351. Wiesel, "Brief Encounter."
352. *New York Post,* February 14, 1966.
353. LoCicero, "Murder in the Synagogue," *Commentary* (June 1966), 49–53.
354. Grad and Roth, 125.
355. Esther Jones, Address at the Annual Meeting of Women's Division, May 12, 1982.
356. Howard M. Sachar, *Egypt and Israel* (New York: Richard Marek Publishers, 1981), 112–119.
357. *DJN,* February 21, 1957.
358. Howard M. Sachar, *A History of Israel: From the Rise of Zionism to Our Time* (New York: Alfred A. Knopf, 1979), 615.
359. Ibid., 616.
360. Trevor N. Dupuy, *Elusive Victory: The Arab-Israeli Wars, 1947–1974* (New York: Harper and Row, 1978), 224–26.
361. Ibid., 226.
362. Sachar, *History,* 620.
363. Nadow Safran, *From War to War: The Arab-Israeli Confrontation, 1948–1967* (New York: Western Publishing Co., 1969), 292–316.
364. Ibid., 312–16.
365. Ibid., 293; Sachar, 626.
366. Sachar, 633.
367. Ibid., 661.
368. *DJN,* June 2, 1967, June 9, 1967.
369. Ibid., June 2, 1967.
370. Ibid., June 9, 1967.
371. Ibid.
372. "Allied Jewish Campaign Results, 1926–Present [1989]," Jewish Welfare Federation internal document, Federation Archives.
373. *DJN,* January 10, 1986.
374. Ibid., June 23, 1967.
375. Ibid.
376. Conot, 491.
377. Correspondence with Harold Norris, December 8, 1987.

378. *Congressional Record*, July 19, 1978.

379. Ibid.

380. *DFP*, April 16 and May 26, 1967.

381. Conot, 522.

382. Grad and Roth, 55.

383. See Sidney Fine, *Violence in the Model City. The Cavanagh Administration, Race Relations, and the Detroit Riot of 1967* (Ann Arbor: University of Michigan Press, 1989).

384. Ibid., 42, 291–93; *DJN*, July 28, 1967; *DFP*, August 12, 1967; *DN*, August 11, 1967.

385. Conot, 531.

386. Fine, 293–94.

387. *DJN*, July 28, 1967.

388. Fine, 295.

389. *DFP*, August 12, 1967; *DN*, August 11, 1967; *DJN*, July 28, 1967.

390. *DJN*, July 28, 1967.

391. Ibid.

392. Conot, 602.

393. Ibid., 603.

Index

514

General Linen Supply, 143
General Motors Corporation, 91, 159, 330
General Zionist Council of Detroit, 275
Gentile American Realtors and Builders Association, 237
German American Bank, 69
German-American Bund, 172, 173, 175, 242, 255
German American Group, 250
German Enlightenment, 21
German Jewish Children's Aid, 248
German Jews (*Yahudim*), 74, 388; anti-Semitism and, 65, 101, 257; and assimilation, 20, 21, 22, 23, 38, 66, 102, 104, 435; and charity, 36, 37–38; and East European Jews, 19, 21–22, 37–38, 41, 59, 162, 397; elitism, 20–21, 36–37; in Federation, 131, 161–62, 188, 363, 373–74; and Jewish Community Council, 212, 213, 223; neighborhood migration, 76, 97; refugees from Nazism, 141, 150, 242, 247, 248–49; religious practices, 22, 104; and Sinai Hospital, 413, 435, 437; and Zionism, 397, 443, 446
Germany: American-Jewish boycott of, 175, 189–90, 221, 248, 254, 496n.139; Ford and, 241–42, 243; Jewish assimilation in, 21, 22; Nazi persecution of Jews, 173, 175–78, 182–83, 234, 240, 241, 254, 255, 257; in World War I, 68–69, 177–78; in World War II, 256, 259
Gershenson, Charles H., 357, 359, 363
Gershenson, Samuel, 358
Gilmore, Horace, 455
Gingold, Marvin B., 137
Ginsburg, Bernard, 23, 26, 35, 60, 65
Ginsburg, Danny, 166
Ginsburg, Mrs. Fred, 137, 249
Ginsburg, Samuel, 36
Girardin, Ray, 463
Girl Scouts, 65
Gitlin, Charles, 436
Gitlin, Esther, 146, 436–37, 439
Gittelman, Mr. and Mrs. H. B., 173
Glantz, Samuel, 29
Glatstein, Jacob, 278–79

Glazer, Rabbi B. Benedict: death of, 395; and Jewish Community Council, 374–75, 376, 391; and race relations, 227, 268, 269, 366–67; as religious leader, 227–29, 263, 272–73; Zionism, 227, 271, 272–73, 274, 397
Glazer, Mrs. B. Benedict, 451
Glazer, Nathan, 22–23
Glowgower, Gertrude, 443
Glowgower, Mrs. Samuel R., 249, 257, 263
Glueck, Nelson, 396
Goldberg, David, 146, 357
Goldberg, Isaac, 23
Goldenberg, Samuel, 159
Goldman, Aubrey, 260
Goldman, Emma, 158, 161
Goldman, Harry, 280–81, 362
Goldman, Harvey H., 341
Goldman, Rabbi Leo, 388, 389, 390–91
Goldman, Nahum, 256
Goldman, Perry, 260
Goldoftas, Movsas, 408
Goldsmith, Max, 357, 404
Goldsmith, Samuel, 37
Goldstein, Charles, 368, 380
Goldstein, Goldie, 246, 285
Goldstein, Rabbi Herbert, 103, 403
Goldstein, Sholom, 402
Goldstick, Nathaniel H., 246, 248, 256, 283, 384
Goldwater, Sigmund S., 412, 434
Gollub, Pauline, 245
Golub, Jacob, J., 437, 441
Goodman, Harold, 238
Goodman, Percival, 392
Goose, David, 281
Gordon, Rabbi Albert, 262
Gordon, Ida, 87
Gordon, Jennie F., 88
Gordon, Max, 33, 91
Gordon, Rose, 87
Gordon, William H., 436, 438
Gorelick, Ada, 215
Goren, Judith, 399
Gorman's Furniture, 464–65
Gorrelik, Rabbi Benjamin, 391, 394
Gould, Arthur, 369

530

532

536